The Goddess as Role Model

The Goddess as Role Model

Sītā and Rādhā in Scripture and on Screen

HEIDI R.M. PAUWELS

OXFORD
UNIVERSITY PRESS
2008

OXFORD
UNIVERSITY PRESS

Oxford University Press, Inc., publishes works that further
Oxford University's objective of excellence
in research, scholarship, and education.

Oxford New York
Auckland Cape Town Dar es Salaam Hong Kong Karachi
Kuala Lumpur Madrid Melbourne Mexico City Nairobi
New Delhi Shanghai Taipei Toronto

With offices in
Argentina Austria Brazil Chile Czech Republic France Greece
Guatemala Hungary Italy Japan Poland Portugal Singapore
South Korea Switzerland Thailand Turkey Ukraine Vietnam

Published by Oxford University Press, Inc.
198 Madison Avenue, New York, New York 10016

www.oup.com

Library of Congress Cataloging-in-Publication Data
Pauwels, Heidi Rika Maria.
The goddess as role model: Sita and Radha in scripture and on the screen / Heidi R. M. Pauwels.
p. cm.
Includes bibliographical references and index.
ISBN 978-0-19-536990-8
1. Sita (Hindu deity) 2. Radha (Hindu deity) 3. Women in Hinduism. 4. Love—Religious aspects—Hinduism. 5. Hinduism—Social aspects. I. Title.
BL1225.S57P38 2008
294.5'2114—dc22
2008009797

9 8 7 6 5 4 3 2 1

Printed in the United States of America
on acid-free paper

Dedicated to my husband

jinha keṃ rahī bhāvanā jaisī
prabhu mūrati tinha dekhī taisī

Everyone perceives the Lord according to his own predisposition.

—Rām Carit Mānas

Preface: An Auspicious Confluence

This book has been in the making for over a decade. It is a *saṅgam,* an auspicious confluence, in more than one sense. First, it brings together two prominent Hindu goddesses, Sītā and Rādhā. Second, it is a confluence of myth and real life, as it is looking at how myth "matters" in presenting role models for women. Third, it looks at the goddesses as portrayed in three different types of texts, Sanskrit, medieval Hindi, and modern film and television series. Thus it brings together "texts" of different provenance.

It was, appropriately, a confluence of circumstances that led to my being in India when the mythological series were first aired on television. This gave me the opportunity to watch them as they unfolded, an opportunity I might have missed had it not been for my Vrindāban guru, the late Shri Baldev Lal Goswami (Choṭe Sarkār), who insisted I spend some Sunday mornings in 1987 watching episodes of the televised versions of the epics with his family at his house. I confess that at the time I did so reluctantly, uneasy about spending my precious time in India watching television—of poor transmission quality to boot. I would have rather read with him the medieval Krishna poetry I had set out to translate and interpret. Now, I am grateful to him for "sowing the seed" *(bīja)* of future works, as good gurus do. He gave me the invaluable opportunity to taste firsthand the influence of these series, and to learn the valuable lesson that, while in India, be focused, but do not close yourself off from the wondrous *līlās* unfolding before your eyes, be they real life or reel life.

The seed came to fruition through another lucky confluence between teaching and research. My first research focused on the goddess Rādhā, and when I got my first teaching job at the School of Oriental and African Studies (SOAS), London, I was finalizing translations for my first book on a Braj reworking of Krishna's dance with the Rādhā and the Gopīs in the woods, the *Rās-pañcādhyāyī*. As I was teaching Avadhī at SOAS, I was reading at the same time with my students from Tulsīdās's *Rāmcaritmānas*—the passages of Sītā's resolve to join Rāma in exile in the woods. While preparing wordlists for the class, I was struck by the similarities in wording and sentiment of Sītā's resolve with that of the Gopīs to join Krishna in the forest. The interest in the televised versions came in that same Avadhī class. The students had been voicing a common sentiment of doubt about the usefulness of reading medieval texts for understanding contemporary India, so I showed episodes from Sagar's *Ramayan* to illustrate the contemporary relevance of the text. When doing so, I was struck by the differences with the texts we had read.

The link with popular Hindi movies came in 1995, when I had a chance to view in a crowded London theatre the full version of the hit movie *Hum aap ke hain koun . . . !* and heard recited the *Mānas* passages we had just read in class! I was delighted to have more evidence to tell my film-loving students how they would benefit so obviously from their hard work in the medieval text class. I am grateful to Munni Kabir for inspiring me with her love for Hindi movies and her message to take them seriously, and in particular to pay close attention to the song-and-dance sequences.

Thus, at the origin of this book is a desire to show the relevance of the medieval texts I love to students of modern India. I feel that my contribution to make is to share my love of these influential classical texts with a wider audience. I hope that I will not be misunderstood as intending to reduce the Hindi film to a mythological Ur-story but that I will instead alert viewers of Hindi films to a wealth of nuances and variants that might otherwise remain unmined. I think his book abundantly illustrates how study of mythology can help to understand contemporary film.

The Sītā parts of three chapters in this book (1–3) are drastically rewritten versions of papers presented at and first written up for Rāmāyaṇa conferences organized by Mandakranta Bose of the University of British Columbia, Vancouver, in 1999 and 2000. I am very grateful for her and Vidyut Aklujkar's encouragement and for the opportunity to sound out my ideas among specialists at an early stage in the development of the book. (These essays are published as Pauwels 2000 and 2004a.) The section on Sītā in chapter 4 in this book was first presented at a South Asia Conference of the Pacific North-West in 1996, and subsequently at a conference in Cambridge, UK, in

1997. (A short article on the topic was Pauwels 2004b.) I am grateful to Lynn Thomas and Jacqueline Hirst for their comments. A summary of chapter 1 was also presented in Paris, when I was visiting at the École Pratique des Hautes Études in 2005. I am grateful for the kind hospitality of Françoise Mallison and Nalini Delvoye and for their suggestions and those of the audience. Finally, the section on Rukmiṇī in chapter 2 is a variant of a paper first presented at the annual meeting of the American Oriental Society in Seattle in 2005 and published in the *Journal of the Royal Asiatic Society* in 2007. However, in the published article I do not touch upon the televised version, and instead compare the Braj version with a Marwari retelling of the story.

I am most grateful to Cynthia Read of Oxford University Press for seeing the book through to publication and for soliciting two superb anonymous readers' reviews, which were both supportive and tactfully critical with excellent suggestions. The reviewers helped me focus my argument and provided even some elegant turns of phrase that I have incorporated in the book. I am very grateful for their comments.

It is a pleasure to acknowledge Carolyn Brown Heinz, for her enthusiastic permission to use the photo on the cover, as well as for sharing with me her vast anthropological expertise on the region of Sītā's birth, Mithilā.

I want to thank especially my good friend and respected colleague Swapna Sharma of Vrindāban for helping me with the translations from the Braj texts. She clarified many obscure passages and saved me from several embarrassing mistakes. More important, in her own devotion to Rādhā, she provided me with an inspiring role model herself. There is no better way to come to understand and love a culture one has not grown up in than through a true friend.

I wish to thank wholeheartedly my colleagues at the University of Washington, especially Michael Shapiro, for taking the time to look through an early draft of this book and offering advice, and also Virginia Van Dyke for great discussions on politics and a reading of some politically relevant portions in this work.

And many thanks to the students at the University of Washington who took my classes on medieval Hindi, Indian literature in translation, Indian goddesses, and *Rāmāyaṇa* in comparative perspective; I am especially grateful to Valerie Ritter (now at the University of Chicago) for many fascinating discussions about Rādhā and Krishna's accosting the Gopīs. Thanks to Prem Pahlajrai for his insightful comments on an early version of the introduction and chapter 6. I thank my students for their enthusiasm, keen interest, and good discussions. This book was largely written during my sabbatical in 2004–5; I am grateful to the University of Washington for teaching relief.

Last but not least, I want to thank my wonderful family, especially my husband: I have been very blessed to enjoy their genuine support and love, much more than I can say. The arrival of our little girl coincided with the sending off of the first draft of this book for review and with Durgā pūjā, so we could welcome a little Devī home as the book of the two great Devīs started its journey in the world. Today, as I prepare to send the finalized version off to press, it is the auspicious occasion of Rādhāṣṭamī.

I have benefited much from stimulating discussions with husband, friends, students, colleagues, and gurus, but all mistakes and shortcomings are my own. I can only hope that the positive points will outweigh the inevitable faults. If any offense is given in the course of this long work, I humbly beg the indulgence of all connoisseurs of the wonderful works cited and the forgiveness of the devotees of the great goddesses who have inspired it.

Rādhāṣṭamī 2007

Acknowledgments

Parts of the first four chapters in this book were published in an earlier form elsewhere. I thank the following publishers and editors for permission to publish material from the following articles.

Mandakranta Bose: "Three Ways of Falling in Love: Tulsīdās's Phūlvārī Episode and the Way It Is Portrayed in Contemporary Electronic Media." In Mandakranta Bose, ed., *A Varied Optic: Contemporary Studies in the Rāmāyaṇa*, pp. 55–100. Vancouver: Institute of Asian Research, University of British Columbia, 2000.

Oxford University Press and Mandakranta Bose: "'Only You': The Wedding of Rāma and Sītā, Past and Present." In Mandakranta Bose, ed., *Rāmāyaṇa Revisited*, pp. 165–218. New York: Oxford University Press, 2004.

Cambridge University Press: "Stealing a Willing Bride: Women's agency in the myth of Rukmiṇī's Elopement." *Journal of the Royal Asiatic Society* 17.4 (2007): 407–41. Reprinted with permission.

Oxford University Press, Jacqueline Suthren Hirst, and Lynn Thomas: "Is Love Still Stronger than *Dharma?* Whatever Happened to Sita's Choice and the Gopis' Voice?" In Jacqueline Suthren Hirst and Lynn Thomas, eds., *Playing for Real: Hindu Role Models, Religion, and Gender*, pp. 117–40. Delhi: Oxford University Press, 2004.

Contents

Abbreviations, xv
A Note on Translation and Transliteration, xvii
Introduction: Sītā and Rādhā, Role Models for Women?, 3

PART I. Getting a Love Marriage Arranged

1. Falling in Love: Sītā in the Flower Garden and Rādhā in the Forest, 49
2. Arranging a Love Marriage: Sītā's "Self-Choice" and Rukmiṇī's Elopement, 95
3. Wedding Promises: Sītā's Wedding and Rādhā's Mock Wedding, 163

PART II. The Challenges of Married Life

4. In Good Days and Bad Days: Sītā and Rādhā Leave Purdah to Follow Their Men, 243
5. The Threat of the Other Woman: Free-Spirited Śūrpaṇakhā and Sophisticated Kubjā, 313
6. Sexual Harassment: Sītā Abducted and Rādhā Accosted at the Well, 379

Conclusion: Approaching Sītā, 497
References, 525
Index, 544

Abbreviations

Abbreviations of Sources

BDS	*Bhāsā Dasama Skandha* by Nanddās (Brajratnadās [1949] 1957)
BhP	*Bhāgavata Purāṇa* (Goswami and Śāstrī [1971] 1982)
BVP	*Brahma Vaivarta Purāṇa* (Śarmā 1970)
NP	*Nanddās Padāvalī* (Brajratnadās [1949] 1957)
RCM	*Rām Carit Mānas* by Tulsīdās (Poddār [1942] 1990)
RM	*Rukmiṇī Maṅgal* by Nanddās (Brajratnadās [1949] 1957)
RP	*Rās Pañcādhyāyī* by Harirām Vyās (Pauwels 1996b)
SS	*Sūr Sāgar* by Sūrdās (Ratnākar 1972–76)
TVR	Televised *Ramayan*, d. Ramanand Sagar (Mizokami and Bakhshi 1992)
TVK	Televised *Shri Krishna*, d. Ramanand Sagar
VR	*Vālmīki Rāmāyaṇa* (Goswāmī 1969)

Abbreviations of Dictionaries

BBSK	Dīndayāl Gupta and Premnarāyaṇ Taṇḍan, eds. 1974. (VS 2031). *Brajbhāṣā Sūrkoś.* Lucknow: Viśvavidyālay Hindī Prakāśan.

EIC Rajadhyaksha, Ashish, and Paul Willemen, eds. 1999. *Encyclopaedia of Indian Cinema*. Rev. ed. London: Oxford University Press.

HŚS Śyāmsundar Dās et al., eds. 1965–75. *Hindī śabdsāgar*. 11 vols. Benares: Nāgarīpracāriṇī Sabhā.

MW Monier Monier-Williams et al., eds. [1899] 1981. *Sanskrit-English Dictionary: Etymologically and Philologically Arranged with Special Reference to Cognate Indo-European Languages*. Rev. and enl. ed. Delhi: Munshiram Manoharlal.

OHED R.S. McGregor, ed. 1993. *The Oxford Hindi-English Dictionary*. Oxford: Oxford University Press.

SBBK Vidyānivās, Miśra, ed. 1985–90. *Sāhityik Brajbhāṣā koś*. 3 vols. Lucknow: Uttar Pradeś Hindī Saṃsthān.

TŚS Hargovind, Tivārī, ed. 1954. *Tulsī-śabdsāgar*. Allahabad: Hindustānī Academy.

A Note on Translation and Transliteration

No translation can do justice to the charming originals considered here, with their elaborate wordplay and playful rhyme and the intertextuality of a whole rich cultural tradition—let alone a translation by someone who is not a native speaker of English. I am woefully aware of my shortcomings. My translations are intended to be functional and to convey the points I want to make. Wherever possible I have given the original in the footnotes, so readers can taste the beauty of these wonderful works for themselves.

In the transliteration, I have followed the standard conventions for the languages concerned (as in *MW* and *OHED*), with the exception of consistently representing all the *anusvāras* as *ṃ*. I have transliterated the final -a for old Hindi, because it matters for the metrical sounding out of the text, but mostly left it out in modern Hindi, unless the language is deliberately archaizing. The Devanāgarī script does not have capitals, so I give lowercase throughout my quotations. I mostly follow the punctuation of the original. However, for the poetry, I consistently give a comma to indicate the caesura and a semicolon for the end of a line, rather than following the at times somewhat ad hoc punctuation of the printed sources.

It is always a difficult decision which words to give with full diacritics and which not. As it is conventional in film studies not to indicate diacritics, I use the conventional Anglicized spelling for titles of films, names of characters and actors, directors, and so on. However, consistent with the rest of the book, I give full diacritics when quoting songs or dialogue.

The Goddess as Role Model

Introduction

Sītā and Rādhā, Role Models for Women?

A Shadow over Sītā on the Wall?

The central question of this book is captured well by the scene depicted on the cover: a little girl in the courtyard of the village of Jitwarpur in Bihar, crying hard, with a wall painting in the background of the goddess Sītā garlanding Rāma as her husband. Is the little girl afraid of Sītā on the wall? Sītā was born in the Mithilā region, the same region as this girl. Sītā got to choose her husband, but not so her little compatriot There is a shadow cast over the painting, as there is over Sītā's life: everyone knows she suffered hardship: first abducted by a demon, whom she resisted, and then abandoned by her husband. What about the little girl? Is she crying because if even goddesses can fall on hard times, surely she will, too? Sītā is often upheld as a role model for women. What good is a role model like Sītā for women? That is a question one hears raised among young women of Indian origin living in the West, as well as in so-called progressive circles in India. Can one generalize that the average Indian woman shares those doubts?

Carolyn Brown Heinz, who took this picture in 1984, carried out anthropological research in the Mithilā area. In her discussions with local women, she came across some strong opinions on this topic. She asked women to comment on the claim that girls from Mithilā get to select their own husbands (seeking to redress a misperception of prevailing matriarchy in the region). One of her informants, Chhaya, wondered whether that claim might be because of Sītā's Svayaṃvara (Self-Choice), "but since her marriage wasn't a successful one, we have stopped that custom. Everything that Sita did, we have stopped doing" (Heinz 2000: 4). "Just how much choice did Sita have, anyway? Her parents had set up the conditions under which she could be won" (5). As it turned out, Chhaya's own marriage had been arranged, somewhat hastily, by her father, who had failed to notice that the household into which she married had significant problems. Continuing about Sītā, Chhaya remarked: "She didn't have a happy married life, she lost everything, she lived in the forest. But sometimes you are more happy in a forest than in a palace. Sita's father-in-law had four wives. All four lived in the palace. Do you think all four of them were happy? No, of course not" (6). Indeed, Chhaya would know, because her own father-in-law had brought his mistress into the house, which made Chhaya's life miserable. "Sita, even living in the forest, she knew that my husband is here, too. He has not taken any other wife. And I think because of that, Sita had a lot of happiness" (7). "But then it was the duty of the king that separated them. . . . It was Rama's job as king that required they live separate. . . . Just like my husband, it's the duty that separates us" (8). Chhaya's husband was a teacher in a college in a different town and only could come home on occasional weekends. Back to Sītā, Chhaya said: "This poor girl, she didn't do anything wrong. Even when she went to Lanka. She's so pure, she didn't go to Ravan no matter what he did to her. She didn't go. Didn't allow him to touch her body. So strong she was in character! . . . I tell you, Sita is *not* a model. But what was her fault? Why *shouldn't* I take her as a model? . . . I am telling you, Mithila seems to be scared of Sita" (8).

Admired at the same time as maligned. Blameless yet blamed. Loved and feared. There is a real ambivalence in this reflection on whether Sītā is or is not a good model for women. Heinz, in her discussion of the personal production of meaning, illustrates with this example how a woman telling her life story may use Sītā's myth to interpret her own life and, conversely, use her own life experience to interpret Sītā's story. Heinz perceptively points out that the situation of real Indian women trying to live up to the model of an ideal woman has its counterpart in some versions of the myth, where Sītā produces a body double, or *chāyā* (shadow), who undergoes the abduction and suffering while the real (that is, the ideal) Sītā remains untainted. Very apt indeed that Heinz gave the woman narrating Sītā's story as her own the pseudonym Chhaya! Could Chhaya be voicing what many of her sisters feel: a strong ambivalence about Sītā as role model for women?

Thus, we could imagine that the girl in the picture is crying because of the shadow hanging over her head, that her life will be a shadow version of Sītā's unhappy story. But maybe not. The wall painting of Sītā garlanding Rāma is considered auspicious. It was purposely painted to decorate the courtyard for a wedding.[1] Still, the place where the wedding night will take place, the part of the house known as *kohbar ghar*, is usually decorated at the entrance with romantic images of another divine pair, Rādhā and Krishna.[2] By contrast to the virtuous, dharma-centered pair of Sītā and Rāma, the erotic, *prema*-centered pair Rādhā and Krishna are not visible in the picture, but they surely are depicted somewhere nearby. Does Rādhā, invisible here, make for an alternative role model for the women of Mithilā? A happier one, of love in fulfillment?

Why, then, is this girl crying? Heinz remembers it was because of her big dark sunglasses, which frightened the girl. Should we extend the metaphor and say that it is not the role model that is the problem but the "glasses," the darkening lens through which the outsider is looking in, the Westernized interpretative position of the observer? Is it only when anthropologists prod that Indian women express ambivalence or burst into tears? Is it only in the books of foreign academics that Sītā as role model becomes problematic? This book will let the most influential texts of the tradition speak for themselves, as it sets out to discover how Sītā functions as a role model for women in contrast to Rādhā.

Mythological Role Models for Love

This book fits within the larger frame of studies that seek to understand the position of women in Hinduism. There has been increasing interest in this field because of the crucial role women play in influencing population dynamics, in setting consumer patterns, and as a vote bank in the democratic process. Women are important agents in these fields; thus we need to understand what they think. How do they make their decisions? What are their ideals and ideologies? Here religion comes in.

The interface of the religious and political has attracted quite a bit of scholarly attention lately because of the political support of Hindu women for the religious nationalist parties in power in the 1990s. This has inspired

1. For photos of the wedding, see Heinz's website about Mithila, www.csuchico.edu/anth/mithila/kanyadan2.htm.

2. For illustrations of the Rajnagar Palace decorated for a royal wedding in 1919, see Heinz 2006: 12-4, ills. 5–7.

several studies on women and Hindu nationalism (e.g., Bhasin, Menon, and Khan 1994, Sarkar and Butalia 1995, Sarkar 2001, Bacchetta 2004, Banerjee 2005).

This book, by contrast, is less about the role religion plays in women's political agency than about their decisions regarding their personal day-to-day life, particularly in the way they cope with issues of love. As one astute observer of popular culture has put it: "Love and romance . . . is a compelling locus to examine womanhood: how does romantic love consitute women? Does this reveal change over time? Discourses on love, romance, sexuality, and the family are sites where women's subjectivity is located, shaping how they are imagined" (Virdi 2003: 126). This book will focus on the mythical heroines who are held up as ideals and influence young women in their partner choices, their matrimonial decisions, and the ways they cope with difficulties and challenges to their marriage and the everyday indignities of unwanted sexual attention.

At this point we should pause to reflect that the term "love" is an ambiguous one. While the emotion may be said to be universal, it is culturally specific in its construction. There is a multiplicity of South Asian codes of love, each with its own history (see Orsini 2006: 1–39 for an overview; for theoretical background see John and Nair 1998). This book engages simultaneously with epic, devotional, and contemporary "lovescapes."[3] Thus, we should be aware that notions of "love," "devotion," "wifehood," "marriage," and "womanhood" are to be problematized as culturally specific categories in a South Asian context, as well as in specific periods in history.

The way women cope with love is not a frivolous topic. It is obviously one of general human interest, but it also can be seen as symptomatic for the discourse of the conflict between modernity and tradition. While in a certain sense a false dichotomy (Kazmi 1999), in common parlance the two are often sharply distinguished. Modernity is often equated with individualism; tradition is seen as privileging the community. Recognition of individual free

3. The epic construct of love may be said to be twofold: (1) sexual liaisons (usually stressing the problematic of the ensuing offspring), and (2) marital bonds in the context of political alliances. However, speaking about "epic love" is itself problematic and complex, as it stretches over a long period, reflecting different sociopolitical constructs, including more or less patriarchal ones and influence from stylized *kāvya* (poetics) conventions of Sanskritic literature. The devotional construct of love is characterized by a conflation of human and divine love, often from a "female" point of view, constantly shifting focus between devotion for husband and for god (or husband-as-god). Key here is an all-consuming passion that defies societal normativity (dharma). At some points, this code seems to be influenced by the Perso-Arab one. Finally, contemporary notions of love may be inspired by all the traditional ones (including the Perso-Arab one), as well as a transnational (or "Western") discourse, which is often associated with the new consumerist middle class (Dwyer 2000).

choice is often contrasted with pride in community and privileging the communal good. This conflict is epitomized in the competing ideals of the love marriage, a union of two autonomous individuals, and the traditional arranged marriage, more a family affair. How women cope with love is indicative of how they position themselves on a scale of modern and traditional. Choosing a love marriage may be seen as a marker of modernity. The way women navigate between these ideals can be taken as a barometer of the inroads of Westernization on a traditional culture.

Often scholars are inclined to discuss the position of women in Hinduism by studying women's legislation in modern India or delving into the ancient so-called Law Books (*Dharmaśāstra*), which lay out the rules of what women should and should not do, what their rights and responsibilities are in given situations. However, one wonders what the currency of theoretical tracts is in actual situations in women's lives. One could well argue that the way prescripts, whether legal or religious, make most impact on the popular imagination is not through dry prescriptions but through the popular stories of Hindu mythology. Many of the heroines of those stories set illustrious examples for a woman's duty (*strī-dharma*). Few women will actually quote the *Dharmaśāstra* with regard to why they act the way they do, but many will cite inspiration from mythological examples. To understand the motivations of Indian women, it may be fruitful to focus on these mythological role models.

Surprisingly few studies have been done on role models for Hindu women.[4] This book is an attempt to help fill that lacuna. Its main goal is to deepen our understanding of the mythological role models that mark the moral landscape young Hindu women have to navigate.

One can say that among the most influential models for Indian women are the Hindu goddesses. Recently, some have turned their attention to the relationship between goddess worship and the position of women (King 1997, Chitgopekar 2002, Sharma 2005). Intuitively, one might surmise that a religion that worships a feminine divine must have some positive implications for women's position in society. However, such an assumption has been problematized in a recent collection of articles aptly entitled *Is the Goddess a Feminist?* (Hiltebeitel and Erndl 2000).[5] That collection (as do the other books

4. A notable exception is a recent work on role models in general (Hirst and Thomas 2004) that includes some articles (a.o. my own) focusing on role models for women. The term "role model" seems not to have been heavily theorized (1–7). Madhu Kishwar also uses it in a recent essay (2003).

5. An earlier variant of this title is Rajeswari Sunder Rajan, "Is the Hindu Goddess a Feminist?" *Economic and Political Weekly*, October 31, 1998, reprinted in Rajan 2004.

already mentioned) explores the issue by turning to the example of the Great Goddess, or Mahādevī. A spate of recent scholarship likewise has focused on the powerful and independent goddesses Durgā and Kālī (Caldwell 1999, Pintchman 2001, Rodrigues 2003). As it turns out, it is by no means clear that goddess worship helps further the position in society of flesh-and-blood women. Even when the goddess is evoked as proof of women's strength, this may be in the service of an ultimate patriarchal goal (Rajan 2004). A related question, of interest here, is whether the Great Goddess is a source of inspiration for women's lives. Again, this is not self-evident. She actually seems not to be a strong role model for women (see Humes 1997).

The contribution of this book is to turn our attention instead toward the more or less great goddesses, who seem to inhabit the domain halfway between women of flesh and blood and the Great Goddess herself. These female figures unquestionably serve as role models for human females, even if the ideal they exemplify is recognized as not always attainable.

Is Sītā a Feminist?

Sītā, the faithful consort of the Hindu god Rāma and heroine of the *Rāmāyaṇa,* undoubtedly functions prominently in the psychology of young Indian women (see, e.g., Kakar 1981: 218; for the diaspora, see Pandurang 2003: 92). As they cope with their daily life and its challenges, women frequently refer to Sītā as a role model.

It is much debated whether that is a good or bad thing. Some feminists strongly believe the latter and consider long-suffering and ever-sacrificing Sītā a restrictive role model that is harmful for women. In February 1988, two well-known Indian feminists, Kamla Bhasin and Ritu Menon, wrote with reference to the televised *Rāmāyaṇa:*

> Eternal mythologies like the Ramayan are revived and popularized via state controlled media at the mass "entertainment" level. . . . With Sita as our ideal, can sati [widow burning] be far behind? It is this overarching ideology of male superiority and female dispensability that . . . accepts the silent violence against women that rages in practically every home across the country. (Bhasin and Menon 1988: 13)

They were writing in the wake of a controversy over a young Rajasthani woman who became *satī,* that is, she was burned on the funeral pyre of her husband. The emotional intensity of the moment may explain the strong wording, but one also hears such evaluations at other times.[6] There is even the term "doormat Sītā" (Derné 2000: 140). Not only foreigners or the Westernized intelligentsia have voiced protest against the Sītā model; a good example of a broader outcry is a letter written by one of the ordinary women readers of an influential magazine for women, *Manushi,* entitled "No More Sītās": "Now we must refuse to be Sitas. By becoming a Sita and submitting to the fire ordeal, woman loses her identity. This fire ordeal is imposed on women today in every city, every home." (translated from Hindi in Kishwar and Vanita 1984: 299)

On the other hand, there are other voices, too. Some stress the opposite and see a self-confident, gracious Sītā as an empowering and inspiring example for women. Interestingly, the founder-editor of *Manushi,* Madhu Kishwar, has been at the forefront of such a more positive evaluation in the past decade. She wrote in 1997:

> My interviews indicate that Indian women are not endorsing female slavery when they mention Sita as their ideal. Sita is not perceived as being a mindless creature who meekly suffers maltreatment at the hands of her husband without complaining. Nor does accepting Sita as an ideal mean endorsing a husband's right to behave unreasonably and a wife's duty to bear insults graciously. She is seen as a person whose sense of dharma is superior to and more awe inspiring than that of Ram—someone who puts even maryada purushottam Ram—the most perfect of men—to shame. (Kishwar 1997: 24)

Kishwar is not alone in her positive evaluation. Multiple articles echo her sentiments.[7] Some point out that the dichotomy between a "traditional" Sītā and a "modern" liberated woman is a false one. A good illustration comes from a radio series intended for high school students in the United States:

> Indian women . . . don't need many lessons from western feminists. The examples and the message of true equality, of a genuine realization of self, are contained deep within India's own cultural

6. Some of the more raw extreme emotional assessments are found on the Internet; see, for example, Sita Agarwal's *Genocide of Hindu Women,* in particular chap. 7, www.geocities.com/realitywithbite/hindu.htm

7. A random example is "Sita—The Silent Power of Suffering and Sacrifice," by Nitin Kumar, which was the article of the month in March 2005 on the website www.exoticindiaart.com/. And projects that are intended to empower women have been named after Sita, e.g. the SITA project (Studies in Information Technology Applications) of Prita Chathoth and Kamalni and Krishna Sane, which began in 1999 (Molina 2002). And there are websites like sitagita.com, which promotes itself as a website for the New Age Indian woman, with a hip blend of tradition and modernity, offering conservative advice for women within a discourse of equality.

> traditions. In that sense, we ask Sita, the heroine of the epic, The Ramayana, to speak, to tell her side of the story, a story that most women know instinctively but have suppressed for too long, a story that has been lost from sight while men retold the story from their perspective.[8]

In turn, such positive interpretations have been problematized as going too far in condemning the insensitive feminist dismissal of Sītā (see Hess 1999: 26). "In appreciating the 'weapons of the weak' we should be careful not to valorize institutionalized weakness. In stepping back from a certain aggressive feminist mode that seems to attack women for not fitting some prescribed 'feminist' model, we shouldn't step right back into the backlash" (27).The issue begs for more scholarly attention.

Who is right? Is Sītā as role model conducive to the oppression of women or to their empowerment? Is Sītā a feminist or an antifeminist? Does it depend on what you call oppressive and what empowering? Is it all in the eye of the beholder? Is this a matter of "Westernized" feminist views against "traditionalist" reactionary ones, as the quotation from the radio series suggests? In the case of Madhu Kishwar, the matter is complicated by the fact that she has declared herself emphatically not a feminist (Kishwar 1990), and she has evolved from something close to "anti" to "pro" Sītā over the past couple of decades.[9] Is she a trendsetter or exemplary of a trend that seeks to rehabilitate Sītā? Should we see this evolution in the context of the conservative discourse of Hindutva, or Hindu nationalism, which is gaining ground in the public sphere?

But are we asking the right questions? Maybe these statements are not contradictory at all. Might different people have different Sītās in mind? Might the Sītā of the television series differ substantially from the Sītā who lives in the hearts of ordinary people? Might the question we should ask be who is Sītā to whom? And when in her story is Sītā empowering, when not?

First, whether one considers Sītā as a negative or positive role model seems to be closely connected with the particular aspect of her story one has in mind. Many feminist-oriented writers have concentrated on Sītā's victimiza-

8. This was part of a ten-part, one-hour radio series *Passages to India* on IBA radio, intended for use in U.S. high schools and colleges, produced in 1991 by Julian Crandall Hollick, in cooperation with Rana Behal, Raja Chatterjee, and Rajasekaran, www.ibaradio.org/India/passages/passages8.htm.

9. For a more extensive assessment of Kishwar's position on Sītā and more in general on the use of Hindu traditional images for the women's movement, see Robinson 1999: 161–7 and 193–7. See also Hess 1999: 25–6. I come back to a more nuanced view of Sītā in the women's movement in the conclusion.

tion: first the fire ordeal (Agniparīkṣā) she has to go through to prove her chastity, and eventually her abandonment notwithstanding the favorable outcome of the ordeal. The fire ordeal is indeed a powerful scene, and the image of Sītā engulfed with flames suffuses popular culture. However, feminists are hardly the first to question the justice of putting Sītā through the test; within the tradition itself there have been voices that object to Sītā's treatment, as differing interpretations in different versions of the story show (Hess 1999). It can even be argued that the scene has a positive effect and that women will rally behind those whose chastity is falsely questioned.[10]

Important as the fire ordeal scene may be, there are other powerful moments in the Sītā myth that have been relatively neglected by scholars. Arguably more relevant in ordinary women's day-to-day life are the stories of Sītā's early life: her falling in love as a young girl, her wedding, and her early married life, where she is faced with some challenges like those women more ordinarily encounter. It is on these episodes from Sītā's early life, up to and including her abduction, that this book will focus. Can Sītā be seen here to be an empowering role model?

Second, who is Sītā to whom? As the debate rages, it becomes woefully apparent how remarkably few academic studies there are about her.[11] It seems that hardly anyone has stopped to study just who Sītā is. Everyone refers to the remarkable impact of the *Ramayan* television series, but there are few studies that analyze how it differs from other versions of the story, and hardly anyone focuses on the portrayal of Sītā (the one exception is Barua 1996). How traditional is Sītā as she appears on television? Or how modern and new? There is

10. Leigh Minturn (1993: 217–9) in her work with Khalapur Rajputs tells of the case of a woman to whom she meaningfully gives the pseudonym "Sita." This poor and low-status (second) wife, falsely accused of being immoral by her husband and beaten, escaped to her parental village, thus "proving" her chastity (if she had indeed had a premarital affair, her father would not have accepted her back). She managed to rally the village's opinion on her side and extract a public apology from her husband. Minturn interprets this incident in the context of the Sītā story, which she considers to provide a role model for the women she studies (9).

11. Sītā has not yet been the topic of an academic monograph, but there are a few important articles. Sally Sutherland Goldman has contributed extensively, with discussion of Sītā in *Vālmīki Rāmāyaṇa* and a contrastive study of Sītā and Draupadī (1989). A recent volume with articles on several Hindu goddesses (Hawley and Wulff 1996) does not feature Sītā at all, though she is featured in the earlier volume on a similar theme (Hawley and Wulff 1982). In 1998, a "Sītā symposium" was held at Columbia University, but only some of the papers were published (Lutgendorf 1999, Hess 1999, Murphy and Sippy 2000, Herman 2000). Still, Sītā has benefited from some of the recent surge in *Rāmāyaṇa* studies: Paula Richman (1991 and 2001) and Mandakranta Bose (2003 and 2004) have each edited volumes on the diversity of the *Rāmāyaṇa* tradition, containing several articles articles touching on Sītā. There is an intense interest in "alternative" Sītās, especially women's folk songs that tell the *Rāmāyaṇa* story from her perspective. This trend is also prevalent in more popular articles in the Indian magazine for women *Manushi*.

an urgent need for a nuanced reading of the messages sent by mass media versions of Sītā. This book is an attempt not to settle the debate but to contribute to a more nuanced understanding of who Sītā is and how she has been understood over time.

The intent of this book is not to join the voices that accuse or defend Sītā. There is no point in dragging Sītā into a feminist court and judging her by alien standards—or in defending her against those norms. She has already had to face more than her fair share of inquiry about her character within the story. She has already been sadly misunderstood many times over. She deserves to be known better. The premise of the book is to make available her voice, to stop and listen to what she has to say, and how she has been allowed to say it, differently in different contexts.

The question asked here then is not simply "is Sītā pro- or antifeminist?" Instead, we will explore *where* Sītā's example may be oppressive or empowering for women. Do the early parts of Sītā's life confirm the negative impression one gets from the fire ordeal? Further, how conservative is the Sītā in the normative Sanskrit text compared to, say, the Sītā of the devotional literature? What happens when Sītā is screened on television?

Chaste Wife or Sensuous Lover: Sītā and Rādhā as Contrastive Role Models

Sītā is not the only role model available to Hindu women. She is best understood in a context of competing messages. The Sītā model is all too often singled out on its own, as if it were the only one present within the Hindu tradition. This may be a case of amnesia: in response to a colonial critique of the Hindu tradition as "vulgar" or "debauched," models perceived to be vulnerable to such critique are suppressed, and "uplifting" models are exalted to the point of obliterating the former. When the pendulum swings back, the older tradition is forgotten and the alternative is instead associated with the West. A case in point is Mira Nair's 2001 movie *Monsoon Wedding*, where the friends of the bride-to-be cynically make fun of the "Sītā-Sāvitrī look," knowing that she is having a premarital affair with a married man. The movie, itself a celebration of hybrid culture, self-consciously seeks to expose some taboos. It uses sexuality to configure modernity, setting up the affair of the bride as modern and at the same time criticizing the traditional example of Sītā as hopelessly old-fashioned—or maybe a hollow subterfuge to trick men who might be so naïve as to believe women can be that way. Such an attitude seems too facile: one does not need to turn to the West for celebrations of women's desires: there are alternative role models within the Hindu tradition itself.

To do full justice to Sītā, we have to study such contrasting models. There are several alternatives,[12] but this book features the consort of Krishna, Vishnu's other avatar. Krishna is as playful as Rāma is serious. He is known for his mischief in breaking the laws of conventional morality (dharma) in the name of love. According to the myth, Krishna spent his youth incognito in the idyllic environs of a cowherding village in Braj, an area between Delhi and Agra. He is famous for his pranks and for his dalliances with the local village belles, the Gopīs, who were milkmaids or cowherdesses. His favorite was Rādhā, and she became a goddess in her own right.

In order to understand Sītā better, it is instructive to compare her with Rādhā. If Sītā is Rāma's wife, Rādhā is Krishna's lover. If Sītā is chastity incarnate (see Rao 2004 on how far this concept can[not] be stretched), Rādhā is sensuality incarnate. She is Krishna's paramour, and in most interpretations, their relationship is a clandestine one. Whereas Sītā is properly married and Rāma's own (*svakīyā*), Rādhā is often understood to be married to another (*parakīyā*), though this is a hotly debated issue (De 1961: 348–51). If the mutual love of Rāma and Sītā is an example of happy monogamy, Rādhā's relationship with Krishna is famously fraught with the issue of his unfaithfulness and her jealousy of his other lovers and wives. If Sītā is a queen, aware of her social responsibilities, Rādhā is exclusively focused on her romantic relationship with her lover. Thus we have two opposite role models. Hindu women then have to navigate between ideals from both ends of the moral universe: the loyal, chaste wife and the adulterous lover.

Still, Sītā and Rādhā have something in common, too. Many events from Rādhā's story can be compared to those in Sītā's. Rādhā, too, falls in love as a young girl. In most versions, she does not get to marry Krishna, but in some, they exchange secret wedding vows. Rādhā's relationship with Krishna is fraught with difficulties, but she, too, stands by her beloved even at the cost of personal hardship. She faces similar challenges including the threat of the "other woman." Her story makes for a good reflection on jealousy, as Krishna is frequently involved with other women, giving Rādhā plenty of occasions to cope with that.

12. Sītā has already been contrasted with Draupadī, the heroine of the other great epic, the *Mahābhārata* (Sutherland 1989). Another potentially fruitful comparison would be with Pārvatī, Śiva's consort, also seen as a devoted wife, but maybe perceived to be less "meek" than Sītā.

In Rādhā and the Gopīs of Braj, we have a set of heroines who seem to challenge the norms that Sītā's example sets. Their potential as role models for women is ambiguous;[13] after all, the divinity of their lovers is central, and many sources hasten to specify that this is not to be read as license for ordinary women to engage in such norm-breaking behavior.[14] Yet they are unquestionably celebrated by men and women alike for their unwavering love for Krishna. The very fact that Krishna is not their husband and hence they have to risk their social security for their love is seen as proof of the strength of that love.

I hasten to specify that I do not seek to retrieve a lost premodern Indian model of free love (John and Nair 1998: 11–4). Like Sītā, Rādhā means and has meant many things to different people; it is too facile to cast her in the role of "liberated lover."[15] As for Sītā, I will explore how she appears over time, taking care to read the different portrayals in their historical contexts. This project aims to understand the production of subjectivity with regard to love and romance in popular culture in India. I look at the discursive and historical processes that position subjects and produce experiences, focusing on these two influential goddesses. This analysis leads to a deeper understanding of the cultural tradition on whose basis modern attitudes toward women are derived, prescribed, and enforced.

We should not forget, in focusing on Sītā and Rādha as role models for women, that they are two much-adored and beloved goddesses, venerated by

13. Minturn (1993: 212–6) also describes a counter-case of "the shameless daughter," to whom she gives the pseudonym "Radha"—a young, educated, wealthy woman who had an affair and became pregnant. This case may well illustrate that Rādhā is perceived to be a counter-model (at least in Minturn's eyes).

14. Even in the classical version of the story, *Bhāgavata Purāṇa* (10.29–33), the role model value of the characters is questionable. The narrator, the sage Śuka, warns King Parīkṣit that Krishna's behavior is not something to be imitated by mere mortals (*naitat samācarej jātu manasāpi hyanīśvaraḥ, vinaśyatyācaran mauḍhyād yathā rudro 'bdhijaṃ viṣam; BhP* 10.33.31). It seems obvious that the same is true for the Gopīs' actions.

15. Rādhā and the Gopīs have been the subject of much scholarship. On Rādhā in Tantra, see Dimock 1966 and McDaniel 2000. On Rādhā in the Bengali classic *Gītagovinda,* see Siegel 1978 and Miller 1977. On Rādhā in *Brahma Vaivarta Purāṇa,* see Brown 1974, and in Sanskrit theological drama, see Wulff 1984. For Rādhā's South Indian origins in Āḻvār poetry as Piṉṉai, see Hardy 1983 and several articles by Hudson (Hawley 2002). An important volume that took Rādhā as the main focus of the study of Hindu goddesses is *The Divine Consort: Rādhā and the Goddesses of India* (Hawley and Wulff 1982). As is the case for Sītā, Rādhā's place is much reduced in the follow-up volume by the same editors, where she has disappeared from the title; *Devī: Goddesses of India* (Hawley and Wulff 1996). Still, sectarian interests, in particular ISKCON, keep fueling publications on Rādhā; the *Journal of Vaishnava Studies* has devoted two special issues to her: 8.2 (spring 2000) and 10.1 (fall 2001). Rādhā also is featured in studies of Braj devotional literature (e.g., Haberman 1987 and 2003; Pauwels 1996b). For a fascinating interpretation of the historical evolution of Rādhā in a Bengali social context, see Sumanta Banerjee 1993. Donna Wulff has written on Rādhā as an empowering role model for women in Bengal (Wulff 1985, 1997).

millions of Hindus: they are Śrī Sītā Devī and Śrī Rādhikā Rāṇī to their loving followers. First and foremost, they are role models for all their devotees, women and men alike, in their ardent devotion to God. We all should emulate their examples and shape our attitude toward God in their mold. Numerous theological works have been written on that aspect.[16]

However, my focus here is limited to how Sītā and Rādhā function as role models for women in day-to-day life. There is no doubt that they have a firm hold on the popular imagination. Their stories are lovingly recounted over and over again, in learned Sanskrit versions and popular bedtime stories alike. Many of these stories focus on their relationships with their divine partners: how they first met the beloved, how they fell in love, and how the courtship evolved; the trials and travails they shared with their beloved, the threats to their relationships, and the ways these got resolved (or remained simmering in the background), crises big and small—in short, how they coped with love. At once, they are larger than life and very much part of the same cycle of life and loving of ordinary Hindu women, or all women for that matter. There are surely lessons to be learned from their examples. If we want to understand how Indian women cope with love, it will be illuminating to focus on the myths of Sītā and Rādhā and how they have evolved over time.

Liberation Theology for Hindu Women?

Notwithstanding their antithetical roles, both heroines function within the strand of Hinduism called bhakti, or devotional Hinduism. Indeed, their consorts Rāma and Krishna are firmly ensconced within the bhakti tradition, so the goddesses, too, are recipients of worship within that tradition. The portrayal of Sītā in bhakti-inspired texts may differ substantially from that in the much older classical Sanskrit text, the *Vālmīki Rāmāyaṇa*. The same holds true for Rādhā. Will that make them more liberating as role models for women?

Often the theology of bhakti is said to bring with it a critical approach to strict hierarchical and patriarchal social relations. Bhakti, then, may potentially be liberating for women (e.g., Lele 1981: 1–15; Vasudevan 2000: 152–3). The main reason for this understanding is that the ideology of bhakti advocates a direct relationship between worshiper and deity, without the intermediary of a Brahmin priest. This allows women to engage in acts of worship that are functionally equivalent to those of men (Robinson 1985: 195–9). Bhakti tends

16. One accessible study of this aspect as exemplified by the Gauḍīya tradition is Haberman 1988.

also to privilege vernaculars over Sanskrit, which makes it more accessible to women. Moreover, one can argue that bhakti, in privileging love over ritual, undermines dharma, which entails a possibility of critiquing its straitjacket hold over women. Indeed, the hagiographical stories of the life of women devotees often feature a rejection of the woman's duty as a devoted wife (*pativratā*) in favor of her calling to God. Thus bhakti can be said to open alternative role models.[17] Finally, bhakti that includes worship of a divine consort has been seen as inherently more conducive to a favorable view of women (Young 1996: 245–50). This positive evaluation is even echoed in the 1975 report from the United Nations for International Women's Year, *Towards Equality*, which was produced by the Committee on the Status of Women in India; it points out that bhakti "brought great solace to women and presented an alternative way of life" (Guha 1975: 43). Will Sītā and Rādhā in bhakti texts be more empowering for women than in other interpretations?

Maybe not. The assessment of bhakti as liberating is not undisputed. Some have blamed bhakti for providing religious sanction for a hierarchical and patriarchal status quo. They see an elite attempt of upper-caste males to co-opt women and condemn bhakti as inculcating obedience, which is disabling in the face of an oppressor (see Guha 1992: 47–60). A more nuanced view splits bhakti up in two camps: *saguṇa* bhakti (worship of God with attributes, especially as one of the avatars of Viṣṇu), which is perceived to be elitist, and *nirguṇa* bhakti (worship of God without attributes, more abstract), which is perceived to be egalitarian (David Lorenzen 1995: 1–32). Devotion for goddesses falls under the former category, so in this case, too, one might not be too optimistic about how Sītā and Rādhā will function as role models for women.

One of the questions addressed in this book is how far bhakti texts can be said to send more or less empowering messages to women in retellings of the Sītā and Rādhā stories. To that end, we will compare vernacular devotional versions of Sītā and Rādhā with their Sanskrit equivalents. Is bhakti a "liberation theology" when applied to women? How about modern media versions?

Sītā and Rādhā on the Small Screen

In 1987, every Sunday morning a country of nearly a billion people came to a virtual standstill, with people congregating around television sets in order not

17. For an ethnographic description of women living out their lives in the footsteps of the Krishna devotee Mīrā, see Martin-Kershaw 1995.

to miss their favorite show: the televised *Ramayan* (TVR), directed by Hindi film director Ramanand Sagar. For a whole nation, for one hour, time was suspended for the virtual timelessness of the epic world. Or was it? How "updated" was this version of the epic? Some have called the series "the soap of the gods," somewhat denigratingly identifying it as a lowbrow modern entertainment version for "the masses." On the other hand, such qualifications came from an elite, deemed Westernized and soon to be scared out of its wits by a resurgence of tradition in the public sphere. Evaluations of the show are cast in terms of tradition and modernity. What is the real identity of these onscreen gods and goddesses? How modern or traditional are they really? And why should we care?

We should care because of the enormous impact of the televised *Ramayan*, which was not limited to the late eighties. In its video and DVD avatar, it is still a best seller, often viewed and reviewed, not only in India but in the whole of South Asia, beyond national and religious borders, as well as by Indians living in Europe and the United States. Furthermore, the trend continued, and in 1988–90 a television series based on the other epic, *Mahabharat,* was even more successful (see Mitra 1993, Majumder 1996). Sagar directed another series, *Shri Krishna* (TVK), on the life of the God Krishna. Though the media landscape had changed a lot since *Ramayan* (see Gokulsingh 2004: 7–26 for an overview) and viewers had much more choice, this series was also a great success. The list does not stop there. Since 2004, Star TV has been broadcasting an abridged version of the original television series, *Sanskshipt Ramayan,* which is doing extremely well (Sternfeld 2005: 203). This shows that its appeal is not limited to the late eighties. Clearly, "soft-soaping" mythology is a trend to stay, and something worth paying attention to. This is especially the case because of the contemporary surge in the influence of Hindutva roughly at the same time, which is often said to be related to the popularity of the *Ramayan* series (Jaffrelot 1996: 388–92, Rajagopal 2001).

Given its popularity (for viewership figures, see Rajagopal 2001: 326 n. 48), it is obvious that the televised Rāmāyaṇa hit a nerve and reflected contemporary ideals.[18] It is significant that most of the "heavy viewers" of the series were women (Rajagopal 2001: 330 n. 72). Thus, it seems reasonable to assume that the message of the series was targeted to some extent toward them, so looking at the televised Sītā as a role model will be rewarding. In the

18. For a brilliant general evaluation of the television series, situating it in its performative context, as well as the media in general, see Lutgendorf 1995.

case of *Shri Krishna* too, its immense popularity proves that Sagar had his finger right on the pulse of what the audience wished to see.

Amazingly, notwithstanding their abiding popularity, very little serious research has been done on these series. While the success of the televised *Ramayan* has sparked academic interest, scholars' concern has been to bring to the public's attention a multiplicity of *Rāmāyaṇa* traditions, paradoxically deflecting attention from the televised version. The pathbreaking studies by Richman (1991) and Thiel-Horstmann (1991) have between them only one article that looks seriously at the televised series (Dalmia-Lüderitz 1991). The only book-length study focusing on the phenomenon of Indian television series, foregrounding the mythological ones (Mankekar 1999), has not all that much to say about the series itself, as it is mainly a reception study. Basically, in terms of scholarly literature attempting to understand the televised *Ramayan* itself, there are only Philip Lutgendorf's two insightful articles (1990, 1995).[19] The situation is yet worse for *Shri Krishna*, which has attracted hardly any scholarly attention.

Twenty years since religion burst onto the small screen, it is time to pay some sustained attention to these series and the trend they set. *Ramayan* deserves special analysis, because of the *Rāmāyaṇa*'s unchallenged importance in providing moral guidance, the televised *Shri Krishna* makes a good comparison. Both are useful as we seek to understand the messages sent to women by the example of Sītā and Rādhā. How have Sītā and Rādhā been "screened" for popular consumption? Are these role models mutually contradictory?

We should keep in mind that the epics were broadcast in the context of soap series, which partook in current debates about such "modern" issues as the advantages and disadvantages of traditional "arranged marriages" and "joint-family living." The epics also shared the screen with news items featuring issues of dowry and "bride burning." All this constitutes the semantic universe in which the televised epics partake. What then do Sītā and Rādhā mean in a rapidly changing social context where the traditional ideals of arranged marriage, unconditional loyalty of wife to husband, and joint family are competing with modern concepts of love marriage, divorce, and nuclear families? Intuitively, we might suppose that these "modern" media represent more "modern" versions of the story and role models that are more "progressive." But is that really the case? This question will hover in the background of the book, and I will deal explicitly with it in the conclusions.

19. More recently there is also an insightful essay by Uma Chakravarti (2005).

Multiforms of Sītā and Rādhā on the Big Screen

The domain where Sītā and Rādhā function does not remain limited to religion and mythology per se. They are ubiquitous in popular Hindi films. Countless film heroines bear their names or variants thereof. These heroines encounter situations similar to those related in the epics, and seem to behave more or less consistently with the epic stories' norms. We could say that we constantly encounter multiforms of the goddesses in popular film. What happens when Sītā and Rādhā spill over into the domain of popular culture?

It is commonplace to relate the prevalence of references to Hindu mythology in popular Hindi movies to the fact that the earliest Indian films were mythological (e.g., Chopra 2005). Their endurance beyond the genre of the mythological is seen as a bit of an anachronism. Some have argued, somewhat cynically, that filmmakers include such references in order to expand viewership in rural areas by bringing those audiences something familiar they can relate to (Derné 1995b: 197).

What do filmmakers themselves have to say on the topic? Raj Khosla, with reference to *Do raste* and *Mera gaon mera desh,* offered the reflection that the epics are "in our blood" and hence unavoidably color his films (Raj Khosla, in Pfleiderer and Lutze 1985: 40). Interestingly, he also points out that he feels the scenarios of the gods are reenacted in his own life, from his spying while girls take their bath in the river to veneration for the eldest brother in the family (39–40). And he indicates that this is not restricted to his own experience: "It is there . . . all over India, in every home" (40). Since the mythological references are such a mainstay of the mix of ingredients of the popular movie, the audience must feel similarly positive about the relevance of such mythological allusions. Indeed, some have articulated as much in interviews (villager interviewees as analyzed in Pfleiderer and Lutze 1985: 69).

Thus, mythological references are worth paying attention to, yet few scholars have done so. Whatever little analysis has been done has tended to be from a psychoanalytical perspective (O'Flaherty 1980, Kakar 1989). Those analyses open up interesting and stimulating ways of thinking about movies, but they may also be perceived as reductionist. Myths tend to be read as universals of human experience, or at least of South Asian experience, which brings a certain timelessness to the movies thus analyzed.

One reason scholars of religion have not been interested may be that these borrowings are regarded as trivial appropriations of the tradition. Hindi films are not seen as a serious source of change of religion (Derné 1995b: 191), and the references are considered "condensed and inexplicit" (212). This is understood to be the case because of censorship, as well as the commercial pressure to appeal to a broad and diverse audience without offending anyone's feelings (191).

It is true that the mythological equivalents of the characters are often flagged in a condensed and stereotypical way. The name Raghuvīra or another epithet of Rāma will set up the audience to expect an obedient son who is ready to place his duty before his personal desires. A scene of a man spying on women bathing or breaking women's pots as they return from the well often signals we are dealing with a Krishna type, often named Birju or another epithet of Krishna. However, it is well worth our while to pay serious attention to what happens to these characters and how they deal with the circumstances they encounter that recall the epics. It is not just that mythological themes are evoked in popular movies; they are appropriated creatively.

One reason anthropologists and social scientists are not paying attention to the epic references in films may be that viewers deny that movie characters are regarded as role models. Often they are regarded to be "mere" entertainment of a "degrading" nature, and interviewees express a sense of guilt about watching them (Derné 1995b, 207–8). Though this may have changed in more recent years, there certainly is a sense that Hindi films are not to be taken seriously; they are mere entertainment. Sometimes it is jokingly said, "You have to leave your brain at home when going out for a Hindi movie." The presumption is that viewers can pick their brains back up unchanged after the movie, that they will not be influenced by what they have seen. However, this discourse flies in the face of the role movies play as trendsetters with regard to such issues as hairstyles, dress, accessories and gadgets, mannerisms, and life styles (see, e.g., Wilkinson-Weber 2005). Certainly, movies help set consumer patterns, and changes in appearances are part and parcel of people's self-understanding and self-expression. Moreover, a certain anxiety about the impact film can have on impressionable young (especially female) minds is obvious in some "metafilms" that are preoccupied with the issue, such as Hrishikesh Mukherjee's *Guddi* (1971), which problematizes a young girl's excessive interest in movie heroes (Taylor 2000: 297–9).

One reason film studies scholars are not interested in mythological references may be that film is felt to be an intrinsically modern medium, which explains the amount of energy poured into studies of film and the modern nation on the one hand and the transcultural implications and borrowings of Indian cinema on the other. However, we do not necessarily need to posit a dichotomy between rupture and continuity of Indian traditional values in film. "Tradition" is of course always a contested category, amply illustrated by the kaleidoscopic shifts within, for instance, the storytelling of the Purāṇas. The difference may be that whereas those texts pose as and are understood to be old, as the name implies, the movies pose as and are understood to be modern. Yet circumstances are always new; they develop and call for new reworkings of old ideas. It should not surprise us that films, too, partake in the grand process of reconstituting a cultural universe, or many multiverses, if you wish. There surely is a coming-to-terms with the challenge of "the modern" in its many historically varying forms, yet this is done in a vocabulary and grammar heavily inflected with "the tradition."

What is going on is not just mixing a preground *masala* into the cocktail or simple-minded "borrowing" to appeal to some unchanging religious sentiment. Rather, we find highly creative reworkings, some serious, others whimsical, intended to delight audiences as well as to push their thinking about how myths can be or ought to be exemplary for daily life. Films at the same time reflect changing attitudes toward religious myths and bring new lines of interpretation by applying them to "reel life" situations. That does not necessarily mean that the messages offered by the movies are widely accepted as such, but if the movie is successful, it still indicates it has hit a chord. If we want to understand fully the message of the television Sītā and Rādhā, we do well to look how that message relates to hit movies from the popular Hindi movie industry. After all the director of the television series, Ramanand Sagar, was a also a director of Hindi film.

Methodology

Siting Sītā and Rādhā

In order to understand what message the mythological references in popular culture carry for contemporary South Asians, we have to start with historicizing. It is a fallacy to speak of Sītā and Rādhā as if they were monolithic characters, unchanging over time. The Sītā of the Sanskrit epic is not the same as that of the televised series. Role models are continually constructed and reconstructed. Epic characters may seem timeless because we cannot always point to one author as their constructor or reconstructor. However, a careful reading with close attention to variables between different versions discloses nuances in how the messages sent to women change over time.

It makes sense to start this process of decoding with the most successful modern media forms, identifying their main sources. In our case, the point of reference is the televised versions of Sītā and Rādhā in Ramanand Sagar's series. In order to investigate what these contemporary texts have to say, we need to determine how exactly their messages refer to, make use of, and differ from those of the earlier ones. I call this activity "siting."[20]

By "siting" I mean the process of uncovering intertextuality. In the first place, this involves studying the way texts "cite" one another. The television versions credit their sources: the older versions of Sītā and Rādhā's stories. More than that, they quote them both verbatim and indirectly. In other instances, they choose not to do so and suppress or pass over certain elements in silence. Yet elsewhere, they appear to be quoting older sources when they are in fact innovating. This complex reworking of earlier versions of the stories needs unraveling. Siting is this process of unraveling some of the threads. I investigate what the contemporary texts have to say by putting my finger on how exactly the contemporary message makes use of and differs from the earlier ones. An important factor to realize here is that such use of sources is never random or value-free. It involves making moral judgments and capitalizing on the authority of the earlier texts while simultaneously feeling free to change and drop material as needed.

At the same time, when I use the term "siting" in connection with role models, I have in mind a process that situates these models, charts them on a geographic site, identifies how they fit on a three-dimensional map. Role models are like landmarks in a moral landscape. Humans travel through such landscapes and use the landmarks to navigate. Like the landscape, the landmarks change over time; they erode, or become more pronounced. Such changes usually happen slowly and are difficult to discern, while in process. To document them, we could take snapshots at different points in time and from different places. Often such changes become even more clear if we compare how they work for two different landmarks. We could, for instance, come to understand how the erosion of one has led to change in another.

What I propose to do in this book, then, is to look at changes in two such landmarks in a moral landscape, the two role models the contrastive heroines Sītā and Rādhā. So as to maximize the comparison, I have chosen snapshots that show them in a similar pose, that is, episodes from their stories that have a lot of similarities and can be fruitfully compared. My theme here is how they cope with love, and I will follow their love stories from their first falling in love (chapter 1) through the process of arranging for matrimony (chapter 2), the

20. No reference intended to Niranjana 1992, whose use of the term is different. On the other hand, my method of siting is comparable to what the historian Romila Thapar has done for the story of Śakuntalā though she does not use this term. My focus here though is not on the colonial intervention but on the relevance of the message sent to women. Thapar says about retold narratives that we should "treat this repetition as a prism through which to view points of historical change" (1999: 1).

marriage (or mock marriage) itself (chapter 3), their decisions to step out of the safety of home and purdah into the dangers of the forest (chapter 4), the challenge of the "other women" seducing—or trying to—their husbands (chapter 5), and finally the challenge of sexual harassment and how they cope with it (chapter 6). As I explain at the beginning of each chapter, all of these moments have everyday relevance for ordinary women today. Studying how the goddesses behave in such situations, as portrayed in the contemporary popular televised texts, helps us understand the moral landscapes ordinary women have to navigate.

For each of these snapshots, I select three points in time to compare. One reason I call this process siting rather than mapping is that I am well aware that I am leaving whole areas blank between the snapshots I discuss. Obviously, one could have looked at many Rāma and Krishna cycle retellings, but within the scope of one book it is impossible to do justice to all the versions. So I have restricted myself here to the three arguably most influential ones: the television, classical, and medieval. In addition, I have provided notes on echoes of Sītā and Rādhā in the vast corpus of popular Indian film. In this way, I am able to identify some of the changes in role models for women that are taking place right now.

In short, through the method of siting, I aim at opening new windows through which to view the "traditional" models that go into the making of contemporary discourses on gender and love in South Asia.

Lessons Learned from Media Research

Since this book takes its point of departure largely from popular television series' depictions of the two goddesses, we should reflect on methodologies of television research. A lot has been written on the impact of television on social behavior (for a good overview, see Asami and Berry 1998). A first lesson is not to regard television—or other texts for that matter—as closed texts, a simple message to be decoded. It is important to consider "what does the viewer do to (or with) television" (Berry 1998: 4). One should not fall into the trap of assuming, for instance, that women are "manipulated by the patriarchal discourses of television." While television programs can be said to create certain "subject positions," viewers can affirm and appropriate or resist and negotiate (Mankekar 1993: 557–8). To explore this issue would be, however, a different study. It is interesting to consider the question of what the impact of mythological series in real life might be. Though that is not the focus of this book, I hope it will be a helpful basis to work from for anthropologists, behavioral psychologists, and social scientists who might consider such questions.

Second, one should keep in mind that the influence of the medium does not unilaterally flow from director to audience. Interaction with the viewers is an important factor for the televised *Ramayan,* even though it occurred before the advent of interactive media. Indeed, it will be clear from my analysis that I am constantly looking for how the director and his team are working with commonly held assumptions about the stories they serialize, some of which viewers communicated to them in correspondence. The viewers' concerns inspired the director to code episodes in certain ways. In fact, this is not unlike the traditional process of interpretation of religious texts, which is a dynamic exchange between the expounder and the listener. The listener may raise doubts and objections (*śaṅkā*), to which the expounder will propose solutions on the basis of his interpretation of the text (*śaṅkā-samādhān*). In retellings of myths, there may be an implicit, unstated "first part" of such questions (*pūrvapakṣa*), to which the author provides a follow-up answer (*uttarapakṣa*) by tailoring the problematic episode in a way to address the issue. The situation does not necessarily need to be a hierarchical one, in which there is a text-expounder or guru guiding his disciples, but can be one analogous to Bible study groups in Protestant traditions, where there is not necessarily a designated authoritative leader. This phenomenon has been studied for other *Rāmāyaṇa* texts (Lutgendorf 1991; Hess 2001), and is particularly relevant here. Sagar has stressed that he himself belonged to a group of *Rāmāyaṇa*-lovers that gathered regularly to discuss and debate passages from the scripture (Sternfeld 2005: 197).

Another insight to take from television studies is the importance of recognizing the medium as an art (Berry 1998: 8). This is particularly important for the televised epics, which are often disregarded as mere derivative, gaudy video versions of ancient texts. In my close viewings of the videos, I have come to respect the amount of creative thinking and originality the director and his team brought to bear on their work. My comparison with the acknowledged source texts is in no way intended to prove the derivational character of the series or to reduce them to faint reflections of the original. Rather the opposite; in paying close attention to detail, I testify abundantly to the creativity of the director.

Finally, there is the issue of the constructed audience.[21] What audience in which circumstances perceived what part of the perceived message? The readings I present are not necessarily the ones that any of the multiple audiences who have watched the series perceived at the time of broadcasting or

21. For a sophisticated analysis of different types of constructed audiences, see Anderson 1998: 214–27; for a historical overview, see Gokulsingh 2004: 78–80.

even have come to perceive after repeated viewing. While there has been abundant evidence that at the moment of its initial screening the series were viewed literally religiously, and with a great degree of undivided attention, of course not all members in an audience perceive things similarly. What I present here is a maximally informed reading, one that takes into account all the details of the source texts. Comparing in such detail is a privileged situation, and few viewers had full access to these source texts during the viewing. It needs to be stressed, though, that many viewers know significant portions of the source texts by heart and thus are in a position to compare to a high degree. While the messages articulated here may well have remain undecoded by the majority of the audience, it is still worthwhile to strive for the maximal reading, as it may uncover some of the director's intentions. What I lay bare here are the potential meanings of the text; the estimation of the realization of these potentialities would be a different study.

The Untenable Lightness of the Popular Hindi Movie

One of the contributions of this work is to incorporate in the analysis mythological references in popular movies. Here, lessons learned from film studies come into play. In the past decade and a half, a sophisticated literature on popular Hindi film has developed (Chakravarty 1993, Prasad 1998, Kazmi 1999, Mishra 2002, Virdi 2003, to name just a few). Here I articulate only the concerns relevant to this study. First, understanding the messages of popular film is not as simple as it might appear; it requires significant sophistication. Recently a lot of work has been done on analyzing visual culture (see for instance, Dasgupta 2006). Theorizers of popular culture have pointed out that Indian viewers and spectators are caught up in an "interocular" field (Appadurai and Breckenridge 1992). We should not forget that they also function in an interaural field, and here, too, "each site or setting for the socializing and regulation of the public gaze" (read also: ear) "is to some degree affected by the experiences of the other sites" (Breckenridge 1995, 12). Analyzing such sites is what my method of siting is designed to do.

Second, following from the first point, studying interaurality is especially important because Indian cinema is dominated by the genre of the musical, and thus centered around songs. Songs evoke other songs. Tunes and words echo back and forth between different milieus, from temple and folk gatherings to movie hall, cassette studio, and back (Manuel 1993). Here the interplay among devotional, folk, and popular culture is particularly relevant. Thus I particulary foreground the film songs and study their intertextuality with the tradition.

Third, we have to guard against treating popular Indian cinema as monolithic. There is a rich diversity. On the one hand, there is something of a hegemonic discourse that reinforces patriarchal values, but at the same time I will indicate "counter-moments," attempts to struggle with challenges posed to such an ideology.[22] It is important to look at both, if we seek to map a narrative of women through Hindi films, as Jyotika Virdi suggests we do (Virdi 2003: 123). Whereas she is mainly engaged in a close reading of the films' intertextually with each other and in conjunction with the underlying "star text" (124), I offer here a reading that is intertextual with the myths and thus reveals the rich texture of these seemingly naïve movies in yet a different way.

Finally, we have to keep in mind that the audience is not merely passively taking in the discourses of the movies. Several recent studies have foregrounded the audience's critical stance and subversion of the values depicted in the movies (Derné 1995b, Uberoi 2001a, Banaji 2005). Still, it is valuable to analyze the movies as text, while being aware of the possibility that the audience comes away with alternative interpretations.

My intent to unpack the mythological references in the movies against the background of other versions of the myths may raise objections. The project falls between disciplines, which is not always welcomed. On the one hand, scholars of religion and religious texts may object. Why look at secular Hindi movies to understand popular religion in India? Scholars of popular culture and film may take offense, too. Why look at epics to understand popular film? This book showcases the need for both. Let me explain briefly the desirability of each in turn.

The interdependence of popular film and religion has been little studied. However, occasionally attention has been drawn to it forcefully, when religious phenomena spill over spectacularly into the domain of popular culture. One example is the case of the "new" goddess Santoshi Ma, who gained rampant popularity in the wake of the unexpected success of the 1975 movie *Jai Santoshi Maa* (studied by Kurtz 1992, Lutgendorf 2002). More recently, suspicions of a growing influence of Hindutva in the visual media have inspired two brief studies, one on nostalgia as manipulated in television advertisements

22. This is along the same lines as what Jyotika Virdi is doing in her chapter "Heroines, Romance, and Social History" in her recent book, though she focuses on "critical readings against the grain" that "destabilize Hindi cinema's hegemonic values" (2003: 121–6). She is keen to detect "lapses" and "leaks" in the prevailing discourse. The elements I discuss in this book, though, are not "lapses," as directors' critical engagement with mythological models is quite deliberate. Moreover, the outcome of the analysis does not unproblematically contest patriarchal values.

(Dasgupta 2006) and another on films engaging with political material (Dwyer 2006).

Obviously, there is some connection that must be more enduring than the spectacular eruptions of the religious into the domain of popular film and television. When we look up close, we find that films frequently play on the religious sentiments of their audience in multiple, sometimes contradictory ways (Kishwar 2003a). Often, filmmakers seem to have their finger on the pulse of popular religion, to show and articulate what audiences are ready to hear and see, and again adopt in their own styles of religious celebration. With regard to politicized Hinduism, it is particularly important to study the link between religion and film. Leaders of Hindutva have been engaged in many ways in the world of popular film and television (Brosius 2005). Finally, we could say that the ubiquitous presence of *filmī bhajanas* in places of pilgrimage virtually shouts it from the rooftops: there is no splendid isolation between the sacred wood of, say, Brindaban and the purportedly secular Bollywood.

On the other hand, scholars of film studies will be quick to raise the objection that an approach of studying films against the background of religious texts reeks of reductionism, something many studies of popular film warn against (see Kazmi 1999: 67, Virdi 2003: 3). They fear that such a study might perpetuate the stereotypes of "epic tropes" and "eternal Indian themes." Of course, we should not lose track of the fact that there is a good deal more going on in Hindi movies than reworking of epic stories. However, one misses out on a lot if one does not understand the playful epic references with which these movies abound. There is no question of "unchanging archetypes" that are simply being reproduced. In fact, we may have to go as far as to say that there are no unchanging archetypes. They are constantly under construction and reconstruction. The epics themselves and their devotional reworkings are full of twists and changes, interesting shifts of focus according to time and place (for reflections on contradictions within Vālmīki's epic itself, see Goldman 2004). As one scholar of myth has put it: "Myth is like palimpsest on which generation after generation has engraved its own layer of messages and we must decipher each layer with a different code book" (O'Flaherty 1980: 4). Film appropriations of myth are no exceptions.

What is needed then is a clearheaded understanding of the multiple shifts and twists in the old texts, as well as in television and movie versions. As I identify the changes from scriptures to screen, I am looking for which notion of tradition is invoked and articulated, and which one is suppressed or altered. I attempt to decode the message of the myths and the allusions to them in popular culture by means of a careful analysis of "what is old, what is new," paying particular attention not only to innovations, significant as they are, but also to what exactly is quoted and what is left out from the earlier versions. I think it is very important to do so; otherwise, we end up ascribing to say, Sagar's *Ramayan,* traits that are much older, and missing elements that are truly innovative.[23]

What This Book Is Not About

Disappointing as it may be, this study has to leave out certain important subjects. One is reception history of the texts studied. For the classical and medieval texts, one can study the commentaries, and I occasionally refer to them. Even so, these are primarily authored by men, and it is impossible to get at the reactions of the women, the main audience of interest here. For the film and television sources, it would be possible to probe audience reaction, with reference to reviews, readers letters in popular magazines, and interviews with directors, actors, and screenplay writers. Another angle of approach is anthropological study of viewers' reactions (e.g., Mankekar's broader study [1999] and Derné's work on Hindi movies [1995a]). In particular, it would be revealing to test how much the audience gets of the quotations from medieval Old Hindi and classical Sanskrit texts. It is commonly assumed that the medieval devotional version of Rāma's story, the *Rām Carit Mānas,* is not easily understood today. However, it is quoted extensively in the televised *Ramayan.* In the course of my study, I have become convinced that the television series' use of the *Mānas* deliberately targets connoisseurs of the *Mānas,* which has led me to suspect that there may be a substantial number of such connoisseurs among the viewers. Still, the audience was much broader, and many of the nuances noted in this book might well have escaped the "average viewer." It would be interesting to see how much of the carefully crafted reworkings of earlier myths in the television series came across in different milieus, but obviously that is a different study that requires a different expertise.

Beyond the narrow issue of the reception of the television series, it would be very desirable to investigate the actual impact of the goddess role models on

23. One fallacy is to conflate particular *Rāmāyaṇa* versions with meta-*Rāmāyaṇa* ideas. Another is to locate ideological aspects of Hinduism in general, and TVR in particular, as originating in or responding to colonial discourse. One has to be careful in doing so. The *Rāmāyaṇa* tradition contains elements with a long pedigree beyond the much-studied nineteenth century. Even so careful an analyst as Purnima Mankekar conflates those when she traces the portrayal of Rāma as embodying both *sannyāsin* and *kṣatriya* to Bankimcandra, whereas, of course, the combination is much older (1999: 205–7).

women. Heinz's study (2000) is a felicitous example of discovering how women make use of the Sītā story when narrating their own lives. I hope this book will be of use to researchers in social studies and women's studies who seek to understand women's responses to and negotiations of, in everyday life, the choices related to love. Recently there has been a lot of interest in how middle-class women partake in traditional and transnational gender discourses, whether in India (Puri 1999) or the diaspora (Rayaprol 1997). In such studies, notwithstanding the high degree of theoretical sophistication, sometimes the "traditional" discourse is seen as monolithic. It is hoped my contribution here will bring a more nuanced understanding, beyond unproblematic equation of the television *Ramayan* with the ancient Indian tradition.

Another limitation of this study is that it focuses solely on the "interaural" aspect of siting. It would take another volume to bring the perspective of visual arts and reveal the "interocular" experience. A comparative study with visual images and earlier films and, further back, miniature paintings, would certainly be a desideratum. An engaging example of such a study with respect to Bhārat Mātā and *śakti* is Geeti Sen's *Feminine Fables*, which touches just briefly on Rādhā (Sen 2000: 79–82).

Finally, related to the issue of audience response, I am not tackling the question of the use of the serialized text by agents engaged in particular political and social action. Given the rise of the Right in Indian politics and of Hindutva-inspired views of gender from around the time of the series, such a study would be very worthwhile, and the topic certainly deserves further exploration by political scientists (in the footsteps of Rajagopal 2001).

Whatever the limits of this study, its investigation of the changes in "the message" from a textual perspective is a logical first step toward understanding contemporary South Asian viewers' reactions to these texts and their political and social implications.

The Sources

There are multiple versions of the myths of Sītā and Rādhā, each important in its own right, but I limit myself here to three. I will take into account, for each episode and each goddess, as far as possible, a classical, Sanskrit version of the story; a medieval, devotional one; and finally the televised version. I also incorporate material from relevant Hindi popular movies. I give specifics about my choices in the introductions to the chapters. I have chosen the classical and medieval sources that are most pertinent to the contemporary versions, in particular the sources that are explicitly acknowledged in the credits of the television series.[24] While the choice is more straightforward for the *Rāmāyaṇa* versions, I have strived to find sources that make for a good comparison for the Krishna stories.

In addition to explaining my rationale for the sources, I will in this section also provide a general contextualization for the three main reference points (classical, medieval, and contemporary), outlining authors' motives, as far as known. For the movies, I provide here a broad overview of trends in the depiction of romance in popular Hindi cinema as a guide for the reader to contextualize the movies analyzed in this work.

Classical Sources

The locus classicus of the Sītā-Rāma story, explicitly announced as one of the major sources of the televised *Rāmāyaṇa,* is undisputably what is known as the *Vālmīki Rāmāyaṇa.* This work, hailed as the first Sanskrit *kāvya* (work of belles lettres) is attributed to the sage Vālmīki.[25] Since Vālmīki is intimately tied up with the main characters, this version has the status of an eyewitness account. Scholarly consensus regards the text as we have it now as a composite, having expanded over time, with a core dating back maybe to the fifth or fourth century BCE, but crystalized in its current form by the second century CE. I will treat the epic as a unified whole, as does the tradition and some Western scholarship (Pollock 1984: 3–6, 15–54). However, one should be aware that another line of scholarship distinguishes within the epic between many individual passages that seem to be later additions, including some passages discussed here (for a full overview, see Brockington 1994 and 1998: 377–97; for a translation of the oldest reconstructable version, see Brockington and Brockington 2006). The text used as a source of the televised version was not the critical but the vulgate edition.[26] Thus, and because of its widespread popularity and availability, references throughout will be to the books (*kāṇḍa*),

24. Taking TVR as a point of departure means, regrettably, that this book is limited to the North Indian sources. A study of the South Indian *Rāmāyaṇas*, taking into account Tamil and other Dravidian language texts as well as films, would make a wonderful contrast.

25. Another wonderful source for the conjugality of Rāma and Sītā would have been the *Ānanda Rāmāyaṇa,* an extremely interesting version focusing on bliss and the domestic joy of the divine pair, see Aklujkar 2001a and b.

26. Note that the critical edition is of course not the final word, as new manuscripts are being discovered (see Bailey and Brockington 2000: 195–217).

chapters (*sarga*), and verses (*ślokas*) in the vulgate edition of the Gītā Press in Gorakhpur (Goswami 1969).[27]

For the story of Krishna and Rādhā, or rather the Gopīs, the equivalent classical authority, acknowledged in the credits of the televised serial *Shri Krishna*, is the *Bhāgavata Purāṇa*, in particular its tenth book (*skandha*), which focuses on the story of Krishna. Authorship of this Sanskrit work is attributed to the prolific sage Vyāsa. Its dating is controversial: current scholarly consensus ascribes the finalized book to the ninth century CE (for a discussion of scholarship on the topic and an argument for an earlier date, see Bryant 2002).[28] Again, the text used for the televised version was the vulgate, (Goswami and Śāstri [1971] 1982).[29] This book is actually shown in the foreground at the beginning of the series, where Sagar welcomes his audience with the greeting "Jay Śrī Kṛṣṇa" from his personal study from behind a pile of books on his desk. So references throughout are to the books (*skandha*), chapters (*adhyāya*), and verses (*śloka* and many other meters) of this edition.[30]

Note that *Bhāgavata Purāṇa* only talks about the Gopīs as a group and does no single out Rādhā by name. Later theologians have done their best to find etymological cues in the text and identify the one Gopī privileged by Krishna during the Rāsa-līlā with Rādhā (Miller 1977: 26–9). In the later poets' vision, too, there is no doubt that Rādhā is the foremost of the Gopīs, and she figures prominently in the medieval sources.

For these two classical sources, the comparison is somewhat marred, since they are widely disparate in place and time. Comparing the classical moments of the Sītā and Gopī stories is anachronistic in that sense. One might have argued instead for comparison with either the *Harivaṃśa* or *Viṣṇu Purāṇas*,

27. I have much benefited from this edition's Hindi paraphrase, as well as the translations and notes of the translators of the critical edition (Sheldon Pollock and Sally and Robert Goldman). Of course, one has to keep in mind that the *Vālmīki Rāmāyaṇa* as received by its audience is not a version using the printed word. Rather it is received in performance, where it is recited and/or visually enacted.

28. Study of the different stages of composition of the text has not been carried out to the same degree of sophistication as for *Vālmīki Rāmāyaṇa*, and one has to be aware of a sectarian interest of some authors who keenly push for an early date for especially the Krishna-related passages.

29. This text, too, is mostly received by its audience not in the form of letters on a page but in recitation or visual enactment.

30. Again, I am much indebted to the Gītā Press translation, as well as as the recent translation of the tenth book in Bryant 2003. It is unfortunate that no critical edition of this important work has been undertaken, possibly because the variants appear to be remarkably scant. No extensive manuscript study has been carried out; though there is a facsimile edition of an old manuscript in the Sharda script (Bechert 1976), hardly anyone has looked at the variants. The only exception is the nineteenth-century French Scholar Eugène Buznouf (and after his death Hauvette-Besnault and R.P. Alfred Roussel) for the French translation [Buznouf 1846.96] 1981). There is also a somewhat opiniated study attempting to reconstruct a "correct" metrical reading (Nadkarni 1975).

both of which are earlier. Rather than choose the earliest version and in that way remain parallel to *Vālmīki Rāmāyaṇa,* I have opted for what is perceived to be the classical version, in which also the Gopī story is more prominent. It is also the first source mentioned in the credits of Sagar's *Shri Krishna,* which read "Mainly based on Shrimad Bhagwat Mahapuran" (under which heading are also listed "Brahma Vaivart Puran, Garg Samhita, Agni Puran"). Only in the next credit frame are "Harivansh Puran" and "Vishnu Puran" listed. And Bhāgavata Purāṇa is privileged within the story: it is the work recommended by none less than Brahmā, the creator god himself, as the sole refuge in Kaliyuga. Thus one cannot underestimate the importance of this source for the *Shri Krishna* series. In effect, the series projects itself as a version of *Bhāgavata Purāṇa.* One has to be aware, though, that the *Bhāgavata Purāṇa* cannot be considered to the same extent the Ur-version of the Krishna story as can the *Vālmīki Rāmāyaṇa* for the Rāma story (though the latter is also problematic; see Richman 1991). It is itself a composite, informed by many other sources (Hardy 1983).

Since the episode discussed in chapter 3 does not occur in *Bhāgavata Purāṇa,* I have taken into account another Sanskrit Purāṇa that is very important for the Rādhā-Krishna story, namely *Brahma Vaivarta Purāṇa.* This book is listed second in the credits at the beginning of Sagar's *Shri Krishna.* It is interesting that this work figures so prominently in Sagar's list of sources, as it is a relatively late text and not very widely known. It seems to be a Śākta-influenced work foregrounding the Krishna story. While it may have an early core, its final redaction, as extant now, is usually attributed to the fifteenth or even sixteenth century (Brown 1974: 1, 37, and 205). I have used the editions of Rānade (1935) and Śarmā (1970); the latter contains also a helpful Hindi translation.

Medieval Sources

For the medieval retellings, I have concentrated on versions that are relatively closer to each other in date and place. For the Sītā story, evidently the choice should be Tulsīdās's influential Old Hindi (Avadhī) reworking, the *Rām Carit Mānas.* Very little is known about Tulsīdās (d. 1623) beyond the fact that he was likely a Brahmin, active in Benares and Ayodhyā (for legends about him, see Lutgendorf 1994). His *Rām Carit Mānas* dates from the latter half of the sixteenth century (it was started in 1564; see Vaudeville 1955: x). It is a widely popular text, quoted and recited ever more eagerly (Lutgendorf 1991) and was extensively used in the televised Rāmāyaṇa. I will again be quoting the most popular vulgate text, of the Gorakhpur Gītā Press, with references to book (*kāṇḍa*), verse-unit (*kaṛavak*), and individual verse line (*caupāī* or *dohā;* occasionally Harigītikā *chand*) (Poddar 1990).[31] I should stress that this work is received by its audience in performance, through recitation as well as the Rāmlīlā dramatical tradition (see e.g. Kapur 1990).

Legend has it that there was strong Brahminical opposition to Tulsīdās's project to translate from Sanskrit. In fact, the text is hardly a translation. While *Vālmīki Rāmāyaṇa* was a major source of inspiration, Tulsīdās abbreviated considerably, and he took significant liberties with the story line, influenced by many different sources, including dramatic reworkings and other Sanskrit *Rāmāyaṇas*, such as the *Adhyātma Rāmāyaṇa* (Vaudeville 1955). He probably also was influenced by the Avadhī romances, most of them Sūfi in inspiration, which are in the same idiom and metrical structure as *Rām Carit Mānas* (Pauwels 2000).

The major point of Tulsīdās's work is expressing and preaching devotion to Rāma. Whether Tulsīdās belonged to the devotional sect of the Rāmānanda-sampradāya or not, there is no doubt about his bhakti agenda. Thus the work concentrates less on narrative and more on glorification, and it exploits every possible occasion to sing Rāma's praise. Notwithstanding the story of opposition by the Brahmin establishment in Benares, Tulsīdās's work is pro-Brahmin, seemingly favoring a status quo of hierarchal relations. Since Tulsīdās lived and worked in Śiva's holy city, Benares, there is also an element of accommodation of devotion to Śiva in Tulsīdās's work. No wonder Tulsīdās has been called a "theological bridge-builder" (Hawley and Juergensmeyer 1988: 151).[32]

For the devotional vernacular perspective on Rādhā, there is an enormous corpus of Old Hindi (Braj Bhāṣā) poetry on the topic from which it is difficult to make a selection. By the end of the sixteenth century, when Tulsīdas ("Tulsī") was composing his *Rām Carit Mānas,* such Braj devotional songs had become widely popular. In fact, many aspects of his work may well have been inspired by them.[33] However, there is no single authoritative retelling in Braj of *Bhāgavata Purāṇa* that would parallel his work. Instead, the Sanskrit classic was

31. My translations are informed by the French translation by Vaudeville (1977) and have much benefited from the English translations by Growse (revised by Prasād, 1978) and Hill (1971). The text of this work is fairly stable, but I have on occasion consulted the critical edition by Śukla, Bhagvāndīn, and Brajratnadās (1973).

32. I treat Tulsīdās's characters in terms of gender roles because of my main interest here in role models for women. There are other possible interpretations, including seeing Sītā as representative of the female self. In an interesting article, Veena Das has argued that through "the distribution of characters . . . the author captures the dramatic nature of the self and the division of male and female within the self" (1998: 67).

33. One work of Krishnaite devotion is attributed to Tulsīdās himself, the *Kṛṣṅagītāvalī;* see McGregor 1976. Notably, the Gopīs' erotic love for Krishna is downplayed in this work.

the inspiration for several short poems more or less loosely based on different episodes. The Braj poets' interest veered away from narrative, concentrating instead on vignettes of love. The closest we get to a narrative is the incomplete attempt to render *Bhāgavata Purāṇa*'s tenth book in Braj by the late sixteenth-century poet Nanddās, sometimes said to have been Tulsīdās's brother. On the other hand, there is the more famous early sixteenth-century poet Sūrdās, who is listed in the credits of Sagar's *Shri Krishna* under "other sources of inspiration."[34] Surdas's poems have been collected to reflect the sequence of episodes in *Bhāgavata Purāṇa,* and are often presented as a vernacular *Bhāgavata.* Finally, the earliest Braj translation and reworking of five famous chapters from *Bhāgavata Purāṇa*'s tenth book, entitled *Rās Pañcādhyāyī,* is by the mid-sixteenth-century poet Harirām Vyās. I will explain in some detail each of these sources, as they are less well known than *Rām Carit Mānas.*

NANDDĀS. One of the earliest attempts at an Old Hindi systematic reworking of *Bhāgavata Purāṇa* is *Bhāsā Dasama Skandha,* composed by Nanddās, who was active around 1570 (McGregor 1984: 85). Nanddās was part of the "new wave" of Krishna poetry in the wake of the "rediscovery" of the Braj area as a center of pilgrimage. He is generally regarded as one of the younger of the canonical "Eight Seals" (Aṣṭachāp) poets, claimed to have been initiated by Vallabha's son Viṭṭhalnāth, and thus connected with the influential Vallabha-sampradāya, or Puṣṭimārg. That he was closely connected with the famous Śrī Nāthjī temple at the time of Viṭṭhalnāth seems to be borne out by his works, as he mentions both the image and the man frequently (McGregor 1973: 31).

The *Bhāsā Dasama Skandha* makes a great parallel to *Rām Carit Mānas* as it is in the same metrical structure (*caupāī-dohā*). Moreover, Nanddās was a contemporary of Tulsīdās; according to Vallabhan sectarian tradition, they even were brothers.[35] The same tradition ascribes the inspiration for the work to Tulsī's example. And like Tulsī, Nanddās is also said to have faced opposition from Brahmins to his "translation" project. However, unlike Tulsīdās, Nanddās did not persist; he obeyed his guru, who requested him to honor the Brahmins' demands.[36] That is the explanation for the incompleteness of his work as extant, which focuses only on the early part of Krishna's life in Braj (up to *BhP* 10.28; in some sources also 29). There is a legend that Nanddās in fact had done a

34. Sagar first acknowledges "Shree Chaitanya Mahaprabhu" and "Mahaprabhu Shree Vallabhacharya."

35. See McGregor 1973: 33–4. For the hagiographic stories, see the Vallabhan hagiography *Do sau bāvan Vaiṣṇavan kī Vārtā, vārtā* 4, *prasaṅga* 1, 3, and 5, in Kṛṣṇadās [1958] 1986b: 34–8, 39–40, and 41–4.

36. The story is found in, *vārtā* 4, *prasaṅga* 4 (Kṛṣṇadās [1958] 1986b: 40–1).

complete translation, which he offered to the Yamunā (i.e., set afloat in the river). Some parts of his work were miraculously saved, and that is why only fragments survive (Brajratandās [1949] 1957: 117). Nanddās indeed also reworked other episodes from *Bhāgavata Purāṇa,* which are usually listed as different works: *Rās Pañcādhyāyī, Govarddhan Līlā, Bhramar Gīt, Rukmiṇī Maṅgal, Sudāmā Caritra.* He himself may not have conceived of them as part of his translation project, as they are in different meters and do not follow the chapter-by-chapter and nearly verse-by-verse translation format of *Bhāsā Dasama Skandha.* I will incorporate one of those works by Nanddās, his *Rukmiṇī Maṅgal,* which is a brilliant work in the *rolā* meter throughout. I give the full quotations in Braj, so those with some ability to do so may enjoy this poet's masterwork.

Who was Nanddās's audience? Contradicting the tradition that ascribes his inspiration to write in the vernacular to Tulsīdās, Nanddās himself attributes it to a special friend who wished to hear Krishna's story but did not understand Sanskrit.[37] A friend is also said to have inspired *Rās Pāñcādhyāyī* and all his works whose titles end with *Mañjarī.* This may be a conventional way of introducing a work (McGregor 1973: 106–7 n. at *Rās Pañcādhyāyī* 58), but there has been speculation about who this special friend was. Popularly it is believed that it was a woman by the name of Rūpmañjarī, who was a fellow-follower of the sectarian Vallabhan tradition (Viśārad 1954: 2). One hagiographic story describes a female "follower" of Viṭṭhalnāth by that name who was said to be a concubine of the Mughal emperor and a devotee of Nanddās (*Do sau bāvan Vaiṣṇavan kī Vārtā, vārtā* 232).[38] There is also a story linking Nanddās's work *Rūpmañjarī* with a woman of that name who seems to be from Gwalior (*gvāḷiyā kī beṭī*) in another sectarian text (*Śrī Nāthjī kī Prākaṭya Vārtā* 59; see Mahārāj and Śāstrī 1968: 41). Whatever may have been the identity of this "special friend," it is interesting that she is understood to be a woman. We may well speculate that the work was perceived as intended for a female audience.

37. He does so in his humble disclaimer at the beginning of *Bhāsā Dasama Skandha: parama bicitra mitra ika rahai, kṛṣṇa caritra sunyau so cahai; sabada saṃskṛta ke haiṃ jaisaiṃ, mo pai samujhi parata nahiṃ taisaiṃ* (*BDS* 1, *caupāī* 1–2).

38. According to the hagiography, she was a Hindu king's daughter but married to the Mughal emperor (Akbar?), though she refused to consummate the wedding. Instead, every night she would visit Nanddās, thanks to a magic ball (*guṭikā*) that gave her stool the power to transport her in the air. One day, the king heard a song of Nanddās and decided to meet him. The saint first met the wife and ate in her quarters *prasād* that Srīnāthjī himself had come to eat. Afterward, he agreed to meet the Mughal, but literally died in his embarrassment of speaking to "one who belongs to a different faith" (*anya-mārgī*). When the emperor told his wife, she, too, suddenly died, much to his consternation (Kṛṣṇadās [1958] 1986b: 461–2). Nanddās is described also as being attracted to a woman before his conversion, in the first *prasaṅga* of his own *vārtā* (4), in the same work (34–8).

Bhāsā Dasama Skandha is a free reworking that takes liberties with the text, yet Nanddās clearly knew the ins and outs of the Sanskrit work and even took into account Sanskrit commentaries, that is, he prefaces his work by paying obeisance to the earliest commentator on *Bhāgavata Purāṇa,* Śrīdhara.[39] One would expect Nanddās also to know of Vallabha's commentary, since he was initiated into Vallabha's sect. However, his readings are not in total conformity with Vallabha's. Still, he attributes the inspiration to "Guru Giridhara,"[40] which is generally seen to be the image of Śrī Nāthjī, which was in Vallabhite hands at this time. *Rukmiṇī Maṅgal* deviates significantly from *Bhāgavata Purāṇa*. It is a free, creative reworking.

Unfortunately, no critical edition of Nanddās's works is available.[41] I will refer to the text of the prestigious Nāgarī Pracāriṇī Sabhā edition by Brajratnadās ([1949] 1957).[42]

SŪRDĀS. The second medieval poet whose works are quoted here, Sūrdās, is one of the most prestigious medieval Hindu poet-saints, and occupies rightfully an important niche in the canon of early Hindi literature. The televised version of Krishna's story cites him prominently as an important source. Sūrdās ("Sūr") is like an older brother to Nanddās, as he is commonly seen as the foremost of the same "Eight Seals" (Aṣṭachāp) poets affiliated with the Vallabha-sampradāya. J. S. Hawley (1984) has shown this affiliation to be a late sectarian development, but to this day, the Vallabhan hagiographies are influential in the way Sūrdās is remembered. The sectarian interpretation of his life is mirrored in the arrangement of the vulgate anthology of his poetry, entitled *Sūr Sāgar* (Sūr's ocean; Hawley 2005: 194–207). The standard edition, again from the prestigious Nāgarī Pracāriṇī Sabhā (Ratnākar 1972, 1976) arranges the poems on the model of the Sanskrit *Bhāgavata Purāṇā,* an arrangement supposedly inspired by Vallabha. However, Hawley has shown that early nonsectarian manuscripts do not arrange the poems in that pattern, and

39. *aru ju mahāmati śrīdhara svāmī, saba granthana ke aṃtarajāmī; tina ju kahe yaha bhāgavata graṃtha, jaisaiṃ dṛhha-udadhi kau maṃtha* (*BDS* 1.4).

40. *jyoṃ guru giridhara deva kī, sundara dayā darera* (*BDS* 1, *dohā* 2).

41. Stuart McGregor carried out a study of the *Rās Pañcādhyāyī* manuscripts, which he reports on (1973: 55–6), as well as of the independent *padas* (McGregor 1992).

42. This edition is based on two older editions (one by Śrīkarmcand Guggalānī and another by Śrī Murārīlāl Keḍiyā) and comparison with a manuscript from Brajratnadās's private collection that he says was about two hundred years old. A first edition from Allahabad University, by Umāśaṅkar Śukla dated 1942, is unfortunately no longer available. There are no published translations of *Bhāsā Dasama Skandha* or *Rukmiṇī Maṅgal* (though there is a brilliant translation of *Rās Pañcādhyāyī* by Stuart McGregor [1973]), so all translations are my own.

indeed that many of the poems are later additions to the ever-growing corpus attributed to Sūr. A major problem in using the vulgate for Sūrdās is that a lot of the poems may well be later—in some cases as late as the twentieth century. A new critical edition of Sūr's poetry is in the works (Hawley and Bryant forthcoming), and I will refer to it as it is appropriate. My references will be to the verse numbers in the standard edition. Most of Sūr's poems that I quote have been paraphrased in Hindi in another edition by Hardev Bahri and Rajendra Kumar (1974: 962–85 for the *panaghaṭa* poems); a few have been beautifully translated in the many articles and books of John Stratton Hawley, and by Dr. Krishna P. Bahadur (1999: 299–303 for the *paṇaghaṭa* poems). When in doubt, I've checked my translation against theirs and the commentary, benefiting from these scholars' interpretations.

HARIRĀM VYĀS. The last Braj work I quote from is *Rās Pañcādhyāyī*, by Harirām Vyās, one of the earliest transcreations of *Bhāgavata Purāṇa* material in Braj. Vyās hailed from the small kingdom of Orccha in Bundelkhand, but moved to Vrindāban in the Braj area of North India in the 1530s. While not formally affiliated with any sect, he was part of the growing community of devotees exclusively devoted to the worship of Rādhā and Krishna. Vyās and his like-minded friends Harivaṃś and Haridās, founders of the Rādhāvallabha- and Sakhī-Sampradāya (respectively), are often classified as "the three Haris" (Hari-trayī), also called "the three connoisseurs" *(rasika-trayī)*.

Vyās's *Rās Pañcādhyāyī* (in *tripadī* meter) has enjoyed some popularity, as is witnessed by manuscript attestation from many parts of North India and its inclusion in the standard edition of the *Sūr Sāgar* (SS 1798/1180).[43] I prefer this text to Nanddās's as the latter does not contain reference to Rādhā.

Again, we need to be clear that the audience of all the medieval Krishna devotional poems was likely to be acquainted with them not through the printed book but through oral performance, in *bhajana* sessions and, popularly, through the theatrical tradition of Rās-līlā (see Hawley and Goswami 1981).

Although these medieval sources for Sītā and Rādhā are closer to one another in time and place than the classical ones, there is a major difference. While Tulsīdās's text is an extended narrative, most of the sources for Rādhā are individual poems/song (*padas*) that do not make a coherent narrative. They

43. I will refer to my own scholarly edition and translation, which also includes a detailed Braj-Sanskrit comparison with *Bhāgavata Purāṇa* parallels (Pauwels 1996b: 163–79). For clarity's sake, I will normalize the irregular spelling of the manuscript, which I reproduced in the text edition in my book.

are like excerpts or moments in the story, known to all, but not told systematically in any source. Thus, the selection of source material is less obvious and less complete, and the choice is more subjective.

The Television Series

The major reference points of this book are the influential televised retellings of the Rāma and Krishna story, both by Ramanand Sagar (né Chopra; b. 1917 d. 2005).[44] Surprisingly, very little has been written about the director, notwithstanding the runaway success of both of his television series. One has to glean facts from the *Encyclopedia of Indian Cinema* (*EIC*), the popular press, interviews, websites, and references in studies of politics and television. Part of Sagar's life reads like a Hindi movie scenario. His father was from a rich family in Kashmir but died destitute when Ramanand was still young, so he grew up in Lahore in the house of his maternal grandparents. He fell out with his grandparents about the marriage that was arranged for him and was thrown out of the house, compelled to sell soap and clean cars for a living. During that period he had his first experience in the film industry with a stint as a clapper boy in a silent movie. He finished his studies, winning gold medals in both Sanskrit and Persian. His first identity was as a creative writer in Hindi/Urdu (this view of himself is apparent from the organization of the official webpage, www.sagartv.com/about.asp). He worked as a journalist and wrote poetry and short stories under several pseudonyms, but his career was jump-started with his *Diary of a TB Patient* in 1942, which was published as a serial in an influential Lahore magazine. After Partition, he fled to India. His story is that of many who had to start all over, penniless (with just 5 annas, according to the website) and only tragic memories to work from. Sagar worked his traumatic experiences into a novel on the horrors of Partition, *Aur insān mar gayā* (And humanity died) in 1948, for which he gained some critical acclaim. He also wrote a drama (*Gaura*), which was produced by Prithvi Theaters. His involvement with the film industry was initially as a writer; his first success was as the story, screen, and dialogue writer for Raj Kapoor's *Barsaat* (1949). Sagar then got off on a film career, writing the script for, and later directing several movies, often with major stars, such as Dharmendra, Rajendra Kumar, Rajesh Khanna, Shammi Kapoor, Rekha, Hema Malini, Mala Sinha.

44. It would also be interesting to compare these to the way the Rāma story is filmed by another director, Ravi Chopra in his *Vishnupuran*, but I have limited myself here to Sagar's series, which came first.

He established his own film production company Sagar Art (in 1953; not to be confused with the earlier Sagar Film Company). His website has it that as a director, "the portrayal of the sensitivity of a woman's love has remained his high point." His penchant for depicting long-suffering heroines who remain steadfast in their love through trials is already clear in his script for *Barsaat,* which contrasts such heroines with flirty, Westernized "Rubies and Lilies." Another film, based on a Hindi novel he wrote, the 1972 *Lalkar* (Challenge), similarly contrasts faithful Indian and flirting Anglo-Indian women. He kept making hit movies (and some flops on the side) until he transcended all that with his runaway success with television (Tully 1991: 127–52, *EIC* 202, www.sagartv.com.).

THE TELEVISED *RĀMĀYAṆA*. The history of the telecasting of the *Ramayan* series is an interesting case of the haphazard road to success. Ramanand Sagar's old friend from his Lahore days, S. S. Gill, was information and broadcasting secretary in the mid-1980s. He personally invited Sagar to develop the idea of a *Rāmāyaṇa* series for television (Rajagopal 2001: 326 n. 48). The first screen script, however, was rejected (327 n. 52). Some claim that it took nothing less than a miracle and a hunger strike by the wife of one of the director-generals (Sternfeld 2005: 199), but eventually the project received the blessings of Rajiv Gandhi on the grounds that it would work to promote national unity (Rajagopal 2001: 327 n. 52). Many would say that this project backfired on Gandhi and instead created an atmosphere in which the BJP (Bhāratīya Janatā Party) could gain prominence on the political scene. It is unclear what Sagar's own political agenda was.[45]

TVR was first shown on what was at the time India's only national television station, Doordarshan, on Sunday mornings at 9:30 from January 25, 1987, to July 31, 1988. As noted, its success was enormous and extended beyond these dates.

Sagar had cast relatively unknown actors in the lead roles: Arun Govil as Rāma and Dipika Chikhlia as Sītā. Soon these actors would be worshiped as representations of the gods, as is common in the dramatic Rāma-līlā tradition (Lutgendorf 1990: 160–3). Divine status would bring with it the responsibilities of exemplary behavior. The whole cast, in fact the whole production site, became strictly vegetarian. Interestingly for our purpose, the actress playing Sītā would see herself compelled to accept only "chaste" roles (163).

45. The issue is too complex to deal with here. I take it up again in the conclusion, but it is really a study for a political scientist.

Regarding the sources Sagar worked with, the credits proclaim that many regional versions were taken into account, but the one most extensively used is like *Rām Carit Mānas* (Dalmia-Lüderitz 1991: 209). Sometimes, the television version seems like a video clip of Tulsīdās's work, which is sung in the background. The director clearly has a very intimate and deep understanding of that text, the fruit of years of close reading and reciting (Sternfeld 2005: 197).

THE TELEVISED *SHRI KRISHNA*. In the wake of the success of *Ramayan*, Sagar came up with a series called *Shri Krishna*.[46] He wrote the screenplay and dialogue himself and directed it with his sons, Anand and Moti Sagar. Doordarshan at first rejected this series, so it started out on a private video circuit, but thanks to viewer interest, from April 1996 the series was shown on Doordarshan channel 2, and due to high viewership, in June 1996 it was moved to the prime channel, Doordarshan channel 1.[47] The DVDs of these series, too, are widely advertised and available in Indian groceries and at websites.[48] The lead actors were, again, rather unknown: Sarvdaman Banerjee as Krishna and Anuradha as Rādhā.

For his *Shri Krishna*, Sagar acknowledges especially *Bhāgavata Purāṇa* as his source. The DVD sleeve says it is "mainly based on Shrimad Bhagvat Maha Puran by Bhagwan Veda Vyas, with material from other puranas and some widely accepted sources." Inside is added: "Inspired by the English rendering of Bhagwat Puran by His Divine Grace Srila A. C. Bhaktivedanta Swami Prabhupadji the Founder Acharya of ISKCON" (International Society of Krishna Consciousness; popularly known as the Hare Krishnas). There may be an element of marketing to an international audience here, including Vedanta, Integral Yoga, and ISKCON followers, who form a sizeable community in the West.[49] In the

46. According to the family, the plan to do a mythological trilogy, with a *Rāmāyaṇa, Shri Krishna*, and *Durga* went back to 1977 (Sternfeld 2005: 200). Sagar also did for television the more children-oriented *Vikram aur Betāl* (before TVR) and *Alif Laila*. A television series, *Sai Baba*, started airing just before his death in 2005. The new mythological series *Durga* was announced in 2004. Details of other future and past serials can be found at www.sagartv.com/serial.asp.

47. It has consequently been dubbed in Bengali as well as several South Indian languages (Rajagopal 2001: 330–1 n. 77).

48. It should be noted that the numbering of the episodes is not consecutively over the different discs. I follow here the numbering on each disc.

49. In the acknowledgment at the end of each episode, ISKCON is mentioned, as well as two America-based people, apparently sponsors: Mrs. Jadoorani Dasi, who was initiated by Prabhupad himself (New York) and Swamini Turiya Sangitananda (Alice Coltrane, jazz musician and widow of John Coltrane, who became a devotee of Swami Satchidananda and later Satya Sai Baba and runs a Vedanta ashram near Los Angeles). Sagar's tapes now are advertised by ISKCON outlets.

introduction to each episode, the specifics of the "widely accepted sources are given": both Puranic and what he terms "folk" sources, appealing to regional sensitivies. Sagar is casting his net wide.

True to Puranic principles, Sagar contextualizes his own text, embedding it in a complex way in a series of dialogues with multiple narrators. In the first episode, he himself appears to address the audience directly. He tells a history of the worship of Krishna from what can be broadly termed a Hindu chauvinist perspective. In a pious India that worships Krishna, the Sanskrit scriptures *Bhāgavata Purāṇa* and *Brahma Vaivarta Purāṇa* are produced. Hinduism spreads first to the east through the Buddha and later also to the west through the saint Ramakrishna of the Ramakrishna Mission, and Prabhupad, the founder of ISKCON. Many devotees of Krishna are inspired by divine visions, which they proclaim to the world, and here the camera shows the woman saint Mīrā and the blind saint Sūrdās. Sagar then introduces the two great pioneers of Krishna bhakti and founders of the most influential movements, or *sampradāyas,* Vallabha and Caitanya, and enumerates a long list of saints from different areas, taking care to include Muslims, such as Rahīm and Raskhān. He discourages narrow parochialism (*sampradāyiktā*). As he stresses love and moral values, he also mentions the need to recognize the value of one's own tradition. What he claims as "his own tradition" is a Hinduism of the broad sweep, including all, prestigious Sanskrit scripture as well as vernacular text. In good Puranic tradition, he takes care to downplay his own innovations and establish the right credentials for his text.

THE TELEVISED *MAHĀBHĀRATA*. Parts of Krishna's story are also told in the televised serial *Mahabharat*, directed by B. R. (Baldev Raj) and his son Ravi Chopra, scripted by Rahi Masoom Raza. Like Sagar, B. R. Chopra was born in what is now Pakistan, studied at Lahore, but fled to India after Partition, in 1948. He founded his own production company, B. R. Films, in 1958 and was a successful director in the sixties with such hit movies as *Kanoon* (1961), *Gumrah* (1963), and *Humraaz* (1968), which were also critically acclaimed with awards. He continued making hit films, most notably *Pati, Patni aur woh* (1978) and *Insaf ka Tarazu* (1980) and received the Dadasaheb Phalke award for lifelong achievement in 1998. His engagement with television started in 1982 with a tele film, and his first television series, *Bahadur Shah Zafar* (1987), was about the last Mughal emperor. Chopra's success with the *Mahabharat* series has remained unsurpassed. First broadcast from September 1988 to July 1990 in ninety-four episodes, this series claims even higher viewership than *Ramayan* (Gokulsingh 2004: 49). It is still a best seller in Indian grocery stores abroad and is now available on DVD.[50] B. R. Chopra received for this series the National Citizen Award from then prime minister Chandra Shekhar.[51]

The story of Krishna figures importantly in Chopra's *Mahabharat,* much more than in the Sanskrit *Mahābhārata* attributed to Vyāsa, where Krishna's divinity is revealed in the *Bhagavad Gītā* but little is said about his life before he met the Pāṇḍavas. The story of his childhood is found first in the later *Harivaṃśa* (Brockington 1998: 315). In the television series, the prominence of Krishna is justified by the cosmic narrator Time (voiced by Harish Bhimani), who is at pains to stress the necessity of understanding Krishna so as to be able to understand the *Mahābhārata,* for instance in the introduction to episode 15 (DVD, vol. 3). This is in the second episode devoted to relating the long prehistory of the "true hero of the Mahābhārata," which in total spans episodes 13–18. I take into account the episode of Krishna's (Nitesh Bharadwaj) elopement with Rukmiṇī (Channa Ruparel) as portrayed in episodes 27–28 (vol. 5) in my discussion of "arranging the marriage" (chapter 2).

Films

As noted, at the end of each chapter, I will bring into the discussion the "echoes" of the Sītā and Rādhā-Gopī characters in popular Hindi movies, and what happens when Sītā and Rādhā leave their sacred woods and go to Bollywood, so to speak. I will refer to Hindi movies from roughly the sixties till now, mostly selected because of their immediate and explicit reference to Sītā and/or Rādhā. Many movie characters have the names Sītā or Rādhā or one of their many epithets, and the situations they encounter are highly reminiscent of the epic ones. Since my main interest is not the episodes of Sītā's trial by fire (Agniparīkṣā) and her banishment while pregnant, I leave out many movies that take up that theme. I have selected instead movies that portray courtship, marriage, and seduction. If these movies include references to the trial by fire I will refer to it, but it is not the main focus. I pay particular attention to the songs that explicitly evoke mythological references.

One movie that comes back again and again in this book is the major blockbuster of the nineties, the 1994 hit *Hum aap ke hain koun . . . !* (What

50. There is a short five-disc version, with fifteen and a quarter hours of film (sold with an essay by James Fitzgerald) and a longer one of sixteen discs (all ninety-four episodes of forty-five minutes each). In addition, a forty-five-episode sequel, *Mahabharat-katha,* contains several subplots that had to be excised from the television version (http://dvdtimes.co.uk/content.php?contentid=12664). Apparently there is even an unsubtitled sixty-four-disc video compact disk version of this epic.

51. Most of this information is from the website www.ultraindia.com/movies/awards/brchopra.htm.

am I to you), directed by Sooraj R. Barjatya (*HAKHK*) starring Madhuri Dixit and Salman Khan. This movie has been much discussed by sociologists and students of film studies,[52] but few have noted its many explicit references to Rādhā and Sītā mythology. The movie figures so prominently in this book because of its tremendous impact. For one, it won many of the Indian Oscars, the Filmfare awards.[53] It grossed an enormous amount of money but, more important, was widely and intensively watched. It was a favorite with members of the artistic elite, including its most ardent fan, the controversial painter M. F. Husain, who reported seeing it more than fifty times. Yet it also appealed to the "general public"; for instance, a college student from Mumbai saw it daily for more than a year (Kazmi 1999: 137).[54] Last but not least, it was a major trendsetter that inspired more "family entertainment" movies in the nineties (see *India Today*, December 25, 2000). Arguably, this movie is the prime example of the new middle-class Indian aspirations.

A similar box office hit, Aditya Chopra's 1995 *Dilwale dulhania le jayenge* [*DDLJ*] also is very relevant here (especially to the material discussed in chapter 2). A recent movie that was not such a box office hit but is important for its critique of the Sītā story is Rajkumar Santoshi's 2001 *Lajja* (chapter 3). I also have occasion to discuss Ashutosh Gowarikar's Oscar-nominated 2001 *Lagaan* (chapter 4).

Some classic movies are also brought into the discussion. Mehboob Khan's 1957 *Mother India* is discussed because of the place it holds in the Indian imagination and the importance of its mythic imagery, including Sītā-Rāma and Rādhā-Krishna symbolism (chapter 6). Several of Raj Kapoor's movies are equally interesting for their creative reworking of mythology, in particular his 1964 movie *Sangam* (chapter 3) and the 1978 *Satyam shivam sundaram* (chapters 5 and 6). I also include several less-known movies, some older, some very recent, that have special relevance.

I do not wish to promote a monolithic approach to myth in Hindi cinema or give the impression that the examples I cite stand for something uniform called "Bollywood" or "Indian popular cinema" in general. There is not space in this book to elaborate on each movie, with data on its production and popularity, complete analysis of its story line, and situating it within the

52. See, for example, Uberoi 2001a, Virdi 2003: 193–7, Raghavendra 2006: 42–6.

53. The movie won four Filmfare awards, including best film, best director, best actress, and best screenplay.

54. The movie also wins out if we gauge its popularity by the quotations in auto-rickshaw inscriptions (Uberoi 2001a: 309).

general trends of Indian popular cinema.[55] However, I feel that at the outset, a general overview of the evolution of the portrayal of romance is appropriate, Film scholar Jyotika Virdi perceptively notes shifts in the "filmī romance" over time. In the sixties, the desire of women is acknowledged, but not allowed to disturb patriarchal status quo (films like *Gumrah, Sangam, Sahib Bibi aur Ghulam;* 2003: 121–44). From the seventies, the heroine is allowed to be sexy and incorporate some elements of the vamp, but even the strong women characters are subjugated into conjugality by the overpowering heroes (films like *Seeta aur Geeta;* 145–59). After a spate of rape movies in the eighties (159–67, 170–7), since the late 1980s films have arrived that happily marry the pursuits of luxury and love and tend to identify the patriarch as the enemy (*Maine pyaar kiyaa, DDLJ;* 192–204). Virdi argues that these movies represent a bourgeois feminist stance that comes at the cost of erasing the low-caste and tribal perspective (205–14). She also points out that the increasing woman-friendly feel of the movies is limited to women's subjectivity, which remains located in discourses on love, romance, and family (126). A similar sentiment was expressed by Tejaswini Niranjana, who also noted the reduction of the Muslim to either terrorist or backward person (2000; speaking of Mani Ratnam's films). While not all movies fit the chronological frame, still this general overview of the changing portrayal of women helps one to understand the multiform and varied approach to mythological goddess archetypes in modern Indian cinema.

After decades of neglect in academia, there has recently been something of an upsurge of studies on popular Indian cinema. In their zeal to rehabilitate this cinema, some observers are keen to attribute a high degree of political correctness to these movies (Kishwar 2003a). Virdi's work questions such quick endorsements by feminists. As with the issue of Sītā's perceived "traditionalism" or "liberating potential," the jury on these movies, too, is out. I hope that certain detailed discussions here will further the debate and show the very uneven and nuanced messages popular movies send to their audiences, both women and men.

Organization of the Book

The main question underlying this study, then, to summarize, is to what extent Sītā's example can be said to be empowering or oppressive for women as they

55. I had hoped to include an appendix with the full information for each movie discussed, but that has not proved practical, given the large size of this book.

cope with love; how that changes at different points in history, and how that contrasts or not with the example of Rādhā. Three subquestions arise. First, are bhakti texts liberating for women, in privileging love above duty and positively valuing women's subjectivity? Second, does the modernity of the medium of television and film result in a more progressive view of womanhood in contemporary screen versions? Finally, how is the increasing influence of Hindutva in the public sphere reflected on screen?

In order to answer these questions, I have organized the argument thematically according to issues of interest to women in their ways of coping with love. The issues are organized into two parts, each with three chapters. Part I focuses on how the goddess deals with premarital love, including falling in love (chapter 1), arranging the marriage (chapter 2), and the nature of the wedding ceremony (chapter 3). Part II addresses how she copes with the challenges of married life, including staying faithful in adversity, that is, coping with setbacks in the husband's carreer or the call to leave purdah to follow one's beloved into the unknown (chapter 4), the threat of the "other woman" (chapter 5) and the "other man," and sexual harassment (chapter 6). Though providing only a fragmentary and incomplete view of women's life cycles, arguably, these are six key points in women's lives when they may turn to role models to find their way through challenges. For each theme, I give snapshots of how Sītā and Rādhā deal with the situation, thus providing, as noted, contrasting landmarks in the moral landscape ordinary women have to navigate.

Obviously, my choice of these themes is informed by contemporary concerns of gender issues. Yet the sequence and division follows also the story of Sītā, up to and including her abduction. For a contrastive analysis, I provide parallels from the story of Krishna's lovers, Rādhā and the Gopīs. In one case, namely the theme of arranging for matrimony (chapter 2), the comparison with Rādhā does not work, since Rādhā—according to most—did not marry Krishna. Instead, I focus on Krishna's first wife, Rukmiṇī, who in the sources considered here eloped with Krishna. This makes for a nice contrast with Sītā's parentally sanctioned wedding and provides possibly an alternative scenario for contemporary women unable to marry the choice of their hearts.

I start most chapters with an analysis of the Sītā story, followed by one of the Rādhā story, comparing for each the three points of reference, namely the classical, medieval, and contemporary versions of the story; I then provide a comparative discussion of the contrastive examples of Rādhā and Sītā. The only exception is chapter 4, where the comparison of the Sītā and Rādhā stories proceeds point by point rather than being split into an investigation of each in turn; the similarities of the situations may not be so apparent at first, and the point-by-point simultaneous approach in itself argues for the validity of the comparison. At the end of each chapter, the film versions are brought in, for an analysis of the multiforms of these role models in popular culture.

The book's conclusion first discusses the woman's movement's engagement with these role models and then, what insights can be drawn for the construction of traditional South Asian "womanhood," as well as how that construction has developed over time, or, one could say, been manipulated by conservators of the tradition. I discuss in turn this book's findings for the devotional and the modern construction of role models of womanhood. The film and television versions are placed in their economic and social political context.

As this book draws together a mass of material from very different sources, it may sometimes be difficult to keep straight what is said where. For that reason I provide tables throughout with comparative overviews of the differences in the sources discussed. If the reader loses track of the general argument through the wealth of detail provided, consulting these tables will reestablish a general overview of what is going on. The material is very complex, but this detailed analysis is intended to contribute to a nuanced understanding of the nature, construction, and reconstruction, and abiding power of South Asian patriarchy—beyond easy generalizations.

PART I

Getting a Love Marriage Arranged

I

Falling in Love

Sītā in the Flower Garden and Rādhā in the Forest

The Right Way to Fall in Love

I start my exploration of mythological role models for women through time with an auspicious moment, when the goddess falls in love. Indeed, Hindu goddesses are not immune to falling in love. The issue of Sītā and Rādhā falling head over heels for their consorts raises several interesting questions. On the theological level, there seems to be a contradiction inherent in the very notion of the divine becoming overpowered by love, but maybe that is exactly the point? When it comes to love, even the gods are powerless!

My focus, though, is on how they set a model for ordinary women. Here we are struck by how goddesses represent a case of tightly controlled letting go. After all, they don't fall for the first or the best guy; they only fall in love when they recognize "Mr. Right," who is none other than God himself. For ordinary women, the question is first how to recognize Mr. Right. What example do the goddesses set in selecting one's mate? Is partner choice preordained? Once the partner is chosen or recognized, the next question is how to handle the situation. How to put out feelers as to whether one's love is reciprocated? Are these goddesses of the shyly blushing, passively waiting type or do they frankly step forward and take the initiative? And once they find their beloved reciprocating, how far do they go in their romantic liaison? Is there any scope for premarital physical closeness?

The issue of falling in love has of course universal human relevance, but what interests us particularly here is the way it is portrayed differently over time. Tracing the multiple depictions of the goddess's love shows us how ideal courtship is understood in contemporary Indian contexts and lets us put our finger on how that differs from earlier interpretations. It can tell us a great deal about the messages sent to young people with regard to how to handle falling in love.[1]

Before we delve into the specific preoccupations of each depiction, we need to pause and look at the broader picture. The theme of falling in love (*pūrvarāga*) in itself is a favorite of Sanskrit belles lettres, known as the *kāvya* tradition. By incorporating this scene into the goddess's story, authors show an aspiration to take part in that tradition. Some elements will be conventional, typical for *kāvya*, yet each author has an individual twist. Our task will be to unravel what is formulaic and what is innovative.

For the devotional versions, it is also important to keep in mind that the love of the goddess stands metaphorically for the love of a devotee for God. While modeled on human love, it also transcends it. Thus we are dealing with something larger than life, larger than "just simply" love itself.

In the modern media versions, the divine courtship functions within the competing ideologies of love marriage versus arranged marriage, often conceived of as a clash of modernity versus tradition, of Western liberal versus indigenous conservative ideas. In that light, we might expect the portrayal in our sources to move over time from a more conservative traditional depiction toward a compromise that incorporates a more liberal interpretation. Let us test that theory by exploring what role models the different versions of the Rādhā and Sītā stories set for women through time.

For Sītā, it is easy to identify the moment to study. The episode of Rāma and Sītā falling in love is part of the first book of the *Rāmāyaṇa* story, the one on Rāma's youth (Bāla Kāṇḍa). The episode is popularly known as the Phūlvārī (or sometimes the more upscale Sanskritic Puṣpavāṭikā), or Flower Garden. It is so named after the romantic setting in which Rāma and Sītā meet each other for the first time before their marriage and fall in love. Rāma and Sītā meet by chance, while she is on her way to a nearby goddess temple for worship, and he is picking flowers for his guru. Of course it is love at first sight, but not much more happens, just mutual beholding.

1. Of course, this is all about the ideal, arguably a middle-class one. For a corrective about lower-caste perspectives, see the interesting work by Jonathan Parry (2002).

The episode figures prominently in the television version (volume 2, episode 6). It is based to a high degree on the medieval version, to the point that it comes across as a video clip of Tulsīdās's *Rām Carit Mānas*, with which comparison is especially fruitful. In Tulsīdās's work, too, the Flower Garden passage is important and is elaborated over several verses (1. 227–36). However, this episode does not occur in the Sanskrit *Rāmāyaṇa* attributed to Vālmīki, so we cannot compare the medieval scene with the classical one. The scene does not even occur in the other major source of Tulsī's work, the esoteric *Adhyātma Rāmāyaṇa* (Vaudeville 1955: 104). Still, its absence does not impede the scene from being an extremely popular one in the contemporary imagination (Lutgendorf 1991b: 94); it occurs frequently in "tableau" (*jhāṅkī*) (105) and in folk (Kajli) singing (332), as well as of course in the popular Rām-līlā theatre.

It is more difficult to select an episode to compare with the romantic feelings of Rādhā and the Gopīs for Krishna. Poets love to elaborate on a first meeting of the two. Most famous is Sūrdās's song "Shyām Asked: 'Who Are You Fair Lady?'" (*Būjha syāma kaun tū gorī, SS* 1291/673). Many theological exegetes have written on the topic (in particular the Gauḍīya theologians Rūpa and Jīva Gosvāmī; see Wulff 1984 and Brzezinski 2000). If we follow the narrative in *Bhāgavata Purāṇa,* we find that the first reference to romantic love occurs when Krishna's flute playing arouses the Gopīs' love (10.21). Thus, the Gopīs fall in love with Krishna in his absence, and their first romantic encounter with him is not till the next chapter, in the so-called Cīraharaṇa or Vastraharaṇa scene, where he steals the Gopīs' clothes (*BhP* 10.22). I have selected for comparison that famous scene, where the Gopīs are engaged in a ritual to worship the goddess Katyāyanī, for which they are bathing in the river. Krishna steals their clothes and climbs up a tree, refusing to give the clothes back until they come out of the water, naked before him. There is clearly a lot more going on here than the chaste mutual beholding of Sītā and Rāma, so it makes for an instructive contrast.

The Vastraharaṇa scene inspired several medieval poets, among them Nanddās, who translates the episode in his *Bhāsā Dasama Skandha* (22). Sagar's televised *Shri Krishna* also features an interesting version of the scene episode (vol. 6, 37), and picks up the theme again later (vol. 7, 57). In addition, Sagar adds a scene of the first meeting of Krishna and Rādhā (vol. 6, 36).

While at first sight the Vastraharaṇa scene may seem very different, still it makes a wonderful parallel for the Phūlvārī episode. Both depict a first articulation of love, described according to sensual conventions of *kāvya* (*pūrvarāga*). All parties seem to be adolescents. The setting of the event is bucolic, and like Sītā, the Gopīs are involved in worshiping the goddess. All our sources are devotional and use the occasion as a metaphor for the meeting of god and his

TABLE 1.1. Comparison of Sītā's Phūlvārī and the Gopīs' Vastraharaṇa

Similarities

First true love (*pūrvarāga*)
Adolescent hero and heroine
Description according to *kāvya* conventions
Bucolic background
Worship of goddess

Differences

Element	Sītā's Phūlvārī	Gopīs' Vastraharaṇa
Setting	Garden	Forest
	Spring	Winter (*hemānta*)
Atmosphere	Dharma	Clandestine
	Serious	Joke
	Proper serenity	Erotic titillation
Outcome	Matrimony	Promise of Rāsa-līlā

devotees, with the central element of mutual beholding, or *darśana*. The scenes are nicely contrastive, mostly in their tone: Sītā and Rāma's meeting is chaste, well within the bounds of propriety, or dharma, whereas Krishna's meeting with the Gopīs is erotic and clandestine. Unlike Rāma, Krishna has no business near the place where the Gopīs are worshiping, and he actually transgresses the rules of dharma by stealing their clothes while they are bathing as part of their religious worship. The episode is decidedly erotic and has an element of titillation, whereas there was no hint of such in the case of Rāma and Sītā. There are also differences in the seasonal context: spring for Rāma and Sītā's meeting and the cold of winter (*hemānta*) for the Gopīs. Finally, the outcome differs too: Sītā and Rāma's meeting leads to matrimony, Krishna promises the Gopīs only to dance the Rāsa-līlā.

I will first compare the medieval versions of the Phūlvārī and Vastraharaṇa episodes before turning to the television retellings and the reverberations of the theme in Bollywood movies. There are multiple echoes of the Phūlvārī in popular Hindi movies; I discuss a scene from the 1994 trendsetting hit *Hum aapke hain koun . . . !* directed by Sooraj Barjatya. As a counterpoint, I will bring into the discussion a scene from the all-time classic *Sholay* (1975), directed by Ramesh Sippy. For echoes of the Vastraharaṇa in Hindi film, I look at Raj Kapoor's 1964 *Sangam,* which has a scene evocative of Krishna stealing the Gopīs' clothes.

Medieval Sources Compared

Hopelessly Devoted to You: Falling in Love à la Sītā

As noted, the Flower Garden scene is one of the major changes to the Sanskrit version that Tulsī introduces in his work. Maybe it is significant in itself that Vālmīki does not mention any premarital meeting between Rāma and Sītā. It may well be that such is not part of the epic universe.

Tulsīdās is not the first to introduce the scene, which has precedents in classical drama: most notably Bhavabhūti's eighth-century *Mahāvīracarita*, and Jayadeva II's thirteenth-century *Prasannarāghava* (Vaudeville 1955: 104; see Pauwels 2000 for an extensive discussion). Tulsī though, seems less interested in dramatic action, than poetic description. He is also pushing his bhakti agenda. His main concern is to set up an example of an ideal relation between devotee and God, and to stress the importance of *darśana* in that relationship. This involves pondering God's beauty, but also an element of reciprocity, since God answers the sincere devotee's love. Appropriately for this bhakti agenda, the tone is less erotic and playful, and but more serene and serious, compared to that in *kāvya*.

Tulsī is, however, not drawing solely on Sanskrit sources. One of the major accomplishments of his retelling is, after all, that it is in the vernacular, Avadhī. By the time he composed his work, there were already several Avadhī romances available, most of them Sūfī in inspiration. When they describe first love, they feature a meeting between the lovers; often the meeting takes place near a temple, usually during a publicly celebrated festival.[2] It may well be that the very medium in which he was working is responsible for at least part of the description of the Phūlvārī episode.

Tulsī must also have been influenced by the Braj poetry celebrating the love of Krishna and Rādhā in a bucolic setting that was so popular by the time he wrote. However, he chose to distance himself from the more overtly erotic Krishna bhakti scenes. For one, Tulsīdās studiously avoids physical contact between the lovers (in contrast also with the Sūfī and *kāvya* poems). Connected with this is the different framing of the whole scene. Much of the Braj mate-

2. As I have discussed at length elsewhere (Pauwels 2000), there are significant differences compared to the Phūlvārī (e.g., the disguise of the Sūfī hero as a holy man, his endurance and fainting prior to the meeting, and the heroines' boldness). The differences are connected to the fact that the allegorical value of the Sūfī romance is the opposite of that of Rāma and Sītā: the Sūfī hero stands for the spiritual seeker, who has to go through different stages before he reaches his goal. In the bhakti tradition, the woman is the model for the human devotee, or *bhakta*, and the beholding of the divine (*darśana*) plays a major role in the worship.

rials derive part of their charm from the titillation of the more or less explicit secrecy of the tryst and its exciting if not downright adulterous, at least illegitimate, nature. Tulsī, on the other hand, seems nearly obsessively concerned with reassuring his public that the meeting is legitimate. Whereas the Krishna bhakti stresses the aspect of eroticism, *śṛṅgāra,* Tulsī makes sure to drench the whole episode in a tone of *maryādā,* or conventional morality.

Tulsī accomplishes his goal by repeated steps toward legitimizing the premarital love of Rāma and Sītā. All possible titillation that might be associated with a scene featuring voyeurism, or at least girls looking at boys and vice versa, is carefully eradicated. Tulsī succeeds in his purpose of keeping sweet first love within the limits of *maryādā* in several ways.

First of all, he makes sure the public is abundantly aware that the protagonists' presence at the scene is totally legitimate, in fact even ordered by their elders. Rāma and Lakshmana are in the garden to pick flowers for worshiping their guru. They have obtained the guru's explicit blessing to do so: "With an eye to the auspicious event (of guru-pūjā), both brothers obtained their guru's permission to go and pick flowers" (*RCM* 1.227.1b).[3] Tulsī even makes it clear they also got permission to pick flowers from the garderners themselves: "They searched in all directions, asked the gardeners, and started to collect flowers and petals with reassured hearts," *RCM* 1.228.1a).[4] In other words, Tulsī is concerned in portraying the brothers as not just "hanging out" in the place. He does the same for Sītā and her girlfriends. They got explicit orders from Sītā's mother to go and worship the goddess whose temple is in the garden: "At that moment Sītā arrived there, sent by her mother to worship Pārvatī" (*RCM* 1.228.1b).[5]

Further, neither Rāma nor Sītā are active agents in bringing about the meeting. They are portrayed as totally innocent; the meeting is absolutely by chance and in no way do they steer toward it. Rāma is first made aware of Sītā's present by the sound of anklets:

> Hearing the sound of bracelet-, belt-, and anklet-bells, Rāma spoke
> to his brother, with wonder in his heart.
> Is the god of love beating his victory drums to announce his
> intention to conquer the world? (*RCM* 1.230.1)[6]

3. *samaya jāni gura āyasu pāī, lena prasūna cale dou bhāī.*

4. *cahuṃ disi citai pūṃchi mālīgana, lage lena dala phūla mudita mana.*

5. *tehi avasara sītā tahaṃ āī, girijā pūjana janani paṭhāī.*

6. *kaṃkana kiṃkinī nūpara dhuni suni, kahata lakhana sana rāmu hṛdayaṃ guni; mānahuṃ madana duṃdubhī dīnhī, manasā bisva bijaya kahaṃ kīnhī.*

It is one of the more adventurous girlfriends of Sītā who takes the initiative to go and look at the boys and drag the other girls along (*RCM* 1.228.4–229, *dohā*). Sītā timidly joins her friends.

Tulsī adds yet another dimension. Sītā only joins her girlfriends in the expedition because she knows this is her "old love" from previous births and because she is reminded of the sage Nārada's prediction that she will marry Rāma, since they are incarnations of Lakṣmī and Vishnu (the prediction itself, is not related in *RCM,* as discussed by Vaudeville 1955: 105–6). Consequently, Tulsī hastens to add, it is pure love (*prīti punīta*):

> With the same dear girlfriend in the lead, they left. Who understands love of yore?
> Sītā remembered Nārada's prediction: the love she felt was pure!
> Agitated she looked all around, like a frightened fawn. (*RCM* 1.229.4b-*dohā*)[7]

Rāma is similarly confused about the strength of his feelings when he sees the girls. Not only does he feel compelled to reflect on his "sinful" feelings, but he confesses them to his brother:

> Praising Sītā's beauty in his heart, the Lord was amazed at his own mental state.
> With pure mind, he spoke to his younger brother words that befit the occasion. (*RCM* 1:230, *dohā*)[8]

Tulsī clearly is eager to stress Rāma's purity of mind (*suci mana*). Rāma then goes on to communicate to his brother how his usually unperturbed mind is now in commotion (1.231.2a).[9] It is not proper for a Rāghava to be so perturbed at the sight of "unrelated" women:

> The Rāghavas nature is never to stray from the path, not [even] in thought.
> [Yet] my heart, which does not even dream of another's wife, is overwhelmed with love! (*RCM* 1.231.5–6)[10]

7. *calī agra kari priya sakhi soī, prīti purātana lakhai na koī; sumiri sīya nārada vacana, upajī prīti punīta; cakita bilokati sakala disi, janu sisu mṛgī sabhīta.*

8. *siya sobhā hiyaṃ barani prabhu, āpani dasā bicāri; bole suci mana anuja sana, bacana samaya anuhāri.*

9. *sahaja punita more manu chobhā.*

10. *raghubaṃsinha kara sahaja subhāū, manu kupaṃtha pagu dharai na kāū; mohi atisaya pratīti mana kerī, jehiṃ sapanehuṃ paranāri na herī.*

Rāma here implicitly justifies his love by reasoning that he, unblemishable as he is, cannot possibly be feeling what he does for a woman who is not his own, so this must be the wife predestined for him.

Clearly, Tulsī feels compelled to justify even his protagonists' "passively going along" with the chance meeting. They both have an inkling that this person is no "stranger" but rather the bride/groom to be, even the intimately close marital partner from previous births or, rather, from their true divine identities as Lakṣmī and Vishnu.

Such concerns of Tulsī are not random. This is in contrast to the Rādhā-Krishna mythology, where there has been a strong hint of adultery, as Rādhā is often understood to be married to another (*parakīyā*). However, in Tulsī's Sītā's case, there is no ambiguity possible. Sītā is safely and soundly Rāma's own (*svakīyā*).

Next, Tulsī ensures legitimacy by avoiding any hint of licentiousness in the meeting itself. Rather, even the visual contact is squarely within the bounds of propriety. There is no question of the flirting, fleeting sidelong glances (*kaṭākṣa*) so celebrated in Sanskrit *kāvya* on the topic. Instead, we could speak of a stability of the gaze, clearly pointing to the theological concept of a steady *darśana*. Rāma's gaze is steadfast (*acaṃcala*; *RCM* 1.230.2b); Sītā's eyes stop blinking (*RCM* 1.232.3c).[11] In fact, Sītā is so overcome that she even closes her eyes (*RCM* 1.232.4a).

Again this has theological significance: Tulsī has combined the typical bhakti theology of *darśana* with an older, more yoga-oriented idea of meditation, or *dhyāna*. Significantly, Sītā has her eyes closed through the head-to-toe (*nakha-śikha*) description of Rāma and his brother that follows (*RCM* 1.233). She does not open her eyes until her friends lure her out of this state of meditation by encouraging her to meditate on the prince before her eyes "instead of meditating on the goddess" (*RCM* 1.234.1b).[12]

In putting it this way, the girls interpret Sītā closing her eyes as a devotional act, which again heightens the atmosphere of *maryādā* instead of eroticism, or *śṛṅgāra*. When Sītā finally allows herself a good look at Rāma's beauty, she immediately interrupts her thoughts by "remembering" her father's oath, namely that she will marry only the one who can break the bow (*RCM* 1.234.2b).[13]

11. *palakanhihuṃ pariharīṃ nimeṣeṃ.*
12. *bahuri gauri kara dhyāna karehū, bhūpakisora dekhi kina lehū.*
13. *nakha sikha dekhi rāma kai sobhā, sumiri pitā panu manu ati chobhā.*

Significantly, too, neither of the protagonists tries actively to prolong the meeting. Again, passivity prevails. Both parties are so overcome by feeling that they become "stunned" and "immobile." The girlfriends once again take the initiative and drag Sītā away, dropping a clever hint suggesting a possible future rendezvous (*RCM* 1.234.3), and Sītā immediately thinks of her mother's worry if she is late (*RCM* 1.234.4a) and is well aware she is in her father's care (*RCM* 1.234.4b).[14] However, Sītā, touchingly, shows some regret, when she follows the Sanskṛt *kāvya* tradition in looking back at Rāma at some pretext or other:

> With the excuse of looking at a deer, a bird, a tree, she turned back again and again
> Gazing at Raghu's hero's beauty, her love grew greatly. (*RCM* 1.234, *dohā*)[15]

Finally, after the meeting, the two lovers do not let go of their composure, not even in the privacy of their thoughts. Sītā goes to the temple to pray for a husband. Her prayer is reported in detail. Matrimony is foremost on her mind, as is clear from the epithets she uses to address the goddess, which are related to the goddess's role as wife and mother: Glory to the princess of the Mountain king, Glory to the one glued to Maheśa's moonface like a cakorī bird. (*RCM* 1.235.3a)[16]

> Among women loyal to their husband-gods, mother, your place is foremost,
> your immeasurable greatness cannot be expressed, [try may] thousand times the goddess of speech or multi-tongued Śeṣa. (*RCM* 1.235, *dohā*)[17]

Still, Sītā does not even in her thoughts express the identity of her groom as Rāma, stressing that the goddess knows her heart anyway. Instead, she humbly prays:

> "You know well my heart's desire, because you eternally dwell in everyone's heart.

14. *bhayau bilaṃbu mātu bhaya mānī* and *phirī apanapaü pitubasa jāne*, resp.

15. *dekhata misa mṛga bihaga taru, phirai bahori bahori; nirakhi nirakhi raghubīra chabi, bāṛhaï prīti na thori.*

16. *jaya jaya giribararāja kisorī, jaya mahesa mukha caṃda cakorī.*

17. *patidevatā sutīya mahuṃ, mātu prathama tava rekha; mahimā amita na sakahiṃ kahi, sahasa sāradā seṣa.*

So, I haven't openly told you the reason [for my prayer]" with these words, the princess of Videha clasped the feet [of the goddess image]. (*RCM* 1.236.2)[18]

This unassuming humble prayer immediately is received favorably with a miraculous sign of approval: "Bhavānī was swayed by this humble love, she slipped down a flower garland and the image smiled" (*RCM* 1.236.3a).[19] This is significant, as it reveals Tulsī's general bhakti agenda with its message that selfless love toward the god will be answered in kind.

To further ensure the propriety of Sītā's feelings for her totally "suitable boy", Tulsī arranges for nothing less then a miraculous divine sanction. Not only does the image smile and shed a flower garland, but Tulsī has the goddess speak her approval very explicitly:

Sītā reverently touched the garland of grace (*prasād*) against her head. Joy filled her heart, as the goddess spoke:
"Listen Sītā, my blessing is true, your heart's desire will be fulfilled." (*RCM* 1.236.2b-4a)[20]

And to ensure total propriety, the goddess, too, refers to Nārada's prediction as a sanctifier of this love: "Nārada's words are always pure truth. You will obtain the bridegroom whom your heart is attached to" (*RCM* 1.236.4b).[21] Tulsī does not leave it at that and elaborates on the business of divine sanction even further in a following *chand* and *dohā*.

Rāma is equally dutiful and does not let his newly awakened love get in the way of his duties in serving his guru. Indeed, Rāma has duly reported the incident to his elder, as Tulsī puts it: so pure is his character that deceit cannot touch it (1.237.1b).[22] In the same way Sītā got divine sanction from the goddess, Rāma receives the blessing of his guru:

The sage performed worship with the flowers, then he gave his blessings to them both:
"May your wishes come true." The brothers were happy to hear this. (*RCM* 1.237.2)[23]

18. *mora manorathu jānahu nīkeṃ, basahu sadā ura pura sabhī keṃ; kīnheuṃ pragaṭa na kārana tehīṃ, asa kahi carana gahe baidehīṃ.*

19. *vinaya prema basa bhaī bhavānī, khasī māla mūrati musukānī.*

20. *sādara siyaṃ prasādu sira dhareū, bolī gauri haraṣu hiyaṃ bhareū; sunu siya satya asīsa hamārī, pūjihi mana kāmanā tumhārī.*

21. *nārada bacana sadā suci sācā, so baru milihi jāhiṃ manu rācā.*

22. *rāma kahā sabu kausika pāhīṃ, sarala subhāu chuata chala nāhīṃ.*

23. *sumana pāi muni pūjā kīnhī, puni asīsa duhu bhāinha dīnhī; suphala manorath hohuṃ tumhāre, rāmu lakhanu suni bhae sukhāre.*

Rāma dutifully discharges all his tasks (*RCM* 1.237.5–6). When he is finally alone, he can reflect on the beauty of his beloved, but again, his musings are highly noble. He does not reflect on Sītā's physical beauty but her noble character, chastizing himself for comparing her with the vile moon.[24]

> The moon rose at the Eastern horizon, which pleased him, happily he saw similarities with Sītā's face;
> But then, he thought by himself, the moon is not like Sītā's face:
> Born from the ocean, its kinsman is poison; in the day it's weak, it has spots!
> How could it be compared to Sītā's face, this poor weak moon? (*RCM* 1.237.4-*dohā*)[25]
> It wanes and waxes, brings sadness to separated lovers, Rāhu grabs it when he finds it nearby.
> It brings sorrow to cuckoos, is the enemy of lotuses. O moon, you have many flaws!
> Comparing Videha's princess's face to the moon, I've made a grave mistake. (*RCM* 1.238.1-2a)[26]

At this point, again, Rāma goes to his guru to massage his feet (*RCM* 1.238.3a). In other words, the whole scene of Rāma's romantic musings is properly sandwiched in between guru-worship.

In short, Tulsī has taken pains to stress that both Rāma and Sītā were in the garden with proper permission of their elders and in a religious context. They met innocently, without prior intent. In addition, the experience of falling in love itself is totally devoid of erotic characteristics; mutual feelings are kept in control by the heroes themselves. Strictly speaking, there is not even a question of "new" love, since this love is in fact an "old" one, dating from previous births. Moreover, it is also duly sanctioned by the proper mother and father figures. Tulsī seems to have set up his scene in conscious contrast to Krishna bhakti, by purging the erotics. In the process, he has transformed the lush Braj-scape into an domesticated and controlled urban environment. It is no coincidence that the setting is not a wild forest bower (*kuñja*) but a neatly

24. This is a clever application of the figure of speech of *vyatireka*, where the traditional object of comparison is one-upped by its subject.

25. *prācī disi sasi uyaü suhāvā, siya mukha sarisa dekhi sukhu pāvā; bahuri bicāru kīnha mana māhīṃ, sīya badana sama himakara nāhīṃ. janamu siṃdhu puni baṃdhu biṣu, dīna malīna sakalaṃka; siya mukha samatā pāva kimi, caṃdu bāpuro raṃka.*

26. *ghaṭaui baṛhaï birahini dukhadāī, grasaï rāhu nija saṃdhihiṃ pāī; koka sokaprada paṃkaja drohī, avaguna bahuta caṃdramā tohī; baidehī mukha paṭatara dīnhe, hoi doṣu baṛa anucita kīnhe.*

groomed and irrigated flower garden, controlled by gardeners at every step. Tulsī's motive for this move is a religious one: he is promoting a bhakti of *maryādā*, fit for his chosen divinity (*iṣṭadevatā*), Rāma, often called *maryādā puruṣottama*, or man of highest moral principles. One could see this as an aspect of Tulsī's theological bridge-building: he seeks to combine the appeal of vernacular Krishna bhakti with the serious serenity more befitting bhakti for Rāma.

Losing Your Clothes: Falling in Love with Krishna

When we move to Krishna bhakti, the scene of Krishna stealing the Gopīs' clothes seems about the exact opposite of the propriety of the flower garden, and this not just because the seasonal setting is winter instead of spring. The very premise of stealing women's clothes is titillating. It involves nudity and lighthearted prank-playing. Not much room here for the seriousness of matrimony, one would assume. Let us analyze in some detail the classical story as told in *Bhāgavata Purāṇa* and the late sixteenth-century Braj recreation by Nanddās.[27]

In *Bhāgavata Purāṇa*, the love of the Gopīs for an adolescent Krishna (*paugaṇḍa*, 10.15.1) seems to follow naturally their maternal feelings of his early years.[28] One of the first references to the Gopīs' romantic love occurs in chapter 15. The focus here is on Krishna's exploits with his friends, the Gopas, but after he slays Dhenuka the Gopīs congratulate Krishna (10.15.42–3). Similarly, during and after Krishna's heroic feats in the next chapters allusions to their romantic feelings follow (10.16.20; 10.19.16), but the romance is not fully developed until later. The stage for romance is set in good *kāvya* style by descriptions of natural beauty, first of the monsoon and then the autumn season (10.20). Then follows the description of the effect of Krishna's flute playing on the Gopīs, who sing about its enchanting power (10.21). At the beginning of the next chapter (10.22), the Gopīs become the heroines of the action. They are observing a vow to the goddess for the purpose of gaining Krishna as their husband.

Nanddās follows *Bhāgavata Purāṇa* chapter by chapter, so he, too, sets the stage via nature description and articulates the Gopīs' love first in their comments on Krishna's flute playing. I will focus here on the differences his

27. The story in *BhP* in turn is an innovation, compared to *Viṣṇu Purāṇa*, and based on Tamil sources, as Hardy has argued (1983: 512–6).

28. On this interesting blending of maternal and erotic love, see Hawley 1983.

rendition of chapter 22 introduces. Notably, he elaborates and spends more time on setting up the scene for Krishna's prank. He individualizes the description by giving a list of the names of the women who partake in the worship, naming Rādhā among others (*Vṛṣabhāna kī nandini, BDS* 22.9).

In contrast to *Bhāgavata Purāṇa*'s ambiguity, Nanddās makes it clear that those women were all married and have relinquished their husbands on account of their love of Krishna:

> Reportedly all the women were married, yet desired the beauty of
> Nanda's son.
> Overpowered, each in turn gave up her husband. While keeping a
> vow, they each had Hari in their heart. (*BDS* 22.3–4)[29]

This is surprising, given that Vallahba, to whose sect Nanddās purportedly belonged, establishes in his philosophical commentary, *Śrī Subodhinī,* that some Gopīs were married and others not and it is the latter whose "marriage" is described in this chapter.[30] Vallabha specifies that in fact the Gopīs are reborn sages, who were anxious not to be given in marriage to anyone but Krishna.[31] Nanddās, however, seems to find it important to stress that the women are married. In doing so, he is maybe not so much seeking to titillate, as to stress that their worship involved an act of renunciation, that is, giving up their marital status. In this concern about renunciation, he is similar to Vallabha, who, however, wants to show the opposite: he says that the whole chapter is to be understood as a test (*parīkṣā*) of the Gopīs to establish that nonrenunciation is superior to renunciation (Vallabha 2003: 2258).[32]

The prayer of the Gopīs though, establishes their very this-worldly goal in their penance. It is reported verbatim: "O Katyāyanī, Great Māyā, Great

29. *jadapi samasta bibāhita āhi, nanda suvana ke rūpahi cāhi; bibasa bhaīṃ pati parihari parihari, karata bhaīṃ brata hiya hari dhari dhari.*

30. See the *Subodhinī* at *BhP* 10.20.1: "and they were twofold: with no other previously and with another previously, the last had gone through the [marriage] ceremony elsewhere . . . that will be told below, and the very ceremonies of those who were not elsewhere promised, is described" (*tāśca dvividhā ananyapūrvā anyapūrvāśca; anyapūrvās tv anyathaiva kṛtasaṃskārāḥ . . . tad uttaratra vakṣyate; anyāsām asaṃskṛtānāṃ saṃskāra eva nirūpyate*). *Ananyapūrvā* is translated as "maiden" and *anyapūrvā* as "married" by T. Ramanan (Vallabha 2003: 2258) in conformity with the next elaboration, or *ṭippanī*, of Viṭṭhalnāth.

31. The commentary reads: "Because of their visionary nature they feared being given away elsewhere and enjoyed in another way, thus they got engaged in this vow"; *tāsām ṛṣitvād anyatra dānam anyathā bhogaṃ cāśaṅkya vratārthaṃ pravṛttaḥ* (Vallabha 2003: 2258–9). This is made more explicit in the commentaries to *Śri Subodhinī* (Vallabha 2003: 2263)

32. *atyāgas tyāgād uttama iti jñāpayituṃ parīkṣā.* Notwithstanding Vallabha's interpretation, one could argue that in *BhP,* too, there is an element of asceticism. It is the cold season (10.22.1), and the Gopīs are bathing at sunrise in the Yamunā.

Yoginī, Empress; Hail to you Goddess, give me for husband the cowherd Nanda's son" (*BhP* 10.22.4).[33] This prayer is at once charmingly naïve and poignant.

Nanddās reports the prayer of the Gopīs as follows:

> Hail, Fair one, Lady, worthy above all, Great Mother, bestower of boons, well-wisher;
> Have mercy, goddess and make it work out such,[34] make Nanda's son my (our) husband. (*BDS* 22.18–9)[35]

There is an important difference from the prayer in the classical text: Nanddās has conveniently transformed the fiercer goddess Katyāyanī into Śiva's consort, Gaurī.[36] We are immediately reminded of the episode of Sītā's prayer to Pārvatī in the temple. There is actually no overlap in the words with Sīta's prayer, except for the reference to the goddess as bestower of boons (*baradāyanī, RCM* 1.2361b), which is generic. Still it may actually not be far-fetched to read in Tulsī's influence, in the light of the tradition that Nanddās composed his work in answer to Tulsī's (see the introduction). In any case, Nanddās leaves out the fiercer, Yoginī aspects of the goddess in his choice of epithets. By using the epithet Gaurī, or Fair One, the Gopīs stress her physical attractiveness, which fits well with the purpose of their prayer. While they still call the goddess Mahāmāī, they hasten to add that she is auspicious (*subhāyaka*) and "bestower of boons" (*varadāī*).

True to the epithet she is invoked with, the goddess answers the women's prayer, granting them their wish: "The goddess, thrilled, uttered these words 'Your wish be fulfilled'" (*BDS* 22.20).[37]

The parallel with the sanctification of Sītā's love is striking, and seems to confirm the theory that the *Mānas* inspired Nanddās's work. Alternatively, Nanddās's invention may be justified with reference to *Bhāgavata Purāṇa*'s assertion that Krishna came by to fulfill the women's vow (*tatkarmasiddhaye*, 10.22.8, "to give completion to their rite").

33. *kātyāyani mahāmāye mahāyoginy adhīśvari, nandagopasutaṃ devi patiṃ me kuru te namaḥ.*

34. I have interpreted *dhar-* as equivalent to *ḍhal-*, following *BBSK*, where *ḍharai* is attested as meaning *anukūl ho, prasanna ho, rījhe, dayā kare.*

35. *aye gavari īśvari saba lāyaka, mahāmāi varadāi subhāyaka; debi dayā kari aisaiṃ ḍharau, nanda-suvana hamarau pati karau.*

36. It may be more correct to say that Nanddās foregrounds the auspicious aspect of the goddess, as he still calls her "Katyāyanī" a few lines later (*kātyāyani teṃ yoṃ bara pāi*, l. 21, "having thus obtained the vow from Kātyāyanī"). Note that in the Sūrdās *padas* on this theme, it is often Śiva himself who is addressed (see SS 1384–5, 1416), who is identified with Ravi-Savitā, the sun (see SS 1386 and 1400).

37. *bolī bacana devi rasa bhāre, pūrna manoratha hohu tumhāre.*

Krishna's arrival on the scene in *Bhāgavata Purāṇa*, has a different flavor: it is more of a joke. First, he is accompanied by his friends ("Having learned of this, Krishna ... with his companions, went there," 10.22.8).[38] In Nanddās's version, Krishna comes by too, but he seems to come alone. A telltale difference is that in Bhāgavata Purāṇa (10.22.11) Krishna calls on his companions to testify to his truthfulness ("Neither have I ever spoken untruth, as these [boys] know";[39] this passage prompts commentary from Vallabha). In Nanddās's version, Krishna does not refer to his companions but simply says: "as all know I have never before spoken untruth" (*BDS* 22.32).[40] This actually scales down the scandalous aspect of the prank, since it is an affair between the women and Krishna, not witnessed by any other males.

Further, in *Bhāgavata Purāṇa*, with Krishna's arrival the tone of the episode, which so far has been solemn and serious, changes. Although the purpose of Krishna's arrival is announced solemnly as fulfilling the women's vow, the prank of stealing the Gopīs' clothes is done in an atmosphere of much banter and joking with his companions (*BhP* 10.22.8).[41] Thus, when he invites the women to come out of the water to pick up their clothes, it is presumably with a big wink that Krishna calls on his friends to prove his words true. The fulfillment of the vow seems a flimsy excuse for what on a folksy level might be read as a prank at the expense of the women.

By contrast, Nanddās's tone remains more serene. He concentrates on describing the beauty of the women in the water from Krishna's vantage point and indulges in wordplay and comparisons—their faces look like golden lotuses in blue Yamunā, their eyes like wagtails on lotuses, and the water drops like pearls dripping from their moon-faces (*BDS* 22.26–8).

Later, too, Nanddās leaves out parts of *Bhāgavata Purāṇa* that are less serene. In particular, he skips the second, sexually intended request Krishna makes as a condition for giving the Gopīs' clothes back to them in *Bhāgavata Purāṇa*: when the women come out of the water, covering their private parts with their hands, Krishna insists they fold their hands above their heads and bow, allegedly to atone for their offense against the river god (*BhP* 10.22.17–21). Nanddās leaves out this whole passage. Instead, Krishna says he has understood them and that they have reached their objectives, returning to a tone of propriety:

38. *bhagavāns tad abhipretya ... vayatyair āvṛtas tatra gatas.*

39. *na mayoditapūrvaṃ vā anṛtaṃ tad ime viduḥ.*

40. *pāchem hūṃ maiṃ anṛta na kabai, bolyau hai ye jānati sabai.*

41. *hasadbhiḥ prahasan bālaiḥ parihāsam uvāca ha.*

> Then the beloved king of Braj spoke: I've understood your intention.
> Come here, don't be ashamed a bit, take each the fruit of your vow
> and go home. (*BDS* 22.44–5)[42]

With this, Krishna comes across as within the realm of dharma. This concern for propriety is doubly interesting in light of the possibility that Nanddās may have composed his work specifically for a female audience (see the introduction).

Nanddās also makes sense of the Gopīs' apparently incoherent answer to Krishna's initial invitation to come out of the water in *Bhāgavata Purāṇa*. They seem to be oscillating between flattery, submission, and threat:

> Do not behave thus, we know you Nanda Gopa's son, as our beloved,
> who is praised thoughout Vraja.
> Dear one, we are trembling. Give back the clothes.
> Handsome dark one, we are your servants and will do as you said.
> Give our clothes. You know what dharma is. Or else we'll speak to
> the king. (*BhP* 10.22.16–7)[43]

Vallabha solves the inconsistency by ascribing different groups of words in these two *ślokas* to Gopīs of different nature, making a ninefold categorization of Gopīs according to the pure (*sāttvika*), muddled (*rājasika*), and opaque (*tāmasika*) nature of the words.

Nanddās's interpretation is simpler, as he distinguishes only two different types of Gopīs, ascribing the first *śloka*, more or less, to one group and the second to another. The first are the inexperienced (*mugdhā*) ones, who take it all seriously and say plaintively:

> Woe, Kānha, don't commit injustice, we beg you show some fear for
> the creator!
> You're the son of Nanda's wife, don't act crazy willingly!
> Give the clothes, the joke has burned up. We're dying immersed in
> this icy cold water. (*BDS* 22.37–9)[44]

The second group are the more mature ones (*prauḍhā*), who can appreciate the joke and speak more boldly:

42. *taba bole brajarāja dulāre, maiṃ samajhe saṃkalpa tihāre; ita āvahu raṃcaka na lajāhu, vrata kau phala lai lai ghara jāhu.*

43. *mānayaṃ bhoḥ kṛthās tvāṃ tu nandagopasutaṃ priyam, jānīmo 'ṅga vrajaślāghyaṃ dehi vāsāṃsi vepitāḥ; śyāmasundara te dāsyaḥ karavāma tavoditam, dehi vāsāṃsi dharmajña no ced rājñe bruvāmahe.*

44. *aho aho kānha anīti na karau, bali bali kachū daī teṃ ḍarau; nandamahari ke pūta rāvare, jāni būjhi jini hohu bāvare; dehu basana bari gaī asa haṃsī, marati haiṃ sīta salila maiṃ dhaṃsī.*

O handsome groom, don't make fun of us. We're all your maidservants.
Whatever you say, we'll do. Give the clothes, we're dying in vain.
If you won't give them to us for passion's sake, we'll go and tell king Nanda. (*BDS* 22.41–3)[45]

The first group refuse to accept Krishna's terms. Note that Nanddās seems to have transferred the epithet *dharmajña* to the first line, by translating it as "show some fear of God" (*kachū daī teṃ ḍarau*). This helps to make his interpretation more consistent: the first group of Gopīs seem to be serious and appeal to Krishna's sense of fairness. They also address him as Yaśodā's son, evoking the possibility they might go and complain to his mother, as they have done in the past about his childhood pranks.

The second group willingly agree to surrender to his demand. They intimate they too enjoy this illicit demand (*rasa bhāi*). In threatening to bring a court case they appeal to Krishna's father rather than his mother, which indicates they see him as more as a man than a child.

In the end the Gopīs are forced to come out of the water. *Bhāgavata Purāṇa* specifies they have been made fun of and are utterly embarrassed.

Seriously cheated and embarrassed,[46] ridiculed and made to dance like playthings,
Plus having their clothes stolen too, still they were not indignant with him, happy with the proximity of their beloved. (*BhP* 10.22.22)[47]

This is translated much more mildly by Nanddās: "They had fallen in the web of the highest love, and played Nanda's son's game" (*BDS* 22.47).[48] It is noteworthy that Nanddās does not make them into "playthings," but rather has them participate in Krishna's play of their own accord.

Finally, in *Bhāgavata Purāṇa,* Krishna sends the Gopīs home with a philosophical bon mot:

The desire (*kāma*) of those whose mind is attached to me does not lead to further desire,

45. *he sundara vara karahu na hāṃsī, hama tau sabai tumhārī dāsī; jo tuma kahahu soi hama karihaiṃ, dehu basana bina kājahi marihaiṃ; jau na deihau rasa bhāi sauṃ, kahihaiṃ jāi nandarāi sau.*

46. Literally: being caused to relinquish "shame" (*trapā*).

47. *dṛḍhaṃ pralabdhās trapayā ca hāpitāḥ prastobhitāḥ krīḍanavac ca kāritāḥ; vastrāṇi caivāpahṛtāny athāpy amuṃ tā nābhyasūyan priyasaṅganirvṛtāḥ.*

48. *parama prema ke phaṃdani parī, nanda ke nandana khela hī karī.*

> Similarly: parched or boiled, the grain as a rule does not go to seed. (*BhP* 10.22.26)[49]

Nanddās has a brilliant transcreation:

> A mind that follows my intent (*biṣaya*), will not return towards the senses (*viṣaya*):
> Just like parched grain in the world, in the same way the seeds will not come to their use.
> Fix your desire on me, and like seed in the earth you will come to fruition. (*BDS* 22.50–2)[50]

He is punning on the meaning of the word *viṣaya*, which can mean "senses" or "object." While preserving the Sanskrit *kāma*, he gives it a more positive meaning than in *Bhāgavata Purāṇa*. Desire attached to Krishna is not barren like porched (*bhuṃjita*) grain, but bears fruit like grain in the earth (*bhūṃ jyau*). Nanddās thus has not less than two puns in his translation.

In both versions, Krishna promises to sport with the women during an autumn night in fulfillment of their vow, which anticipates the Rāsa-līlā. As the women return to Braj, Nanddās throws in a nice observation: "They got their clothes but not their hearts. Their hearts went with the thief of hearts" (*BDS* 22.55).[51]

What can we conclude? First of all, Nanddās's work is not a pedestrian translation, as it is sometimes said to be, but a creative recreation, with elisions and elaborations. Second, even though he adds a passage stressing that the Gopīs were *parakīyā*, still overall he has toned down the "scandal" of the classical version. To some extent, he is following the irenic tone of Vallabha in his *Śrī Subodhinī*, but there are also important discrepancies with that text. So it will not do to describe Nanddās's work as a Vallabhan reflection of the Sanskrit text. Maybe it is indeed Tulsī's influence that can be discerned in this Braj version of the *Bhāgavata Purāṇa*. The epiphany of the goddess and her Gaurī-like characteristics definitely seem to point into that direction.

Comparing Bhakti Role Models for Falling in Love

Tulsīdās and Nanddās seem to have a common agenda that could be somewhat disrespectfully characterized as cleaning up the goddess's act. Everything is

49. *na mayy āveśitadhiyāṃ kāmaḥ kāmāya kalpate, bharjitā kvathitā dhānā prāyo bījāya neśyate.*

50. *mere biṣaya ju mati anusarai, su mati na bahuri viṣaya saṃcarai; bhuṃjita dhāna jagata meṃ jaisaiṃ, bīja ke kāma na āvahi taisaiṃ; e pari jo mo icchā hoī, bhūṃ jyau bīja nipaji parai soī.*

51. *basana paye pai mana nahiṃ paye, mana manamohana gohana gaye.*

TABLE 1.2. Vastraharaṇa in *Bhāgavata Purāṇa* and *Bhāsā Dasama Skandha*

BhP	Bhāsā Dasama Skandha
No Rādhā	Rādhā present
Marital status unclear	Married Gopīs
Prayer to Katyāyanī	Prayer to Gaurī
Krishna fulfills wish	Goddess promises, but Krishna fulfills wish
Gopas present	No Gopas present
Folksy joke	Serene atmosphere
Request that Gopīs lift up hands	No request to lift up hands
Gopīs humiliated	Gopīs choose to join the fun

cast in the light of propriety. Divine sanction of the mother goddess seems to be a sine qua non for love. The erotic aspect of first love is downplayed. In both cases, the devotional allegorical aspect is foregrounded and Sītā and the Gopīs are cast as model devotees. They have become closer in the process. Definitely, the change is in the Gopī characters. They have come to resemble Sītā.

Does the Krishna tradition recognize something of this Sītā-izing of Rādhā? As noted (in the introduction), the Vallabhan hagiographers acknowledge that Nanddās was inspired by Tulsīdās's example in composing a "translation" of the Sanskrit scripture. However, that is as far as they go. In their view, not surprisingly, their own brand of devotion is far superior, as is Krishna to Rāma, and Rādhā to Sītā. There is no question of Nanddās shaping his Rādhā on Sītā's model.

In the sectarian story of Nanddās's life, there is an explicit comparison between Krishna and Rāma with regard to their attitude to women. I translate the story here in full:

> So this Nanddās did not leave Braj to go anywhere else. Then, Nanddās's big brother, Tulsīdās, who lived in Kāśī heard that Nanddās had become a disciple of Śrī Gusāī Jī. Then the thought occurred to Tulsīdās that "Nanddās has as much as given up his fidelity to the husband [*pativratā dharma*]." For him Śrī Rāmcandra jī was his Lord. So with this in mind, Tulsīdāsjī wrote a letter: "Why have you given up fidelity to your husband and worshiped Krishna?" When this letter reached Nanddāsjī, he read it and wrote the answer: "Śrī Rāmcandrajī has taken a vow to have one wife, so how can he take care of another wife? He could not even take care of his one wife without interruption, who was abducted by Rāvaṇa. Krishna is the Lord of innumerable wives: those who have become his wife don't

> have any type of fear left. And he gives bliss to innumerable different wives at the same time. For that reason, I have made Krishna my Lord, so you'll know." When the letter written by Nanddāsjī reached Tulsīdās, he read it and pondered: "Nanddās's heart has been lost there, so he won't come now. Indeed, his resolve is stronger than mine. I have left Ayodhyā and will live in Kāśī, but Nanddāsjī won't leave Braj to go anywhere. So his resolve is bigger than mine." In this way Nanddāsjī was a great devotee filled with grace of the Lord. (252 *vārtā* 4, *prasaṅga* 3; see Gaṅgāviṣṇu Kṛṣṇadās 1986b: 39–40)

Strong language indeed. The Vallabhan hagiographers are never afraid to offend in their criticism of others and never shy in their affirmation of their own superiority. What is of interest to us is the gender terms in which the debate is cast. The devotee is compared to a woman. Doubt is cast on Nanddās's "fidelity to the husband," and he has to defend himself in those terms. Of course, the perceived infidelity is only apparent. Thus, according to the Krishna tradition, Tulsīdās draws his own (somewhat disconnected) conclusion and recognizes that Nanddās's devotion to Krishna is superior to his own to Rāma. Nanddās does not waver, he is indeed like a good loyal wife, devoted to just one husband-god.

Note, however, that Nanddās subtly changes the terms of the debate from the question of the woman's faithfulness to the man's prowess to take care of the wife (or many wives). Rāma loses of course. In this sectarian Krishna bhakti view, Rāma's monogamy is decidedly inferior to Krishna's merry polygamy. This is exactly the opposite of what we find in the modern electronic media, where the pendulum has swung back: Rāma's monogamy is touted as superior, and it is again the woman's faithfulness that figures most prominently, as we shall see in the next chapters.

Converging Modern Trends in Sagar's Televised Texts

Outdoing Tulsī in Propriety

What happened when these episodes from medieval bhakti texts were adapted in a contemporary context? At first glance, changes are few. The Phūlvārī episode of the television version seems to be mainly an enactment of sung extracts from *Rām Carit Mānas* (or seemingly from it), interspersed with some minimal Hindi dialogue. It is nearly a video clip of the *Mānas*, or rather a series of tableaux, Rām-līlā style. However, a careful comparison shows that certain elements are singled out for emphasis, and some innovations have been made.

The television *Ramayan* shows first, while the introductory music is playing, a procession of Sītā and her girlfriends traversing the garden on their way to the Pārvatī temple. The girls enter the temple and get ready for *bhajana* singing and *pūjā,* while the camera zooms in on the image of the goddess. Then the recitation starts with a *dohā* from Tulsī's epic (*RCM* 1:232) describing how Rāma and Lakshmana appear from the bushes; appropriately, the next shot is of the two brothers entering the garden. After some lines of dialogue in which the brothers ask the gardeners for permission to pick flowers, the action shifts back to the girls in the nearby temple, with equally minimal dialogue. One "adventurous" girl from Sītā's retinue has seen the boys: her report is sung in a pseudo-Avadhī verse (*TVR*: 86).[52]

Tulsī's lines about the friends showing Sītā the two princes from the cover of the bushes (*RCM* 1.232.2a) are enacted, while Sītā is shown being very reluctantly dragged along. From now on, no more mundane Hindi is spoken. In contrast to Rām Carit Mānas, Sagar first shows Sītā beholding Rāma, who is quite unaware of this attention. Meanwhile, *Rām Carit Mānas* is recited in the background. The first quotation expresses Sītā's confused inner feelings and her inkling about this being foretold by Nārada (*RCM* 1.229, *dohā,* translated earlier). Interestingly, while the singer chants the words "sacred love" (*prīti punīta*), Sagar offers his audience a glimpse of the divine couple Vishnu and Lakṣmī, thus commenting in images, so to speak, on the recited text. On the other hand, while the next part of the verse describes Sītā as fearfully looking in all directions (a remnant of the different sequence in Tulsī's text, where the verse occurred before she spotted Rāma), the camera belies this by showing a happy Sītā steadily gazing at one object only, Rāma. Clearly, the only reason for quoting this particular *dohā* lies in the first line. And the importance of this allusion to eternal love was compelling enough for Sagar to include the *dohā,* even though it did not fit the situation well.

Only when Sagar has thus established the *maryādā* context of this act, by turning the new love into an old, eternal and divine one, comes the quotation of Tulsī's verse on Sītā's eagerness to behold her beloved more, yet stressing that it seems to her that she is seeing a recovered treasure ("Her eyes were eager to behold his beauty, rejoicing as a man who has found his lost treasure," *RCM* 1.232.25).[53] Meanwhile, Rāma himself has looked up and is returning Sītā's gaze. Lakshmana has conveniently left the scene just a few minutes earlier so as to leave Rāma and Sītā in privacy. The camera then freezes on Rāma and

52. *bāga bilokana rājakuṃvara dou āe, e sakhī unake atula rupa kī sobhā kahiyo na jāe.*

53. *dekhi rūpa locana lalacāne, haraṣe janu nija nidhi pahicāne.*

Sītā beholding each other against the background of some pseudo-*Mānas* singing:

> Their hearts can not get enough of beholding each other
> Rāma engrossed in Sītā, Sītā engrossed in Rāma. They show one single form. (TVR 87)[54]

This verse is sung over and over, quite elaborately. Meanwhile, the camera keeps zooming in on Rāma and Sītā in turn. Lakshmana returns and looks in amazement at his brother and then at Sītā. Like Lakshmana, the audience is mainly intent on watching the divine pair beholding each other, they have become one form indeed, as the object of our and Lakshmana's gaze. (This moment could be fruitfully cited in the project to identify how the "gaze" of Indian cinema differs from the much-discussed Hollywood "gaze.")[55]

Next is recited, appropriately, the *Mānas caupāī*, comparing Sītā and Rāma to the *cakora* bird and the moon (1.232.3). Then Sītā closes her eyes, on cue from the corresponding line from *Mānas* (1.232.4a). This apparent getting into a trance causes Sītā's friends to interfere and "wake her up," but Lakshmana understands how it expresses the purity of her love and pays obeissance with a little devout bow. The girlfriends then lead Sītā away, while the *dohā* about Sītā turning back again and again is sung (*RCM* 1.232, *dohā*).

The scene in the Pārvatī temple is then enacted, while a shortened form of Sītā's prayer from *Rām Carit Mānas* is sung (1.235.3 and 236 1b-2). Sagar uses the lines where Sītā says she will not ask for anything explicitly because the all-knowing goddess is sure to know her heart's desire anyway. Tulsī's lines follow describing how pleased the goddess is with Sītā's humble devotion (1.236.3a). While the rest of Tulsī's text is recited (1.236.3), the miraculous shedding of the garland is enacted. Finally, Pārvatī's blessing of Sītā's wishes (1.236.4 and the *harigītikā chand*) is sung, not in chorus but by a single voice, as if articulating the words from the image's lips. While the *chand* ends, Sītā exits.

Finally, this episode is wound up with two parallel scenes. In one, Rāma is shown musing about the similarity of the moon to Sītā's face in Lakshmana's company, with some dialogue, to which we will come back, and quotations from *RCM* (1.237.4 and *dohā*). The camera then shifts back once again to Sītā's girlfriends, who similarly compare Rāma's face to the moon. Sītā is portrayed

54. *ika dūje ko nirakhata mana na aghāe; rāma siyā maya, siyā rāma maya, eka hī rūpa lakhāe.*

55. A seminal study with regard to the concept of visuality in India is Babb 1981. Important studies seeking to differentiate Hindi films' Indian scopic regime with reference to Laura Mulvey's theories of "visual pleasure" are Rajadhyaksha 2000 and Taylor 2002.

as lost in dreams; she does not say a word. This scene has no equivalent in *Rām Carit Mānas.* The episode ends when one of the girlfriends voices doubt whether such a delicate prince as Rāma will be able to lift the bow, hereby announcing the next episode.

Superficially then, the television episode appears to follow Tulsī very closely and may not seem to warrant much further investigation. However, a close analysis shows some interesting shifts in focus, revealed when we look at what Sagar chooses to preserve of *Rām Carit Mānas,* what he discards, and where he innovates.

First, the whole Flower Garden scene is viewed mainly from Sītā's perspective: most of the quotations from *Rām Carit Mānas* are verses to that effect. Rāma's musings to his brother about his feelings are simply skipped, at least for the time being (till the next scene makes them explicit). Rāma hardly looses his composure, the way Tulsī had suggested he did in his text. He sports an all-knowing smile of superiority on his face throughout.

If Rāma's feelings are hardly touched on during the scene proper, it is Sītā's reaction that is important. Whereas in Tulsī's text, Rāma spots the women first, Sagar has Sītā and her friends spying on a completely unaware Rāma. The result is that the audience identifies with Sītā's perspective. This stress on the devotee rather than the object of veneration is most obvious from the fact that Sagar leaves out the whole *nakha-śikha* description of the brothers. This omission may have to do also with the conventions of the medium he is using. He is, after all, a Bollywood movie director, and in the popular film, the camera tends to linger on the woman's body rather than the man's. However, we do not see a fully erotic evocation of Sītā's beauty either, as, for instance, in the *kāvya* texts. Nor does the camera end up voyeuristically lingering on Sītā's physical beauty. Camera movement remains well "above the belt" and mainly concentrates on Sītā's eyes meeting Rāma's. Sagar may be working in a secular genre, but he keeps his text free from vulgar eroticism.

The gaze of Sagar's camera, then, is, like in Tulsī's text, directed to the gazing of the protagonists themselves, to their mutual *darśana.* This stress on *darśana* fits well with traditional theatrical convention and has been noted for the epic as a whole (see Lutgendorf 1995: 230–31). *Darśana* is also apparent in the reactions of the other characters: the girlfriends stare at Sītā, Lakshmana gazes at Rāma gazing at Sītā. The subservient characters are portrayed as interested in their brother's or friend's falling in love rather than the other sex per se. Clearly, the audience is invited to identify with them rather than with Rāma, or even Sītā. This is well illustrated by the pseudo-Avadhī verse that is repeated over and over again while Sītā and Rāma behold each other. It goes quite a bit further in theological interpretation than the *Mānas* itself, as it suggests a unity between Rāma and Sītā. As the divine pair melts together, it is the audience beholding the pair rather than the pair beholding each other that takes center stage.

What I said earlier about the absence of Rāma's perspective needs to be modified in the light of the romantic scene following the Flower Garden scene. Here, while the brothers are gazing at the moon, the issue of Rāma's reaction is addressed. On the one hand, Sagar did not want his "beholding" scene interrupted by it, but apparently he considered the matter too important to be left in Avadhī, the point of which might conceivably escape his audience. As in Tulsī's text, Rāma confesses his unusual feelings to his brother, but here, after the Flower Garden scene proper and in Hindi. The same business of the inappropriateness for a Rāghava to gaze on "unrelated women" is raised. In Sagar's version, Lakshmana makes explicit the clue only hinted at in Tulsī's: he surmises that Sītā is destined to be Rāma's wife. Rāma answers that only God knows, an ironic statement, since the audience is of course very well aware that Rāma is in the end God himself. This scene seems to be designed according to the commentatorial tradition of countering objections (*śaṅkā-samādhān*), here with regard to the possiblity of inappropriate behavior by Rāma (for the tradition, see Lutgendorf 1991b: 393). Indeed, a major concern of Sagar is to affirm that Rāma's love for Sītā is of the *svakīyā* type.

It also pays off to look closely at the careful selection Sagar has made from the eight or so *kaṛavaks* that constitute the Flower Garden episode proper. He has in effect concentrated mainly on two passages from Tulsī's text, namely *kaṛavaks* 232 and 236–7, and, significantly, added only one *dohā* from 229. His selection is partly driven by narrative concerns (the verses describe the action, such as there is) but also reveals his main agenda. This is especially clear from the exceptional quotation from 229, which is about the purity of Sītā's love and its being in accordance with Nārada's prediction. As noted, this *dohā* is taken out of context, and its second line does not fit what Sagar's camera shows. Clearly, it is the first line with its legitimizing aspect that is its raison d' être. We conclude that Sagar has been attracted especially to the passages where Tulsī stresses the legitimacy of the meeting of the hero and the heroine: the rest of the quotations stress Sītā's shyness and her bashfully closing her eyes. Most important, he chose to show completely the scene where Sītā receives the blessing of Pārvatī, the divine mother, for her choice of groom.

In two scenes introducing the Phūlvārī one, Sagar has provided even more justification for the legitimacy of the young people being in the garden. Before the Flower Garden episode proper, Rāma and Lakshmana are shown taking leave from their guru and getting proper permission to go and pick flowers for *pūjā*. In Sagar's version, it is Viśvāmitra himself who directs the boys to go to the garden near the palace's Gaurī temple (TVR 86). Here Sagar is satisfying a possible objection one might have were one inclined to doubt the purity of Rāma's motives. In Sagar's version, the princes are present in that very flower garden because their guru has ordained it, and one might speculate that the guru in his omniscience, foresees what will happen. Even more blessing from the elders, courtesy of Sagar.

Just before that, Sagar introduces another innovation in the same vein, this time for Sītā. She is shown being sent by her mother to the garden to worship Pārvatī. This is portrayed as directly connected with the ceremony of choosing a groom (Svayaṃvara) that is to take place the next day. Sītā and her girlfriends receive the plates with worship materials from their elders, and they even ask whether some older lady should accompany them as chaperone (TVR 85).[56] However, the answer they receive is that worship of Pārvatī as virgin, or Kumārī, is only done by virgins (*kuṃvārī kanyā*). No such stress on the virginal status of the goddess or her devotees comes up in Tulsī's text. Sagar seems to have gone out of his way to ensure a proper *maryādā* atmosphere. What he is doing in this extra scene is countering yet another possible objection one might raise were one inclined to doubt the purity of Sītā's motives. She did not on her own account venture out without elder chaperone. Even the absence of the elder is ascribed to the command of the elders.

Thus, from studying selections of *Rām Carit Mānas* and the innovation of the introductory and, concluding scenes, it is clear that Sagar was interested in situating the blossoming of love within the boundaries of *maryādā*. He says as much explicitly during a sermon at the conclusion of volume 3 of the video series, while commenting on the later occasion of the Svayaṃvara scene (Dalmia-Lüderitz 1991: 224–5).

Of course, he is not the first commentator to stress these matters. One of the famous *Mānas* commentators, Rāmkiṃkar Upādhyāy, stresses the same point. He speaks explicitly about this episode being set in *maryādā* like a jewel in gold (1974: 1:288) and calls Tulsī's treatment of this scene of prenuptial love a golden median between too much stress on either duty or love (189). The commentator who reportedly influenced Sagar most is Morārī Bāpū, a guru from Gujarat, belonging to the Nimbārka Sampradāya (Lutgendorf 1995: 228, see www.iiramii.net/en/sggt.htm), who similarly stresses in his works the *maryādā* aspects of the scene. He makes much of Rāma's insistence on asking permission from the gardeners to pick the flowers, though Lakshmana finds it

56. *āp bhī calkar pūjan karāie na kākī jī.*

natural that as guests of the king they should just go ahead (Bāpū 1986: 239). And he stresses that Rāma and Sītā meet in the morning, not in the evening, as young people nowadays do, to the dismay of their parents (240), clearly linking the scene with modern-day dating concerns and setting up Rāma and Sītā as a model for young pre-maritally dating couples. Bāpū also gives a "spiritual" interpretation of the scene that is in line with treatment of Sītā as metaphor for the *bhakta* (devotee). He even assigns the "bold" girlfriend the role of the guru, since she is the one who will give Sītā *darśana* of Rāma, and Lakshmana becomes the *pūjārī*, who dresses Rāma up for *darśana* (241–2). (Note that Bāpū sticks to Tulsī's scenario, where Rāma first sees his devotee before the devotee spots him). He makes much of Sītā closing her eyes, as if she wants to stick with the spritual and has no more need for the rest of the world (242–3). Finally, Bāpū also stresses *maryādā* elements, such as the blessing of the goddess, and both Sītā's and Rāma's immediate confessions to their elders of what has happened (245).

If Sagar, then, shared Tulsī's and traditional commentators' stress on *maryādā*, the question is what his motive was. One may well doubt whether his agenda was as theological as Tulsī's. After all, Sagar is not working in a context where erotic Krishna bhakti is predominant and needs to be downplayed in favor of more serene and stern Rāma bhakti. Rather, Sagar's universe of operation is a profoundly secular one.

As a popular movie director, Sagar was working against the backdrop of the eroticism of the Hindi popular cinema genre. In fact, the whole scene fits well within its clichés, in that the action is halted to allow the emotions of hero and heroine to be marked with a song-and-dance sequence. Usually, such scenes are set in a fantasy-scape of the outdoors, and the flower garden setting fits well.

However, in contrast to the Hindi popular movie, we don't have a hip-gyrating heroine; Sītā does not venture to dance. In avoiding that, Sagar marks his product as distanced from commercial voyeurism. In contrast to the couples of the popular cinema, who could be said to represent teenagers' dreams, Sītā and Rāma model a love that can be approved of in religious terms, that incorporates at the same time the dream of the teenager and the ideal of the parent-elder.

Sagar was also working against the background of the secular soap series on Doordarshan. His *Rāmāyaṇa* indeed started out as a "soap opera of the gods" (*Sunday*, quoted in Mitra 1993: 85), designed to be a mythological counterpart to successful secular series like Ramesh Sippy's *Buniyād* and Kumar Vasudev's *Hum Log*. Such soaps had functioned as a mixture of didactic and entertainment programs on Doordarshan since the eighties (36–8, 78–89). Their main function seems to have been addressing middle-class family concerns against a backdrop of national integration (99). One of the social issues given airtime in these series is that of marriage, in particular the issue of the legitimacy of the love marriage as compared to the more traditional arranged marriage.

When viewed in this context, Sagar's concern for *maryādā* takes on different dimensions from Tulsī's. It seems obvious that Sagar is engaged in situating romance within *maryādā*, in sending the message to the younger generation that prenuptial meetings are okay only within strict *maryādā* control. This message, that love and dharma must be made to cohere rather than conflict, is of course not new to Sagar. It conforms with one of the central imperatives of the Hindi movie: the heart (*dil*) is valued and is a sine qua non for the hero, and needs to be brought into harmony with duty and principles (*kartavya, usūl*; see Thomas 1995).

Innocent Krishna, Meek Gopīs

What happened when Sagar filmed the Rādhā-Krishna romance? Little surprise: he managed to make even such erotic heroines as the Gopīs remain within *maryādā*. He accomplishes this by a clever device: splitting up the Vastraharaṇa story into two episodes and adding another one to explicitly address the first meeting of Rādhā and Krishna. The first Vastraharaṇa scene shows it as a prank of the child Krishna, well before adolescence (TVK vol. 6, episode 37). The second one is the religious observance, or *vrata*, of the adolescent Rādhā and Gopīs to the goddess Pārvatī (vol. 7, episode 58). Sagar adds a scene of *pūrvarāga* proper, the first meeting of Krishna and Rādhā, which occurs in the episode before the Vastraharaṇa (vol. 6, episode 36).

In the scene of the first meeting (TVK vol. 6, episode 36), Rādhā is just a little girl of about seven or so, and Krishna a little boy of the same age. The meeting does not take place in the forest but in the domestic atmosphere of Krishna's house. Rādhā arrives with her father, Vṛṣabhānu, who has come to arrange the upcoming Holī festivities with Krishna's father. Yaśodā, Krishna's mother, suggests that while the men talk, little Rādhā can play with Krishna, and Vṛṣabhānu gives his parental blessing. Yaśodā then introduces the little boy and girl to each other and suggests they go play outside. She adds that Krishna should hold her hand when they come near the Yamunā lest she fall into the river, to which Krishna charmingly responds by asking if he can hold her hand right away. Mother smilingly consents, adding he should not let go of her hand later. Little does she know what love affair is in the offing, or rather, in the past.

When the children are finally alone, they take on their eternally young adult divine form. Krishna immediately starts chiding Rādhā for coming to his house before the time has come. Rādhā claims she could not stand missing him. Krishna gives her a long lecture about what is appropriate and how they need to sacrifice for the sake of mankind, to which she meekly consents with a submissive "whatever you command" (*jo ājñā prabhu*). At this point a song starts:

> They have been companions in age after age, but act as if it is their first meeting
> What a marvelous play this is: acquainces of old, again are getting acquainted.[57]

Sagar's stress on the eternal aspect of the young persons' love echoes his depiction of Sītā and Rāma in the Phūlvārī episode. What is striking in this episode is also the surfeit of parental consent for the first meeting. Sagar leaves nothing up to the children; even their holding hands is in obedience to Mother Yaśodā cautioning them. Everything is safely within the boundaries of *maryādā*. Again, this evokes the careful legitimization of the Sītā-Rāma love affair. Rādhā is also strikingly submissive, which seems more Sītā-esque.

How does Sagar get around the eroticism of the scene of Krishna stealing of the Gopīs' clothes, which is tougher to bring into *maryādā* boundaries? Krishna's prank playing is portrayed in the next episode (vol. 6, episode 37), and it is immediately apparent that he is still a small child and so are his friends. The Gopīs are all adult women, and they are all married, as will become clear in the course of the scene. Rādhā is not one of the Gopīs, since she is still a little girl, as we have just seen. As in *Bhāgavata Purāṇa,* Krishna has brought his friends along, who are witness to the scene. Krishna's motives however are non-sexual, he is not really out to expose their nakedness; rather, the episode is portrayed as a move in the battle for butter the boys have been waging with the milkmaids. The boys are hoping with this prank to accomplish in one stroke everything they want: to make the women apologize for telling on their butter thievery of the past and promise not to tell on them any more and give them a "fair share" of butter daily. Krishna is the mastermind behind the plan, and he does a marvelous job of acting the innocent toward the Gopīs. He startles them by playing his flute in the tree near where the women bathe. When they discover their clothes are gone, they ask him for help, but like a typical child he refuses to help them because he is enjoying playing his flute. When they catch

57. *yuga yuga ke sāthī haiṃ donoṃ, pratham milan jaisā abhinay hai; yah adbhut līlā hai kaisī, cir-paricit pai phir paricay hai.*

a glimpse of their clothes, of course he is shown not to have been innocent at all; still, he is portrayed as truly innocent of erotics. In fact, he preaches about the impropriety of bathing naked, pointing out that the women should not assume they are alone anywhere, because God is everywhere. There is of course much irony in this statement, as Krishna himself is God. Soon the Gopīs will be even more shocked to find out that they were also being spied on by all Krishna's friends who were hidden nearby. They will eventually blame these companions for having a bad influence on Krishna, while in their eyes Krishna is free of guilt.

Krishna's childish innocence of erotics is stressed in several other ways. The main condition for getting their clothes back is a promise to feed the boys butter daily. And when the women are asked to bow to Krishna (*praṇām*), he does not insist on their lifting their hands above their heads. It ends up being a very prudish little act of obeisance; nothing is exposed. Further, when the Gopīs are about to come out of the water to get their clothes, after they have assented to all Krishna's demands, he and the Gopas leave the scene, and Krishna urges his friends to cover their eyes and not look back.[58]

Not only have Krishna and his friends gained in innocence in this version; the Gopīs have lost a fair bit of their free spirit. They readily agree that they have committed an offense by bathing naked, and though they sputter a bit about promising Krishna anything, they come around quickly. They give in to all his demands once he and his companions threaten to take the clothes to their husbands and tell them their wives are running around naked in the woods. It is quite ironic how Sagar has succeeded in making the Gopīs submit to Krishna's prank exactly because they are good submissive wives, concerned about their good name in the village! Gone is all the illicit titillation. They are *parakīyā* indeed, but foregrounded is the women's desire not to bother their husbands with their foolishness.

In contrast to Krishna and Rādhā's first meeting, there are no elder relatives setting boundaries of what is proper. There is no divine sanction from the

58. This episode occurs also in B. R. Chopra's *Mahābhārata* (DVD, vol. 3, episode 15), where it is treated similarly; it is told as a flashback by Rohiṇī (who was present in Braj) to Vasudeva and Devakī (Krishna's birth parents) in jail. Krishna is not accompanied by his friends. He faces away from the women and turns in their direction only when they call him. Though he asks them to come out of the water, this does not happen. Instead, the scene ends with Krishna scolding the girls for having gone in the water naked. When they protest there was no one around, he points out that the natural elements where there. Turning toward the audience, he adds a rhetorical question as an aside, wondering where he is not present. The scene thus ends on the emotion of wonder and amazement at God's marvels (*vismaya-adbhuta bhāva*).

goddess as in Nanddās's version. In fact, the Gopīs' worship of Katyāyanī is mentioned only in passing (by Krishna, as he proposes the plan to his friends) and is never shown. More precisely, full treatment of the worship is postponed till later, when Rādhā has become adolescent and can participate in the rite.

The second half of Sagar's Vastraharaṇa is a scene just preceding the Rāsa-līlā (TVK vol. 7, episode 58). Here the Gopīs' and Rādhā's *vrata* to the goddess is developed in parallel with Sītā's prayer to the goddess in the television *Ramayan*. The raison d'être for this scene is that Rādhā and the Gopīs, too, will get divine sanction for their desire for Krishna.

Like Nanddās, Sagar identifies Katyāyanī as Śiva's consort, Gaurī. In a proceding scene, Sagar has one of the sages in conversation (with Akrūra) refer to the Gopīs' Katyāyanī *vrata,* but the scene of devotional worship that is shown just prior to Rāsa-līlā is Gaurī Pūjā, which the Gopīs are shown performing in order to obtain Krishna as a husband. This is a master stroke. In the first place, Gaurī Pūjā is popular and a part of the experience of the women in Sagar's modern audience. Next, since it is usually carried out by unmarried girls, Sagar strengthens the impression that the Gopīs who partook in the Rāsa-līlā were young virgins. This contrasts with the controversial aspect of their *parakīyā* status, which Nanddās stressed. Moreover, *Gaurī Pūjā* is geared toward the consort goddess Pārvatī rather than the independent Durgā, adding an occasion for reflection on what constitutes a good wife, even in this context. What becomes very clear in comparison with the *Bhāgavata Purāṇa* scene is that Sagar has managed to turn an erotically charged scene into a purely devotional one, illustrative of *strīdharma*.

The Gopīs perform this *pūjā* in traditional Bollywood film style, reminiscent of, for instance, the highly succesful *Jai Santoshi Maa*. There is no mention of bathing in the river, as Sagar has already treated this episode earlier as one of the pranks of the child Krishna, before puberty. The *vrata* scene is thus divorced from the bathing and the stealing of the clothes.

In Sagar's *vrata* scene, Krishna does not appear at all. Instead the goddess, Pārvatī, appears to give *darśana* as a result of the Gopīs' efforts. She grants them the boon of partaking with Krishna in the Rāsa-līlā. This sets a totally different tone to the event. Whereas in *Bhāgavata Purāṇa* the atmosphere is one of sexual arousal and secret excitement, in Sagar's scene dharma is central.

The goddess responding to the Gopīs *vrata* is clearly Pārvatī, though she is multiarmed and looks like Durgā. However, she is addressed as a consort goddess, and mainly in her capacity of securing fitting husbands. This becomes clear when Rādhā formulates (in fittingly Sanskritic Hindi) on behalf of all the women what boon they seek from the goddess. She says:

> O embodiment of *śakti,* Mother Gaurī, you are the best among all women, and you are the goddess devoted to her husband, who knows the secret of the husband,
> O mother, you are the most elevated happily married woman, and grant others happiness in marriage too.
>
> For that reason, we ordinary women who live on this earth's surface, keeping your *vrata,* ask from you the following boon: in the same way as you obtained by your penance Śrī Śaṅkar Bhagavān, the groom you desired in your heart, for your husband, in that same way, may that we too, by doing penance for you, obtain for a husband the one whom each of us desires in her heart. In the same way as you are Śrī Śankar Bhagavān's dearest beloved, let us all also be the beloved of the groom we desire in our hearts. O mother, grant us this blessing that we all, according to our desire, might obtain our own best husband.[59]

The effect of this speech on the audience is clear: it reinforces the impression that the Gopīs are unmarried girls. It is of course helped by the fact that most of the women shown are girlfriends of Rādhā, with whom the audience is acquainted from previous episodes. Their seeking a good husband is a perfectly dharmic thing to do. In case the audience missed this, it is stressed by the parallel between the women's *vrata* and Pārvatī's asceticism.

The prevailing feel of dharma is also reinforced by the body language of the actors. Throughout the scene, Pārvatī looks and acts much like a schoolteacher, making eye contact with each of the girls, who smile back demurely, looking very much like students. This body language, together with the women's devoutly kneeling and bowed position, again serves to imbue the scene with the atmosphere of *maryādā.*

59. *he śakti svarūpinī, gaurī mātā, āp sab nārioṃ meṃ śreṣṭha aur pati kā marm jānevālī pativratā devī haiṃ; he mātā āp param saubhāgyavatī, aur dūsroṃ ko saubhāgya pradān karnevālī devī haiṃ. isīliye is dharātal par rahnevālī, ham māmūlī nāriyāṃ āpkā vrat dhāran karke, āp se yahī vardān māṃgtī haiṃ ki, jis prakār āpne tapasyā karke apne manvaṃśita var śrī śankar bhagavān ko patirūp meṃ prāpt kiyā thā, usī prakār āp kī pūjā ke phalsvarūp hameṃ bhī vahī pati mileṃ jis kī kāmnā har sab ke apne apne man meṃ hai. jis prakār āp śrī śankar bhagavān kī parampriyā haiṃ, usī prakār ham sabhī apne apne manvaṃśit var kī priyā hoṃ. he mātā hameṃ āśīrvād do ki ham sab kī kāmnā ke anusār ham sab ko apnā apnā śreṣth pati prāpta ho.*

Like Sītā, Rādhā and the Gopīs also get the benefit of receiving explicit divine sanction for their love. It is not Krishna who assures them that their wish is fulfilled. In fact, Krishna is nowhere on the scene. However, the goddess herself is shown to be pleased with the women's humble worship and grants them the boon they ask for.

To top it off, after Rādhā's plea and the goddess granting the boon, Pārvatī addresses Rādhā's divine form (which, on request of the goddess, had risen from her kneeled position). She makes it clear that Rādhā has called herself an ordinary woman and has acted as she has to instruct women, for the sake of people's education (*lok śikṣā*) and women's welfare (*nārī kalyān*), as she puts it. In short, Sagar has succeeded in surrounding the Gopīs' *vrata,* which is traditionally associated with the stealing of the clothes, instead with an aura of social respectability and *maryādā.*

The prevalence of the dharma character of the scene in *Shri Krishna* is all the more remarkable when compared to the same episode in an earlier movie on the topic of Krishna's early life, *Shri Krishna Leela* (1970), which was produced and directed by Homi Wadia for Basant Pictures and starred Master Sachin, Hema Kumari, Jayshri Gadkar, Padmarani, and the comedian Tun Tun. Striking, first, is that Rādhā is older and decidedly more mature than Krishna (an echo of this is still found in B. R. Chopra's *Mahabharat*). This allows for a certain ambiguity about Krishna's feelings, which seem more innocent than hers. Rādhā is also shown to be married to another man, here named Aney. In fact, her very first meeting with Krishna is cut short because her husband rushes by in a bullock cart, complaining that he got no breakfast because she did not return in time from the well. She repents and offers to come home right away, but he drives off in a huff. This is an interesting permutation of the *parakīyā nāyikā,* showing her to be a duty-minded housewife after all!

The first meeting in this movie is beautifully introduced by Krishna hearing the jingling of anklets, which attracts him irresistibly to Rādhā on her way to the well. This is reminiscent of Tulsīdās's Rāma first hearing the sound of Sītā's anklets. In contrast to Rāma, though, Krishna has no second thoughts about meeting Rādhā alone and enchanting her with his flute playing to the point of making her dance to his tune.

The Vastraharaṇa episode comes later in this film, after the love of Rādhā and Krishna is well established. Here, too, it is the magic of Krishna's flute that is foregrounded as the Gopīs' clothes are magically conjured up into the branches of the tree by Krishna's flute playing. The scene features Krishna's friends as appreciative audience for the prank, but they tactfully leave the scene before the Gopīs come out of the water. There is also an older lady on the scene, who was appointed as guardian over the Gopīs' clothes. Her presence adds an element of chaperoning, as well as comedy as she vociferously protests Krishna's prank. Krishna does not ask the women to lift up their hands above their head in obeisance. The director preserves propriety by showing only the Gopīs' naked lowerlegs as they step out of the water. In the next scene, the Gopīs, rightfully outraged, complain with Yaśodā, Krishna's mother. Yaśodā punishes Krishna with a good thrashing—so good that it elicits in turn complainers' protests! Thus, Wadia, too, is mindful of propriety and restores dharma, but not until after letting the scandal build to the full.

In comparison to this older version, Sagar has a much bigger dose of *maryādā*, and he has worked hard to all but erase the scandal from the clothes-stealing episode. The love of Rādhā and Krishna in any case has been purged of titillation and firmly rooted in *maryādā*. Of all versions, this is the one that extols Rādhā most clearly as a goddess, in particular through constant intrusions in the narrative of her divine form. Yet, at the same time, this is also the version in which she is most clearly domesticated. The more she is extolled, the less room there is for *parakīyā*. It seems that the price of her deification is to become more like Sītā.

Comparing Television Role Models for Falling in Love

The conclusion is inescapable: Sagar outdoes the medieval poets in cleaning up these potentially problematic scenes. Dharma and *maryādā* are writ large all over. In contrast to Tulsīdās, Sagar is less concerned with a devotional agenda, than with the message sent to young people regarding falling in love. He makes this explicit in his afterword to the scene; but just from this close

TABLE 1.3. Overview of Innovations in Sagar's Vastraharaṇa

Episode 1.	*First Meeting*
	Parental consent stressed
	Rādhā and Krishna's love is "old love"
Episode 2.	*Vastraharaṇa Proper*
	Rādhā does not participate
	Gopīs are married women, mindful of husbands
	Innocent, childish prank rather than erotic titillation
Episode 3.	*Vrata to Goddess*
	Gaurī is described as supermatrimonial
	Unmarried Gopīs praying for husband
	School-like atmosphere
	Rādhā uplifted above others as goddess

reading, it is apparent that Sagar's Sītā outdoes Tulsī's in perfectly toeing the line of propriety.

The biggest difference between medieval and contemporary sources is in the portrayal of Rādhā. It is remarkable how Rādhā has come to look like Sītā. She has lost the very playfulness Krishna loved so much in her. She is preoccupied with setting a good example for the edification of woman (*lok śiksā*). She stays away from pranks like Vastraharaṇa and avidly partakes in devout goddess worship. As a reward for her proper behavior, she gets to be elevated herself to the status of Great Goddess. The more like Sītā she behaves, the more adorable she becomes. The price of divinity, it appears, is conformity!

Falling in Love à la Sītā or Rādhā in the Movies

There is of course no dearth of falling-in-love scenes in the colorful world of the popular Hindi movie. Many movies portray the lovers' meeting in a romantic natural setting, whether a park, the modern equivalent of the Phūlvārī, or a forest area in a hill station, swimming pool, or beach, the latter-day equivalents of the woods of Braj and Yamunā's banks. The dawning of love is invariably celebrated in song, the setting and action of which is often related to the main narrative only in a very tangential way. It seems that love immediately transports its subject and object to a world beyond, the world of myth.

Filmī courtship has many echoes from the erotic Rādhā-Krishna tradition. At the outset, we should take note of the reduction of such romances to a "mono-sound," in that most of the songs are performed in the ubiquitous Lata Mangeshkar's shrill adolescent girl falsetto style. This has been interpreted as "domesticating," "infantilizing," and "naturalizing" the potentially threatening free-agent woman cavorting in the public sphere (Srivastava 2006: 130, 140, 146). Thus the apparently free and unencumbered Rādhā-like movie heroine is immediately "tamed" by the sound overlay.

The falling-in-love scene in many movies evokes the Rāsa-līlā, or moonlit circle-dance of Rādhā and Krishna. The hero and heroine cavort in a bucolic setting with lots of other dancers around, whether all female dancers, who evoke the Gopīs, or couples, which suggests Krishna multiplicating and dancing with the Gopīs. Often the hero is portrayed as a lover-boy, a playful Krishna type. In many movies, he spies on the heroine while she is bathing, reminiscent of Krishna's behavior in the Vastraharaṇa scene. Following *kāvya* conventions, falling in love is often associated with the onset of the monsoon or spring, even though this may not, strictly speaking, fit in the narrative frame.

Here, too, one may read in echoes of the Krishna-Rādhā tradition, with its plethora of seasonal poetry.[60]

It is not always clear whether such scenes and the bucolic surroundings are just a matter of *kāvya* convention or whether the Sītā or Rādhā model is specifically being evoked. In some cases, though, the reference is explicit, and one can read with much profit the film scenes in question against the nuanced understanding we have gained of the multilayered myths. An unambiguous evocation of the Vastraharaṇa episode is found in Raj Kapoor's 1964 movie *Sangam* and one of the Phūlvārī episode in Sooraj Bharjatya's 1994 *Hum aap ke hain koun . . . !* I will analyze in some detail how these movies creatively appropriate these mythical scenes.

Pestering Rādhā: Raj Kapoor's Vastraharaṇa in "Sangam"

Raj Kapoor's *Sangam* has many direct references to the Rādhā-Krishna mythology and the Vastraharaṇa episode in particular. To begin with, the heroine (played by the actress Vyjayanthimala) is called Radha, and the man she is in love with (Rajendra Kumar) is named Gopal, a famous epithet of Krishna. However, the movie is about a love triangle, and the real hero is actually the third party, Sundar (Raj Kapoor), who is also in love with Radha. He persists and devises pranks to make her yield to his advances in very Krishna-like manner. One could say that he usurps the role of Gopal and is the true Krishna of the movie. This is apparent in a scene early in the movie wherein the heroine, Radha, goes swimming, and Sundar steals her clothes. The impression of a modern version of Krishna's Vastraharaṇa is strengthened when Sundar, sitting in a tree like Krishna, puts a peacock-like feather behind his ear as he starts a song. A good dose of humor is added as Sundar hauls up the heroine's clothes with a fishing rod. The director has updated, or maybe cosmopolitized, his Krishna, who plays bagpipes rather than the flute, and Rādhā, who wears a trendy bathing suit. All this just adds to the audience's delight.

60. In particular, many movies use the festival of Holi as a backdrop because it evokes the liberty of sexual approach, which is also exploited by the bhakti poets celebrating Rādhā and Krishna's love. A well-known example in film is *Sholay*, where Veeru and Basanti are playing Holī, while Jay and the widow Radha exchange longing glances. Another example of the hero declaring his love for the heroine in the context of Holi, occurs in the second half of *Hum Tulsi tere aangan ki*. Here, the hero leads a procession to the house of the girl he has fallen in love with and challenges her to come out and play Holi with him, much as Krishna does with Rādhā. There is even an explicit reference to Rādhā-Krishna mythology, as the hero brings actors dressed up as the divine pair. His beloved acts delighted, though she stays safely behind the closed windows of her mansion, but his persistence wins her over, and in the next scene we see the two as a romantic pair.

Kapoor exploits the reference fully: Sundar asks Radha to imagine he is "Gopal," that is, Krishna,[61] as he puts the peacock-like feather behind his ear. At the same time, there is a double entendre, because Gopal is also the name of Radha and Sundar's mutual friend, with whom Radha is really in love. The reaction shot of Radha at this point shows her startled, which betrays clearly that she thought immediately about the third, absent party, the man Gopal, whom she loves. Sundar remains oblivious, casting himself in the role of Krishna-Gopāla, and the audience gets to enjoy the joking reference to the mythological Krishna.

Like Krishna in the myth, Sundar tries to get something out of the heroine for the return of her clothes, but–cleverly circumventing the censors–he does not require her to emerge naked from the water. Sundar is rather insisting on getting yes for an answer (*jab tak hāṃ na kahogī ye kapṛe nahīṃ mileṃge*). What the question is is elaborated in song, the refrain of which comes down to "Come on, let's get together." Appropriately for the setting at the river, Sundar's song uses the metaphor of the confluence of rivers, the *sangam*, which is also the title of the movie. The song thus at the same time serves to cleverly establish the theme of the whole film. It is worth examining in detail.

Say, Rādhā, say:
Will my heart's Ganges,
And your heart's Yamunā
Unite together? Won't they?
(Rādhā: no, never!)[62]

Hundreds of years have gone by
Alas, in making you see!
Is there in this world
Anyone as patient as me?
Will the burden on my heart
Ever lighten up? Won't it?
(Rādhā: Get lost!)[63]

For you, I'm in agony like
The earth thirsts for the monsoon.

61. *mān lo rādhā ek minute ke liye maiṃ sundar nahīṃ maiṃ gopāl hūṃ aru gopāl tum se kuch kahtā hai.*

62. *bol rādhā bol: mere man kī gaṅgā, aur tere man kī jamunā kā, bol rādhā bol: saṅgam hogā ki nahīm? (nahīṃ, kabhī nahīṃ).*

63. *kitnī sadiyāṃ bīt gaī haiṃ; āy sūjhe samajhāne mem. mere jaisā dhīraj vālā, hai koī aur zamāne meṃ? dil kā bhār bojh kabhī kam hogā ki nahīṃ. (caicā!)*

"Rādhā, Rādhā" is the one prayer
Of my rising and falling breath.
A stone may melt, but will your heart?
(Rādhā: Get lost, why are you pestering me. Yes, yes, yes.)[64]

This scene comes close to the *Bhāgavata Purāṇa* in its atmosphere of scandal: the hero and heroine are not married to one another; in fact Radha loves someone else, so she is, we could say, *parakīyā*. There is no matrimonial agenda underlying the prank: Sundar's words have a strong sexual undercurrent. And of course there is no parental sanction for this meeting.

In contrast to the classical Vastraharaṇa episodes I have discussed, it is immediately apparent that the roles are reversed: Sundar may be stealing her clothes, but he is the one praying to "the goddess", that is, Rādhā, to fulfill his dream of love. The irony of this reversal is brought out explicity in the song. In the last verse, Sundar refers to the chant of his breath, "Rādhā Rādhā," which the audience recognizes instantly as a mantra to the goddess. Thus, the male lover is the devotee, and the woman is adored like a goddess. This is also underscored by the second verse, where Sundar describes himself as a "patient" lover.[65]

What is interesting for our purpose is that in the course of the song, Rādhā's answer seems to be transformed from a decided negative into a vexed yes. She exasperatedly seems to give in to Sundar's will.[66] Persistent pestering, it seems, wins the girl over. However, Kapoor cleverly overturns this outcome by having Radha turn the tables in a move worthy of her mythological namesake: she steals back her own clothes and then turns Sundar's own weapons against him: with his own fishing rod, she pulls his bagpipes into the river,

64. *terī khātir maiṃ taṛpā jyuṃ, tarase dhartī sāvan ko; rādhā rādhā ek ratan hai, sās kī āvan jāvan ko; patthar pighale dil terā namra hogā ki nahīm? (jāo na, kyoṃ satāte ho, hogā hogā hogā).*

65. There is of course more to this song, in reference to the title of the movie. Sundar eagerly presents the union of Radha and himself as natural and inevitable by comparing it to the confluence of the Ganges and Yamunā. However, there is a subtext that is not lost on the audience: everyone knows that the famous pilgrimage site at Allahabad constitutes the *sangam*, or confluence of the Ganges and the Yamunā, as well as a hidden third river uniting with the other two, the mythical Sarasvatī. The unmanifest third party alluded to is of course Gopal, evoked unwittingly by Sundar by urging Radha to see him as Krishna, or as "Gopal," as he says. Rādhā's first understanding is to think about the third, absent party, the man Gopal whom she loves. While Sundar remains oblivious to this interpretation of his words, the audience is privy to Radha's way of decoding and is thus sensitized to the "undercurrent" in the song that follows. This foreshadows the ending of the movie, where Gopal commits suicide to make room for the happy union of Sundar and Radha, saying: "after its confluence, the Ganges belongs to the Yamunā, and for the sake of union, the Sarasvatī has to disappear" (*saṅgam kar gaṅgā jamunā kā hī hotā hai, aur saṅgam ke liye sarasvatī ko lupt honā hī paṛtā*).

66. One could argue that Radha's answer may be interpreted as only to the last line of the verse, which posed the question "Will my heart's burden be lightened?" rather than to the refrain's persistent "Come on let's get together."

Sundar himself following. A reversal of roles compared to the myth, much to the audience's delight.

Still, notwithstanding this playful ending, Sundar has succeeded in pestering Radha into giving in to him. Though this long-awaited "confluence" does not immediately take place, Sundar seems to have forced fate to give him his deal, as he will eventually marry Radha. Thus, the devotee's prayer is heard and his desire fulfilled. Up to a point, though: Radha never really reciprocates his feelings, but once married she will devote herself completely to him. She becomes an incarnation of the devoted wife Sītā perforce. This becomes clear toward the end of the movie, when Sundar has at last become aware of his wife's feelings for Gopal before their marriage and in a fit of jealousy packs to leave the house. Radha basically asks for a "fire ordeal": "What can I do to make you trust [me]? Let me take an oath that ever since we got married, not even the shadow of another has come into my heart!"[67] Ironically, it is Gopal who speaks up to clear Radha of all blemish in a climactic final meeting: "The day Radha set foot in your house, she was holy like the Ganges, and now too, when she left your house she was holy like the Ganges."[68] One might have suspected a more explicit reference to Sītā, but perhaps in view of the title of the movie and the recurring theme of rivers meeting, the reference to the Ganges is not surprising. This brings to fulfillment what the song foreshadowed in putting Radha on a pedestal, as a goddess to be worshiped. As was the case in Sagar's mythological series, the more Rādhā grows in stature as the goddess, the more she starts to resemble Sītā.

Yet it is important to qualify this. At the same time Radha is idealized as Sītā, she is neglected as woman. To her devotee, her feelings seem not to matter. This is abundantly clear throughout the movie; neither Gopal nor Sundar seem to care at all about Radha's feelings. Sundar is totally oblivious, and Gopal places his friend's interests before his own, without stopping to ask Radha. It has been a given that for both friends, duty toward the male friend comes before romantic love.[69] At the same time, for the woman, too, marital duty prevails over romance. Though she is the victim of this dictum, Radha herself has bought into it. At the end, in her defense of her chastity, she offers:

67. *tumheṃ viśvās dilāne ke liye maiṃ kyā karūṃ. kasam le lūṃ jab se hamārī śādī huī mere man meṃ kisī dūsre kī parchāī bhī nahīṃ āyī.*

68. *rādhā ne jis din tumhāre ghar meṃ pāṃv rakhā, vah gaṅgā kī tarah pavitra thī. aur āj us ne tumhāre ghar ke bāhar pāmv rakhā, tabhī vah gaṅgā kī tarah pavitra thī.*

69. Of course much can be and has been made of their rivalry over the female as valorizing male homosociality (in the wake of Eve Sedgwick's work). However, what is of interest here is the broader discourse of duty prevailing over love.

> Love is something beyond human control, it just happens.
> Marriage is a duty, which man abides by. And I have abided by it."[70]

Thus, love is subordinated to duty. The former is independent of human volition, but the latter is subject to human agency, hence there is a responsibility to act. Marriage is safely divorced from love. Premarital romance brings nothing but trouble; this is clearly the message.

Rādhā's Phūlvārī: Madhuri Dixit Drops by the Temple in "Hum aap ke hain koun . . . !"

Creative appropriation of the Phūlvārī episode is most conspicuous in the trendsetting 1994 hit *Hum aap ke hain koun . . . !* (Who am I to you!), directed by Sooraj R. Barjatya (*HAKHK*). This movie celebrates the love of two brothers and two sisters. The eldest brother, Rajesh (Mohnish Bahl), is the Rāma type, and the story of his love for Pooja (Renuka Shahane) is permeated with *Rāmāyaṇa* references, including celebration of the engagement at the Rāma shrine of Rāmṭek.[71] The younger brother, Prem (Salman Khan) is more the Krishna type, and when he falls in love with Pooja's sister Nisha, the relationship is much more *masāledār,* or spicy.[72] In this movie, the names are not epithets of the gods the characters are inspired by, yet one could argue that Pooja, which means "worship" (*pūjā*) is an apt name for a Sītā-like character, and Nisha, which means "night" (*nīśā*) is appropriate for Rādhā, whose epithet is often *śyāmā,* or "the dark one." Prem is a bit of a prankster and flirt throughout the film, and plays the mandoline in lieu of the flute. The reference to Prem as Krishna is also made explicit in one of the songs of the movie, the poignant "goodbye" (*bidā*) song at the end of Pooja's wedding:

> My father-in-law is now my father,
> My husband is my god,
> My brother in law is like Krishna.[73]

70. *pyār ek majbūrī hai, pyār ho jātā hai, vyāh ek dharm hai jo ādmī pāltā hai aur maiṃ ne pālā hai.*

71. See p. 142 for more on the shrine.

72. This relation possesses some of the daredeviltry, spice, and charming assertiveness of the Gopīs. An important parallel is the crossdressing motif (on which more in ch. 5). Often the mood evoked (*rasa*) is humor, or *hāsya,* rather than romance, as in the scene where the swimming-pool is a proper Yamunā substitute. This scene has all the ingredients for romantic declaration of feelings yet ends on a humorous tone, with Prem falling in the water and Nisha running off laughingly—at which he delivers the immortal line "Shit! I love her." Very Rādhā-Krishna-like all this.

73. *mere sasur jī pitā haiṃ, pati devtā haiṃ, devar chavi kriśan kī.*

True to Hindi popular film stratagems, the first confession of Prem and Nisha's love is enacted in the usual escapist pseudofolk harvesting scene (with the song *yah mausam hai jādū kā mitvā*). Prem and Nisha dally, he "steals" her flower bouquet, and she in revenge his beloved mandoline. However, and here it gets particularly interesting for our purpose, this love also receives divine sanction. After their rural excursion, Prem and Nisha drop by again at the Rāmṭek temple where their brother and sister's engagement was celebrated.[74] During their visit, while Prem half-jokingly pays his respects to the temple manager, Nisha prepares a *diyā* (oil lamp) to be lit and set afloat in the temple pond, just as her sister did for her engagement. What is recited in the background is precisely the scene from *Rām Carit Mānas* where Sītā gets sanction in the temple from Pārvatī—the end of Sītā's prayer to the goddess, where she modestly refrains from naming the man she desires for husband. Of course, that is Rāma, whom she has just met in the flower garden. The goddess is impressed both by Sītā's love and her humility, and grants her wish. In *HAKHK*, these lines are recited in the background while the banter with the manager is going on, and the passage that is foregrounded, as Nisha and Prem worship and do the rounds of the temple (*parikramā*), is the following:

> "Listen, Sītā, my blessing is true, your heart's desire will be fulfilled.
> Nārada's words are always pure and true: you will get the groom whom your heart desires.
> The one your heart desires, you will get for your groom, truly handsome and dark,
> Compassionate, understanding, skilled, your love is known to be."
> Having thus heard Pārvatī's blessing, Sītā and her friends rejoiced in their heart.
> Tulsī says: worshiping the goddess over and over, they left the temple with happy heart. (*RCM* 1.236.4-*harigītikā chand*)[75]

Prem's worship is halfhearted, and he even tries to sneak one of the sweets on the offerings tray, which quick-witted Pooja prevents with a playful slap on his hand. He is his pranking Krishna self as he follows her around while she

74. This scene is cut in the shorter versions of the movie, but is included in the full version (which also has the song "Chocolate, Lime Juice").

75. *sunu siya satya asīsa hamārī, pūjihi mana kāmanā tumhārī; nārada bacana sadā suci sācā, so baru milihi jāhiṃ manu rācā. manu jāhiṃ rāceu milihi so baru, sahaja suṃdara sāṃvaro; karunā nidhāna sujāna sīlu, sanehu jānata rāvaro. ehi bhāṃti gauri asīsa suni, siya sahita hiyaṃ haraṣīṃ alī; tulasī bhavānihi pūji puni puni, mudita mana maṃdira calī.*

worships. However, Nisha is serious and seems to understand the lines as they are recited: she smiles, pleased about this auspicious promise that her wish will be fulfilled. The audience understands that her wish is to get Prem for her husband, as she looks back at him at the right moment. The spectator enjoys fully the irony of Prem's careless strolling around as the line praising the promised groom's compassion, understanding, and skill is recited.

Is it coincidence that this is the very episode foregrounded in Sagar's television series? Can we speak of a trend developing? It is not just a particular scene from Tulsī's work that becomes popular. There is a concept of love that goes with it. Clearly, *maryādā* is seen as a necessary complement of love. The scriptwriter has skillfully picked up on the right lines from *Rām Carit Manas* to get this conservative point across, and the director in picturizing the song with a nonchalant Prem injects just the right amount of humor to make the scene work.

There is another parallel with Sagar's Phūlvārī. Just before they worship, Prem asks Nisha why she is lighting the *diyā*. She answers truthfully that her mother told her to do so, as indeed, she did before Nisha and Prem set out on their trip. We are reminded of Sagar's Sītā, whose presence in the garden was justified by her mother's command to perform *pūjā* of Pārvatī. Again, the movie seems to pick up on a clue from Sagar's television version.

In short, the seemingly *masālā* heroine Nisha has received for her choice of partner a double blessing, one maternal, one divine, and this with quite explicit reference to the model of Sītā. Such intertextuality with *Ramayan* does not remain limited to this particular scene but, as we will see, sets the tone for the romance of Nisha and Prem, which progresses with its due serving of Bollywood *masālā,* but always within bounds of happy, playful *maryādā*. Rāma presides even over this relationship. Rādhā has once again been pressed into a Sītā mould.

Conclusions: Keep Your Cool

What have we learned in tracing the portrayal of Sītā and Rādhā falling in love from classical and medieval devotional through contemporary film and television versions? Our analysis shows two marked trends, one to do with the goddess and her status, the second to do with the message sent to women about premarital romance.

First, we revisit the issue raised at the beginning of this chapter, of the paradox of the divine goddess overpowered by love. Does this detract from her power, hence her status as a goddess? Implicitly, the answer seems to be yes, because the poets and directors are hard at work to show that the goddesses never lose their cool. Especially in the contemporary versions, Sītā and Rādhā alike are shown to know perfectly well what they are doing. There is no being swept off one's feet, no head-over-heels, undeliberated surrender. What we see instead is how they seriously ascertain that love is in line with *maryādā* for the instructional benefit of (wo)mankind. It seems that not for a minute do they lose sight of their position. They are constantly aware of their responsibility as goddesses to set an example. They may fall in love, but not "head over heels."

More than that, these goddesses are venerable, in that they are determined and dedicated devotees of God. Paradoxically, they worship the Great Goddess so as to be successful in love. That may seem a sign of their inferiority, but it works the other way around. It is in worshiping both the Great Goddess and their husbands-to-be that these goddesses are venerable. The more subservient to others, it seems, the more exalted they become. This is most dramatically the case for Rādhā, who has to leave behind her passionate playfulness and acquire a stronger sense of duty and responsibility. The most marked trend is that Rādhā becomes more venerable, at the cost of resembling Sītā more and more.

The second trend regards the role model function of goddesses for women. I formulated a theory that the portrayal of the goddesses' first love would become more liberal over time. Is that the case? Decidedly not. In all our versions, starting with the medieval ones, we found a clear concern with embedding love within the bounds of conventional morality. However, the trend gets more marked in the contemporary versions. Poets and directors are at pains to establish legitimacy for the heroines' behavior by stressing that they act with parental approval, even divine sanction, and that the men they fall in love with are in fact their predestined partners. The only good premarital love is in fact marital love, "old love" from past births and/or matches preapproved by the elders. Presumably the two overlap, it is in any case difficult to determine one's previous birth's partner. Observing vows (*vratas*), in particular to the goddess, might help clarify matters as well as provide divine sanction.

There is more to *maryādā* than partner choice. Even with the right partner, premarital contact is to be avoided. Both parties involved should refrain from arranging it, and if others arranged it for them, they should remain completely passive. They should deny their own desires and steer away from the meeting as far as possible. If an actual meeting is to take place, they should avoid close contact. Eroticism is a big no-no. "Clean" romance is imposed even on Rādhā and Krishna.

Interestingly, we can see this trend at work already in the medieval versions. Tulsī's agenda was a theological one: promoting devotion for *maryādā-puruṣa* Rāma and possibly countering the erotic tone of the Krishna bhakti counterpart. Nanddās may have been coy in addressing a female audience. That seems definitely to be Sagar's concern. He is very concerned about the message he is sending to the younger generation, in particular young women. His worries are not of a theological but of a social nature. He seeks to guide the younger generation as they grapple with the Western model of romantic love. The film directors seem to have very much the same thing in mind, even as they seek to titillate with such romance. The answer seems to be unequivocally: Rādhās are fine, as long as they end up behaving like Sītās.

It would not be right, though, to end the matter on this note. Hindi movies are not speaking in one voice. There is in fact a wonderful counterpoint to Sītā's Phūlvārī in the cult movie *Sholay* (1975, d. Ramesh Sippy). The movie has an unusual heroine, the village belle Basanti (Hema Malini), who is, however, not at all of the "tais toi et soi belle" type. She has a penchant for actually talking *too* much, but while her character is comical, she is not a fool. She is marked as an "emancipated woman" because she has taken up the "male" profession of tonga driver (with the argument that if a mare can pull the tonga, why can't its driver be a girl). She certainly knows what she wants and is not about to be cheated out of it. The hero's best friend, Veeru (Dharmendra), admires her spunk and falls in love with her. She is somewhat attracted to him, but also diffident, as he is not a villager. Veeru is also not the rich groom she is hoping to marry. For that purpose, she decides to undertake a series of vows (*vrata*s) on Mondays. Here is where the parallel with Phūlvārī comes in: her first visit to the Śiva temple in her village makes for a wonderful persiflage of Sītā's worship of Pārvatī.

Like Sītā, Basanti had a request to make, which she, too, prefaces with the apologetic statement that of course God knows everything: "Lord, there is nothing in the world that remains hidden from you. You know everything."[76] In contrast to the passive Sītā, Basanti is prepared to take agency, much to the delight of the audience: "Look, I'm not saying that you'll forget, but it's good to speak up for oneself."[77] In contrast to Sītā, Basanti is very down-to-earth, which renders the desired comical effect. She shows the Shiva image her hands,

76. *prabhu, saṃsār meṃ aisī koī bāt to hai nahīṃ jo tum se cupī ho. tum to sab jānte ho.*

77. *dekho maiṃ to yah nahīṃ kahtī hūṃ ki tumheṃ yād nahīṃ hogā lekin phir bhī apnī tarah se kah denā acchā hotā hai.*

hardened by the reins of her tonga, and asks him for a groom who will be rich enough so she can abandon her trade: "For you it's no trouble at all! Just get negotiations going in such a place where Basanti will rule like a queen. That way, I'll get fun in life. For the rest, your will be done."[78] She hastens to end on a humble note, like Sītā.

Basanti, too, gets a miracle: the image starts speaking. She's delighted when the voice reveals that Shiva has found her a groom. "In just one Monday, you've found him! Wonderful, Lord!"[79] While Basanti is getting excited, we are made privy to the source of the miraculous voice, which is actually none other than Veeru's. He is standing behind the image, speaking through a tube to create a miracle effect. When Basanti eagerly asks for the name of the groom Śiva has found her, he predictably gives his own, Veeru. Her reaction is not submissive, though. "Lord, this is a question of my life, don't be so rash."[80] Veeru alias Śiva insists: "If you don't do as I say, you will remain a spinster your whole life long!"[81] Basanti acts submissively, but she is not going to take that lying down and starts to argue vociferously, as is her wont; but at that point, Veeru's friend approaches her and, signaling to her to be silent, leads her behind the image. Now she sees Veeru, who does not realize he has been exposed and keeps up his rant. He is really getting into his theological sermon: "From today it is your duty to honor Veeru, because your heaven is at his feet. If you please him, I will be pleased, if you anger him, you have angered me."[82] Basanti just interjects, "Well! Well!" It takes Veeru/Śiva a second to realize he has been exposed before he backs down.

This humorous episode playfully appropriates the divine intervention theme that is so serious and all-important in the sources reviewed earlier. Both hero and heroine take initiative. While Basanti is observing a vow, the tone of the scene is not solemn but one of intimate conversation with God, with a simplemindedness that is endearing to the audience. When Veeru usurps the voice of Śiva, he casts everything in a high-register language (though he betrays himself with some small dialectic pronunciations (*ādra* for *ādar*). He spouts language of propriety and women's duty but clearly in a self-serving way, so that discourse is deflated, and again the (counter) hero is endearing to

78. *tumhāre liye kyā muśkil hai? bas aisī jagah bāt lagāo prabhu ki basantī rāṇī jaisī bankar rāj kare. yoṃki mazā ā jāe zindagī kā. āge jaisī tumhārī marzī.*

79. *ek hī somvār meṃ ḍhūṛh liyā, vāh prabhu!*

80. *prabhu yah merī zindagī kā savāl hai jaldī se kām mat lenā.*

81. *yadi hamārī ājñā kā pālan nahīṃ kiyā to sārī umr kuṃvārī baiṭhī rahogī.*

82. *āj se vīrū kā ādra karnā tumhārā dharm hai. is liye ki usī ke caraṇoṃ meṃ tumhārā svarg hai. yadi tumne use prasanna kiyā to ham prasanna ho jāeṃge. yadi tumne use krodhit kiyā to ham krodhit ho jāeṃge.*

the audience. Best of all, Basanti is not fooled by Veeru's self-serving plot but gives him a good thrashing at the end. In the very end of the movie, of course, she will come around to be his beloved, and give proof of her absolute dedication in a "trial by fire" type of dance on broken glass. So there's no escaping Sītā's model in the end. But that does not mean that the whole serious business of love cannot be made fun of along the way.

2

Arranging a Love Marriage

Sītā's "Self-Choice" and Rukmiṇī's Elopement

How to Marry One's Groom of Choice

Chapter 1 concentrated on the moment where the goddess falls in love, and chapter 3 focuses on her wedding. This chapter studies the transition between the two. How does initial, private love culminate in the public celebration of the wedding? We are looking at the divine counterpart of the stuff Bollywood films are made of: boy has met girl, they have fallen in love, now how will they get their parents to agree to the match? In other words, how does one get a love marriage arranged?

Judging by the prevalence of this theme in the popular media and in literature,[1] it must be a problem that occupies many young women's (and men's) thoughts. This is the case in the diaspora as well as India. Newspaper articles on Indian marriage in the United States talk about love-cum-arranged marriage, also known as "assisted" marriage, seeking to "combine" the best of both types (see Belafante 2005). In India, too, interviews reveal that for upper-class women, a combination of the two is the ideal (Puri 1999: 183–43, addressing the false dichotomy of love and arranged marriage). Although women

1. This is the case for both ends of the spectrum: on the one hand prestigious literature in English, such as, say, Vikram Seth's 1993 novel *A Suitable Boy,* on the other hand the romances of popular fiction from women's magazines, as discussed in Uberoi 2001b.

may prefer for their parents to arrange the marriage, they unhesitatingly view the companionate marriage as the ideal (135–53). These are not only the preoccupations of the urban and privileged. Anthropological literature reveals the anxieties of rural and less privileged women around arranged marriages, eloquently summed up in the refrain of a folk song: "Don't marry me to a plowman!" (also the title of a sociological study: Jeffery and Jeffery 1996).

In short, many girls are concerned about being married off to an unwanted groom, and if they have found a suitable boy on their own, are concerned with somehow convincing their parents of his suitability. The taboo on talking with elders about one's own future match does not make things easier. If there is no possibility of the love match being approved by the parents, elopement might be considered as an option, though an inferior one.[2] Here the issue of the woman's agency becomes tricky, with parents often arguing that the girl was "abducted" rather than that she "eloped" (see e.g. Chowdhry 2004). Interestingly, contemporary informants sometimes justify their elopement with reference to the ancient normativity of the *Dharmaśāstra* (Mody 2006: 332).

If we look at the context in which the televised *Ramayan* was aired, we find that the popular soap series preceding it had extensively reflected on and caused reflection on this very issue. A wonderful example is the soap *Hum Log* (aired on Doordarshan 1984–85; written by Shyam Manohar Joshi), which followed the ups and downs of a lower-middle-class joint family. The arrangement of the marriage of the oldest daughter, Badki, who had a boyfriend, caused a lot of consternation, judging by the correspondence Doordarshan received on the topic. Moreover, it appears that many young women made it a point to visit the actress in her home to advise her on the need to marry her boyfriend. Apparently, the outpouring of audience displeasure with the arranged marriage caused the scriptwriter to break off the engagement. When the love marriage was celebrated, the public responded by sending cards of congratulations to the couple (Gokulsingh 2004: 33). This emotional reaction to the issue of a woman caught between a secret love interest on the one hand and the match her parents are arranging on the other betrays that it is a real-life concern for many women. It will be well worth our while to assess how the goddess acts when she is caught in a comparable situation to determine what kind of a role model she makes.

For Sītā, there is a straightforward parallel with the plight of the young marriageable girl. I will analyze the episode following the falling-in-love scene

2. For elopement among Satnamis in Chattisgarh, see the interesting work by Parry (2002).

that leads up to Sītā's wedding—known as the Svayaṃvara or "self-choice". This episode is crucial for the narrative. While the central action is told in just one chapter in *Vālmīki Rāmāyaṇa,* important chapters precede and follow (*VR* 1.66–8). Tulsīdās devotes ten *kaṛavaks* to the event (*RCM* 1.227–36). Sagar stretches the central event over two episodes, in good cliff-hanging tradition, and adds a bit of the aftermath in the third one (vol. 5, episodes 7–9). In the Savayaṃvara, Rāma has to prove himself eligible as Sītā's groom in a public ritual. He succeeds in lifting the bow of Śiva, now in the possession of Sītā's father, the king of Mithila, and thereby wins the hand of princess Sītā.[3] This episode could be said to correspond to any ordinary wedding's first step, sometimes called *vadhū-vara-guṇaparīkṣā,* or examination of the qualities of bride and groom (Kane 1974: 531). However, in contrast to the norm for modern weddings, in the epic it is the groom who is on the spot, not the bride. In the modern context, this episode raises issues related to partner choice—what constitutes "a suitable boy" and how a "proper match" is made.

In the Krishna mythology, the Gopīs' falling in love does not culminate in matrimony; the Gopī-Krishna relationship is typically clandestine, and legitimacy is out of the question. I will return to that issue in chapter 3; for now, for a contrasting episode, we will look instead at how Krishna marries his first wife, Rukmiṇī. Here we have a case where the bride has been promised to a man she does not wish to marry. She instead invites the man she has set her heart on, Krishna of course, to abduct her.

The elopement of Krishna and Rukmiṇī has been popularly cited as an example of the flexibility of "ancient Hindu culture" and its perceived openness for women. For example, a commercial flyer advertising the comic book of the story in Anant Pai's Amar Chitra Kathā series reads: "Rukmini is a perfect foil to Krishna in this idyllic tale. It is she who though coy, makes the first move by confidently revealing her heart to her lover. She plans the details of their escapade too and proves how high the status of resourceful women was in ancient India."[4] On the other hand, one wonders whether this mythological example might be considered applicable in the modern context. Does it legitimize elopement as a plausible option for women trapped in an unwanted engagement? One suspects there is a discrepancy between what is applauded about ancient India and what is condoned today. Comparing different versions

3. I skip the incident during the Svayaṃvara where Rāma is challenged by Paraśurāma (Bhārgava Rāma or Rāma Jāmadaghnya), which is less of interest here. For the Vālmīki version of this episode, see Sutherland-Goldman 2004.

4. See www.exoticindiaart.com/book/details/ACL23.

of the Rukmiṇī story will help us to understand what message is being sent to young women. Would a feminist reading of Rukmiṇī's example find support for women's defiance to patriarchy? Do the most recent retellings support such a reading?

Two chapters of *Bhāgavata Purāṇa* are devoted to this episode (*BhP* 10.53–4).[5] They were recreated in Braj by Nanddās in 133 *rolās*, or distichs, in his *Rukminī Maṅgal*. As far as televised retellings go, the *Shri Krishna* series ends with Krishna's education and does not depict his life as a king, so does not include the incident. I will look instead at the episode in B. R. Chopra's *Mahabharat*. While the story of Krishna (Nitesh Bharadwaj) and Rukmiṇī (Channa Ruparel) might be considered a minor aside in view of the epic narrative, it is given two full episodes (DVD, vol. 5, episodes 27–8) of the complete series.

The contrast between Sītā's and Rukmiṇī's weddings corresponds to that between two types of wedding as laid down in the treatises of *Dharmaśāstra:* Svayaṃvara and Rākṣasa-vivāha. Sītā's wedding is often styled a Svayaṃvara, or "Self-Choice," wedding. This is somewhat of a misnomer, since in fact the bride is given to the man who wins a contest or accomplishes a feat. The epic Kṣatriya Svayaṃvaras, however, generally deviate from what is outlined in the Śāstras (see Kane 1974: 2.1, 523–4), whose authors apparently interpreted the Svayaṃvara as a form of Gāndharva-vivāha, or "wedding of the nymphs," a mutual-consent-only wedding that required no parental involvement. This type of wedding is nowadays often equated with "love marriage." In Vālmīki's story, however, some elements of the more prestigious "gift of the virgin" (*kanyādāna*) type of marriage are present.[6] Rukmiṇī's wedding could be classified as a Rākṣasa-vivāha, or "demon-style" wedding (not to be confused with the Āsura-vivāha, which is basically the sale of a bride), where the groom abducts the bride to make her his. Actually, the latter applies best to the Rukmiṇī's wedding as told in *Viṣṇu Purāṇa,*[7] but the way it is told in *Bhāgavata Purāṇa* may be best described as a combination of the Rākṣasa- and Gāndharva-vivāha types. Indeed, such as combination is described as a procedure acceptable for Kṣatriyas (Olivelle 2005: 45; Manu 3.26). The name Rākṣasa makes it obvious that this type of wedding is not prestigious but carries a stigma.

5. A handy translation of these chapters is in Coleman 2003.

6. For a full discussion of the evolution of the Svayaṃvara from the epics to the Śāstras, see Brockington 2000.

7. I am grateful to Peter Scharf of Brown University for bringing this to my attention. A study of the evolution of the Sanskrit story will be part of a forthcoming work by Tracy Coleman.

Both types of wedding revolve around a public spectacle that establishes the prowess of the groom. Thus, both stories are replete with *vīra rasa,* or the heroic mode. In both instances, too, the bride appears in public, and there is an element of free choice for the bride-to-be; yet it is limited. It is also contrary to what one might expect just from the names: one might think of the Svayaṃvara as a prochoice option and the Rākṣasa-vivāha as victimizing the bride. In the case of the Svayaṃvara, notwithstanding the name, the bride's choice is in fact severely limited by the condition or contest, whose terms she has not set. For instance, in *Rāmāyaṇa* Sītā's father has set the condition of lifting Śiva's bow. In the case of the Rākṣasa-vivāha, there is a possibility of agency on the part of the bride; she may have actively sought out the groom and proposed to him that he abduct her, as indeed Rukmiṇī did. Still, the limitation is that she is of course dependent on her chosen groom's willingness to undertake this dangerous enterprise for her sake, with all the ensuing political implications. Rukmiṇī makes use of the services of a messenger, a Brahmin, who functions as a matchmaker, whereas in Sītā's case there is no question of an intermediary. The major difference between the two types of wedding is that in the first there is parental consent for the match, while the second proceeds against parental wishes. And in the first case, the groom is one of many wooers, all having equal chances, while in the second, there is another legitimate groom to whom the parents have given preference and who hence holds a right over the bride. Finally, whereas the violence in the second type of wedding is inevitable and often bloody, in the first type it is channeled into a contest.

At first sight, these may seem quaint, antiquated praxes with little contemporary relevance. However, both types of wedding have modern resonances and abound in novels, movies, and real life anecdotes. In scenarios à la Sītā-Rāma young men have to prove their mettle to qualify in the eyes of their (richer or higher-class) beloved's father. Similarly, Rukmiṇī's elopement brings to mind newspaper stories of unwilling brides eloping before the appointed wedding day with the boy of their hearts. Our goddesses have a role model function even today.

In this chapter, I will first discuss Sītā's Svayaṃvara, comparing its classical, medieval, and televised versions, and then do the same for Rukmiṇī's elopement. Finally, I will discuss how the "test of the groom" and "elopement" scenarios are treated in popular Hindi movies. I will revisit *Hum aap ke hain koun . . . !* and discuss movies that have a "test of the groom" scenario, such as Sooraj Barjatya's 1989 hit *Maine pyar kiya,* or the "elopement" scenario, such as Aditya Chopra's 1995 *Dilwale dulhania le jayenge.*

TABLE 2.1. Comparison of Svayaṃvara and Rākṣasa-vivāha

Similarities

Vīra rasa
Prowess of hero central
Public spectacle
Bride appears in public
Bride's agency limited

Differences

Svayaṃvara	*Rākṣasa-vivāha*
Seems to allow woman's choice	Seems to cast woman as victim
Woman has less initiative	Woman can take initiative
Agency limited by condition for contest	Agency limited by hero's willingness to fight
No intermediary	Messenger-"match-maker"
Parental consent	Against parents' wishes
Many rival wooers	One legitimate groom as rival
Violence between wooers	Violence between groom's and bride's families
Violence deflected in contest	Violence and ensuing abduction

Sītā's Svayaṃvara

Dhanuryajña: Did Sītā Get to Choose Rāma?

Right from the beginning, our investigation encounters the need for nuance. The terms "Svayaṃvara" and "Dhanuryajña" (bow sacrifice), as this episode is commonly referred to, do not apply very well to the story of Rāma stringing Śiva's bow as told by Vālmīki in the Bāla Kāṇḍa (1.66). Here, when Rāma arrives in Mithilā, Janaka is performing a nonspecified Vedic sacrifice; it is not identified as Dhanuryajña or as a preparation for a Svayaṃvara. Viśvāmitra and his two wards happen to drop by and ask to see the famous bow. There is no question of Rāma having any competition from other kings on this occasion. The unsuccessful Svayaṃvara proper seems to have taken place long ago, well before Rāma arrives on the stage. Janaka relates to the sage and the princes, in the past tense, how the disappointed kings after their failure to string the bow laid siege to Mithilā but were eventually expelled (*VR* 1.66.16–25). There is no question of Sītā "choosing" Rāma. It is not even clear whether she witnessed his feat, and she does not get to lay a victory garland (*jayamālā*) on his shoulders. Her father chooses for her by simply declaring that Rāma is now entitled to his daughter's hand (1.66.21–3). Thus, notwithstanding the common understanding of Sītā's wedding as a Svayaṃvara, that concept does not correspond to the description in the Vālmīki version.

That is not the whole story, however. There is a slightly different and shorter version of the Svayaṃvara story later in *Vālmīki Rāmāyaṇa,* at the end of the Ayodhyā Kāṇḍa. Interestingly, it is put in the mouth of none other than the bride herself. Thus it provides a version of the Svayaṃvara from Sītā's perspective. It occurs in the context of the meeting of Sītā with Anasūyā, the sage Atri's wife.[8] At Anasūyā's request, Sītā relates the events leading up to her Svayaṃvara. She starts with the story of her "birth" from the earth and her adoption at Janaka's court (*VR* 2.118.27–33). Then, she dwells on Janaka's worries when she came of age and he had to find a suitable groom for her (2.118.34–7). According to Sītā, these worries made Janaka decide to hold a Svayaṃvara and set the test of the bow as the condition for her marriage (2.118.38–42). Many kings failed, but "after a good long time," Rāma appeared and succeeded (2.118.43–9).

This version fits better with the common understanding of how the wedding came about, as it allows for the possibility that Rāma was present at the Svayaṃvara ceremony proper and that the "sacrifice" he came to see was indeed the Dhanuryajña. Vālmīki thus offers two slightly different interpretations of what happened. In the first one, it is an all-male affair, and Rāma just by chance happens to be able to lift the bow, long after the Svayaṃvara proper. Only in the second version, as told by Sītā, is there scope for the interpretation that Rāma won Sītā's hand in a competition. What is most striking in Sītā's version is the poignancy of her father's plight, a concern that many girls are able to identify with; I take this up again in the next chapter.

The Svayaṃvara setting and the competition element are a given for Tulsīdās and the televised version. Tulsī seems to have borrowed it from the Sanskrit dramatic tradition (Vaudeville 1955: 108–9). One minor difference in the television version compared to *Rām Carit Mānas* is that the arrival of the sage and the princes is no mere coincidence. In an earlier episode we learn that Janaka has sent an invitation to the sage for the event and is pleased to learn that Viśvāmitra has come (TVR 77).

Tulsīdās fully exploited the background of competition to demonstrate the greatness of Rāma, and Sagar follows suit. While Rāvaṇa is not present at the competition proper, Tulsīdās has the bards in their introduction to the bow mention that "Great warriors like Rāvaṇa and Bāṇāsura looked at the mighty bow and forewent the opportunity" (*RCM* 1.252.1b). The appearance of Rāma in this public setting becomes a major occasion for *darśana*. When Rāma enters

8. For a full analysis of this passage with its explicit instruction to women, see Pauwels 2001. In the oldest layers of the text, Sītā does not tell the story, but Anasūyā instructs her in dharma (Brockington and Brockington 2006: 69–70).

the hall where the contest is to take place, Tulsī makes this explicit in his famous line "Everyone saw the Lord's image according to his own predisposition" (*RCM* 1.241.2b).[9] In the television version, this line is quoted, and the camera registers the reactions of the different parties present. Tulsīdās goes on to describe several feelings (*rasas*) in which Rāma is seen by different groups of spectators, to create, one could say, a multidimensional *darśana*. He then provides a head-to-toe (*nakha-śikha*) description of the two brothers (*RCM* 1.242 *dohā*–244.1). Sagar's camera lingers on the image of the brothers to provide a *darśana*, but there are no further quotations from *Rām Carit Mānas*.

Tension Mounting: Who Loses His Cool at the Svayaṃvara?

Notwithstanding the background of the contest, in Tulsī's *Rām Carit Mānas* there is never any real doubt that Rāma will win, either for the audience or for Rāma and his party.[10] On the morning of the contest, Lakshmana predicts that "someone on whom Viśvāmitra's grace [*kṛpā*] rests" will be the winner (1.240.1b). Sagar reworks this incident in modern Hindi and adds a short scene before it in which Lakshmana tells Rāma how eager he is to attend the Svayaṃvara. Rāma, however, keeps his cool and gives his brother a *Gītā*-esque lesson in detachment, saying, "At the time of a test one should not be excited, one should only concentrate on one's action" (TVR 93).[11] By doing so, Sagar reinforces the sense of predestination and sets up Rāma as a model for disciplined human behavior. The contest is not a real test but a blueprint, an occasion to set an example.

The only one to doubt the outcome, is Sītā, yet she also displays exemplary disciplined behavior. Recall that in Vālmīki Rāmāyana, Sītā is nowhere on the scene. She does not even seem to merit a description of her beauty; only the miraculous story of her "birth" is recounted by Janaka (1.66.13–4), and that in the same breath as the history of the bow (1.66.8–12). In contrast, Tulsīdās provides a full *darśana*. While he spends many more words on the beauty of Rāma than of Sītā, Sītā is very much on the scene. Tulsī gallantly uses a whole *kaṛavak* (1.247) to say that there is no comparison to her, and calls her Jagad-

9. *jinha keṃ rahī bhāvanā jaisī, prabhu mūrati tinha dekhī taisī.*

10. Tulsī is inspired by the *Adhyātma Rāmāyaṇa*, in which predestination is palpable in every line. This work is usually dated to the fourteenth century and seen as one of the major sources of Tulsī's *RCM*; (see Vaudeville 1955 and Whaling 1980). The wedding episode in this work starts out following *VR*: Viśvāmitra asks for Rāma to see the bow, which, it is well known, others have seen, too. Still, there is a definite Svayaṃvara flavor to the episode: Rāma is said to string the bow "in the assembly of the kings," and Sītā is present and "crowns" him with a *svarṇamayī mālā* (*Ādhyātma Rāmāyaṇa* 1.6.29, edition by the Ramakrishna Math: Swami Tapasyananda 1985).

11. *parīkṣā ke samay uttejit nahīṃ honā cāhie. keval apne karm par dhyān rakhnā cāhie.*

ambikā (*RCM* 1.247.1a) and Jagata-jananī (1.248.1b), both meaning "Mother of the World." Notwithstanding these exalted titles, Sītā is a character of flesh and blood. Whereas Rāma does not lose his cool, Sītā shows the signs of love. After all, she is the ideal *bhakta*. Tulsī describes how her anxious eyes scan the room for Rāma (1.248.4). Still, Tulsī hastens to stress her self-control: out of respect for her elders (*gurujana lāja*), she turns her eyes to her friends, while keeping Rāma's image locked in her heart (1.248 *dohā*). Sagar does not miss this occasion to make the heroine conform to *maryādā*. His Sītā enacts this scenario while these very lines from *Rām Carit Mānas* are cited (TVR 95).

In case the message did not get across clearly, Sagar seems to have felt the need to appear on the screen in person to explicitly address the issue of appropriate behavior. On the video, after episode 9, the director appears and comments on the events he has portrayed (not transcribed in the Mizokami edition). He does not quite apologize for the preceding Phūlvārī episode, where Rāma and Sītā are portrayed as falling in love, but apparently feels compelled to clarify some issues. He stresses first that the love of the divine couple is eternal, and that this was just their first meeting since they had descended to earth. Moreover, he stresses that while they feel romantic love, their behavior remains fully within conventional morality (*maryādā kā pūrṇa ācaraṇ*). He stresses that at every step the *Rāmāyaṇa* teaches conventional morality and discipline (*maryādā* and *saṃyam*).[12] I think Sagar is trying to warn the young and eager that Sītā and Rāma's courtship is no justification for "love marriages."

Tulsī uses the Svayaṃvara contest to create dramatic tension.[13] He fully exploits the irony of the avatar, who acts like a human but is in fact God himself. Whereas Tulsī's audience was of course aware of Rāma's divinity, most of his characters act as if they are unaware of it, including Sītā. Tulsī provides a window into the minds of all present at the contest and their personal worries and desires about the outcome. This outpouring of emotions works well within *Rām Carit Mānas's* general agenda of promoting emotional devotion or bhakti. Sagar pretty much follows suit, but there are some interesting differences. I will explain in detail the reactions of the different parties in so far as they are relevant for our perspective.

12. This has also been noted by Dalmia-Lüderitz 1991: 225.

13. This is in contrast to the *Adhyātma Rāmāyaṇa*. The *RCM* creates tension also in its description of the reaction of the people once the Rāghava boys and Sītā have arrived in the public space of the contest. There is an element of predestination, in that people just know that Rāma is the right match for Sītā (1.249.1). On the other hand, they see Janaka's condition for winning Sītā's hand as an obstacle to the outcome (1.249.2–3). The television version's treatment is more dramatic, as it owes much to the theatrical conventions of Hindi theater and movies, as noted by Dalmia-Lüderitz 1991: 211

First, when the kings see handsome Rāma, they figure that Sītā will choose him even if he does not break the bow (*RCM* 1.245.2). In the television version, they even consider this foul play on the part of of Janaka, and they voice the opinion that the marriage match is prefixed (TVR 94). This is doubly ironical, given that the match was indeed made in heaven, so to speak. To some extent this is underscored by an implicit equation of the bow with Sītā. The bow will not yield to anyone but Sītā's rightful husband. Tulsīdās has suggested as much in the scene where all the kings try and the bow refuses to budge, by likening the bow to a *satī*, or virtuous woman, who does not give in to a suitor's pleas (*RCM* 251.1b).[14] Significantly, this line is recited in the television version (97). Sagar must have been aware of the implications of the comparison, and they suit his purpose of providing further legitimization of Sītā's love for Rāma.

In *Rām Carit Mānas,* when all the kings are defeated, Janaka expresses his despair of ever finding a real male (*vīra*) who can lift the bow and be a true match for his daughter (1.251.3b–252.3). There is irony here, too, in that the audience knows he is about to obtain the best match of all. Sagar follows Tulsī and stresses even more explicitly Janaka's moral quandary. Either he is to break his vow or not marry off his daughter: "If I break my word, I'll be called a blemish on my family name and I'll destroy all the good deeds of my ancestors. If I keep my word, my daughter will remain a virgin for this whole life, and the sin of rendering her life useless will be on my head" (TVR 98).[15] Sagar's Janaka is concerned with the wider repercussions, not just for himself but for his whole lineage.

By comparison, no such despair is voiced in the Bāla Kāṇḍa by Vālmīki's Janaka. In that version, the other kings have pressured Janaka into organizing a Svayaṃvara (predating Rāma's visit) (*VR* 1.66.17–8). In Tulsī's fourteenth-century source text, the *Adhyātma Rāmāyaṇa,* Janaka is not worried at all, which he himself explains later, after the wedding: long ago Nārada disclosed to him that Sītā, who is really Lakṣmī, was only to be married to Rāma, who is really Vishnu. This disclosure was the reason for his strict condition on Sītā's marriage (*Adhyātma Rāmāyaṇa* [1.6.58–75]).

The contrast of these relatively unworried Janakas with Sagar's Janaka is striking. One might speculate that the stress on a girl's father's plight in the television series strikes a chord in a contemporary environment, where the requirement of a high dowry makes it problematic to marry off daughters to truly "suitable boys." Ironically, in the real-life situation, the frustration of the father

14. *ḍagai na saṃbhu sarāsanu kaiseṃ, kāmī bacana satī manu jaiseṃ.*

15. *agar maiṃ yah pratijñā toḍ dūṃ to kul kā kalaṅk kahlāūṃ, pūrvajoṃ ke sukṛt naṣṭ karūṃ aur maiṃ apnā praṇ rakhūṃ to merī putrī ājanma kuṃvārī rahegī, uskā jīvan viphal karne kā pāp mere sir caṛhegā.*

with finding the right match for his daughter is caused not by any inability on the part of the groom but rather the inability of the bride's family to meet the groom's party's financial demands.

To return to the story, in both *Rām Carit Mānas* and the television version, Lakshmana takes strong offense from Janaka's words, especially his claim that there seem to be no true men or heroes left on earth. Eventually, he is calmed down by his brother and his guru, and Viśvāmitra urges Rāma to lift (or rather break) the bow. In *Rām Carit Mānas,* when Rāma steps up to the plate to lift the bow, Sītā's mother vents her worry about this tender boy being able to pull off such a task (1.255 *dohā*–256.3a), in turn providing the occasion for one of the ladies-in-waiting to reflect on deceiving appearances with several examples from mythology (256.3b–257.2a).

Sagar seems to have particularly liked the perspective of the girl's mother, Sunayanā, because he has her vent her worries twice, once during the futile operations of the kings (TVR 7.97) and later, as in *Rām Carit Mānas,* when Rāma takes his turn (TVR 99). The second occasion is modeled after *Rām Carit Mānas* with the difference that it is her sister-in-law, Kuśadhvaja's wife, who tries to comfort her with the platitude that whatever is to be will come true. In Sagar's version, Sunayanā is not happy with that answer, musing that the king seems to have gone mad to let such a young boy try and lift the bow. For more ironic effect, Sagar also has the other assembled kings ridicule Rāma for his apparent immaturity. Finally, Sagar heightens the dramatic tension by breaking off the episode just before its climax. Doordarshan spectators had to wait a week before the tension would be relieved by Rāma actually lifting the bow.

Rām Carit Mānas and the television version also provide a window into Sītā's thoughts at the moment of Rāma's test. She is prey to serious doubts, apparently having forgotten all about his divinity. In a touching episode, Sītā ardently beseeches the gods to make the heavy bow lighter so that Rāma can lift it and she can become his (*RCM* 1.257.3–4). The television version quotes these lines, while the camera focuses on Sītā. Then comes a series of cuts from her worried face to pictures of Śiva-Pārvatī and Gaṇeśa (TVR 100).

The singers in the television version then jump ahead a few verses in *Rām Carit Mānas* to Sītā's humble voicing of her desire: "If in body, mind, and words, my vow is true, that my soul is attracted to the dust of Raghupati's feet; Then, Lord, who dwells in everyone's heart, make me the maid-servant of Raghuvara" (*RCM* 1.259.2b–3a).[16] Special stress is placed on these lines by singling out the

16. *tana mana vacana mora panu sācā, raghupati pada saroja citu rācā; tau bhagavānu sakala ura bāsī, karahi mohi raghubara kai dāsī.*

first and last half-verse for repetition (TVR 100). The last line is further stressed by being delivered in declamation, not sung like the rest. Such humble voicing of her desire may seem out of place in a contemporary context, and one might have expected these lines to be dropped, but Sagar chose to quote them rather emphatically. This is no coincidence. As we shall see, Sagar later explicitly updates the traditional view of wife as servant (*dāsī*) of the husband, yet even on that occasion, he in effect portrays Sītā as ready to play the subservient role. In the televised version, the ideal woman sees herself as subservient to her husband, her lord.

These lines are explicitly set up as having general relevance—the next verse quoted from Tulsī reads: "Who truly loves, will get his true love, there is no doubt about it" (*RCM* 1.259.3b).[17] The catch here of course is the stipulation "a love that is true" (*satya sanehū*). Sītā's submissive attitude is generalized, and the message is that this will be the one that is rewarded in the end. We should remember here, too, how the bow was earlier compared to a *satī*, unyielding to anyone except her righteous husband. The image of the *satī* merges with the idea of true love, or *satya sanehu*. At this point Sagar adds flashback images of the goddess Pārvatī, who granted Sītā the boon of the groom of her choice in the previous episode. These images reinforce the legitimacy of her desire.

We should also note what Sagar leaves out. In the ardor of the moment, Tulsī allows Sītā in her thoughts a split second of rebellion against her father's harsh condition for her marriage: "Alas, what terrible insistence of my father! Can he not tell benefit from harm?" (*RCM* 1.258.1b).[18] She goes on to criticize in her thoughts, as her mother has done out loud, the ministers and learned men present for not stopping such a tender boy from taking on such a big task. She muses that the bow should have become light for Rāma to lift, now that its obtuseness (*jaṛatā*, "lifelessness" or "stupidity") seems to have been transferred to everyone present (1.258.4a). Tulsī's Sītā does not shy away from criticizing the whole gathering of venerable elders as dull-witted (1.258.3b).[19] Not so in Sagar's text. He does not allow his Sītā even that much loss of decorum in her thoughts, and leaves out these verses altogether. Whatever Sītā's private wish in favor of Rāma, in the television version she submits fully to parental authority. Far from getting to speak out to her confidantes about her private preferences, the very thoughts are suppressed.

17. *jehi keṃ jehi para satya sanehū, so tehi milai na kachu saṃdehū.*

18. *ahaha tāta dāruni haṭha ṭhānī, samujhata nahiṃ kachu lābhu na hānī.*

19. *sakala sabhā kai mati bhai bhorī.*

Why Does Rāma Lift the Bow?

In both the television version and *Rām Carit Mānas,* we also get a window into Rāma's feelings and an interesting perspective on what prompts him to action. In *Vālmīki Rāmāyaṇa,* there is not much psychological background. Significantly, though, it is Rāma himself who takes the initiative to lift the bow and string it, though he proceeds to do so only after having received the permission of his guru and the king. Tulsī's and Sagar's Rāma is much less keen to act. He rather meekly follows the command of his guru. Again, the irony of the incarnation is central: God the Almighty defers to mere mortals. To top off the irony, Tulsī's Rāma prays to Gaṇeśa before lifting the bow (*RCM* 1.255.4). Sagar leaves out this line but shows Rāma bowing his head respectfully as he prepares for the task.

In both the television version and *Rām Carit Mānas,* the scene is stretched out to build tension, but ultimately it becomes clear that what prompts Rāma to lift the bow is compassion for Sītā. He acts really to save Sītā from the horrible tension she is going through (*RCM* 1.259.3–4 and 260*dohā*--261.2; the latter are quoted in TVR). Tulsī's bhakti agenda is to highlight Rāma's compassion as the motivation for his actions, notwithstanding his total Self-sufficiency as God Supreme. Central to the episode is the irony that this all-powerful God has to go through the motions of proving himself. In that limited sense, the scene could be seen as a counterpart to Sītā's Agniparīkṣā or fire ordeal. Here Rāma is on trial and has to prove himself publicly worthy of Sītā, though we know all along that there is no doubt he is.[20] The main point, though, is that Rāma acts for the sake of his devotees.

Sītā may prompt Rāma into action, but it would be a mistake to interpret that as a move to turn Sītā into *śakti,* the female empowering principle. True, Sītā is called Mother of the World, as noted, yet it is not her power that propels Rāma but rather her powerlessness. The thoughts that flash through Rāma's head just before he lifts the bow are not very lofty and quite down-to-earth. In fact, it feels like a proverb that he quotes; it is not flattering to Sītā, as he compares her with a corpse: "When a thirsting man, for want of water, has died, what use is a lake of nectar for his corpse? What's rain when all crops have dried up? Why let the moment pass and be sorry afterwards?" *RCM*

20. Only in this limited sense can we speak of a parallel. There are also many differences. For one, in *RCM*, Rāma's trial is "more real" than Sītā's, which is undergone by a shadow-Sītā. Moreover, Sītā is supportive and concerned that Rāma may win his trial, whereas Rāma "speaks some harsh words" during Sītā's trial. In terms of audience reaction, also, as Vidyut Aklujkar has rightfully pointed out (personal communication, June 2000), Rāma's trial does not come even close to eliciting the same emotional response as Sītā's.

1.261.1b–2a).[21] While these lines have strong dramatic force, they may seem a bit matter-of-fact for romantic love. It is surprising, then, that Sagar singles out these verses for quotation (TVR 100); yet he does something interesting with them. He succeeds in making the reference of these lines less pointedly Sītā by focusing the camera in turn on her, her father, and her mother, thus managing to suggest that Rāma acts out of grace toward the whole Mithilā family—without changing an *akṣara* of Tulsī's work.

In his editorial comment, Sagar voices an emphasis that is in fact the opposite of Tulsī's. Tulsī wanted to highlight Rāma's compassion and so stressed that his action was inspired by Sītā's despair. Sagar, in his editorial comment, stresses that Rāma acts only on his guru's command, although he knows Sītā's state of mind very well (not in the Mizokami transcription).[22] Sagar clearly is not as interested in Rāma's compassion as in his obedience to his elders.

To Touch or Not to Touch the Husband's Feet

Once the bow is broken, Tulsī describes the reactions of all present, and Sagar's camera registers the joy on all the faces, though without quoting *Rām Carit Mānas* this time. Tulsī then lovingly describes how Sītā honors Rāma with the *jayamālā*, or garland of victory, an element, we remember, that was totally absent from *Vālmīki Rāmāyaṇa*. Obviously, this moment lends itself well to a tableau-like scene (*jhāṅkī*), of which Sagar makes full use. The camera moves from Sītā to Rāma and back again. We behold them beholding: *darśana* all around. Surprisingly, Sagar does not orchestrate the scene with any of Tulsī's lovely phrases, such as "Outwardly hesitant, but inwardly ecstatic, love so deep no one can fathom" (*RCM* 1.264.2a).[23] Instead, Sagar inserts a "women's song," "Put on the Victory Garland" (*pahanāo jayamālā*, TVR 101), probably following Tulsī's lines: "The clever girls instructed her, seeing [her being lost]: put on the beautiful Victory Garland" (*RCM* 1.264.3a).[24]

The instances where Sagar chooses to deviate from Tulsī's lead are few, but usually significant. Here is an important one. Tulsī's Sītā does not touch Rāma's feet, even when her girlfriends remind her to do so (*RCM* 1.265.4b). The reason for this, Tulsī says, is that Sītā knows that the adultress Ahalyā

21. *tṛṣita bāri binu jo tanu tyāgā, mueṃ karai kā sudhā taṛāgā; kā baraṣā saba kṛṣī sukhāneṃ, samaya cukeṃ puni kā pachitāneṃ.*

22. *hālāṃki sītājī kī adhīratā aur vivaltā ko acchī tarah se dekh rahe haiṃ, aur samajh rahe haiṃ.*

23. *tana sakocu mana parama uchāhū, gūṛha premu lakhi parai na kāhū.*

24. *catura sakhīṃ lakhi kahā bujhāī, pahirāvahu jayamāla suhāī.*

was delivered when she came in contact with Rāma's feet and shrinks in fear from such powerful feet. Tulsī adds that Rāma understands and just smiles at Sītā's extraordinary love (*RCM* 1.265 *dohā*).[25] Sagar's Sītā, however, does not suffer from such subtle qualms. She can't help but touch Rāma's feet. During the episode, Sagar instead concentrates on showing Sītā's feet and stresses how shyly and reluctantly they move (as noted by Dalmia-Lüderitz 1991: 218–9). The breach of decorum of Tulsī's Sītā did not find favor with Sagar; he keeps his Sītā neatly within the boundaries of traditional *maryādā*.

Finally, to return to *Vālmīki Rāmāyaṇa*'s second version of the Svayaṃvara story, where Sītā sums up her wedding description to Anasūyā: "Thus I was given away to Rāma there at the Self-choice ritual" (*VR* 2.118.54a);[26] she adds, "I am devoted to the best of the brave, my husband by dharma" (*VR* 2.118.54b).[27] This may seem contradictory to a modern audience. Contemporary discussions tend to pit "love marriages" against "arranged marriages," yet Sītā has the magical combination; a "self-choice" ritual in which her father sets the terms and gives her away and a lawful husband to whom she is genuinely devoted. Interestingly, Vālmīki's Sītā provides here a neat summary of what Sagar's series promotes. It was all already in Vālmīki after all.

Parental Approval for "Self-Choice"

After the bride has been won, the groom's parents need to be informed of the match and their permission for the wedding secured. All versions contain the subepisode of the message to Ayodhyā to inform Rāma's parents, which could be said to correspond with an ordinary wedding's phase of the "suing" (classical *varapreṣaṇa*), although that usually means the suing by the groom's party for the bride (Kane 1974: 531–2). In contrast, here we have the party of the bride bringing the proposal to the groom's family.

In *Vālmīki Rāmāyaṇa*, Janaka takes the initiative to send a message to Daśaratha, but makes sure to procure the blessing of Viśvāmitra (67.24–5). This does not totally square with *Vālmīki Rāmāyaṇa*'s second description of the Svayaṃvara at the end of the Ayodhyā Kāṇḍa where Sītā says that Janaka was ready to give her away to Rāma on the spot and even had a vessel of water (*jalabhājana*) handy for the ritual transaction but Rāma insisted on first securing the permission of his father (2.118.50–1). This alternative reading,

25. *gautama tiya gati surati kari, nahiṃ parasati paga pāni; mana bihase raghubaṃsamani, prīti alaukika jāni.*
26. *evaṃ dattāsmi rāmāya tathā tasmin svayaṃvare.*
27. *anuraktāsmi dharmeṇa patiṃ vīryavatāṃ varam.*

highlighting the respect of Rāma for his father, is not taken up by either *Rām Carit Mānas* or the television version, at least not at this point. In *Rām Carit Mānas* and the television version, neither Rāma nor Janaka takes the initiative. Instead, Janaka asks Viśvāmitra what to do next, and the sage suggests sending messengers to Daśaratha (*RCM* 1.286.3–287.1; TVR 8.108). Still, Sagar takes up Rāma's insistence to ensure his father's permission before marrying a bit later in the story, at the beginning of the wedding negotiations between Janaka and Daśaratha. When Śatānanda formally proclaims the wedding proposal, he states that Rāma did not wish to marry without having secured his father's permission (TVR 120).[28] This reinforces Sagar's stress on obedience to elders and on making love marriages conditional on parental approval.

The reception of the message in Ayodhyā is related in a straightforward way in *Vālmīki Rāmāyaṇa* (1.68; the chapter is only nineteen *ślokas* long). Tulsī "devotionalizes" the passage by turning the message into a hymn of praise to Rāma (*RCM* 1.291 *dohā*–293.3). He also adds an interesting incident. When Daśaratha seeks to reward the messengers bringing the good news, they refuse, considering it "improper" (*anīti*) to accept a gift (1.293.4b). Everyone approves of the messengers' sense of propriety. Sagar duly follows Tulsī's example, explaining that the messenger cannot accept anything from his "daughter's" *sasurāl* (in laws) (TVR 114). This betrays the concern for the relative status of the bride's and the groom's parties, which as we will see in the next chapter is even more foregrounded during the wedding itself.

In all versions, of course, Janaka's proposal is happily accepted. In *Vālmīki Rāmāyaṇa*, the king suggests immediately that the proposal should be accepted, if his councilors (i.e., Vasiṣṭha, Vāmadeva and the other ministers) approve of the appropriateness of the match (1.68.14). Tulsī's Daśaratha humbly seeks his guru Vasiṣṭha's advice, but there is hardly any doubt about the verdict. Vasiṣṭha elegantly says that the king naturally deserves the good luck he gets, given his extensive service to guru, Brahmins, cows, and gods (*RCM* 1.294). Sagar, too, is careful to have Daśaratha properly consult Vasiṣṭha first (TVR 113).[29] Sagar's Vasiṣṭha immediately uses the situation to put a megapolitical spin on the matter, describing the match as an appropriate alliance between two major "Aryan" political forces (113).[30] Finally, preparations

28. *pitā kī ājñā milne par hī sītā kā pāṇi-grahaṇ karūṃgā.*

29. *gurudev apnā nirṇay pradān kareṃ. usī ke anusār kārya kiyā jāe.*

30. *mithilā aur ayodhyā kā yah sambandha baṛā hī śubh hai. is sambandh ke dvārā āryāvart kī do mahān śaktiyoṃ kā milan hogā.*

TABLE 2.2. The Svayaṃvara Scene in Vālmīki's, Tulsī's, and Sagar's Versions

Element	VR	RCM	TVR
Setting	Heroic sentiment	Devotional sentiment	Obedience to guru/elder
	Heroic feat central	*Darśana* of Rāma central	*Darśana* of Rāma central
	No competition	Competition	Competition
	Rāma's party dropping by	Rāma's party makes casual visit	Purposeful visit by invitation
	No other kings present	Kings see Rāma as ideal groom	Kings suspect match is fixed
Sītā	No Sītā on scene	Sītā called Jagadambinī	*RCM* quoted
		Sītā shy (*gurujana lāj*)	*RCM* quoted
		Sītā prays to be Rāma's *dāsī*	*RCM* quoted
		Sītā pleads her love is true	Flashback to Pārvatī's boon
		Sītā critiques elders in mind	No such critique
Svayaṃvara	Janaka feels humiliated (in Sītā's retelling only)	Janaka angry	Janaka's quandary described at length
		Lakshmana upset	Lakshmana upset
		Rāma remains cool	Rāma remains cool
	No women on the scene	Sunayanā's misgivings	Sunayanā's misgivings (2x)
	Rāma acts with permission	Rāma acts at guru's command, out of compassion for Sītā	Rāma acts at guru's command, out of compassion for family
	No *jayamālā*	*Jayamālā*	*Jayamālā* and song
	No Sītā	Sītā does not touch Rāma's feet	Sītā touches Rāma's feet
Message to Ayodhyā	Rāma seeks father's permission (Sītā retelling)	Viśvāmitra suggests they seek Daśaratha's permission	Viśvāmitra suggests they seek Daśaratha's permission
	Daśaratha happily accepts, stipulating: if gurus accept	D. accepts; song in Rāma's praise; seeks first approval guru	Family banter in Ayodhyā
			Guru gives political spin
		Messengers refuse gift	Messengers refuse gift from their *sasurāl*
	No queens	Gift-giving of queens	Gift-giving of queens
			Kauśalyā reassures Sunayanā

are made for the "procession to the bride's house" (*barāt;* classical *vadhūgṛhagamana;* Kane 1974: 532).

In *Vālmīki Ramayaṇa,* we are never informed about the reaction of the queens of Ayodhyā. Tulsī describes their joy at the news and how they immediately celebrate, with charity for Brahmins (*RCM* 1.295.4), a typical combination of bhakti and caste dharma. Sagar duly includes an episode where Kauśalyā reports on her gift-giving. New is that she gives a rationale for her actions by saying that a king cannot celebrate any private festival if even one of the subjects in his kingdom is in pain (TVR 115).[31] Another innovation of Sagar here is that Kauśalyā sends a message to Sunayanā, Sītā's mother. She gives her assurance that Sītā will be treated like a daughter (*beṭī*) rather than a daughter-in-law (*bahū*) and will be taken under her own wing.[32] Kauśalyā's message sets the tone for the wedding scenes proper, where sympathy of the groom's party (*vara-pakṣa*) with the plight of the ritually inferior bride's party (*kanyā-pakṣa*) is a major concern.

Comparing Svayaṃvaras

What can we conclude from this analysis? First of all, we have to recognize that contrary to appearances, Sītā's so-called Svayaṃvara is not really a self-choice, and certainly not a love marriage in the modern sense. In Vālmīki's version, she is not even present on the scene as Rāma lifts the bow, there is no contest, and there is no question of her offering Rāma a victory garland. In Tulsī's version, and even more so in Sagar's, she is present but her role is passive. Though she gets to formalize the decision by garlanding the hero, she does not get to choose her groom. She had no say in the nature of the contest. Her father has set the test Rāma has to undergo, and to her mind the outcome is far from certain. She undergoes real agony thinking that he may fail, and she touchingly and humbly prays for his victory.

In which ways does the television series follow and differ from its sources, and what does that tell us about its biases? If classically Svayaṃvaras were seen as Gāndharva-vivāha, Sagar is most emphatic in subverting this. As with the Phūlvārī, here, too, he does all he can to make it clear that though Sītā and Rāma may have fallen in love at first sight, theirs is no love marriage. He even makes an editorial appearance to explicitly make the point. He is very concerned to communicate clearly that in the ideal epic world, love marriages are out. As a consequence, in the modern world, too, parental approval, if not determination of the match, is central.

Particularly striking in the televised version is the stress on obedience to elders and on male dominance. At every step, Sagar is keen to highlight the submissive attitude of his characters to paternal and elder male authority. Even

31. *jis rājā ke rāj meṃ prajā kā ek bhī prāṇī duḥkhī rah jāe, unheṃ apnā koī utsav manāne kā adhikār nahīṃ hotā.*

32. *kauśalyā kī mamatā ke āṃcal meṃ saṃtān ke samān hī sthān pāegī.*

Rāma himself sets a good example. He acts to lift the bow only after receiving the command of his guru, and says he will marry Sītā only after he receives permission from his father. This was already the case in *Vālmīki Rāmāyaṇa* and had become more explicit in *Rām Carit Mānas,* but it is emphasized most strongly in the television version.

Sagar definitely goes furthest with regard to the need for a woman's submission to male dominance. This is clear from his omission of Sītā's rebellious thoughts about her father's condition for her wedding, as well as from the reversal of Tulsī's scenario with respect to her touching Rāma's feet after the Svayaṃvara. Whereas Tulsī says she refrained from doing so in awe of their mysterious saving power, Sagar's Sītā feels compelled to touch them. Modesty in front of elders is another form of respectful behavior Sagar favors. He singles out for quotation verses from *RCM* that stress Sītā's modesty during the Svayaṃvara ceremony.

Sagar's message to the young then stresses the need for private desires to be submerged and made secondary to dharma and *maryādā*. He values positively the lack of agency of Rāma and Sītā in having their love sanctified in marriage. In his editorial comment, he stresses that Rāma makes no move to lift the bow until commanded to do so by his guru, although he understands, Sītā's agony full well. Such self-effacing silence is typical of the idiom of the Hindi movie. While the *Rāmāyaṇa* tradition is often blamed for the morality that glorifies the submergence of individual desires for the common good, paradoxically, the contemporary television version allows for much less agency than *Vālmīki Rāmāyaṇa* itself.[33]

Rukmiṇī's Elopement

Sagar's Missing Television Version

When we turn to Rukmiṇī's elopement, we find that the Sagar series does not treat this topic. That may be surprising, as there are, for instance, several movie versions of the story, the earliest one by Dadasaheb Phalke (1927).[34] One could argue that he follows, *Bhāgavata Purāṇa* which reserves this story to its second part. The DVD packet follows scriptural conventions and at the end of the

33. In *RCM*, too, Rāma has less agency than in *VR*, but the stress here is on the irony of the avatar, a typical bhakti theme. In the TVR, by contrast, the exemplary function of Rāma is stressed, as Sagar makes explicit.

34. There is also a famous film on the topic by Baburai Painter (1946). Most film versions date from the 1930s and 1940s; see *EIC*, S. V. *Rukmini* (*-Haran*, *-Kalyanam*, and *-Swayamvar*), and *Shri Krishna Rukmini*.

episode's summation says: "The first part of the deeds of divine incarnation ends here." While affirming authenticity, this allows of course for a sequel, were the series to prove a success. So nothing would impede Sagar or his sons from indeed tackling the second part of Krishna's life cycle, including the Rukmiṇī story. Still, notwithstanding such success, no such sequel has been forthcoming. One may suspect that Krishna's flirtations with the Gopīs taxed Sagar's dharma concerns enough, and that he may have chosen not to let himself in for the thorny issues of Krishna's multiple weddings later and what moral message might be extracted from them.[35] It is not for lack of airtime that Sagar quits after (significantly!) relating the education of Krishna and Balrāma and their "fee to the guru," or *gurudakṣinā*. The first and the two last volumes of the DVD contain quite a bit of material extraneous to the Krishna story itself. It is all brought together under the rubrique of Krishna's education, with the guru relating summaries of the other classical avatars of Vishnu. Sagar dwells in particular on the Rāma incarnation. The Svayaṃvara and wedding of Rāma and Sītā are related again at much length (at the end of episode 88, on vol. 11). The choice to redo a Sītā-Rāma type of wedding in preference to continuing on and venturing into the Rukmiṇī episode may have been a practical one of being able to fill up the airtime (or DVD) with material already available and with proven popularity. In fact, the retelling of the Rāma story as part of Krishna's education is a kind of "greatest hits from the series" summary, interestingly excluding Sītā's fire ordeal but dwelling lovingly on the Svayaṃvara. Whatever Sagar's practical reasons may have been, one suspects that his selection also reflects a strong preference for one type of wedding over the other.

Luckily, the equally popular televised serial *Mahabharat,* directed by B. R. Chopra, does include the story: it spans vol. 5, episodes 27–8. This interpolation of Krishna-related events is an interesting innovation by Chopra in the *Mahābhārata* story—neither the story of Krishna's childhood nor the Rukmiṇī episode figure prominently in the classical Sanskrit version attributed to Vyāsa.

Thus, for the Rukmiṇī story, I compare the classical Sanskrit version of *Bhāgavata Purāna* 10.52–3 with the devotional Braj version of Nanddās's *Rukminī Maṅgal* and the depiction of the episode in Chopra's *Mahabharat.* There are many subtle differences in these versions, but before turning to them, I shall enumerate what they have in common in comparison to Sītā's Svayaṃvara. Immediately apparent is the focus on the heroine, Rukmiṇī. She

35. Of course, the focus on the first part of *BhP*, in particular the Braj episodes of Krishna's life, reflects a preference similar to the medieval period under the influence of the Braj renaissance.

is in no way passive, as Sītā is so increasingly in the three versions we have studied. It is refreshing now to turn to a woman heroine who is keen to act and make decisions of great impact. In the Rukmiṇī story, the subjectivity of the heroine is much more important than that of the hero. The episode is mainly shown from her point of view; even though politics matter, she is no mere puppet in the political games of the men but an agent with her own agenda of personal happiness.

Male Politics versus Female Subjectivity

Notwithstanding these common traits, there are major differences in tone between Bhāgavata Purāṇa, Nanddās, and the televised version. While the emphasis remains on the heroine, in *Bhāgavata-Purāṇa* the story is strongly embedded in politics. Just before it comes the episode about Krishna's enmity with Jarāsandha of Magadha, whose daughters were married to Kaṃsa. After Krishna kills Kaṃsa, Jarāsandha attacks and fights Krishna and Balarāma, eventually causing them to take flight (10.50–2; with the interesting intervening story of a Yavana attack on Mathurā). Right after this story (from 10.52.15 onwards), the narrator shifts to how Krishna took Rukmiṇī for his bride when she had been promised to the Cedi king Śiśupāla, of whom Jarāsandha was an ally. It is indeed Jarāsandha who leads the party pursuing Krishna (10.53.57), whereas Śiśupāla remains rather passive throughout the affair. This stress on politics is even stronger in the televised version, where the cosmic commentator-narrator at the beginning of the episode situates it within the political buildup of the enmity between the Kauravas and Pāṇḍavas, reducing the marriage to a tactical alliance proposed by Jarāsandha as a move in the political dice game he is playing to overcome Krishna. He hopes to gain in one move the alliance of the Cedi king and his sons, as well as to win Bhīṣmaka's son Rukmī for his cause. Indeed, the story of Rukmiṇī starts with a scene where Jarāsandha comes to suggest the match to his old friend Bhīṣmaka, a proposal that is accepted wholeheartedly by both Bhīṣmaka and Rukmī but not by the younger son Rukma (TVK vol. 5, second half of episode 27).

In contrast, Nanddās's story stands on its own with hardly any reference to the main story. Nanddās takes little interest in politics. The title of his work, *Rukminī Maṅgal,* has totally different connotations: it evokes the joyous and auspicious wedding celebrations of the women rather than the heroic-political world of the men. The word *maṅgala* also occurs several times in the concluding verses:

Whoever sings this auspicious song, attentively listens or makes others listen,
He will obtain all auspiciousness, as it pleases the heart of Hari and Rukmiṇī.
What pleases Hari and Rukmiṇī's heart, pleases everyone.
Nanddās sings of the eternal auspiciousness of his Lord (*RM* 132–3).[36]

So here the stress is on the auspiciousness of the wedding; such seems counter to the general understanding of the abduction, which is classified generally as a Rākṣasa-vivāha. In Nanddās's version, the loving feelings between the bride and groom ripple into cosmic happiness. This mutual love, sustaining the devotional love of the devotee, is of course totally in agreement with Nanddās's bhakti agenda.

Defying the Arranged Marriage: Defense of Women's Rights

The *Bhāgavata Purāṇa* devotes minimal *śloka* time to set up the story. Bhīṣmaka of Vidarbha and his five sons and one daughter are introduced in just two verses (10.52.21–2). The situation is sketched briefly: Rukmiṇī wants to marry Krishna, and he her (10.52.23–4), but her brother Rukmī thwarts these plans out of enmity for Krishna (10.52.25). This upsets Rukmiṇī, who promptly dispatches a Brahmin to talk to Krishna (10.52.26). The focus then is mainly on the delivery of the message to Krishna, shown from the Brahmin's perspective, and describing Krishna's exemplary welcome service (*satkāra*) to Brahmins (10.52.27–36).

In the televised series, the main focus is again on the political world of the men. An innovation is a "good brother, bad brother" routine. Rukma is the good brother, who suggests, out of genuine love for his sister and appreciation of her being the most unusual woman in the known world (except for Draupadī), that only someone like God (Nārāyaṇa) should marry her, and Krishna is the one. Rukmī vehemently shuts up his younger brother, on the ground that this is an insult to their guest, Jarāsandha, who has come with an alternate proposal and is an enemy of Krishna. Rukmī also points out that it is not clear what Krishna's lineage is and he would never allow his sister to be married to such a pedigree-lacking person. One brother is shown to care about his sister's marital happiness, the other only about the family honor.

36. *jo yaha maṃgala gāya, citta dai sunai-sunāvai; so saba maṃgala pāvai, hari-rukamini mana bhāvai; hari rukamini mana bhāvai so, saba ke mana bhāvai; naṃdadāsa apane prabhu kau, nita maṃgala gāvai.*

Nanddās seems to assume we know the story already, and he jumps in right in the middle. One might surmise that some initial material is lost, because there are only two verses of invocative material, which are incidentally not in all manuscripts (see Brajratandās [1949] 1957: 175 n.1). Nanddās's first story line is:

> When Rukmiṇī heard "They will give her to Śiśupāla,"
> She froze like a picture: "What fortune has now befallen (me)?"
> (*RM* 3)[37]

In Nanddās's version, the focus is on the subjectivity of the heroine, Rukmiṇī. He has a long, charming description of her state of mind, how that is reflected in her appearance and behavior, and how she has no one to confide in (4–17). We are privy to her thoughts (18–23), which inspire her to make a decision and write a letter to Krishna (24). This look at a woman's subjectivity, mediated of course by the male devotional poet, is especially interesting for our purpose because it makes her work through her decision and look for a justification. Rukmiṇī is portrayed as justifying her defiance to patriarchy with reference to the example of none else than the Gopīs of Gokul!

> She would turn this around in her mind over and over: "now what to do?
> My image for the world, observing family honor, to me it's all damaged.
> A follower of Lord Krishna has to be obstinate and keep it up.
> Mother, father, and brother, relatives, may they all burn in the fire!
> This shame wrecks my life: may it catch fire and burn up
> (*RM* 19–21)[38]
> It's what keeps me separate from handsome Nanda's prince, the mountain lifter.
> Leaving their husband, worshiping Hari, that's what did the Gopīs of Gokul.
> Even them, he hid in every way, made them shine in the passion of the highest love.

37. *sisupālahi koṃ deta, rukminī bāta sunīṃ jaba; citra likhī sī rahī, daī yaha kahā bhaī aba.*

38. *karata bicāra manahi mana, abha dhauṃ kaisī kījai; loka lāja kula kāni kiye, mohiṃ sarabasu chījai; jyoṃ piya hari anusarauṃ, soī aba jatana karauṃ haṭhi; māta tāta aru bhrāta bandhu,-jana sabai parau bhaṭha; āgi lāgi jari jāhuṃ lāja, jo kāja bigārai.*

> Even today, it's the dust of their lotus feet to which aspire
> Sanaka, Sanandan, Śiva, Sarasvatī, Nārada, "impassioned."
> (*RM* 22–3).[39]

Rukmiṇī, making her difficult decision to defy patriarchy in the form of her brother's matchmaking and family honor, cites the Gopīs as an example and takes heart from their experience. She could easily be quoted as a role model for women forced to marry against their choice. Nanddās is not judgmental about Rukmiṇī's defiance: he does not comment and seemingly does not disapprove. From his perspective, the main point is that Rukmiṇī is acting out of love for God. Still, in this fine description of the psychology of a young girl in love, Nanddās betrays that the Gopī model could inspire women to act against their parents' wishes, choosing husbands of their own.

In the televised series, Rukmiṇī's feelings are important, but things are different. For one, she has a "real" Svayaṃvara, in which she will be able to choose her groom and garland him as a sign of her choice. However, before the event, her brother asks her to cooperate and select Śiśupāla. Interestingly, he introduces the request by saying "Here's a suggestion that may limit your rights somewhat."[40] Rukmiṇī remains respectful to her brother (*bhrātāśrī*) but cautiously inquires about a hypothetical case in which she might not consider Śiśupāla worthy, if she were to have her mind set on someone else. Twice her brother answers that even so, she must obey his and their father's wishes. This scene seems to reinforce the power of patriarchy. Rukmiṇī does not even get to voice her own choice to her brother; she can only obliquely suggest she might have an alternative scenario in mind. In this version, the woman's desires are crushed before they are even allowed to be articulated.

At the same time, patriarchy is undermined. If Rukmiṇī is not able to speak up, the cosmic narrator is. As if in answer to Rukmī's suggestion, and in an outspoken criticism of it, Time considers the matter from a social point of view (*samājśāstra kī dṛṣṭibhūmi se*, TVK vol. 5, episode 28). He points out that the old Indian practice, now forgotten, was that a woman got to choose her groom, contrasting the groom-selection (*varamālā*) of old with modern-day bride-selection (*vadhūmālā*). If she does not want to marry Śiśupāla, it will not happen, even if Krishna himself has to come to the rescue: "Society has

39. *suṃdara naṃdakuṃvara, nagadhara soṃ aṃtara pārai; pati parihari hari bhajata, bhaīṃ gokula kī gopī; tinahuṃ sabai bidhi lopi, parama premai rasa opī; jinake carana kamala raja, ajahū bāṃchana lāge; sanaka sanaṃdana siva, sārada nārada anurāge.*

40. *tumhārā ek adhikār thoṛāsā sīmit karne kā prastāv hai.*

no right to snatch this privilege from woman's hand."[41] Krishna acts to defend women's rights: "It establishes that in Indian society woman was not dependent, but she had the full privilege to make decisions about her own life."[42] The narrator then declares himself totally in favor of Rukmiṇī's decision: "For that reason, I respectfully bow to Rukmiṇī who through her letter showed the light on the threshold of society."[43] This point of view is made more explicit by the characters within the series themselves, notably Krishna and Baladeva, as we will see. The television version then explicitly supports Rukmiṇī's choice and her agency; however, what it shows from her actions actually suppresses her voice. She does not admit to choosing Krishna as a groom, not even to her friends. Instead, her younger brother chooses the deviant option for her. In her conversation with her older brother, she does not get to express her feelings either. When she tentatively asks her brother about other options, she is shut up in no uncertain terms. Her protest is silenced even before it is uttered as a hypothesis. Rukmiṇī then may be hailed as a path-blazer at the surface level, but the actions she carries out are hardly an inspiring example. Nanddās's Rukmiṇī is a much stronger agent, even though the fact that she reacts against patriarchal decisions is downplayed.

Three Ways to Write an Invitation to Elope

Once she has made up her mind, Rukmiṇī is to communicate her resolve to Krishna and invite him to elope with her. In the Sanskrit and Braj version, she chooses a Brahmin to go to Dwaraka and deliver the message (*BhP* 10.52.26; *RM* 25–6). Nanddās dwells lovingly on the marvels and wonders of Dwaraka (*RM* 28–39), whereas *Bhāgavata Purāṇa* spends few words on it (*BhP* 10.52.27) and concentrates instead on the warm welcome Krishna extends to the Brahmin, with exemplary humility and courtesies (10.52.28–35). Nanddās's Krishna, too, welcomes the Brahmin warmly (*RM* 47–51).

In both cases, the Brahmin then proceeds to convey Rukmiṇī's message, whose exact contents we get to know. The message is conveyed orally in *Bhāgavata Purāṇa*, but Nanddās's Rukmiṇī sends a letter written by her own hand. Krishna receives the letter, which the Brahmin has kept in the hem of

41. *nārī ke hath se samāj ko yah adhikār cīnh lene kā adhikār nahīṃ hai.*

42. *yah siddh kartā hai ki bhāratīya samāj meṃ nārī adhīn nahīṃ thī, use apne jīvan ke viṣay meṃ nirṇay lene kā pūrā adhikār thā.*

43. *is liye maiṃ rukmiṇī ko sādar praṇām kartā hūṃ jisne samāj kī dahlīj par us patra kā dīyā jalāyā.*

his coat (*RM* 52)[44] and which has a seal Krishna has to break (53).[45] The reason for introducing the device of a written letter seems to be that it allows for an opportunity to demonstrate emotional fervor: Krishna presses the letter to his heart (54),[46] and there is a dramatic culmination, an emotional catharsis, when Krishna gives the letter back to the Brahmin, "first sprinkled with Rukmiṇī's tears, now by those of Krishna" (55).[47] In the end, excessive love impedes Krishna from reading the letter himself, and he asks the Brahmin to read it to him. There is much more suspense with this longish introduction to the message, facilitating a very bhakti-like reveling in emotions.

Rukmiṇī's message in *Bhāgavata Purāṇa* is quite business like: she tells Krishna why she has chosen him (10.52.37–8), establishes that the king of Cedis should not get her instead (10.52.39), points out her merits (10.52.40)[48] on whose grounds he should really save her, and offers a practical plan to allay his potential misgivings about the bloodshed involved (10.52.41–2). She finishes up by declaring she will surely die from austerities if he does not come to her rescue, but she will keep hoping for him in a next birth (10.52.43). Her tone is that of someone who knows what she wants, who negotiates as an equal with Krishna and is in no way self-deprecating.

Nanddās's Rukmiṇī writes a much more passionate letter, without any practical details, and is more self-deprecating. She repeatedly calls herself his maidservant (*anucari, RM* 58a; *paricārī*, 61b; *dāsī*, 69b). In *Bhāgavata Purāṇa,* Rukmiṇī says Krishna is unique in pedigree, disposition, beauty, wisdom, age, opulence, and glory.[49] Nanddās's Rukmiṇī's reasons for selecting Krishna are more metaphysical: she points out that he alone brings bliss, all others only sorrow (*RM* 62b-63). Both Rukmiṇīs compare Śiśupāla to a jackal about to touch what is rightfully Krishna's (*BhP* 10.52.39; *RM* 70).[50] Nanddās likes to dwell on that type of imagery: his Rukmiṇī also calls Śiśupāla a defiling crow (*RM* 67).[51]

44. *taba rukamini kau kāgara, nāgara neha navīnoṃ; basana chori taiṃ chori, bipra śrīdhara kara dīnoṃ.*

45. *mudrā kholi guvindacanda, jaba bāṃcana āṃce; parama prema rasa sāṃce, acchara parata na bāṃce.*

46. *śrī hari hiyo sirāvata, lāvata lai lai chātī; likhī viraha ke hātha, supātī ajahūṃ tātī.*

47. *hiya lagāya sacu pāya bahuri, dvijabara kauṃ dīnī; rukamini aṃsuvana bhīnī, puni hari aṃsuvana bhīnī.*

48. Her self-stated merits include Brahmin worship: "If the Lord, the almighty, has been sufficiently fulfilled by merit, sacrifice, alsmgiving" (*pūrteṣṭa-datta-niyama-vrata-devavipragurvarcanādibhir alaṃ bhagavān pareśaḥ*).

49. *kula-śīla-rūpa-vidyā-vayo-draviṇa-dhāmabhir ātma tulyam.*

50. *mā vīrabhāgam abhimarśatu caidya ārād gomāyuvan mṛgapater balim ambujākṣa.*

51. *hai yah tumaro bhāga, kāga sisupāla biḍārau.* He also makes a comparison with hunter's imagery: "When a dove drops from the sky, (can the hunter stand) seeing it in the hand of another?" (*RM* 68): *parata parevā nabha taiṃ, parakara dekhata yākauṃ.*

In *Bhāgavata Purāṇa*, Rukmiṇī assures Krishna that she will die if he does not help her (10.52.43b).[52] Nanddās's Rukmiṇī speaks plainly of suicide by fire if Krishna does not save her (*RM* 69),[53] and she ends her letter cursing with clever rhyming wordplay that she would rather burn herself than that let that jackal Śiśupāla touch her (70).[54] Here we get more of a Rajput ethos, reminiscent of the *satī*. Although Rukmiṇī is never called to prove her willingness to die to stay pure for Krishna, still she declares herself prepared to undergo a type of Agniparīkṣā if she is approached by another man.

Things are quite different in the televised series. Rukmiṇī's letter is sent to Krishna without intermediary, straight from the heart. Krishna is of course able to feel the distress of his devotee. For realism's sake, there is a suggestion that birds might have transmitted the letter, as they figure prominently in the picturization of the song:

> Listen to my plea, O Lord,
> Lord of my heart, Hari, Play-boy,
> With peacock crown and yellow sash,
> Śrī Krishna Murārī will come.
> This is a connection of birth after birth,
> Its witness is the starry sky.
> Counting every breath, hope assures,
> Śrī Krishna Murārī will come.
> Eyes unblinking in continuous waiting
> O Bridegroom, Savior from Sorrow!
> You are welcome, now give occasion to welcome.
> My eyes are like worshipers, you are their refuge.
> What else can I say, you dwell within,
> You are the Lord of my body and soul, my wealth and life.
> Tell me when you arrive, respectfully,
> That you agree to my request.[55]

It is immediately apparent that the tone of this song is subservient. The refrain, returning again and again, sets up the song as one of humble sup-

52. *yarhi ambujākṣa na labheya bhavat-prasādaṃ jahyām asūn vrata-kṛśāñc catajanmabhiḥ syāt.*

53. *jo nagadhara naṃdalāla, mohi nahiṃ karihau dāsī; to pāvaka para jarihauṃ, barihauṃ tana tinakā sī.*

54. *jari mari dhari dhari deha, na paihauṃ sundara hari bara; pai yaha kabahuṃ na hoya, syāla sisupāla chueṃ kara.*

55. *binatī suniye nātha hamārī, hṛdayeśvara hari hṛdaya-bihārī, mora mukuṭa pītāmbaradhārī; janama janama kī lagī lagana hai, sākṣī tārā bharā gagana hai, gina gina śvāsa āsa kahtī hai, āeṃge śrī kṛṣṇa murārī; satata pratīkṣā apalaka locana, he bhava bānā vipati vimocana, svāgata thā abhi avakāra dījiye, śaraṇāpaṭa hai nayana pūjārī; aura kahūṃ kyā antaryāmī, tana mana dhana prāṇoṃ ke svāmī, kara ādara ākar yah kahiye, svīkārī binatī svīkārī.*

plication. This is a letter of a devotee to her Lord, not a passionate letter from a woman in love. Like Nanddās's, this Rukmiṇī does not offer any practical suggestions for how Krishna can go about the abduction; there is no presumption to tell God what to do, just total trust in his ability. In contrast to Nanddās, we have no suicide threat, just confident reliance on God's saving power. Of course, Rukmiṇī's trust is not misplaced. The song ends on a recitation of two lines in a form of Old Hindi:

> Hari kept reading her letter, listening to her call of love,
> Every word showed openly the flow of love.[56]

The picturization of the song shows both lovers, each in his or her own house, overcome with emotion—she in her plea for his love, he endeared by her feelings, supernaturally aware of her agony, even though far away. We see Krishna dreamily pondering the letter, as his brother Balarāma appears and asks him what is the matter. This is different from both our other sources, where Krishna acts immediately without bothering to discuss the matter with Balarāma. Clearly, the director of the television series felt that was a mistake. He feels the need for permission from the elder brother for the younger to go on his adventure, and stresses their hierarchical relationship through some banter between the brothers, reminding the audience that Krishna is the younger one. In any case, Krishna tells his older brother he is going to Vidarbha because he has received a call for help, and he explains Rukmiṇī's situation.

The scriptwriter here could have made the most of the Vidarbhans' failure to invite Krishna to the Svayaṃvara. This would naturally have excited irrascible Baladeva to fume and rage about the slight and ensured his support for Krishna's cause. However, that issue does not come up here; we will find out only later that Krishna was not invited. Instead, Baladeva wonders: "do they not regard the woman's permission important in Vidarbha (when they arrange their marriages)?"[57] Krishna retorts that it's not a regional peculiarity, simply an ideosyncracy of the royal family. Naturally, Baladeva comes to the desired conclusion that they need to teach the Vidarbhans a lesson in how to treat their women: "We're obliged to go to teach the royal family a lesson in Indian culture and civilization."[58] Krishna protests that he does not need Baladeva or the Yādava army, but Baladeva is adamant that he does not want his brother to

56. *bāṃca rahe hari patrikā, sunake prema pukāra; akṣara akṣara dekhake, khulā prema kā dhāra.*
57. *vidarbha meṃ nārī kī anumati kā mahatva nahīṃ?*
58. *vidarbh ke rāj parivār ko bhāratīya sanskṛti aur sabhyatā kī śikṣā dene ke liye calnā hī paṛegā.*

face the Vidarbhans on his own. Thus, the television version not only ensures total approval from his elder for Krishna's action but also establishes that Krishna would have been willing to face it alone.

More important for our purpose is how Krishna is shown not to abduct Rukmiṇī out of personal interest. Far from being politically motivated to thwart his enemy, his action is for the greater cause. He is actually disinterested, simply intent on furthering the noble cause of spreading Indian culture—or at least one flattering understanding of Indian culture. The abductor here is shown to be not just the knight on the white horse saving the damsel in distress but actually a staunch defender of women's rights avant la lettre!

The Unbearable Tension of Awaiting an Answer

In *Bhāgavata Purāṇa,* we rush along to Vidarbha, and witness the auspicious wedding preparations going on in the city, complete with recitations of Vedic priests to protect the bride (10.53.7–13) and rites welcoming the groom's precession (*barāt*) (10.53.14–9). Śiśupāla's party is anticipating Krishna's intention of abducting Rukmiṇī and ready to impede him if that were to happen (10.53.18–9). Balarāma, out of love for his younger brother, joins Krishna with a huge army (10.53.20–1).

Still, the subjectivity of the heroine is foregrounded in *Bhāgavata Purāṇa,* which devotes several verses to Rukmiṇī's state of mind: her anxious awaiting the return of the Brahmin and her worry that Krishna might have found fault with her. (10.53. 22–6). She somewhat defiantly blames the gods for not being on her side: "Neither the creator, nor Śiva is on the side of unlucky me! Or is it the virtuous [*satī*] goddess Gaurī, Śiva's spouse, born of the mountain who is averse?" (10.53.25).[59] Nanddās this time does not make us privy to Rukmiṇī's thoughts, but he describes her state, how she wanders aimlessly through her quarters (10.53.76–7), and he adds a quaint comparison: "like a mosquito in a drab of water, oppressed by the heat of the sun" (10.53.76b).[60]

In both versions, Rukmiṇī's limbs start to throb, which is a good omen (*BhP* 10.53.27; *RM* 78), and indeed immediately afterward the Brahmin shows up. From his face she can tell that he has been successful in his mission (*BhP* 10.53.28–9; *RM* 79). *Bhāgavata Purāṇa*'s Rukmiṇī has the wherewithal to speak smilingly with the Brahmin (*samapṛcchac chucismitā,* 29), but Nanddās's Rukmiṇī is still tense with doubt ("will he revive her with nectar or will he burn

59. *durbhagāyā na me dhātā nānukūlā maheśvaraḥ, devī vā vimukhā gaurī rudrāṇī girijā satī.*
60. *rabi tejahi soṃ dukhitta, machari thore jala jaiseṃ.*

her body with poison?" *RM* 80b)[61] and in good emotional bhakti fashion is unable to speak. In both cases, the Brahmin quickly informs her that Krishna has come (*BhP* 10.53.30; *RM* 81), and Rukmiṇī is overjoyed. She wishes to reward the Brahmin for his services, but unable to find anything appropriate, she simply bows down to him (*BhP* 10.53.30; *RM* 82). Nanddās elaborates on the significance of the moment:

> Gods and men keep serving her over and over, but cannot catch her.
> That goddess, Lakṣmī, at his feet, she fell. How to describe his fortune? (*RM* 83)

Next, Nanddās describes the reaction of the townspeople, who are all charmed by Krishna. He gives a long head-to-toe (*śikha-nakha*) description of how different people are transfixed by different parts of his physique (*RM* 84–93); this corresponds to just one verse in *Bhāgavata Purāṇa* (10.53.36).

The popular vote on who should be Rukmiṇī's groom is of course immediately in Krishna's favor (*BhP* 10.55.37–8; *RM* 93–5). *Bhāgavata Purāṇa*'s townsmen pun on Krishna's grace being etymologically linked with the verb for grabbing the hand of the lady ("may Acyuta have mercy [on us] and grab the hand of the Vidarbha-princess," 10.55.38).[62]

> Nanddās uses folksy Braj to express popular opinion:
> "Some said: 'That is a hero, worthy of our Rukmiṇī!
> That wretch Rukmī is a party-pooper: tying a lovely jewel around a monkey's neck!" (*RM* 94)[63]

Bhāgavata Purāṇa is more interested in the reaction of the bride's father to Krishna's arrival, first describing how Bhīṣmaka greets the newly arrived Krishna and Balarāma with a special welcome (*madhuparka*) as if they were the groom's party (10.53.32–4). Nanddās leaves this out, but he instead mentions that the kings were worried about Krishna's presence (96–7). In his story, it is the reaction of the man in the street that is foregrounded.

That is totally different from the televised version, where there is of course no question of a Brahmin returning. We simply see Rukmiṇī anxiously awaiting word from Krishna against the romantic background of the full moon. She wonders out loud whether he will come: "you will honor my waiting and

61. *kai amṛta soṃ sīṃca kidhauṃ viṣa deha dahaigo.*
62. *anugṛhṇātu gṛhṇātu vaidarbhyāḥ pāṇim acyutaḥ.*
63. *koū kahai yaha nāyaka rukaminī yāke lāyaka, mani bāṃdhī kapi kaṃṭha sumahu rukmī dukhadāyaka.*

my free partner choice, won't you?" (*merī pratīkṣā, mere varamālā kā mān rakhoge, na?*). Next, we have a shot of a great army approaching, immediately followed by one of a lone chariot carrying Krishna. Tension mounts as the arrival of a guest is announced with a long list of epithets that could apply to either Krishna or Śiśupāla, but it is revealed finally that it is Śiśupāla. He is received with great pomp and show. The main focus of the scene is the reaction of Rukmiṇī's family, not the people of Vidarbha. The scene ends with a shot of Jarāsandha's wily smile of pleasure that his self-serving plans are working. In the television version, then, the political context again eclipses the airtime given to emotions, whether those of Rukmiṇī or the people of Vidarbha. Paradoxically, the version aired in by the democratic state–controlled television channel is the least democratic in its approach.

Princess Leaving Purdah

We now turn to an interesting parallel with the Sītā story: Rukmiṇī's prayer to the goddess. Just like Sītā prayed to Pārvatī to get Rāma as her husband, here Rukmiṇī pays a temple visit to Gaurī and ardently prays for her groom to be Krishna. In both cases, the women receive nearly instant gratification of their prayers.

The classical and medieval versions of Rukmiṇī's story make it clear that she is well protected with a special escort of bodyguards and other retainers who accompany her procession to the temple of the goddess with much fanfare (*BhP* 10.53.39–45; *RM* 98–100).[64] The main difference is that Nanddās does away with the Brahmin women and the ritual details that play an important role in the orthodoxy-loving *Bhāgavata Purāṇa* (*dvijapatnyaḥ* 10.53.42, *viprayoṣitaḥ*, 10.53.45, *viprastriyaḥ*, 10.53.48).[65] Nanddās simply says that her worship is "orthodox"—(*vidhivat*), but her prayer to the goddess is presented as entirely hers; whereas in *Bhāgavata Purāṇa* it seems to be dictated to her by the Brahmin women. In *Bhāgavata Purāṇa*, it is a formulaic one-liner, more of a mantra:

> "I bow to you again and again, o Ambikā, auspicious, accompanied by your offspring.

64. The goddess is named as Ambikā in *BhP* (*ambikālayam*, *BhP* 10.53.39) and identified as Śiva's wife (*bhavapatīm*, 10.53.45). Nanddās also mentions Ambikā first (*RM* 98, 103), but in her prayer Rukmiṇī will propitiate her as Gaurī and Īśvarī (103).

65. He also fails to mention the girlfriends and the "courtesans" (*BhP* calls them *vāramukhyāḥ*, 10.53.42), and the bards of different types (*sūta-māgadha-vandinaḥ*, 10.53.43).

May my husband be Lord Krishna, please find favor with that" (*BhP* 10.53.46)[66]

Nanddās gives only a slightly longer prayer:

O Goddess, Ambikā, Gaurī, Our Lady, Blessed among all,
Great Māyā, Bestower of boons, Śiva is your hero.
You know every heart's secret, how can I conceal it from you?
Please let me obtain for a husband the moon of Gokul, Govinda, son of Nanda (*RM* 103–4)[67]

Remarkable here are the resonances with Sītā's prayer in the Phūlvārī: the goddess is explicitly addressed as the wife of Śiva, matrimonial and auspicious. Rukmiṇī, too, mentions that the goddess knows the wish one cherishes in the heart, just like Sītā, but rather than shyly repressing her desires, she states explicitly who her beloved is, making sure to give three different epithets to avoid confusion!

It gets even more Sītā-esque when Nanddās provides immediate gratification in the form of a divine response to Rukmiṇī's prayer:

Pleased, Ambikā said: "Pretty Rukmiṇī,
You'll get your Govinda-moon imminently, do not despair in your heart" (*RM* 105).[68]

None of this has any precedent in *Bhāgavata Purāṇa,* rather, Nanddās seems to be inspired by the Sītā-script of Tulsīdās.

Suspense is building as Rukmiṇī exits the temple in procession, in full view of the assembled kings. She eagerly scans the assembled crowd for Krishna. The spectacle is lovingly described in the classical and medieval sources. *Bhāgavata Purāṇa* lingers over her incipient feminine features as voyeuristically observed by the kings (e.g., her expanding breast, *vyañjatstanīṃ,* 10.53.51), adds a theological gloss on her beauty's effect as *māyā* (10.53.51a),[69] and ends the description by revealing that this whole spectacle of the procession has been a ruse to offer a vision of her beauty to Hari (10.53.53b).[70]

66. *namasye tvām ambike 'bhīkṣṇaṃ svasaṃtānayutāṃ śivāṃ, bhūyāt patir me bhagavān kṛṣṇas tad anumodatām.*

67. *aho devi aṃbike gauri īśvari saba lāyaka, mahā māya baradāya su saṃkara tumare nāyaka; tuma saba jiya kī jānati tuma soṃ kahā durāūṃ, gokulacaṃda gubiṃda naṃdanaṃdana pati pāūṃ.*

68. *hvai prasanna aṃbikā kahata he rukmini suṃdari, paiho abahiṃ guviṃda caṃda jiya jina biṣāda kari.*

69. *devamāyām iva vīramohinīṃ.*

70. *yātrāc chalena haraye 'rpayatīṃ svaśobhām.*

Nanddās spins this out further and in the process accords agency to Rukmiṇī in several ways. First he stresses how she deliberately slows down, though her retinue urges her to hurry (*RM* 106–7), how she is fearless under the gaze of the assembled kings (109), how she even actively opens her veil to that male gaze (110), but for her own purposes: to distract them and render them incapable of battle. Nanddās unravels the long Sanskrit string of epithets for Rukmiṇī from *Bhāgavata Purāṇa,* adding a consistently sustained set of metaphors of his own: he equates different aspects of Rukmiṇī's beauty with weapons disarming the kings: her earrings are like the tusks of elephants piercing them (112), her glances are like arrows aimed at killing them (113). With no little irony, he describes the desired effect of incapacitating all the great heroes, to the point that they swoon on the spot (114). Thus, while Rukmiṇī opens herself to the male gaze and thus exposes herself to objectification, she does so purposely, in Nanddās's version, to render the men impotent. An interesting way of returning that gaze.

In the televised version, Rukmiṇī leaves the palace without an escort, with only two girlfriends. On the way to the temple, she bumps into her brother, who asks her where she is going, but she manages to deflect his suspicion by displaying of devotional sentiment. She tells him she is going to worship God (*prabhu*), a nice double entendre, as we know she intends to worship Krishna, but as her husband, not an image in the temple. She does indeed go out to the temple, but the image there is that of the goddess, immediately recognizable as Pārvatī, as she is portrayed as a mother with her son Gaṇeśa on her lap. This is reinforced by the invocation in the song, where Ambikā is identified as Gaṇeśa's mother. The beginning of the song is in Sanskritic Hindi, evoking a Sanskrit mantra–like invocation:

> Hail to the goddess, mother of Gaṇeśa,
> Reflection of Śiva, the Highest God.
> Hail to the moonlight of the moon on Śiva's face.
> Hail, hail, Mother of the World,
> Give me a boon, Bestower of boons!
> Giver of husbands, of the Lord [remover] of obstacles.[71]

At this point Rukmiṇī spreads out her sari border in supplication and has a day dream of putting the *varamālā* around Krishna's neck, thereby making him her groom.

71. *jaya jaya janani śrī gaṇeśa kī, pratibhā parameśvara pareśa kī, jaya maheśa mukha candra candrikā, jaya jaya jaya jaya jagata ambikā; vara de mā varadāna-dāyinī, barudāyikā vārikeśa kī.*

Listen to my humble plea:
May Hari come, make me his own, take me away!
May the auspicious blissful time come, Mother,
Of entering his house in blissful wedlock.[72]

At this point, the goddess responds to Rukmiṇī's ardent prayers and grants her the boon:

Listen and know, take the boon:
Take your handsome groom, Pretty Rukmiṇī!
He will be your husband,
The one who creates the world in every age.
He will come and take you
Respectfully to his city.
He's the enchanter of the world, you a hero's daughter
You'll give birth to heroes, Pretty lady.[73]

What stands out here is the stress Rukmiṇī puts on not so much a romantic union with Krishna as a matrimonial one. She wishes to "enter his residence," and the goddess grants that she will be a "mother of heroes." The scene in the temple, then, while superficially at a romantic level, has in fact undertones of patriarchy, privileging entrance into the house of the in-laws (*sasurāl*) and procreation over a romantic union. Moreover, the maternity of the goddess herself is foregrounded, as it is an image of Pārvatī with Gaṇeśa that is shown.

The Elopement and Ensuing Battle

Rukmiṇī then leaves the temple, looking eagerly for her savior, Krishna. In *Bhāgavata Purāṇa*, all agency is his. No sooner has she spotted him than he takes over. He immediately grabs her as she is mounting her own chariot and installs her on his, before abducting her "like a lion taking his share from among jackals" (*BhP* 10.53.55–6).[74] Nanddās allows her more agency, and does so in lovely internal rhyme describing her state of mind (after he has just said it is impossible to describe, *RM* 115):

In a flurry, she seemed to be swooning. Nothing could keep this lady under control.

72. *suvinaya vinatī suna, hari āe apnāe le jāe, śubhada sukhada velā āe mā, sarva sumaṅgala griha praveśa kī.*

73. *suni jāni de varadāni le, suvara le varanā rukamiṇī, honge vahī tere dhanī, juga juga jagat jina kāriṇī, vah āeṃge le jāeṃge, ādara sahita apnī pūrī, viśvamohana vīrakanyā, vīrajāyā sundarī.*

74. *sṛgālamadhyād iva bhāgahṛddhariḥ.*

> Her body did not grow wings, or else she would have flown to her beloved. (*RM* 116)[75]

Nanddās also stresses Rukmiṇī's slow gait and the drugged-like state of the kings as a consequence of her seductive behavior, implying that this is what makes the abduction possible (*RM* 117–8).

Krishna seizes the opportunity and swiftly grabs his bride, puts her on his chariot, and speeds off in the direction of Dwaraka. *Bhāgavata Purāṇa* uses the epithet Mādhava (*BhP* 10.53.55b), and Nanddās, never one to spurn an opportunity for a clever play on words, is inspired to come up with a pun: Mādhahā, with a double meaning of Killer of Madhu (synonymous with Mādhava) and Honey-Eater.

> The clever mountain-lifter ran off with his bride:
> Like a honey-eater [bear] (Madhuhā) with honey, throwing dust in the eyes of the bees [in pursuit] (*RM* 119).[76]

True to his bhakti agenda, Nanddās offers us a nice opportunity for *darśana* while Hari runs off with his newly conquered bride:

> Together with the handsome dark one, the beauty shone splendidly,
> As if near a fresh cloud the pretty moon is shining forth. (*RM* 120)[77]

In the televised version, neither kings nor bodyguards are on the scene as Rukmiṇī exits the temple. She slows down and looks around, searching for Krishna. Her friends ask her what she is looking for. She answers she's looking for her future (*apnā bhaviṣya*), and just then of course a chariot approaches, and it is Krishna arriving.

Thus, in *Bhāgavata Purāṇa*, the heroine becomes the object of the gaze of the suitors (and the audience), though her beauty is really a ruse to attract Krishna, who is the real agent. In Nanddās's story, she fearlessly returns the lustful gaze of the kings, and assumes agency in her own abduction. This works within the context of his bhakti agenda, where the devotee is irresistibly drawn to God.

75. *arabarāi murajhāya kachū na basāya tiyā paiṃ, paṃkha nāhiṃ tana bane, nataru uḍi jāya piyā paiṃ.* Note that this line is not in all manuscripts; see Brajratnadās [1949] 1957: 183

76. *lai cale nāgara nagadhara navala tiyā koṃ aise, māṃkhina āṃkhina dūri pūri madhuhā madhu jaise.*

77. *lasata sāṃvare suṃdara saṃga suṃdari ābhāsī, janu nava nīrada nikaṭa cāru caṃdrikā prakāsī.*

This passage of Rukmiṇī's procession in the classical and medieval source shows some parallels with Sītā arriving on the scene of the Dhanuryajña in Tulsī's version. Here, too, we had a prized bride appearing in public, to be seen by men. However, Tulsīdās had treated the scene as one of *darśana* rather than voyeurism, calling Sītā "Mother of the World" (Jagadambikā). Nanddās instead turns Rukmiṇī's sexuality into a weapon, instrumental in bringing about her plan. Like Nanddās, Tulsīdās also chooses to focus on Sītā's subjectivity and her anxious searching for Rāma, which is a nice parallel with Rukmiṇī scanning the faces of the kings for Krishna. However, Tulsī has his Sītā deferentially lower her eyes out of respect for the elders (*gurujana lāja*). This is in great contrast with bold Rukmiṇī, who opens her veil to better show off her face and stun the men, all to facilitate her self-solicited abduction.

By contrast to the two older versions, the television story does not bring the heroine out of purdrah. She is never seen in public in front of men. Instead, the elopement is a private affair, witnessed only by women. The director's concern is with a question hovering in the background, namely, who is really to blame for the abduction. Chopra's Rukmiṇī has the film heroine routine down, and as she sees Krishna approaching on his chariot, she acts coy and shy, but she is also "irresistibly" drawn to him. He welcomes her: "You are welcome on my chariot Princess."[78] She asks, somewhat worried whether he has come alone, and he says gallantly that if she joins him, he will no longer be alone. He offers her his hand, in which she puts hers, aware of the gravity of the moment. He leads her onto his chariot. "How can I show you my gratitude?"[79] she says, but he assures her there is no question of her being under any obligation. In good *Gītā*-esque fashion he clarifies: "If anyone truly calls for me then I just have to come."[80] He adds that this is his greatest joy. Then Krishna asks her to give him the command (*ājñā*) to leave, in a seemingly lawyer-conscious act to transpose the responsibility for the abduction to the lady thus taken. He rubs it in: "You were the one who called me. How can I leave from here before you give me formal permission?"[81] In addition, Krishna makes it a point to blow his conch, explaining to the worried Rukmiṇī that though he has come unannounced, it would be cowardice to leave without notice. He specifies: "I'm not abducting you, I'm just taking you with me."[82] This seems to be in answer to an implicit objection that Krishna might have acted in a cowardly way by

78. *mere rath par tumhārā svāgat hai, rājkumārī.*

79. *maiṃ apne ābhār kaise prakaṭ karūṃ?*

80. *yadi mujhe koī sacmuc pukārtā hai to mujhe ānā hī paṛtā hai.*

81. *mujhe tumne bulāyā. jab tak tum ājñā na doge maiṃ yahāṃ se kaise cal saktā hūṃ?*

82. *maiṃ tumhārā haraṇ nahīṃ kar rahā hūṃ. tumheṃ le jā rahā hūṃ.*

taking Rukmiṇī away by stealth. As we have seen, the issue does not come up in the other versions, as he takes her away in the middle of the day, right in front of her bodyguards and the assembled kings. One wonders why Chopra avoided such a scenario in his own version. Part of the answer may lie in a changed environment where elopement has new connotations. This attitude of the would-be abductor giving his action a twist and calling it by a different name seems to be a distinctly modern phenomenon. As we will see, it is in tune with some contemporary attitudes expressed in hit movies, most notably the 1995 *Dilwale dulhaniya le jaenge.*

With this, the main story is over for Nanddās; he has just ten verses left to deal with all the rest of the story, which now gets really action packed. *Bhāgavata Purāṇa* in contrast, is far from done and even starts a whole new chapter to describe at length the ensuing battles, including Baladeva's defeat of Jarāsandha (10.53.57 and 54.1–9; summarized in *RM* 122–4),[83] and the fight with the enraged Rukmī, who feels his honor is at stake (*BhP* 10.54.18–31, shortened to a statement with a couple of apt comparisons in *RM* 127–9). When Krishna is about to kill her brother, Rukmiṇī interferes and pleads for his life (*BhP* 10.54.32–4), and Krishna obliges, merely giving vent to his anger by shaving off part of Rukmī's hair and moustache (10.54.35). Still, shaving a man's facial hair is considered a serious insult, so Krishna's action is not all that merciful—for which Balarāma duly chides him (10.54.36–7). Balarāma also feels compelled to ask Rukmiṇī for forgiveness for this rash act of his brother, but does so in philosophical terms, pointing out the ultimate irreality of enmity and other feelings (10.54.38–49). This supposedly appeases Rukmiṇī (10.54.50). In the end, Rukmī is released, but he cannot return home because he has sworn not to do so without bringing his sister back (10.54.51–2).

Nanddās does not give Rukmiṇī any voice here; Krishna acts out of self-restraint and leaves even Rukmī's honor intact:

> Krishna did not give full vent to the anger in his heart:
> He only shaved his head, keeping his honor and hairtuft intact.
> Then he let him free. (*RM* 130)[84]

With Rukmī out of the way, the stage is clear for the official wedding to be celebrated. *Bhāgavata Purāṇa* describes the festivities in Dwaraka at some length" (*BhP* 10.54. 53–60); in the words of the translator, this part is entitled

83. This is followed by a lengthy philosophical argument intended to comfort Śiśupāla in *BhP* (10.54.10–17), presumably to explain why Jarāsandha gave up without fighting. No philosophy is given in *RM* (125–6).

84. *jitika chohu hari hiyaiṃ huto, tetika nahiṃ kīne; mūṃḍ mūṃḍi sata-cuṭiyā rakhi, puni chori ju dīne.*

"The Espousal of Rukmiṇī by Shri Krishna Solemnized" (Goswami and Sāstrī [1971] 1982: 2.1301). Nanddās simply says the wedding was properly (*vidhivat,* also in *BhP* 10.54.53b) celebrated in Dwaraka. As we have seen, he ends his work on the happy note of resonating auspicious wedding songs (maybe echoing *BhP* 10.54.59).

In the television series, the riveting battle scenes take up quite a bit of screen time. We have seen that after he installs Rukmiṇī on his chariot, Krishna blows his conch to announce his presence. Śiśupāla hears this as he is in the middle of a game of dice with Rukmī. When they consequently receive the news of the abduction, Śiśupāla exclaims: "Such guts for a cowherd."[85] Here the caste issue surfaces that is submerged in the other versions. We had seen that in the television series Rukmī initially objects to Krishna on the grounds that his pedigree is unclear and hence his caste is in question. Now Śiśupāla voices a similar caste prejudice: the insult of the abduction is worsened by the fact that Krishna is not a Kṣatriya. In contrast to *Bhāgavata Purāṇa*'s, this Śiśupāla is immediately ready to fight, but Rukmī urges him to tackle Baladeva and his army and leave Krishna for him.

Rukmī challenges Krishna by saying he cannot just grab a woman as if she were a plaything. Here Chopra seems to incorporate feminist discourse that women are not to be treated as material possessions. However, that does not translate into more agency for Rukmiṇī: she just helplessly stands by as the men fight it out. Needless to say, Krishna here, too, easily defeats Rukmī. When he asks Krishna to kill him, Krishna does not oblige, nor does Krishna shave his hair. Instead Krishna acts extremely graciously and fights without any anger, as if in play. He sets a wonderful example of disinterested action by a ruler when he grants Rukmī his life, saying he sees no cause for the death penalty. Rukmī has only done his duty in protecting his sister, and now Krishna will do his duty and let him live.[86] Rukmiṇī does not need to say a word; she looks at times apprehensive but generally proud of her new husband. Krishna rides off with her in the distance, off to a new life.

So there is no need here for Balarāma to chide Krishna for unchivalrous behavior. We see Balarāma angry in the next episode, set in Dwaraka, but it is because of a perceived slight perpretated by others (the Pāṇḍavas on their *digvijaya* tour neglect to come and visit Dwaraka). In this case, Rukmiṇī and Krishna work together to deflect his anger. The televised version then restores full agency to Krishna. Rukmī is humiliated by admitting his own defeat, so

85. *us gvāle kī yah himmat!*

86. *maiṃ tumheṃ jīvandān de rahā hūṃ, kyoṃki yah merā kartavya hai.*

there is no need for Krishna to rub it in, and he can grandly let him off the hook. Krishna is not chided by his elder brother but instead is shown as the more mature of the two, deflecting Balarāma's anger about a minor slight. Rukmiṇī is not given any personal opinion in the matter. She seems proud of whatever her new husband does.

In conclusion, *Bhāgavata Purāṇa*, through Balarāma's chiding, problematizes Krishna's treatment of Rukmī, but leaves it hanging, unsolved. Nanddās is happy to let Krishna off the hook without fraternal chiding, stressing his great grace in not killing his foe. The modern version feels the need to clean up Krishna's act. Here, Krishna is completely disinterested and does not disfigure Rukmī. At the same time, this version cannot see Rukmiṇī as having her own feelings; not even yet properly married, she already totally identifies with her new husband, even against her own brother.

Aftermath

Nanddās's work ends here, but *Bhāgavata Purāṇa* has an interesting, little-noticed coda in the form of a conversation between Krishna and Rukmiṇī that is reported a few chapters later (*BhP* 10.60). In the intervening chapters, Rukmiṇī gives birth to a son, whose story is told (10.55), and meanwhile Krishna has contracted many more marriages—among others, to Satyabhāmā (10.56–7), eight other ladies (10.58), and the thousands of princesses he rescues from Naraka's tyranny (10.59). Krishna seems to have grown in stature from a minor monarch to an important one, and Rukmiṇī has something of a record number of cowives.

At the beginning of chapter 60, the scene is one of conjugal bliss, a moment of intimate togetherness between Rukmiṇī and her husband. At a certain point, he queries Rukmiṇī as to why she chose him, "a loser," as he describes himself, someone who because he made enemies of powerful people, had to leave his throne and "hide in the ocean" (*BhP* 10.60.12). He warns her, somewhat belatedly, that her decision to elope with him will bring her nothing but sorrow. This is worded in a general way, as a proverb, so the warning is to all women who might choose unconventional marriage partners: "O pretty-browed lady, generally women sink low when they follow the track of men whose path is not clear and who are aspiring other than the beaten path" (10.60.13).[87]

87. *aspaṣṭavartmanāṃ puṃsām alokapatham īyuṣām, āsthitāṃ padavīṃ subhrūḥ prāyaḥ sīdanti yoṣitaḥ.*

He then shifts from self-deprecation to an aggressive mode. Claiming that marriage should be between equals (*BhP* 10.15), he encourages her to choose another husband (10.17) and tops it off by saying he eloped with her not for her sake but for political reasons, or rather to break the pride of the kings involved (10.19). After all, he adds, I am self-sufficient and need no women (10.20).

There is an echo of *Vālmīki's* Rāma's famous "harsh words" to Sītā here, after he has recovered her from her abductor, Rāvaṇa. Rāma, too, offers Sītā the choice of another husband (*VR* 6.115.22–3) and claims his actions were not inspired by love for her but for political reasons (6.115.15–6). The difference is that Rāma does not remember he is a god and needs the intervention of the Vedic gods to remind him of his divinity (6.117), at which point he immediately comes around and reveals it was all intended as a test to satisfy his subjects (6.13–7). Krishna, by contrast, uses his divinity as proof that he did not act out of love.

In Krishna's case, his words are explained as a joke, to enhance the joys of marital bliss (it is given the title "A Sweet Quarrel" in one of the editions (Śāstrī 1983: xiv). However, it is difficult not to read in some resentment. It sounds like the scenario of a conjugal conflict where a man has married a woman of higher rank and consequently climbed up the social ladder, and is embarrassed by the memories of his earlier inferiority. His high-status first wife has become a reminder of his earlier lower status, and he wants to hurt her for this perceived slight. In that scenario, Rukmiṇī's reaction can be read as a model of how to deal with such a husband without losing his love.

The first thing to do is to burst into tears, which Rukmiṇī does promptly. This causes the husband to feel gracious. Indeed, Krishna, in his compassion, seeing her suffer in the power of love and "unable to get his mature humor" (*BhP* 10.60.25),[88] proceeds to console her. Now he claims that it was just a joke (*kṣvelyā 'caritam* 10.60.29) and that he wished to see her pretty, angry face and hear her retort (10.60.29–30).

The second step is to give the schoolbook answer of the devoted wife, which is not to deny but rather to confirm that of course he is right. Rukmiṇī says as much: indeed, theirs is an unequal match, but because he is so much greater than she. After all, he is God, she is only *prakṛti* (10.60.34). She elaborates the point and specifically addresses his inferiority feelings in the form of his self-description as a loser, making the point that he did not at all need to flee to the ocean given that he defeated all those kings when he abducted her

88. *tad dṛṣṭvā . . . priyāyāḥ premabandhanam, hāsyapraurhim ajānantyāḥ.*

(10.60.40). She makes it clear that choosing a human mortal husband over Him, the immortal, is utterly foolish (10.60.45). A woman married to a mortal husband might still take a cue here and make sure that indirectly the root of the problem is tackled and his feelings of inferiority are properly allayed.

Finally, Rukmiṇī declares her total submission to patriarchy by explicitly supporting male discourse. She is not upset that he might have accused her indirectly of being unchaste. She says that though he was obviously the best choice among her suitors, still she does not consider his doubts foolish, because women might love someone other than the one they are married to and then do not deserve to be kept by their husbands:[89]

> Even when married, the mind of a nymphomane transgresses to each new man [she meets].
> An alert man should not maintain an unchaste woman, because maintaining her, both are fallen (*BhP* 10.60.48).[90]

This rather misogynistic statement is put into the mouth of a woman who is herself being tested for the steadfastness of her love. Her strategy to prove her own chastity seems to be to ensure her accuser that she totally buys into the patriarchal paradigm that refuses support to women perceived to be fickle.

Her response pays off. Krishna is quite pleased with her submissive words and says that was what he wanted to hear (10.60.48). He has tried to test her love for him and her chastity (*patiprema pātivratyaṃ ca*), but she has not gotten disenchanted with him (10.60.51).[91] He now compliments her on her choice of himself above others and lauds her for her initiative in their elopement (10.60.54) as well as her readiness to die for him (10.60.57). He even makes it a point to say that he has noticed and appreciated her swallowing the insults he perpetrated on her brother and never reproaching him for it (10.60.56). He ends his speech: "We are well pleased in return" (10.60.57).[92] What more can a woman expect from a husband? They promptly proceed to love play.

89. Here she gives, interestingly, the example of Ambā, who loved someone else (*BhP* 10.60.47). This seems a rather complex example, because in contrast to Rukmiṇī, Ambā was not abducted on her own initiative but was carried away by Bhīṣma for his brother. Notwithstanding the abduction, she remained in fact true to her first love, but was spurned by him.

90. *vyūḍāyāś cāpi puṃścalyā mano 'bhyeti navaṃ navaṃ, budho 'satīṃ na bibhṛyāt tāṃ bibhrad ubhayacyutaḥ.*

91. *na dhīr mayyi apakarṣitā.*

92. *vayaṃ pratinandayāmaḥ.*

Needless to say, this little coda distracts quite a bit from the potentially inspiring example for women of Rukmiṇī's defiance to patriarchy. Yes, she actively rejects the marriage her male relative arranges for her, and seeks out her groom herself, taking the initiative to encourage him to abduct her and actively working to make it possible. But she pays a price for this choice. For one, she has to swallow the insults to her brother. Moreover, her husband seems to harbor some resentment against her, which she has to work hard to allay. Ultimately, she, too, has to maneuver within the code of submission to one's husband to bring him around—not to mention the many cowives. Unconventional love clearly has its price. One may be able to defy one kind of patriarchy but ends up submitting to another.

Such is at least the feeling one comes away with from reading *Bhāgavata Purāṇa*'s full version of the Rukmiṇī elopement story. It seems meaningful that Nanddās has left out the coda in his version,[93] though it may be mostly a technical matter of restricting his transcreation to one episode only. This seems in tune with his stronger stress on Rukmiṇī's agency.

Comparing Elopements

Clearly *Bhāgavata Purāṇa* and the television *Mahabharat* focus much more on politics than Nanddās's version does. Male agency is central in the oldest as well as the most recent version; only the medieval version exclusively focuses on the woman's subjectivity. At the same time, that version stresses woman's agency most and is the most defiant of patriarchy. On the surface, the modern version may seem to be defiant with its rhetoric that stresses the right of women to have a say in the choice of their partners, but in fact Rukmiṇī is not allowed even to voice her alternative choice to her relatives.

It is not so simple, though, that we can say Nanddās's version consistently shows a more assertive Rukmiṇī. In fact, the tone in her letter to Krishna is much more self-deprecating than in *Bhāgavata Purāṇa*. Maybe what surfaces here is something of the coda of *Bhāgavata Purāṇa*, where Rukmiṇī acts submissively and is self-deprecating. And in the letter as drafted by Nanddās, Rukmiṇī talks like a Rajput woman, threatening suicide as a *satī*, if Krishna won't save her from the disgrace of submitting to Śiśupāla. Here we detect the intrusion of a profoundly patriarchal discourse that sees women's purity as central to male honor.

93. Of course, the indomitable Sūrdās tradition includes a version of this episode, aptly entitled "Rukmiṇī-parīkṣā" (*SS* 4813/4195).

TABLE 2.3. Rukmiṇī's Elopement in Bhāgavata Purāṇa, in Nanddās, and on TV

Element	BhP	Nanddās	TV Mahabharat
General	Politics central (Jarāsandha)	Auspiciousness central	Politics elaborated
	Defiance of patriarchy	Strong defiance of patriarchy	No open defiance, but commentator pro women
		Gopīs as role model	Krisna defends women rights
Focus	Brahmin's message	Rukmiṇī's feelings	Rukmiṇī's feelings
	Krishna welcoming Brahmin	Beauty of Dwaraka	Krishna's reaction to letter
Rukmiṇī's letter	Brahmin recites message	Brahmin reads letter	Letter; no intermediary
		Krishna can't read for emotion	Krishna emotional
	Businesslike, short	Passionate, longer	Song of longing
	Rukmiṇī speaks as equal	Rukmiṇī speaks as *dāsī*	Rukmiṇī humble as *pūjārī*
	Outrage: Śiśupāla is jackal	Outrage: Śiśupāla is jackal	Outrage: Śiśupāla is jackal
	Rukmiṇī has elopement plan	Rukmiṇī has no elopement plan	No elopement plan
	Vague threat of dying	Threat of suicide as *Satī*	Trusts in eternal connection with Krishna
Krishna's reaction	Checks with Brahmins	Immediate departure	Receives brother's permission
Rukmiṇī waiting for news	Extreme anxiety; blames gods	Less *viraha*, excited waiting	*Viraha*, trusting in savior
	Upon return of Brahmin Rukmiṇī falls at his feet	Upon return of Brahmin Rukmiṇī falls at his feet	Tension mounts: Śiśupāla arrives first
Reaction to Krishna's arrival	King welcomes Krishna	King welcomes Krishna	King welcomes Śiśupāla
	Subjects delighted	Subjects get *darśana*	Unobserved arrival of Krishna
	Śiśupāla's party worried	Śiśupāla's party worried	Śiśupāla's party unaware
The procession to the Devī temple	Public procession	Public procession	Private party visits temple
	Brahmin ladies central in ritual	No Brahmin ladies, less ritual	Only friends for simple *pūjā*
	Short mantra-like prayer	Sītā-type prayer	Song seeking heroic sons
	Detailed ritual ceremonies	Goddess grants wish	Goddess grants wish
	Kings gaze at Rukmiṇī	Her beauty is like weapon	No kings present
	Woman as object	Woman as bold agent	Woman as shy agent

(continued)

TABLE 2.3. (continued)

Element	BhP	Nanddās	TV Mahabharat
The elopement	Krishna has exclusive agency	Rukmiṇī has more agency	Krishna denies it is abduction
	Krishna scoops her up	Rukmiṇī would fly to him	Krishna stresses Rukmiṇī comes of her own free will
The battles and humiliation of Rukmī	Krishna fights off others	Kings under Rukmiṇī's spell	Krishna and Balarāma fight
	Fight elaborately described	Much less stress on fight	Fight elaborately shown
	Rukmiṇī pleads for brother's life	Rukmiṇī has no voice	Rukmiṇī has no voice
	Krishna spares brother's life but humiliates him	Krishna has self-constraint	Krishna has self-constraint; Krishna talks dharma
	Baladeva chides Krishna	No chiding	No chiding
	Bladeva asks Rukmiṇī for forgiveness	No asking for forgiveness	No asking for forgiveness
	Wedding in Dwaraka	Wedding only one verse	Wedding not shown
	Coda: Krishna tests Rukmiṇī	No coda	No coda

The argument of what a disgrace it would be to Krishna if Śiśupāla got to marry Rukmiṇī is left out in the television series. Rukmiṇī there simply asks Krishna to make her his, without mentioning the circumstances. Still, her letter there is close to Nanddās's, very much that of a devotee asking her Lord to help her. She does not threaten suicide, though, as the older versions have her do. Throughout she seems confident that Krishna will save her.

In both Nanddās's version and the televised one, the visit to the temple is not just a ruse, providing an occasion for Krishna to abduct her. In both versions, it also has the function of legitimating Rukmiṇī's abduction. We could read in an echo of the Phūlvārī in Nanddās's version, something Chopra happily takes over. Just like Sītā's, Rukmiṇī's prayer is answered by the goddess. Thus, while defying patriarchy, Rukmiṇī is still ensured divine parental (albeit maternal) endorsement of her actions. That the opinion of the people of Vidarbha is on her side may also be interpreted as an extra legitimation for her behavior (this is the case in both older versions). In addition, *Bhāgavata Purāṇa* has Rukmiṇī's parents initially approve of the match. In all cases, it is really the brother who is the villain, and the role of the parents in the fatal choice of the unwanted groom is downplayed, so one could argue that Rukmiṇī is not really opposing her parents, only her misguided brother.

The television version deviates from the other two in that it makes the abduction a private affair and goes out of its way to attribute agency to Rukmiṇī. Care is taken to justify Krishna's actions and remove any question whether he might have acted in a cowardly way. The fights receive a lot of airtime.

Nanddās is least interested in the battle scenes. His focus has been on Rukmiṇī's feelings, so it is remarkable that he does not let on how she might feel about the consequences of her actions for her family. This may be explained with reference to his bhakti agenda, where love for God overshadows all other sentiments. The determination to attain the ultimate goal suppresses everything else. In the joyful harmony of wedding songs, there is no room for discord. The tension of the young woman's feelings, torn between her family and her romantic love, surfaces only in *Bhāgavata Purāṇa,* where she interferes to save her brother's life. Also relevant is the consequent mediation by Balarāma, who anticipates Rukmiṇī's feelings upon the humiliation of her brother and asks her for forgiveness. His ultraphilosophical arguments apparently convince her. Krishna himself does not ask for forgiveness, but he later, in the coda, compliments her on forgoing reproaching him for that humiliation. He says he appreciates that she has swallowed her feelings out of love for him, which hints at her efforts to adapt to the circumstances and a purposeful move on her part to put her husband's interests before those of her natal family. Thus in *Bhāgavata Purāṇa,* while Rukmiṇī's feelings about her brother are taken more seriously, the conflict is still settled in a conservative way. The woman's husband's interests come before those of her parental family. The television version seems to take that as an unproblematic given, and Rukmiṇī does not even seem to be troubled by her brother's plight.

Finally, most interesting for our purpose, Nanddās shows his Rukmiṇī thinking through her decision to defy her arranged marriage and taking courage from the example of the Gopīs of Gokul. This confirms my conjecture that women, now as in the past, are understood to navigate their own moral course with reference to mythology, taking for role models the divine lovers of Krishna, as well as Sītā. The power of the example of the Gopīs is illustrated in Rukmiṇī's story. In turn, Rukmiṇī's story can magnify this subversive potential for women who have to cope with the conflicts between arranged and love marriages. This story may well justify the elopement option in the eyes of young women.

Sītā and Rukmiṇī Compared

In contrast to their falling in love, where the heroines' actions resembled each other, in getting their marriages arranged, Rāma's and Krishna's consort are at the opposite ends of a range of possible approaches. Sītā has the good luck that her beloved fulfills her parents' conditions for the groom. She can afford to remain fairly passive. There is some tension before the qualifications of the groom become apparent, but on the whole she manages not to let her feelings get the better of her. Throughout, she is dignified and respectful to her elders. She is rewarded with a happy ending. What is surprising is that in the television version, Sītā has become yet more passive than in the medieval one. The message to the girls in the audience is to wait, have faith, and be submissive to the elders' wishes. Permission is crucial, not only from all parental parties but also from the family gurus. This fits with the general stress on marriage as an affair between two families rather than two individuals, as is explicitly stated in Sagar's text.

However, what to do when the happy ending is not forthcoming? Rukmiṇī is a potential role model for those confronted with the nightmare scenario where the parents have settled on a different groom. She chooses elopement and takes an active hand in the proceedings, to the point of suggesting the strategy to carry out her wish, and of course cooperating fully with the abductor in creating distractions. Significantly, in the devotional and televised version, she gets divine sanction for her actions from the goddess. The devotional version also presents the example of the Gopīs as a justification of her dharma-transgressing initiative. However, it is difficult to speak of a happy ending, though Nanddās certainly ends on a happy, auspicious note. Though he may try to suppress it, still it is clear that the sacrifices Rukmiṇī has to make are large. Her husband has to fight her parental family and their allies. Marriage, indeed, cannot fail to become a family affair: if there is no alliance, then it becomes a point of rupture. Vendetta ensues inevitably. And Rukmiṇī through her elopement totally allies herself with her groom and his family, alienating herself from her parental family to the point of giving up even the right to be concerned about them. Total submission to patriarchy remains a given; while defying her own family, she will still be submissive to her husband. The words of Baladeva and the coda in *Bhāgavata Purāṇa* make that explicit. Nanddās and Chopra choose not to deal with any of this and abbreviate significantly or cut out the negative consequences. Chopra is careful to portray Krishna as acting completely fairly toward Rukmiṇī's family. For Nanddās, the overpowering love for God overshadows everything else. Both these texts are more concerned with absolving Krishna from all blemish, than pointing out the negative consequences for the women.[94] All in all, none of the versions can be read as an unproblematic endorsement of the elopement scenario for women caught in a bind. How far does that fit or contradict what we see in the movies?

Arranging a Love Marriage in Popular Movies

If any of our themes are prevalent in popular culture, it certainly is the one of how to arrange a love marriage. It is pretty much the major theme of the Hindi popular film: boy and girl have met and fallen in love. After a celebratory song and dance, the real action starts: they encounter obstacles, and the rest of the movie is devoted to their struggle to see things through to the happy ending of their marriage. One of the most common obstacles is parental disapproval of the match from one side or another, usually the richer and higher-caste one. Matrimony must ensue; the question is just how. One of the problems is the young lovers' inhibitions about talking with their parents about their preferences. Subtle hints don't get understood, other matches are made, the parents find out and disapprove. Will the lovers then conform to the Sītā scenario—

94. Indeed, *Bhāgavata Purāṇa* was also engaged in such a clean-up project; unlike the straightforward robbery of a bride in *Harivaṃśa Purāṇa*, it introduces the motif of Rukmiṇī's invitation. (See a forthcoming work by Tracy Coleman; I am grateful to Peter Scharf for alerting me to this work.)

wait and trust that their parents will somehow arrange for them the marriage they want? Or will they, in their despair, elope?

"Hum aap ke hain koun . . . !": Duty before Love

We find Sagar's concerns about establishing the legitimacy of a love match echoed in this popular movie. As noted, this romance of two rich, orphaned brothers with two sisters has many *Rāmāyaṇa* references. The explicitly *Rāmā-Sītā*-style engagement is that of the older brother, Rajesh to the older sister Pooja, while that of the younger brother, Prem, and the younger sister, Nisha, incorporates more of the Rādhā-Krishna romance.

Conforming to Bollywood conventions, the brothers have been raised by their bachelor uncle (*kākā*), Kailāśnāth, their late father's younger brother. He has the responsibility of arranging Rajesh's wedding, and does so in an enlightened way. He has prospected a match that suits the family best, without concern for dowry, and found a suitable bride in the form of Pooja, the delightful daughter of his old school friend, who is an impoverished (relatively speaking) professor. In order to ensure Rajesh's personal happiness, he seeks to arrange for him a premarital meeting with his bride-to-be so that the two can get to know each other before the big step. Rajesh is not aware of the plan being arranged for him, and is lured along on the pretext of a pilgrimage to Rāmṭek, where Pooja happens to be holidaying with her family. Like Rāma and Sītā's, Rajesh and Pooja's premarital meeting is in no way engineered by the young people themselves.

It is significant that the setting of the first meeting between Rajesh and Pooja is Rāmṭek, a shrine devoted to Rāma. In the movie, it is a beautiful modern Hindu temple complex (much too clean to be real, according to many viewers); in the main shrine is the familiar marble *filmī mūrti* of Rāma flanked by Lakshmana and Sītā. When the camera catches its first glimpse of the temple complex, *Mānas* recitation is heard in the background, to set the proper devotional atmosphere.[95] Several other explicit references to *Rām Carit Mānas* ensue, suggesting that the filmmaker deliberately framed his story within a traditional context, guided by models from the *Rāmāyaṇa*, and in particular Tulsīdās's version of the story.

95. The verses recited are 7.90, *dohā* k: "Without faith there is no devotion, without it Rāma does not melt, without Rāma's grace, even in a dream, a human soul cannot reach peace" (*binu bisvāsa bhagati nahīṃ tehi binu dravahi na rāmu, rāma kṛpā binu sapanehu jīva na laha biśrāmu*), and 1.112, *caupāī* 4: "Abode of auspiciousness, remover of inauspiciousness, playful child in Daśaratha's courtyard, have mercy on me" (*maṃgala bhavana amaṃgala hārī, dravaü so dasaratha ajira bihārī*).

As could be expected, given the essential love story content of this movie, it is in particular the model of Rāma and Sītā falling in love that looms large in the background. The love story of Rajesh and Pooja gets off to a good start. The match for Rajesh is an arranged one, but during the holiday, both parties actually fall in love. They get acquainted very much in accordance with *maryādā*, with lots of scope for sweetly shy bashfulness on the part of Pooja and controlled yet growing interest on the part of Rajesh. Several elements of the scene where the couple meets the first time are reminiscent of Rāma and Sītā's first meeting as shown in the televised version. Pooja and her sister look at the brothers from behind the kitchen doors, like Sītā and her girlfriends from behind the bushes. When called on to appear before her future fiancé, Pooja first hesitates, and has to be pushed forward by her sister. Rajesh is equally modest. The scene immediately following the first meeting is reminiscent of the one with the moon-gazing brothers in the televised *Ramayan*. Prem is massaging his elder brother's legs, an ideal moment for confidences. He has to ask Rajesh quite explictly whether he liked the girl he met or not, and Rajesh does not even answer; he just smiles, upon which Prem draws his own conclusions, congratulates his astonished brother, and spreads the news. Clearly, the protagonists act just as inhibited as Sītā and Rāma, and it is their brother and sister confidantes who actively promote their moments of togetherness and encourage and voice their feelings. There are major differences, too, of course, especially in the form of the presence of the elders. However, that confirms only the similarity of the major message: love flourishes within *maryādā* boundaries. This fits well with what popular women's magazines advocate: "In no case is courtship and marriage an affair between two souls: they are merely units within the wider family to which they belong, and their desire must be subordinated to their responsibility to the family collectivity" (Uberoi 2001b: 183).

This message is well epitomized in the song "Vāh vāh Rāmjī" ("Congratulations, Lord Rāma"), which accompanies the engagement celebrations. Just the first few lines, part of which also function as refrain, say it all:

> Well-done, Lord Rāma! What a match have you made [in heaven]!
> To my brother and sister-in-law, congratulations, congratulations.
> The best of all ceremonies, is the one in which hearts get
> engaged.[96]

96. *vāh vāh rāmjī, joṛī kyā banāī! bhaiyyā aur bhābhī ko, badhāī ho badhāī. sab rasmoṃ se baṛī hai jismeṃ dil se dil kī sagāī.*

It could hardly be put more explicitly: marryng traditional values (*maryādā*) with love is the theme the filmmaker wants to promote with the movie. At the same time, these categories seem to be connected to tradition and modernity, and to some extent with East and West. I will explore this further in the next chapter.

For the second, more Rādhā-Krishna-like couple, mutual love arises before there is a question of marriage. Yet, as noted, even the love story of Prem and Nisha is marked by divine sanction and explicit references to the Phūlvārī. How do they manage to have their love sanctified in matrimony? While the younger siblings have been falling in love, Pooja has given birth to a baby boy. Family happiness is nearly complete, and now it is time to raise the issue of Prem's marriage. Pooja herself brings up the matter when she and her baby are about to get into Prem's car, on their way to her maternal home (*maikā*). The head of the family, Prem's paternal uncle, says he will feel very lonely without them, which prompts her to say that he needs another daughter-in-law.[97] Prem jumps up and down, hardly able to contain his happiness, exclaiming in Hindi and English: "*Kyā bāt hai bhābhī!* Well said!" Uncle sighs that the times have changed, meaning the old ways of elders' strict control in those matters, and he puts the matter entirely in young Pooja's hands. Pooja does not suspect Prem is in love with her sister, but Prem is delighted with this development.

Once alone in the car, Pooja probes Prem privately about his preferences. She wonders whether he prefers "love marriage" or "arranged marriage." His reply is: "A love marriage that has been set up to be arranged for you."[98] Again, the language is a mix of Hindi and English, mirroring the answer proposed, which is a hip blend of tradition and modernity. None of the youngsters in the audience is going to miss the point: these matters are not to be discussed openly with elders, but some initiative is fine. Enlisting siblings' help is permitted. Needless to say, Pooja is delighted when she finds out that Prem's chosen bride is her very own sister, Nisha. She promptly sanctions their love in song and dance (with "Lo calī maiṃ apne devar kī bārāt leke," "Look, I'm heading my younger brother-in-law's wedding procession"), and gives her own necklace to her sister as a token of her approval. If the movie ended there, already the message would be clear. The filmmaker's solution for premarital love is sanctification by the elders' approval. Love-within-*maryādā* is writ large all over the place, if not actually on Prem's car, which proclaims the only allowed public face of love: "I love my family."

97. *ab hamāre liye devrānī le āiye, na!*
98. *bhābhī, "love marriage"* [*sic*] *jo āp ko arranged karā dī hai.*

Nonetheless, the love of Prem and Nisha will be seriously tested. Disaster strikes: Pooja dies suddenly in an accident before she can tell anyone of Prem and Nisha's love. The elders decide that the baby needs a mother, so Rajesh should remarry. And who could care better for the baby than his Aunt Nisha? So Nisha is betrothed to the widower, Rajesh, the brother of the man she loves. Both lovers suffer silently but are willing to forsake their love in a grand sacrifice for their family's sake. The climax comes when the wedding of Rajesh and Nisha is about to take place.

At this point, when *māryādā* is threatening to smother love, none else than Śrī Krishna is the one to be invoked. This is not Krishna's first appearance in the movie. As the preferred deity (*iṣṭadevatā*) of the sister's parental home, he has figured importantly at the time of Pooja's wedding, when Prem and his party successfully prayed to the large Gopāl-Krishna image in the bride's house in order to win the playful tug-of-war about the groom's shoes. Naturally, a prankster like Krishna prevails in the shoe-wars (or wars of the sexes). However, this time, playfulness is not the main mood; *maryādā* prevails again. Lalloo, the trusted servant and confidant of Prem, is the only one who is aware of Prem's agony. In despair, he again seeks refuge with Krishna. He prays to the Krishna image, complaining that Prem has bound him with a vow of silence, so he cannot speak out. But he continues: "He made me helpless, but you aren't helpless! Work such a miracle that people's belief in you will grow even stronger in this world."[99] At this point, a devotional song (*bhajan*) resounds: "Rādhe Krishna, Gopāla Krishna," reminding the audience amply how Krishna is the god of happy fulfillment in romantic love.

The camera lingers on the smiling image with its flute, then shows shots of the family dog, Toffee, and again shots of the image of Krishna. This suggests divine inspiration for the dog's next action. Toffee sets off in a hurry on a mission to Nisha's room. The bride is getting ready, melancholically sitting amid her jewelry, but Toffee looks for a necklace that is in one of the drawers. Nisha watches on with disbelieving eyes as Toffee picks up the very necklace Pooja gave her as sanction for her and Prem's love. She takes the necklace, looks at her sister's picture, and on an impulse writes a note to Prem: "Prem, This is the necklace with which my sister adorned our love. She wanted for her sister-in-law to wear it. I am returning it to you. Nisha."[100]

99. *majbūr kiyā hai, lekin āp to majbūr nahīṃ hai. aise camatkār kījiye ki saṃsār meṃ logoṃ kā āp ke prati viśvāś aur baṛh jāe*

100. *prem, hamāre pyār ke bandhan ko jījī ne is hār se sajāyā thā. cāhā thā ki hār unkī devrānī pahane. ise lauṭā rahī hūṃ. Niśā.*

Toffee is to deliver the necklace and the letter, tied in a handkerchief, to Prem. The dog sees Prem, but hesitates. Prem is playing with his little nephew, laughing hard to cover up his pain. Shot of dog hesitating. Shot of Prem laughing. Shot of Rajesh, who is being invited to take the groom's place near the sacred fire. The wedding is impending now. Back to the dog, Prem, Rajesh. Tension is mounting. Suddenly Toffee changes direction and walks up to Rajesh, delivering the message to him. Oof, it's saved. Rajesh reads the letter and confronts Nisha and Prem with it. Of course he would not want Prem to hide such an important matter and to make such a big sacrifice. He says to Nisha, "You crazy girl, you were on your way to give up your whole life, all your happiness."[101] His is a voice that privileges love over sacrifice, so it seems.

The rest of the family now comes in to witness this spectacle. One of Rajesh's uncles feels compelled to stress the nobility of the way the lovers have suppressed their own feelings: "you should be proud of them. Whatever they did, they thought was their duty, son."[102] Rajesh then says he has a duty to carry out, too—to realize his late wife's dream.[103] Love prevails, but it comes to be cast in terms of duty! Dharma does not suffer. After all, as an aunt, Nisha will love the little baby just as much as she would as a mother. All is well, and the wedding of the true lovers is celebrated with song and dance, of course. The song allows Lalloo to thank Krishna for the happy resolution: "Today We Have All Come to Respect You,"[104] but—wink of the director—he decorates not the image with the garland but Toffee. That is a little *līlā* Krishna might enjoy indeed. In the last shot, the riddle of the movie's title is finally resolved: the title appears on the screen—*Hum aap ke hain koun* ("What am I to you?")—and the last word flashes, until it is dropped and only the phrase *Hum aap ke hain!* ("I am yours!") remains. Finally, the problem of premarital love has been settled with sacred matrimony. Willingness to sacrifice and placing duty first is what purifies love and eventually sanctifies the wedlock.

If we were to summarize this dramatic turn of events, we could say that Krishna stopped the *līlā*—not quite in character—and duly responded to prayer by resolving the emotional tangle. True to character, though, Krishna does it in a whimsical manner by selecting the dog Toffee as the instrument of catharsis as well as comic relief. Thus, Krishna himself is needed to solve the conflict between dharma and love. He does so effortlessly and playfully, in

101. *are paglī, sārā jīvan, sārī khuśiyoṃ tyāg karne calī thī.*
102. *tum ko in par nāz honā cāhiye. inhoṃne jo kuch bhī kiyā apnā farz samajhā, beṭā.*
103. *mujhe ek farz purā karnā hai, māmājī. pūjā kā adhūrā svapnā.*
104. *āj tumheṃ ham sab ne mānā.*

characteristic *līlā* style. It is important to note that his devotee is the servant Lalloo, and the worship is semiserious. Moreover, Krishna is the preferred deity (*kul devatā*) of the bridal family and, by association, of lower status than the groom's family deity, Rāma. Subtly, then, the movie exalts Rāma over Krishna. Order prevails over chaos; *maryādā* has to be in place before love can blossom. And, appropriately, all women fall into the Sītā mold, giving up whatever Rādhā-like spunk they might have possessed. The path to love leads always through sacrifice.

Most interesting for our purpose is how explict references to the mythological model get linked up with contemporary concerns. The message to young people is that the ideal that renders a maximum amount of happiness is a love marriage that receives the parents' blessing and preferably even coincides with the match arranged by them. Modernity and Hindu tradition do not need to be in conflict. Compromise is just around the corner. If the love is true, that is, the lovers are willing to sacrifice for the family's sake, not expecting any selfish happiness in love, then it will be sanctioned by the elders in the end. That is, with a bit of patience, obedience, faith, and clever helping out of fate.

A Groom Is Tested: "Maine Pyar Kiya"

Another possible scenario of arranging a marriage that has close Sītā resonances involves the test of the prospective groom. In this type of scenario, the families of the groom and bride are inimical. The boy of the girl's choice somehow falls short of expectations. The parents reject him, and he is determined to prove his mettle and measure up to their expectations, showing he is a suitable boy after all.

An interesting, prolonged test of a prospective groom occurs in the second half of another film directed by Sooraj R. Barjatya, his 1989 hit *Maine pyar kiya* (I have fallen in love).[105] Prem (Salman Khan) and Suman (Bhagyashree), the son and daughter of two estranged friends, have fallen in love. The main problem is the class difference between the former friends: Prem's father (Ajit Vacchani) is a rich industrialist, and Suman's father (Alok Nath) is a car mechanic. When his father objects to the match, Prem runs away from home and sues for Suman's hand on his own behalf. He has the blessing of his

105. In the first half of the movie *Dil* there is an interesting reversal of the Sītā-Bhavānī temple scenario: the fathers of the hero and heroine vist a Durgā temple and pray for a proper match for their children. Interestingly, in this movie it is the men who visit the temple, and the tone is only ostensibly humble prayer to God but in fact exploitation of this occasion for display of wealth.

mother Reema Lagoo, who is of course named Kaushalya after Rāma's mother, in the material form of auspicious bangles and a red shawl. When he arrives in the mountain village where Suman lives, she is delighted, but it is now her father's turn to throw obstacles in the way of matrimony. He cannot forget the insults he had to swallow, dealt by his former friend, and is not willing to accept Prem in his house.

At this point, the song sequence "Dil divānā" ("The heart is crazy") interrupts the action. Toward the middle of the song, we see Prem go to a local temple, followed by Suman. At first this seems to be a shrine to Śiva, as suggested by close-ups of a Naṭarāja (Lord of the Dance) image. The reference to Śiva's destructive dance (*ṭāṇḍava*) fits with the image of out-of-control lover evoked in the refrain of the song:

> My heart is crazed: without my beloved, it does not listen!
> It is mad, even if lectured, it refuses to see reason![106]

However, the Śiva temple seems to be a minor shrine; the major temple in the complex is a Rāma temple. While the images (presumably Sītā and Rāma) never come clearly into focus, the walls of this temple are inscribed with the mantra *Śrī Rāma* and with verses from *Rām Carit Mānas*. While Suman lingers in the background, Prem is shown first rolling in front of the temple, then dancing and praying in front of the images, to the song lines

> In love, I've lost everything, but not my courage.
> Tell the world that it should not stop the way of the heart.[107]

Interestingly, the shot of Prem joining his hands in a gesture of prayer is taken from just behind the images of the deities. This suggests his love receives divine blessings. Only after that does Suman join Prem in a dance suggesting ecstasy with balletic apotheosis. The music stops, and threatening musical notes announce a change of tone. The next shot of the couple is taken from between the legs of an onlooker in a threatening posture: Suman's father has caught them red-handed. He slaps his daughter and is about to give Prem a sound thrashing, when Prem falls to his knees and begs for mercy. In flashback, we see how this scene reminds the father of the child Prem he knew long ago, before he fell out with Prem's father. His heart melts. The thrashing is

106. *dil divānā bin sajanā ke māne na, yah paglā hai samajhāne se samjhe na.* Interestingly, this song's tune with a Sītā text "*sone kē mṛgeyā le kar raghuvīro āo ne*" (catch the golden deer and come to me Raghuvīr) was promoted on cassette during the Ayodhya crisis (Basu et al. 1993: 98).

107. *pyār meṃ sab kuch hār diyā par himmat kaise hāre, kah do duniyā dil kā rāstā roke na.*

thus avoided. Prem gets a chance to articulate that he wants to live independently from his father. In front of the Rāma and Sītā images, he spreads out the red shawl and adds the golden bangles, formally suing for Suman's hand. The Sītā-Rāma resonances are again visually explicit.

However, Suman's father points out that Prem is destitute without his father's financial backing. In order to marry Suman, he must prove he can earn enough to support her, even if it is as "modest" a living as the father himself makes. He says to Suman: "If his love is true then let him prove it."[108] The goal of earning 2,000 rupees in one month is set and becomes the preoccupation of the hero for the next thirty days.

Thus our hero, like Rāma, is being tested. We get an interesting socialist twist to the Rāma scenario, as pampered Prem, previously keen on riding motorbikes in a leather jacket and boxing in his private gym, now seeks to make a living, first as a lorry driver, then as a laborer (*mazdūr*) in a stone quarry. He starts to sport an artfully disheveled, rough and tough appearance, with ample scope for showing off his muscles. A notable line in one of the song-and-dance sequences that illustrate this process is "Lovers are not afraid of labor, those who are don't love."[109] All along, long-suffering Prem is of course lovingly adored by his bride-to-be.

At the end of the month, Prem has succeeded in accumulating the desired sum of money, through sweat and hardship, and he sets out on his way to wedlock. However, an evil uncle intrigues to have his Westernized evil son kill Prem and to transfer the blame to Suman's father. A group of *goondas* waylays the hero on his way to the heroine's house. "Look we've all come for your wedding as guests to join the groom's procession. Come, friends, adorn our groom, tie a groom's headgear on his head."[110] They beat him up and leave him for dead after he falls into the nearby waterfall. But Prem of course survives and succeeds in bringing his soaking-wet wad of rupees to his father-in-law-to-be. In the denouement, Prem's father comes to realize that Suman's father is a true friend, and after their embrace, we are immediately shown the bride and groom finally united in marital bliss.

In this film, the test of the groom is explicitly framed in mythological Sītā-Rāma references. Prem's test is arguably quite a bit harder than Rāma's: rather than simply lifting a bow, he has to swallow humiliations by his father-in-law-

108. *agar iskā pyār saccā hai to use yah sābit karne de.*

109. *dilvāle mehnat se ḍarte nahīṃ haiṃ, ḍarte haiṃ ve pyār karte nahīṃ haiṃ;* in the song "Maiṃne pyār kiyā."

110. *dekho ham sab āe tumhārī śādī par barātī bankar. calo barātiyo, dūlhe ko sajāo iske sir par sehrā bāndho.*

to-be, sweat and toil to make money, survive through hardship, suffer a beating from villains, and survive a fall in a waterfall before he can take his prized bride. Love may take some convincing of one's in-laws before it can be transformed into happy matrimony. In conformity with the message of the televised epics, the ultimate consummation of love can only take place in a patriarchal context. Only when the inimical families, in this case the fathers, have been reconciled is sanctification possible. No doubt about it, in the end, dharma has to prevail.

Elopement in Bollywood

There is no dearth of cases of elopement in Bollywood hit movies. One of the most famous is in Raj Kapoor's 1973 cult film *Bobby*, where the minor boy and girl elope on a motorcycle.[111] Their immature attempt to strike out on their own quickly leads to disaster, as the hero is incapable of defending the heroine against villains, though the ending is happy. It is significant that this movie is characterized by a remarkably strong defiance of parental authority. The hero openly and publicly challenges his father about the match that has been arranged for him. We should hasten to add that the parents are of a type branded "modern" and "Westernized." The defiance is justified by portrayal of the parents as selfish and unloving. To make this abundantly clear, the match they arrange for their only son is obviously inspired by greed, to the extent that it is with a mentally retarded girl. These rich, Westernized parents of the hero are contrasted to the lower-class and uncouth but loving father of the heroine and her very Indian (though Christian) white sari–donning grandmother, also the hero's governess, who is the true Indian mother. The happy ending in this movie then involves, significantly, a change of heart on the part of the rich parents in the face of the real possibility of losing their child. The final images of the movie show not the embrace of the couple but that of the fathers with their future son and daughter-in-law. Not only is romantic love reconciled with parental authority, the latter is transformed into Indian-style parental benevolence.

In the 1980s, elopement scenarios tend to lead to disastrous endings, as in the aptly titled and highly successful 1988 *Qayamat se qayamat tak* (From doomsday to doomsday), directed by Mansoor Khan. This movie is a Romeo and Juliet story wherein the main obstacle between the star-crossed lovers is the enmity between their families. The young people are portrayed as Westernized, living in the surreal enclave of coed colleges, complete with camps

111. For a brief discussion of this movie, see Virdi 2003: 179–81.

where the sexes freely mix without parent supervision. This world, where love is about individuals and physical attraction, clashes dramatically with the feudal viewpoints and caste interests of the parents (in this case Rajputs), for whom marriage is about family loyalties and tactical alliances. The hero and heroine are inarticulate about communicating their love to their parents. Still, they persist in it to the point of dramatic death. Here the hero's initiative to abduct is thwarted at first; it ends up being the girl herself who takes the initiative. She manages to escape, disguised as one of the singers at her own engagement party, and arrives at the hero's house. These lovers elope on a motorcycle, too, and they run into some of the same problems as Bobby and her beloved, notably *goondas* who are after the girl. However, in this case, the lovers succeed for a while in leading an independent life. They establish an idyllic household in bucolic environs, reminiscent of Rāma and Sītā's forest hut (Pañcavatī). The ending here is unhappy, as the title warns. There is a false hint of a possibility of reconciliation with the estranged parents, but the feudal machinations they set in motion run their course and lead to the death of the couple. By the end of the eighties, it seems, elopement in the movies spelled disaster to the point that conventional happy endings were turned into tragic ones.

One Must Not Abduct the Bride: "Dilwale dulhania le jayenge"

By the mid-1990s, we see a remarkable twist in and strong comment on the elopement scenarios. For more detailed comparison with the Rukmiṇī story, I have selected Aditya Chopra's widely popular 1995 *Dilwale dulhania le jayenge*.[112] The very title suggests elopement: it literally means "the one she loves will carry off the bride" (official English translation: The brave-heart will take the bride). This immediately sets the love marriage against the arranged marriage, while suggesting a happy resolution. Significantly, though, the expectation of an elopement scenario raised by the title is not fulfilled.

It is not till the second half of the movie that the elopement theme comes to the fore.[113] Simran (Kajol) has been promised by her father to the son of her father's friend, whereas she has given her heart to a nonresident Indian (NRI), Raj (Shah Rukh Khan). She is at first not sure whether Raj loves her, and she reluctantly agrees to the arranged match out of love for her father. Confiding

112. For a brief discussion of this movie, see Virdi 2003: 197–9; see also Chopra 2002.

113. The movie has the extra complication of being a "diaspora movie," discussed at length by Patricia Uberoi (1998). I concentrate here on the second part (after the intermission), so far as it is relevant for its take on the Rukmiṇī trope.

in her mother, she affirms patriarchal discourse: "If Dad is my father, he has always considered my happiness. Can I now for the sake of his happiness not make one little sacrifice?"[114] With her permission, then, her father takes the whole family to Punjab, where the wedding is to take place imminently. Thus, this heroine abides by her father's decision and seems prepared to forsake her love to submit to patriarchy.

However, Raj arrives on the scene and calls her—in good Krishna fashion—to a secret moonlight tryst by playing his characteristic melody on the mandoline. They meet and confess their enduring love. Simran now turns into a Rukmiṇī character. She asks Raj to arrange for an elopement. Since her father will never go back on his promise to his friend to have his son marry his daughter, she says there is no other way: "We'll just have to flee from here!"[115] However, this Krishna character refuses to do the deed by force, arguing: "No Simran, I have not come to take you away by fleeing or stealing, I have come to make you my bride and will take you from here only when your dad himself will place your hand in mine."[116] When she argues her father never will and persists in her request to elope, he calms her down and pateronizingly says she needs to trust him and pretend she does not know him and he will take care of everything.

In order to make his bid for the approval of the bride's family, Raj enters Simran's house under disguise and works hard to endear himself to everyone. He succeeds first with the bride's mother. She even unsuspectingly blesses him, saying that he will get the wife of his dreams. This can be read as a nice reversal of the more usual situation where the girl receives blessings from the mother-goddess, as in the Sītā and Rukmiṇī myths. By the time Simran's mother finds out what is really going on, she has come to appreciate Raj. She encourages the couple to elope, even assembling a bundle of jewelry for their expenses. However, Raj again refuses, stating: "I do not wish to snatch Simran away but to nurture her, not to steal her but to look [you] in the eye when taking her away."[117] He quotes his deceased mother who always encouraged him to seek the difficult but right path, and Simran and her mother acquiesce.

114. *agar bāū jī mere pitā haiṃ, unhoṃ ne hameśā merī khuśī ke bāre meṃ socā haiṃ. kyā maiṃ unkī khuśī ke liye ek choṭī sī kurbānī nahīṃ kar saktī hūṃ?*

115. *hameṃ yahāṃ se bhāgnā hī hogā!*

116. *nahīṃ simran maiṃ tumheṃ yahāṃ se bhagākar yā cuṛākar le jāne nahīṃ āyā hūṃ. maiṃ yahāṃ tumheṃ apne dulhan banāne ke liye āyā hūṃ aur tumheṃ yahāṃ se le jāūṃgā tabhī, jab tumhāre bāūjī khud tumhārā hath mere hath meṃ deṃge.*

117. *maiṃ simran ko cīnnā nahīṃ, pālnā cāhtā hūṃ. maiṃ usko cuḍākar nahīṃ, āṃkh milākar le jānā cāhtā hūṃ.*

Raj seems to be sailing toward success, winning over almost everyone, but not Simran's father. Raj has clearly proven his mettle by now. While he has not had to break a sacred bow, he has passed extensive testing. In everyone's eyes (including the audience's) he is the more worthy suitor, compared to Simran's fiancé, who cannot be trusted, having declared already in an off-guard moment his intention to cheat his future wife. Raj is understood to be morally far superior. It is interesting that the question of the morality of carrying out a secret affair with a girl by abusing her family's hospitality does not seem to be an issue. Raj's morality is exclusively focused on achieving a proper marriage.

Nonetheless, the wedding day is fast approaching, and Simran's father has not come around. The situation is hopeless. Even Raj's father (who has meanwhile arrived on the scene) suggests elopement, but Raj steadfastly refuses. The whole matter comes to a climax when Simran's father finds a photo of Simran and Raj together and confronts Raj. Accusing Raj of having played with his honor, he gives Raj a sound beating. Raj does not fight back and takes it like an obedient son. In effect, he turns it into a demonstration of his Indian respect for authority.

At this point Simran appears, runs to Raj, and begs him again to elope with her, right in front of her father's (and future in-laws') eyes. You would think this would force the situation, since such a public demonstration leaves her no way back into the marriage planned for her. Yet Raj does not oblige. He gives her a lecture in parental obedience that is actually aimed at her father, in a last bid to convince him that Raj is the truly worthy groom: "These are our elders, our father and mother. They nurture and raise us all our life. They give us immeasurable love. They can make the decisions of our life better than we. We have no right whatsoever to fulfill our own happiness by hurting them."[118] With this, he gives her back to her father, thus returning the daughter to the parental authority. Of course he can do that easily and walk out to get on with the rest of his life. All she can do is fall at her father's feet and forever be spoiled goods in his eyes and everyone else's. Her life is ruined. Raj's sense of duty has destroyed the woman he claims to love.

Raj has undoubtedly established himself as a champion of respect for elders. Still, that does not mean he gets the girl yet. It is not until he has proven total disinterest in the outcome of his actions that this can happen. Raj

118. *ye hamāre buzurg haiṃ, hamāre mātā-pitā haiṃ. ye pūrī zindagī hameṃ pālte haiṃ, poste haiṃ, ham ko desāha pyār dete haiṃ. ye hamāre zindagī ke faisle ham se bahtar kar sakte haiṃ. ham ko koī hak nahīṃ pahunctā ki ham unko dukh pahuncākar apnī khuśiyoṃ ke mehat khaṛe kareṃ.*

despondently has boarded the train back home and is about to leave. Simran, on the station platform, begs her father to let her go. Only then will her father acquiesce, in a very passive way: he lets go of her hand. Were it not for his words, we might not believe he has actually let go, but he indeed encourages her to join Raj, somehow finally convinced that the young man loves his daugher truly. She has to run to catch up and nearly misses the train, but finally Raj manages to pull her aboard (a nice replay of their first meeting).

All this is an interesting permutation of the Rukmiṇī elopement scenario. Finding herself in the plight of having to marry the man she does not love, the heroine takes agency, but her agency is complicated by several factors. At first, when she is unsure of Raj's feelings for her, she acquiesces in her marriage. When Raj shows up, she encourages him to elope with her, but when he refuses she simply waits, leaving the initiative to him, as he asks her to. On two counts, then, she delegates action to those she perceives to be her male protectors. However, when push comes to shove and her father finds out the truth, she takes action and publicly chooses Raj. Her male protector, Raj, lets her down, though, again refusing to take her with him. In the end she just barely secures parental consent. Her lover is already on his way out, and she has to run to catch up with him. Thus, far from being abducted in a passive sense, actually she has a kind of do-it-yourself abduction with a minor helping hand from the reluctant lover, just enough to pull her onto the departing train. It is in sharp contrast to Krishna's eloping with Rukmiṇī, but maybe not that out of tune with the television version, where Rukmiṇī in the end is asked to shoulder the responsibility for her abduction.

We certainly have a very reluctant abductor here. Raj does not spare an occasion to preach against abduction, which he casts as an impatient act by someone unwilling to wait. Instead he advocates the longer, slower way of winning parental approval. The feasibility of this path is hardly supported by the fact that the ending is so unbelievable. The outcome of patient waiting when the bride is engaged to another cannot be happy because once the ritual transfer of the bride has taken place it is irrevocable. Still, the film's message is loud and clear: elopement is a big no-no.

This was explicitly acknowledged by the director, who also wrote the story and at least part of the screenplay (Uberoi 1998: 311 n. 13). He articulated his reasons for making this movie as follows:

> I'd been quite troubled by watching those love stories in which the boy and the girl elope. I'd wonder how can they just cut themselves off from their parents who've done so much for them? How can they be so callous. They have no right to break the hearts of

> their parents. I wanted to say that if your love is strong enough, your parents will be convinced about your love ultimately. (*Filmfare*, April 1996, quoted in Uberoi 1998: 312).

This sentiment was echoed by Shah Rukh Khan, the actor who played the hero and who in an interview alluded to the difficulties he faced in "arranging" his real-life intercommunal love marriage. He managed to push through with the permission of the girl's parents. When the interviewer asked him whether he had ever thought of eloping, Shah Rukh Khan answered:

> No, like Raj and Simran we never wanted to go against the wishes of our parents. The thought of running away from home never crossed our minds. But we knew we'd get married for sure. When I met Gauri's parents, I just couldn't get myself to say that I loved their daughter. That, I thought, was a stupid thing to say... because I could never love their daughter as much as they loved her. They had given birth to and brought up Gauri.... My love would never be a substitute for their love. (*Filmfare*, April 1996, quoted in Uberoi 1998: 321)

Similar ideas were in the air in the nineties. Other movie directors followed this lead of letting parental sanction prevail. Hrishikesh Mukherjee, for example, in an interview about his film *Jhooth bole kauwa kaate*, voiced a similar sentiment:

> It is a very simple story. It's about this man who is very simple and very down to earth.... He brings up his daughter like he would a son. He imparts all his love and values to her. He gives her complete freedom to do what she wants. Even sends her to the city for higher education. But he lays only two conditions. That she should never lie to him and she would marry a boy of his choice.
>
> But the girl falls in love. Now the dilemma is how to convince her father and she doesn't want to hurt him. So she asks the boy to come to the hill station and convince her father of his good intentions. She tells him that in our society marriage doesn't happen between two individuals, but between two families. Though the boy suggests they elope and marry, she refuses. So the boy comes to the hill station and tries to win over the father....
>
> The father is a hard nut to crack and the boy keeps bungling all the time. The boy keeps telling the girl that her father is a very old fashioned man and that since she is educated, she should be more sensible. The girl is not convinced since she loves her father and

believes in the values that her father gives her. (www.rediff.com/entertai/1998/dec/04hrish1.htm)

In this case, of course, it is the girl who puts her foot down and refuses to elope. It supports again the thesis, that the elopement scenario as a vehicle for voicing defiance of parental authority has fallen out of favor. Movie directors of the nineties[119] seem to have been on a crusade to discourage young people from going against parental wishes. It was considered all right to work to gain parental approval for a love match, but this is portrayed as a difficult path and inferior to the arranged marriage. The preferred option seems still to be to get married first, then fall in love.

Conclusions: Family Comes First

What are the lessons learned from mythology about how love marriages get "arranged"? We have traced through our sources the Sītā-Rāma wedding scenario and contrasted it with the elopement of Rukmiṇī. First we found that Sītā's so-called self-choice was not really a choice—her father set the breaking of Śiva's bow as a condition for her marriage. In *Vālmīki Rāmāyaṇa* she does not even witness Rāma's feat. In the later versions, she is present and prays that Rāma may win, but she tries hard to keep her cool out of respect for her elders. Tulsīdās allows the princess some rebellious thoughts, but not Sagar. The televised *Ramayan* stresses most strongly of all versions that young people's amorous feelings are not and should not be a deciding factor as far as matrimony is concerned. Family comes first. Parental sanction is absolutely vital, and sanction of the family gurus is a sine qua non. This scenario is prominent in popular movies, which often revolve around exactly this plot. Young lovers might get their way if and only if they are prepared to put family before their individual needs, duty before love. Only when tested and found prepared to deny love, is love obtained. Miracles may be needed, though, to resolve the family complications. The deity who resolves all problems in the end may be Krishna, but even he is subservient to the higher order of family values. Even with Krishna's intervention, love can only be victorious to the greater glory of the family.

119. Movie directors of the twenty-first century seem to have a different outlook. There is a penchant for Hollywood remakes with "bad girl" heroines. Interestingly, actresses seem to have a hard time playing such roles, which compel them to abandon the Sītā mold (Chopra 2005).

The elopement scenario of Rukmiṇī represents, one could say, the emergency option for brides engaged to someone other than the person they are in love with. It is an inferior solution, as it pits the family of the bride against that of the groom and thereby violates the very raison d'être of marriage, alliance between families. Still, if not preferable, it is a valid option in the classical source, and in Nanddās's work Rukmiṇī's course of action acquires even divine sanction. In *Bhāgavata Purāṇa* and the televised *Mahabharat*, the story is embedded in politics, Krishna is the main agent, and things are looked at predominantly from a male perspective. In *Rukminī Maṅgal*, the subjectivity and agency of the bride are stressed from a more female perspective. In all cases, the woman's agency is severely limited by a voluntary submission to patriarchal values be they of a husband of her own choice. Elopement, for the bride, entails forsaking her own family. Such a marriage comes at a substantial cost. Nanddās, concentrating on the glory of love for God, conveniently leaves out the negative sides. The television version makes sure to keep Krishna's actions impeccable, even turning him into a champion of women's rights, a defender of women's independent choice. Rukmiṇī is given full responsibility for the elopement. The echoes of the elopement scenario we find in popular Hindi movies are by and large not happy ones. The movie directors of the nineties judged elopement negatively, truly as a demonic option. The heroes of this type of movie do all they can to seek parental blessing and steadfastly oppose the elopement scenario against all odds. Somehow a happy ending is forced. The didactic intent of these movies is marred by the unbelievable last-minute turns of the story. We could conclude that in the Bollywood of the nineties, the elopement is a truly *rākṣasa* situation and even Rukmiṇīs are compelled to act like Sītās.

In sum, in the movies, we see multiple ways of making sense of Sītā's Svayaṃvara and Rukmiṇī's elopement. The first seems to have shifted into a test of the mettle of the groom, sometimes of the bride, too. They have to prove to their future in-laws their worthiness to be included in the family. Merely professing love for the girl is not enough. Modern movie heroes regularly outdo Rāma's lifting of the bow in that respect. But the main point they have to establish is their loyalty to family dharma. The elopement scenario on the other hand is not even a measure of last recourse. It seems that under no circumstances should lovers even think about going against their parents' wishes. True love will prevail to be properly sanctioned.

Again, in order to avoid the trap of homogenizing the wonderfully diverse world of Bollywood, I would like to bring in some counterpoints to the Sītā-Svayaṃvara model. In Raj Kapoor's *Ram teri Ganga maili* (Rāma, your Ganges is dirty, 1985),[120] the mountain village heroine Ganga (Mandakini) invites the visiting city-boy hero Naren (Rajiv Kapoor) to attend a full-moon Svayaṃvara rite, during which young girls can choose their grooms.[121] Naren happily obliges, though his friend warns him that those village rites will not be recognized by his rich industrial father back in Calcutta. The rite is depicted as a public affair in which the whole village, including the elders, participate, though of course the young women take center stage in the famous song-and-dance number "Sun sahibā sun" ("Listen, sir, listen"). At the end of the song, Ganga, decked out with bridal veil, garlands Naren with the victory-wedding garland (*mālā*).

There is a rival suitor, a distant relative, to whom Ganga's deceased father promised her. Ganga's brother (Tom Alter) is keen that she should choose this fellow, but when she does otherwise, while displeased, he still endorses his sister's choice and personally sanctifies the wedding by accompanying the couple to a ruined temple decked out as a bridal chamber. In a remarkable reversal of the Rukmiṇī scenario, the brother then single-handedly fights the gang of the spurned suitor, who have set out to turn his sister's night of love (*suhāg kī rāt*) into a bloodbath (*maut kī rāt*). Kapoor intersperses the racy (especially for Hindi film standards at the time) love scenes with the violent fight, during which Ganga's brother dies. Amazingly, Ganga's reaction to his death is not registered. Like Rukmiṇī in the television version, she seems to have totally transferred her loyalty to her husband, to the point where her brother's fate becomes insignificant.

This movie presents an interesting variation on the Svayaṃvara scenario, here interpreted as truly a self-choice, and there is no test or condition for the hero to fulfil during the ritual itself. Though the male relative of the girl does not agree with her choice, he feels duty bound to abide by it, in this case even by fighting off contestants till he is killed. The potentially Rukmī-like brother here has turned into a brother who defends his sister's choice against his own interests. The televised *Mahabharat* had a similar Svayaṃvara scenario for Rukmiṇī's wedding, but there the brother did not even allow the sister to express a choice. Chopra had Time, the commentator, explicitly reject this as disrespectful to women, and presented Krishna as the defender of women's

120. The reference is in fact not to the god Rāma but to the modern Hindu saint Rāmakrishna, after whom the protagonist is also named; see Bakhshi 1998: 114–5. An overview of this movie's mythological references is available in Derné 1995b: 203–7.

121. She specifies that this rite is customary among the mountain people (*pahārī*). It's a great move on the filmmaker's part to make this unusual procedure believable to a modern audience by casting it as a quaint folk rite.

choice. Yet in the end, Rukmiṇī was not in fact allowed much of a voice. Kapoor is more liberal than Chopra, notwithstanding Chopra's rhetoric. In both cases, however, the woman's reaction to her brother's defeat is bypassed. There can be no remorse or regret for women once they have made their choice. They simply abide by the patriarchy of a different man.

More recently, Hindi movies have included some whimsical persiflages of the Svayaṃvara theme. One spoof is found in the 2000 comedy *Dulhan hum le jayenge* (I'll take the bride), directed by David Dhawan, wherein the hero Raja (Salman Khan), to realize his ideal match, first has to impress the heroine Sapna (Karisma Kapoor) and then not less than three maternal uncles who have brought her up. Each uncle requires a special test. One of the uncles is, in the film's parlance, a *pūjā-pāṭh* freak, or religious zealot, but Raja effortlessly brings him around by singing a one-line *bhajan* about Krishna's Rāsa-līlā with the Gopīs[122] and by mouthing the appropriately devout Sanskritic register of the Hindi language. For the other two uncles, Raja manages the appropriate amount of disco dancing and wrestling, respectively. There is only one rival on the scene, who is, however easily outsmarted.[123]

The point of the film is its intertextual references to other movies, including *Dilwale dulhania le jayenge*. Interestingly this hero's inclination resembles that of the hero in *DDLJ*. In the denouement, the uncles find out that their niece's suitor has been fooling them, and they reject him. However, the hero refuses to elope with her, saying in good *DDLJ* style that each uncle is like a mother and father to her and knows best. He goes even further: later, when his parents regret that the match has fallen through, Raja comforts them, stating explicitly that he loves his parents more than Sapna. In a reversal of the usual Hindi film scenario, he even encourages his parents to arrange his marriage with someone else. In fact, Raja set out on his quest to win Sapna's love at the behest of his parents: his mother was longing for a daughter-in-law, and his father preapproved the match with Sapna, even attempted to arrange for it with the uncles. Of course, everything is solved in a happy ending, and the two who are "made for each other" get to marry after all. Again, the hero's quest for love is safely bracketed within paternal authority.[124]

122. *muralī manohara rādhikā kānhā jamunā kināre gayau, nandalāla rāsa race brija kā gopāla.*

123. Part of the comedic appeal of the movie is that the party of the bride—i.e. the uncles—are so haughty as to reject splendid marriage offers for the girl and require the groom to undergo several tests. Another comical irreal aspect is that there is no mention whatsoever of dowry (see also chapter 3 on this).

124. Note also that the happy ending does not come to pass till after the party of the girl has been profoundly humiliated and made amends in front of the party of the groom. The status quo is emphatically reestablished. See also chapter 3 on this.

The "test of the groom" theme is whimsically taken up, with explicit *Rāmāyaṇa* references, in Subhash Ghai's *Pardes* (Foreign land; winner of best screenplay and best actress Filmfare award of 1997).[125] Yet another Ganga (Mahima Chaudhary) is wooed by two parties, one local and one "foreign," (*pardesi*) in this case a Non Resident Indian. When the parties of the two suitors start fighting it is decided that a formalized competition between the two is needed to settle matters: the winner will get the girl. This is called a Svayaṃvara, with explicit references to the mythology of Sītā's Svayaṃvara. The village head says: "Well, to get Sītā, even Rāmcandra had to lift a bow."[126] The NRI father responds: "My son is ready to lift any bow for the sake of Ganga."[127] The local (*desī*) candidate gets to choose the medium of the fight and settles, cleverly, on the Indian game of *kabaḍḍī*.[128] The NRI team is thus at a disadvantage, as—much to the hilarity of the audience—some of them do not even understand whether they are winning or losing.[129] This combination of humor and suspense is similar to that in Sītā's Svayaṃvara in the television series, with the difference that it is the good guy who is made fun of. Tension mounts. Unlike Sītā, Ganga is shown to be openly rooting for Rajiv. No divine intervention is forthcoming, but Ganga appeals to Rajiv's friend and adopted brother, Arjun (Shah Rukh Khan), who is closely associated with Krishna in this movie.[130] After the necessary setbacks, of course, Arjun succeeds, and the NRI team wins.

125. From the beginning of the movie, there are references to mythology. The setting at the beginning is the riverbank (presumably of the Ganges) near Ganga's home, where a group of women is engaged in a ritual of setting oil lamps afloat on the river. For the first time we glimpse the face of the heroine, in the mirror, as she is combing her hair and dreaming of a groom. As the lines become audible, we hear the women sing: "A bride approaches her father, who's going to ask [a groom's] hand [for her]? Father, choose such a groom, look all over, like for Rādhā there was Śyāma and for Sītā, Rāma" (*bannī bābājī ke pās jo hāth māṃge jāe bannī bābājī ke pās; bābā aisau vara ḍhūṃrh jī hazārī bār ḍhūṃrh lo, jaise rādhā jī ko śyām, jaise sītā jī ko rām*).

126. *are sītā jī ko pāne ke liye rāmcandrajī ko bhī dhanuṣ uṭhānā paṛā thā.*

127. *merā beṭā gaṅgā ke liye har dhanuṣ uṭhāne ko taiyār hai.*

128. This is interestingly reversed in Ashutosh Gowarikar's Oscar-nominated *Lagaan* (2001), where the game chosen for the central competition is the British game of cricket and thus the Indian team is at a disadvantage.

129. As in *Dilwale*, care is taken all along, to affirm that the foreign (*pardesī*) candidate and in particular his best friend, who in the end will get the girl, are not really foreigners *firaṅgī* as the other party contends but Indian at heart. The rival is shown to be a superficially Westernized fellow. Still, at this point the confrontation remains in terms of East versus West.

130. Arjun is associated with Krishna throughout the movie. We first get acquainted with him as a pop star who is interviewed in the movie. When asked where he is from, he says that he was born and raised in Mathurā. The interviewer links him with Krishna, but Arjun points out that his name is not a reference to Krishna but to, Krishna's advisee in the great war of the *Mahābhārata*. Implicitly, he says he does not have anything to do with the playboy reputation of Krishna but rather with the more high-minded Krishna who teaches the *Bhagavad Gītā*'s lofty philosophy, a reconciliation of bhakti and dharma. This is silently reinforced

This irreverent approach to the Sītā Svayaṃvara theme has a nationalistic twist to boot, yet gadgets that are Western imports abound also in this film. The same hip blend of East and West noted in *HAKHK* becomes apparent in the images accompanying the ensuing engagement ceremony song. The focus is on joy and celebration of the occasion, with much display of abundance and imported luxury goods. Brahminical rites do not figure at all; instead, playfulness, especially on the part of the bride-to-be, is central, until of course the final, tearful farewell (*bidāī*) scene. At the airport, where the father of the bride and groom say their goodbyes, the father of the groom says, in a spoof of *filmī* dialogue: "Now you'll say I should take good care of Ganga. And I'll say that Ganga is my daughter now, so what right do you have?"[131] This is intended to show the exemplary total identification of the groom's father with the plight of the bride and his desire to allay all possible misgivings, with an indirect promise to treat the newly gained daughter-in-law (*bahū*) as a daughter in his own house. This depicts an ideal, in sharp contrast to the the real-life anxieties of the bride's situation in her in-laws' house. Such exemplary behavior on the part of the groom's father echoes the noble sentiments of Daśaratha at Sītā's wedding, as depicted by Sagar—the topic of the next chapter.

by images of the chariot on which Krishna and Arjun sit, which are interspersed throughout the movie. Notwithstanding his best efforts, the identification of Arjun with Krishna's lover aspect sticks. When he first arrives at Ganga's house, ahead of Rajiv, the children announce him as "not Rāma but Śyāma." Moreover, as a musician, he is seen on occasion playing the flute. In the end, though, Arjun sticks to principles of dharma, in the form of unswerving loyalty to his adoptive father, who has asked him to actively promote the match between Ganga and Rajiv. If anyone, it is Rajiv who incorporates Krishna's playboy character, flirting with Western girls and with many girlfriends in his past, while Arjun aspires to a monogamous wedding as well as a Rāma-like loyalty to his father and remains firm to his principles.

131. *ab tū kahegā ki gaṅgā kā khyāl rakhnā aur maiṃ kahūṃgā ki gaṅgā ab to merī beṭī hai terā kyā haq hai?*

3

Wedding Promises

Sītā's Wedding and Rādhā's Mock Wedding

How to Wed in Style

In this chapter we will concentrate on the construction of ideal love and gender relationships as expressed in the wedding ceremony itself. Whether a love marriage or an arranged one, this rite of passage is unquestionably a major event in the lives of South Asian men and women individually as well as for the communities in which they live. The wedding ceremony is of particular interest, in that it is a public ritual in which values are articulated and tradition is constructed in a way meaningful for the participants. For one, it encapsulates what is understood to constitute love and its relationship to the matrimonial bond. In close connection with that, it reflects gender ideologies. It illustrates the process of the transfer of authority over women. It raises the question of who transfers her to whom and how.

It is important to note that a wedding ceremony consists of different layers. A Brahminical ritual layer is at the heart of the ceremony, with a Vedic fire, chanting of Sanskrit mantras, and an officiating Brahmin priest. However, regional folk elements figure importantly throughout, especially in the preparatory and concluding rites. One could in fact easily miss the Brahminical center in the cacophony of folk rites surrounding it. Significantly, the folk rites involve the participation of women (i.e., auspiciously married women). The ceremony then provides an occasion to articulate gender relationships from different angles. While the Brahminical formulae tend to be quite unabashedly patriarchal, the women's voices are multiple and ambivalent (see Raheja 2003: 182–205, Raheja and Gold 1994: 73–148).

Ceremonies function in a wider social world of hierarchical relationships that are affirmed (or constructed) in the course of the ceremony. Center stage goes to the relationship between the families of the bride and groom, which is what I will concentrate on, but also of importance are the intercaste relationships of the community, e.g., the traditional roles of barbers, potters, and other lower caste members in the ritual exchanges. Wedding ceremonies are the major occasion for a family to establish its respectability within the community (*izzat*), and the families have a lot at stake to maintain or enhance their prestige. One important way this is done is through an elaborate exchange of gifts (for which see e.g. Raheja and Gold 1994: 82–6).

In the mythological descriptions of Sītā and Rādhā's weddings, some aspects of the real-life wedding are missing, but others are there. Unquestionably, the wedding of Sītā and Rāma is of prime importance as a paradigm. In many areas, the enacting of the wedding as "Sītā Kalyāṇam" is celebrated as an auspicious event (for example in Chennai; see Singer 1966: 100).[1] It is no coincidence that an extremely popular mythological movie on the early exploits of Rāma is called not *Rāma's Childhood* ("*Bāl kāṇḍ*" or some such) as one might expect but, synecdochically, *Seeta's Wedding* (*Seeta svayamvar*, d. Bapu 1976).[2] This movie has immense popularity including in the diaspora.[3] That the exemplary nature of this divine wedding ceremony is to be taken quite literally is suggested by anecdotal evidence that shortly after the episode on the wedding of Sītā and Rāma was aired on televsion, actual wedding ceremonies were modeled after it. At least in the Delhi region, it became fashionable to hire wedding consultants who advertised a designer wedding called Sita-Ram Vivah.[4] As a first step in investigating what makes this lavish style of public

1. I am grateful to Indira Peterson of Mount Holyoke College for drawing my attention to the phenomenon of enactment of mythological weddings in South India.

2. I am grateful to William Smith for first drawing my attention to this movie, which seems to be a remake of the Telugu *Sita Kalyanam*, and has been dubbed in several Indian languages (see www.imdb.com/name/nm0052677/). Sattiraju Lakshminarayana, "Bapu," has done several mythological movies and, according to the afore mentioned website, is currently working on a television series for ETV called *Bhagavatham*. Even the "socials" of this director are replete with references to mythological names and situations. His films merit in-depth study, as is shown by Philip Lutgendorf's analysis of Bapu's *Hum paanch* (1980), which has many *Mahābhārata* references (2007).

3. For an ethnographic description of its viewing in a Southall family in Britain, see Gillespie 1995: 355–8.

4. I am grateful to Julie Mehta for personal communication during the conference entitled "Mediating Culture," University of British Columbia, Vancouver, June 26 2000.

ritual so attractive today, I will analyze how exactly the televised version of the wedding of Sītā and Rāma differs from its classical and bhakti counterparts.

A counter-example to the Sītā-Rāma wedding is the mythological non-wedding, or mock wedding, of Rādhā and Krishna. According to most interpretations, they are the archetypal lovers who never marry.[5] The fervor of their passion is often felt to be antithetical to the social institution of marriage. Thus, there is no hint of a wedding between them in the *Bhāgavata Purāṇa,* or in the televised *Shri Krishna.* However, the medieval bhakti traditions have filled in the blank. Some poets imagine a straightforward marriage in local Braj style, celebrated with much verve, lots of emotion, and little attention to ritual correctness. Others are even less conventional but delve deeper into the secret meanings of Rādhā and Krishna's play. Their poetic vision detects secret wedding rites in the Rāsa-līlā or other song-and-dance exploits of the divine pair. These interpretations can be read as subtle subversions of social conventions. Doubts about the conjugal nature of Rādhā and Krishna's love have in any case not stopped the popular staging of their wedding as "Rādhā Kalyāṇam," understood as an occasion as auspicious as the "Sītā Kalyāṇam" (e.g., in Chennai, see Singer 1966: 97).

The bulk of this chapter is devoted to the wedding ceremonies of Rāma and Sītā, as they figure so prominently and are described at length in most versions. My reference point will be the televised version, in which the wedding is shown with all its minutiae in three episodes (vol. 3–4, episodes 9–11). At first glance, the television version follows the older accounts closely for all episodes. There is some dialogue, but mostly the wedding is enacted against the backdrop of songs and recitation, often from Tulsī's text, with occasionally also quotations from Vālmīki's. For that reason, I stick to those two texts in my analysis, though I could also have taken into account other fascinating vernacular descriptions of Sītā and Rāma's wedding, such as *Janakī Maṅgal* and *Rām Nahchū,* also ascribed to Tulsīdās (analyzed by Stasik 1995, 1999).

Though the televised version seems very derivative of its Sanskrit and vernacular sources, it is important to keep in mind that the contemporary retelling of these traditional episodes takes place against a changed backdrop of modernity. As I stressed in the introduction, the medium on which the television *Ramayan* is broadcast puts it in the context of current debates about issues of dowry and "bride burning," which are discussed in the media all the time. Whereas the traditional subject of the series does not leave much room to

5. On the issue of the debates about Rādhā's status as "wedded wife" (*svakīyā*) or "adulterous lover" (*parakīyā*), see Brown 1974: 201–2, De 1961: 348–51.

explicitly discuss these issues, they still loom large in the background. It is helpful to keep this in mind to understand some of the emphases of the television version.

In a second, shorter section, I will contrast these orthodox proceedings with the secret wedding vows of Rādhā and Krishna. Since the *Bhāgavata Purāṇa* does not contain such an episode, we have to turn to another Sanskrit text, the much later *Brahma Vaivarta Purāṇa,* and its chapter on Krishna's incarnation (Kṛṣṇajanma Kāṇḍa 15).[6] There are other sources I could have chosen—most prominently the Sanskrit narratives of the *Gauḍīya Sampradāya,* including Rūpa Gosvāmī's drama *Lalita-mādhava* and Jīva Gosvāmī's *Gopālacampū.* I have chosen the *Brahma Vaivarta Purāṇa* because it is mentioned explicitly as one of the major sources on which Sagar based his *Shri Krishna.* This source also falls within the same Puranic paradigm as *Bhāgavata Purāṇa,* my classical reference in the other chapters of this book. As for the vernacular poetry, again, out of many choices, to be consistent with the other chapters, I have concentrated on the poems ascribed to Nanddās (*Padāvalī* 58–60) and Sūrdās (*Sūr Sāgar,* 1:498–502).[7] Other possible sources would have been from the so-called *rasika* tradition of Vrindāban, a strand of Krishna worship that pays special attention to the wedding rites, to the point that even today the wedding festival (*vyāhulau utsava*) is celebrated, particularly in Rādhāvallabha temples.[8] The poetry produced within that context is substantially similar to that translated here.

Finally, I will look at how these mythological marriage ceremonies spill over in popular culture. There are many interesting wedding and mock-wedding episodes in popular movies, and since the mid-1990s we can speak of something of a wedding wave: many popular movies have weddings as their frame stories. I have analyzed only the ones most pertinent to my subject. For the private (mock) wedding, I analyze Shakti Samanta's *Aradhana* (1979) and Indra Kumar's *Dil* (1990). For a public, societal wedding, I focus in particular

6. Elsewhere in the same text, Rādhā is said to have been married to a man named Rāyaṇa, who is Krishna's maternal uncle (brother of Yaśodā). However, the text immediately disqualifies this by stating on the one hand that it is only a shadow (*chāyā*) of Rādhā that is married to him, and on the other that he is really a part (*aṃśa*) of Krishna (see Brown 1974: 22 and 202, see *BVP* 15.40.32–8). Moreover, Brahmā himself officiated at Krishna and Rādhā's lawful wedding (*BVP* 15.40.39).

7. It should be specified that none of these poems from *Sūr Sāgar* occur in the oldest sixteenth-century manuscripts. I am grateful to Jack Hawley for sending me a correspondence list of the poems in *SS* with the poems from the forthcoming edition by Kenneth Bryant.

8. For a discussion of the wedding poems by Harirām Vyās, see Pauwels 1996a: 39–41. Hit Harivaṃś frequently uses the terms *dūlaha* (groom) and *dūlahin* (bride) for Krishna and Rādhā. Svāmī Haridās, too, uses the terms on occasion. For a translation of Rādhāvallabhan *Vyāhulau utsava ke pada,* by Dhruvdās, see Beck 2005: 86–90.

on Kumar Santoshini's subversive *Lajja* (1999), a film that is self-consciously modeled after the *Rāmāyaṇā*,[9] and compare it with some wedding wave films like *Hum aap ke hain koun . . . !* and Isshaan Trivedi's recent spoof *7 1/2 Phere* (2005).

The Wedding of Sītā and Rāma

This is undoubtedly one of the most important and popular scenes in the Sītā-Rāma mythology. Sagar seems to have been very pleased with his depiction of it, spread over no less than three episodes. We can tell, because he recycles the material in his other series; for example, he incorporates highlights of it in his *Shri Krishna* series. This scene then warrants close attention. Like the television version, the classical and medieval sources, too, provide a lengthy depiction, which is all the more reason to take the event seriously.

In terms of sequence, the nuptials of Sītā and Rāma, like any marriage, include first the groom's procession (*barāt*), and preparatory ceremonies, then the wedding ceremony (*saṃskāra*) proper, the leave-taking at the bride's house (*bidāī*), and finally the arrival of the new bride in the groom's house (*vivāha*, in the etymological sense). Elsewhere, I have given a full comparison of the epic, medieval and television version in chronological sequence and provided a comparative chart (Pauwels 2004). Here, I will organize the analysis thematically and foreground elements that are of interest for the comparison to the Rādhā-Krishna mock wedding.

The discussion in this section first looks at the construction of the hierarchical relationship between the bride-givers (*kanyāpakṣa*) and bride-takers (*varapakṣa*), which can be read as a dramatic enactment of what constitutes matrimony. Then I study the nature of the rituals and the interaction between Brahminical and women's rites which is instructive for the message sent about gender ideologies. Next, I raise the issue of the adjustment of new brides (*bahūs*) in the joint family of their in-laws (*sasurāl*). Finally, I look at what exactly the wedding vows are, those publicly declared as well as those made in private. This is revelatory in regard to gender equality between the marriage partners.

Relationships between the Bride's and Groom's Parties

In general, what is striking about the depiction of the wedding in Sagar's Television version is its overwhelming concern with balancing the relative

9. I am grateful to Vidyut Aklujkar for alerting me to this fascinating movie.

status of the groom's party and the bride's party. Care is taken that the bride's party is not treated as inferior and the groom's party is shown as sympathizing with its difficulties. This preoccupation implies that this is exceptional and opposite to what normally would be the case. Indeed, in real-life weddings, everything is structured such that the family of the girl is on the spot to perform. They take great pains to show their love for their daughter (and demonstrate the family's prestige) by taking care that every detail of the hospitality shown to the guests is lavish and perfect. The other party is in the role of inspector, ready to judge the quality of the hospitality extended and, sad to say, often bent on fault-finding and criticism.

Sagar seems to have an educational agenda in affirming the equality between both parties. His groom's party behaves humbly and shows respect for the bride's party. Sagar is keen to set a good example for real-life families of brides and grooms. One might consequentially wonder whether he is working to put men and women on a more equal footing. We will investigate the question whether Sagar is actually carrying out a reformist agenda in these series, which is usually understood as heralding a return to ultraconservative Hinduism.

SĪTĀ'S "LAPSE" AND A NEW INTERPRETATION OF THE BĀLA KĀṆḌA CEREMONIES. If we study the episode carefully, we find, surprisingly, that a concern with putting bride's and groom's parties on a more equal footing is not new, and can be traced back all the way to *Vālmīki Rāmāyaṇa*. For our source on this episode, we usually go back to *Vālmīki Rāmāyaṇa's*. Bāla Kāṇḍa, where the actual happenings are related. However, as we have seen, there is a different version of the story in the flashback when Sītā tells her story to Anasūyā in the Ayodhyā Kāṇḍa.[10] One of the most striking aspects of her story is that Sītā lovingly portrays Janaka's worries when she comes of age, and sympathizes with his fears of losing prestige in having to look for a groom. Apparently it was already then a well-known truth that "in the world, the father of a girl experiences ill-treatment from equals and inferiors, be he similar to Indra on earth" (*VR* 2.118.35).[11] We heard nothing of the kind in the Bāla Kāṇḍa, where indeed we were following the events from the point of view of the party of Viśvāmitra and Rāma. The focus there was mainly on the history of Śiva's bow, and no

10. For a full analysis of this episode, see Pauwels 2001. The retelling of the wedding is not part of the earliest textual core.

11. *sadṛśāc cāpakṛṣṭāc ca loke kanyāpitā janāt, pradharśaṇam avāpnoti śakreṇāpi samo bhuvi.*

reason for Janaka's decision to make it a prerequisite for Sītā's marriage was given. In Ayodhyā Kāṇḍa, we hear the story instead from Sītā's perspective.

We could read this as a small "lapse" that affords us a look behind the scenes. It sheds new light on the more public story related in Bāla Kāṇḍa. Not only do we find out about the reasons behind the condition of bow-lifting but also we learn about the underlying dynamics of the wedding ceremony itself. If we read the whole ceremony against the background of this new information, the way Vālmīki relates it seems polemical. We now have an inkling that there is an unarticulated criticism the author seeks to address by telling his episode a certain way. Sītā gave us the *pūrvapakṣa*, or problematization: the inequality of bride-givers and bride-takers. The way the wedding is portrayed in Bāla Kāṇḍa lays the problem to rest. The stress there on Daśaratha's generosity in treating Janaka as an equal can be read as a solution to this implicit problem. Thus, Vālmīki already foreshadows Sagar's reformist agenda.

The concern for equalizing the two parties is apparent in the exchange between Janaka and Daśaratha on first meeting one another, when the groom's procession (*barāt*) arrives in Mithilā. The episode corresponds to the traditional lavish reception of the bride-groom's party at the bride's house (*madhuparka*) (Kane 1974: 532). As behooves the father of a bride, Janaka goes out of his way to welcome Daśaratha respectfully to his hometown. What is surprising is that Daśaratha reciprocates in kind. He humbly responds with a proverb, "Who receives is obliged to the giver" (*VR* 1.69.14),[12] specifying "we shall do as you will say, o wise man" (1.69.15).[13] Though the proverb is a polite formula, meaning that one does not refuse a gift (Goldman 1984: 387), still the answer is considered surprisingly humble for the father of the groom. The text itself calls this answer surprising (*vismayam*, 1.69.1).

The proverb, interestingly, is one of the few literal quotations from *Vālmīki Rāmāyaṇa* in Sagar's version of the episode (TVR 116). The quotation occurs in a longer passage of niceties exchanged by the two rulers on their first meeting. Janaka welcomes Daśaratha humbly, and expresses his joy at this match with the prestigious Raghu family. Daśaratha says that he is tied by the strings of love.[14] His guru, Vasiṣṭha, specifies that the match and alliance between Mithilā and Ayodhyā is all God's wish (*parameśvar kī icchā*). When he calls this connection one of equals (*barābar ke saṃbaṃdhī*), Janaka feels compelled to

12. *pratigraho dātṛvaśaḥ*, literally "The receiving [party] is in the power of the granter."

13. *yathā vakṣyasi dharmajña tat kariṣyāmahe.*

14. *prem kī ḍor meṃ baṃdhe.*

protest that he, as father of the bride, is the subordinate (*dās*) of Daśaratha. Daśaratha then turns the tables and insists that he is like a beggar who has come to Janaka's door to ask for alms.[15] He quotes the Sanskrit proverb from *Vālmīki Rāmāyaṇa* (*pratigraho dātṛvaśaḥ*) to prove the point that it is the giver who is in charge, and he humbly offers to carry out Janaka's wishes.[16]

Tulsī, too, is preoccupied with the exceptional situation where the in-laws (*samadhī*) are treating each other as equals. He expresses this clearest of all three versions. In Tulsī's account of the proceedings, the *barāt* sing the praise of their host (*RCM* 1.307.1). This is a striking difference with current practice, where the groom's party often feels justified in belittling and criticizing the hospitality extended by the bride's family. Small wonder, then, that even the gods comment: "Since the creation of the world, we have seen many weddings; but such preparations and attendance, equal in all ways, such balance of in-law parties, we've seen only today" (1.320.3).[17] It appears that even the gods are surprised when the girl's party is treated on equal terms.[18]

Sagar does not miss any chances to drive that point home extradiegetically. He makes another "editorial appearance" at the end of episode 9 and comments on this anomaly of equity between the two parties. He explicitly sets it up as an example for the audience. Here, he quotes the full *śloka* from Vālmīki wherein Daśaratha expresses his eagerness to carry out Janaka's command. Sagar singles out Daśaratha's forgoing the prerogatives of the *vara-pakṣa* as exemplary for today's society, and reflects on how, if that behavior found imitators nowadays, many tensions would disappear from Indian society. An environment of love would come about, and the *Rāmāyaṇa* story would come true.[19] Interestingly, the verbal form he uses (*ho jātī*) is the "irreal" or coun-

15. *ek yācak, ek bhikhārī—jo āpke dvār par āpkī kanyā kā dān māṃgne āyā hai.*

16. *āp jo ājñā kareṃge, vah hameṃ śirodhārya hogī.* This stress on the relative status of bride-givers and bride-takers in this episode of the television epic has also been noticed by Lutgendorf, who translated this passage (1990: 150).

17. *jagu biraṃci upajāvā jaba teṃ, dekhe sune byāha bahu taba teṃ; sakala bhāṃti sama sāju samājū, sama samadhī dekhe hama ājū.*

18. This theme returns at the beginning of the actual nuptial ritual. In *VR*, Vasiṣṭha goes to see Janaka and announces very humbly and politely that the groom's party is ready, again using a variant of the aforementioned politeness formula stressing the equivalence of donor and receiver (*dātṛpratigrahītṛbhyāṃ sarvārthāḥ sambhavanti hi, VR* 1.73.12a). Janaka, well aware of the courtesy thus extended by the other party, answers equally humbly that his kingdom is theirs, and leaves up to them the decision of the moment to start. In Tulsī's version, it is the bride's party that takes the initiative, or more precisely, the Brahmins exhort Janaka to fetch the *barāt* from its quarters (*janavāsa*). Tulsī keeps the girl's party in a more humble position than does Vālmīki. Sagar does not follow either version here: at the beginning of the wedding proper, the groom's party is shown to arrive and enter the palace, it is not clear on whose initiative (TVR episode 10). Sagar, then, misses another chance to stress his reformist agenda at the diegetic level.

19. *rāmāyaṇ kī kathā sārthik ho jātī.*

terfactual, implying the impossibility of the condition being fulfilled. One could conclude that the mythological example implicit in Vālmīki's text is articulated more clearly in the television series, yet without much hope that after millennia, there is a chance for change.

THE MEANING OF MATRIMONY: PRIVATE AND PUBLIC PERSPECTIVES. In other respects, Sagar is fundamentally different from the other texts. He introduces several innovations in his depiction of the preparation to the wedding, including a private and a public commentary on what a wedding is all about. For the private commentary, he introduces Rāma himself confiding to his brothers what matrimony means to him. The scene starts with Lakshmana passionately reporting to Bharat and Śatrughna about Rāma's state of mind after the first meeting with Sītā whom he refers to as "sister-in-law" (*bhābhī*) (TVR 119–20). Rāma arrives unexpectedly, and Lakshmana sheepishly admits what he was talking about.[20] Śatrughna teasingly asks Rāma where he got this love-education (*prem kī śikṣā*), since gurus don't teach *prem-śāstra*. Rāma's answer is dead serious. He lectures about "primordial love" that cannot be forced by man.[21] Rāma insists that his love for Sītā came about in the same way that nature (*prakṛti*) teaches mothers to love children, brothers to love brothers, and the waves of the ocean to be attracted by the moon. Love for a spouse is preordained by God (*vidhātā*). So when man meets his mate, all he has to do is to put full trust and love in her, so that afterward even his attention will not turn elsewhere.[22]

In this scene, Sagar is working hard to come to terms with a possible objection (*pūrvapakṣa*) raised in the Flower Garden scene (discussed in chapter 1): that the marriage of Rāma and Sītā is really a love marriage, albeit one sanctioned by the elders. By giving Rāma's private perspective, Sagar manages to stress that the match was "made in heaven," that it was not a matter of the girl's or the boy's initiative. Even this divine wedding is an arranged, or rather preordained, one. Rāma thus voices a perspective on marriage as a union between parties predestined to be spouses, at once natural and primordial. Free choice does not figure at all here; it is not a matter of individuals choosing partners.

20. *bhābhī ke pahle darśan kaise hue.*

21. *pahle se hī nirdhārit . . . jo manuṣya ke banāne se nahīṃ bantā.*

22. *manuṣya ko cāhie ki jab us se bheṃṭ ho to apnā sampūrṇa viśvās, sampūrṇa prem use sauṃp de jis se uske paścāt jīvan meṃ kisī dūsrī or dhyān hī na jāe.*

The public angle is highlighted in the next scene, showing a full court meeting of Janaka and Daśaratha with their councilors (TVR 120–1). Vasiṣṭha takes the floor for a longish lecture on the meaning of marriage. He starts out by saying that a wedding is not a personal affair, but a social sacrament. It is not just a matter of a man and a woman tying the knot; joined with them are their societies, their families, their religions.[23] One could say that, according to Vasiṣṭha, rather than a meeting of hearts, it is a meeting of families (*do kuloṃ kā . . . saṃgam*).

Both innovations serve the same intent: to transmit the message to the younger generation that this is no love marriage, but, as Janaka's guru, Śatānanda, has put it, a "gift of a bride" according to custom and religion (*vidhipūrvak aur dharmpūrvak kanyādān*). In case anyone would miss this point, Sagar in his editorial appearance repeats that a wedding is not a personal affair but a societal and familial tie.

If marriage is a contract between families, an important part of the ceremony has to be the recitation of the lineages of the parties. In the classical source, the better part of two chapters (*VR* 1.70.19–45, 71.1–15) is devoted to each family guru doing so. It sounds like an oral legal contract, a model document for kings who wish to intermarry their offspring. Janaka adds to his family history a "disclosure" about the particular geopolitical situation of his kingdom (1.71.16–19).

Sagar, too, accommodates some recitation of the ancient genealogy of the Raghu family in his version. It fits in well after Vasiṣṭha's sermon on marriage being in essence a union of two families. Naturally, then, the family tree of Rāma is relevant. This stands in contrast to Tulsī, who cuts out such dry parts to make room for more bhakti moments. Tulsī prefers to focus on different auspicious moments of high emotional content, which he underlines by switching to a different meter (*chand*). Much later, in the midst of the actual nuptial rituals, Tulsī simply remarks in passing that the gurus recite the lineages (*RCM* 1.324, *chand* 3.a).[24]

What we see is an unself-conscious assumption that wedlock is mainly a genealogical family affair, according to Vālmīki, which is downplayed by Tulsī in emphasizing love and devotion. Sagar revisits the issue, but he is operating within a different context. He is concerned to counter the alternative ideology of the love marriage. Thus, Sagar feels compelled to elaborate on the traditional

23. *vivāh vyaktigat kārya nahīṃ hai, yah ek sāmājik saṃskār hai . . . keval ek strī aur ek puruṣ ke gaṭh-baṃdhan ko hī vivāh nahīṃ kah sakte, kyoṃki un donoṃ vyaktiyoṃ ke sāth, unkā samāj, unkā kul, unkā dharm juṛā hotā hai.*

24. *sākhocāru dou kulagura karaiṃ.*

versions and rearticulate their implicit ideology. His innovative scenes confirm what was once taken for granted, namely that marriage is not a matter of individuals choosing a partner but is preordained and mainly about the meeting of families, not the meeting of hearts.

The Ceremony: Balancing Bhakti and Dharma, Traditions Great and Little

The foregoing observations bring us to the issue of the technicality of the rites and the tone that pervades the ceremonies. Often TVR has been described as a feast of *darśana* and a paradigmatical bhakti *Rāmāyaṇa*. To what extent does that hold when we compare it with the other versions? Is the wedding ceremony overwhelmingly a joyous celebration of love or does it partake more of the solemnity of dharma? Related to that, what is the role of male gurus in the legalities of the events? Are the rites mainly Vedic and patriarchal or is there room for women's rites that may voice a different perspective? Where does Sagar come out in the balance, when all is said and done?

WHO OUTDOES WHOM IN LOVING DEVOTION? In Vālmīki's and Sagar's versions, as already suggested by the welcoming ceremonies, a solemn tone prevails during the wedding ceremony. This is strikingly different from Tulsī's version, where spontaneous joy is the order of the day. Tulsī stresses emotion rather than Brahminical exchanges of civilities. For example, when the two parties catch a glance of one another, they are overjoyed and run into each other's arms (*RCM* 1.305.4-*dohā*). All this abundance of emotions fits well with Tulsī's bhakti agenda and contrasts with Sagar's stress on recitation of genealogies.

Tulsī and Sagar (episode 10) have in common that they have turned the whole wedding event into an occasion of mega-*darśana*. Whereas *Vālmīki Rāmāyaṇa* is short about the actual wedding ceremony, Tulsī and Sagar don't miss a nuance of the ritual that can be exploited for *darśana*. In *Rām Carit Mānas*, this is underscored by a plethora of lyrical meters (*chand*) that interrupt the more action-oriented *caupāī-dohā* rhythm. The TVR happily does the equivalent in its visual medium, alternating action with extended moments of *darśana*, deriving from the tableau (*jhāṅkī*) tradition. Significantly, Sagar uses Tulsī's lyrical meters as background music.

Both Tulsī and Sagar exploit several occasions to halt the action and provide *darśana*. For example, Tulsī lovingly dwells on how Sītā's parents wash the feet of the groom (*RCM* 1.324.4b–*chand* 2), using the occasion for a hymn of praise to Rāma. Sagar also dwells lovingly and at extraordinary length on the feet-washing episode.[25] While parts from Tulsī's *chands* play in the background, Sagar's camera underscores their words. Accompanying a recitation about Janaka washing the lotus feet whose pollen "sages and yogīs served, their minds turning into bees, to attain the salvation they desired" (TVR 133),[26] Sagar's camera registers the beatically smiling faces of the gurus of Ayodhyā.

The climax, the actual nuptial rituals, are a feast of *darśana* in the televised series. Sagar shows the ceremonies of "taking the hand" (*pānigahanu*), "walking around the fire" (*bhāvaṃrīṃ*), and "filling the parting of the hair" (*seṃdura*), with much recitation from Tulsī (*RCM* 1.324, *chand* 3–325.5). Sagar also singles out for recitation Tulsī's verses comparing the wedding to those of the goddesses Pārvatī and Śrī (1.324, *chand* 4a–b). However, Sagar then turns to Sanskrit recitation, while showing Sītā's hands being daubed with paste by her mother. This is surprising, as such women's rites are typically accompanied by folk songs in the vernacular. The Sanskrit text used is a hymn in praise of Nārāyaṇī from the *Durgāsaptaśatī* (TVR 134). The inclusion here seems calculated to stress Sītā's divinity and to interpret this occasion as a wonderful *darśana* of the goddess incarnate.

Finally, Tulsī says that on Vasiṣṭha's bidding, the newlyweds sit next to one another, which provides yet another wonderful occasion for *darśana*, this time by Daśaratha, who rejoices at the sight (*RCM* 1.325, *chand* 1). Sagar shows Sītā and Rāma paying obeisance to the gurus and their parents before sitting down again to give *darśana*.[27]

Notwithstanding this common stress on *darśana*, there is a difference between the medieval and television versions. This is apparent the moment we first get a glimpse of Sītā's procession approaching the wedding pavilion (*maṇḍapa*) and of the rites she carries out on arriving (*RCM* 1.322–3). Tulsī describes how Sītā and Rāma behold one another (1.323, *chand* 2c).[28] This may be seen as a reference to the rite wherein bride and groom gaze at each other for the first time, the *parasparasamīkṣaṇa* (Kane 1974: 533). Significantly, Sagar does not quote this verse, and with the exception of one brief glance Sītā casts

25. This episode is reportedly very popular with the audience of the Rām-līlā as performed in Rāmnagar (see Kapur 1990: 72).

26. *kari madhupa mana muni jogijana je sei abhimata gati lahaiṃ.*

27. Another example of *darśana* is the groom's procession. Vālmīki uses only a few *ślokas* on the topic of the *barāt* (*VR* I 69.1–6). Tulsī provides a wealth of physical details about horses, chariots, and even amphibious cars that can traverse water and land (*RCM* 1.298–302). It is as if we witness the event. Interestingly, Sagar does not portray the *barāt* with horses and chariots but shows the grooms and their party only when they arrive in the palace halls on foot. Budget limitations may have played a part here. Still, in general, TVR shows lavish—though by Bollywood standards low-budget—sets for the wedding scenes.

28. *siya rāma avalokani parasapara premu kāhuṃ na lakhi parai.*

on her groom-to-be on arrival, the two do not behold each other at any point during the whole ceremony.[29] There are, though, many close-ups, suggesting that everyone else is beholding the couple with much tender love.

Similarly, at the end of the ceremonies in Mithilā, the newlyweds pay a visit to the site of the divinity presiding over the wedding (*kohabara*). Tulsī does not care for the formalities of the occasion. Instead, he concentrates on Sītā's feelings. In a beautiful verse he hints at her being torn between decorum and love. She acts shy, but feels eager: "Looking at Rāma again and again, Sītā withdraws, but her heart does not withdraw. Her eyes, thirsty for love, surpass the beauty of pretty fishes" (*RCM* 1.326, *dohā*).[30] Pointedly, Tulsī does not describe the deity they are worshiping. Instead, we could say that he gives a full description of the deity Sītā worships, her new husband. Tulsī merrily inserts a top-to-toe (*nakha-śikha*) description of Rāma (1.327.1–*chand* 1a). This might be interpreted as a view from Sītā's shy perspective, but at the end Tulsī broadens it into a public view, with a description of the joy of all witnesses at the event. Tulsī has again managed to get maximal benefit from the opportunity to sing a hymn of praise to Rāma and to provide a reverential *darśana* for the devotee.[31]

Sagar treats this scene quite differently. He shows the procession, with the couples striding forward solemnly, restrainedly smiling, but not looking at each other. In the background, a rather pedestrian folk song is sung, which ends by quoting only one *dohā* from *RCM* (1.327, *dohā*). Sagar passes up the chance to quote Tulsī's beautiful description of Sītā's feelings. Instead, the focus is on decorum. The folk song says that the clan goddess (*kuladevī*) confirmed all ritual activity that had been going on (*sāre kāraja siddha bhae,* TVR 137), and we have a shot of everyone bowing to her image. The focus is on the

29. Elsewhere, Tulsī's text says: "Hearing the melodious singing, holy men abandoned their asceticism, and Cupid and cuckoos were ashamed" (*kalagāna suni muni dhyāna tyāgahiṃ kāma kokila lājahiṃ, RCM* 1.322, *chand*). While this verse is sung in TVR, the presiding gurus are shown with their backs to the women, and do not even so much as glance in their direction (TVR 132). This illustrates well the amount of hypercorrection Sagar has applied to *RCM*.

30. *puni puni rāmahi citava siya, sakucati manu; sakucai na; harata manohara mīna chabi, prema piāse naina.*

31. Tulsī does not stop with the conclusion of the wedding ceremonies. When the newlyweds arrive in Ayodhyā, there is yet more scope for *darśana*. Vālmīki simply mentions that the queens carry out the ritual reception of the new daughters-in-law (*vadhūs*) (*VR* 1.77.10–13). Tulsī elaborates, weaving in as much gift-giving, devotion, and love as will fit in verse. He stresses the jubilant joy of the queens who are anticipating Rāma's *darśana* (*RCM* 1.346) and that of the citizens of Ayodhyā when enjoying *darśana* of Rāma (1.347–8). The climax in *RCM* is the queens' auspicious welcome ceremony (*parachani*) (1.349). Sagar has concentrated on this scene, quoting two *dohās* from RCM, and suggesting the happiness of everyone in the city in the accompanying song "Ayodhyā nagarī dhanya bhaī" (TVR 146). The queens of Ayodhyā, too, get their chance to wash the feet of brides and grooms (*tinha para kuṃvari kuṃvara baiṭhāre, sādara pāya punīta pakhāre, RCM* 1.350.1b) and continue *pūjā* in great joy.

gods worshiping according to the rules, and it comes at the cost of our *darśana* of Rāma. Sagar has cut out Tulsī's hymn of praise to Rāma.

Thus, while Sagar is fond of halting the action for *darśana,* he does not always incorporate Tulsī's hymns of praise for Rāma. Another significant difference is that he follows Tulsī in presenting Rāma to the audience's gaze, but does not allow Sītā to gaze at her groom. The cultural code that a bride is to be shy and does not glance at her groom outweighs religio-aesthetic concerns. Sagar seems to judge that this propriety must be preserved even at the cost of the loss of some beautiful poetry. There can be no doubt that Sagar allows us to feast our eyes on multiple *darśanas*; however, Tulsī gets the prize for loving devotion.

DIVINE SANCTION. Tulsī further enhances his moments of *darśana* by having the gods participate in the occasion. Vālmīki is much more restrained in that respect, allowing only once for the gods to shower flowers over the bride and groom;[32] Tulsī intersperses the events at regular intervals with vistas of the gods in heaven showering flowers. The density grows during the actual nuptial rites.[33] The gods thus are shown to overwhelmingly approve of the match. They don't restrict themselves to throwing flowers on stage from the balcony, either. They become active participants in ensuring that the rites are carried out properly.

In *Rām Carit Mānas,* when Sītā arrives at the altar, the gurus have her do a *pūjā* of Gaurī, Gaṇapati, and the Brahmins. The gods reward her by bestowing blessing in person (1.323, *chand*).[34] The sun god, Ravi, who is the dynastic patron of Rāma's family, instructs the ritual agents at the ceremony about what to do (1.323, *chand*). At the time of the libations in the fire, the god of fire becomes manifest, and the Vedas take the form of Brahmins to give correct ritual advice (1.323, *dohā*). Sagar, somewhat surprisingly, does not follow Tulsī. The closest parallel is when the newlyweds go to pay their respects to the clan-divinity (*kuladevatā*), when the accompanying song stipulates that everything was approved (*siddha*) by her (TVR 137).

Significantly, it is not only the divine patriarchs that show their approval. In Tulsī's version, the gods' wives actually participate in the wedding cere-

32. Only during the actual circumambulation of the fire are the heavenly flowers said to rain down (*VR* 1.73.37). For text-critical remarks, see Goldman 1984: 391.

33. The gods are described as showering flowers on Sītā's arrival (*RCM* 1.323.3a), on Sītā's mother's arrival (1.324.4a), when Rāma's feet are washed (1.324, *chand* 1b), on the cermony of the circumambulation (*bhāvaṃrī*) (1.324 *dohā*), and when the *barāt* leaves the altar (1.326, *chand* 4).

34. *sura pragaṭi pūjā lehiṃ ehiṃ asīsa ati sukhu pāvahīṃ.*

monies. They are disguised as married mortal women (*RCM* 1.318.3a–*chand*) who participate in the singing for Sītā on her wedding day (1.322.3–4). The gods follow their wives to the party and join the *barāt* disguised as Brahmins (1.321.3b–4). Neither party is recognized in the general joy, except by Rāma, who honors the gods with a seat in his heart (1.321, *chand* c).[35] Sagar follows Tulsī's lead in having divine guests for the wedding, but he has Śiva and Brahmā descend before the ladies do. Rāma nods smilingly to the gods disguised as Brahmins, while they make their obeisance with folded hands.

The gods have a sanctifying function as participants in the rites, but there is also a humorous element: they act like self-important VIP wedding guests. Tulsī portrays them as country bumpkins arriving in the big city from their own regions (*lokas*). Brahmā himself does not recognize his creation (*RCM* 1.314.4b). Śiva is described as something of a rural tour guide, who exhorts his ox to move on, after he has explained to his bewildered covillagers that this society wedding is a major cosmic event (1.314 *dohā*--315.2a). In tune with the bhakti agenda, Śiva's speech is really a hymn glorifying Rāma.

Sagar's gods, too, are portrayed as somewhat rustic. That is clear from their speech, which is remarkably different from the *atiśuddha* Hindi the noble human characters speak. When the gods perceive that preparations for the wedding are taking place, Śiva comments, rather colloquially, "I've been keen on seeing it for ages. So, goddess, let's go?" (not transcribed in Mizokami's transcription).[36] The contrast is all the more remarkable because this scene is preceded by the lofty Sanskrit recitation of the *Yajurveda* by Janaka's Brahmins. So in both *Rām Carit Mānas* and the television version, by making the gods actors in the rites, two purposes are accomplished. Divine sanction is ensured, and the superiority of Rāma is affirmed, as he effortlessly upstages the other gods.

A BALANCING ACT BETWEEN BRAHMINICAL AND WOMEN'S RITES. Whereas *Vālmīki Rāmāyaṇa* focuses naturally on Vedic ceremonies, a striking innovation of Tulsī is that he makes room for folksy ones. The incorporation of folk elements is an important aspect of the bhakti tradition, as is well exemplified by the projection of folk rites onto the Krishna mythology (Entwistle 1987: 46). One wonders whether this inclusion of folk, in particular women's, rites might undercut patriarchy. Is there an element of critique here? Can we see evidence of a power struggle?

35. *sura lakhe rāma sujāna pūje mānasika āsana die.*
36. *ham to kab se utāvale ho rahe haiṃ, kyoṃ devī, caleṃ?*

Close study reveals that Tulsī is very concerned to be evenhanded and to balance both Brahminical and folk ritual; he stresses that everything is carried out according to both great and little tradition. Frequently he uses a variant of the phrase "Everything was done according to Veda and popular rites."[37]

A good example is the preparation of the wedding site. *Vālmīki Rāmāyaṇa* describes the wedding altar or *vedi,* which is brimming with Vedic sacrifical references (*VR* 1.73.20–4, not retained in the critical edition). Tulsī, on the other hand, has an elaborate description of the *maṇḍapa*'s beauty that has little to do with sacrifical sites (*RCM* 1.287.2–89, 320 *chand*). Interestingly, Sagar first shows the *maṇḍapa* while the priests are busy purifying the site, engaged in sacrificial preperatory activities, and reciting Sanskrit mantras from the *Yajurveda* (TVR 130). Immediately afterward, the camera turns to women's rites. Sagar thus harks back to Vālmīki's emphasis on Vedic sacrifice but incorporates some of Tulsī's interest in women's rites. This illustrates how Tulsī's championing of folk rites is somewhat reluctantly followed by Sagar.

The main agents of the folk rites are women. Tulsī lovingly describes the rituals the women of the bride's family conduct, including the *pūjā* of the groom (*parachani*) (*RCM* 1.318–9.2), the singing of *maṅgala gīta* at the *maṇḍapa* (1.323.4), and so on.[38] He seems to consider these female participants just as crucial as the male Brahmins. Often he mentions both in one breath; for example; "Auspiciously married women sing their songs, holy Brahmins recite the Vedas" (1.313.2b).[39] Sagar also balances the two by showing closeups of sacrificial activity by Brahmins as well as women's rites. The sound track of the wedding ceremony also is an attempt to balance the Sanskritic and the vernacular. Sagar certainly does his best to work in a lot of Sanskrit recitation.[40] Brahmins recite from the *Yajurveda* during the tying of the knot, from the *Viṣṇu Sahasranāma Stotra* while Sītā adorns Rāma with the *mālā* and from *Durgasaptaśatī* when he reciprocates.[41] The wedding ceremony is presented with shots of Brahmins reciting, performing sacrifices in the fire, and blessing

37. Some examples are: *kari kula rīti beda bidhi rāū* (*RCM* 1.302.1), *beda bihita aru kula ācāra, kīnha bhalī bidhi saba byavahārū* (1.319.1b), *kari baidika laukika saba rītiṃ* (*RCM* 1.320.1a).

38. To some extent, one could argue that Tulsī strives for a popularization of the wedding with full participation not only of women but also of low castes. In one line, the presence of *nāīs*, *bārīs*, *bhāṭs*, and *naṭs* is mentioned as recipients of money distributed by Rāma; see *RCM* 1.319, *dohā*.

39. *subhaga suāsini gāvahiṃ gītā, karahiṃ beda dhuni bipra punītā.*

40. Reportedly, the wedding ceremonies of the Rāmnagar Rām-līlā too are conducted in Sanskrit, as exemplified in the performance of September 10, 1979 (see Kapur 1990: 70).

41. Surprisingly, the exchange of the *mālās* is not mentioned by Tulsī, and indeed seems not to be part of the classical wedding ceremony descriptions (not in Kane 1974: 533–4).

the couple. On the other hand, the actual *agnipariṇayana* or *pherā* (circling of the fire) and *māṃg bharnā* (adorning of the parting of the woman's hair) is performed by young women and accompanied by a folk song that describes the general joy (TVR 135).[42]

Most real-life weddings include a lot of folk rituals after the ceremony proper. Vālmīki has little to say on this topic. Tulsī again brings folk rites to the forefront by stating that folk rituals (*laukika rīti*) are carried out (*RCM* 1.327, *chand* 2b-4). He describes a big feast (*jevanāra*), to which Janaka invites the *barāt*. This gourmet meal is served swiftly on exquisite dishes and described in much culinary detail (1.328–9). While they have dinner, the guests are entertained with the traditional "insult songs" (*gāri*, 1.329.1a, 3b–4a), which they much relish.[43] Tulsī even specifies that these songs are "personalized" (1.329.3b).[44] This practice (both the meal and the *gālī* performance) is depicted, and relished by the audience, at the Rām-līlā of Rāmnagar (Kapur 1990: 72). Similarly, when describing the happiness in Ayodhyā on the return of the *barāt*, Tulsīdās mentions the women of the city singing auspicious *gārī* (1.358.1b). While the television version also gives much airtime to women's songs, they are neatly sanitized. Sagar does not feature any of the *gālī* type of songs. He may be catering to the sensitivities of "reformed" Hindu tastes of the more prudish middle classes.[45]

On returning to Ayodhyā, there are more rites, nearly exclusively carried out by women. There is a welcome ceremony for the new brides (*parachani*) (*RCM* 1.349). Sagar dwells lovingly on this scene, suggesting the happiness of everyone in the city in the accompanying song, "Ayodhyā nagarī dhanya bhaī" (TVR 146). Tulsī stresses that the rites follow both great and little traditions (*nigama nīti kula rīti, RCM* 1.349, *dohā*), but he clearly relished the women's rites. Sagar quotes two *dohā* s from *Rām Carit Mānas,* one of which stresses the ultraorthodoxy of the rites.

Vālmīki says that the new brides worshiped in local temples, and Sagar follows suit, showing Sītā and her sisters joining a *pūjā* of Ayodhyā's royal family's *kuladevatā,* the sun god. This is a patriarchal affair, affirming the lineage of the groom's family. Sagar throws in some more Sanskrit mantras recited by Vasiṣṭha, who blesses all present.

42. "Siyā raghuvara jī ke saṃga parana lāgīṃ."

43. For examples of *gālīs* from Rajasthan, see Raheja and Gold 1994: 45–7 and 49–50, 57–62.

44. *jevaṃta dehiṃ madhura dhuni gārī, lai lai nāma puruṣa aru nārī.*

45. An explicit rejection of the practice can be found in the *Rādheśyām Rāmāyaṇa* (Kathāvācak 1971: 1.4.19–20). For the general context of such cleaning up of folk practices in colonial India and its communal anti-Muslim overtones, see Gupta 2001.

Tulsī first focuses on playful activity: the royal women engage the newlyweds in games designed to break the ice between bride and groom and to determine who will be the dominant one in the relationship (this is usually called *juā khel*). He reports that all the young people act shyly but that Rāma smiles secretly (1.350, *dohā* 2).[46] Only after these rites does Tulsī briefly mention worship of the gods and ancestors, which is instantly rewarded (1.351.1–2a).

Sagar reserves the icebreakers (*juā khel*) for after the formal worship (TVR 146–7). Perhaps following Tulsī's hint, the shyness of the participants is highlighted, but the voluptuous images in the background evoke an atmosphere of *śṛṅgāra,* suggesting auspicious fecundity. Kauśalyā and Kaikeyī preside over a ceremony, called here *dūdh-bhāt,* wherein bride and groom feed each other. It is only at this point that Sītā and Rāma look at each other shyly. Kaikeyī whispers something in Sītā's ear, which is instantly understood by Bharata, who warns his brother that his new bride may well use the occasion to bite his finger. Sītā, though, just smiles away blissfully and does not do any such thing. Sagar may well have been inspired here by an earlier passage in Tulsī featuring *lahakaura.* Right after the nuptial ceremonies, Tulsī describes how the newlyweds go to the *kohabara* for folk ceremonies and how Pārvatī instructed Rāma, and Sarasvatī took Sītā's side (*RCM* 1.327, *chand* 2c). The most significant difference, though, is that Tulsī reports a lot of merrymaking and joking on the occasion (*hāsa vilāsa,* 1.327, *chand* 2d; *vinoda pramoda,* 1.327, *chand* 3c). In contrast, Sagar features a rather solemn and serene atmosphere. This may be a consequence of his having chosen to concentrate on the games played at the groom's house rather than at the bride's paternal home.

In the television version, a contest follows involving finding an object in a bowl of liquid. This object looks like a ring but is called *kaṃganā.* Again, the participants smile beatifically, this time without looking at one another, while their hands search in the liquid. Sagar passes up the chance to quote Tulsī, who says that Sītā is so eager to behold Rāma that she remains transfixed by her rings, which reflect Rāma's face (*RCM* 1.327, *chand* 3a–b). In Sagar's version, neither of the two is engaged in the competitive element; they both have to be encouraged to start the game. Sītā wins, smiling shyly. Lakshmana, of course, true to character, blurts out that Rāma has let her win, but Bharata counters that it is not bad that at least at some point Rāma loses. Everyone savors the irony of Sītā winning over Rāma. Sagar may well be drawing his inspiration here from the myriad folk songs for wedding rituals that often

46. *loka rīti jananīṃ karahiṃ, bara dulahini sakucāhiṃ; modu binodu biloki bara, rāmu manahiṃ musukāhiṃ.*

feature Rāma and Sītā as the bride and groom (see, e.g., Archer 1985: 90, 101–5, 114). Some of these songs irreverently make fun of the exemplary Rāma as a clumsy groom who is unable to untie the wedding knot, whereas breaking Śiva's bow was easy for him. Sagar has transformed the situations sketched in such songs so that they portray more solemn occasions, while still allowing for some role reversal. His scene is not irreverent but merely reinforcing of the irony of the incarnation.

However, something else is also going on in this episode of the television version. Throughout, the emphasis is on women's solidarity. The mothers-in-law take the side of the new brides against their sons. This is made explicit by the encouragements they give during the test of finding an object in liquid (*kaṃganā ḍhūṃṛnā*), and is commented on by Lakshmana, who says "Now the daughters-in-law are counting for more than the sons" (TVR 147). To this the reply is "What's that label 'daughter-in-law'? Rather, they are our daughters!" (147).[47] Clearly, Sagar is taking up the earlier message of the gracious behavior of the girl's in-laws toward her. The mother-in-law, her traditional enemy, is here transformed into an ally. This women's solidarity, however, is well entrenched within the patriarchal frame.

Anxieties about the Welfare of Daughters in Their Sasurāls

This brings us to the next element prevailing in Sagar's depiction of the wedding. At several points, he voices an outspoken anxiety about the plight of a young bride in her new home. In real life, the wedding ceremonies at the bride's house end with the tearful leave-taking ceremony (*bidāī*), which anticipates these anxieties.[48] The new *bahū* will often find herself at the bottom of the food chain in her new home. She is watched carefully and critically, is put to work hard as a Cinderella, and basically has to prove her character. Unless other women she knows have married into the same village, she finds herself far away from family and friends in a strange environment that might be hostile. There may also be pressure for her to seek financial assistance from her parents for her husband's family. In short, the young woman does not have an easy time.

Foremost on everyone's mind is of course the vexed issue of the dowry. While officially illegal in modern India, still, the bride's party often "volunteers"

47. *"ab betoṃ se baṛhkar bahueṃ ho rahī haiṃ bhayyā!" "kyā bahū-bahū lagā rakhā hai? are, hamārī beṭiyāṃ haiṃ!"*

48. For some examples of folk songs from Rajasthan, see Raheja and Gold 1994: 99–103.

to give gifts. The dowry is seen as a compensation for the new family's expense of caring for the girl (no matter how hard she will work to "earn" her living, the perception remains that she is a "burden"). Against that background, the dowry functions as a kind of insurance for the good treatment of the girl by her in-laws. Similarly, the *bidāī* ceremony is sometimes interpreted as a chance for the bride's family to show how much they care for her, so as to send a message to her in-laws that they should treat her well.

Sagar is at pains to show the exemplary behavior of Sītā's in-laws in making things easier for her. This may be regarded as an attempt to reform the tradition. At the same time, he works within the traditional means of the bride's family in ensuring her welfare by suggesting that a large dowry has been given, stressing the presence of "sisters" married into the same family, and portraying a display of sadness at her departure to demonstrate how much her family cares for her. An important element that provides us a glimpse in Sagar's agenda is the advice that the bride receives from her parents when leaving for her *sasurāl*. I will take up each of these points in turn.

ALLIES FOR THE NEW BRIDE AND A BIG DOWRY. First, Sītā is not going alone to her new *sasurāl*. At the same time she married Rāma, her sister and two cousins also married Rāma's brothers.[49] Thus, four "sisters" will go to the same house, a welcome situation for most brides, as they will have natural allies in their new home.[50] The match is arranged by the elders, all men, of course, and strictly to address patriarchal concerns.[51] Sagar's camera registers the surprise and happiness of the other parties at learning this good news. Kuśadvaja and Lakshmana are shown to be happy with the proposals in a dignified way. More abundant is the joy of the women, first Sunayanā and Kuśadvaja's wife, then the girls themselves. There is much joy on hearing that the four "sisters" will go to the same *sasurāl*. Interestingly, in Tulsī's version, the suggestion of the fourfold wedding comes first from the women of Mithilā,

49. This is not an innovation of Sagar, though the situation is somewhat ambiguous in *VR*, may be due to the multiple layers of the text. Whereas officially there is only mention of Rāma marrying Sītā, at a certain point Janaka does preparatory rituals for both his daughters (1.69.19), which indicates that Lakshmana is to marry Janaka's other daughter, Urmilā. However, it is not till the public meeting in Mithilā that Vasiṣṭha sues for both Janaka's daughters (1.70.45), and Viśvāmitra then proposes a fourfold wedding, in which also Bharata and Śatrughna are to marry the daughters of Kuśadvaja (1.72.1–8).

50. For an an anthropological description about the role such considerations play in arranging marriages among Khalapur Rajputs, see Minturn and Kapoor 1993: 47–8.

51. The reasons given for the fourfold wedding are slightly different in TVR. In *VR*, Viśvāmitra seeks to strengthen the alliance between the two houses, whereas in TVR, Viśvāmitra judges that it is not proper that two of the four brothers should remain bachelors. Concern for the welfare of Sītā is not acknowledged to play a role.

when they behold the arrival of the *barāt* (*RCM* 1.311, *chand*). One could say that in *Rām Carit Mānas*, the wedding parties are expanded on popular demand. Tulsī has a more democratic sensibility; he gives much attention to the people of Mithilā, stressing their comments approving of the match (1.309.4–311).

How do the versions differ regarding the issue of dowry (*dahej*), which figures so importantly in the bride's plight? There is reference to a lot of gift-giving in all the versions, but there are interesting twists.[52] In Vālmīki, Janaka sends the groom's party back with a huge gift for his daughters. This is referred to by the technical term "girl's wealth" (*kanyādhana*). This seems to be part of the woman's property, or *strīdhana:* "what a woman receives at the nuptial fire, what she receives when she is taken away" (as defined in *Mānavadharmaśāstra* 9.194; see Olivelle 2005: 169). Vālmīki then describes the contents in detail. Tulsī, too, describes the gifts of Janaka in detail (*RCM* 1.326.1b–3), but he speaks of a dowry (*dāija,* 1.326.1b, 1.333 *dohā*) instead of *kanyādhana.* This is a significant change, as the focus now is not on what is given to the bride as her personal property but on what is given to her in-laws. The issue comes up twice, once just after the wedding ceremony proper and again at the time of leaving. The first time, Daśaratha is said to accept everything but promptly divide it among the beggars (1.326.4). This illustrates well that the gift is meant for the in-laws, not for the bride. Tulsī's intention is probably to illustrate how Daśaratha was generous beyond bounds and how there is no concern with personal enrichment. One can say that this sets an example that the groom's party should accept *dahej* without any greed. On the other hand, in a modern context, the father-in-law's passing on the gifts might be misunderstood, as the groom's party might thus try to make a point that the gifts are defective or inferior. In that context, giving away what is received from the bride's party to beggars might be intended to be offensive and illustrate once again the superiority of the groom's party. Needless to say, that is far from Tulsī's intention, but Sagar does not show this, maybe to avoid the misunderstanding.

Sagar skillfully dodges the dowry issue, not even mentioning the word *dahej*. He makes only one reference to gifts by the bride's family in passing.

52. In *RCM,* the whole ceremony is replete with descriptions of gift-giving. After the wedding, when the *barāt* leaves for Ayodhyā, Tulsī describes elaborate gift-giving by Daśaratha (*RCM* 1.339.4). Later, when Ayodhyā is preparing for the newly wedded couples, Tulsī adds more gift-giving to Brahmins (1.345, *dohā*). After the *barāt* is dismissed with proper gift-giving, Vasiṣṭha orders that the Brahmins be honored and fed (1.352.1–2). After that, finally, it is time for paying the fee to the guru. The king offers great wealth to Viśvāmitra and Vasiṣṭha. Significantly, though, they only take their traditional fee (*nega*) (1.352.3–353.2a). What is meaningful is that Tulsī adds that the joy of all this is too much to describe (1.355.1–3). Sagar, somewhat surprisingly, shows none of the dismissal of the gurus, maybe to avoid the delicate issue of how much payment gurus should accept and how much decline.

This occurs in episode 11 where Sunayanā gives her final advice to her daughters. It is worth looking in detail at this passage. Sunayanā refers only obliquely to a dowry, carefully avoiding the word *dahej*. She says that while a father may give a lot of material wealth, which engenders surprise in the three worlds (may be a reference to *RCM* 1.333, *dohā*), all a mother has to offer is advice on how a woman should behave (TVR 142).[53]

It seems to me that Sagar has masterfully dealt, or rather avoided dealing, with the issue. Sunayanā's passing remark intimates that there must have been a big *dahej*, without saying so explicitly or calling it by name. Placed in the context of the leave-taking ceremonies (*vidā*), it gets conflated with the more acceptable practice of sending away visitors with a gift. At the same time, Sagar downplays the importance of the material dowry, privileging instead the mother's gift of "spiritual" advice. Given all the controversy about dowry—its condemnation in the media (and the law) and abiding (even expanding) prevalence in practice—it is not surprising that Sagar avoids the issue. It is surprising rather that he manages to let this much slip by without condemning the practice, all the more on an official government channel of communication. One has to remember that some of the soap series aired on Doordarshan at the time were working to counter this "social evil." In any case, dowry is not tackled head-on, but the message that is sent confirms a common-sense understanding that surely loving parents will give their daughter a generous dowry, as well as sound advice to the bride on how to behave with her in-laws.

TEARFUL PARENTAL FAREWELL. In Vālmīki, the leave-taking ceremony is dealt with rather swiftly, in just eight *ślokas*. Daśaratha asks permission to leave, Janaka sends him with the gift for his daughters, and there's nothing more to it. The other versions, however, go literally through a whole song-and-dance at this point. Tulsī's Janaka is reluctant to let the groom's party leave. Affectionately, he makes Daśaratha stay (*RCM* 1.333.1b).[54] It seems that a strong liking for the in-laws is at the root of his reluctance. This impression is reinforced during the actual leave-taking, where the majority of the verses are devoted to Janaka's saying goodbye to Rāma and his brothers (1.341.1b–342), and Viśvāmitra (1.343.1–3). In his eagerness to make the groom's party stay just a bit longer, Tulsī's king is acting by popular consent (1.333.2b).[55] It is not until

53. *pitā ne tumheṃ itnā diyā hai ki tīnoṃ lok meṃ uskī śobhā ho rahī hai, par maiṃ to tumheṃ nārī-dharm kā jñān hī de saktī hūṃ, jo jīvan ke har moṛ par tumheṃ kartavya aur dharm kā rāstā dikhāegā.*

54. *dina uṭhi bidā avadhapati māgā, rākhahi janaku sahita anurāgā.*

55. *nita nava nagara anaṃda uchāhū, dasaratha gavanu sohāi na kāhū.*

Viśvāmitra and Śatānanda intercede that the *barāt* finally gets the go-ahead. The royal women, too, share the king's feelings and are unhappy when they are informed that the *barāt* is about to leave. They entrust the girls to their husbands, taking the opportunity to praise Rāma (with a *chand,* 1.336.4–337.1).

Sagar follows Tulsī's main lead and elaborates further in episode 10. His Janaka pleads very politely with Daśaratha that the *barāt* should stay on for some time. Sagar's Janaka does not act so much out of a liking for the groom's party as out of love for his beloved daughter, and he says as much. The groom's father understands the bride's father's plight and promises to wait till Janaka tells him to go, and the two kings embrace (TVR 138–9).[56] Sagar thus dwells on the chivalries of the two parties and takes up again the issue of the exemplary gallantry of the groom's party (*varapakṣa*) toward the bride's party (*kanyāpakṣa*). To drive his point home, he adds a new scene. At the beginning of episode 11, he shows the queens in Ayodhyā getting impatient when the *barāt* does not return (140). While Kauśalyā is the voice of reason and understanding, the impatient Kaikeyī argues that after all, the bride's party should respect the wishes of the groom's party (140),[57] and she sends a message to that effect to Daśaratha. However, he reacts very negatively to such reasoning and refuses to force the bride's party to do anything against their wishes. Nevertheless, it is clear that he must return home at some point. The scene ends with a Realpolitik argument by his councilor that carries more weight: a king should not stay away from his responsibilities too long.

On the other side, Janaka is finally convinced to let the *barāt* go by Viśvāmitra and Śatānanda, just as in *Rām Carit Mānas.* But in Sagar's version, we get the full argumentation. Viśvāmitra points out that Janaka is setting a bad example by giving in to his emotions so much, and should pull himself together and help protect the ways of proper conduct (*nīti kī rakṣā,* TVR 142). Śatānanda tells Janaka that once the girl is given away, she belongs to someone else (*parāī*). This finally prompts Janaka into action.

Why does Sagar dwell on these protracted leave-takings? As in *Rām Carit Mānas,* there is definitely a bhakti sensibility; loving devotion seeks to linger in the proximity of the beloved. It is significant, though, that Sagar's Janaka is portrayed as acting less out of love for Rāma than for his daughter. Sagar taps a universal (at least within this culture) sentiment when he has us wallow in the emotional state of the father who has to bid farewell to his beloved daughter.

56. Daśaratha says emphatically that this is "Daśaratha's promise," an element of foreshadowing of later more dramatic happenings having to do with Daśaratha being held to keep his promise to Kaikeyī.

57. *ham var-pakṣ vāle haiṃ, ham jaisā cāheṃge kanyā-pakṣ vāloṃ ko vaisā hī karnā paṛegā.*

This is well illustrated in the next scene, where Sagar follows Tulsī in giving airtime to the view of the people of Mithilā. Tulsī's public, like its king, has relished the presence of the *barāt*. Sagar's focus is different. He has some people sympathize with Janaka's state of mind on the general human principle that it is difficult to send one's daughter away to her in-laws. The *ḍolī*- makers, while preparing the palanquin in which the brides are to be taken away, phrase quite poignantly the dilemma a girl's parents face: "Any father and mother wish not to send her, and yet, they cannot keep her" (TVR 141).[58] Following the tradition of the classical drama (and the Hindi film), the "people" speak a rustic language, not Modern Standard Hindi, although the latter is used for a more philosophical remark by one of the workers: "A daughter is the true manifestation of what they call illusion" (141).[59] They add that even a king like Janaka will forget all his asceticism, which may be an echo of *Rām Carit Mānas* (1.338.3a).[60] While the people's words capture well the king's emotional state, and for that matter that of every parent, they consitute a different type of popular endorsement of the king's actions than in *Rām Carit Mānas*.

There is so much stress on the sincerity and depth of the emotion that one might start wondering whether all this might be an elaborate show put on to make the in-laws understand how dear the bride is to her parents. That would miss the point. The pathos of the situation is real and deeply felt. Its elaboration is perhaps better understood in reference to the melodramatic mode of the whole series, which indulges in closeup, zooming in on every shade of emotion portrayed.

The plight of the parents of a bride is not exhaustively treated with reference to Janaka's sorrow alone. It comes to its full climax with the description of the farewell in the women's quarters, which gives Tulsī the opportunity to fully exploit the emotional depths of the sentiment of tragedy, or *karuṇā rasa*, as he himself puts it: "All men and women, the queens and the ladies-in-waiting, were overwhelmed with love. They seemed to have turned the city of Videha into a dwelling for pathos and farewell" (*RCM* 1.337, *dohā*).[61] Tulsī touchingly describes the goodbyes of the women: "Again and again, they embraced Sītā, blessed her and gave her advice" (1.334.2a).[62] The parting words of the queen-mothers are first of all a blessing: "May you always remain your

58. *kauno bāp-mahtārī kā na bheje ko jī karat hai aur na rakh sakat haiṃ.*

59. *vah jise māyā kahte haiṃ na, uskā asalī rūp hī biṭiyā hai.*

60. *sīya biloki dhīratā bhāgī rahe kahāvata parama birāgī.*

61. *premabibasa nara nāri saba, sakhinha sahita ranivāsu; mānahuṃ kīnha bidehapura, karunāṃ birahaṃ nivāsu.*

62. *puni puni sīya goda kari lehīṃ, dei asīsa sikhāvanu dehīṃ.*

husband's darling, we bless you to live a long, happily married life" (1.334.2b).[63] The advice proper is very short: "You should look after the needs of your mother- and father-in-law, and the guru. By just looking at your husband's facial expression, carry out his command" (1.334.3a).[64] Tulsī further describes the goodbye of the girlfriends: "Overwhelmed with extreme love, the clever girlfriends whisper instruction on women's duty" (1.344.3b).[65] The next verse again returns to the goodbye of the mothers, who cannot get enough of embracing the girls. Interestingly, they curse the fate of women: "They said: 'why did the creator create women?' " (1.344.4b).[66] Following the *kāvya* tradition, even the birds raised by Sītā share in the general outburst of tears: "The parrot and mynah that Sītā had helped hatch, kept in a golden cage, and taught [to speak], desperately cried out: 'Where's Sītā?' When they heard this, no one could remain dry-eyed" (1.338.1).[67]

Sagar, too, exploits the dramatic possibilities of the scene and its *karuṇā rasa*. He adds an episode wherein Sunayanā confides in the wife of the royal guru about her sadness at losing a daughter (TVR 137–8). She does not quite curse the fate of women, but her words are bitter nevertheless: "It is as if someone is getting away with wounding someone, and then plundering their all" (137).[68] She despairs at the charade a mother has to go through in blessing the groom, the very one who is taking away her dearest (137).[69] This sentiment seems quite counter to anything Tulsī would say with reference to his beloved Rāma. Sagar seems to be carried away from the bhakti agenda here in his sympathy for the mother's plight.

After having given full airtime to the mother's poignant feelings, Sagar feels compelled to temper this with the voice of reason, here the guru's wife. First, she says that this is just the way of the world (TVR 137).[70] Sunayanā protests "What a way is that? That a mother and father have to bring up a daughter lovingly for so many years, and then send her off to a strange house, by their own doing?" (137–8).[71] The guru's wife then reminds Sunayanā that

63. *hoehu saṃtata piyahi piārī, ciru ahibāta asīsa hamārī.*

64. *sāsu sasura gura sevā karehū, pati rukha lakhi āyasu anusarehu.*

65. *ati saneha basa sakhīṃ sayānī, nāri dharama sikhavahiṃ mṛdu bānī.*

66. *kahahiṃ viraṃci racīṃ kata nārīṃ.*

67. *suka sārikā jānakī jyāe, kanaka piṃjaranhi rākhi paṛhāe; byākula kahahiṃ kahāṃ baidehī, suni dhīraju pariharai na kehī.*

68. *jaise kisī ko ghāyal karke koī sab kuch lūṭ karke jā rahā hai.*

69. *māṃ ke hṛday kī kaisī viḍambanā hai, jo uskā sab kuch chīn kar le jā rahā hai, use āśīrvād de rahī hai.*

70. *saṃsār kī yahī rīti hai.*

71. *kaisī hai yah rīti ki mātā-pitā itne baras pāl-pos kar beṭī ko baṛā karte haiṃ aur phir ek din use apne hāthoṃ parāe ghar bhej dete haiṃ?*

things won't be that bad, and that Sītā, after all, will have her husband to confide in, just like Sunayanā herself now has Janaka. Still, Sunayanā finds it hard as a mother to let go of her daughter: "A mother's heart does not understand the language of reason, it knows only the delusion of intense love" (*mā kā hṛday jñān kī bhāṣā nahīṃ samajhtā, keval mamatā kā moh jāntā hai,* 138). The guru's wife, then, points out that such concern with matters of the world is not fitting for a queen, especially the consort of the king of Videha. Here she is punning on the literal meaning of *vi-deha,* "detached from the body." '[72] Sunayanā confesses that the king of Videha himself is caught in this web of affection, he, too, feels *mamatā* that is so strong that he cannot let go of his daughter. To be sure, Sunayanā gets the last word, but still, in comparison with Tulsī's version, the atmosphere of *karuṇā* is tempered by words of wisdom. While giving full range to the shades of pathos, Sagar seems eager to warn his public against the excesses of emotion. Nothing seems to work better to exorcise this demon than to let it run its full course.

BALANCING IDEAL BRIDES AND IDEAL IN-LAWS. Notwithstanding all Sunayanā's pathos in the scene with the guru's wife, her farewell to the young brides is remarkably restrained in comparison to Tulsī's version. Whereas Tulsī's queen-mothers embrace the girls over and over again, blessing them, and sending them off with just one line of instruction, Sagar's Sunayanā gives a long Sanskritic sermon to instruct the girls. Throughout, she acts like a stern schoolteacher, and the young brides listen deferentially, with bowed heads. She has prepared her speech well, and it is worthwhile to take a close look at how she instructs the girls about the duties of married women.

First, a woman's husband is her god, equal to no other. A woman does not need to worship (*pūjā*) anyone but him. A woman's first duty is to give up her own self-interest (*svārth*) and to be concerned only with what fosters her husband's welfare (*kalyāṇ*). That is the only self-denial (*tapasyā*) required of a woman. A woman who is fully, in thought, word, and deed, devoted to her husband (*pativratā*) does not need anyone else's blessing; even God himself is compelled to carry out her wishes (*uskī ājñā ke adhīn*). A woman should be her husband's moral partner (*sahadharmiṇī*) in carrying out his duty. Her highest duty (*uttama dharma*) is to honor her husband's parents. She should only speak after having checked her husband's facial reactions, because even if her

72. Sagar may well have been inspired by Tulsī's pun to that effect in the context of the *pānigahanu* ceremony of Rāma: "How could Videha's king pay his respects, when the image of the dark one [Rāma] had taken him beyond his body [*bidehu*]" (*kyoṃ karai binaya bidehu kiyo bidehu mūrati sāvaṃrīṃ, RCM* 1.324, *chand* 3c).

words would be true, she may be speaking at the wrong moment, with dire results. Finally, she should consider her in-laws' house (*sasurāl*) to be her home, she should never even hint that her own paternal home (*maikā*) is better, and she should even try to forget it altogether (TVR 142–3).

This is a remarkably conservative view of women's duty for a popular series on contemporary television. One can hardly imagine a more explicitly patriarchal statement, and that in the mouth of a woman, the bride's mother. It is apparent that Sagar is keen to explicitly send a conservative message to mothers and young brides, especially if one considers that at this point, there is nothing equivalent in the other source texts discussed here. This stern speech is strikingly different from Tulsī's emotional farewells, and Vālmīki does not mention anything of the kind. Sagar incorporates the one line of advice from the *Mānas,* explaining the suggestion that a woman should read her husband's facial expression and obey his command. For the expansion of the advice, Sagar can claim sanction from a later passage in the *Mānas,* after the exile, where Sītā meets the venerable female ascetic Anasūyā. Much of Sagar's Sunayanā's sermon is reminiscent of Anusūyā's words to Sītā (in *RCM* 3.5).[73] In any case, Sagar works to bring some *Mānas* credentials to the sermon, and throws in a quotation from another later passage, the scene where Rāma tries to dissuade Sītā from following him into exile and says her duty is to serve her mother- and father-in-law (2.61.3a; quoted in TVR 143).

In short, my comparison reveals an important fact. Sunayanā's conservative sermon in Sagar's version is deliberately constructed to look as though it was lifted straight out of the medieval text. Actually, it is based on a single line in Tulsī's corresponding version, which is expanded to the effect that it has become an innovation. Paradoxically, the most modern version here is the most conservative one.

If women are urged to completely subordinate themselves to husband and in-laws, Sagar does not forget to address the other side of the issue, and to stress that in-laws should treat young brides well, even with respect. The scene of Janaka's farewell makes that clear. Janaka pleads with Daśaratha to be patient with the girls, who are after all very young and will need to adjust to the ways of their new environment. Sagar may well be following Tulsī's lead

73. There are some different emphases in Anasūyā's speech. Appropriately for the occasion, she stresses also that a woman should never leave her husband in bad days. She also colorfully describes the dire consequences of any trespasses, including becoming a child widow in one's next birth (*vidhvā hoi pāi tarunāī*). She even gives a classification of the different types of wives, and she also stresses that though a woman may be impure (*apāvani*), she still can reach the highest good (*śubh gati*) via service of the husband.

here again, because Tulsī has a similar scene at the end of the nuptial ceremonies proper.

Janaka asks Daśaratha to treat the new brides generously, and to give these "servants" a place "at his feet" (TVR 144).[74] Daśaratha counters that his new daughters-in-law are goddesses of good luck (*ghar kī lakṣmī*) and that as such their place is rather at the head (114).[75] He promises to treat them as the future queens of Ayodhyā. Janaka lauds this great generosity of the groom's father. As earlier, the stress here is on the graciousness of the groom's party and its lack of display of superiority. That was apparent already at the beginning of the scene when Janaka wanted to touch Daśaratha's feet in subservience and he chided him gently for doing so.

Notwithstanding the plea to treat young brides well, the scene ends again on a note of female subjugation. Tulsī's Janaka simply "instructed his daughter manifold, taught her about women's duty and family ways" (*RCM* 1.339.1a).[76] Sagar's paternal farewell to Sītā is much shorter than Sunayanā's but highlights again the ultimate subordination to a patriarchal system: the bride's conduct must never bring disgrace to the father's or in-laws' good name (TVR 144).[77] Though Janaka has shown concern for his daughters' wellfare, the fear of female sexuality binging dishonor to the family surfaces in these last moments of farewell. After her father's words, a closeup of Sītā's face suggests to the audience all that is to come, and how indeed Sītā will be accused of breaking these rules and be seen as a disgrace to the family.

Finally, Sagar returns to the sentiment of *karuṇā,* or pathos. A proverb is quoted that sets the tone, and is followed by a wedding song of the farewell type called *Bābula.* In this song, the line "Ruthless creator, explain just this: why did you create daughters?" (TVR 145)[78] echoes Tulsī's queens' poignant lament of women's plight (*RCM* 1.344.4b).[79] Paradoxically, by narrowing the lament down to the fate of daughters rather than women in general, the bitter statement in the song is actually opened up to incorporate not only the perspective of the women but also that of the father, as is traditional in the North Indian wedding songs. This is reinforced by the camera showing at this moment Janaka addressing Daśaratha, the latter empathizing with Janaka's plight, and the two embracing.

74. *āpke caraṇoṃ meṃ sthān dījiegā.*
75. *lakṣmī kā sthān caraṇoṃ meṃ nahīṃ, sir-māthe par hī hotā hai.*
76. *bahubidhi bhūpa sutā samujhāīṃ, nāridharmu kularīti sikhāīṃ.*
77. *tumhāre kisī bhī ācaraṇ se tumhāre pitā kī lāj aur sasurāl kī kīrti ko dhakkā na lage.*
78. *niṭhura vidhātā itnā batā de kāhe ko biṭiyā kī jāta banāī.*
79. *kahahiṃ viraṃci racīṃ kata nārīṃ.*

While the voices that sing are female, the camera widens the perspective. During this song, the camera registers the pathos on the faces of all participants, in particular a dignified type of sadness on the part of Janaka, who alone follows the palanquins just a few steps further and then returns despondently, to retreat to the inner quarters of the palace, followed by Sunayanā. Meanwhile, a verse is quoted that voices the sorrow of all participants, but stresses Janaka's: all his happiness, it is said, now belongs to another (TVR 145–6).

In *Rām Carit Mānas,* too, Janaka has followed the *barāt* on its way home for a while, and the exemplary *samadhī* relations and extreme courtesy of both parties has been highlighted. Daśaratha sends Janaka back repeatedly, before he finally returns. The difference is that Tulsī shows Janaka's sadness to be about taking leave of Rāma. When Janaka says goodbye to Rāma, Tulsī turns the farewell into a hymn of praise to Rāma (*RCM* 1.340.4b–342.3a). Clearly, the spirit of bhakti prevailed.

Thus, there are significant differences between Tulsī's and Sagar's texts. Both are drenched in the sentiment of pathos. However, in Tulsī's text, the main concern is an expression of bhakti for Rāma. Sagar is more focused on drawing the audience in by capturing the feelings of a bride's parents, yet at the same time reining in excessive emotion with reference to duty. Even more so than his ancient and medieval sources, Sagar inserts moralizing sermons that seek to reinforce unapologetically a patriarchal normativity. While superficially similar to the older source texts, this version makes a significant shift toward a conservative view of gender relationships.

Sagar, to his credit, also emphasizes the other side of the coin. If *bahūs* are expected to be totally submissive, their in-laws have a responsibility, too, which is to treat them well. This aspect is elaborated in several scenes.

In *Rām Carit Mānas,* King Daśaratha urges his queens to take good care of their new daughters-in-law: "The brides are just girls arrived in a strange house. Take care of them the way eyelids protect the eyes" (1.355.4b).[80] Sagar transforms the scene into a private conversation between Daśaratha and Kauśalyā (who is engaged in sewing) (TVR 148–9). Daśaratha muses about Janaka's worry over sending off his daughters. Kauśalyā points out that the mother must feel even worse. Daśaratha confirms that "only a woman can understand a woman's pain" (148).[81] This nod to the women's perspective is typical for Sagar, and is in line with the scene where Sunayanā talks about her plight to the guru's wife—an innovation, compared to *Rām Carit Mānas.*

80. *badhū larikanīṃ para ghara āīṃ, rākhehu nayana palaka kī nāīṃ.*

81. *strī kī vedanā strī hī samajh saktī hai.*

Sagar's Daśaratha then tells Kauśalyā that he has promised Janaka that the girls will never be uncomfortable at their in-laws' household. It is, he says, Kauśalyā's task to help him keep his word (TVR 148). Kauśalyā, sincerely hurt, asks whether he seriously fears anything less than good treatment. Daśaratha hastens to say that that is not the case, but that they need special care, having arrived in a new environment, and that they need to be loved even more than when they were at home. So mere lack of bad treatment is not enough; special care is required. He echoes Tulsī: "Just like the pupil of the eye is protected between the eyelids, take these four girls under your wings of love" (148).[82] Kauśalyā assures him that this will be done and that within a few days the girls will have forgotten their old home.

In this way, we have come full circle: Sītā's mother instructed her that it is a woman's duty to forget her parental home. In the ideal scenario, this might conceivably be the case, because of the extra love and care of the women in the husband's home. Sagar's point is clearly that if all play their parts the way they are supposed to, a woman's position is enviable indeed. He stresses that women should submit to patriarchy, but he also urges the representatives of patriarchy to reciprocate. If everyone holds up his or her end of dharma, this world will be truly a better place. While feminists may not like Sagar's ultra-patriarchal advice to the women, one has to admit that he balances it with a good example for in-laws.

Promises: Public and Private

Finally, we turn to the issue of gender equality between bride and groom. A significant innovation in the television version is an episode featuring Sītā and Rāma's wedding night as the setting for Rāma's vow of monogamy (*eka-patnīvrata*). There is no exact equivalent for this scene in any of the other *Rāmāyaṇas* I consider. Here, surely, Sagar seems to be progressive. Or is he? I will contrast this scene of a private vow with the formal vows taken at the nuptial ceremony itself in earlier versions.

THE PUBLIC WEDDING VOW. Before looking at Rāma's private wedding vow, I shall revisit the actual nuptial ceremony and analyze the public wedding vow taken there. In *Valmīki Rāmāyaṇa,* Janaka gives Sītā away with the words:

82. *jaise palakoṃ ke bīc āṃkh kī putalī ko sambhālā jātā hai, usī tarah in cāroṃ ko apne pyār ke āṃcal meṃ lapeṭ ke rakhnā.*

"This, my daughter Sītā, is your partner in dharma *[sahadharmacarī]*. Accept her. Take her hand in yours. She has great fortune, is devoted to her husband, and will always follow you like a shadow" (1.73.26b–27b).[83] This formula is spoken just before the ceremony of the groom taking the hand of the bride (*pāṇigraha*) and the circumambulation of the sacred fire. There does not seem to be any corresponding promise from the groom or his father.

The *pāṇigraha* ceremony is one of the rare occasions when Sagar quotes directly from Vālmīki: his Janaka solemnly and theatrically recites the same Sanskrit *ślokas*. In choosing to quote Vālmīki, Sagar is conservative. He does not even use the classical formula that is used even today in wedding ceremonies. In that formula, the father of the bride urges the groom, not to be false to her in dharma, *artha*, and *kāma* (*dharme cārthe ca kāme ca nāticaritavya*, Kane 1974: 519 n. 1209), and the groom has to respond that he will not transgress (*nāticarāmi*, 533).

Whereas Vālmīki and Sagar give the actual wedding formula, Tulsī is silent on that matter. He is instead preoccupied with the feelings of the fathers during this exchange, in particular Daśaratha (*RCM* 1.325, *dohā*). Janaka's touching paternal love and his humility are made explicit as, concerned for the welfare of his daughters in the new house, he addresses Daśaratha: "Make these girls your servants, and cherish them with ever-new forgiveness" (1.326, *chand* 3a).[84] He also asks for forgiveness for his own insistence on establishing the match (1.326, *chand* 2b).[85] Daśaratha returns the civilities. Sagar, too, has Janaka apologize for possible mistakes (TVR 136). As we have seen, he also takes this paternal concern up in the leave-taking rituals. The scene ends with an embrace of the in-laws. Tulsī's wedding ceremony is more a transfer between the fathers of the parties and involves an exchange between them only. Sagar, as we have seen, is elsewhere concerned about the welfare of the new *bahūs*, but he does not make that part of the wedding vows. Instead, he follows the ultratraditional formula of Vālmīki. The woman is promised as a partner in ritual, yet she is self-effacing to the point of becoming his shadow. The groom is not expected to promise anything in return in public.

83. *iyaṃ sītā mama sutā sahadharmacarī tava; pratīccha caināṃ bhadraṃ te pāṇīṃ gṛhīṣva pāṇinā, pativratā mahābhāgā chāyevānugatā sadā*. The same formula is repeated for the other couples. The grooms then take the hands of the brides, and with them circumambulate the fire, the altar, and Janaka and the sages (*VR* I 73.37–39). Incidentally, this formula is foregrounded in the replay of Rāma's wedding in Sagar's *Shri Krishna* Series (vol. II, episode 83).

84. *e dārikā paricārikā kari pālibīṃ karunā naī*.

85. *aparādhu chamibo boli paṭhae bahuta hauṃ ḍīṭyo kaī*.

THE PRIVATE WEDDING VOW. As if to redress this imbalance, Sagar complements the public wedding vow with a private one, spoken by Rāma voluntarily, though only overheard by the audience. We get to voyeuristically view the beginning of the divine couple's first wedding night. As he arrives in the room, his bride is decked out and waiting for him. Rāma tells her that he sees her as an equal, and he promises to be monogamous. There is no precedent for this in either of the other versions. Let us first look at how Vālmīki and Tulsī deal with the wedding night.

In contrast to some other versions,[86] Vālmīki does not report on the wedding night but simply states that after they fulfilled all their obligations, the new brides got to enjoy themselves in private with their husbands (*VR* I 77.13–4). Tulsī's version is surprisingly different. After Daśaratha retires, the queens spread out a wonderful bed, described in loving detail (*RCM* 1.356.1–2), on which they invite Rāma to sleep. Rāma has to repeatedly insist that all the brothers retire for the night, for they are keen to massage his feet. However, if we expect to witness the first wedding night (*suhāg kī rāt*) once he enjoys privacy, we are disappointed. Instead, Tulsī foregrounds the queens' emotions, which are convincingly those of all mothers. We nearly hear them whisper, while they glance at Rāma dozing off, that they cannot quite fathom how their tender boy could have accomplished all the feats they have heard tonight he did, such as killing the terrible demons and breaking the bow (356.4–357.4).[87] Surely this must be the guru's grace. The mothers stay with Rāma till he falls asleep, and Tulsī adds a loving description: "In his sleep too his very handsome face looks like a golden lotus at dusk" (1.358.1a).[88] In the background, we hear songs coming from every house in Ayodhyā (1.358.1b). Finally, the queens go to bed themselves, taking their *bahūs* with them.

What is going on? Tulsī avoids any hint of erotics (*śṛṅgāra rasa*) in favor of vivid motherly feelings (*vātsalya rasa*). The contrast with Krishna bhakti is too obvious to miss. It seems that Tulsī quite consciously seeks to distance himself from the eroticism of the Braj poets. Still, he makes sure bhakti is central. The queens' motherly words form yet another hymn of praise to Rāma.

In the television series, Sagar chooses to ignore Tulsī's *vātsalya* angle, perhaps because there such a portrayal could evoke a hint of child marriage

86. I have in mind the *Mahānāṭaka*, the entire second act of which is devoted to the love play of Sītā and Rāma.

87. This is also the scenario depicted in the Rām-līlā of Rāmnagar; see Kapur 1990: 74–5.

88. *nīdaūṃ badana soha suṭhi lonā, manahuṃ sāṃjha sarasīruha sonā.*

(a much-debated issue with regard to *VR;* for references, see Brockington 1998: 432). Next to dowry, this is another much-debated problem and is an embarrassment to "reformed" Hindus. Middle-class opinion holds that the practice is pretty much confined to unenlightened villagers, so it would not be fitting at all for a leading Kṣatriya family. That is likely why, instead of following Tulsī, Sagar shows the beginning of Rāma and Sītā's wedding night (147–8).

We see Sītā, decked out in all her jewelry, seated on the flower-decorated wedding bed (*phūl-sej*), waiting for her groom to arrive. A *dohā* from *Rām Carit Mānas* is recited that contains Daśaratha's command before he retires: " 'The boys are tired, and overpowered by sleep, go and put them to bed.' Saying thus, the king retired to his bedroom, meditating on Rāma's feet" (*RCM* 1.355, *dohā*).[89] That is totally out of context in the bridal chamber, but Sagar seems to be betting in this case that his audience will get just enough of the *dohā*, thus taken out of context, to think that the meditation on Rāma's feet refers to Sītā. While the reference to Rāma's feet is made, Sītā's meditative face lights up, as she apparently hears his footsteps.

When Rāma enters, they look at each other and smile. She gets up and ever so slowly walks to him and stoops to touch his feet. He stops her, and asks why she does so. Now Sītā gets to speak her very first words in his company. She speaks very emphatically, like a child eager to pronounce clearly. She says that her mother told her that he is her lord (*parameśvar, TVR* 147). Rāma then teases her mildly: "Okay, so you have taken your mother's instruction to heart. Will you also listen to one of my instructions?" (148).[90] Sītā demurely answers, bowing her head: "Please command me, because I am your slave-girl" (148).[91]

The rest of the scene consists of a long sermon by Rāma. First, he redefines the meaning of what a wife should be: not a slave but a partner. He says: "In that case, my first command is that you should not remain my slave (*dāsī*). Be my better half (*arddhāṃginī*), my friend (*mitra*), my mate (*sakhā*), my companion (*sāthī*), walking by my side" (TVR 148). Rāma's word choice is interesting, in that except for the first, all these epithets are masculine. One might speculate that equalization entails a desexualization of the wife. Rāma goes on to explain what the woman's companionship involves: "Take part in every good work I carry out, and if you ever see me lose track of the right path,

89. *larikā śramita unīda basa, sayana karāvahu jāi; asa kahi ge biśrāma gṛha, rāma carana citu lāi.*
90. *māṃ kā upadeś to sun liyā, ab merā ek upadeś sunogī?*
91. *ājñā kījiye, maiṃ to āpkī dāsī hūṃ.*

keep me from getting astray. That is the duty of a true friend, of a real companion" (148). There is some irony in Sagar putting these words in Rāma's mouth. After all, he is *maryādāpuruṣa,* a paragon of virtue, himself. Since Sagar's Rāma is set up as an example, we should also consider the real-life implications of this statement. In effect, he is saying that women are to keep their men on the right track. This transfers the burden of responsibility for the man's moral character to the woman's care!

Rāma continues with a promise: "Mother Kaikeyī told me that I should make sure to give you a present to keep the memory of the first meeting alife. I have brought a gift. It is not one of pearls or diamonds. By way of gift, I give you today a promise. [You know that] kings have the custom to take many queens, but in Rāma's life there will never be anyone but you. This is Rāma's oath. Do you know when I first took this oath? When I saw you for the first time in the flower garden, just this way!" (TVK 148). Sītā does not receive any spectacular diamond ring or set of pearls. Instead, she gets the most valuable thing for a woman, namely a vow of fidelity from her husband.

Sagar's Rāma is quite in character here with his earlier statement of marital faithfulness in the company of his brothers. Of course, Rāma is popularly considered to have taken just one wife, as is expressed by the epithet "monogamous by vow" (*ekapatnīvratadhara*). Vālmīki does not describe a scene where Rāma takes such a vow, though in his story Rāma does not take another wife after banishing Sītā, and of course, throughout the epic Rāma and Sītā are very devoted to one another (Brockington 1998: 433). Still, there is some debate about whether there are hints at other wives of Rāma in *Vālmīki Rāmāyaṇa* (Brockington 1984: 173). Tulsī never uses the term with reference to Rāma, which is surprising. He must have been aware of it, since it was current at least since the ninth century: it occurs in *Bhāgavata Purāṇa* (9.10.55). One may infer that Tulsī did consider Rāma monogamous, because he says later that all males in Rāma's kingdom (Rāmrājya) took a vow of monogamy (*eka nārī vrata;* he hastens to add that the women, too, were devoted to their husbands in deed, word, and thought, *RCM* 7.22.4). Still, it seems that nowhere in *Rām Carit Mānas* is it described how Rāma took that vow, certainly not during the wedding night. In short, Sagar manages to make his scene look traditional, but again, this is an innovation.

At first sight, the scene sends a positive message. Certainly, Rāma's tenderness and wonderful tact on the first wedding night set a great example. And all what he says is politically correct. Woman is explicitly lifted in status from subordinate to equal to man. Marriage is a bond between companions, not a subordinating relationship. To top it off, there is Rāma's promise of if not quite explicitly fidelity at least monogamy. Women might rejoice over Sagar's portrayal of this excellent example for mortal men.[92]

However, there is a catch; the linking of woman's partnership and her custody of the man's morality with the man's faithfulness is in itself a tricky proposition. Does the former become a condition to be fulfilled before the latter is imperative? If the final responsibility for the husband's morality is in the woman's, not the man's, hands, does that mean that he cannot be blamed? In other words, does she first have to deserve his fidelity before it can be granted, and is she then, too, the one who has to wakefully secure it? And has she only to blame herself if he goes astray?

It is also significant that the promise is prefaced very emphatically by Sītā's own attitude of self-subjugation. Implicitly, it seems, this is set up as a sine qua non. Deserving women, that is, women who are prepared to play the subordinate role, are promised a monogamous relationship. It does not take much imagination to see the other side of the coin: women who are not subordinate do not deserve such consideration. The way the episode is portrayed seems to reinforce the old stereotype after all.

Finally, it is striking that Rāma lifting Sītā from a state of *dāsī* to that of *arddhāṃginī* explicitly takes the form of a command (*ājñā*). Is it not a contradiction in terms that a man commands his wife to be his equal? Rāma's tone is patronizing: he knows what is best (for them, if not for her). Sītā does not get to answer; she merely smiles, presumably overcome with happiness about everything he says. Obviously, it is not expected that she will reciprocate his promise. That would be totally superfluous. If his monogamy is a gift, hers is a given.

Comparing Sītā's Wedding Ceremonies

What can we conclude from the detailed analysis of the wedding ceremonies of Sītā and Rāma? How does the television version follow and differ from its sources? Sagar is well in tune with Tulsī in the main. Tulsī's version of the wedding is itself an attempt to wed dharma and bhakti. Hymns of praise and expressions of deep emotion are interspersed with references to obeisance to elders and gurus, zeal for ritual precision, and strict observation of caste

92. Moving beyond gender issues, one could say that the scene also has an apologetical ring to it. Sagar's linking of these issues is typical for a discourse of modernity: "In the old days, when women were regarded as slaves, polygamy was the norm. Now, women can become full partners, so monogamy prevails." At the same time, it enforces a Hindu chauvinist discourse—that even in those unenlightened days, when other civilizations still practiced polygamy, Rāma got it right.

TABLE 3.1. Versions of Sītā's Wedding Ceremony Compared

Element	VR	RCM	TVR
Relation between bride's and groom's party	Equality stressed	Amazement at equality	Amazement at equality, stressed in editorial comment
Nature of matrimony	Lineage recitation	Lineage mentioned only in passing	Family matter; preordained love
Mood of ceremony	Solemn	Loving informality	Solemn
Devotional tone	Little	*Darśana;* praise of Rāma	*Darśana,* but not for Sītā
Divine sanction	Gods shower flowers 1x	Many flower showers Gods present	Gods present
Nature of rites	Vedic/Brahminical	Vedic and folk/women	mixture; sanitized
Dowry	*Kanyādhana*	*Daheja* described	Gifts mentioned, not shown
Farewell	Matter of fact	Tearful, emotional	Restrained, didactic
Advice to bride	No advice	One line of advice	Long sermons for bride; balanced with in-law assurance
Vows	Stress on bride's obedience	Vow not stated	*VR* quoted
Monogamy	Not mentioned	Not mentioned	Rāma's wedding gift
Wedding night	*śṛṅgāra* in private	*Vātsalya* of queens	Sītā's shyness and humility; Rāma's uplifting sermon

dharma. Sagar, too, tries to have it both ways. Many have remarked on Sagar's bhakti agenda and the way he exploits the medium of television to provide multiple occasions for *darśana.* However, what is less commonly realized is that in comparison to Tulsī's medieval version, the balance has shifted away from emotional bhakti and toward strong endorsement of dharma.

Sagar's privileging of dharma over bhakti is clear from the many occasions where he turns down Tulsī's emotional pitch and gives more airtime to preaching dharma. *Darśana* is balanced with *śravana,* moral instruction. This becomes very apparent if we add up how many of Tulsī's hymns in praise of Rāma have been dropped and replaced with moralizing sermons. On several occasions, Sagar suppresses Tulsī's *darśana* verses in favor of reinforcing dharma. One example is the adoration of the *kuladevī* after the wedding ceremonies are over, where Sagar substitutes Tulsī's *nakha-śikha* description of Rāma with a pedestrian song stressing the *dhārmika* nature of the event.

Sagar's bhakti, in other words, is suffused with dharma. Sagar's message is that emotional devotion needs to be restrained and disciplined, and emotional excess strongly discouraged. This is perhaps most striking on the occasion of the leave-taking of the *barāt,* where Tulsī's scenes are drenched in pathos, or *karuṇā rasa,* and he indulges in a description of all Sītā's relatives crying their full. Sagar instead uses the occasion to warn against excessive emotions. One example of now he innovates to make this point is the scene where Sunayanā confesses her trepidations about her daughter to the guru's wife and gets chided for not restraining her emotions better. Another example is the scene of her farewell sermon to Sītā. Hardly any emotion is allowed to surface till after a long lecture on women's dharma.

Of all the classical types of bhakti, it seems, Sagar has worked deliberately to stay safely away from the *śṛṅgāra* mode. Instead, he favors modes like serenity (*śānti*) and servitude (*dāsya*). The latter comes to the fore most strongly in the wedding scene where Janaka washes Rāma's feet. Sagar dwells on the scene for a comparatively long time, which seems significant in assessing his bhakti preferences.

Sagar's privileging of dharma over bhakti is most apparent with regard to Sītā, and has also its repercussions for the way she functions as a role model. Everything she does is always with due respect for elders, and her attitude toward Rāma is one of unquestioning subordination. She gets to consider herself to be his partner rather than his slave, but it is only by his command that she consents to do so. As in Krishna bhakti, the ideal loving devotee is God's beloved, yet Sītā's conjugal love seems light years away from Rādhā's *śṛṅgāra,* and shows more affinity with *dāsya* bhakti.

Comparing Sagar to Vālmīki, it is apparent how much more the latter focuses on women's rites and women's perspective. Again, he has this in common with Tulsī, but one should also refer to the context. Sagar's series was shown on Doordarshan, where several previous serials had women-oriented narratives (Mankekar 1999: 104). These serials were set in a joint-family context (110), and Sagar's "soap opera of the gods" turns out also to be family focused. This perspective, one we do not find in Tulsī, seems to have inspired many of Sagar's innovations. It seems to be in response to the new ideological push towards forgrounding individuality that he repeatedly stresses that the wedding is a family and not an individual affair.

Sagar's picture of the joint family is very rosy. In his ideal epic world, there is no tension between the bride's party and the groom's party or between mother-in-law and daughter-in-law (or, for that matter, between cowives). Interestingly, stress on unusual harmony of these traditional dyads is not new and is already present in *Vālmīki Rāmāyaṇa.* What is new is that in his editorial comments, Sagar explicitly recommends following the epic example. The message sent to the groom's family is to treat the bride's family with respect and the new brides, once they arrive, with loving understanding. In his editorial comments, Sagar says that if people followed this example a lot of tensions would disappear from "our society" and the *Rāmāyaṇa* story would come true. Is he suggesting that the tensions are later accretions, whereas the pure Hindu ideal does not insist on the inequalities? In fact, my analysis of *Vālmīki Rāmāyaṇa* has shown that already in the earliest text there is a hint of those tensions between the givers and takers of brides.

When Sagar asks his audience to follow the royal house of Ayodhyā's example, he chooses to tacitly pass over one of the key problems in contemporary weddings, the issue of dowry. By mentioning Sītā's dowry obliquely, in passing, he seems to condone the practice, or at least he does not condemn it, and he classifies it in the category of auspicious elements that constitute a successful wedding. This unwillingness to confront the issue directly is all the more suspect because Sagar does show the problem of the plight of the father of the bride, by dwelling on Janaka's despair. He does so without ever touching on the issue of dowry, which remains a specter hovering in the background. Probably he considered it too hot to touch. Certainly it would be hard to please all parties: the issue is not welcomed in Hindutva discourse, and it would be difficult to appease feminist misgivings, too.

As Sagar portrays it, the secret of the happy joint family is obedience to elders and male dominance. At every step, Sagar is keen to highlight the submissive attitude of his characters, even of Rāma himself, toward paternal and elder male authority. To some extent, this was already the case in *Vālmīki Rāmāyaṇa*, and more so in *Rām Carit Mānas*. However, Sagar definitely goes furthest. His characters show impeccably respectful behavior and obedience to elders in thought, word, and deed. During the whole wedding ceremony, Sagar's Rāma and Sītā are shown not to look at each other out of respect for decorum, whereas Tulsī explicitly added a verse to describe their beholding of each other.

So what kind of role model has Sagar set up? First, his message to the young stresses the priority of the family over the individual. This is clear in several of his innovations, most explicitly in Vasiṣṭha's lecture about the social importance of a wedding. Sagar is very explicit: a wedding is a meeting of families, not of hearts.

Further, the message to young women about their marital duties is remarkably conservative. Notwithstanding all the stress on women's perspectives and the airtime given to women's rituals, which creates the illusion of empowerment of women, Sagar's characters endorse unabashedly patriarchal values. Sunayanā's instruction (*upadeśa*) to the young brides and Janaka's parting words to Sītā are quite explicit statements to that effect. Sagar's emphasis is all the more remarkable because, contrary to what one might suspect, he does not base these passages directly on his sources.

Another example of Sagar being more conservative than Tulsī is the wedding vow scene. Sagar follows Vālmīki and solely refers to the bride's duties, without adding the groom's corresponding promise, as prescribed in the classical sources, not to transgress against his wife in dharma, *artha,* and *kāma.* Sagar seems concerned to stress women's duties rather than women's rights. One could argue that Sagar makes up for this in the wedding night scene, where Rāma makes his promise of monogamy. However, the husband's exclusive commitment to the woman is not presented as her right but as a favor.

More than Vālmīki or Tulsī, Sagar seems to promise that if (and only if) a young bride is ready to subjugate herself to her husband's family, she will encounter love and understanding. Ditto for the relationship between husband and wife. If she is prepared to unconditionally obey him, his command will be that she should be his equal, his partner, rather than a *dāsī.* He may even promise to return her exclusive devotion. In both cases, the outcome for women seems liberating, but in both cases it is actually predicated on the condition of a woman's subjugation. A woman's subjugation is always a given, whereas anything she receives in return is portrayed as a gift. In Sagar's world there is lots of scope for women's rites, but not women's rights.

The Love-Marriage Rites of Rādhā and Krishna

If Sītā and Rāma's wedding is the ultimate parentally sanctioned society wedding, the secret love marriage of Rādhā and Krishna can be seen as its opposite. The problem here is that not all sources depict their nuptials, because the tradition overwhelmingly understands Rādhā and Krishna's love as illicit, exemplary in the fervor of its passion, which is exactly heightened by its lack of societal sanction. Thus, neither *Bhāgavata Purāṇa* nor the television series *Shri Krishna* has a comparable episode. Nevertheless, the tradition is not unequivocal, and some sources read wedding ceremonies into the relationship of Rādhā and Krishna in some way.

One Sanskrit source, *Brahma Vaivarta Purāṇa,* describes the wedding in unusual terms. The Braj Bhāṣā poems are of two types, those that speak of a secret or even subversive wedding and those that describe an actual wedding ceremony, which comes closest to Sītā and Rāma's nuptials. In several *Sūr Sāgar* poems, the poet reads secret wedding vows into the Rāsa-līlā. Others (including all Nanddās's poems on the topic) have a more straightforward description of a wedding celebrated by the whole community.

In *Sūr Sāgar,* the wedding poems are all collected under the rubric "Śrī Kṛṣṇa Vivāha Varṇana," a subsection of poems in the midst of the Rāsa-līlā section. This title is a bit of a misnomer: there are not many poems explicitly about the ceremony, and some of them merely have an isolated reference to Rādhā and Krishna as bride and groom. And most of the marriage poems are not found in the earliest manuscripts we have for Sūrdās (Hawley 1984: 86–8).

Since the sources dealing with Rādhā and Krishna's marriage are so diverse, it seems most appropriate to deal with them one by one, instead of with an item-by-item comparison as for the Sītā-Rāma wedding. I will first discuss the absence of reference to a wedding in Sagar's *Shri Krishna*, then describe the wedding episode from the Sanskrit *Brahma Vaivarta Purāṇa*, and finally analyze the lovely vernacular versions attributed to Sūrdās and Nanddās.

Sagar's "Shri Krishna": Lovers Do Not Marry

The first point to establish regarding the marriage of Rādhā and Krishna is that it is a contradiction in terms. Rādhā and Krishna are nearly by definition unwed sweethearts. They are usually imagined as eternally young and pubescent, at the tender age of first love and its sweet, passionate fervor. Rādhā's love is supposedly unmarred by considerations of matrimony, in fact heightened by the tension between the role of "adorable daughter" (*lāṛilī*) at home and secret lover during trysts. Interestingly, that is the way Sagar portrays Rādhā in his *Shri Krishna*.

Three episodes (TVK vol. 7, episodes 53–55) deal with the blossoming love between Rādhā and Krishna. We see them grow up, in the course of a song (halfway episode 53), from childhood to adolescent sweethearts. After the song we witness the rather chaste conversation of the now adolescent pair by the river, where they have a tryst. They are—by contemporary film norms—quite innocently sitting together holding hands. Even so, Rādhā is concerned about propriety. This comes to the fore as they are interrupted by Rādhā's mother calling out to her. When asked where she was, Rādhā's friends cover for her (episode 54). They say that they were all playing near the river and Rādhā nearly fell in when a cowherd from Gokul grabbed her hand just in time. This faint hint at Rādhā's romance is luckily not understood by the mother, who is preoccupied with a meeting the elders are having about the upcoming festival of Holī.

Next we see the celebration of this festival of color and passion, which provides the occasion for Rādhā and Krishna to publicly display their newly aroused feelings for each other. To some extent, this can be seen as a substitute for the wedding ceremony, in that it constitutes a public ritual introducing the intimacy between the two lovers. While the images remain fairly chaste, the song vocalizes some of the sexual desires beneath the surface, and indeed, this scene is followed immediately by Rādhā and Krishna's first "night" together. That scene, too, is chaste; we are merely witnessing a reluctant Rādhā being urged by her friends to join Krishna, who walks her to a bower while a song vocalizes what is going to happen. We do not get to witness any of the lovemaking; we just see the couple after the fact, engaged in playful, presumably postcoital, banter (beginning episode 55).

In the light of Sagar's elaborate legitimations of the couple's first love, it might be surprising that he does not attempt to sanctify their union with the propriety of a marriage, especially because he cites the *Brahma Vaivarta Purāṇa* in his list of credits at the beginning of each episode, and that Purāṇa does make room for a wedding ceremony. Instead of a Rādhā-Krishna wedding, Sagar provides in his later episodes a repetition of the wedding of Rāma and Sītā. As noted, this occurs in the context of Krishna's education, where Krishna's guru relates summaries of the other classical avatars of Vishnu, especiallty Rāma. Sagar could for the purpose recycle material from his *Ramayan*, and one can see this as his selection of "greatest hits" from it. Significantly, the retake excludes Sītā's fire ordeal but dwells lovingly on the wedding ceremony (TVK vol. 11, end of episode 88).

The lack of marital sanction for the Rādhā-Krishna romance is compensated for by the fact that the whole romance takes place as a flashback, or rather is witnessed as it occurs by the divine couple in heaven. Thus, while the earthly Rādhā and Krishna are allowed to be unwedded secret lovers, as tradition overwhelmingly demands, a measure of legitimacy and sanction is ensured by the presence of the divine eternal couple fondly witnessing their own play on earth. This stratagem may well be inspired by the *Brahma Vaivarta Purāṇa*, as will become clear in the next section. The episode of the wedding there, though, takes a totally different line of interpretation, which merits some closer study.

An Unusual Wedding in "Brahma Vaivarta Purāṇa"

THE CHILD GROOM AND THE MATURE BRIDE: VĀTSALYA AND ŚṚṄGĀRA. In *Brahma Vaivarta Purāṇa*, the story of the wedding occurs in the midst of Krishna's childhood exploits. At the outset, he is portrayed as a child, while Rādhā is a young woman. The point of departure is the same as in Jayadeva's famous twelfth-century *Gītagovinda*, though the scene is evoked much less poetically and less ambiguously. While Jayadeva masterfully condensed much information into his first verse, here the situation is sketched in several rather pedestrian verses. Krishna's father, Nanda, is taking his little boy out to the woods to let the cows graze (*BVP* 15.40.1–2), but a storm is brewing

(15.40.3–5).[93] As little Krishna acts frightened, Nanda wonders what to do. Should he leave the cows and take Krishna home for safety (15.40.6–7)? The solution is the same as in *Gītagovinda:* Rādhā will take Krishna home, and it is on the way home that their love blossoms. This depiction of Rādhā as older than Krishna has elicited much comment (on the first verse of *Gītagovinda,* see Miller 1977: 16–7 and ns.). Of course, the issue can be explained away by the fact that Krishna and Rādhā are eternal and their ages during their *līlā* on earth do not matter against that background. However, in a post-Freudian world, the issue seems fraught with controversy. Though some early movies follow the convention of portraying an older Rādhā (notably Homi Wadia's *Shri Krishna leela*), most contemporary versions shy away from this potentially controversial portrayal. Still, the age difference is culturally not an unfamiliar phenomenon. One can think of folk songs about women married to child grooms—for example, in cases where widows are remarried to their husband's younger brother (Chowdhry 2005: 118–21).

In *Brahma Vaivarta Purāṇa* already we sense some uneasiness with the issue of an affair between a child and an adult woman. This manifests itself in many ways. First, after the initial situation is established, with the description of Krishna afraid in a storm, the tone changes to the miraculous and deviates markedly from *Gītagovinda* (though the words may be chosen to allude to that famous first verse). Rādhā appears in all her luster, a timeless goddess rather than an adult cowherdess. Nanda immediately recognizes her as the Great Goddess, mother of the universe, and he addresses her as such, specifying that he knows, thanks to the sage Garga, that she is Lakṣmī, the darling of Hari (*BVP* 15.40.8–10).[94] One could see in this recognition of Rādhā as Vishnu's darling an attempt to justify the unusual erotic desires of the adult woman for the young child.

Further justification follows. Nanda is fully aware of what will happen once Rādhā and Krishna are alone: he makes it clear that he also knows the identity of little Krishna as Vishnu (*BVP* 15.40.10b), and he asks her not to take little Krishna home but instead to fulfill her desire, and give him back to him after that (15.40.11).[95] Rādhā accepts the baby (15.40.12) and addresses Nanda: he is to guard this secret (*rahasyakam*) that he knows as the result of his good

93. In this Purāṇa's didactic style, nothing is left to the devotee's interpretation; the storm is explicitly said to have been caused by Krishna's *māyā* (15.40.3).

94. *jānāmi tvāṃ gargamukhāt padmādhikapriyāṃ hareḥ.*

95. *paścād dāsyasi matputraṃ kṛtvā pūrṇaṃ manoratham.*

luck in previous births (15.40.13). Though preordained by Garga, this secret (*gopya*) course of action of Rādhā and Krishna should not be put into words (*akathya*). Somewhat at odds with the story line, she adds that he should return to Gokul, and she gives him a boon (15.40.14–5). Nanda asks to be eternally near her and Krishna, and she grants his wish (15.40.16–20). Thus, there is no question of Rādhā abusing Nanda's trust by becoming erotically involved with the child entrusted to her care. Rather, at the story level, all parties recognize the divinity of the pair. Moreover, the sage Garga foretold what would happen. Care is thus taken to keep Rādhā blameless. At the same time, there is an acute awareness that the noninitiated might find a hint of scandal. Thus the precaution is taken of articulating this as a secret (*rahasya*).

With all doubts removed, Rādhā can be portrayed as taking Krishna far away, to Vrindāban, as it turns out, holding him at her breast, kissing him again and again, which is said to *remind* her of the Rāsa-līla (*BVP* 15.40.21–2), which, of course, is yet to come in the story. But as Rādhā is divine, one can say that ordinary linear time does not apply. Next Rādhā has an elaborate vision of the youthful (*kiśora*) Krishna in a pavilion (*maṇḍapa*, 15.40.23–9). It is not clear whether this is merely a vision (whether of the future or a memory of the past) or involves an actual transformation of Krishna, but the latter seems to be the case. At this point, Krishna addresses her for the first time:

> Rādhā, do you remember what happened in Goloka, in the midst of the gods?
> Today I will fulfill what I agreed to before, o my love. (*BVP* 14.40.30)[96]

As in the television series, this evokes the same image of the eternal pair seated in Goloka hovering over the two lovers. However, the roles are reversed: here the couple on earth remembers divine incidents rather than the other way around. Actually, instead of fondly remembering, Krishna turns theological, stressing his ontological connection with Rādhā. He elaborates on the identity of the two of them with a long set of comparisons (*BVP* 15.40.31–3) and calls her his *śakti, prakṛti,* and so on (15.40.34–6). Rādhā confirms this, and—in rather humble terms for a Great Goddess—asks him to bring her sorrow of separation from him (*viraha*) to an end (15.40.37–41). Krishna asks her to be patient, arguing that they have to wait for the right moment that the creator has preordained (15.40.43–5), a rather deterministic argument. This whole conversation is perfectly in accord, though, with the tone of the divine pair's

96. *rādhe smarasi golokavṛttāntaṃ surasaṃsadi, adya pūrṇaṃ kariṣyāmi svīkṛtaṃ yat purā priye.*

conversations in Sagar's televised series, where Krishna has a definite penchant for theological monologues and Rādhā is mostly humble in her rejoinders. Rādhā often complains about the pangs of separation she suffers, and Krishna keeps reminding her of her divine duty and not to act before the time is right.

THE MOST ORTHODOX OFFICIANT: BRAHMĀ HIMSELF. She does not have to wait long. Hardly has Krishna mentioned predestination before the creator god, Brahmā, appears on the scene, wedding garland (*mālā*) and vessel with sacred water (*kamaṇḍalu*) in hand (*BVP* 15.40.46–7). The implication clearly is that he is ready to perform a wedding ceremony, although that is not commented on. Rādhā has only asked for an end to suffering *viraha,* but it is obviously interpreted as a desire for wedlock.

In Brahmā's presence, things turn very formal. Several verses describe his proper obeisance: he respectfully bows to Krishna first, then to Rādhā (*BVP* 15.40.48–50). However, he sings a hymn of praise for Rādhā alone, whose vision, he relates, he has obtained, thanks to a boon of Krishna after many centuries of *tapas,* or penance (15.40.51–9). Rādhā in turn now grants him a boon, and he asks for bhakti for both of them, which is granted (15.40.60–2). Brahmā's is a careful balancing act of cosmological precedence: yes, he bows to Krishna first, but yes, he states that Rādhā's vision was the hardest to get, and he has Krishna to thank for it. He also wisely asks for bhakti of both together.

At that point, without Rādhā being asked whether she wants to marry Krishna, the marriage ceremony starts: Brahmā lights a Vedic fire (*BVP* 15.40.63–5), makes Rādhā and Krishna go around it (15.40.66), arranges for the *pāṇigrahaṇa,* or ceremonial taking of the hand of the bride, reciting the appropriate mantras (15.40.67–9), and has them put the garlands around each other's necks (15.40.70–1); finally he seats Rādhā to Krishna's left, reciting further from the Veda (15.40.72–3). A comparison follows: that Brahmā turns towards Krishna like the bride's father (15.40.74).[97] The gods then appear on the scene celebrating the occasion with much fanfare, playing instruments (*dundubhi, ānaka,* and *muraja*) and showering flowers (15.40.74–5). Celestial beings sing and dance (15.40.76). Brahmā asks for his sacrificial fee (*dakṣiṇā*) and once again wants *bhakti* for the divine pair, which is granted again, and then he departs (15.40.77–80).

97. *kanyakāñca yathā tāto bhaktyā tasthau haraiḥ puraḥ.*

What to make of this unusual ceremony? For one, *Brahma Vaivarta Purāṇa* has come up with a wonderful legitimizing stroke for Rādhā and Krishna's love making—not only by arranging their wedding ceremony but also by making none other than Brahmā himself preside over it, consequently allaying all doubts of its legitimacy. If Brahmā presides, it must be a superorthodox wedding ceremony. We see echoes here of Sītā and Rāma's wedding, where the Vedic gods were also said to help in performing the rituals. The gods are ever-ready to celebrate the event with flowers showering from heaven, as they are in Tulsī's description of the Sītā-Rāma wedding and, as we shall see, in vernacular traditions of the Rādhā-Krishna wedding. Interestingly, Brahmā shows the same lack of greed about the fee he receives as the gurus in Tulsī's version of Sītā's wedding. An interesting difference from Tulsī, though, is that all the rites are Vedic; there is no mention of women's rites.

In *Brahma Vaivarta Purāṇa,* Brahmā has a double role to play: he acts both as officiant of the marriage ceremony and as the father, giving away the bride. In its wording, the text evokes the ceremony of *kanyādāna* rather than Gāndharva-vivāha. Thus full legitimacy is ensured for any forthcoming love-making between the lovers. That is indeed the main concern, and Brahmā is dismissed immediately after he has received due payment for the wedding.

THE WEDDING NIGHT: AN ANTICLIMAX. Once Brahmā is gone, we expect the lovemaking to proceed. Rādhā certainly seems to do so, too, as she gets excited and shy and prepares the bed for lovemaking (*BVP* 15.40.81–3). However, there is an unexpected turn of events again, because Krishna abruptly turns into a crying child (15.40.84–5). Disappointed, Rādhā also bursts out in tears and asks

> How come, O lord of illusion, that you delude a maid-servant like me? (15.40.87)[98]

This reversal to a child at the moment of the consummation of the wedding invites psychoanalytical analysis with reference to male anxieties it may bespeak. And Rādhā's reaction is telling. In contrast to earlier, now the mood of erotics (*śṛṅgāra rasa*) is considered incongruent with that of motherly feelings (*vātsalya bhāva*). Whereas earlier Rādhā had kissed the child Krishna and been reminded of their erotic union, now the crying child spoils the fun, so to speak.

Only a divine voice can save the situation, and thus happens. A voice in the sky reprimands Rādhā: she should stop crying and meditate instead on Krishna's lotus feet. Basically she is asked to behave in an enlightened way and

98. *māyāṃ karoṣi māyeśa kiṃkarīṃ katham īdṛśīm?*

return home (that is to say: place her body double (*chāyā*) in her home). She is promised she will sport with Krishna at the night of the Rāsa (*BVP* 15.40. 88–90). As a token of things to come, the stage all set for the Rāsa appears. When Rādhā sees this, she picks up the baby without further ado (15.40.91–2), leaving Vrindāban for Gokul, where she gives the child back to Yaśodā and hurries on home (15.40.93–7). Yaśodā promptly puts the crying baby at her breast, while Rādhā gets back to work (15.40.98). The chapter ends with a formulaic verse (15.40.99).

At the end of the *Brahma Vaivarta Purāṇa* episode then, there is a strong split between the lover and mother figures. Once Krishna turns into a crying baby, Rādhā hurriedly delivers him to Yaśodā, who is the one who will comfort him by laying him at her breast. In this text, the role of lover seems to preclude that of mother and taking care of the infant's needs. All of these problems are avoided by having the lovers be of similar age in the televised version as well as in the medieval ones.

At this point, one is reminded of the portrayal of the wedding night of Sītā and Rāma in Tulsīdās's epic. There, too, the tone shifted to one of maternal love (*vātsalya bhāva*), with the mothers marveling of how their little Rāma has grown. The contrast with the erotic mood (*śṛṅgāra rasa*) there is not as abrupt, though. The role of mother and lover is not confused. And there is no question of an incongruence in age, as there is between Rādhā and Krishna in the *Brahma Vaivarta Purāṇa* episode. Tulsī's main point was the promotion of bhakti. In *Brahma Vaivarta Purāṇa*, rather, the intent is didactic. Delayed gratification seems to be the important lesson taught here. That is indeed also the case in Sagar's *Shri Krishna*. Though Rādhā is portrayed as reluctant about the first rendezvous, at other meetings she takes the initiative to see Krishna and is reprimanded by him for her impatience to be with him.

In conclusion, even in *Brahma Vaivarta Purāṇa* we detect an uneasiness about incorporating the consummation of the wedding while Krishna is still a child. One wonders whether this, and the disturbing factor of the age difference between Rādhā and Krishna, might be the reason the passage lacks popularity and indeed Sagar chose not to include it. In any case, it is a significant difference with the vernacular sources, in which, at the time of his wedding, Krishna is more mature, an adolescent boy (*kiśora*), and Rādhā is of similar age (*kiśorī*).

Secret and Folk Wedding Ceremonies: The Bhakti Songs

GĀNDHARVA-VIVĀHA: SUBTLY UNDERMINING BRAHMINICAL RITES. The medieval bhakti traditions are quite different, yet pick up the faint connection with the Rāsa-līlā, also made in *Brahma Vaivarta Purāṇa*. That fits the bill well for the compilers of *Sūr Sāgar*, who had to decide where to include the wedding episode, as of course it does not fit their scheme of following *Bhāgavata Purāṇa*'s sequence for ordering the poems. Since the scripture does not include the episode, the compilers had to resort to some ingenuity and ended up including the poems in the midst of the Rāsa-līlā.[99]

In doing so, the compilers may be following hints in the poetry itself, or the other way around—the very first poem may well have been created for the purpose of making *Sūr Sāgar* fit the *Bhāgavata Purāṇa* straitjacket:

> What Vyās describes as the Rāsa
> Is a Gāndharva Wedding, if one pays attention. Listen to the
> different sports. (*SS* 1689/1071)[100]

The ritual of the wedding is superimposed on the Rāsa-līlā itself. The suggestion is that the discerning eye ("if one pays attention") will find underlying all the elements of the Rāsa, aspects of a secret wedding ceremony. Thus, there is more to the Rāsa-līlā than meets the eye. Luckily we have a good guide, who has a discerning eye. Though he may have been blind to the physical world, Sūrdās was attuned to the nuances of Rādhā and Krishna's love play. Significantly, he signs off at the end of the first poem with the epithet *rasika*, or connoisseur:[101]

> Taking in the passion of that passionate Rāsa, is the connoisseur
> Sūrajdās. (*SS* 1689/1071)[102]

This signature has to be understood against the view that the interpretation of Rāsa-līlā as a Gāndharva wedding rite is for those who pay attention, for "connoisseurs" only. Our *rasika* poet is able to identify for us the different parts of the secret wedding ceremonies, and he does so in detail in this and the following poems. I quote here selectively, following the chronology of the wedding ceremonies.

99. If we look closely at the poems included under the heading of *vivāha* (*SS* 1:498–502), we find that only the first five are unambiguous wedding songs, and those are the ones I will discuss here. The others are actually just poems on Rāsa themes, describing the couple, but not explicitly referring to a wedding in any way. Some include references to symbols of married status (*SS* 1694/1076 contains a reference to *sindūr*), but most (*SS* 1077–80) are generic song-and-dance poems (poems 1081–4 are more erotic, and thus seem unlikely candidates to be included under the "wedding ceremony" rubric).

100. *jākauṃ byāsa baranata rāsa; hai gaṃdharba bibāha cita dai, sunau bibidha bilāsa.*

101. In calling himself *rasika*, the poet places himself in the Rasika tradition of Vrindāban, which produced a substantial amount of poetry on the topic for the festival celebrating Rādhā and Krishna's wedding.

102. *leta yā rasa-rāsa kau rasa, rasika sūrajadāsa.*

The first and obligatory stage has to do with the astrological calculations to determine the correct moment to perform weddings. So, the auspicious date of the wedding is stressed, which is of course the full moon of autumn:

> They established the marriage for the night of autumn. After due determination,[103] the guru performed the Rāsa. (*SS* 1689/1071)[104]

Then follows a difficult task: we need to read into the Rāsa-līlā evidence of the groom's procession (*barāt*). Luckily, Sūr fills us in on that:

> Cupid's soldiers were in the groom's party, the trees in the forest rejoiced in unprecedented ways;
> Gods, like bards, got together to sing praise; the Thunder god [Indra] drummed blissfully away. (*SS* 1690/1072) [105]

Sūrdās is quite clever in his interpretation with fancy wordplay. He finds evidence of the rite of welcome extended to the groom, involving oblation of honey (*madhuparka*), in the way the Gopīs offer the honey from their lips (*adhara-madhu*):

> They receive the groom with honey (*madhuparka*): the oblation is the nectar from their lips; their faces smile. (*SS* 1689/1071)[106]

Of course a wedding requires a bridal pavillion (*maṇḍapa*) and an altar, but not to worry, Rādhā's girlfriends, the *sakhī* s took care of that:

> They spread with flowers the bower-pavillion, and made an altar on the riverbanks. (*SS* 1690/1072)[107]

In case anyone would worry about Vedic hymns, no problem, in fact the women's ritual singing upstages the chanting of the Vedas:

> They sang sacred songs of many kinds, a beautiful sound agreeable to the Vedas. (*SS* 1690/1072)[108]

Finally, no wedding is complete without the seven turns around the fire, or *sāt pherā,* and the poet helps us see this in the pirouettes of the round

103. The verb *sodh-* can mean in Braj "to determine an auspicious date" (*OHED*).

104. *dharī lagna ju sarada nisi kī, sodhi kari guru rāsa.*

105. *manamatha sainika bhae barātī, druma phūle bana anupama bhāṃtī; sura baṃdījana mili jasa gāe, maghavā bājana anaṃda bajāe.* This is one of the few wedding poems that can be found in an old manuscript, dated 1641, from Bikaner, but Hawley conjectures that it might have been an addition by a manuscript compiler in need of an introductory verse for the section on Rādhā and Krishna's *śṛṅgāra* (1984: 87 n. 28)

106. *adhara-madhu madhuparaka kari kai, karata ānana hāsa.*

107. *chāe ju phūlani kuṃja maṃḍapa, pulina maiṃ bedī racī.*

108. *gāe ju gīta punīta bahu bidha, beda ruci suṃdara dhvanī.*

dance: with the flashing of their jewelry, it looks like they are whirling around a sacred fire:

> They are pirouetting as if around the fire which is provided by the splendor of their jewelry. (*SS* 1689/1071)[109]

Striking is the prominence of the role of women in the wedding proceedings. They take over the Sanskritic rituals. We have already seen that in real-life weddings, and indeed in the *Rām Carit Mānas* and television portrayals of Sītā's wedding, auspiciously married women play an important role. So do the bride's girlfriends. In order to make that work for the Rāsa-līlā, it requires that the round dance is not interpreted as an orgiastic feast of love in which all the women of Braj are Krishna's lovers, but rather as a rite of love of the divine pair Rādhā and Krishna, assisted by *sakhīs*, or girlfriends. Their role is limited to assisting the pair. It is parallel to that of the bride's girlfriends during the wedding. One can, of course, consider this reading of Rāsa-līlā farfetched, but that is missing out on the fun and playfulness of discovering the clues. After all, picking up on divine clues is what *rasika* bhakti is about.

DIVINE SANCTION FOR A SECRET WEDDING. Sūr says explicitly that the wedding rites are of the Gāndharva variety, not involving parental presence. What is central is the "bond of the heart," as expressed in another line of the same poem: "When the knot of souls is made, who would give that up, no mother- or sister-in-law nearby," (SS 1689/1071).[110] This is of course in stark contrast to the stress on the tie of the families in the descriptions of Sītā's wedding. There is no need to balance the status of the parties of the bride and groom, which so preoccupied the poets describing the latter, as here there are indeed no relatives present.

Still, Gāndharva-vivāha or not, Sūr does not leave the divine couple without official sanction. He makes a link with the Vastraharaṇa episode, foregrounding the vow to the goddess that Rādhā/the Gopīs undertook to secure Krishna for a groom.

> First they kept the vrata of the virgins, and trusted him in their hearts.
> "Give Nanda's son for a husband, O goddess, fulfill our heart's desire."
> Then she [the goddess] bestowed her grace (*prasāda*) to all, to their heart's delight.... (*SS* 1689/1071)[111]

109. *phirata bhāṃvari karata bhūṣana, agni manau ujāsa.*

110. *jiya perī graṃthi kauna chorai, nikaṭa nanada na sāse.*

111. *kiyau prathama kumārikani brata, dhari hṛdaya bisvāsa; naṃdasuta pati dehu debī, pūji mana kī āsa; diyau taba parasāda saba kauṃ, bhayau sabani hulāsa.*

The union of Rādhā and Krishna is thus a direct result of the goddess's wish-fulfillment. This is also expressed in the next poem:

> With that vow in mind they worshiped the goddess, no other desire was in their hearts:
> "Make Nanda's son my husband, if your grace is with me."
> She [the goddess] then gracefully granted the desired groom, when the maidens had done penance for a year:
> The most handsome man in the three worlds, unequaled in beauty and qualities.
> Here, the friends massaged her,[112] adorned her with a forehead mark and brought the princess to the altar.
> The Creator granted the moment as she had kept her vows according to the rules. . . .[113]
> When he heard this, Sūrdās too was delighted and worshiped the goddess who fulfills the heart's wish. (*SS* 1690/1072)[114]

For Sītā's wedding, we have seen that divine sanction from the goddess played an important role. We see the same for Rādhā. Moreover, as for Sītā, the gods in heaven also bestow their blessings:

> The women from heaven came to this marvel, giving up the company of husbands and sons. (*SS* 1689/1071)[115]

This is a clever reversal, or an echo, of the Rāsa-līlā, where the Gopīs are said to have come to Krishna after leaving their families, husbands, and children. Still, the goddesses may have left behind their families, but the gods are not far behind:

> The gods showered flowers from their hands, watching on from the thirteen heavens. (*SS* 1689/1071)[116]
> Resounding instruments and all gods in the sky rained down flowers with their hands.

112. Note here a nearly imperceptible shift from a group of Gopīs to Rādhā alone as the bride, which is possible in the Braj text, where pronouns can remain indetermined.

113. I am interpreting *bāniyau* as a rhyming variant for the fem. ppp. of *bān-* ("to fix," *BBSK*).

114. *yaha brata hiya dhari devī pūjī, hai kachu mana abhilāṣa na dūjī; dījai naṃda-suvana pati meraiṃ, jau pai hoi anugraha teraiṃ; taba kari anugraha bara diyau, jaba baraṣa juvatini tapa kiyau, trailaukya-bhūṣana puruṣa suṃdara, rūpa-guna nāhiṃna biyau; ita ubaṭí khori siṃgāri sakhiyani, kuṃvari caurī āniyau; jā hita kiyau brata nema-saṃjama, so dhari bidhi bāniyau . . . suni sūradāsahiṃ bhayau ānaṃda, pujī mana kī sādhikā.*

115. *nāri-divi kautukahiṃ āīṃ, chāṃḍi suta-pati-pāsa.*

116. *varaṣi surapati kusuma aṃjuli, nirakhi tridasa akāsa.*

> Their chariots stopped in the sky, and sages rejoiced, shouting
> "hurray." (1690/1072)[117]

Thus, goddesses and gods are all present, lending their legitimizing prestige to the ceremony. This resounding approval from the gods substitutes for the absent family. Music making and social commentary, normally performed by the bride's and groom's family members and friends are here taken over by divine and mythological beings. The community celebrating here is not the village community but that of heavenly beings.

CELEBRATION OF LOVE, NOT SOLEMN POMP. So far I have discussed only one set of poems, which read secret wedding vows into the Rāsa-līlā. There is another set of poems in which we get a more straightforward interpretation of the divine wedding. All of Nanddās's poems on the topic fall under this rubric and some from *Sūr Sāgar*. These poems depict a local wedding between the son of Nanda of Gokul and the daughter of Vṛṣabhānu of Barsānā. Thus, the couple's relatives are involved, but even so the tone is very informal, in contrast to Sītā's wedding (at least in the Vālmīki and television versions; Tulsī is closer in this respect). If we look at real-life parallels, we might reason that such informality is inspired by the proximity of the villages of the bride and the groom. They know each other well, as do their parents. Another factor may be the relatively lower status of the families. This is no high-society event that signals the alliance between two royal houses but rather a rural affair, celebrated with local verve.

In any case, the mood is not solemn. The main focus is abundant celebration, manifest in many joyous vignettes. The description is not driven by a narrative of ritual action; instead, everything is focused on emotion. The honors of seating arrangements and presents for the guests are foregone for the bliss of beholding the pair.

> When they meet and give their hearts, they seat everyone on thrones
> of joy, everyone surrenders their eyes as presents. (*SS* 1690/
> 1072)[118]

In these poems (in contrast to the previous set), the poet's function is not to delve for deeper meaning behind the surface description. Rather, he creates snapshots of the events for us to behold and cherish in our hearts. In the

117. *bājahiṃ ju bājana sakala, sura nabha puhupa-aṃjali baraṣahīṃ; thaki rahe byoma-bimāna, muni-jana jaya-sabada kari haraṣahīṃ.*

118. *mili mana dai sukha asana baise, citavani vāri kiye saba taise.*

following poem from Nanddās's *Padābali,* we get an elaborate description of Krishna as he arrives on his horse, and then little vignettes of the main moments of the celebration:

> The groom is splendid darling Mountain-lifter, the bride is fair Rādhā.
> Spectators' hearts are overcome with awe, such a wonderful couple!
> His groom's turban is studded with jewels, he has a pearl garland on his neck.
> Seeing the face of handsome Śyāma, the women of Braj are enchanted.
> Madanamohana regally rides his horse, accompanied by the rest of the procession.
> Drums of all shapes and sounds resound everywhere.[119]
> Together they arrive at Vṛṣabhānu's door where all are gathered.
> He receives his forehead mark, is worshiped with *ārtī,* and seated in the pavilion.
> Brahmins from all over are reciting the Vedas, everyone is pleased.
> When Hari takes Rādhā's hand, beautiful auspicious songs are sung.
> After the wedding, Yaśodā congratulates Mohana:
> "Long live this pair on this earth." Nanddās can only bow his head.[120] (*Padābalī* 60)[121]

Interestingly, the poem ends on a moment of mother love (*vātsalya*). The climax is reached when Yaśodā congratulates her own son as now as a mother she tastes the bliss of seeing her son's wedding day. That is the perspective we saw in Sītā's wedding in a more restrained manner at the moment of the welcoming ceremony in Ayodhyā. At this point, the poet holds up the action and invites us to participate and rejoice from the perspective of the new mother-in-law of Rādhā. He reports Yaśodā's words as if he were an eyewitness, present at the scene in Gokul.

119. Particular instruments are mentioned: *damāma* and *upaṃga.*

120. Literally: "Nanddās surrenders."

121. *dūlaha giridhara lāla chabīo, dulahina rādhā gorī; jina dekhī mana meṃ ati lājī, aisī banī yaha jorī; ratana jaṭita koṃ banyo seharo, ura motina kī mālā; dekhata badana syāma suṃdara kauṃ, mohi rahīṃ braja-bālā; madanamohana rājata ghoṛāpai, auru barātī saṃgā; bājata ḍhola damāmā cahuṃ-disi, tāla mṛdaṃga upaṃgā; jāya jure bṛṣabhānu su paurī, utahū sabamili āe; ṭīko kari āratī utārī, maṃḍapa maiṃ padharāe; paṛhata beda cahuṃ-disi tai vipra-jana, bhae sabana mana bhāe; hathalevā kari hari-rādhā soṃ, maṃgala-cāra gavāe; byāha bhayoṃ mohana koṃ jabahīṃ, jasumati deti badhāī; cirajīvo bhūtala ihi jorī, naṃdadāsa bali jāī.*

Another noteworthy element in these poems is the celebration of the display of wealth involved in the proceedings. It is not called dowry, or explicitly said to enhance the prestige of Vṛṣabhānu's family. Nor is there a question of the formal "giving of cows" *(godāna)*. Rather, the wealth, mainly herds of cows, is a sign of auspiciousness and an indicator of spontaneous joy and amazement that accompanies the divine wedding. Another example:

"Friend, I can't contain my joy!
Vṛṣabhānu in Barsānā has fixed the wedding time and sent the letter to Nanda's village.
Everywhere are resplendent cows of every color: white (*dhaurā*) and grey-red (*dhūmarā*).
Of jewelry and precious stones there is no end, I'm stunned to witness this wealth.
The bride has enthralled the cowherd gathering, I'm immersed in singing her praise."
Nanddās says: "I'm in the thrall of darling Giridhara's bride." (*Padābalī* 58)[122]

Thus we get another eye witness report from the events, which bring us along, too, to witness the abundant joy. This time the focus is on the beautiful bride. We feel as though we are right there. In this case, we witness the engagement rituals. Elsewhere, it is as if the wedding procession passes by right here and now, as Nanddās shows it in another poem:

"Friend, let's go and see the groom!
Behold handsome Śyāma, charm incarnate, our eyes will be gratified."
The young women of Braj came all together, smiling in Mohana's direction
A peacock feather tied on his head, earrings in his ears, his decorated face all happy smiles.[123]
He's wearing a brocade outfit. Jewels on every limb, attracting all eyes.
Splendid is the groom's procession. Excitement spreads wherever it goes.

122. *sajanī ānaṃda ura na samāūṃ; barasānaiṃ vṛṣabhānu lagana likhi, paṭhaī hai naṃda-gāūṃ; dhaurī dhūmari dhainu bibidha raṃga, sobhita ṭhāūṃ-ṭhāūṃ; bhūṣana mani-gana pāru nāhiṃnai, so dhana dekhi lubhāūṃ; gopa-sabhākari lagana ju līnī, magana hoi guna gāūṃ; naṃdadāsa lāla-giridhara kī, dulahina pai bali jāūṃ.*

123. The word used is *maravaṭ*, which refers to painting the face of bride with *rolī* (*OHED*). Here the description seems to be of the groom, though.

Nanddās's Gopīs have eyes like bees: they ride the waves in the lake
of cowherd-faces,
Keen to land on this exquisite, blossoming lotus. (*Padābalī* 59)[124]

We are among the women witnessing the procession coming by. This is not an exclusive wedding behind closed palace doors but one open to all. And we happily peek in and revel in the joy. We can all be part of it, and find a way to join the guests. In fact, Krishna has invited us with meaningful glances as he has passed by in his procession, and Sūrdās has taken the hint and encourages us to do so, too:

"I'll go to see the groom!
On the road, his hints registered.[125] Under what pretense will I get
to see him?"
"I'll braid flowers into a garland, and will go as a flower girl."
"I'll take a betel leaf for Nanda's dear son."
"As a whisker girl,[126] I'll go and look at him to my heart's
content."
"To the Moon of Vrindāban, I'll take jewelry I've crafted myself:
As a goldsmith lady I'll go and look at him to my heart's content."
"For my very own Gopāla, I'll design an outfit:[127]
As a tailor lady, I'll go and look at him to my heart's content."
Sūr will take sandalwood, aloe, and saffron:
"As a perfume lady, I'll go and look at him to my heart's content."
(*SS* 1693/1075)[128]

Who is speaking in this poem? It is ambiguous, but we seem to hear the voices of the women of Braj, all eager to go and look at Krishna to their hearts' content. They all find some excuse to get close to him. Sūr himself takes on the

124. *arī cali dūlaha dekhani jāṃya; suṃdara-syāma mādhurī mūrati, aṃkhiyāṃ nirakhi sirāṃya; juri āīṃ braja-nāri navelī, mohana disi musikyāṃya; maura baṃdhyoṃ sira kānana kuṃḍala maruvaṭa mukhahi subhāṃya; paharaiṃ jarakasi paṭa ābhūṣana, aṃga aṃga naini rijhāṃya; taisīya banī barāta chabīlī, jaga-maga raṃga cucāṃya; gopa-sabhā saravara meṃ phūle, kamala parama jhapaṭāṃya; naṃdadāsa gopina ke dṛga-ali, lapaṭani ko akulāṃya.*

125. The verb *utarnā* can mean "to be registered [for mental impression]" (*OHED*).

126. I am interpreting *colini* as *cāmar* + *inī*, but have not found this attested.

127. *Bāgā* is a wedding garment for the groom and his party (*OHED*).

128. *dūlaha dekhauṃgī jāi, utare saṃketa baṭahiṃ, kihiṃ misa lakhi pāuṃ; phūla gūṃthi mālā lai, mālini hvai jāuṃ; naṃda naṃdana pyāre kauṃ, bīrā kari leuṃ; colini hvai jāuṃ nirakhi, nainani sukha deuṃ; bṛṃdābana caṃda kauṃ maiṃ, bhūṣana gaṛhi leuṃ; hvai sunāri jāuṃ nirakhi, nainani sukha deuṃ; apane gopāla ke maiṃ, bāge raci leuṃ; darajini hvai jāuṃ nirakhi, nainini sukha deuṃ; caṃdana aragajā sūra, kesari dhari leuṃ; gaṃdhani hvai jāuṃ nirakhi, nainani sukha deuṃ.*

role of one of these women. He participates by taking on a double disguise: first that of one of the women of Braj, then in a ritual role appropriate for the circumstances. This song clearly takes its inspiration from traditional wedding songs that articulate the participation of different castes in wedding ceremonies. However, here the point is not so much expressing village solidarity of all castes, as expressing the formation of a bhakti community around Krishna. In his presence, it is suggested, we are all women and of the service castes to boot. But it does not matter, because all such distinctions get dissolved in the simple act of beholding, in the bliss of *darśana*. Sūr invites us to participate in this bhakti community over and over again in the refrain.

FOLK RITES AND WOMEN'S CEREMONIES. The wedding is informal, also in that the Brahminical ceremonies do not receive as much attention as do the more folksy rites. That is so even when the reporters are the gods themselves:

> They know: the sage Nārada, Sanaka and his brothers, the gods Śiva and Brahmā.
> The gods announce with kettle drum and drum the choice news:
> "Hari was anxious to break the suspended doorgates."[129]
> According to all the customs of Braj, the wedding has taken place in Barsānā
> All women have come running to see the ceremony of disentangling the bracelets.
> The girlfriends run to and fro, chests extended, unable to contain their joy.
> The groom sways down the path, like an elephant placing his feet on the earth,
> Peacock feathers dangling, naturally turning his turban[130] into a groom's headdress (*sehrā*),
> Beautiful with his bride at his side. A splendid spectacle!
> Elephant and horse chariot adorned, gorgeous whisks and umbrellas.
> The bride, Vṛṣabhānu's daughter is beautiful in every respect,

129. I am interpreting *torana* as a verb and *bārana* as the plural of *bāra*, "door." One could also read *torana* as "garland" and *bārana* as "elephant," but that does not render much meaning. The reference seems to be to the custom where the arriving groom breaks the doorway decoration that has been put up for this purpose at the bride's house (*toraṇa*).

130. Literally: "peacock feathers dangling naturally from his head like a *sehrā*," taking *bhāu* as *svabhāv* (*BBSK*).

And look, Sūrdās, at the splendor of the groom: the king of Braj.[131]
(*SS* 1692/1974)[132]

The gods explicitly state that the divine pair got married according to Braj folk tradition. We get a vignette of Krishna breaking the doorway decoration (*toraṇa*), and then immediately afterward of one of the ice-breaker women's rites, *kaṅkaṇa* (discussed at more length later). We hear nothing about the altar and fire or recitation of the Vedas. Even though the folk rites are mentioned, the focus of the poem is again a *darśana*, a glimpse of the divine pair, as seen through the eyes of the female wedding guests.

Among the rites that are mentioned is the singing of *gālī*, or customary teasing jokes that are sung by the women at the expense of the groom's party, which can get rather risqué. We will remember that Tulsī did mention them, but the television version leaves out all reference to these juicy songs. Sūrdās includes them:

Up there the cuckoos created an uproar, here gathered all the women of Braj,
As wedding guests from both parties, joyfully sang the *gālīs*. (*SS* 1690/1072)[133]

A lot of attention is paid to the informal rites that take place after the ceremony proper and are meant as ice-breakers between the newlyweds. One such rite involves the *kaṅkaṇa*, a bracelet consisting of a thread with mustard seeds, iron rings, and so on, which is tied around the wrists of bride and groom.[134] To be sure, there are references to *kaṅkaṇa* during the wedding of Sītā and Rāma, but there it is the ceremony of "tying the knot," before the marriage proper (in the Sanskrit epic, see *VR* 1. 73.7–9, 15b; see the notes by Goldman 1984: 391). The focus in the Rādhā-Krishna material is instead on the

131. The word translated as "splendor" is *śrī*. There might be a reference here to Rādhā as an incarnation of Śrī, Vishnu's consort.

132. *sanakādika nārada muni, siva biraṃci jāna; deva-duṃdubhī mṛdaṃga, bāje bara nisāna; bārana torana baṃdhāi, hari kīnha uchāha; braja kī saba rīti bhaī, barasānaiṃ byāha; ḍorani kara chorana kauṃ, āīṃ sakala dhāi; phūlī phiraiṃ sahacari ura, ānaṃda na samāi; gaja bara gati āvana maga, dharani dharata pāu; laṭakata sira seharo manu, sikhi sikhaṃḍa bhāu; sobhita saṃga nāri aṃga, sabai chabi birāji; gaja ratha bājī banāi, caṃvara chatra sāji; dulahini bṛṣabhānu-sutā, aṃga aṃga bhrāja; sūradāsa dekhau śrī, dūlaha brajarāja.*

133. *uta kokilā-gana karaiṃ kulāhala, ita sakala braja-nāriyāṃ; āīṃ ju nevate duhūṃ taiṃ, detiṃ ānaṃda gāriyāṃ.*

134. That is the definition given in *BBSK*. A description for Khalapur Rajputs is found in Minturn 1993: 51. It seems to be a variant of the ceremony (also known as *kautuka-bandhana*), described by Kane which is subsumed under the set of rites called *ārdrākṣatāropaṇa* (mutual showering of bride and groom with wet, unbroken rice grains). This ceremony involves the bride and groom tying (rather than undoing) a thread with turmeric on each other's hands (Kane 1974: 536).

more informal follow-up ceremony, where bride and groom have to undo each other's bracelet after the marriage ceremony. There is a playful atmosphere here and a competitive element, in that onlookers will comment on the skill with which the groom is able to untie the bride's *kaṅkaṇa* and vice versa. Apparently, this is an occasion for the women of the bride's party to make fun of the groom, by tying the bride's *kaṅkaṇa* in ingenious ways so he has a hard time loosening the knots. Sūrdās devotes a whole poem to this marvelous little *līlā:*

> First the wedding takes place according to the rules. Now think about nice *kaṅkaṇas*!
> With much cleverness and effort they braided them, the clever young women of Braj.
> "When you are big, you can disentangle them, king of the whole cowherd settlement!
> You might have to plead with folded hands, or touch Rādhikā's feet.
> This is not like lifting the mountain, listen, prince, Lord of Braj!
> You call yourself big, but your hands start to tremble."
> All the Braj women stick closely together and stare intently at the knots:
> "Give up quickly or call your mother Yaśodā and bring her here."
> With his cool tender hands, Hari carefully disentangled it effortlessly.
> All Śyāma's friends burst out laughing: "Now you disentangle his, pretty princess."
> She was defeated, so how come she did not give up, tied in the knot of love?
> Looking at the ways of these two, the girlfriends smiled, averting their faces.
> "Now don't help her, friends, stop that cleverness.
> The bride is to disentangle the groom's *kaṅkaṇa*," said Vṛṣabhānu.
> Describing her lotus hand, and the lotus hand of our friend's darling,
> Now how about this simile:[135] their hairs on end are like thorns on a lotus stalk!
> The secret of the play of darling Gopāla is the *rasa* the connoisseur utters.

135. Literally: "the lineage of poets finds its true calling."

> "May that couple remain for ever tied up, I'd bow my head over and over,"[136] says clever Sūr. (*SS* 1691/1073)[137]

This charming poem makes the most of the irony of the incarnation. Rādhā's girlfriends try to one-up the god of the universe, who once lifted the mountain. But the task he is presented with now, the untying of Rādhā's *kaṅkaṇa,* they say, is a totally different game. What they are implying is that great heroes may not always be adept in love. Interestingly, we have an echo of *Brahma Vaivarta Purāṇa,* when they belittle him, treat him as Yaśodā's little baby, insisting he might need Mom's help to do the trick. However, Krishna succeeds with flying colors, and it is Rādhā who bungles, much to the delight of Krishna's party. Or does she really have trouble untying the knots? Isn't some secret "under the table" thing going on there? The poet cleverly puns that she is tied in the knot of love. She cherishes the excuse to touch Krishna's hand, and so does Krishna. And Vṛṣabhānu does not get it, he just sees the competition element and does not want to be seen to favor his daughter. Only the girlfriends see through it. They have to turn away their smiling faces. Now what can a poor human do? This is beyond the poet's bag of tricks, similes can only be absurd, and all Sūrdās can do is surrender. Such *līlā* can only be savored by a few who are initiated; no wonder Sūr here uses the epithet "connoisseur" (*rasika*) for himself.

Comparing Rādhā's Wedding Ceremonies

The wedding of Rādhā and Krishna is difficult to fathom, for "connoisseurs" only. At the surface level, there may be no wedding at all, as is the case literally with the televised *Shri Krishna.* Both medieval vernacular poets and *Brahma Vaivarta Purāṇa* indicate that the wedding of Rādhā and Krishna is a secret, not intended for the ordinary observer. In the *Purāṇa,* it takes place in absolute isolation, deep in the forest. There are no mortal witnesses, and Rādhā declares it to be a secret herself. In the Braj poems one has to become a *rasika* and read

136. Literally: "I surrender to them again and again."

137. *prathama byāha bidhi hoi rahyau, ho kaṃkana-cāra bicāri; raci raci paci paci gūṃthi banāyau, navala nipuna brajanāri; baḍe hohu tau chori lehu jau, sakal aghoṣa ke rāi; kai kara jori karau binatī, kai chuvau rādhikā-pāi; yaha na hoi giri kau dharibau ho, sunahu kuṃvara-brajanātha; āpuna kauṃ tuma baṛe kahāvata, kāṃpana lāge hātha; bahuri simiṭi braja-suṃdari saba mili, dīnho gaṃṭhi ghurāi; chorahu begi ki ānahu apanī, jasumati māi bulāi; sahaja sithila pallava taiṃ hari jū, līnhau chori saṃvāri; kilaki uṭhīṃ taba sakhī syāma kī, tuma chorau sukumāri; pacihārī kaisaiṃhu nahiṃ chūṭata, baṃdhī prema kī ḍori; dekhi sakhī yaha rīti duhuni kī, mudita haṃsī mukha mori; aba jini karahu sahāi sakhī rī, chāṃḍahu sakala sayāna; dulahini chori dulaha kau kaṃkana, boli babā bṛṣabhāna; kamala kamala kari baranata haiṃ ho, pāni priyā ke lālā; aba kabi kula sāṃce se lāgata, roma kaṃṭīle nāla; līlā-rahasa gupāla lāla kī, jo rasa rasika bakhāna; sadā rahai yaha abicala jorī, bali bali sūra sujāna.*

TABLE 3.2. Versions of Rādhā's Wedding Ceremony/First Night Compared

Element	BVP	SS and NP	TVK
Context	Bālā-līlā	Rāsa-līlā	Childhood sweethearts adolescent first night
Age difference	Krishna child; Rādhā goddess	Both *kiśorī*	Both *kiśorī*
Accessibility	Secret (*rahasya*)	For connoisseurs only (*rasika*)	Offscreen
Legitimization	Rādhā goddess Predicted by sage Brahmā presides	Boon from *vrata* Goddess's permission *Sakhīs* preside	Divine pair witnesses own *kiśorī līlā* *Sakhīs* arrange for tryst
Astrology	Brahmā preordained	Full moon night	Not mentioned
Role of families	Brahmā as father of bride	Family in Braj, wedding songs	Not mentioned
Role of gods	Play music	Play music	Not mentioned
Mood ceremony	Solemn	Loving informality	Morning after Holī
Nature rites	Purely Vedic	Mostly folk/women	No rites strictly speaking
Vātsalya	Tension with *śṛṅgāra*	For mother only	Not mentioned
Wedding night	Delayed	Celebrated	offscreen

between the lines of Rāsa-līlā, or one has to be transformed in a Gopī to be able to witness. Interestingly, it is through the eyes of women that the ceremony becomes manifest.

One reason for all this secrecy may lie in the potential scandal ensuing from the fact that Krishna is portrayed as a child. The overwhelmingly erotic feelings connected with the wedding somehow are in competion with the chaste ones of motherly love. Counter to expectation, this is most problematically the case in the pre-Freudian *Brahma Vaivarta Purāṇa*. Here the line between the mother and the lover is blurred, and apparently this is felt to be problematic. To resolve the tension, Rādhā is denied her wedding night, and Krishna returns to Yaśodā's exclusively maternal love. In the medieval songs, there is only a vague hint of this issue, when Krishna is taunted by Rādhā's party with the name "Mommy's boy." Surprisingly, in some modern (post-Freudian) film versions, notably the movie *Shri Krishna leela*, there is not felt to be a problem, and the age difference between the two is unself-consciously upheld. If we look for comparisons with the Sītā-Rāma wedding, we notice a similar switching of sentiments from erotic to motherly just before the wedding night, though only in Tulsī's *Rām Carit Mānas*. There the mode had switched to *vātsalya* of the mothers, but there was no blurring between mothers and lovers. Maybe we should not worry too much about all this; after all, whether erotic or maternal, what counts is the strength of the emotion toward God. Bhakti has room for love of all kinds.

To return to the wedding ceremonies of Krishna and Rādhā, while we find that divine sanction for the wedding is stressed in the Sanskrit as well as in the vernacular sources, the prevalence of women in the medieval sources is intriguing. Does this subtly undermine Brahminical authority? Do the secret rites subvert the official wedding rites? Certainly the vernacular Rāsa-līlā songs seem to make a mockery of priests and Vedic chanting. Even the more straightforward folksy wedding celebrations don't attend much to the Brahminical aspect of things. Women are in the foreground, as are their songs and playful rites. We have already noticed the same phenomenon in the vernacular versions depicting the Sītā-Rāma wedding. It is tempting to speculate that the foregrounding of women is connected with the bhakti discourse, where indeed women are valued as role models for the devotee. In that respect, it is important to note that the *Brahma Vaivarta Purāṇa,* which is roughly contemporary to the vernacular sources, has none of that and features only ultraorthodox rites presided over by Brahmā. It certainly reinforces doubts about the alleged connection of this text with the bhakti *sampradāyas* of North India (Brown 1974: 201–5).

If we compare the scenarios of Sītā's public and Rādhā's secret wedding, we find that the descriptions of both have in common over time an increasing prominence of folk rites and women's songs, as well as a strong interest in legitimization through reference to gurus and divine intervention. In both cases, the bhakti versions display more loving devotion than the televised ones, which revert to the Sanskrit sources and add a level of sermonizing and preoccupation with dharma. The major difference between Sītā's and Rādhā's weddings is obviously the stress on family concerns in the former, with all the anxieties that entails about the two parties' relative status and the bride's plight in her new home. The love marriage obliterates all these concerns, or maybe it is safer to say that it ignores them, as common sense and consensus has it that problems will occur with a vengance. A look at popular cinema will abundantly illustrate this.

Love and Society Weddings in Popular Film

Many popular films have at least one wedding episode. This may be the case partly because a wedding is auspicious, and the Indian film business loves to frontload its movies with signs of auspiciousness.[138] It may also be partly for

138. This includes the rituals surrounding the making and release of the movies, with ground-breaking ceremonies, as well as careful calculations of auspiciousness in the title, and the convention of framing the movie with an invocation to God, a device, taken over straight from the textual tradition, called *maṅgalācaraṇa.*

commercial reasons, because the sound track associated with a wedding episode can become a bestseller, used for background music and played by bands at actual wedding ceremonies. In the nineties, this phenomenon became even more common, and one can speak of a new trend that framed movies explicitly as wedding movies. *Hum aap ke hain koun . . . !* was a trendsetter of the genre, closely followed by *Dilwale dulhania le jayenge.* I have already discussed certain scenes from these movies; here I will look at the nuptial ceremonies proper in *HAKHK.*

I will contrast this with a look at filmic representations of secret ceremonies. The Gāndharva weddings in two movies, Shakti Samanta's *Aradhana* (1969) and Indra Kumar's *Dil* (1990). The latter is particularly interesting because it involves a critique of the dowry system. Finally, I will also look at a movie that problematizes the "traditional wedding" and the dowry system, and does so in the context of explicit *Rāmāyaṇa* references: Rajkumar Santoshi's *Lajja* (2001).

The Filmī Gāndharva Wedding: "Aradhana" and "Dil"

Whether the Gāndharva-vivāha, or marriage by mutual consent only, fully sanctioned by the scriptures, is acceptable in real life in modern times or not, it plays a significant role in the imagination as evidenced by popular culture. Before filmī lovers can celebrate their first night together, they have to make their inevitable stop at the village temple to perform the sanctifying rites.[139] The problem with such secret rites is that there are no or few witnesses (who anyway have an unfortunate tendency to die or be otherwise unavailable when push comes to shove). Thus, notwithstanding the sanctity of the witness of the sacred fire or the images of the god (often, appropriately, a Śiva *liṅgam*), the validity of the rite is questionable. Mostly, in the rest of the film, the protagonists struggle with this problem, ending up suffering heroically through the ensuing misunderstandings and complications. The message inevitably is that the lovers, in particular the women, end up paying dearly for the transgression.

The classic filmī Gāndharva wedding episode is undoubtedly the one in Shakti Samanta's *Aradhana* (1969).[140] The mountain village belle Vandana

139. An interesting exception is the Raj Kapoor film *Bobby,* where the "first night" of the couple takes place without any such reference. However, even there, in a later scene, just before they elope, they take a pseudo-Christian wedding vow in which Rāju, the Hindu boy (Rishi Kapoor) asks Bobby, the Christian girl (Dimple Kapadia): "Will you be at my side? In happiness and sorrow? In good times and bad times? In living and dying? For always? (*tum mere sāth dogī? dukh sukh meṃ? acche buṛe vaqt meṃ? jīne marne meṃ? hameśā?*).

140. For a brief discussion of this movie, see also Virdi 2003: 147–51.

(Sharmila Tagore) and her pilot beau Arun (Rajesh Khanna) are properly engaged, yet they succumb to the temptation to consummate their love before their wedding day. Still, the (mostly offscreen) lovemaking is preceded by a Gāndharva wedding. The episodes have been insightfully and delightfully summarized by Philip Lutgendorf:

> Arun and Vandana pay a visit to a Shiva temple where, at the prompting of a cheerful priest, they impulsively exchange garlands and "marry before God." A sudden storm then forces the lovers into a nearby bungalow where they doff their wet clothes—she substituting an artfully wrapped blanket for her soaked sari, and he building a fire. The blanket is red, and the firepit resembles a Vedic altar; eyeing each other hungrily, they circle the blaze while (substituting for a mantra-chanting priest) an amorous young man in an adjacent room sings the sultry *Roop tera mastana* ("Your beauty intoxicates me"). The film's most erotic song picturization thus simultaneously manages to encode the key elements of a perfectly dharmic Hindu marriage ritual, although it necessarily remains a scandalous secret, unsanctioned by family and "society." (www.uiowa.edu/~incinema/Aradhana.html)

This description, especially with its clever reading of allusions to ceremonial elements, immediately evokes Rādhā and Krishna's Rāsa-līlā interpreted as wedding (discussed earlier). The improvised fire to stay warm becomes a sacred fire, the red towel stands for the red wedding sari, the song stands for for Vedic chanting. Like Rādhā and Krishna's, Vandana and Arun's "Rāsa-līlā" is coded to be read as a secret wedding ceremony.

In addition, this has been preceded by a more explicit mock wedding. The exchange of *mālās* in the Śiva temple, sanctioned by a Brahmin priest, is complemented by other wedding-like elements: a "wedding photo" taken by the local photographer, who is addressed by the family term *cācā*. Finally, a vow is shouted out in the mountains, echoing over the vale: he says: "Vandana, you are mine" (*Vandanā, tum merī ho);* she replies: "I'm yours" (*maiṃ tumhārī hūṃ).* Plus, there is a keen, legitimizing desire for offspring: he insists they will have a boy as their firstborn. All these elements constitute a conscious playacting of a mock marriage.

While the sacred fire scene gained a lot of notoriety and was probably for many the highlight of the movie, the film is really about the tragic consequences of this premarital encounter. In contrast to Rādhā and Krishna's secret ceremony, which is not regretted or regrettable, the Gāndharva wedding in the movie leads to ruin for Vandana. For one, she gets pregnant (never an issue for the divine pair), and moreover Arun dies before the "real" wedding ceremony can take place. She is forced to abandon her illegitimate child—a son of course—and is doomed to lead the stark ascetic life of a widow, without ever having enjoyed marital happiness. As a widow, she is always sexually suspect and vulnerable to unwanted male attention, which leads to many humiliations. As a mother, she will sacrifice everything for her son who has been adopted and she manages to get hired as his nanny. She will even go to jail for him. Yet while suffering the sacrifices of motherhood, she cannot taste its joys, unable as she is to publicly recognize her son, who does not know she is his mother.[141] A tough curse indeed. While the movie has a happy ending, and her years of sacrifice bear fruit,[142] the message is clear. Those who venture to subvert the traditional wedding ceremony will come to no good. This example, while delightfully subverting the traditional ceremony, in the end squarely comes down on the side of affirming the ultimate legitimizing value of the patriarchal society wedding.

A counterexample is another impromptu wedding ceremony, in Indra Kumar's *Dil* (1990). This wedding is improvised just before the star-crossed lovers elope. This film combines the Gāndharva scenario with the elopement one, which is fitting in a movie that portrays (in contrast to many other movies of the nineties) a defiance of parental authority, reminiscent of the *Bobby* scenario.[143]

The ironic plot of this movie itself turns conventions upside down. Madhu (Madhuri Dixit) and Raj (Aamir Khan) are sworn enemies, but their rich fathers have settled their marriage. First they defy their fathers and flatly refuse the match, insulting their would-be in-laws. However, afterward they fall in love, of course, just when their fathers fall out. The mock wedding occurs at the point that the movie reverts to a Romeo-and-Juliet scenario.

When Raj hears that Madhu's father plans to take her abroad, he is propelled into drastic action. He enters Madhu's bedroom and locks the door. Her father (Syed Jaffrey) cannot enter the room, but he observes the goings-on through the open window. In front of her abhorred father, Madhu and Raj

141. In connection with the alternation between *śṛṅgāra* and *vātsalya* I have noted for some Sītā as well as Rādhā versions, it is interesting that after her release from prison, Vandana meets her now grown son, who is of course the spitting image of his father, and played by the same actor. He is a pilot, too, and when his plane is lost in war, she prays to none other than Krishna, stressing that she has never asked him for anything, but if he takes her son's life, she will not consider him God but a stone. Of course, under such threat, Krishna has to make sure that everything comes out all right in the end.

142. *barasoṃ kī ārādhnā saphal ho gaī*—this explains the movie's title.

143. For a discussion of this movie and reports on interviews to fathom audience reaction, see also Virdi 2003: 184–92.

"commit" a marriage. The soundtrack features the tolling of bells while Raj breaks a wooden stool for firewood and sets it aflame. He ties Madhu's shawl to his outfit, and they circumambulate the "Vedic" fire. Appropriate chanting is played on the sound track, which drowns out Madhu's father screaming bloody murder (as he literally does audibly just seconds before the bells start to toll). Madhu happens to be wearing a red outfit, which fits the occasion, Raj happens to have a *maṅgalsūtra* handy, and for *sindoor,* he just cuts his finger and uses the blood, a romantic gesture, staple of many a Hindi movie. They have just enough time to perform the ceremony before father finally bursts into the room with a gun, followed by the paternal grandmother (*dādīmā*), who struggles to prevent disaster. Madhu protects her new husband with her body, and her father cannot bring himself to shoot her. Apparently the marriage is now recognized by all as fait accompli. The father cannot prevent them anymore, and the lovers escape. When they arrive at Raj's house, his mother is sympathetic to their decision. Her rite-savvy reflexes lead her promptly to ask the servant to bring a tray for worship (*ārtī*), ready to perform the welcoming ceremony. In this scenario, though, the ritual cannot be carried through as Dad arrives and gives the newlyweds a welcome of a different kind. He promptly disinherits his son and sends the couple out of the house.

Significant in this movie is the centrality of the dowry issue, from the point of view not of the bride's family but of the groom's greedy father. At the surface level, the film critiques the practice of "selling grooms." Raj's father (Anupam Kher) is portrayed as a miser, thinking only about money. He is determined to arrange his son's marriage to the daughter of the highest bidder, looking well beyond his status. We could politely say he is in the recycling business, but the Hindi word for his profession is pejorative: *raddīvālā* or *kabāṛī* (scrap-merchant). Right from the start, we find he is not only a cheapskate but also a cheater, and sure enough, once he sights the prospective party of his dreams, in the form of a millionaire's only daughter, he resorts to all kinds of tricks to arrange the match. When things turn sour, he tries another wealthy party, this time settling for a daughter-in-law who is mentally disturbed. We have encountered this twist in the scenario earlier. As was the case in the earlier movie *Bobby,* here, too, the son's rebellion against his father is justified because the father is not the benign father who has his children's interest at heart, but rather a mean man who is only interested in money.

In the Hindi movie, it seems a son can rebel only against a father who is willing to blatantly sacrifice his child's happiness for financial gain. Dowry is bad when it becomes an obsession at the expense of the happiness of the parties to be married. This is the avowed didactic message in the movie. It comes to the fore most poignantly when, at the engagement ceremony with the mentally disturbed girl, Raj does not show up. Instead, the police bring in a corpse that is presumed to be his. Everyone suspects suicide. The shock is too great for Raj's mother (not incidentally named Savitri), who bursts out in front of everyone with an accusation to her husband of killing her son. She gets a few good lines: "Now you guys can take his corpse to the market and put it up for sale. Perhaps you'll get some money from it."[144] But of course the corpse is not really Rāj's. He has been waiting in the wings and has overheard everything. Now he can confront his father: "What am I to you? Just a saleable commodity?"[145] He disowns his father and runs off to get his true love back, and of course a happy ending is forthcoming, in which everyone is reconciled with everyone.

Fathers of grooms, then, should not see their children as saleable commodities, lest they lose their love. Excessive greed is bad. However, there is an interesting twist. The hero's father in *Dil* is not a Westernized character, as was the father in *Bobby*. So the point is not to blame rampant Westernization and the evils of Western-style materialism. By the time *Dil* comes around, the zeitgeist has changed. Rather, the hero's father is a comic character. His excessive greed is portrayed as a caricature and is coded as comic right from the start, where he is dreaming about a downpour of rupees and wakes up to find it's only the cotton from his mattress he has been inundated with. This helps quite a bit to take the sting out of the message; it is difficult to take it seriously in the face of repeated comic twists. Still, one might say the point is made, and it may linger on in people's minds. Arguably this romantic comedy may be engaged in its own kind of awareness raising.

Subversion and Affirmation of the Traditional Wedding: "Lajja"

I have looked at some mock weddings that seemingly undermine traditional Hindu wedlock. However, we can find also the opposite scenario: a portrayal of a societal wedding that is used to question tradition, in particular the dowry system. The example for analysis here is from Rajkumar Santoshi's *Lajja* (2001), a film self-consciously construed such that the frame story as well as the stories within it are all variants of what we could term a Sītā scenario turned sour.[146]

144. *ab āp log is lāś ko bhī bāzār meṃ jākar bec ḍālo. śāyad iske bhī kuch paise mil jāe.*

145. *maiṃ kyā hūṃ āp ke liye? sirf ek bikāū cīz.*

146. A short summary with illustrations can be found at Philip Lutgendorf's home page, www.uiowa.edu/~incinema/Lajja.html.

The main character in this movie is Vaidehi (Manisha Koirala), who was married to an NRI in New York, but the marriage has turned sour. Now pregnant, she is fleeing an abusive husband all across India. During her flight, she gets involved in the life of three women consecutively, all of whom are multiforms of Sītā, as is indeed Vaidehi herself, which is clear from their names, which are all epithets of Sītā. I concentrate here on the first episode, which features the wedding of Maithili (Mahima Choudhry).

In her flight, Vaidehi has narrowly escaped her husband's flunkies with the help of a crook (Anil Kapoor). To escape her pursuers, she then seeks refuge in the crowd at Maithili's wedding in a nearby reception hall and finds her *ajnabī* (unknown) savior doing the same thing. They team up, pretending to be in the bride's party. Soon he finds out Vaidehi is pregnant, which causes him to comment on cultural praxes of boy preference and obsession with complexion of the skin. Encouraging her to eat more coconut for a fair complexion of the child, he says: "In this nation, no matter how black the groom, he still wants a fair bride."[147]

Their noncommittal observation of the wedding scene gives much further scope for criticism. There are a lot of comments on the abuses of the arranged wedding system, in particular the dowry and the skewed relationships between bride-givers and bride-takers. Upon her wonder at his ability to tell who belongs to the groom's and who to the bride's party, the crook reveals that "those who move around with bowed head and folded hands are in the girl's party, those who move around arrogantly, chest swollen with pride, are in the groom's party."[148] Meanwhile, we witness vignettes of the groom's party criticizing the arrangements made for the wedding, as well as the costly gifts the bride's party distributes, which are promptly passed on to others, an insult the other party silently swallows.

As Vaidehi and her savior bluff their way into the reception hall, they get more and more involved with the bride's story. Vaidehi gets to chat with Maithili and finds out that the wedding is half a love marriage (*ādhā ādhā*). That is to say, bride and groom had fallen in love in college, and luckily their parents have agreed to the match. However, everything is not happy. The dowry demand is excessive. As it turns out, the father of the bride is 5,000 rupees short of the required cash. Throughout the episode, there is a fear of the deal being canceled at the last minute and the father-in-law "getting up" (*uṭh jānā*) from the arrangement. The despair of the father of the bride, who is

147. *is mulk meṃ laṛkā bhale kālā bhūt kyoṃ na ho, dulhan use gorī hī cāhiye.*

148. *jo log hāth joṛe jhuke cal rahe haiṃ ve laṛkīvāle, jo log sīnā tāne akaṛ cal rahe heiṃ ve laṛkevāle.*

trying to arrange for last-minute loans, is palpable. When all fails, he breaks down and admits his utter defeat, the defeat of a lifetime's work: "Each father, as soon as his daughter is born, gets absorbed in the preparation for this day."[149]

Vaidehi suggests that Maithili talk to her groom-to-be and ask him to talk to his father about the dowry, but he turns out to be a "yes-Daddy guy," unwilling to stand up for their love. Meanwhile, the crook who saved Vaidehi has been hiding in Maithili's room and has overheard her plight. He has a change of heart and decides to donate the money he has stolen. The reason for this unusual generosity is relevant, too. He has shortly before witnessed a row in a brothel in which a woman confessed to working there only to collect a dowry for her sister. Convinced now of the evil of the dowry system, which is humiliating to women, he decides to lend a helping hand.

Unfortunately, the ploy turns against the crook turned savior. The groom's party finds out that the money is stolen and accuses the bride's father of the theft. The thief tries to save the day by heroically revealing himself as the culprit, but that, too, backfires. Now it is found that he spent some time in Maithili's room, which compromises her and causes a big scandal. The father of the groom now bigheartedly agrees to go through with the wedding notwithstanding, but of course under the understanding that the dowry now will have to go up yet higher.

The spectator's outrage now has reached levels of unbearability, and the film director provides a beautiful catharsis. So far, the bride has been seated, veiled and quiet, near the sacred fire. All at once she speaks out. Maithili tells her father to accept the new proposal of her father-in-law-to-be. Sarcastically she says that if one man can leave 5,000 rupees after spending an hour in her room, they'll have two come tomorrow and get the extra 10,000 rupees required by her future in-laws.

The bridegroom's father is scandalized, and her groom stands up and commands her to keep her mouth shut, but she adds oil to the flames: "Better become a *satī* than get a husband like you."[150] And that is only the beginning. Maithili demands that the groom's party give back all the much-criticized presents they have received. With the glow of the fire on her red sari, she shouts all the good lines the audience has been burning to speak out in great outrage. Her love for her parents is what causes her most consternation: "As if

149. *har bāp beṭī ke paidā hote hī isī din kī taiyārī meṃ to lag jātā hai.* This concern (and consequentially the undesirability of the female child) is also uttered in folk songs (Archer 1985: 96–7).

150. *tere jaise pati hone se satī bannā acchā hai.*

by giving birth to a girl, they had committed a great sin!"[151] While the wedding guests leave in disarray, some comment approvingly, including our crook, before going to jail: "Today a girl became free of all of society's burdens of custom."[152] And her paternal aunt (*cācī*) lauds her: "It may be you had to suffer trouble, but girls everywhere will find courage, great courage. Well done, daughter, well done."[153]

Maybe it was the director's intent to have us chime in with this aunt, but there is a contradictory message: at the end of the scene, Maithili is left alone, totally ruined. We all know she is now thoroughly "spoiled goods" and her future is bleak. Women who speak out forgo their own personal happiness; this is surely the message we come away with. The director may have tried to counter that: at the end of the movie, Maithili's story is resolved happily. Vaidehi, by now reunited with her husband and back in New York, has a chance encounter with the former crook, now turned taxi driver in New York. He turns out to have married Maithili. So there is a happy ending, and Maithili has found someone prepared to marry her even after her disastrous nonwedding. Not only that, the man she has married has made his way to the United States and can provide some relative prosperity. Still, this scene is short and comes long after we are left hanging with an utterly devastated Maithili in our minds. It does not do enough to contradict the impression that a woman who speaks up will come to no good.

Several elements here are in stark contrast to the mythological Sītā's wedding. Most notable is the imbalance between the bride's and groom's parties. This is foregrounded in many ways in the movie, from the comments of the crook on how easy it is to tell the two parties apart by their body language to the poignant scenes where the groom's family insults the bride's by spurning the costly gifts they receive and passing them on to their servants. It seems that Sagar was quite right to put his wishful thinking about equity between the two parties in the counterfactual mood.

Further, in contrast to Sītā's wedding, here the dowry issue is openly dealt with and the abuses of the system are laid bare. The problems with the dowry follow from the imbalance between the two parties. The bride's people are nervous that the deal may be called off at the last minute, which would bring a stigma to the girl, but not to the boy. The groom's father even boasts that he has several times "gotten up" from marriages of his other sons. He feels entitled to

151. *jaise laṛkī ko paidā karke unhoṃ ne baṛā pāp kiyā ho.*

152. *āj ek laṛkī samāj ke sāre gārevāle rīti rivāz ke bandhan se āzād ho gayī.*

153. *ho saktā hai ki tujhe taklīf sahnī paṛī lekin laṛkījāt ko himmat milegī, baṛī himmat milegī, śābāś beṭī, śābāś.*

demand his price, even at the cost of much anxiety for his relatives-to-be. When actions compromising the bride are found out, he uses this as blackmail to raise his demand even higher.

We never get to the *bidāī* ceremony, but the sorrow and anxiety of the parents of a daughter is palpable throughout. Maithili's worry about her father and his ordeal is a beautiful reminder of Sītā's way of telling her wedding's story to Anasūyā, with her loving sympathy for her father's plight. There is a difference, though. In the movie, the worry is mostly financial. Parental love here is compromised by the burden of having to raise a dowry. The focus is exclusively on how, from the moment of a girl's birth, her parents are scheming about how to raise enough money to ensure a good groom. This seems to crowd out love, and it may be significant that the film does not address the worry about the welfare of the daughter at her *sasurāl*. We can easily imagine how her greedy father-in-law would pressure Maithili into bringing in more money afterward, but there is only a hint that they might mistreat her.

Another marked difference with Sītā's wedding is the fall from grace of the groom. We started out with the knowledge that he was Maithili's choice, but we end up being as disappointed in him as she is. Maithili flatly refuses her love match now, saying somewhat incongruously that it's better to become a *satī* than to marry a weak man like him. Why does the scriptwriter have her say that? Obviously, she cannot become a *satī* without marrying. The implicit threat is that she would burn herself, committing suicide by jumping in the wedding fire. By evoking the image of the woman burning in flames, the director raises the specter of dowry deaths in the audience's mind, and thus the potential ill-treatment of a woman in her *sasurāl* is hinted at implicitly.

All in all, this episode in *Lajja* seems like the other side of the coin of Sītā's wedding. Here we have explicitly the problematization (*pūrvapakṣa*) unspoken in Sagar's television version. The film brings to the fore a feminist agenda, indicting the dowry system and the inequality of bride-takers and -givers. Sagar tried hard to address the latter especially, by giving a positive example. *Lajja* shows the consequences of less-than-noble behavior, but ironically, it is the courageous bride who comes out on the losing end. She does not commit suicide, but we wonder what will become of her. Some may commend her action, and the public is certainly made to feel good because she speaks up. But the bottom line is that we know her future marriage chances are utterly ruined. She ends up being rather the opposite of a role model.

One wonders what is accomplished by this elaborate mise-en-scène and by framing this as Sītā's wedding turned sour. On one level, the director seems to wish to raise the issue of hypocrisy underlying so-called holy wedlock in Hindu society. On another, he seems to indicate that the root of the problem is

Hinduism itself, in particular the *Rāmāyaṇa,* which is portrayed as an inherently patriarchal text. The first intent, that of demasking hypocrisy, is a commendable one. As long as greed can pose as righteousness, things cannot improve. The root problem, as shown so bitterly-comically in *Dil,* is of course human greed. This is unfortunately difficult to change. One may well argue that the rhetorics by which such greed can be allowed to take its course can be more easily remedied by deflating it. The perception that the groom's party has a right to feel superior over and to make demands of the bride-givers enables recurrence of the problem.

However, if the director wishes to suggest that this is a problem created by religion, or the *Rāmāyaṇa* story in particular, he is misleading us. Rather, as we have seen, it is one whose inequity even Vālmīki's text seeks to address in its efforts to show the parties' exemplary behavior. The root of the problem does not lie with religious texts but rather with the concept of honor (*izzat*), which is what prompts the urgency to find a suitable groom, lest the bride remain unmarried, and what informs the dowry and gift-giving. The problem is not Sītā, or Vālmīki, or the *Rāmāyaṇa* tradition, or for that matter Hinduism. I hasten to add that the problem was there well before the birth of Islam and the arrival of the British so should not be blamed on either of those either. The problem lies in a culture that turns a marriage into a public display of something other than a promise of mutual love and affection between bride and groom and their families.

The Wedding Wave of the Nineties

This wedding scene in *Lajja* remains an exciting instance of traditional unstated privileges being tackled head-on. However, this movie, though much hyped, turned out to be a flop. The cash grossers are instead the feel-good movies of the 1990s, such as *HAKHK* and *DDLJ*. I will here focus on the wedding ceremonies proper in the former and put them in the larger perspective of gender relations. I will also bring to bear a recent offbeat film that reflects and comments on the trend, *71/2 Phere,* by Isshaan Trivedi.

The feel-good movies of the nineties often are framed completely as traditional wedding movies. Even the NRI directors Mira Nair and Gurinder Chadha cashed in on the trend with *Monsoon Wedding* (2001) and *Bride and Prejudice* (2004), explicitly indicating in their titles that they were getting on the bridal bandwagon or, if you want, surfing the wedding wave.

What makes these films so attractive? For one, they are good fun. Standards of production are high; everything is suffused with song and dance, beauty and wealth. Weddings are also, on the screen, great occasions for showing off, and they make for great entertainment. All this can be watched without embarrassment in the company of little children. Thus they are family films in the true sense of the word.

There is more. The films quite explicitly state they are family value oriented. They are proud to be celebrations of joint family living. All or nearly all members are loving and committed to their families first and foremost. In contrast to the "reflexively rebellious youth" films of the Amitabh Bachchan period, these films feature not confrontation but reconciliation.[154] Children are respectful to their parents, parents love their children. Individual choice is allowed, but individuals always choose for the family. One could say we find the psychological equivalent of free market theory in the vein of the *Economist*'s dictum: leave it up to the free market (here choice), and everything will be for the greater good in the end. Consequently, in these movies there are hardly any villains—free agents choose well. There are only misunderstandings and unfortunate circumstances.

Of course it helps that the joint families in the movies are rich, with no lack of space or resources. They have at their disposal plenty of consumer goods; everyone is aware of Western lifestyle niceties; but all this is effortlessly integrated in an Indian lifestyle, which is coded as basic. No matter how fancy the cars they drive and the houses they live in, all characters are supposed to be Indian at heart and proud of it, too. Everyone feels good in his or her own skin and exudes self-confidence. No more lingering postcolonial angst. No more hangovers from India's engagement with communism or leftover guilt about excessive consumption while the poor masses starve. The movies show a guiltless Westernization and consumerist lifestyle. A good example of confluence of Western elements and Indian traditions in a wealthy setting is the engagement ceremony of Pooja and Rajesh in *Hum aap ke hain koun . . . !*

We have already seen that though their marriage is arranged the traditional way, the enlightened family patriarch wishes the couple to meet before anything is finalized so they can have their say, too. This trendy mix of "Indian-style arranged" and "Western-style love" marriage is reinforced in the rites that take place during the engagement ceremony. Mostly they are traditional: feeding the groom-to-be, lighting of a *diyā* and setting it afloat in the temple tank, and other pūjā rituals recognizable to the middle-class audience, yet celebrated with great luxuriousness. At the same time, there is an easy, elegant incorporation of Western influence, in the form of the rings that are

154. One could argue that Amitabh Bachchan, now in the role of the family patriarch, remains the troublemaker, but now it is in his insistence on maintaining family traditions.

exchanged. Of course, all this takes place in the temple at Rāmṭek, so the surroundings are safely Indian dharma, Rāma-sanctioned, as the song repeats over and over ("Vāh vāh Rāmjī").

The wedding wave movies' effortless integration of Western and Indian style is particularly apparent in the way these movies portray women. The heroines featured are traditional Hindu women with a modicum of spunk and a veneer of modernity. They are equally comfortable in jeans as in a sari, but prefer the latter. They may be computer engineers, yet at the same time, they are firmly rooted in dharma. They are playful, but they always choose submission. They are allowed a measure of freedom and can be endearingly strong in their opinions, yet they are basically deeply committed to their joint families, who reciprocate. These women are shown to be deeply loved by their men and in-laws. The joint family is portrayed as a happy, harmonious group. There is no conflict for the women in their *sasurāl*. In *HAKHK*, the father of Pooja and Rajesh's *cācā* are old friends. The potentially divisive issue of dowry is cleverly bypassed by having a greedy aunt raise the issue, only to be put down by the enlightened patriarch (Kazmi 1999: 145). The niceties the friends exchange are reminiscent of the bride-takers and -givers of Sagar's version of Sītā's wedding. Ramesh's uncle never makes his old friend feel he is inferior because he is the father of the bride. After the birth of Pooja's son, her family comes to visit their daughter. After a few happy days, they feel that they have stayed too long, but her in-laws firmly deny this and insist on them canceling their tickets back home.

During Pooja and Rajesh's wedding ceremony at her house, all the tension between the party of the bride and that of the groom is transferred to playful interaction between the young men who came in the *barāt* and the young women who are "sisters" of the bride. The focus is the teasing by hiding the groom's shoes and demanding a fee for revealing where they are hidden. In this movie, the whole issue of the families' rivalry is transformed to a war of the sexes, famously dealt with in the song "Jūte de do paise le lo" ("Give the shoes and take the money"). The whole weighty issue of the party of the groom's superiority to that of the bride is here made light of and playfully turned into a hit song.

Finally, the portrayal of the wedding ceremony itself is significant. As in Sagar's version of Sītā's wedding, there is a marked foregrounding of women's rituals. Of course, in the movie industry, that gives the opportunity for many a song-and-dance sequence, and in the interest of providing *masālā*, the sexy scenes are not edited out. While we do not witness the singing of saucy *gālīs*, we do have some risqué all-women ceremonies (of the type called *khoṛiyā;* see Raheja and Gold 1994: 94), for example, the celebrated song-and-dance sequence of "Dīdī terā devar divānā" ("Sister, your brother-in-law is crazy"; more on this scene later).

The Brahminical ceremonies are shown on the screen, but they are made light of. While they are the ritual heart of the wedding, certainly the real interest of the protagonists as well as the audience lies elsewhere. During Pooja and Rajesh's *sāt phere,* for instance, the brother-in-law is preoccupied with preventing the party of the bride from stealing the groom's shoes. Just before the auspicious occasion (*muhūrt*), he and his friend discover they've been cheated. While throwing flowers on the newlyweds who are circumambulating the fire, they chime in with the Sanskrit mantra chanting, but instead chant *Ham ullū ban gaye* ("We've been made fools of"). The Brahminical heart of the ceremony is thus not taken very seriously in these movies, but that does not undermine the importance of the traditional marriage. Rather, it can be taken as a hip positioning, more of a fashion statement than a profound rejection.

This wedding wave has now matured to the point that it has spawned its own spoofs. One example is the comedy *7½ Phere* (2005). The (anti)heroine of the movie is Asmi (Juhi Chawla), a dedicated but somewhat clueless young aspiring television director who gets a chance to get ahead by directing a reality television show. The topic is to be "wedding" (*śādī*), and it has to be the traditional joint-family-style wedding. Unfortunately, the show is planned for a time outside of the astrologically auspicious season, and in all of Bombay there is only one family that is planning a wedding that can be broadcast live. Another obstacle is that the family of the bride refuses to be filmed. Asmi and her team then manage to install secret cameras with the connivance of one family member, *cācā* Manoj (Irfan Khan). Manoj is in love with her, and Asmi exploits him mercilessly, though somewhat clumsily.

The reality show provides lots of occasions to show wedding rites, nearly all of which are of non-Brahminical nature and are carried out by the women. In fact, the men are markedly absent from the center of the action. After having settled the match, it seems, they withdraw. The patriarchs of the family are not portrayed in a flattering way—they are unmasked as oversexed and hypocritical. But their wives are no sweethearts either. Everyone is more interested in watching television, and the melodrama on the screen drowns out that of reality. Ironically, it is the melodrama in their own family, which they are not interested in, that will be the material for the next television series. This joint family is not an ideal one, and some tensions are hinted at. However, this is not elaborated on, and whatever criticism there is in the first few scenes soon gets drowned in the plot of Asmi's efforts to get the show going.

Still, throughout, there is occasion to reflect on the nature of wedlock. The bride is encouraged to be Sītā-like. The impending wedding tends to bring out memories of others, missed love marriages and non-religious court marriages that brought strife and estrangement to the family. Neither love nor arranged marriages are advocated. Everyone is shown to have ended up in a loveless situation.

Things get complicated when it turns out that the "reality" bride is planning an elopement. Now the Rukmiṇī scenario comes into play. When the uncle, Manoj, finds out about the elopement through the hidden camera, he immediately rushes off to try to persuade the reluctant bride to go through with the wedding. His impromptu advice for his niece nicely summarizes a common-sense piece of advice: "What's all that love-shove. Look, look at the other people. After a year of marriage everything is over, they've all become alike.... Whether it's a love marriage or not, they all start with love and afterwards it's all over, kids and the lot, household, all that."[155]

Of course his niece denies that her love will be of that type, but the uncle wisely says: "Is your love so special? Everyone says something like that."[156] The tone of the perspective offered is one of experience and world-weariness, which is incongruent for this clumsy, unmarried uncle. Still, this line is singled out as profound, repeatedly replayed by the television directors and repeated in other situations. No doubt the repetition is meant to rob it of its sting, to reveal it as commonplace—seemingly profound yet banal.

In the same conversation, we find an interesting reference to another movie. Manoj tries to cheer up his niece by saying that the groom she does not want looks a lot like Aamir Khan in *Qayamat se qayamat tak* (1988) and she will look like the heroine, Juhi Chawla, next to him. She points out that in that film, the lovers' families did not let them marry either and they died for their love. This is an interesting use of another film as a kind of justification for a "real-life" scenario. We are reminded of Nanddās's Rukmiṇī, who was following the example of the Gopīs when she planned her elopement with Krishna. In any case, the incident confirms that film perceptions of true love and the legitimacy of elopement are part of the discourse about marriage, but not everyone gets the film's message straight. Uncle is quoting the other movie to justify what he sees as the right action, but he conveniently neglects its main message. It is a

155. *kyā hotā hai yah pyār-vār. dekh, bāqī ke logoṃ ko dekh. śādī ke ek sāl bād sab khatm ho jātā hai sab ekse ho jāte hai . . . love marriage ho na ho sab pyār se śurū karte haiṃ bād meṃ sab khatm ho jātā hai bacce-kacce ghar-bār sab.*

156. *"merā pyār vaisā nahīṃ hai." "terā pyār koī anokhā hai? sab aise hī bolte haiṃ."*

timely reminder for our study of messages sent by popular media: they are not necessarily received as we might think. Movies with subversive messages may still be read to support the status quo.

The possibility of elopement initially excites Asmi and her team. However, dramatic as it may be, it ruins the plan of a "traditional wedding show." Asmi's producers (two impossibly caricaturized Westernized women) are adamant that without a wedding, there can be no show. The television team then becomes involved in construing its own reality and does all it can to discourage the elopement, resorting to all kinds of illegal and immoral means.

This disgusts Manoj. When he finds out what tricks are being played on his family, he refuses to cooperate any longer. He cleverly turns the tables on Asmi to make her understand that she's playing with a woman's life. Asmi remains committed to the cause that the show must go on, but he seems to have gotten through, as her interference now is limited to watching the action unfold. On the day of her wedding, the bride still manages to elope, with the help of *cācā* Manoj, but this lover is no Krishna ready to save the damsel in distress. He stands her up, and she is promptly shuttled back just in time for the arranged ceremony. This is an interesting variant on the *DDLJ* scenario: willing bride but groom with cold feet. Here the lovers do not get to marry, but the bride is allowed to return within the magic circle of arranged matrimony.

When the bride arrives back at her wedding, unbeknownst to most, there is a moment of comic relief. We see the pundit in front of the sacred fire muttering complaints about the quality of the firewood and the ghee to be poured on it. In the whole movie, this is the sole glimpse of the Brahminical aspect of the wedding, and it is not a flattering one. The bride's party puts the officiant in place, reminding him that they are the ones who will pay him his fee, so he should not criticize them as if he belonged to the groom's party. This hints at the inequality between the bride and groom parties. Although we don't get to see any direct evidence of such behavior, still it is understood to be there in the background. Yet the bride's family feels confident enough to joke about its inferior status, which may be a sign of some societal change.

Next, we get to listen to the Sanskrit formulae uttered by the pundit, but suspense rises as the bride keeps crying throughout the ceremony and the groom halts the action for a private talk with her. After the proper confession, he is—to everyone's relief—ready to go through with the ceremony. The action now goes in fast-forwarded to the farewell ceremony. Pathos is prominent, as it should be, but this is contrasted comically with Asmi's great relief that her show did come through as a wedding show. She succeeds in selling the show to her bosses, but has a last-minute change of heart and cuts up the tapes. No more compromised reality for Asmi.

The film is highly self-reflexive, with lots of inside jokes and references to the lead actress', Juhi Chawla, role in *Qayamat se qayamat tak* and to the movie *Kabhi khushi kabhie gham*. This intertextuality brings to the fore how life imitates the movies and the movies in turn imitate life.

In any case, we have come full circle here, from television back to television: from *Ramayan*'s society wedding of Rāma and Sītā, which aimed to change societal praxis, to a movie about a television reality show about a real wedding failing to conform to society's demands for entertainment. In the process, several levels of reflexivity, irony and self-criticism are added. It seems that after the trendsetting Sītā-Rāma-*vivāha* came a decade of wedding films of the rosy *HAKHK* type, which happily fulfilled, at least on celluloid, the prophecy of the happy joint family that Sagar predicted in the counterfactual mood. Now, after the serious soul-searching and self-criticism of the *Rāmāyaṇa* tradition in *Lajja*, finally things are balanced out, and we see actual weddings as reality shows, replaying the drama of movies and mythology alike, but coming out on the side of the status quo nevertheless.

Conclusions: A Warm Welcome for the Submissive Bride

The gender ideology expressed in mythological and filmī marriage ceremonies has remained remarkably constant over time. The examples of the secret love marriage do not truly challenge that status quo. The ideal of the traditional wedding is still the norm. There may be more participation of women in the modern depictions and even some lip service to selected feminist ideas, in particular a critique of the excesses of dowry; however, at the core, the television and most film versions turn out to be even more patriarchal than the older ones.

This is best illustrated by the example of Sītā's wedding as portrayed in the television version. Often, it is taken for granted that the television version is a bhakti text, just like *Rām Carit Mānas,* the main difference being that it is electronically mediated. The wedding ceremony would be an excellent example, as there is plenty of *darśana* going on with recitation of *Rām Carit Mānas* on the soundtrack. It is undeniable that Sagar has exploited the medium of television very well for the sake of providing maximum *darśana*. However, my comparison shows that he also leaves out crucial bhakti elements. Generally, he disregards loving devotion in favor of moralizing sermons. Notwithstanding some innovations that seem progressive at first sight, such as the *ekapatnīvrata,* on the whole, Sagar's version seeks unapologetically to reinforce a patriarchal normativity, more even than his ancient and medieval sources. In comparison to its sources, Sagar's text, then, is didactic, more dharma- than bhakti-oriented, and more explicit in subjugating women to patriarchy.

This is very similar to the message of quite a few Hindi movies. Parentally sanctioned matrimony remains the sine qua non. The Rādhā-Krishna scenario is present in the form of secret wedding vows of the Gāndharva-vivāha type, but they do not constitute the full sanctity of wedlock, and women who engage in them typically fare badly. Only prolongued, self-sacrificing suffering can redeem them in the eyes of society. In the end, parental approval is the determining factor of the couple's ultimate happiness, both morally and materially, as these tend to go hand in hand.

The abiding popularity of both television *Rāmāyaṇa* and wedding wave movies—as opposed to more feminist movies like *Lajja*—seems to indicate that their formula hits a nerve. There is a strong desire among women to carve out an identity for themselves that allows for both a measure of Western-style emancipation that entails some freedom and the safety net of a strong family basis. Maybe we should also look at it from the other side, and say that men like to be seen as acting enlightened toward their womenfolk, yet at the same time also be assured of their subservience? Clearly, these series and movies put their finger right on a need. There is a strong yearning to overcome the dichotomy between modernity and tradition and to find a symbiosis of both in a hybrid identity to be proud of. Not incidentally, against the backdrop of commercial television stations on which all this is broadcast, this allows for uninhibited, seemingly boundless consumption of consumer goods (this aspect has been much commented on; see e.g., Uberoi 2001b on *HAKHK*). In other words, like the television version, the movies show how you can, so to speak, have your wedding cake and eat your *laḍḍū* too.

PART II

The Challenges of Married Life

4

In Good Days and Bad Days

Sītā and Rādhā Leave Purdah to Follow Their Men

Leaving Purdah for the Forest

I have traced the culmination of romantic love in matrimony. But after the wedding, what? For our goddesses, the story was not "They lived happily together ever after," nor of course is such the case for ordinary women. In the following chapters, I will explore some of the difficulties the goddesses face. How do they respond to challenges in their marriages? What can ordinary women learn from this?

In this chapter, I look at the first test of the marriage. What happens when the going gets tough? How do women react when their men fall on hard times? The wedding promise was for good days and bad days. What happens when the hardships arrive? The story of Sītā and the Gopīs include comparable situations when women abandon home and hearth to join their men in times of sorrow.

For Sītā, we look at her resolve to follow her husband into the hardship of his exile to the forest (*vanavāsa*, or Hindi *banvās*). After the wedding, a "happily ever after" seems quite possible. Sītā and Rāma are joined in conjugal bliss, living in the royal palace in Ayodhyā. Rāma has a bright future ahead, set up to be the next king. However, fate decides differently. On the eve of his coronation, Rāma's stepmother, Kaikeyī, becomes worried and schemes to get her own son, Bharata, on the throne. She manages to seduce her husband, Daśaratha, into promising her that whatever she asks will be fulfilled. She asks that Bharata may be crowned in Rāma's stead, and that Rāma will be exiled for twelve years. Daśaratha is appalled but finds himself trapped, unable to take back his promise. Rāma, paragon of filial piety, takes this turn of fate with remarkable equanimity. He declares himself prepared to help his father keep his promise and voluntarily makes preparations to leave. After comforting his father, he first says goodbye to his mother, and then breaks the news to Sītā. I will examine in detail her reaction. What is important is her instinctive, courageous decision to take the big step out of purdah and follow her husband into a life of penance in the woods. The episode takes several chapters in *Vālmīki Rāmāyaṇa* (*VR* 2.26–30) and is also treated elaborately by Tulsīdās (*RCM* 2.57–68). Sagar dispenses with it rather swiftly, spending only part of one episode on its retelling (vol. 5, episode 15, TVR 201–3).

This episode of the *Rāmāyaṇa* story has attracted little scholarly attention,[1] but it is arguably a moment of great intensity and significance for the rest of the story. Moreover, it may well bear a more direct relevance to ordinary women's lives than the rather exceptional "proof of purity" situation, because it portrays a woman's moral quandary and independent decision making to resolve it. Sītā's action could potentially function as a positive, empowering example. Her decision to leave behind the comfort of the palace shows a willingness to step out of confinement "within four walls" (*cār-divārī*). It can be seen as a guiding light for stepping out of purdah and courageously braving the public gaze for a cause. Such an interpretation can have empowering effect. One major example of such a liberating application of Sītā's example would be Mahatma Gandhi, who used it to encourage Indian women to come out of the house and fight for indepencence (Kishwar 1985).

Sītā's eagerness to join her husband in his forest exile has an interesting parallel in the mythology of the Gopīs. I have in mind the episode of Krishna's round dance, or Rāsa-līlā, his sporting with the Gopīs on the full-moon night in the autumn month of Kārttik. A parallel with Sītā's resolve is the decision of Rādhā and the other Gopīs of Braj to join the village charmer, young Krishna, in the forest. The description of the Rāsa-līlā takes five chapters in *Bhāgavata Purāṇa* (10.27–32), and the medieval transcreations are hence called *Rās Pañcādhyāyī* (The five chapters of the Rāsa). We will look at the earliest vernacular reworking—by the *rasika bhakta* Harirām Vyās. In Sagar's *Shri Krishna*, the scenes are split: the Rāsa-līlā proper (vol. 7, episode 59) is preceded by a preparation or rehearsal (vol. 7, episode 56).

1. There are two important exceptions, though: Sutherland (1989, 1992) and the rhetorical analysis by Renate Söhnen-Thieme (1980: 47–96).

The comparison may seem flawed at first sight. Indeed, the stories of Sītā and the Gopīs are different in more than a superficial way. Most prominently, their motives are radically different. Sītā, being a loyal wife, feels that it is her duty to follow her husband into the forest, and she argues dharma. The Gopīs, being adulterous lovers, forsake their duty toward their husbands to follow Krishna in the forest. He will invoke dharma to send them back, but of course they do not listen.

Notwithstanding these fundamental differences, the similarities make for a fruitful comparison. In each case, women make an independent decision on a moral issue pertaining to their lives. It is for each a courageous decision, in that it involves, in a sense, a coming out of purdah, leaving a relatively comfortable and protected environment for the unknown forest "out there." In each case, too, the women face opposition. The males are initially unwilling to let them carry out their intent and argue on the grounds of dharma that they should stay home or go back home: that is where their heaven lies, and following the men will be hell. The women react strongly, threatening suicide in more or less outspoken ways, but they also show that the men's arguments of dharma do not apply. They show courage in their willingness to defy conventional norms. In the end, the women prevail, by showing that love, or *prema,* is stronger than dharma.

Their resistance to the men's suggestion they stay home makes it clear that the women leave the world of convention and traditional roles prescribed for them by their own choice. Their main motivation to do so is their love for their men, which they value more highly than conventional duty. This choice fits well in the context of bhakti, where love for God takes precedence over everything else, even the worldly concerns of conventional morality. I will investigate whether in the televised versions love is still valued over dharma.

This chapter is organized differently from the previous ones. Instead of first treating the Sītā story and then that of Rādhā, or following the sources chronologically, the discussion proceeds thematically. I discuss both goddesses together with respect to different narrative moments. I will discuss first the setting of the women's decision, then the initial reaction of the males to the women's resolve, then the way the women push through their intents, and finally the outcome of their decisions. These differences need to be seen against the general background of bhakti, especially the differences between Tulsīdās's Rāma bhakti and Harirām Vyās's Krishna bhakti.

Finally, I compare these versions with some popular Hindi movie evocations of the Rāsa-līlā and of Sītā's decision to accompany Rāma to the forest. For the latter, I will look at K. S. Sethumadhavan's 1977 *Yahi hai zindagi,* and

TABLE 4.1. Overview of Similarities between Sītā's and the Gopīs' Resolves

General intent	Moral quandary Leaving comfort for forest Out of purdah Decision goes against elders
Opposition	Initial rejection by beloved Men argue in terms of dharma Men promise heaven, threaten hell
Women's arguments	Love is stronger than dharma Defying *maryādā:* courageous Suicide threat
Result	Women get their way, men yield
Interpretation	Love prevails over dharma Model for bhakti

for the former again at *HAKHK,* as well as K. Ravishankar's 1992 *Meera ka Mohan* and Ashutosh Gowarikar's 2001 *Lagaan.*

Sītā and Rādhā Go to the Forest

Setting the Stage

In both stories, the women choose to move from the world of civilization and conventional morality (*maryādā*) to the uncivilized habitat of the forest. Their decision involves a transformation from a comfortable, well-established role-pattern into a totally new persona. It is a move into unfamiliar domain, a jump into the unknown. What is different for Rādhā and Sītā is he background of this transformation, as well as its relation to *dharma*. The authors of the medieval and contemporary texts have taken care to define the tone of the episode by setting the stage carefully.

BACKGROUND: JOYOUS UNION OR TEARFUL EXILE. The most significant differences between the two stories lie in the background against which the women make their decisions. For Sītā, the trip to the forest is not a happy occasion. Her husband Rāma, the erstwhile crown prince, has been exiled, a reversal of fortune, brought about by palace intrigues. In Vālmīki's version, Rāma comes to Sītā to break the news to her "on the way to the forest," as Rāma puts it (*VR* 2.26.19–24). When she sees him come in, she is as yet ignorant about the situation. Seeing her husband's drop of spirits, she worries and charmingly tries to cheer him up (2.26.6–18). Remarkably, her reaction to the news of the exile per se is never registered. Instead the focus is on her forceful reaction against his assumption that she will stay home. In the *Mānas*, too, Sītā reacts only to Rāma's intent to leave her behind. This overwhelms all other thoughts, and she does not comment on the injustice of Kaikeyī.[2] In this reversal of circumstances, Sītā is faced with a Hobson's choice: either staying comfortably home yet missing Rāma, or accompanying her husband on his exile to the threatening forest. In that context only, the forest has some attraction. In the words of Kauśalyā, the forest has become auspicious now that Rāma is going there, and Ayodhyā will be inauspicious without him (*RCM* 2.56.3a).[3] The pathos of the occasion is brought out well in Tulsī's story: when Sītā appears on the scene, her mother-in-law is lamenting her loss.[4] Sagar's television version, too, features a lot of wailing on the part of the women in the palace, in Kauśalyā's words: "How come the hour of doom has arrived?" (TVR 201).[5]

The Gopīs' excursion to the woods, on the other hand, is a happy and auspicious occasion. Its purpose is a rendezvous with Krishna, the long-awaited fulfilment of their dreams, as the Braj poet puts it (*maṃna ciṃtyo pāyo baru nāhu, RP* 2.1b). For the Gopīs, the forest is right from the start a romantic place. The tone is set immediately in the first lines of Vyās's work:

> The bright night of autumn came.
> All over the forest lotuses bloomed open....
> The banks of the Yamunā with moonbeams adorned.
> Trees dripping with nectar from flowers and fruit.
> The breeze, thrice pleasant, burnt sorrow away (*RP* 1.1a–b)[6]

This conforms with his source text, *Bhāgavata Purāṇa* (10.29.1–3), and follows the conventions of Sanskrit literary theory. The desired sentiment is to be created by an appropriate setting, the technical term for which is *uddīpana vibhāva*. In the case of romantic emotion (*śṛṅgāra rasa*), a romantic portrayal of the forest forms an appropriate background. In Sagar's television version of the Rāsa-līlā too, the romantic mood is emphasized. The episode has been introduced previously (vol.7, episode 58) with shots of Gopīs suffering from

2. This is left up to the people of Ayodhyā. Their reaction to the news is described at length (*RCM* 2.46.4–51.3): "Some put blame on Fate, who shows nectar, but serves poison" *(eka bidhātahi dūṣanu dehīṃ, sudhā dekhāi dīnha biṣu jehīṃ,* 2.49.1a). One metaphor, interestingly, uses the image of the forest: "Hearing the news all men and women became upset, like trees and creepers seeing a forest fire" (*suni bhae bikala sakala nara nārī, beli biṭapa jimi dekhi davārī,* 2.46.4a).

3. *baṛabhāgī banu avadha abhāgī, jo raghubaṃsatilaka tumha tyāgī.*

4. *dāruna dusaha dāhu ura vyāpā, barani na jāhiṃ bilāpa kalāpā.*

5. *kaisī pralay kī ghaṛī ā gaī hai?*

6. *sarada suhāī āī rāti, dasuṃ disa phūli rahī banajāti... sasi gomaṃḍita yamunā kūla, bariṣita biṭapa sudhā phala phūla, tribidhi pavana dauduṣa bhayo.*

separation (*viraha*) from Krishna. The women are sighing in eager anticipation of the rendezvous, they are tossing and turning at night, and they frequently gaze longingly at the phases of the moon in the sky. With the romantic mood thus set up, episode 59 of the Rāsa-līlā proper starts out with shots of the appropriate *uddīpana vibhāva* (enhancing characteristics of a particular mood), such as the full moon, in which Krishna appears as in a medallion. The camera plays with the reflection of the moon on the river, and adds some romantic stars. The effect of Krishna's flute playing on the Gopīs comes next (classical *anubhāva*), and the women are shown setting out on their trip to the forest, in full dress, flowers in their hair, and making their way through the park-like forest with pretty flowers in bloom. Throughout the song that follows, the women are depicted as classical *abhisārikās*, or "women sneaking off to a secret tryst." According to classical literary theories, this erotic mood can be supported with the right dosis of suspense (*bhaya*) as a supporting emotion (*vyabhicāri-bhāva*). For the *abhisārikā nāyikā,* there are several potential dangers lurking in the forest. Interestingly, Sagar shows only Rādhā overcoming dangers on her way, in the form of a cobra on her path. She brushes breezily past the snake, which is depicted in *vismaya bhāva*—forgetting to attack her, as it were, and just turning to stare at the disappearing girl.

Thus, in all versions, Sītā's choice is portrayed as one made in a difficult and sad situation, with the predominant *bhāva* of sorrow (*śoka*). For the Gopīs, on the other hand, the choice is a welcome opportunity, an occasion of great joy. They are operating within a romantic context, with the predominant *bhāva* of erotic love (*śṛṅgāra*).

SĪTĀ IS SVAKĪYĀ, BUT HOW PARAKĪYĀ ARE THE GOPĪS? The status of the heroines is also quite different. Sītā is, of course, married to Rāma; she is his legal wife (*svakīyā*). The Gopīs, on the other hand, do not have any such legal bond with Krishna, rather the opposite; he is their paramour, and they leave their legal husbands behind to meet him (*parakīyā*). The choice to leave the world of *maryādā* for the forest is thus a much more drastic choice for the Gopīs than for Sītā. Their departure involves a radical reversal: from dutiful wives they are transformed into adulterous lovers. They put the salvation of their souls at stake.

In comparison with Sītā, it is even before they get a voice that the Gopīs have irrevocably made their choice. The medieval version stresses this strongly, as a significant part of Vyās's work is devoted to the description of the Gopīs rushing off, emphasizing all they leave behind (*tripadī* 1–5, which is one-sixth of the work). Giving up *maryādā* means, for one, transcending the world of village gossip:

> In their growing excitement, they forgot the honor of the family (*RP* 2.1a).[7]

From the outside world, Vyās moves to the Gopīs' more immediate environment. He stresses that they give up all material aspirations, and, more important, all family ties, even the strongest for a woman: that with husband and children:

> They gave up their interest in kine and in kin, causing frustration to husband and cattle (*RP* 2.1b).[8]

First, they forget to care for themselves. This is described in *Bhāgavata Purāṇa* (10.29.6–7), and the Braj poet follows suit:

> Unconcerned with food and drink, or bodily [needs] (*RP* 2.3a)
> Application of collyrium and makeup,
> Garments, jewelry, and coiffure disheveled. (*RP* 2.3a–4b)[9]

The lack of concern with sustenance of the body could be seen as asceticism, which is nicely parallel with Sītā's giving up the comforts of palace life for an ascetic life in the forest. The giving up of garments, jewelry, and makeup also is reminiscent of Sītā forgoing the lavish costume she is used to. However, whereas Sītā trades such for the simple outfit of the ascetic, the Gopīs do not don birch-bark garments, their lack of concern with attire serves another function. It is a convention of *kāvya* that women in love lose all awareness of what they look like. That becomes clear in the following lines:

> One forgot to apply kohl to her eyes,
> Another put her bodice on her hips, her skirt around her chest,
> Another wound her necklace around her feet.
> Earrings worn upside-down in their ears,
> Amulets adorning the string of their skirt. (*RP* 4.1–2b)[10]

The image of the woman rushing off to a tryst in disarray is a cliché in *kāvya*. What is meaningful here is that the Gopīs are depicted as forgetting about all the traditional signs of being a happily married woman (*sumaṅgalī*),

7. *ghara ḍaru bisaryo baṛhyo uchāhu.*
8. *dūdha pūta kī chāḍī āsa, godhana bharatā kiye nirāsa.*
9. *ṣāna pāna tana kī na saṃbhāra . . . aṃjana maṃjana aṃga siṃgāra, paṭa bhūṣana sira chūṭe bāra.*
10. *āṃjata eka nayana bisaryo, kaṭi kaṃcukī ura lahaṃgā dharyo, hāra lapeṭyo carana su; śravanani pahire ulaṭe tāra, tiranī para caukī sinagāra.*

so important in ordinary women's day-to-day concerns. Yet they are explicitly called auspicious in precisely this context, and this apparent contradiction (*virodhābhāsa*) is explained by their having found something more basic in life than even fulfilling a woman's dharma:

> Forgotten their oil-massages and toilet.
> Yet fortunate women they were: they had found the essence of life.
> (*RP* 3.4a–b)[11]

It is exactly in this respect that Sagar's television version differs. Here the Gopīs are all decked out carefully when they set out on their tryst. True, the accompanying song mentions that they lose all awareness and good sense and are in disarray:

> Their hair open, not tied up, they did not care about their clothes.[12]

At this point the camera focuses on one Gopī with her hair streaming down on her shoulders, and another one plucking at her clothes as if she is too hot. However, after this lip service to the classical scene of disarray, the women we get to see are all impeccably dressed. Maybe the actresses were not too keen to leave their toilets incomplete, or maybe Sagar felt it would break the mood if he showed them in disarray, as it might inadvertently insert a comic element (*hāsya rasa*), which would be out of place here. Whatever the case may be, modern sensibilities do not seem to favor this classical image.

There is another, most important difference with the televised version. The medieval text stresses that the women next give up all aspects of domestic dharma. It contrasts their choice of Krishna with the choice of home and hearth:

> This frenzy freed them from domestic chores. (*RP* 2.3b)[13]

The next verse, *Tripadī* 3 seems to be a mapping out all traditional tasks of women, only to stress how the Gopīs dropped them. The women give up their task of looking after the cattle[14] (*RP* 3.1a) and of cooking and feeding the family (*RP* 3.2).[15] Vyās stresses this strong reversal of a woman's dharma by specifying:

11. *tela ubaṭanu nhaibo bhūlī, bhāganī pāī jīvaṃna mūlī.*
12. *keśa khule bāndha nahiṃ basana sambhāla nahī.*
13. *hilaga chuḍāī gṛha vyauhāra.*
14. *eka duhānuṃ chāḍeṃ calī.*
15. *uphanata dūdha na dharyau utāri, sījhī thūlī cūlhaiṃ dāri, puruṣa tajyo jeṃvata huto.*

They left, putting down the child they were breastfeeding
Care for the husband was totally neglected (*RP* 3.3a–b)[16]

Again, the Braj poet is following *Bhāgavata Purāṇa*, where the women leave while serving food and feeding milk to their babies (*BhP* 10.26.6a).[17] The point is clear: rejection of conventional norms (*maryādā*) is the sine qua non for the Gopīs' forest excursion.

This is quite different in Sagar's television version. Amazingly, he manages to avoid a sense of conflict. True, the song that accompanies the Gopīs setting out on the tryst duly mentions that they give up conventional morality:

When they heard the flute, the Gopīs lost their awareness and good sense.
They set out, leaving their domestic chores and concern for worldly conventions.[18]

And, further on, the song specifies:

One gave up milking the cow, one gave up her food,
one left her bed, and came, singing *bhajanas* they came[19]

Nevertheless, it is notable that even this song avoids any hint that the Gopīs might be leaving their husbands or children. Furthermore, the images that accompany the song do not show any conflict between the Gopīs' tasks at home and their leaving for their tryst. The audience is given the impression that all this happens late at night, when the Gopīs have finished their housework anyway. One of the women is shown eating in the kitchen, which strengthens the impression that everyone has already been fed, if we project onto ancient times the social habit that women always take their meal last. In that case, the Rāsa-līlā can be seen as a simple late-night pastime for the Gopīs, not something that interferes with their household duties.

Sagar is here manipulating the technique of discrepancy between word and image. Something similar has been noted as a strategy to circumvent difficult issues for the *Amar Chitra Katha* comic strips (Hawley 1995: 115–8, 126, 128). The narrator of *Bhāgavata Purāṇa* resorted to a different device. He could explicitly allay doubts (*śankā-samādhāna*) by having the interlocutors of the story, sage Śuka and king Parīkṣit, moralize about the issue of how it can be

16. *cuci pyāvata bālaka dhari calī, pati sevā kachu karī na bhalī.*
17. *pariveṣayantyas taddhitvā pāyayantyaḥ śiśūn payaḥ.*
18. *bāṃsurī suni to gaī sudha budha gopina kī, calī gaī griha-kāja loka-lāja tajake.*
19. *gāu kalhoana choṛā kisī ne bhojana choṛā, kisī ne śayana choṛā, āī bhaja bhaja ke.*

that adulteresses, mired in the sensual world, can be liberated by God (*BhP* 10.29.12–6). Sagar uses that technique elsewhere (on Sagar's role as expounder of scripture, or *kathāvācaka,* see Lutgendorf 1995).

To be sure, Sagar in fact has already shown a bit more of the conflict in a previous episode. He has introduced a kind of rehearsal, or pre-Rāsa-līlā, earlier (vol. 7, episode 56).[20] The context is that Rādhā, in a fit of jealousy, challenges Krishna to prove his claim that other women love him as much as she does. She claims that she is special because she has flaunted all conventional morality for his sake. Krishna accepts the challenge. Before the test begins, Rādhā draws a line around Krishna, stipulating that no woman can come closer to him than this line, unless she would love Krishna as much as she does. This is reminiscent of the line Lakshmana drew around Sītā to protect her, the so-called Lakshmana Rekhā (more on this in chapter 6), but the roles here are reversed: it is the woman who draws the line around the man, and the goal is protecting not him but her claim on him (*adhikāra*) from other women.

Now Krishna calls the other Gopīs by playing his flute. Next we see the effect of the sound of his flute on the Gopīs. The women here are shown to be at work: one is churning butter, another is pounding grain, a third is massaging the feet of an elderly man (suggesting he might be her father-in-law rather than husband), a fourth stands near the cowshed with a pot in her hand, a fifth is shown to be about to leave the kitchen with a plate of food in her hand, presumably to serve to her family. Interestingly, the women are not shown to run off but to split up: while their bodily form remains on the spot of duty, their "soul" sails off, flying in the air, straight to Krishna.

What Sagar has managed to do here is avoid any hint of women really quitting their household tasks, by splitting the Rāsa-līlā in two: one "illusory" rehearsal and one "real" Rāsa-līlā. The first is only a meeting of "souls" and does not really involve any conflict with a woman's duties, since the Gopīs' bodies stay behind to carry out the tasks they were engaged in. The second and "real" Rāsa-līlā, it is suggested, takes place at night, after the Gopīs have carried out their duties anyway. Clearly there is a concern here to avoid giving the women in the audience ideas! Sagar's Gopīs thus have come to ressemble Sītā, and the inversion of the Lakshmana Rekhā only serves to underline that ressemblance.

20. A pre-Rāsa-līlā scene in which Krishna tests the depths of the Gopīs' feelings occurs also in Jīva Gosvāmī's *Gopāla-campū* (Brzezinski 2000), which may have inspired Sagar; however, the resonances of Sītā's Agniparīkṣā are totally absent in the older text.

Sagar adds yet another reference to the Sītā story, when he makes the Gopīs undergo a kind of trial by fire (Agniparīkṣā). When the Gopīs appear and approach the line Rādhā has drawn, it becomes enflamed, presumably by Rādhā's jealousy. The women slowly draw closer to Krishna, and although they remain at a little distance and do not really interact with him, they are able to withstand the fire unharmed. This proof of purity is highly reminiscent of Sītā's Agniparīkṣā, although it is Rādhā, not Krishna, who puts the women through this ordeal, whereas in the Rāma story usually Rāma himself is understood to command the trial.[21]

Another parallel with Sītā's fire ordeal is that the women who undergo the test are perhaps not real. It is only the spiritual forms of the Gopīs, their body doubles, that have approached Krishna and stepped across the line. In Tulsī's version of the Sītā Agniparīkṣā, the woman who undergoes the test—and indeed the one who was abducted—is not really Sītā but a mere body-double (*chāyā*) Sītā (*RCM* 6. 108–9; I will revisit this issue in chapter 6). Tulsī had taken his cue from another scripture, *Adhyātma Rāmāyaṇa* (Vaudeville 1955: 191). In Sagar's *Shri Krishna,* too, the burning Gopīs are not real, only shadow forms. And Sagar, too, has sound theological precedent. The Gauḍīya theologian Jīva Gosvāmī elaborates in his *Krishna-sandarbha* on this matter, in connection with nothing less than the weighty issue of the theory that the Gopīs were really Krishna's wives (*svakīyāvāda*). In order to support the claim of his uncle, Rūpa Gosvāmī, that the Gopīs were all properly married to Krishna, Jīva came up with the theological safety valve of *māyā:* illusory forms of the Gopīs were married to the Gopas, illusory Gopīs were engaged in housework (De 1961: 348–51).[22] One could argue that Sagar has reversed the roles: it seems to be the real forms of the women that continue doing the chores; while their spiritual forms fly off to Krishna and succeed in passing the fire ordeal set by Rādhā. None of these body doubles, though, gets to dance with Krishna: their function is merely to illustrate his philosophical discourse, which follows. After that, at a mere gesture of his hands, they disappear. Sagar's Gopīs thus have become less *parakīyā* than their predecessors and they have come to ressemble Sītā.

A CHANCE TO SPEAK ONE'S MIND. With Sītā, there is no issue of her going against dharma as she decides to leave for the forest. Unlike the Gopīs, she

21. In fact, in several versions, among them *Vālmīki Rāmāyaṇa,* it is not really Rāma's idea that Sītā undergo a trial by fire. Sītā herself offers to as proof of her purity.

22. I am grateful to Carol Salomon, University of Washington, for reminding me of this point.

does not flaunt defiance of social norms. Her speech is set in the palace, and she is shown in her well-defined role of young queen-to-be, conscious of observing family and court decorum. Tulsīdās stresses her obedience and compliance with the rules in placing her squarely in the midst of *maryādā*: the setting is Kauśalyā's quarters. Sagar has followed suit, and throughout the episode the presence of Sītā's mother-in-law looms large. Sītā does not get to be alone with Rāma to talk matters through. Instead, she has to remain within the bounds of her role as a humble daughter-in-law while speaking her heart.

By contrast, in Vālmīki's Sanskrit *Rāmāyaṇa,* the conversation with Rāma takes place in the privacy of their own appartments (*svaveśma, VR* 2.26.5). Sītā can afford to be confrontational, and she roundly rejects his advice to stay at home ("Why do you say such words, which I should ridicule on hearing, best husband among men?" 2.27.2).[23] She as much as says that what he has said is not worth listening to and unworthy of a true man (2.27.3).

In the television version, Sītā remains completely within *maryādā:* she turns to her mother-in-law before even addressing her husband and first seeks her blessing. Initially, Kauśalyā misunderstands Sītā, assuming that her daughter-in-law proposes to return to her parental home (*maikā* or *pīhar*). She affectionately asks her not to leave her alone in these tough times. However, when Sītā explains that she proposes to leave with Rāma instead, Kauśalyā immediately changes tracks and lends her active support to the decision, even using maternal authority to urge Rāma to take Sītā along on his trip.

Why this misunderstanding that has no base in the older *Rāmāyaṇas*? It allows for reflection on where a woman's loyalties should lie. Sītā makes it clear—with the family-in-law. She stresses that on marrying, her mother instructed her that all ties (*nātā*) with her natal kin had now been severed. "When I was saying goodbye in my bridal palanquin, my mother told me that I had no affiliation anymore with Janakpur" (*TVR* 201).[24] Sagar may be working here from Sītā's words according to Vālmīki, where she speaks to Rāma about the exclusive love of a women for her husband: "Neither father, nor son, or soul, nor mother or girlfriends: here and in the herebeyond, women have only their husband for refuge" (*VR* 2.27.6).[25] However, Vālmīki's Sītā made that a reciprocal relationship when she pointed out that for men, too, relatives ultimately are not as close as the wife. They do not share a man's reversal in fortune, only she does: "Noble Lord, father, mother, brother, son, daughter-in-

23. *kim idaṃ bhāṣase rāma vākyaṃ . . . yad apahāsyaṃ me śrutā naravarottama.*
24. *jab maiṃ ḍolī meṃ baiṭhkar vidā ho rahī thī to māṃ ne kahā thā, janakpur se terā koī nātā nahīṃ rahā.*
25. *na pitā nātmajo vātmā na mātā na sakhījanaḥ, iha pretya ca nārīṇāṃ patir eko gatiḥ sadā.*

law, each serve their own destiny according to their own merits. Only a woman shares her husband's fate, bull among men" (*VR* 2.27.4–5a).[26]

Sagar's script differs from both other versions of the story, in that it does not concentrate on Sītā's choice to stay in the palace or leave. Instead he sets up a contrast between a woman's reflex to return to the safe haven of the parental home when there is trouble at her in-laws', and her loyalty to the husband even in difficult circumstances.[27] Sītā's choice, then, for the modern audience, has been transformed into one between parental and in-law kin.

In the *Mānas*, on the other hand, Sītā not only has to make her case in the restraining presence of her mother-in-law but also has to contradict her husband's mother openly. The passage starts out with Kauśalyā speaking for Sītā and, though loving and well-intentioned, she says exactly what the girl does not want to hear. Kauśalyā here understands perfectly what Sītā wants ("That [delicate] Sītā wishes to go with you to the forest," 2.59.4a).[28] However, she recommends that Sītā stay home because she is so dear to her in-laws (2.58.4b–*dohā* and 59.1–2), to whom she will also be a support (2.60.4a). Kauśalyā also worries that Sītā's delicacy may not withstand the dangers and discomforts of the forest (2.59.3–*dohā* and 60.1–3).

The art of Tulsīdās in this passage is that he manages to make Sītā's concerns resonate through Kauśalyā's speech. One instance is when Kauśalyā asserts that Sītā will be unable to suffer the hardships of the forest, comparing her delicate daughter-in-law to the partridge (*cakora*), which is unable to suffer contact with the sun, because of its being a connoisseur (*rasika*) of the moon (*RCM* 2.59.4b).[29] The partridge is a traditional symbol of unswerving love, since it cannot stand to be separated from its beloved moon for even a moment. This image, then, also hints at how impossible it will be for Sītā to survive Rāma's departure, suffering love in separation (*viraha*). What is going on? Tulsīdās is basically working at several levels at once here: on the most obvious level, Kauśalyā's words give the mother-in-law's rationale for keeping Sītā back in Ayodhyā. Her speech is drenched in tenderly motherly feelings (*vātsalya*), which is in keeping with the preceding scene in which Kauśalyā uttered her feelings for her son Rāma. At the same time, the poet has weighed the words so

26. *āryaputra pitā mātā bhrātā putras tathā snuṣā, svāni puṇyāni bhuñjānāḥ svaṃ svaṃ bhāgyam upāsate; bhartur bhāgyaṃ tu nāryekā prāpnoti puruṣarṣabha.*

27. Sagar may also have been inspired by Vālmīki's Sītā's line when she asserts: "I'll live as comfortably in the forest, as in the house of my father" (*sukhaṃ vane nivatsyāmi yathaiva bhavane pituḥ*, *VR* 2.27.12 and similarly in 2.27.22).

28. *soi siya calana cahati bana sāthā.*

29. *caṃda kirana rasa rasika cakorī, rabi rukha nayana sakai kimi jorī.*

as to undermine Kauśalyā's discourse by evoking images from another kind of love, this time erotic love in separation (*viraha*). Notwithstanding Sītā's silence, the poet manages to conjure up for the audience a suggestion of what Sītā's plight must be while listening to her mother-in-law's words.[30]

Elsewhere, too, Tulsīdās undermines the mother-in-laws' speech. Kauśalyā makes the point that Sītā is so delicate and pampered that her feet have not even touched the earth (*RCM* 2.59.3a).[31] Tulsīdās's audience is well aware of the story of Sītā's birth from the Earth (and her eventual reabsorption into the womb of her mother), so these words must sound ironic. That irony is even more enhanced because Kauśalyā uses the poetic and unusual *avani,* which is frequently part of one of the titles of Sītā, namely Daughter of the Earth, or Avanikumārī (used by her husband Rāma just a bit later in 2.64.2b). It seems as if the audience can read Sītā's mind through the poet's subversion of her mother-in-law's words!

Thus, we can read in an undercurrent of silent protest by Sītā. However, we should not lose track of the fact that while the poet is at pains to show the plight of the heroine, at the same time he keeps stressing her exemplary obedience. Sītā's body language throughout the episode testifies to her deference: throughout Kauśalyā's speech, she sits with head hanging down:

> At that moment, Sītā, who had heard the news, had become apprehensive.
> She went to her mother-in-law, paid obeisance to her lotus-feet, and sat down with head bowed.
> Her mother-in-law blessed her tenderly, and observing the exceedingly young girl, she became distressed.
> Sītā sat with bowed head, worried, an image of beauty and pure love for her husband. (*RCM* 2.57, *dohā*–58.1)[32]

Sītā is dumbstruck by decorum—she cannot speak in front of her mother-in-law. The only sound she produces is the tinkling of her anklets as she shuffles her feet. Interestingly, the poet accords her at least that much of a

30. On yet another level, there is ironic foreshadowing of later events in Kauśalyā's words. The all-knowing audience will easily recognize references to the demon Rāvaṇa, who will kidnap Sītā (*RCM* 2.59, *dohā: nisicara carahiṃ duṣṭa jaṃtu bana bhūri*), to the ascetics that Rāma and Sītā will visit on their trip (2.60.2a), and to Hanumān (2.60.2b: *citralikhita kapi dekhi ḍerātī*, "She is afraid of even a monkey drawing").

31. *palaṃga pīṭha taji goda hiṃḍorā, siyaṃ na dīnha pagu avani kaṭhorā.*

32. *samācāra tehi samaya suni sīya uṭhī akulāi, jāi sāsu pada kamala juga baṃdi baiṭhi siru nāi. dīnhi asīsa sāsu mṛdu bānī, ati sukumāri dekhi akulānī, baiṭhi namitamukha socati sītā, rūpa rāsi pati prema punītā.*

voice in explicitly interpreting this as a plaintive sound, with a hint of despair that leads to suicide.

> With the nails of her pretty feet she draws circles on the floor, the sweet sound of her anklets is described by the poets:
> As if, in the power of love, they are begging: "Let Sītā's feet not leave us behind." (*RCM* 2.58.3)[33]

The Gopīs, too, circle their toes in the dust in despair in *Bhāgavata Purāṇa* (10.29.29). However, their situation is quite the opposite from that of Tulsī's Sītā. In the first place, the Gopīs can freely speak for themselves. They get rid of their family members long before they address their beloved. Vyās's Gopīs, even more emboldened than their *Bhāgavata Purāṇa* counterparts, curse their entire families:

> Mother, father, and husband stood in their way,
> They could not bear this bar to meeting their lover
> And insulted each and every one of them. (*RP* 5.1)[34]

In terms of body language, too, the Gopīs do not conform to paradigms of deference and respect. They are portrayed as openly displaying amorous behavior:

> The ladies of Vraja approached their beloved
> With meaningful glances and eyebrow-play (*RP* 6.2a–b).[35]

Vyās does not hesitate to have his Gopīs show a frank erotic interest ("Support our gourd-like breasts," *RP* 9.2c)[36]... and lack of interest in moral issues ("We're all weak women, not knowing dharma," 11.1c).[37] Thus, in the medieval sources, we find a strong contrast between Sītā, who is restrained in speaking out by the presence of her mother-in-law, and the Gopīs, free to speak their minds, unhesitatingly privileging love over dharma.

However, when we compare the television version Gopīs with Sītā, we find that things have changed. Sagar has managed to make even such erotic heroines as the Gopīs remain within *maryādā*. While the Gopī story does not allow for any in-laws, Sagar manages to include divine parental sanction for their

33. *cāru carana nakha lekhati dharanī, nūpura mukhara madhura kabi baranī; manahuṃ prema basa binatī karahīṃ, hamahi sīya pada jani pariharahīṃ.*

34. *mātā pitā pati rokī āna, sahatī na piya darasana kī hana, sabahiṃ ko apimāna kiyo.*

35. *brija banitā āī piya pāsa, citavati sainani bhrikuṭi bilāsa.*

36. *kuca tumbani avalamba de.*

37. *hama abalā nahi jānai dharma.*

play with Krishna. It is not the mother-in-law but none other than the Divine Mother who is the larger-than-life role model of the devoted wife, Śiva's consort, Gaurī. She does not figure in the Rāsa-līlā itself but in the episode immediately preceding it (vol. 7, episode 57), where the Gopīs are shown to perform Gaurī Pūjā in order to obtain Krishna as a husband (described in detail in chapter 1).

To sum up, in the episodes as related by medieval poets, Sītā and the Gopīs are on opposing ends of dharma. Sītā, the *svakīyā* heroine, makes her bid for personal happiness from within *maryādā,* whereas the Gopīs, *parakīyās*, can only make theirs after having squarely forsaken all conventional morality. Regarding attitude, the Gopīs are portrayed as active agents, quickly finding their own voices when challenged. Sītā, on the other hand, remains quite passive in demeanor. Though in *Vālmīki Rāmāyaṇa* she gets to speak in private with Rāma, in Tulsī's work, she is silenced by her mother-in-law's presence. Notwithstanding the poet's best efforts to let her voice resound in her mother-in-law's words, her protest initially remains a silent one.

In the televised *Ramayan,* on the other hand, Sītā gets to speak for herself immediately, but in a sense her voice is then taken over by her mother-in-law. Her plea is supported by Kauśalyā, but her decision to accompany Rāma is portrayed as woman's loyalty to her in-laws rather than parental kin. Sagar has turned the scene into a reflection on women's duties toward her husband's family. Here Sītā's voice has been hijacked in a subtle way for a patriarchal agenda.

The Gopīs in the television version are more like Sītā than Vyās's Gopīs. Sagar succeeds in downplaying their flaunting of *maryādā* in the Rāsa-līlā scene. He allows for only a symbolic quitting of houshold tasks in the spiritual rehearsal of the Rāsa-līlā. Moreover, he gives the Gopīs' love for Krishna a *svakīyā* aura by elaborating on the *vrata* they take for Gaurī, which is compared with Pārvatī's performance of ascetic activities to obtain Śiva for a husband. Sagar even has them go through a test, a trial by fire of sorts.

The Initial Rejection by the Males

In the medieval versions, Sītā and the Gopīs both have to face an initial rejection by the males they are about to sacrifice so much for. Even before they get a chance to speak, their men are already bent on discouraging them from carrying through with their intent. Male intuition may be responsible for Rāma and Krishna's immediate and correct assessment of their women's intent, but the males do not seem to have such great hunches when it comes to finding good reasons to keep the women home. Their arguments, which revolve around women's dharma and the dangers of the forest, wind up not being very convincing.

SERIOUS RĀMA AND AMBIGUOUS KRISHNA. Tulsī's Rāma and Vyās's Krishna differ most in terms of their tone, their treatment of dharma, and their ways of presenting the dangers of the forest. In the *Rām Carit Mānas,* Rāma's tone is all grave and earnest. In tune with the *maryādā* atmosphere sketched earlier, Rāma first agonizes about the propriety of speaking to one's wife in front of one's mother. However, invoking basically a case of emergency (Skt. *āpat*), he proceeds anyway: "hesitating to talk in the presence of his mother, he spoke anyway, silently thinking it to be a proper occasion" (2.61.1a).[38] This simple introduction helps sustain the tone of gravity and seriousness pervading the passage.

Rāma is quite clear about his advice, and does not leave his Sītā much choice: "Princess, listen to my advice, and don't count anything else in your heart" (*RCM* 2.61.1b).[39] Yet he uses inclusive language to introduce his command: "If you wish both your own and my good, take my word for it and stay home" (2.61.2a).[40] Tulsī is basically in agreement with Rāma's words in *Vālmīki Rāmāyaṇa,*[41] although there, Rāma has started out with the assumption that Sītā would stay home, and had already proceeded with advising her on how to behave in his absence so as to survive under the sway of his brother (*VR* 2.26.29–38). In all versions, Rāma is quite clear about his intentions.

In contrast, Krishna's reaction to the Gopīs' initiative is ambiguous, both in *Bhāgavata Purāṇa* and in the Braj poet's text. On the one hand, Krishna seems to encourage the women: "You have done well, coming along the way" (*RP* 6.3a);[42] but in the same breath, he reproaches them: "Ladies of good family shouldn't go out after dark" (6.3b).[43] The Gopīs are left to interpret this either as reproach or as a subtle congratulatory remark on their difficult task of giving up worldly honor and negotiating the dark forest to come near him.

However, Krishna is just set on confusing them: he seems encouraging when he obligingly asks "What can I do for you, who are worthy?" (*RP* 6.3c),

38. *mātu samīpa kahata sakucāhīṃ, bole samau samujhi mana māhī.*

39. *rājakumāri sikhāvanu sunahū, āna bhāṃti jiyaṃ jani kachu gunahū.*

40. *āpana mora nīka jauṃ cāhahū, bacanu hamāra māni gṛha rahahū.*

41. "Act here according to dharma, so that my mind will find peace" (*ihācarasva dharmaṃ tvaṃ yathā me manasaḥ sukham, VR* 2.28.3b), "Sītā, you should act as I will tell you, weak woman" (*sīte yathā tvāṃ vakṣyāmi tathā kāryaṃ tvayābale,* 2.28.4a), and "Please understand I'm saying this with [your] welfare in mind" (*hitabuddhyā khalu vaco mayaitad abhidhīyate,* 2.28.6a).

42. *nīkeṃ āī māraga mājha;* corresponding to *svāgatam, BhP* 10.29.18.

43. *kula kī nāri na nikasai sāṃjha;* corresponding to *rajanī neha stheyaṃ strībhiḥ, BhP* 10.29.19.

but the same phrase may also be read as "What can I do [about it]? You are capable [of doing anything]."[44] Then he again goes on to ask them about the family they have just left behind ("Tell me, fortunate wives, how Vraja is faring," 6.4a) and the motive of their coming ("Why have you come, happily married ladies?"),[45] as if making small talk at a tea party. All the while, he keeps interspersing his speech with references to their married state (*baṛabhāga, subhaga, suhāga,* in both texts), which they have just thrown overboard for his sake. And then he apparently unambiguously advises them: "You'd better return to your homes at once" (7.1a).[46] Is Krishna testing the women? Do they have to read double entendres in all he says, as some philosophical commentators suggest?[47] What is clear in the midst of all this confusion is that the tone of Krishna's speech is whimsical and lighthearted, not at all like Rāma's serious straightforwardness.

MEN ARGUING DHARMA. Both heroes take the trouble to explain the advice they give, and do so with reference to dharma. They slip relatively easily into the role of the pundit providing instruction in *Dharmaśāstra.* In the *Mānas,* Rāma says to Sītā: "There is no other higher dharma than this: respectfully worship the feet of your father- and mother-in-law" (2.61.3a).[48] He takes a carrot-and-stick approach, promising Sītā excellent karma as a result of following the short-cut dharma he has pointed out, and predicting terrible trouble otherwise, invoking mythological examples.[49] Rāma ends his speech on a threatening note: "who does not do respectfully what spontaneous well-wishers as guru and husband advise, will regret with heavy heart, because for sure

44. *kahā karo tuma jogu ho.* In *Bhāgavata Purāṇa,* Krishna is somewhat less inviting and more formal: "What can I do to please you?" (*priyaṃ kiṃ karavāṇi vaḥ, BhP* 10.29.18a).

45. *brija kī kusala kaho baṛabhāga, keū āī tuma subhaga suhāga;* corresponding to *brūtāgamanakāraṇam BhP* 10.29.18.

46. *ajahuṃ tuma apaneṃ gharu jāhu;* corresponding to *pratiyāta vrajaṃ, BhP* 10.29.19b.

47. See the commentary by Vallabha for this passage, i.e., *BhP* 10.29.18–27, as translated in Redington 1983.

48. *ehi te adhika dharamu nahiṃ dūjā, sādara sāsu sasura pada pūjā.* Here the *Mānas* deviates from Vālmīki's *Rāmāyaṇa,* where Rāma is mainly concerned with pointing out the dangers of the forest (2.28.4–25). He refers to *dharma* only in the beginning, pointing out that she should fulfill her *dharma* at home so that he may have peace of mind (2.28.3).

49. "The fruit of dharma, conform to the guru and sacred scriptures, is obtained without any problem" (*śruti saṃmata dharama phalu, pāia binahiṃ kalesa*); "When possessed by obstinacy, many hardships were endured by Gālava and King Nahuṣa" (*haṭha basa saba saṃkaṭa sahe gālava nahuṣa naresa, RCM* 2.61 *dohā;* see also 2.62.2). Interestingly, only one of the examples from mythology he quotes is considered evil: Nahuṣa, who usurped Indra's throne and tried also to borrow his wife. One could argue that Gālava endured hardship for a worthy cause, namely in service to his guru, as he fulfilled the guru's command with much forebearance and single-mindedness (see Citrāv 1964: 190). Tulsī's examples may indicate that Sītā's wish is not necessarily illegitimate, at the same time stressing the primary importance of obedience.

their well-being will be damaged" (2.63, *dohā*).[50] Clearly Rāma has two points in mind: a woman needs to serve her in-laws, and she should obey her husband instead of obstinately following her own advice.

Krishna, too, assumes the role of pundit, a rather ill-fitting one for him, and holds forth about woman's dharma both in *Bhāgavata Purāṇa* and in the Braj text. He stresses her responsibility to home, husband, and children: "Only a young lady can grace the house with virtue, without her husband and son are all sad, this is what the Creator ordained" (*RP* 7.3a–c).[51] The carrot Krishna offers is nothing less than a promise of *mokṣa:* "Attending one's husband is the key to happiness, by shunning deceit, *saṃsāra* falls away" (74.a–b).[52] Ironically, Krishna makes it a point to condemn adultery, describing types of husbands one should not leave (8.1; See *BhP* 10.29.26). To make sure the women abide by such rules, he comes up with the stick, the threat of hell:

> If she abandons her husband and indulges in a lover,
> such a woman cannot be noble.
> Without a shred of honor, she falls into hell. (*RP* 8.2)[53]

All this punditic sermonizing seems terribly out of place in the mouth of Krishna, to the point of raising suspicion of a charade. Indeed, the whole speech is undermined by one clever admonition at its beginning: "Consider your husband to be the supreme Lord" (*RP* 7.1c).[54] Taken at face value, it validates the whole sermon and admonishes the Gopīs to go back home and worship their husbands instead of Krishna. But this statement has a double meaning: "Krishna as the Supreme Lord is to be known as the true husband." In that case, it is to be taken as an admonition to stay with Krishna, who is each human soul's true Lord. Harirām Vyās has set up his audience for such a reading by stressing earlier that the Gopīs "obtained their heart's desire: the Lord for a husband" (2.1b).[55] Krishna's appeal to dharma, then, is not sincere. His speech may be read as a test for the Gopīs. Or the whole sermon may be an inside joke for connoisseurs (*rasikas*) only. The sermon is full of irony intended to amuse the Gopīs and the audience alike.

50. *sahaja suhṛda gura svāmi sikha, jo na karaï sira māni, so pachitāi aghāi ura, avasi hoi hita hāni.*

51. *juvatihi dharamu ghara mai phabai, jā bini pati suta duṣita sabai, yah bidhanā racanā racī;* See *BhP* 10.29.22.

52. *bharatā kī sevā suṣa sāru, kapaṭa tajeṃ chūṭai saṃsāru;* See *BhP* 10.29.24.

53. *taji bharatā rahi jārahi līna, hoi na aisī nāri kulīna, jasa bihune hi naraka parai.*

54. *jānahu paramesura kari nāhu.*

55. *mana cīṃtyo pāyo baru nāhu.*

THE DANGER ZONE OF THE FOREST. To justify their rejection, both Rāma and Krishna voice a second argument, allegedly for the good of the women: the dangers and hardships of living in the forest. In the *Mānas*, Rāma does this elaborately, pointing to meteorological circumstances (2.62.2b), the bad road conditions (2.62.3–4a, 63.1.b), dangers from wild animals (2.62.4b, 63.2) and robbers (2.63.2), as well as problems of outfit and equipment (2.62, *dohā*). Taking a cue from his mother, he claims that all that is hard to overcome, especially for a delicate palace-raised lady like Sītā. Tulsī is following *Vālmīki Rāmāyaṇa*, where the hardships of the forest are the main objection Rāma raises, hammering his words home with repetition, ending all the lines in his speech with "the forest means hardship" (*duḥkhataraṃ vanam*) or a variant thereof (*VR* 2.28.6–25).

Tulsī's Rāma also resorts to more subtle means to make his point. In his eagerness to show the proposed project impossible, he is clever in a tender—though to twentieth-century sensibilities rather paternalistic—way. To make the point that Sītā just is not up to the forest trip, he addresses her with traditionally flattering terms for women, and then proceeds to subvert these compliments and use them to underline her weakness. He calls her "doe-eyed," only to stress the skittishness implied in the epithet, to make the point that she is by nature easily frightened (*RCM* 2.63.2b).[56] He addresses her as "swan-gaited," only to turn around and claim that like a swan, she does not belong in the woods (2.62.3a)[57]—and that a swan raised on sweet water from Lake Mānsarovar can never subsist on the salt water of the ocean (2.62.3b).[58] Further flattering her with a comparison to a cuckoo, he continues that cuckoos of course do well in gardens, where they find the nectar to live on, not in the thorny bushes of the forest (2.63.4a).[59] Rāma here appears as the master of compliments with a cutting edge, turning them into deterministic statements of character.

Tulsī's text is extremely rich. Just as he does with Kauśalyā's speech, he works some irony into Rāma's argumentation by having him unknowingly foretell the disasters that will indeed befall them. For one, he refers to kidnapping demons (*rākṣasas*) who can take on many guises (*RCM* 2.63.1a). In addition, gossip will ensue, and people will blame him for her hardship (2.63.3a).[60] This sensitivity of Rāma to his subjects' views may also be a foreshadowing of the

56. *mṛgalocani tumha bhīru subhāeṃ.*
57. *haṃsagavani tumha nahiṃ bana jogū.*
58. *mānasa salila sudhāṃ pratipālī, jiai ki lavana payodhi marālī.*
59. *nava rasāla bana biharanasīlā, soha ki kokila bipina karīlā.*
60. *suni apajasu mohi deihi logū.*

events to follow, which will lead to Sītā's fire ordeal (and in versions other than the *Mānas,* her eventual exile).

Whereas Rāma stresses that the forest is a place fraught with danger, for Krishna it is mainly the setting of a romantic rendezvous. Krishna does not dwell on explaining the dangers; he voices only a minor threat: "Don't stay in the woods at night" (*baṃna maiṃ basiai nīsa nahī, RP* 7.1c). In tune with his earlier whimsical tone, he proceeds to treat the Gopīs as if they were out for sightseeing and he their botanical guide:

> "You've come and had a glimpse of the basil grove:
> The delightful white lilies have bloomed open
> In Yamunā's waters, cool and deep" (*RP* 7.2)[61]

Here again, the medieval poet is following Sanskrit scripture (*BhP* 10.29.21). Krishna's references to the forest are hardly frightening. They leave much to the imagination of the Gopīs, and he could be stirring up their fear to enhance the erotic mood (*vyabhicārī-bhāva*)—something not unbecoming to the king of the *rasikas*.

TELEVISION THEOLOGY. The modern versions by Sagar follow quite a different course. Where Vyās has his Krishna give an ambiguous speech for the sake of enhancing *rasa,* in the television version no one gets to speak at all during the Rāsa-līlā, which consists only of mime, dancing, and singing. The camera concentrates on *abhinaya,* when the Gopīs arrive on Yamunā's banks. They look around for Krishna, who is initially nowhere to be seen. However, he arrives pretty soon, having made sure in his privileged position as "the Lord within" (*antaryāmī*) that the women's devotion is pure. So it says in the accompanying song:

> When the "dweller within" saw that he alone was abiding
>   in each woman's heart
> and that with the intention of undying union, the friends desired
>   him alone. . . .[62]

The singing and dancing starts pretty much immediately after Krishna's descent amid the Gopīs, so there is no occasion for him to lecture. The lecture has been transposed to a different location: the "pre-Rāsa-līlā" episode (dis-

61. *briṃdābana tuma deṣyo āī, suṣada kumodana kusamita jāī, jamunā jala sītala ghane.*

62. *jab antaryāmī ne dekhā har antar meṃ vahī vās kare, liye amar milan kī abhilāṣā sakhiyāṃ un se hī ās kare.*

cussed earlier) in which he calls out the Gopīs' spiritual forms with his flute playing. On this occasion, Krishna lectures Rādhā; but the topic does not touch on dharma. He transposes everything to a philosophical level and explains to his little jealous mistress that all these other women are only forms of her, and in fact, in the whole world there is nothing else but Krishna and Rādhā. Krishna presents this as the secret of *dvaita* (dualism) and *advaita* (monism). Such an explanation makes the raising of issues of dharma totally irrelevant.

Sagar apparently felt that to be insufficient. At the beginning of episode 60, he appears in person on the screen and gives a full punditic explanation of the scene himself (not in the DVD version.) Just as his Krishna has done, he concentrates on philosophical categories. He stresses that it is all about a meeting of the human soul with God.[63] He calls the Rāsa-līlā a contradiction in terms,[64] and he comes up with a whole set of equations of Krishna as Puruṣa with Rādhā as Prakṛti, and so on. Thus, Sagar manages to avoid any allusion to dharma or a conflict between it and bhakti.

How about Sagar's television *Rāmāyaṇa?* He follows Tulsī to some extent, but there are some important differences. For one, Rāma does not give a whole speech before Sītā gets a chance to answer. They actually have a dialogue with each other, but that does not mean that Sītā is treated more as an equal. Rāma, though tender, treats her very much like a child who does not know what she is talking about ("Do you know what it means to go with me to the forest?" *TVR* 201–2).[65] and has no idea what hardship means ("You have never seen any troubles that were hard to bear, Sītā," 202).[66] Rāma is content with pointing out the difficulties of the proposed *banvās* and does not trot out dharma; the closest he gets is when he says that the forest is not for women (203).[67]

Sagar's script has an interesting reversal of roles: here the women claim to have the authority of dharma. Kauśalyā interferes to support Sītā's claim by urging him to be consistent. She exclaims: "Rāma, you have just held forth about women's duties (*strīdharma*) to me, saying that a wife's whole good lies at her husband's feet. So now, how can that model, that dharma, be different for Sītā?" (*TVR* 203).[68] There is much *rasa* to be had from this little role reversal,

63. *jīvātmā aur paramātmā kā milan.*

64. "Asceticism in enjoyment and enjoyment in asceticism" (*yog meṃ bhog aur bhog meṃ yog*).

65. *van meṃ sāth jāne kā arth jāntī ho?*

66. *duḥsah duḥkhoṃ ko tumne kabhī dekhā nahīṃ hai sīte.*

67. *vanvās striyoṃ ke lie nahīṃ hai.*

68. *rām! tū mujhe abhī strī kā dharm batā rahā thā ki strī kā sarvasva pati ke caraṇoṃ meṃ hotā hai. phir sītā ke lie vah ādarś, vah dharm dūsrā kaise ho saktā hai?*

not only between women and men with regard to dharma but also in that the mother-in-law takes up the case of her daughter-in-law against her own son. Truly different from our Kaliyuga television era!

In conclusion, we can say that the crucial difference between the medieval and the television versions of the men's words is that, on television the men no longer object to the women's intent on grounds of dharma, but instead preach theology. The difference between Krishna and Rāma is that while Rāma is serious and grave, Krishna is joking. His speech in support of dharma in the medieval poetry is a charade, a way to test the Gopīs or to delight them with a good taste of *rasa*.

The Women's Voices

In the classical and medieval texts, it is not until after the men are done preaching that Sītā and Rādhā get a chance to speak their minds and voice their feelings. The men have already made it clear that they reject them, the women acknowledge the men's point of view, but nevertheless ask them to change their mind. The speech of both heroines has the character of a plea; the Gopīs explicitly call it so (*binatī, RP* 12.4a). Still, there are substantial differences between Sītā and the Gopīs, in their body language and tone of their speech, and in the content of their message.

THE WOMEN'S TONE AND BODY LANGUAGE. Countering he husband is not something an ideal wife should do. We can expect, then, that Tulsī's Sītā will find this difficult and that it will show in her body language. She remains always aware of decorum, no matter how strong her feelings. Vaudeville has already remarked on the "délicatesse" of her sentiments (1955: 134). Sītā gets tears in her eyes (*RCM* 2.64.1a);[69] and we get a glimpse of the storm raging in her heart when Tulsīdās poetically says that her beloved's words leave her wondering how his cold instruction can burn the way the cool autumn moon burns the *cakavā* bird who has to suffer *viraha* from its mate (2.64.1b).[70] The implicit reference to *viraha* is reminiscent of and confirms the undercurrent in Kauśalyā's speech I discussed earlier. Notwithstanding this glimpse of her subjectivity, it is again Sītā's passivity that is underlined: she is speechless at first. Distressed, she cannot utter a single word at the thought that her beloved

69. *suni mṛdu bacana manohara piya ke, locana lalita bhare jala siya ke.*
70. *sītala sikha dāhaka bhaï kaiseṃ, cakaïhi sarada caṃda nisi jaiseṃ.*

lord would be willing to leave her (2.64.2a).[71] Overall, Sītā does not get to express the vehemence in her feelings with any passionate flair.

That is quite different from Vālmīki's heroine, who is clearly indignant at the beginning (*saṃkruddhā VR* 2.27.1b).[72] The poet does not disapprove but stresses that she deserves to be treated with sweetness, as she is a sweet-spoken woman herself (*priyārhā priyavādinī*, 2.27.1a). Like Tulsī's Sītā, she also has tears in her eyes throughout her speech, but it is not till the end that she gets to shed her long-restrained tears (2.30.23b),[73] at which point the poet invokes some wonderful metaphors to describe her extreme anguish (2.30.22–5).

Vyās's Gopīs, however, do not display any such heroic control of their feelings. Their reaction is much more extreme: immediately after Krishna's speech, they swoon and fall to the ground (*RP* 8.4a–b);[74] *Bhāgavata Purāṇa*'s Gopīs are much closer to Tulsī's Sītā: they sob and sigh and write in the dust with their feet (10.29.29). Lest this be construed as passivity, it needs to be pointed out that their swooning does not render them speechless by any means. Like the Gopīs in *Bhāgavata Purāṇa*, they immediately speak, and their tone is an uninhibited cry from the heart: "By dire dismay we're completely overwhelmed" (*RP* 9.1a); "We have cried a swelling deep river" (9.2a).[75]

In contrast, Sītā's sense of decorum does not allow her to "make a scene." She remains in total control in the televised version. In Tulsī's text, too, she patiently swallows her tears (*RCM* 2.64.2b).[76] Her first act is again in tune with *maryādā:* she touches her mother-in-law's feet and folds her hands in supplication (2.64.3a).[77] Her first words are already apologetic about the defiant stance she is going to take: "Please grant me pardon for my great insolence" (2.64.3a).[78] And she starts out by confirming her unswerving faith in her husband's advice being for her own good (2.64.3b).[79] It is not until the end of her monologue that she complains that his words are cruel, and then again, she sounds nearly apologetic for not having died on the spot: "Hearing such

71. *utaru na āva bikala baidehī, tajana cahata suci svāmi sanehī.*

72. Tulsī's Sītā's situation is somewhat different from *Vālmīki Rāmāyaṇa*, where the order is reversed. Rāma's arguments to discourage her from her intent to accompany him come only after Sītā has made it clear what she wants.

73. *cirasaṃniyataṃ bāṣpaṃ mumoca.*

74. *piya ke bacana sunata duṣa pāī, byākula dharanī parī murajhāī.*

75. *dārūna cittā baṛhī na thora . . . rudana karata vaṛhī nadī gaṃbhīra.*

76. *barabasa roki bilocana bārī, dhari dhīraju ura avanikumārī.*

77. *lāgi sāsu paga kaha kara jorī.*

78. *chamabi debi baṛi abinaya morī.*

79. *dīnhi prānapati mohi sikha soī, jehi bidhi mora parama hita hoī.*

harsh words, if my heart did not break, then, O Lord, this shallow life of mine will suffer the severe pain of being separated from you" (2.67, *dohā*).[80] In the televised version, too, Sītā acts very humbly and repeats polite epithets throughout (*nāth, āryaśreṣṭh, svāmī,* see *TVR* 202).

Vyās's Gopīs, on the other hand, do not show much regard for decorum. They do not sound apologetic at all, and they make not bones about confronting Krishna with the effect his words have had on them and how he has let them down: "Young son of Nanda, you've spoken cruel words! Yet, no other refuge comes to mind but you" (*RP* 9.1b–c).[81] They are assertive, complaining that there is nothing they have done to deserve such treatment: "Beloved, we had much hope in you, but you reject us without our slightest offense" (9.3a–b).[82] Rather than addressing Krishna humbly and respectfully, they call him a rogue (*kitaba,* 9.3c). They do not introduce their plea with polite acknowledgments that he must surely have the best for them in mind. Instead, they reproach him: he does not know what he has done to them. And they are not inclined to let him off the hook: how come Hari cannot fathom the depth of their sadness, though he supposedly is the ferryman who helps people across the pain of *saṃsāra* (9.2b)?[83]

Of all this sweet assertiveness, however, very little remains in the televised version. As indicated before, all actors remain mute during the Rāsa-līlā, which robs the Gopīs totally of a voice. But even elsewhere, the women of Braj behave demurely, nearly Sītā-like. Even Rādhā, who shows the most assertiveness of them all, acts as the charmingly shy wife, not the assertive lover. As we have seen, Sagar has provided the little girl from Barsānā with a divine alter ego, which shows up at several occasions throughout the story. This alter ego of Rādhā puts all the events into a different perspective, as they are flashbacks shown while she and the divine Krishna are reminiscing nostalgically about their youth, their time on Earth. This renders the events in Braj irreal compared to the eternal present of Goloka, the divine heaven, where Rādhā and Krishna are for ever enthroned. In Goloka, Rādhā is never separated from Krishna; she is his consort, and, significantly, addresses him with respect and humbleness (using the pronoun *āp* and the honorific forms of the imperative;

80. *aiseu bacana kaṭhora suni, jauṃ na hṛdaū bilagāna; tau prabhu biṣama biyoga dukha, sahihahiṃ pāvaṃra prāna.*

81. *krūra bacana kahe naṃdakisora; aura sarana nahī sūjhahī.*

82. *tiharī bahota hutī piya āsa, bina aparādhahi karata nirāsa.*

83. *hari kariyā nahi jānai pīra.* It is to be noted, though, that this is slightly different from *Bhāgavata Purāṇa,* where the Gopīs are somewhat less assertive (Pauwels 1996b: 178; see also 232–6 for a line-by-line comparison). For example, instead of calling Krishna a "rogue," they call him "difficult to obtain" (*duravagraha*).

he addresses her with *tum* and familiar imperatives). Her earthly counterpart has more freedom of address (using *tum* and the familiar), but still her behavior shows more than once the respect accorded to a husband.

Vyās's Gopīs pose a challenge to Krishna, but there is a hint of irony as well in their words. They match Krishna's playfully teasing words with equally clever wordplay and double entendres. They challenge him, pointing out that his actions are contradictory. How can he, the master (*nātha*), deprive his own servants of their master, or literally, make them orphans (*anātha*) (*RP* 9.4)? The Gopīs continue this type of assertive challenge with blackmail. They point out that Krishna is famous for being graceful; after all, he is called Dīnadayāla ("compassionate toward the poor"). So he is only detracting from his own epithet if he does not show his grace to them: "You have disgraced yourself by insulting us.... And your fame lies in pitying the poor!" (12.4b, 13.1a).[84] They challenge him to show his grace or else be called a miser: "Destroy our agony in the embrace of your arms, the way an artist shows off his artistry. A miser would not do so, even when prompted!" (13.1c-2b).[85]

Tulsī's Sītā in her speech refers to Rāma's fame for mercy, too, calling him "abode of mercy" (*karunāyatana*). However, she does not do this ironically; she is only trying to strengthen the case she is making (to him and to her mother-in-law) about how rightfully miserable she will feel when he is gone: "Lord of my life, Abode of Mercy, handsome and adroit provider of bliss, without you, the lotus of the Raghukula family is bereft of its moon, and heaven will be hell" (2.64, *dohā*).[86] Toward the end of her speech, she calls him "graceful" again (*kṛpānidhāna*, 2.66.3b) and, like the Gopīs, says he is her very self, the one dwelling in each heart (Skt. *antaryāmin*). Again, her tone is not ironic but rather bespeaks an unshakable confidence when she says: "Why should I elaborate my plea, My Lord? You are full of grace, and already dwelling in each one's heart" (2.66.4b).[87]

Tulsī's Sītā is much meeker than Vālmīki's. In the Sanskrit version, Sītā increasingly uses strong language when she feels Rāma is not budging; she challenges nothing less than his very manlihood. For one, she makes it clear that he would be a woman in a man's body if he left without her! She says: "Or

84. *hai apajasu kīne apumāna ... birada tumhāro dīnadayāla.*

85. *bhuja daṃḍani ṣaṃḍahu bithā, jaiseṃ gunī diṣāvai kalā, kripana karai nahi halaï bhalā.* Here they are following similar pleas in *Bhāgavata Purāṇa*, e.g.,"Have mercy on us, destroyer of sins" (*tan naḥ prasīda vṛjanārdana*, *BhP* 10.29.38a; see also 10.29.41).

86. *prānanātha karunāyatana, suṃdara sukhada sujāna; tumha binu raghukula kumuda bidhu, surapura naraka samāna.*

87. *binatī bahuta karauṃ kā svāmī, karunāmaya ura aṃtarajāmī.*

otherwise, did my father, Vaideha, the king of Mithila, O Rāma, obtain a son-in-law who is a woman in a man's body?" (*VR* 2.30.3).[88] More than that, she calls him something of a pimp, who would hand over his wife to the care of others: "[I'm] your bride at puberty, who lived with you a long time, who is true to you; do you yourself wish to hand me over to others, like a dance-troupe leader?" (2.30.8).[89] Tulsī chose to excise such strong arguments from his Sītā's speech. No way that mother Kauśalyā's ears should listen to such language! Needless to say, Sagar does not choose to give airtime to any of this either.

To sum up, Tulsī's Sītā is the opposite of Vyās's Gopīs. Her humble and self-composed tone contrasts with their challenging tone, which is dripping with irony, determined as they are to let Krishna know how miserable his rejection makes them feel. The difference in attitude fits with the difference in marital status of the women. Sītā remains conscious that Rāma is her husband, and although she is about to press her will through against his, she bows to her lord and husband in respect, conforming to *maryādā*. The Gopīs see Krishna as a lover and have no place for these niceties and formalities. Only love counts. A love that has no boundaries. A love that is so strong it does not even care about *maryādā*.

Still, the married Sītā in Vālmīki's *Rāmāyaṇa* minces no words. Tulsī is more conservative than the text that inspired him, and Sagar has followed suit. This difference in attitude and tone, to be sure, has its theological significance. Sītā's attitude is the model for Tulsī's Rāma-bhakti: respectful worship of God, emotional and unswerving, but controlled and within the limits of propriety. Theological interpretations see the Gopīs as ideal examples of Krishna bhakti: rather than be marred by God's different status, his majesty, or *aiśvarya*, they go straight for sweet intimacy, or *mādhurya*, which, it is felt, is what Krishna prefers.

THE WOMEN'S COUNTER-ARGUMENTS. Since my concern is mainly with Sītā and the Gopīs as role models, it is important to analyze their arguments. How do the women convince their men? Let us first concentrate on how they justify their rejection of the men's powerful evocation of *strī-dharma*. Tulsī's Sītā does not address the matter directly. However, when she mentions that without Rāma even heaven seems like hell (*RCM* 2.64, *dohā*),[90] she indirectly rejects his "carrot": a shortcut to heaven is not appealing, if it means being without him.

88. *kiṃ tvām anyata vaidehaḥ pitā me mithilādhipaḥ, rāma jāmātaraṃ prāpya striyaṃ puruṣavigraham?*
89. *svayaṃ tu bhāryāṃ kaumārīṃ ciram adhyuṣitāṃ satīm, śailūṣa iva māṃ rāma parebhyo dātum icchasi.*
90. *tumha binu... surapura naraka samāna.*

Vālmīki's Sītā says pretty much the same thing (*VR* 2.27.21). But she also addresses the matter more directly. A woman belongs with her husband; that is her greatest dharma. She quotes the authority of gurus for her decision to stick with him (2.29.5a)[91] and predictions by Brahmins and ascetics to the effect that this is her destiny (2.29.8–14). She puts the scriptures to good use for her purpose by saying that if a husband is a woman's god, surely she should follow him, which implies no sin if it is done with love and sincerity (2.29.16).[92] Sītā even throws in what seems to be a quotation from the scriptures on the topic: "The woman who is given [in marriage] properly [with water] by elders following their dharma in this world, O strong one, belongs to the man also in the hereafter" (2.29.18).[93] Thus she makes her point that if a woman should follow her husband in the hereafter, certainly she should follow him in exile! And Sītā cleverly turns the question around and inquires what Rāma's dharma is. Instead of asking why she wants to come along, Rāma should ask himself why he does not want his devoted, unblemishable wife along (2.29.19).[94]

In the television version, too, Sītā, turns the tables on Rāma. Her argument goes something like this: with all this talk about his father keeping his promise to Kaikeyī, what about Rāma's own dharma? Hasn't he made a promise to Sītā? Surely Rāma should also be held to his wedding vow of keeping her always by his side! So if he is so true to his word, there simply is no way around him taking her along to the forest. And surely, if he gets to do his dharma, he should not stand in the way of her doing hers! It would not even cost him anything, rather, they get, so to speak, double dharma merit for the price of one. Sītā says: "O Lord, bound to promise to keep me with you lifelong, wouldn't it be called *adharma* if you went alone to the forest? O son of nobility, let me keep my dharma at the same time that you keep yours" (*TVR* 202).[95]

Clearly, it is Rāma who needs instruction on what dharma is; Sītā is quite confident she knows about her own! She goes on to insist that of all the relatives in a man's life, it is only his wife who gets the prerogative of sharing his fate (*TVR* 202).[96] Here again, Sagar is returning for inspiration to Vālmīki's Sītā's words: "O son of a noble man, father, mother, brother, son and daughter-in-law reap their own merit and have their own destiny. Only the wife

91. *tvayā ca saha gantavyaṃ mayā gurujanājñayā.*

92. *śuddhātman premabhāvāddhi bhaviṣyāmi vikalmaṣā, bhartāram anugacchantī bhartā hi paradaivatam.*

93. *ihaloke ca pitṛbhir yā strī yasya mahābala, adbhir dattā svadharmeṇa pretyabhāve'pi tasya sā.*

94. *evam asmāt svakāṃ nārīṃ suvṛttāṃ hi pativratām, nābhirocayase netuṃ tvaṃ māṃ keneha hetunā?*

95. *nāth! jīvan-bhar sāth rakhne lie vacan-baddha hokar kyā āpkā akele van meṃ jānā adharm nahīṃ kahlāegā? he ārya-śreṣṭh! apne dharm ke sāth mujhe bhī apne dharm kā pālan karne dījie.*

96. *mātā-pitā, bhāī bahan, sāre nāte pīche rah jāte haiṃ. keval strī hī svāmī ke bhāgya kā anusaraṇ kartī hai.*

gets the fate of her husband, O bull among men, so by that reckoning, I am obliged to dwell in the forest indeed."[97] And she continues: "I have been instructed by my mother and father about various means of support [available for woman], so today, I do not need to be told how I should behave."[98] Is Sītā turning women's dharma into women's rights? Is she invoking her right to stay with the one she married? Sagar's version has gone back to Vālmīki's in showing a strident Sītā: she is the one who lectures on dharma, not Rāma!

How do the Gopīs counter Krishna's lecture on dharma? Characteristically, Vyās's Gopīs address the matter head-on. They simply inform Krishna that his sermon on women's dharma is wasted on them—precisely because they are women. Are not women stupid, according to his dharma books? So what's the point in instructing them? He should have known better. "You have instructed us in ethics, of which we've failed to grasp the essence: we're all weak women, lacking in wit" (*RP* 11.1).[99] One could reflect that if anything, it is certainly not wit these Gopīs are lacking.

In fact, the Gopīs give Krishna a perfectly good serious response. They point out that matters of morality just do not apply for those who love Krishna. "Those who love you faithfully feel no suffering, worldly nor spiritual. Sin and merit don't apply to them" (*RP* 11.3).[100] Morality, with its contrast between good and bad, virtue and sin, is still part of the world of duality. Love for Krishna goes beyond that; it is transcendent.

This argument is even more sophisticated than the one in *Bhāgavata Purāṇa*, where the Gopīs point out that Krishna is everyone's true Self (*ātmā*, *BhP* 10.29.32b), in whom everyone should naturally rejoice, and compared to whom everything else pales ("What's the use for husbands, sons, and so on who bring only sorrow? *patisutādibhir ārtidaiḥ kim*, 10.29.33a). The Gopīs in that version also make it clear that they are not so easily to be shaken off: if Krishna will not answer their love in kind, they will still follow him by means of meditation (10.29.35b).[101] And they declare themselves unable to stand anyone else's company (10.29.36). They humbly call themselves maidservants (*dāsyaḥ*, 10.29.37b) in search of the dust of his feet (10.29.37).

97. *āryaputra pitā mātā bhrātā putras tathā snuṣā, svāni puṇyāni buñjānāḥ svaṃ svaṃ bhāgyam upāsate; bhartur bhāgyaṃ tu nāryekā prāpnoti puruṣarṣabha, ataś caivāham ādiṣṭā vane vastavyam ity api* (*VR* 2.27.4–5).

98. *anuśiṣṭāsmi mātrā ca pitrā ca vividhāśrayam, nāsmi samprati vaktavyā vartitavyaṃ yathā mayā* (*VR* 2.27.10).

99. *hama su tuma upadesyo dharama, tā kau hama nahi jānyu marama, hama avalā mati hīna sava.*

100. *tuma su prīta karaiṃ jai dhīra, tinahi na loka beda kī pīra, pāpa puṇya tina ke nahī.*

101. *dhyānena yāma padyoḥ adavīṃ sakhe te.*

Vyās's Gopīs, though, turn the tables and place the *onus* of whatever dharmic mistake they may have made squarely on Krishna's shoulders. After all, it was he who called them to come out into the woods, and on account of whom they left the path of virtue! (*RP* 12.1a–b and 2b).[102]

Sagar's Gopīs do not argue with Krishna at the time of the real Rāsa-līlā, but after the pre-Rāsa-līlā (described earlier), Rādhā gets into a philosophical argument with Krishna. This is after the other Gopīs' trial by fire, by means of which he has deflated her claim of being unequalled in her love for him. As noted, at that point Krishna provides text and explanation in a philosophical lecture on monism (*advaita*). What is Rādhā's response to Krishna's philosophy? Just like that of Vyās's Gopīs, it centers on the meaning of love. When Krishna claims that in the whole world there is nothing but Rādhā and Krishna, she interrupts him to say there is one other thing, namely love.[103] Rādhā goes on to say that love is crucial, the basis of the world: "Without it, what would your world be based on?"[104] Clearly, for Sagar's Rādhā, as for Vyās's Gopīs, love is the plain and simple way to answer Krishna's claims, be they of dharma or of *advaita*.

What do the arguments of Sītā and the Gopīs have in common? In all versions, the women's answer revolves around love. When confronted with the option, they are strongly opposed to the idea of gaining heaven for one's afterlife at the cost of separation from the beloved (*viraha*). They argue in different ways and in different degrees of assertiveness, but the point is the same: love is stronger than whatever dharma may prescribe for them.

The women's rejection of *strī-dharma* minimalizes the whole world of dharma, which is characterized by social relations. The Gopīs and Sītā both make the point that nothing matters to them except the man they love. Both stress they do not care for any other relationship in life, including the strong bond with parental kin. More than that: they call all other relationships a source of stress. Their language is much the same. Tulsī's Sītā says:

> Mother, father, sister, dear brother, dear family, circle of friends;
> mother- and father-in-law, guru, in-laws, supporters, even sons may
> be handsome, adept, and enjoyable;

102. *baina bajāī bulāī nāri, āī sira dhari kula kī gāri... āraja paṃtha tajai suni gāna*, similar to *BhP* 10.29.34a.

103. *"ek cīz hai." "kyā?" "prem. rādhā aur krishna kā prem."*

104. *uske binā tumhārā saṃsār kiske āsre par ṭikegā?*

> But when it comes to love and relationship, My Lord, for a woman without her beloved, these [bonds] burn hotter than the sun. (*RCM* 2.65.1–2a)[105]

Interestingly, Sītā refers here to Rāma as her beloved (*piya;* possibly for internal rhyme with the following *tiya*) rather than husband (*pati*). It is to be noted that there are no such statements by Sītā in *Vālmīki Rāmāyaṇa.* In the beginning, she stresses something similar, but with reference to Rāma, not herself. She says that a woman is the only party who sticks by a man, not his other relatives (*VR* 2.27.4–5). Later on, she will repeat several times that for her the forest will be as comfortable as her father's house (see e.g., 2.27.12 and 22).

The Gopīs argue in much the same vein as Tulsī's Sītā: to them nothing matters, but their love. All other relationships are insignificant.

> Husband and son, guru and brother: nothing but sorrow they bring. . . .
> Who can be dearer than you? (*RP* 11.2a, c)[106]

The major difference between these lists of secondary relationships is of course that the Gopīs' list includes the husband as a source of sorrow. This fits their *parakīyā* nature. The Gopīs' list is also much shorter. It seems that their leaving their relatives behind, which has been already described in the beginning of Vyās's *Rās Pañcādhyāyī* (*RP* 2–5), enables them to reduce the list to some bare essentials, as they have already established their credentials. Indeed, they have abandoned the children they were breastfeeding (3.3a). They point this out themselves: "With your flute playing you summoned us women, we came with insults of the family on our heads" (12.1a–b).[107]

Sītā's enumeration of relatives is longer and sounds formulaic. At this point in the story, she has not yet given up anything although the audience of course knows she will make good on her words. Even her reference to her willingness to give up her children will come true. At this point in the narrative, Sītā is not even pregnant, but the audience knows about the versions where later on she will raise her twin boys alone, only to leave them at their father's when they come of age and disappear herself, returning to her mother Earth.

105. *mātu pitā bhaginī priya bhāī, priya parivāru suhṛda samudāī; sāsu sasura gura sajana sahāī, suta suṃdara susīla sukhadāī; jahaṃ lagi nātha neha aru nāte, piya binu tiyahi taranihu te tāte.*

106. *duṣadātā pati suta gura baṃdhu . . . tuma se prītama avara ko?* Vyās is following *kurvanti hi tvayi ratiṃ . . . nityapriye patisutādibhir ārtidaiḥ kim, BhP* 10.29.33a.

107. *baina bajāī bulāī nāri, āī sira dhari kula kī gāri.*

Countering her husband and mother-in-law, Sītā says it is the palace and its comforts that will be painful for her, not the forest:

> My Lord said there are many discomforts of the forest: fear, despondence, and embarrassments of the worst kind;
> but even all those together don't count up to just a second of separation from the beloved, O ocean of grace. (*RCM* 2.66.3)[108]
> Body, wealth, house, land, city, kingdom, without my husband, are like a mourning assembly;
> Pleasures [will seem] like illness, jewelry a burden, the world will seem like Hell [Yama's torment]. (2.65.2b–3a)[109]

Sītā's words are typical for the *virahiṇī* for whom every sweet memory of her beloved has become painful. She continues with classical comparisons:

> Lord of my life, without you, in the whole world, nowhere is there anything comfortable;
> A body without life, a river without water, similarly, Lord, is a woman without her man. (*RCM* 2.65.3b–4a)[110]

The Gopīs make the same point, but without elaborating. They are again much more concise, and simply say:

> Without your grace all aeons lack insight. (*RP* 11.2b)[111]

In short, both Sītā and the Gopīs argue that the forest cannot possibly be as bad as the comforts of home without their beloved. When countering their men's objections regarding dharma, the women univocally argue that it does not apply in the case of love. Love is stronger than dharma: the laws of love must prevail over those of propriety. In the bhakti context, the message is clear: love for God takes precedence over all else. It is ultimately the only relation that matters.

A SYLVAN VISION FOR THE FUTURE. Having deconstructed thoroughly their men's objections on grounds of dharma, the women move on to a constructive

108. *bana dukha nātha kahe bahutere, bhaya biṣāda paritāpa ghanere; prabhu biyoga lavalesa samānā, saba mili hohiṃ na kṛpānidhānā.*

109. *tanu dhanu dhāmu dharani pura rājū, pati bihīna sabu soka samājū; bhoga roga sama bhūṣana bhārū, jama jātanā sarisa saṃsārū.*

110. *prānanātha tumha binu jaga māhīṃ, mo kahuṃ sukhada katahuṃ kachu nāhīṃ; jiya binu deha nadī binu bārī, taisia nātha puruṣa binu nārī.*

111. *tumharī kripā vina saba juga aṃdhu.*

phase. They readily describe an alternative to being left behind; they come up with a blueprint, a vision for the future. Sītā does a great job of working up enthusiasm for the trip into the unknown. She counters the claim that she will not be able to survive the dangers lurking in the forest. From her feminine perspective, the jungle takes on a different dimension. She sees everywhere possibilities of transforming the potentially dangerous into something helpful, and comes up with an elaborate project for domestication of the forest.

Tulsī's Sītā addresses her husband and mother-in-law's argument that the forest is a dangerous and uncomfortable place point by point. She answers their concerns by turning each potential discomfort into its opposite. In this respect, she follows Vālmīki's heroine (*VR* 2.30.11–6, foreshadowed in 2.26.13–22). The picture she conjures up is an idyllic one. Through a process of appropriation, Sītā manages, at least in her fantasy, to "domesticate the forest"—to transform the totally other into something familiar:

> Birds and deer will be my friends, the wood my city, birch-bark clothes my spotless silks.
> [When I'm] with my lord, the hut of leaves will seem a source of joy, like heaven! (*RCM* 2.65, *dohā*)[112]
> The *kuśa* grass and sprouts will make a pretty bed, with my husband, it becomes not less than a mattress for Cupid. (2.66.1a)[113]
> Beets, roots, fruits will be a gourmet dinner, the mountains will seem like hundred [towering] palaces of Avadh. (2.66.2a)[114]

In contrast to what American sensibilities might expect, Sītā does not look forward to possessing a greater freedom of movement in the forest. Interestingly, she readily finds substitutes for those guardians of *maryādā,* her in-laws:

> The forest deities, male and female, are friendly and will take care of me like fathers- and mothers-in-law. (*RCM* 2.66.1a)[115]

This may be taken as calculated to appeal to Kauśalyā, and in fact Sītā is repeating her mother-in-law's earlier reassurances to Rāma ("The forest deities will be your father and mother, birds and deer the servants of your lotus feet," *RCM* 2.56.2a).[116] Since Sītā is not yet present during this part of the conver-

112. *khaga mṛga parijana nagaru banu, balakala bimala dukūla; nātha sātha surasadana sama, paranasāla sukha mūla.*

113. *kusa kisalaya sātharī suhāī, prabhu saṃga maṃju manoja turāī.*

114. *kaṃda mūla phala amiā ahārū, avadha saudha sata sarisa pahārū.*

115. *banadebīṃ banadeva udārā, karihahiṃ sāsu sasura sama sārā.*

116. *pitu banadeva mātu banadevī, khaga mṛga carana saroruha sevī.*

sation of Rāma and Kauśalyā, she cannot be held responsible for echoing purposely her mother-in-law's words, but clearly the poet has in mind again to stress Sītā's extreme sensitivity to decorum and matters of *maryādā*. Though she may be naïve about the pleasures of sporting with her husband in the forest, she cannot be accused of seeking to escape the stifling duties of the palace for the freedom of life unencumbered by in-laws.

Sītā is not just trying to convince Rāma and Kauśalyā; underneath her words, the skilful poet Tulsīdās is simultaneously addressing the audience's concerns. Uppermost in the minds of all who know the story is the threat of her abduction. Tulsīdās has Sītā address the prediction of her abduction that which has so alarmingly reverberated through Rāma's words. She reassures him that no one will dare to touch her if he is around:

> Who would cast his eye on me when I am with my lord, like a hare or jackal on a lion's wife? (*RCM* 2.67.4a)[117]

Sagar's Sītā duly echoes these words: "When my Lord is with me, then who would dare to cast an eye on me?" (*TVR* 202).[118] Vālmīki's Sītā even mentions the potential for people to gossip if Rāma will not take her along. Here Vālmīki counters the reproach that had she not gone, she would not have been abducted, by implying that people would gossip about Rāma anyway (*VR* 2.30.4).

Tulsī's Sītā's speech, in its final part, projects a happy fantasy of life together in the forest. The focus here shifts from a strong affirmation of her ability to bear the hardships of the forest to Rāma's travails to come. Her concern here is to make it clear to Rāma that she will not be a burden but rather an asset. Sītā's vision of the future is concerned with Rāma's comfort and pleasure; she promises to serve him (*sevā*) and make the trip easier in every way she can, she will fan him, wipe his sweat, massage his feet:

> In all ways, my love, shall I serve you, I'll take away all exhaustion caused by the trip.
> Washing your feet, I'll sit in the shade of a tree, I'll fan you with happy heart.
> Seeing your dark body with beads of sweat, how can there be time for sorrow, if I see my beloved?

117. *ko prabhu saṃga mohi citavanihārā, siṃgha badhuhi jimi sasaka siārā.* Here too Tulsīdās has precedent in Vālmīki (*VR* 2.26.14).

118. *mere prabhu sāth hoṃge to merī or āṃkh uṭhāne kā sāhas kaun kar saktā hai?* Compare also with *VR* 2.29.3–4 and 6.

> I'll spread a bed of grass and leaves on an even spot, and will massage your feet all night, like a maidservant. (*RCM* 2.67.1b–3a)[119]

What is going on here? Sītā is answering the objection that she is too delicate for the forest. Is she tactfully pointing out that Rāma, too, might have a few tough moments in his exile and that he would be in trouble without a devoted wife at his side? Are these words addressed to Rāma, or is she signaling to her mother-in-law that she can make herself more useful by attending to her son in the woods than by staying back in the palace? Whatever the case, she ends on a very strong note by reversing his words again. Instead of not being worthy of asceticism or yoga, she puts it that when he is gone, she will not capable of enjoyments or *bhoga*:

> Am I so delicate, and my lord good for the forest? Are austerities only good for you, and comfort for me? (*RCM* 2.67.4b)[120]

Underlying this statement are two assertions. After all, the dharma laws stipulate that a woman should share her husband's fate, and if his is *tapas* then hers should be, too. Moreover, women are usually supposed to undergo fasts for the benefit of their husbands. Now how does that rhyme with Rāma's concern to keep her comfortably at home while he undergoes austerities? Though one can read Sītā's words as ironic, the tone of the whole passage does not call for such an interpretation, rather for one where she painstakingly stays within *maryādā*.

What a difference with the Gopīs! Since Krishna has not stressed the dangers of the forest, Vyās's Gopīs are not compelled to answer that objection. However, they, too, share happy visions of the near future. They do not stress much the sylvan character of the togetherness they envision, but rather the erotic elements: "Calm us by granting the nectar from your lips" (*RP* 10.2b);[121] "Place your hand on our breasts to protect us" (13.1b.).[122] Strikingly, whereas Sītā is eager to look for ways to do *sevā* for her husband, the Gopīs are adept at finding ways Krishna can serve them!

Given the bhakti context, it is not surprising that both Sītā and the Gopīs stress *darśana* or visual experience of God. They react vehemently against the

119. *sabahi bhāṃti piya sevā karihauṃ, māraga janita sakala śrama harihauṃ; pāya pakhāri baiṭhi taru chāhīṃ, karihaūṃ bāu mudita mana māhīṃ; śrama kana sahita syāma tanu dekhe, kahaṃ dukha samau prānapati pekhe; sama mahi tṛna tarupallava ḍāsī, pāya paloṭihi saba nisi dāsī.*

120. *maiṃ sukumāri nātha bana jogū, tumhahi ucita tapa mo kahuṃ bhogū?*

121. *adhara sudhā de kari viśrāma.*

122. *kuca para kara dhari karo pratipāla.*

most cruel part of the males' proposed solution, because it implies that the women have to miss the sight of the beloved. Sītā says:

> Lord, all happiness lies with you, in beholding your impeccable autumn-moon face. (*RCM* 2.65.4b)[123]
>
> Every moment, gazing at your lotus feet, I will remain happy, like a Kokī bird by day. (2.66.2b)[124]
>
> Marching on the roads, I won't feel tired: I'll gaze at your lotus feet every moment. (2.67.1a)[125]
>
> Seeing your soft countenance time after time, I won't feel the blazing hot wind. (2.67.3.b)[126]

The Gopīs argue in a similar vein:

> Gazing at your face, our eyes find contentment. (*RP* 10.1a)[127]
>
> From the moment we saw these feet,
> ever since, no one else can please us. (10.3a–b)[128]

In conclusion, we can say that the vision for the future of both sets of heroines revolves around enjoying the vision of the beloved (*darśana*). Sītā has to answer the objections regarding the dangers of the forest, and she proposes a sort of forest-domestication project. The Gopīs do not have any such objections to answer and hence do not make any such plans. Finally, Sītā's vision of the future is one of subservience; she is looking for ways to do *sevā* for her husband. The Gopīs are more interested in proposing ways Krishna can relieve them. They say so ironically: after all, it is his job, as God, to come to the rescue of those in need.

THE CLINCHING ARGUMENT. No matter how Sītā argues about the superiority of love over dharma, no matter what lovely vision of the future she draws, Rāma remains unconvinced. He does not come around until harsher measures are threatened. Only downright blackmail with the threat of suicide seems to work.

123. *nātha sakala sukha sātha tumhāreṃ, sarada bimala bidhu badanu nihāreṃ.*
124. *chinu chinu prabhu pada kamala bilokī, rahihaüṃ mudita divasa jimi kokī.*
125. *mohi maga calata na hoihi hārī, chinu chinu carana saroja nihārī.*
126. *bāra bāra mṛdu mūrati johī, lāgihi tāta bayāri na mohī.*
127. *muṣa deṣata suṣa pāvahi naina.*
128. *jaba taiṃ hama deṣe ai pāi, tava tai hamahi na avara suhāi.*

Taking the lead from Vālmīki (*VR* 2.27.6; 29.7, 21; 30.18–21), Tulsī has his Sītā threaten suicide in her speech. When she first does so, she calls Rāma *Dīnabandhu* (friend of the poor) to shame him into compassion: "If you keep me in Avadh for the period of exile (*avadhi*), you know my life-breaths won't stay, O friend of the poor, handsome one, bestower of joy, wise one, embodiment of love" (*RCM* 2.66, *dohā*).[129] This statement is elegantly phrased with a wordplay on Avadh and "period of exile" (*avadhi*) to underscore how her formerly happy *sasurāl* has now become a place with "limitations" (*avadha* in that meaning). It brims with Sītā's respect for her husband, in the use of several flattering epithets.

Notwithstanding her moments of assertiveness (described earlier), Tulsī's Sītā just does not seem able to shake off her apologetic demeanor. The last *dohā* of her speech comes back to the suicide threat, and sounds like an apology for having not already died:

> "If my heart is not broken just by listening to such cruel words,
> Then, O lord, my vile life breaths will be able to stand the pain of separation!" (*RCM* 2.67, *dohā*).[130]

Sagar's Sītā has more of an edge to her character and, incidentally, a great sense of dramatic effect. When even Kauśalyā's support fails to convince Rāma, a despondent Sītā announces he will have to stay back in Ayodhyā longer if he refuses to take her along. "Why?" he asks. She answers with a question: "Who will light my pyre?" (*merī citā ko agni kaun degā? TVR* 203). This provides enough of a shock for Rāma, but the author's concern for *maryādā* prompts him to make sure that it is Mother Kauśalyā's confirmation that propels Rāma into action: "She's speaking the truth, Rāma. If you wish to protect Sītā's life, then you should take her with you" (203).[131]

What is the clinching argument for Krishna? In contrast to Rāma, it is not the threat of suicide, which is not even mentioned in *Bhāgavata Purāṇa*. To be sure, Vyās's Gopīs, too, refer to suicide, but if it is a threat at all it is a veiled one, and hidden in a pun. They say, perfectly earnestly, it seems: "What should we do, back in Braj? . . . Turning away from from you, beloved, is suicide" (*RP* 10.4b).[132] The ironic undertone lies in the word they use to indicate suicide:

129. *rākhia avadha jo avadhi lagi, rahata na janiahiṃ prāna; dīnabaṃdhu suṃdara sukhada, sīla saneha nidhāna.*

130. *aiseu bacana kaṭhora suni, jauṃ na hṛdaü bilagāna; tau prabhu biṣama biyoga dukha, sahihahiṃ pāvaṃra prāna.*

131. *yah ṭhīk kah rahī hai, rām! agar sītā ke prāṇoṃ kī rakṣā cāhte ho to ise apne sāth le jā.*

132. *tuma bimuṣa piya ātama hāna.*

"harm to the self" (*ātmahāni*). This has a philosophical ring: the Self (*ātman*) of all human beings is of course none other else than Krishna. So under the pretext of threatening suicide, they actually teach Krishna a lesson. How can he, who is their very Self (*ātman*), turn them away? They have caught him in a contradiction. For the *rasikas*, this pun enhances the *rasa* of the Gopis' speech, making it not a threat but a treat.

Arguably, it is the combined effect of this speech, with all its puns and charming assertiveness, that blows Vyās's Krishna's mind. However, the last line of the speech, the one he seems to fall for, is their declaration of exclusive love for him: "Our goal is always only you" (*RP* 13.3c).[133] As it has become clear, their love is of a special kind. In the end, it is their willingness to trade a spot in heaven for one in his arms, their insistence on their love for him against all odds, and their true complaint of broken hearts over his harsh words that make Krishna come around. This is consistent with *Bhāgavata Purāṇa,* where it is their sincere despondence that brings him around (*BhP* 10.29.42).[134]

That Krishna falls for love is the message propagated insistently by Sagar's television version. At first view, in the pre-Rāsa-līlā, Rādhā loses out. Krishna succeeds in meeting the challenge she has set Krishna to demonstrate that the other Gopīs' love for him is as strong as hers. She actually falls on her knees, folds her hands, asks for forgiveness, and admits that she has been defeated: "Mistakenly I thought that only I had 'rights' in you. Today, my pride is shattered. Rādhā is defeated."[135] However, as we have seen, in the ensuing discussion she corrects his musings about *dvaita* and *advaita* by stating that what really makes the world tick is neither he nor she but love. Now it is Krishna's turn to admit defeat: "With just one word, you have shaken off all my long-winded argument. Today I've lost again."[136] Savoring the moment, she insists he admit he lost, which gives him the occasion to hammer the message home: "Yes, only before love alone even God is defeated."[137]

Notwithstanding this lip service, Sagar's Krishna never loses his cool or indeed his little superior smile of the one who knows it all best. And Sagar has had us again and again witness how Krishna teaches Rādhā what love really means. When she tries to assert her rights over him on account of her unique love, he says that love does not seek rights but is only concerned about giving: "In love there's no demanding, only giving, Rādhā" (also in TVK vol. 7,

133. *tumahi hamārī gati sadā.*

134. *iti viklavitaṃ tāsāṃ śrutvā.*

135. *maiṃ ne bhūl se keval tum par apnā hī adhikār samajhā thā. āj merā ahaṃkār ṭūṭ gayā. rādhā hār gaī.*

136. *hamāre itne lambe caure tarkoṃ ko tumhāre ek śabd hī se haṭā diyā tum ne. āj ham phir hār gaye.*

137. *"to bhagavān ne hār mān lī?" "hāṃ, ek prem ke āge hī to bhagavān bhī hārte haiṃ."*

episode 55).[138] Elsewhere, when she complains about the village gossip when he courts her too openly, all comfort he offers is that true love does not care about what people think: "Look Rādhā, if you're afraid of gossip, you should not walk the path of love" (in vol. 7, episode 53).[139] So for all his admitting defeat in the face of love, Sagar's Krishna keeps up his superiority.

Another interesting contrast with Vyās's scene is that Sagar's Krishna falls for the theoretical issue that love is the basis of everything, not that love is stronger than dharma. That issue does not come up. Rather it is asserted that, philosophically speaking, love is the first principle, the basis (*ādhār*) on which everything rests. Vyās's Gopīs, by contrast, win not so much because of convincing theorizing. Their philosophy lies mainly in wordplay; they never take themselves seriously. When they convince Krishna, it is not so much by what they say as by the way they say it: their charming ways and their demonstration of the principles they profess. In their obstinate will to stay with Krishna, no matter what the moral implications are, they prove by their actions that love is stronger than dharma.

To sum up, the women's attitudes are quite different: Sītā remains demure and aware of decorum; the Gopīs react vehemently and challenge Krishna repeatedly. The arguments of both revolve around the idea that love overrides dharma. In addition, they depict a vision of the future, in the case of the Gopīs one tinged with eroticism, in the case of Sītā one that involves a domestication of the forest. Sītā's vision is one of sylvan servitude to her beloved, whereas the Gopīs dream about how happy he can make them. What convinces the males is again quite different. Rāma finally gives in because of Sītā's suicide threat. Krishna is convinced by the Gopīs' point that love overrides dharma, which is not only a theoretical issue for them but one they have lived.

The Final Outcome

Eventually, the men give in and allow the women to join them in the forest. Not only what causes them to change their minds, but also the way they grant permission are radically different. The authors' concerns turn out to be diametrically opposite.

138. *prem meṃ māṃgnā nahīṃ, denā hotā hai rādhe.*

139. *dekho rādhā, jo nindā se ḍare, use prem kī ḍagar par nahīṃ calnā cāhiye.*

After the threat of suicide, Tulsī's Rāma finally comes around to letting Sītā have her way. His answer is short, and, as Tulsī stipulates, inspired by certainty that Sītā will die without him:

> Seeing her state, Raghupati knew in his heart: "she won't survive if kept home by force."
> So the graceful Lord of the Solar Race told her: "rejoice, and come along to the woods." (*RCM* 2.68.1a)[140]

Tulsī's concern is to point out that Rāma has the capacity to correctly assess the situation and that he is true to his reputation for being compassionate. Tulsī does not want to end too abruptly here, and has Rāma console Sītā some more. However, not too many words are spilled on that. Clearly, it would be inappropriate for Rāma to devote too much attention to his wife in the presence of his mother, so the mood switches nearly immediately back to the parental feelings (*vātsalya bhāva*) the passage started out with:

> With sweet words, he consoled his beloved. Then he touched his mother's feet and received her blessings. (*RCM* 2.68.3a)[141]

This is quite different from Vālmīki's hero, who seems sincerely swayed by his wife's arguments, and basically tells her that he cannot stand to hurt her for the sake of dharma: "I find no delight even in heaven by causing sorrow to you" (*VR* 2.30.27a).[142] He goes as far as to admit she is right, even calls her idea brilliant (*atiśobhanam,* 2.30.41). It is indeed his dharma to take her along (2.30.30) and her destiny to go to the forest (2.30.29a; as noted, she pointed out that this was prophesied to her long before her marriage). Vālmīki's hero even declares a reciprocity in love by saying that for him, too, heaven without her loses its attraction (2.30.42b). And to top it off, he invites her to be a "partner in dharma" (*sahadharmacarī,* 2.30.40b). In contrast, Tulsī's depiction of Rāma as a chivalrous yet exalted husband clearly has to do with his eagerness to demonstrate to the devoted public Rāma's graciousness toward his devotees and at the same time his keen sense of propriety.

As we have seen, Sagar, too, takes care to construe Rāma's actions in conformity with his mother's command. Sagar's Rāma, however, does not take the time to calm down his excited wife. He immediately shifts gears and starts

140. *dekhi dasā raghupati jiyaṃ jānā, haṭhi rākheṃ nahiṃ rākhihi prānā; kaheu kṛpāla bhānukulanāthā, parihari socu calahu bana sāthā.*

141. *kahi priya bacana priyā samujhāī, lage mātu pada āsiṣa pāī.*

142. *na devi bata duḥkhena svargam apy abhirocaye.*

ordering her around to get ready to join him (*ṭhīk hai sīte! calne kī taiyārī karo,* TVR 203). It seems as if he wants to show that he is in perfect command, notwithstanding having given in to her wishes! Immediately afterward, brother Lakshmana bursts in on the scene, and the audience is distracted by a new outburst of feelings.

In both the medieval and televised *Rāmāyaṇa* versions, the authors take care to make it clear that while Sītā gets her way, Rāma remains in control. The same point is totally reversed in Vyās's Rāsa-līlā episode. Here Krishna is moved to tears: "When the young ladies spoke humble words, he was embarrassed, tears streamed from his eyes" (*RP* 13.4a–b).[143] What is more, Krishna admits defeat at the hands of the women. The body language of Vyās's Krishna is significant: he folds his hands and impersonates a beggar or a *sādhu,* a religious mendicant. He is said explicitly to cast off all majesty: "Hari spoke, holding out his hem with a smile, his hands joined, all majesty cast off" (14.1a–b).[144] And then he makes it clear that he, the self-professed *sādhu,* got it morally totally wrong, and is actually not a *sādhu.* The women are the real *sādhus*, the ones who have morality on their side: "I am the bad guy, you are the good ones, all of you" (14.3c).[145] This is a clever transformation of a line in *Bhāgavata Purāṇa,* where Krishna says "I am not able to repay (*svasādhukṛtyam*) you, endowed with innocence as you are. You have left behind the shackles of domestic life, may that repay you properly (*sādhunā*)" (10.32.22).[146] In his translation, Vyās incorporates the play on the word *sādhu* of the original but transformed the statement, paying less attention to who is indebted to whom than to the Gopīs' moral superiority, in their love beyond borders (see also Pauwels 1996b: 166). In *Bhāgavata Purāṇa,* though, Krishna utters this line after the episode of his disappearance during the Rāsa-līlā, which, he explains, was a test the Gopīs passed, thanks to their selfless devotion to him.

Vyās's Krishna does not do any such testing; Vyās chooses to leave out this episode from his version. His Krishna reacts only to their argumentation about the need for their desires to be fulfilled on the grounds of their selfless devotion. Vyās's Krishna explicitly grants the Gopīs that not only is the point of

143. *dīna vacana juvatina jaba kahe, taba sakuce nainani nīra bahe.*

144. *haṃsi bole hari olī oṛi, kara jore prabhutā saba choṛi.*

145. *huṃ asādha tuma sādha saba.* In comparison with the Rāma story, we could point here to another interesting parallel, that Rāma, too, is a *sādhu* in disguise, and takes on the yellow robes of the ascetic during his exile (*banvās*).

146. *na pāraye 'haṃ niravadyasaṃyujāṃ svasādhukṛtyaṃ vaḥ . . . gehaśṛṅkhala saṃvṛścya tad vaḥ pratiyātu sādhunā.*

their arguments well taken but also they have demonstrated it. Conventional morality fades when compared to their love: "For my sake you have become fearless, worldly and spiritual sanctions proved powerless and poor" (*RP* 14.2a–b).[147] He admits that he has behaved poorly, but that they have withstood it perfectly: "I've been taken in by you effortlessly; I abused you, but you did not waver" (14.3a–b).[148] Immediately he proceeds to play with them.

Vyās's Rāsa-līlā proceeds to a happy ending in total equality. In the dazzling round dance that follows, Krishna's characteristics become totally mixed with those of the Gopīs (*RP* 17.3–19.3). Krishna and Rādhā are shown to be dancing together in perfect harmony. The total reciprocity of their love is exemplified by their sharing each other's betel leaves (27.3b) rather than her chewing his leftovers as a sign of devotion (as in *BhP* 10.33.13). Vyās sums it up: "they are one breath in two bodies" (*RP* 27.3c).[149] At times, the roles are even reversed, as when he lifts her up when she is tired, and he wipes off her sweat (28.4a–b). He is portrayed as unable to follow Rādhā's intricate dance patterns (21.2a). Vyās even has it that *he* finds happiness kissing *her* (27.2). In his most spectacular deviation from *Bhāgavata Purāṇa,* Vyās does not depict the disappearance of Krishna and the Gopīs' ensuing *viraha.* Instead, the episode has a happy ending, or rather, depicts an eternal merry-go-round. The night never ends.

What happens in Sagar's television version? Interestingly, he also leaves out the episode of Krishna's disappearance. Instead, he depicts the Gopīs' *viraha* before the Rāsa-līlā, during the waiting period after their Gaurī Pūjā. Some of the charming reciprocity of Vyās's Krishna and his Gopīs can be seen also on the television screen. When the Gopīs are about to get a bit jealous, as expressed in their *abhinaya,* by pouting and staring dreamly at Krishna and Rādhā in the middle of the circle, Sagar intervenes with the miraculous multiplication of Krishna (following *BhP* 10.33.3). In that sense, there is reciprocity, namely, in that Krishna answers their desire by multiplying himself, so that each Gopī can have him close by. Sagar's Mahārāsa is a long Bollywood song-and-dance number involving Gujarati-style stick dancing (*daṇḍiyā rāsa*) with several multiplication camera-effects.

Also relevant regarding the reciprocity of the love between Krishna and Rādhā is an earlier episode (*TVK* vol. 7, episode 55) that depicts a scene of cross-dressing—appropriately enough, immediately after the Holī celebrations.

147. *mo kārana tuma bhaya nisaṃka, loka beda bapurā ko raṃka.*
148. *binu damakai huṃ līnū mola, karata anādara bhaī na lola.*
149. *aika prāna doya deha hai.*

Rādhā reproaches Krishna that he has been expressing his affections too openly, thereby giving away their secret liaison to the whole of Braj. He has besmirched her good name. When he says he does not care what the world thinks, she points out that he has it easier because he is a man. If only he were she, he would understand. He declares himself prepared to become her, and as she happens to have an extra skirt and blouse handy, he immediately acts on the impulse. We witness a lovely scene in which Rādhā helps Krishna into her woman's attire. He claims now to know what it is to be Rādhā: "I've become Rādhā completely haven't I?"[150] But she inquires about his heart: does he perceive the same beating, the same strong currents of love? He is only Rādhā in appearance, not in feeling.

Truth be told, says Rādhā, he can never pay off the debt he owes her for her true love.[151] Here Rādhā has picked up the line from *Bhāgavata Purāṇa* where Krishna expresses that sentiment: "I am not able to repay you" (10.32.22). We recall that Vyās wrote: "I am the bad guy, you are all good ones" (*RP* 14.3c). Note, however, that Sagar has changed the dynamics completely, because in his version Krishna does not admit this; it is Rādhā who ventures the sentiment. Krishna actually contests her statement.

At this point, the camera shifts to Goloka, where divine Krishna applauds divine Rādhā's words, yet is eager to point out to her that, in the end, he and she are both one, and all this is nothing but illusion. He advises her to stop being upset about things and just sit back and enjoy the "play of illusion" (*māyā kā khel*). That gets a rise out of his otherwise so meek divine consort. She indignantly refuses to put love and *māyā* in the same existential category: "Whatever you mean with 'illusion'... what they call love is not a mere game, nor a lie, it is the highest truth, and it is the very basis of your world."[152] Without love, she points out, there is no devotion or bhakti, and without bhakti, of course, there is no God or Bhagavān. Oops, that is quite convincing. And even Krishna has to admit defeat: "God is defeated only when he is confronted with love, that's why devotees always win."[153] While he speaks those words, though, nothing in his tone or behavior is in agreement with the statement. Far from acting like a beggar, he continues to wear his smile of superiority. He even comes up with a nice deus ex machina (or should we say avatar ex machina) to save the day: in

150. *ban gayā na pūrī Rādhā?*

151. *prem kā jo riṇ hai use tum kabhī nahi cukā paoge.*

152. *māyā jo bhī ho... jise prem kahte haiṃ vah na khel hai na jhūṭh, vahī param satya hai aur vahī āp ke jagat kā ādhār hai.*

153. *prem ke āge hī to bhagavān hārte haiṃ, isī liye sadā bhakt kī hī jīt hotī hai;* this will be echoed in the later episode of the pre-Rāsa-līlā, described earlier.

Kaliyuga, he says, he will come down to earth in a form that feels love for Krishna as Rādhā does, namely as Caitanya Mahāprabhu. Thus Krishna ends up once again having the last word.

To sum up, the outcome of the Gopīs' and Sītā's pleas to join their beloved in the forest is the same in that they get what they want. The way each male gives in is quite different, though. Rāma simply grants Sītā permission to come along, and goes on immediately to other matters. Tulsī takes pains to show how he behaves perfectly "correctly," in accordance with his duty as gracious God. At the same time, he also behaves in accordance with decorum as a son toward his mother, who is present throughout the whole scene. In Sagar's version, Rāma seems to feel the need to prove that, even though he has given in to his wife, he has not lost in manliness; he does so by ordering her around.

Krishna not only gives the Gopīs what they want but also admits defeat. He takes their argument seriously and grants their point. In Vyās's version, he does so unconditionally, playfully impersonating a beggar in front of them. Sagar, however, cannot quite let his Krishna lose face that much, and grants him the last word and the last laugh.

Sītā and Rādhā Compared

What can we conclude from this detailed analysis? The different approaches of Sītā and the Gopīs in the medieval versions can be categorized following classical theological categories, as *svakīyā* and *parakīyā,* with *aiśvarya* and *mādhurya* as the most important flavors. These differences fit of course the general bhakti agendas that Tulsīdās and Harirām Vyās wished to promote.

However, what is under investigation here is not this more general bhakti interpretation but whether, and if so how, Sītā and the Gopīs function within a narrower domain, namely that of *strī-dharma*. They can be seen as illustrating or commenting in word and deed on what is proper for women to do and what not. Notwithstanding the differences, their words hold a common conviction: that love is stronger than dharma. Might this potentially liberate women from the straitjacket of *strī-dharma*?

Is Sītā's example empowering for women? Vālmīki's Sītā surely speaks her mind and gets what she wants. Tulsī's Sītā is a different case. There seems to be a contradiction at the heart of this episode. How can Sītā at the same time argue that dharma is meaningless for her, yet take all the proper steps to remain within *maryādā*? When she says that love is the only thing that matters, her body language and register of speech remain studiedly within *maryādā*. Her stance is not an antinomian one but one that seeks to reconcile love and duty.

TABLE 4.2. Overview of Differences between Sītā and the Gopīs' Resolves

Element	Subelement	Gopīs in Vyās	Sītā in Tulsīdās
Context:	Mood	Happy: *śṛṅgāra*	Sad: śoka, *karuṇā*
		Union long-awaited	Exile thwarts long-awaited coronation
	Forest	Romantic	Threatening
	Marital	*Parakīyā:* join lover (downplayed on TV)	*Svakīyā*: join husband
	Bhakti	*Mādhurya*	*Aiśvarya*
	Dharma	Defying *maryādā* (downplayed on TV)	Within *maryādā* (more voice on TV)
		No in-laws present (mother figure Gaurī on TV)	Mother-in-law present (choice between in-laws and parental loyalty on TV)
Rejection:		Whimsical	Serious
		Krishna is ambiguous	Rāma is straightforward
		Dharma is a joke/test (Gopī Agniparīkṣā on TV)	Dharma is serious (Rāma is taught dharma by women on TV)
		Forest = *uddīpana vibhāva*	Forest = difficult
Protest:	Tone	Strong; challenging; playful	Self-composed; humble; serious
	Argument	Clear	Implicit
		Dharma does not apply	Heaven and hell matter less than *viraha*
	Goal	Making love (erotic): reciprocal	Sevā: subservient
			Forest domestication project
	Suicide	Implicit threat	Repeated threat
	Final point	To reward love they have demonstrated	To avoid her suicide
Outcome:		Krishna admits defeat	Rāma gives in gallantly (commanding Rāma on TV)
		No in-laws	Approval of mother-in-law

With regard to the Gopīs, one might more easily argue that the preponderance of love could prove liberating for women. However, does it really do so? Their argument is still male-focused. It seems that women can afford to break through dharma stipulations only in demonstrating their love for a male. Even so, it is quite clear, they cannot expect immediate understanding and support from their beloved in return. The very male for whom the women sacrifice their good names will turn around and argue dharma and *maryādā*, condemning their actions. The very male who leads them on will refuse to take the responsibility for their self-sacrifice, masquerading as a *sādhu* and spokesperson for dharma! Only if they are willing to sacrifice everything unconditionally, without expecting anything in return, will they be applauded as having stood the test. And even so, even if the Gopīs manage to overcome Krishna's initial resistance and he grants them their wish, his admission of defeat lies exactly in the fact that he does not love them as much as they love him. There is a limit to reciprocity, even in Vyās's text.

The Gopīs secure a victory, but is it not one of the famous Pyrrhic kind? Does not the victory deflect attention from the real issues? Have women been fooled again, told they are so great . . . in their self-surrender and self-sacrificing love, which suits the men fine after all?

If we cannot see these bhakti models as bringing liberation from patriarchy, perhaps we need to keep in mind that the women are portrayed as using dharma as it suits them in argumentation, turning the tables, insisting that it is the men's dharma to take them along. Sometimes, it seems, dharma can be seen not as women's burden but instead as women's rights. This point may be strongest in the medieval versions, but it is definitely still present in the modern texts. Maybe the liberating potential of the stories lies more in providing a role model for maneuvering within a patriarchic frame.

Not surprisingly, the modern television version continues the trend of downplaying the scandalous element by depicting the Gopīs who partake in the Rāsa-līlā as unmarried. This is never explicit, but the Gaurī Pūjā episode especially seems geared to establish the Gopīs' desire for Krishna as socially acceptable. Sagar does his best to bring the Gopīs in line with dharma. He has left out reference to their potentially objectionable quitting of domestic chores, keeping their mortal forms at work while their souls can fly to Krishna, and showing them leaving for the Rāsa-līlā only after all the housework is done. Moreover, their strident assertiveness has disappeared. In particular, Rādhā has been tamed. She listens attentively when Krishna takes to lecturing her, and whenever she comes up with a good point, she is treated like a good student, without in the least denting Krishna's sense of superiority. He grants her the point but keeps his superior smile. Rādhā may pout a little and have flashes of brilliance, but like the good heroine of the Bollywood film industry, she always knows her place. Would it be far-fetched to say that in Sagar's version the Gopīs and Rādhā have become *maryādā*-ized?

Similarly, Sītā's character is different in the television version. While Sagar's Sītā has more edge to her, she is depicted as an ideal daughter-in-law even more than in Tulsī's text. Her mother-in-law is in perfect agreement with her. Sītā's choice has become a statement of loyalty to the husband, as opposed to the woman's own native family. In some respects, however, Sagar has modeled his Sītā after Vālmīki's more strident heroine; hence she ends up being more assertive, to the point of telling Rāma what his dharma is. However, much of this gets lost when the passage ends on a blunt command by Rāma. Vālmīki's reciprocity is totally bypassed.

While Tulsī and Vyās's heroines seem to occupy opposite ends of the spectrum, Sītā and the Gopīs in the contemporary versions are much more alike. The Gopīs have been domesticated. Even Sītā seems to have slid more to the right, identifying emphatically with her in-laws and being snubbed by her commanding husband at the end. Are we witnessing an ever more reactionary model being forged for women?

Finally, we should not overlook what is obviously the main message: in times of hardship, women unquestionably are to follow their husbands. The husbands may actually want to dissuade them from doing so, but the women should persist in carrying out this dharma, no matter what. None of the texts shows a split second of doubt in the heroines about whether they should follow their men or not.

Also interesting is the question what might the differences in the reactions of Rāma and Krishna have to tell us about male role ideals? The more Krishna argues *advaita*, the less he and his Gopīs are truly equal, it seems, judging by the television version. The more air time Rāma allows his Sītā, the harder it is for him to graciously let her have her way, and the more he feels compelled to balance his giving in to her with giving her a command—again in the television version.

It is of course too simple to see the differences in the medieval and modern versions as a unidirectional phenomenon. I have not been able to begin to do justice to the many other versions of the stories, of medieval times, as well as now. Tulsī's version is without any doubt a dominant one, but Vyās's cannot be claimed to be representative. Many other versions of Rāsa-līlā, including Nanddās's, boast much less assertive, meeker Gopīs (Pauwels 1996b: 163–79).

Nonetheless, another contemporary version of the Rāsa-līlā has elements very similar to Sagar's: B. R. Chopra's *Mahābhārata* sequence, retelling the Krishna story (DVD, vol. 3), which also splits the Rāsa-līlā in two parts. The first (in episode 15) portrays a very cleaned-up first version of the Rāsa-līlā. Here we see the boy Krishna playing his flute and growing up into a preadolescent boy. The Gopīs, also grown up, are irresistibly drawn to him. They get into a trance-like state when they hear his flute playing. Limited elements from the *Bhāgavata Purāṇa* Rāsa-līlā are incorporated: one of the Gopīs is boiling milk but starts pouring the milk next to the pot absentmindedly; another puts on her make-up wrong. There is no hint, though, that these women are married with children, though the possibility is left open. The women flock to Krishna and walk around him swaying as if in trance, but nothing erotic happens. The accompanying song, entitled "Muralī madhura bajāī" ("The flute resounds sweetly"), seems to be a variant of Vallabha's famous *Madhurāṣṭakam*, a Sanskrit poem in which the adjective *madhura* is applied to different features of Krishna over and over again. In this case what is repeated is the word *nirmala* (pure stainless), which is related to different features of the Gopīs and nature. Only toward the end of the song does the action take on a Holī-like, playful character, but even so things remain quite tame. Nevertheless, in this series, in contrast to Sagar's, Rādhā looks a little bit older than the very young preadolescent Krishna, who, it is said elsewhere, is just eleven years old. The second version of the Rāsa-līlā comes in the next episode (vol. 3, episode 16). After the Govardhana-līlā, just as in *Bhāgavata Purāṇa*. Interestingly, in this interpretation, Rādhā is being made fun of by the other Gopīs, who see her as a stranger, not a resident of Nandgaon. And it is in response to her boasting that Krishna plays only for her that the Gopīs approach him with the request he play his flute for them, too. He promises to do so and sinks into a reverie when they have gone off. The ensuing Rāsa-līlā could thus be interpreted as a dream of Krishna, and in any case the focus is on the celebration of his flute playing; thus the Rāsa-līlā becomes a celebration of his "Magic Flute". In addition, somewhat contrary to expectations, Rādhā is the first who appears on the screen in the Rāsa-līlā, and the song stresses the inseparability of the divine pair. This Rāsa-līlā is a non-erotic, though late-night, folk-dance scene, wherein the Gopīs use sticks. Krishna and Rādhā are in the middle of the circle, dancing as well as taking on poses as in a tableau (*jhāṅkī*). The language of the accompanying song is very Sanskritic and ends in a chant of "Rādhā Krishna." Visually, there is much duplicating of the images of Krishna and Krishna and Rādhā. There is no hint of the Gopīs leaving their home for the occasion. Right after the Rāsa-līlā, Rādhā and Krishna are shown alone. She has a foreboding of the coming events and asks him to play for her alone. However, Balarāma interrupts and reminds Krishna of his duty to work for the salvation of the world, at which Krishna promptly leaves. Thus we see here, too, a tendency to clean up the Rāsa-līlā and edit out the less dharmic aspects of the Gopīs' devotion.

If we compare Sagar's *Ramayan* to earlier movie versions, we find significant differences. In Babubhai Mistry's 1961 *Sampoorna Ramayan*, strikingly, Sītā acts very differently.[154] As soon as she hears Rāma break the news of his upcoming exile to his mother, we see Sītā's reaction of pain, and then we see her rush off. After his conversation with his mother, Rāma finds her in his quarters. She has taken off all her jewelry and is dressed like a devotee, ready to

154. Mistry had worked with Vijay Bhatt in the 1940s on mythologicals that were influential during the independence movement. He was a consultant for the televised *Ramayan*, so bridges the early and later periods.

go with him; she has immediately taken decisive action according to her best judgment.

Now follows the debate between husband and wife in private. This movie shows Sītā using very submissive language yet respectfully disagreeing with her husband and winning each argument. He tries to convince her that the hardships of the forest will be too much for her. However, she counters that it is his pain and separation from him that she will not be able to suffer.[155] He says that time will teach her how to do so. She cleverly counters that that is just what she would say: as time goes along, watching his smile, sitting at his feet, she'll be able to put up with the hardships of the forest and find her heaven.[156] He seems convinced but tries to find another authority that might come in the way, arguing that her following him would be against Kaikeyī's command. She says it would be against Kaikeyī's command to go alone, because a woman is a man's *ardhāṅginī,* so without Sītā he would be following Kaikeyī's command with only half his body. At this point, the camera cuts to the *ardhanārīśvara* image in the background as if to illustrate her point. Rāma does not give up yet; he plays on her feelings of concern for his good name, arguing that he will get a bad name by taking her along because people will say he took her to make his hard time easier. She counters in kind, saying that if she does not go along, people will say that Sītā stayed true to Rāma in good days but when times got tough she did not go along.[157] She asks him whether he would let her be so dishonored,[158] and he of course has to reply he would not. That argument clinches it, and Sītā and Rāma embrace; she sighs happily "Lord" (*nāth*), and he calls her tenderly by name ("Sīte"). In the background of the embrace the *ardhanārīśvara* image looms large, wonderfully illustrating the tone of the whole scene, in which man and woman are on equal terms. This scene from the sixties is more liberating for women than Sagar's from the late eighties.

Thus, a detailed analysis shows that overall, Sagar's texts are a step back; they offer more *maryādā*-abiding role modes for women. There is only limited "wiggle room" to make their choices when countering those of their husbands. Still, Sagar was successful. It seems that his view is a hegemonic one. How far do we find this confirmed in the world Sagar comes from, that of non-mythological Bollywood movies?

155. *sab kuch sah lūṃgī par āp ke liye pīṛā mujhse nahīṃ sahī jāegī.*

156. *yahī to maiṃ bhī kahtī hūṃ svāmī! āp ke hoṃṭhoṃ ke madhu muskān dekhkar maiṃ apne sāre dukh bhulā dūṃgī, āp ke caraṇoṃ meṃ baiṭhkar maiṃ apnā svarg basā dūṃgī.*

157. *to vehī log kaheṃge sukh ke samay sītā raghunāth ke sāth rahī aur jab banvās kī gharī āyī to usne apne pati kā sāth nahīṃ diyā.*

158. *svāmī kyā āp merī badnāmī sahan kareṃge?*

Love and Dharma in Bollywood

Bollywood movies often have Rāsa-līlā-like scenes. Love is unfailingly celebrated in a song-and-dance number with the hero and heroine cavorting in a bucolic setting, often with lots of female dancers suddenly joining the pair. Often the hero is portrayed as a lover-boy, a playful Krishna type, who calls the heroine out from her home for a meeting in a romantic, bucolic place, whether by playing the flute or, more prosaically, calling her on the phone. One example is the 1995 *Dilwale dulhania le jayenge.* When Simran (Kajol) is awaiting her impending, unwanted wedding, the man she really loves, Raj (Shah Rukh Khan), arrives in the Punjabi village she is staying. He calls her out in the fields to a secret moonlight tryst by playing his characteristic melody. In this case, there are no others present, but the Rāsa-līlā connotations are clear.

I single out here for detailed analysis a Rāsa-līlā scene from a lesser known 1992 movie, *Meera ka Mohan,* directed by K. Ravishankar, and another one from Ashutosh Gowarikar's Oscar-nominated *Lagaan* (2001).

Surprisingly, few Hindi movies elaborate on the issue of following the husband into the hardship of exile. Reportedly, this is a common motive in early Bengali movies, where wives regularly accompany their husbands posted in interior villages, but this theme is not taken up by Hindi directors (Gayatri Chatterjee, personal communication, March 2 2006). There is, though, an interesting counterpoint, where the wife does not follow her husband. *Yahi hai zindagi* (1977), directed by K. S. Sethumadhavan. Finally, I will return to the 1994 blockbuster *Hum aap ke hain koun . . . !* and how it illustrates the relationship between bhakti and dharma with reference to Rāma and Krishna mythology.

Sītā-Radha Stays Home While Her Husband Moves in with Her Father: "Yahi hai zindagi"

An interesting variant of Sītā's decision to follow her husband can be found in the delightful 1977 movie *Yahi hai zindagi,* directed by K. S. Sethumadhavan.[159] This movie is a rags-to-richess farce with the message that wealth does not make one happy. In this movie, the women are the sane, loving, and pious characters, and the heroes are agnostic, deluded by ambition and false images of self-importance and jealousy. The movie is drenched in Krishna mythology, as Krishna himself makes frequent appearances in his form of the flute-player.

159. This director worked mainly in Malayalam and Tamil film; this is one of his few Hindi movies.

The main character is Anand (Sanjeev Kumar), a waiter in a local restaurant who does not believe in the supernatural or fate but in the power of his own brain and labor. He scoffs at the superstition of his wife, who is an avid Krishna devotee, arguing that he is working himself into a sweat while "that flute-player" is just vegetating. In some delightful humorous scenes, Anand is irreverent toward ideas of fate and belief in miracles and the gods, Krishna in particular. He is the everyman in whom we can recognize ourselves, at the same time that we keep our distance from him by laughing at his simple stubbornness and the disrespectful familiarity with which he treats the gods. While the movie gives a lot of time to Anand's refusal to believe in miracles and his insistence on common sense, it actually undermines his point of view by poking fun at it.

Anand regularly fills out puzzles in hopes to raise enough money for the education of his children and the wedding of his daughter. To his chagrin, his eldest son, Madhu, has to give up his college studies due to lack of money for the tuition fees. Madhu's fellow student, Radha, who is secretly in love with Madhu, offers to pay for the fees. She is the daughter of Anand's employer, so Anand's family feels they cannot accept such an offer. One day Anand takes money for his puzzle submission out of the donation box of the Krishna image that is worshiped in his house. His wife has collected the money to celebrate Krishna's birthday and she protests that God will not let him rest in peace until he has put the money back. Anand says that after all, it is money he has earned himself, so it really is his. That night indeed Krishna appears to Anand, who is astonished but remains unconvinced of Krishna's power. After a delightful conversation, Anand extracts from Krishna the promise that he will be rich, in return for donating a set percentage of money to Krishna. Krishna wagers a bet that the wealth will not make Anand happy, but he is keen to prove the opposite. Krishna agrees to the bet and disappears. When Anand tells about the *darśana* he has received, no one in the family believes it could be true that their agnostic father would be thus honored. However, a few days later the dream comes true when Anand wins the lottery and his family is suddenly propelled into wealth.

Initially all goes well. Anand behaves nobly toward his former friends, sharing his newfound wealth generously. Madhu marries Radha, and the family gets richer and richer. However, soon the trouble begins. Radha's father, Anand's former employer, is jealous and does what he can to wreck the family's happiness. He leads Madhu into dubious deals involving dishonest money-making. Anand wishes to remain an honest businessman, and it pains him greatly when he finds out that his son has abused his confidence and grown corrupt. He tries all he can to turn things around, but to no avail. After a major fight with his father, Madhu goes as far as to leave the parental house, choosing to live with his father-in-law instead.

At this point, the *Rāmāyaṇa* discourse emerges. Radha has tried to make Madhu see reason, only to be slapped in the face. Now again she tries to stop him, but her father counters with something worse than a slap—parental disapproval and the accusation that she is not a good wife: "I'm ashamed of you. Your husband is going into exile, and you, instead of going with him, you're lecturing him! I had thought that when the time came my daughter would show herself to be a Sītā-Sāvitrī."[160] That this crook dares argue *Rāmāyaṇa* to his wonderful daughter is ironic. He is a gambler and has lost everything; only thanks to Radha's marriage to Madhu has the father been saved from penury. It is then totally appropriate that at this point, Madhu's mother quickly intervenes to argue that the mythological example does not apply. Madhu is leaving because of a tiff with his father, not for any noble reasons: "There's no question of her becoming Sītā. She was born Sītā indeed, in your house. It's only my son who has not turned out to be a Rāma."[161] Radha, the good *bahū,* thus stays on at her in-laws, whereas her corrupt husband goes to live with her father.

Like much else in the movie, this exchange illustrates a playful turning of mythological stories upside down. Here, Madhu-Rāma is not an obedient son but a corrupt figure, and his Radha chooses not to follow him in his self-imposed exile from the parental house. We get a valuing of dharma over love, but this time the type of dharma that prevails is not that of wifely duties but the universal dharma of honesty over corruption. Radha does not feel compelled to follow her beloved into the realm of vice and is strengthened in her resolve by her in-laws, who also value honesty above their love for their son. It is significant, though, that her father is portrayed as the cause of the evil in her husband, and that her holding true to dharma breaks her loyalty toward her own parent but not that toward her in-laws. It seems that a woman's first duty is always toward the in-laws, even before that toward her husband.

After he has lost his son, Anand's health starts to deteriorate, and it gets worse, as he is also disappointed in his other children. By the end of the movie, Anand has to admit to Krishna that he has lost the wager; his wealth has caused

160. *mujhe śarm ā rahī hai tum pai. tumhārā pati vanvās jā rahā hai, aur tum uske sāth jāne ke bajāy unheṃ bhāṣan de rahī ho. maiṃ ne socā thā ki kabhī samay ā gayā to merī beṭī sītā sāvitrī banke dikhā degī*

161. *sītā banne kā kyā savāl hai. āpke ghar meṃ to sacmuc sītā hī janam liyā hai, merā beṭā hī rām nahīṃ nikalā.*

his children to go astray and has not made him happy. He accepts defeat, and Krishna teaches him that his fault is in his pride (*ahaṃkāra*). Anand takes the lesson to heart and decides to withdraw from the world, which causes a tearful apotheosis in which he is reconciled with his children.

Though the dominant tone of this movie is one of irreverent playfulness, very much in sync with Krishna bhakti, as indeed fits the emphasis on Krishna as the main deity (*iṣṭadevatā*) of the family, in the end what prevails is undoubtedly dharma, with a hierarchic return to dharmic order more in sync with Rāma's *maryādā*.

Rādhā-Mīrā Turns into Sītā: "Meera ka Mohan"

K. Ravishankar's *Meera ka mohan* (1992) was not very successful, but it is interesting in many respects. It refers explicitly, both in its title and in its lyrics, to the Rādhā-Krishna myth, or more precisely the Mīrā variant of Rādha. Mīrā was a legendary sixteenth-century Rajput princess to whom are attributed many devotional songs to Krishna. Her legend stresses the persecution she suffered for her love for Krishna and the way she unconventionally acted out this love without keeping the rules of propriety for a princess of her standing. In her willingness to give up dharma rules for the sake of her love, Mīrā seems to be following the Gopīs.

The story of *Meera ka Mohan* is a variant of what we could call the *Andaaz* theme: the impossibility of friendship between a man and a woman, as it inevitably raises doubts and suspicions to the point of destroying the marriage of the woman involved. In this case, the central character, Priti (Ashwini Bhave), is the daughter of a classical musician and is herself an aerobics teacher, which marks her as quintessentially modern—not your traditional Sītā type.

Priti has several chance encounters with an attractive young man, Ravi (Avinash Wadhavan), who rescues her from several troubles. First, he restores a music award to her father by exposing corruption underlying the selection of another music teacher. The victory is celebrated in a song-and-dance sequence called "O Krishna." Ostensibly, this song is in honor of Krishna as patron of music, but the prevalence of a giant Krishna image on a chariot evokes rather Krishna's role as advisor in the *Bhagavad Gītā*. There is a hint that Ravi is metaphorically linked to Krishna, as a savior-avatar of Vishnu, who descends to help his devotees whenever they need him. This becomes more explicit later in the movie when Ravi rescues Priti from an attempted rape. She is grateful to him, and they get together on other occasions.

Ravi—and with him the audience—misunderstands Priti's intentions, and he falls in love with her. This love is celebrated in several song-and-dance sequences, in which the couple cavorts happily. However, they turn out to be just Ravi's dreams. One of these scenes features a Rāsa-līlā-like dance, foregrounding Krishna's bucolic character: his flute playing is mimicked by the dancers in *abhinaya,* and if that were not enough, the lovers dance on a giant flute. Interestingly, also shown is a filmī fantasy of Rajasthani-style folk dance, with a corps de ballet, all women, suggestively dancing in circles, evoking the Rāsa-līlā. Halfway through the song, out of nowhere, the theme of Holī emerges—another popular theme of Krishna *bhajanas*. The festival of colors involves not only orgies of colored powder but also fountains of fluids, creating the famous wet-sari effect. The erotic visual possibilities are further exploited in waterfall scenes, another convention of the Hindi movie by this time. Interestingly, in the song the love of Ravi and Priti is explicitly likened to that of Krishna and Mīrā:

> She:
> When you stole my heart,
> I gave up all sense of propriety:
> I've become crazy with love for you!
> I'm Mīrā, you Mohan,
> I'm the body, you're my life,
> My beloved, come![162]
>
> He:
> When you stole my heart,
> I gave up all ritual connections.
> There was tumult in my heart:
> You're my heartbeat,
> I'm your heartbeat!
> My beloved, come![163]
>
> She:
> May I stay every moment with you,
> That's my heart's only wish.
> He:

162. *tūne prīt jo mujhse corī, maiṃ ne lok lāj sab choṛī; pyār meṃ tere pāgal huī, maiṃ mīrā, tū mohan, maiṃ kāyā tū jīvan, mere mitvā ā jā!*

163. *tūne prīt jo mujhse corī, maiṃ ne rīt-rasm sab toṛī; man kī nagarī meṃ halcal huī, mere dil kī tū dhaṛkan; tere dil kī maiṃ dhaṛkan, mere mitvā ā jā!*

What do I expect from the world?
You alone are my world![164]
(Refrain)

He:
Seven heavens, seven seas,
Seven lives together we have.

She:
Sweeter than the seven notes,
Is the song of my life.[165]

The explicit references to Mīrā are underscored iconographically. At a certain moment in the dance sequence, the lover bows over his backward-leaning beloved in a scene reminiscent of the iconography of Mīrā in the popular *Amar Chitra Katha* comic strip. The drawing there is of Mīrā's total surrender after being saved by Krishna from her attempt at suicide by drowning (Hawley 1995: 118–20). In this movie, the image is rather one of ecstatic love in the waterfall, and there is no question of the heroine's suicide or forsaking a husband for the sake of this lover. The movie will actually be the reverse scenario.

Several lines in the lyrics are reminiscent of popular ideas about Mīrā's *bhajanas*, including the theme of her giving up all chastity (*lok lāj*) for the sake of her love, and self-avowed craziness in love. The movie song is no *bhajana*, however, and a significant difference is the alteration of the male with the female voice. It is not just her giving up everything for him but also his vowing to do away with customary rites for her sake. Whereas Mīrā's devotional songs focused on the eternally unanswered longing of the woman, the movie song shows a reciprocal relationship between the hero and the heroine. Maybe it is no coincidence that this song-and-dance sequence will turn out to be not really a celebration of love but just Ravi's dream of it. It is slightly ambiguous at this moment but becomes clear all too soon that in fact Priti does not reciprocate his feelings.

Indeed, all this emphasis on the Mīrā theme is quite surprising and sits uncomfortably with the plot up to this point. First, the hero is crazy for Priti rather than vice versa, whereas in the Mīrā story, Mīrā is perennially longing for Krishna and complaining that he does not respond to her love. Indeed, one could read the title of the movie slightly differently. *Mīrā kā Mohan* means literally "Mīrā's Krishna," or "Mīrā's enchanter," a phrase associated with the

164. *har pal tere sāth rahūṃ maiṃ, mere dil kī yahī hai tamannā; jag se mujhe bhī kyā lenā hai, tūhī hai merī duniyā.*

165. *sāt gagan haiṃ, sāt haiṃ sāgar, apnā sāth hai sāt janam kā; sāt suroṃ se bhī hai surīlā, gīt mere janam kā.*

poetry attributed to Mīrā, but may imply "the one who is crazy for Meera." This is a role reversal of sorts, more in tune with the Rādhā-Krishna than the Mīrā paradigm. Second, the theme of love against all odds is hardly applicable. As we understand the story up to this point, the two young people have actually no obstacles in way of their possible love affair. As in *Andaaz,* we have been encouraged to identify with the hero's growing feelings for the heroine, and with him we have been led to believe that she reciprocates. Moreover, the dream is shown from Ravi's perspective, who is—as are we—at this point unaware of Priti's unavailability. The lyrics thus appear to be extradiegetical. At this point, the audience may well dismiss the Mīrā-Krishna references as another of the absurdities of the Bollywood genre, and take the song for a visual feast with slightly incongruent lyrics.

It is not till later in the story that we come to know that the heroine has a preexisting engagement. She is in love with the son of an influential judge, who desires to marry her, though his parents oppose the match. There is definitely an element of socially upward mobility in Priti's choice of this rich and high-status partner over the apparently poor Ravi. In any case, when we find out about Priti's true love, the Mīrā theme of the song sequence can retrospectively be reevaluated as hinting at the transgressive character of Ravi and Priti's love since she is to be married to another. However, the theme of breaking dharma for the sake of one's love is downplayed and becomes no more than the love-song convention of saying one is prepared to disregard all propriety for the other's sake.

What transpires in the rest of the movie sends the opposite message. Priti gets to marry her rich hero, but her friendship with Ravi comes back to haunt her. Circumstances lead her husband to believe she may have a relationship with Ravi, and he seeks to divorce her. The story now reverts to a Sītā scenario. Priti's painstaking abiding by the rules of propriety, her acceptance of her fate, and her willingness to sacrifice her happiness for what she perceives to be her husband's is only upstaged by Ravi's total commitment to the sanctity of the matrimonial bond. Ravi now is the sole advocate of the reunion of Priti and her husband. He cannot understand why her husband has rejected her, a woman as pure as Sītā. Priti's answer is revealing: "In this degenerate age there are no Sītās nor Rāmas. They appear only in calendars or on wedding invitations."[166]

The climax of the movie follows in the next song, wherein Priti prays to God to save her husband, as he is about to get remarried to a woman who is in

166. *is kaliyug meṃ na sītā haiṃ na rām. ab to ye donoṃ sirf calendars meṃ nazar āte haiṃ yā śādī ke cards par.*

fact only after his money. Priti's last resort is God himself. She leads a *bhajana* session in front of the Rāma image, but her song is directed to both Rāma and Krishna:

> Long live Lord Rāma, who helps people across this world
> Long live Dear Krishna, who staged the Rāsa in this world. . . .
>
> Where is the Rāma of the Rāmāyaṇa? Where is the Dark hero of the Gītā?
> Where are Rāma's commandments? Where are Krishna's messages? . . .[167]
>
> Priest:
> "Whenever virtue turns dim, O Arjuna,
> and the tide of evil rises, I emanate myself [in the world]" [*Bhagavad Gītā* 4.7][168]
>
> Where is the support of the world? Where are life's sacraments?
> Where is Raghuvīr, the killer of foes? Where is the hero of the Solar dynasty?
>
> Since I have called you witness of my love,
> Upholder of virtue, Rāma, listen![169]

The intervention of the priest who recites from *Bhagavad Gītā* gives patriarchal sanction to Priti's desperate plea for divine intervention. It is Ravi, though, who acts as the agent of the divine to save the day. Through his decisive action, he succeeds in thwarting the remarriage of Priti's husband. Predictably, he dies for the cause, and in extremis manages to bring about the final reconciliation of Priti and her husband. He forces the villain who caused all the trouble to give testimony of Priti's purity before breathing his last in front of the sacred wedding fire: "Priti is pure like the water of the Ganges" (*prīti gaṅgājal kī tarah pavitar*). Another Agniparīkṣā has taken place. Maybe it is a test of Ravi's love, of Mīrā's Mohan, of a friend's sincerity. In the end, though, it is Priti's purity, the woman's chastity, that has been at stake. In this movie, Mīrā has undergone a fire sacrifice, and her choice is not for the lover, her Mohan, but instead for the

167. *jai jai rām ramaiyā, jag ke pār lagaiyā, jai jai krishna kanhaiyā, jag meṃ rās racaiyā; rāmāyaṇa kā rām kahāṃ haiṃ? gītā kā ghanśyām kahāṃ haiṃ? rām ke vah ādeś kahāṃ haiṃ? gītā ke sandeś kahāṃ haiṃ?*

168. *yadā yadā hi dharmasya glānir bhavati bhārata, abhyutthānam adharmasya tadā 'tmānaṃ sṛjāmy aham.*

169. *duniyā kā ādhār kahāṃ haiṃ? jīvan meṃ saṃskār kahāṃ haiṃ? duṣṭadalan raghuvīr kahām haiṃ? sūryavaṃś kā vīr kahāṃ haiṃ? jab iśq meṃ mānā tumko, dharmavīr raghuvaṃśī sun lo!*

sanctity of matrimony. It is no accident that with all its Krishna imagery, in the end the image that she prays to and the force that prevails is that of Rāma.

The Gopīs Reject Their Krishna for the Sake of the Children: "Hum aap ke hain koun . . . !"

One may object that *Meera ka Mohan* was not a success and that the scenario it represents thus cannot be said to be a popular one. Maybe the movie flopped, but there is no dearth of reformed Gopīs in successful Hindi movies. The message of love-within-dharma is writ large in the domain of popular culture. This is best illustrated by revisiting one more time the popular hit movie *Hum aap ke hain koun . . . !*

As already discussed, there are several interesting reworkings of mythology in this story of two brothers and two sisters. Nisha (Madhuri Dixit) is the real heroine of the movie, and she possesses some of the spice and charming assertiveness of the Gopīs, in addition to being marked as modern by the trappings of her roller-skating (that is how we see her first in the movie) and studying the computer. An important parallel with the Gopīs is the cross-dressing motif. At the beginning of the movie, Nisha dresses up as a man (the manager of the Rāmṭek ashram), and that is how she first meets her beloved Prem (Salman Khan). More significant in its Krishnaite inspiration is the famous cross-dressing scene with the hit song "Dīdī terā devar divānā" ("Sister, your brother-in-law is marvelous"). There are plenty of Krishnaite elements in this scene, which evokes something of a drag Rāsa-līlā, posing as the (glamorized) woman folk genre *khoṛiyā* (see Chowdhry 2005: 112–4). This involves a riotous celebration of the pregnancy of Nisha's sister and Prem's sister-in-law. Nisha dresses up like her pregnant sister, and Rita, Prem's spurned girlfriend impersonates Prem.

The scene starts out as an all-women affair, with the hero marginalized. Prem himself tries to gain access dressed as a woman but is found out. Later though he gets to enjoy the spectacle on the sly, in tune with his Krishna-like role. He is shown to be snacking vigorously throughout, with Coca-Cola and Seven Up substituting as the consumer equivalents of Krishna's favorite buttermilk. When he is inevitably found out again by the women, a riotous scene ensues, reminiscent of Braji Holī situations. Prem punishes Rita and is on the verge of spanking Nisha, when he suddenly changes gears. Like Krishna before his Gopīs, he takes the position of the inferior begging Nisha to punish him as she wishes. The climax of the scene is the voyeur's punishment: he is dressed up as a pregnant woman, again a wonderful reversal of roles.

Though very Krishna-like, this ladies-only function is portrayed as perfectly legitimate within the movie. Poking fun at the brother-sister-in-law (*devar-bhābhī*) relationship is common in folklore. Potentially such a scene is against *maryādā;* however, the director has cleverly inserted this piquant scene in the context of a socially sanctioned rite connected with life-cycle rituals, in this case a pregnancy celebration.

The overwhelming mood, the *rasa,* of this scene is humorous, (*hāsya*) rather than romantic (*śṛṅgāra*). This continues in the next scene, where Nisha and Prem meet at the swimming pool, a proper Yamunā substitute. This tête-à-tête has all the ingredients for romantic declaration of feelings, but still ends on a humorous tone. Prem falls in the water, and Nisha runs off laughing—at which he delivers the impeccably Hindi line "Shit! I love her." All this is very Krishna-like. Interesting, too, is that Krishna's pranks are suffused with markers of modernity. It is as if his capricious *līlā* is best suited to become a vehicle for the legitimization of the consumerist and free-love behavior that is perceived as the essence of Westernization.

Still, for all its celebration of Krishna and Westernization, the movie is at pains to show that at its heart lies a Rāma-like dharma, as is well illustrated by what happens just after disaster has struck and Nisha's sister Pooja has died. When the well-intentioned elders of the family, unaware of the blossoming romance between Prem and Nisha, decide that for the baby's sake, Nisha is to be betrothed to the widower, Prem's brother Rajesh, they ask for Nisha's permission, but she thinks that she is to be given in marriage to Prem. She does not discover whom she is to marry until she sees the engagement invitations. At this point, love can no longer proceed within the boundaries of *maryādā,* and a classical conflict between duty (*farz*) and love (*prem*) ensues. This conflict is epitomized in a (sung) phone conversation between Prem and Nisha. She says: "I will extinguish the fire of love from my heart. I will give up everything in service of my duty."[170] He has all along abided silently by the decisions of the elders and supports her in her choice: "You have to carry out your duty. How can I ever repay my debt to you? I have to bow my head worshipfully for you now."[171] Note again the reference to the lover's "indebtedness" but here because of her forsaking love for others. Fareed Kazmi has pointed out that now, after the sacrifice, Nisha becomes like a goddess to him (1999: 150). This fits with what we have seen in Sagar's series: Rādhā grows in

170. *maiṃ pyār kī āg dil se miṭā dūṃgī, maiṃ farz kī ghabil sab kuch bulā dūṃgī.*

171. *tujhko nibhānā hai jo farz hai, terā kaise cukāūṃgā maiṃ qarz hī terā, sajde meṃ ab tere ki sir jhukānā hai.*

stature, becomes a great goddess, once she submits to patriarchy and loses her spunk.

There is another Krishna reference that has not been noticed; In the background of this sung conversation between Prem and Nisha, we see at Nisha's house the image of Krishna looming large, though it remains out of focus. In the foreground, Nisha is holding and kissing the baby. She has been deliberately cast as the very opposite of a latter-day Gopī. Notwithstanding her house-worship of Krishna and all her dallying with her beloved, she is prepared to sacrifice her love for her perceived duty. This Gopī would not drop the baby for the sake of love, rather, the other way around.

The next time we see this Krishna image again in full focus is at the climax of the conflict, when the wedding is about to take place and Krishna has to save the day (as discussed in chapter 2). At this point, Krishna is the one to be invoked, and indeed, all the problems are solved, and Nisha is free to wed Prem in the end. When love has prevailed and the wedding of the true lovers is celebrated, Rāsa-līlā-style dancing ensues.

Superficially, it is Krishna who has the last word, but (as the analysis in chapter 2 has shown) in the end Rāma is the ultimate winner. He is the higher, more serious deity. It is his dharmic order that prevails over chaos, and his *maryādā* has been confirmed before love can blossom. Rāma's victory over Krishna automatically entails Sītā's over Rādhā. Superficially we can equate Pooja, whose name means "worship," with Sītā, and Nisha, whose name means "night," with Rādhā-Śyāmā, "the dark one." However, my analysis demonstrates that both heroines actually are designed to fit the model of Sītā. Both are allowed some degree of initiative, but both can be trusted to remain within the bounds of *maryādā*. Their love never makes them forget their duties, rather the opposite. Nisha has to go through the fire ordeal. Her willingness to sacrifice for the family's sake takes the form of the wedding with the wrong brother. This "Gopī" can only celebrate her love after being ready to drop her beloved for the baby. Even spunky Nisha turns out to be a *maryādā* girl after all.

Neither Rādhā nor Rukmiṇī: Lagaan's Heroine Supports Her Freedom Fighter–Cricket Star

References to Krishna mythology are recurrent even in Ashutosh Gowarikar's *Lagaan* (2001), best known as a cricket movie with an anticolonial theme. There is much going on in this empire-strikes-back celebration of India's growing confidence on the international scene. The basic story line is that an Indian village team scores a cricket victory over an imperial British one and thereby succeeds in escaping an unreasonable tax (*lagān*) levied on the villagers during times of drought. Most important, the team also scores a moral victory that sends the British packing. This victory is ascribed to several factors. First, there is the villagers' determination and courage to fight for their rights, which goes hand in hand with their camaraderie and village solidarity across caste and religious lines. And there is their willingness to undergo a rigorous regime of yoga-cum-cricket training.[172] On the other hand, they receive help from an English lady, the sympathizing sister of the villainous British captain who represents the colonial government. However, the victory is far from sure, and as the game extends over several days, suspense mounts, and the good guys are on the verge of loosing. At that point, divine intervention is needed. The whole village community appeals to none other than Krishna, singing a collective *bhajana* in front of the village shrine.[173] Krishna of course obliges, and not only is victory won but on top of it the long-awaited monsoon arrives. Thus Krishna is quite central even to the movie's main theme. It is remarkable that the choice fell on Krishna rather than Rāma in a film that so emphatically asserts Hindu pride against foreign domination.

For my purpose, the most interesting use of Krishna mythology in the film are the references to Krishna's relationship with Rādhā, which include Rāsalīlā evocations. Krishna's philanderous inclinations are applied to the love triangle of the hero, Bhuvan (Aamir Khan), his village sweetheart, Gauri (Gracy Singh), and the English *memsahib,* Elizabeth (Rachel Shelley), who is in love with him, too. The movie takes full advantage of the ambiguity of which of the two girls is to be cast in the mold of Rādhā.

From the beginning of the movie, we find that Gauri has *svakīyā* aspirations; she hopes to marry Bhuvan. We encounter her first when her fortune is being read by the village madman. She asks whether she will marry the prince of her dreams (*man kā rājkumār*), and he answers: "If you do penance with a true heart, than you will wear his marriage bangles and his toe-rings."[174] Gauri is pleased and reports to Bhuvan, hinting that he is her chosen one, but he pretends not to notice.

Gauri sticks with her man, though, even when the whole village declares him mad for accepting the arrogant captain's challenge to a cricket game. That night, when Bhuvan is lying awake on his bed, worried about the future, he hears the sound of anklets and investigates. Gauri has become the *abhi-*

172. This is celebrated in the song "Bār bār hāṃ bolo yār hāṃ hamarī jīt ho unkī hār hāṃ" ("Say 'yes' over and over again, friend, 'yes' may we win, 'yes' may they lose").

173. This is the song "O pālanahāre, nirguṇa o nyāre, tumhare bina hamarā kaunu nahīṃ" ("O sustainer, O transcendent, aloof God, we have none but you").

174. *jab sacce man se tapasyā kaī hai to usī ke kaṃgaṛā pahanegī usī kī bichiyāṃ.*

sārikā, as she has ventured out late at night to Bhuvan's house, but not for a romantic tryst, like Rādhā and the Gopīs, but to express her support for her man in times of hardship, as a married woman would. Like Krishna, he enquires somewhat indignantly what she's doing there late at night.[175] She answers she wants to let him know she's with him: "I've come to meet you. I want to tell you that I'm with you. I have faith in you, in your courage. That's all I wanted to say."[176] With that she returns to her home. No Rāsa-līlā, no illicit affair here.

In the next scene, Bhuvan tries to win the villagers' support for his cricket game by demonstrating in front of all how cricket is easy, like *gillī-ḍaṇḍā.* When he misses a hit, he asks Gauri to pick up the ball, but her dad calls her back and tells her to go and heat water in the house. This Gopī obediently goes back into her house, and Bhuvan has to pick up his ball by himself. When he hits the ball next, it flies right to the temple and hits the bell, as if to invoke Krishna: an auspicious beginning that brings the villagers around. My point here, though, is that Gauri is shown to be a *dhārmika* Gopī. She obeys her father, even if her heart tells her be to be with Bhuvan. As Bhuvan gains the villagers' support for his project, we see Gauri steadily at his side, as a good loyal woman, but this is no infraction of parental obedience, as her father is shown to come around and approve of his daughter's choice.

Meanwhile, Elizabeth, the English lady, has taken a fancy to Bhuvan and teaches him and the villagers how to play cricket. The special features of the movie include some scenes that were cut in the final editing, which make the play on the Krishna-Rādhā mythology explicit. Here Gauri is identified as the jealous party. First we see Elizabeth bringing the villagers brand-new cricket equipment. They are grateful, and Bhuvan wants to give her something in return, offering his family's pair of oxen. At first she does not want anything, but she hints at his being virile like an oxen, a statement with sexual undertones, though Bhuvan seems not to get it. When he insists that he wants to give her something, she asks for his amulet, which he, somewhat crestfallen, gives her. All this is keenly observed by a jealous Gauri. When Elizabeth has left, she confronts Bhuvan and asks him what went on between them. Sensing her jealousy, and keen to make fun of her, he makes up a story that the white lady thought he was handsome and strong and wanted to elope with him. Gauri gets really upset, so he confesses he's been teasing her. She is indignant and

175. *gaurī, tū yahāṃ kyā kar rahī hai?*

176. *maiṃ tose milan āī thī. tohe ī batāne āī thī ki maiṃ tore sāth hūṃ. bharosā hai mohe tujhpe torī himmat pe. bas itnā hī kahnā āī thī.*

puts it this way: "I'm neither Rukmiṇī, nor Rādhā. I'm Gauri, and I'll stay just Gauri."[177] This explicit rejection of both the *svakīyā* and *parakīyā* Krishna consort models is very interesting. Gauri does not want to be the mistress, nor does she want to be the wife who is cheated. She insists on being instead herself. Her name of course is one of the auspicious titles of Śiva's consort Pārvatī, who is typically understood to be happily married, even if the world considers her husband a madman. Thus what she actually is reacting against is that Bhuvan is acting like a Krishna, having fun and playing with women's hearts. What she wants him to do is settle down in a steady relationship. In other words, she does not want Krishna but Śiva for a husband. It gets even more interesting when Bhuvan counters: "Come on, you alone are my Rādhā as well as my Rukmiṇī."[178] He then insists on his Krishna role. Women may want their men to act responsibly, but the men do not necessarily comply.

A scene with explicit reference to Rāsa-līlā is the performance of the song "Rādhā kaise na jale" by Asha Bhosle, Udit Narayan, and Vaishali. This song—appropriately—comes just after Elizabeth has visited the Krishna temple for the occasion of the Janmāṣṭamī festivities. She asks Bhuvan what the images represent, and when told, wonders whether Rādhā was Krishna's wife. Bhuvan explains that the divine pair was not married: "Krishna married Rukmiṇī and Rādhā Anay. But they had such a deep love that it remains an example till this day. You can understand it like a dewdrop on a lotus leaf. Not one, but not separate either. For ages now, their worship has continued to this day."[179] At this Elizabeth gazes enchanted at the images, but Gauri burns with jealousy, expressed by her moving quickly to have the *pūjārī* make her *tilak* right after Bhuvan's, and to ring the temple bell right after Bhuvan, just as Elizabeth is about to do so. Gauri tries to forestall a divine sanction for the love she senses Elizabeth is feeling for Bhuvan.

Immediately following this scene, a beautifully choreographed dance sequence presents a kind of Rāsa-līlā or round dance of Krishna-Bhuvan with Gauri, now clearly identified as Rādhā, and her friends as the Gopīs. The song itself is a wonderful exploration of the subjective experience of jealousy as perceived differently by the perpetrator and the victim:

177. *nā maiṃ rukmiṇī hūṃ aur na maiṃ rādhā. maiṃ gaurī hūṃ aur gaurī hī rahūṃgī.*

178. *are tūhī hamarī rādhā hai aur tūhī hamarī rukmiṇī.*

179. *kisanjī kī śādī to rukmiṇī se huī aur rādhā kī anay se. lekin donoṃ meṃ bahut gahrā prem thā jo ek misāl banke rah gayā, āp samajh lo kamal ke patte par sabanam kī būṃd jaisā ek bhī nahīṃ hue aur alag bhī nahīṃ. jug jug se donoṃ kī pūjā hotī calī ā rahī hai.*

Gauri:
When Krishna meets with a milkmaid in Madhuban,
smiles at her, teases her, talks with her,
how could Rādhā not be jealous,
her body and soul on fire?[180]
Bhuvan:
Well, Krishna may meet with a milkmaid in Madhuban,
But in his heart are blooming only the flowers of Rādhā's love,
Why would Rādhā be jealous,
without trying to understand?

The milkmaids are stars, Rādhā is the moon,
why then would she have little faith?[181]

Gauri:
When Krishna's attention wanders here and there all the time,
How can poor Rādhā have faith in herself?[182]

Bhuvan:
The milkmaids come and go, but Rādhā is Queen of the heart
Day and night, at the banks of the Yamunā,
Krishna calls out for Rādhā alone.[183]

Gauri:
If anyone puts their arms like a garland on Krishna's neck.
how could Rādhā not be jealous,
her body and soul on fire?
If Krishna has taken Rādhā to stay in his heart
then why did he not tell her?[184]

Bhuvan:
Love has its own separate way of talking, its own language,
But his eyes tell it all, that's Krishna's hope.[185]

180. *madhuban meṃ jo kanhaiyā kisī gopī se mile, kabhī muskāye kabhī cheḍe, kabhī bāt kare, rādhā kaise na jale? āg tan man meṃ lage!*

181. *madhuban meṃ bhale kānha kisī gopī se mile, man meṃ to rādhā ke hī prem ke haiṃ phūl khile; kis liye rādhā jale? binā soce samjhe! gopiyāṃ tāre haiṃ cāṃd hai rādhā, phir kyoṃ hai usko bisvās ādhā?*

182. *kānhājī kā jo sadā idhar udhar dhyān rahe, rādhā becārī ko phir apne pe kyā mān rahe?*

183. *gopiyāṃ ānī jānī haiṃ rādhā to man kī rāṇī hai, sāṃjh savere jamunā kināre, rādhā rādhā hī kānha pukāre*

184. *bāhoṃ ke hār jo ḍāle koī kānha ke gale, rādhā kaise na jale, āg tan man meṃ lage; man meṃ hai rādhā ko kānha jo basāye, to kānha kāhe ko usse na batāye?*

185. *prem kī apnī alag bolī alag bhāsā hai, bāt nainoṃ se ho kānha kī yahī āsā hai.*

Gauri:
Those eyes of Krishna
Have robbed the milkmaids of their peace of mind
When he casts his glance, she goes mad,
any fair milkmaid would![186]

Bhuvan:
If love for Krishna grows in the heart of a milkmaid,
Why would it bother Rādhā?[187]

The song starts as a stick dance (*ḍaṇḍiyā rāsa*)—appropriate for Rāsa-līlā celebrations, as well as expressive of the pent-up aggression in Gauri. Throughout the song, the refrains the lovers repeat make clear the way their positions are radically opposite: he cannot comprehend why she would be jealous, but she finds it natural that she would be, considering his behavior. The irony of course is that the trope used here to express Gauri's jealousy is that of the Rāsa-līlā, in which Krishna dances with the other village girls, but we know that her main worry is about one of the spectators outside of the magic circle, the English woman, Elizabeth. This perspective is brought in with shots of Elizabeth, who is seated next to Bhuvan's mother in the audience. It is suggested that she, too, is becoming jealous of Gauri, though only mildly so. The additional angle of the jealousy of another villager, a suitor of Gauri, is also brought into the picture with shots of his jealous face.

In between the verses, we see Rādhā draw her Krishna away from the other village women, but at other moments, the dance turns into a war of the sexes. Bhuvan and his party wonder why the girls doubt them, while Rādhā and her friends point out that they have good cause. This brings out the ambiguities inherent in the concept of Rāsa-līlā, the jealousies that are never explicitly spoken, and the antagonism between male and female perspectives on love. The song takes on a Punjabi character, featuring big drums, toward the end. Rādhā-Gauri gets the last word, with her rhetorical question "How could Rādhā not be jealous?" Her last pose is not of self-confidence but of self-doubt. At that point, Elizabeth—not Bhuvan—applauds her and compliments her in comically English-accented Hindi—at which Gauri regains her composure and straightens her shoulders in pride. Notwithstanding all the anti-English rhetoric of the movie, it is the praise of the English woman that inspires the native

186. *kānha ke ye jo nain haiṃ cīne gopiyoṃ ke cain haiṃ, milī nazariyā hoī bāvariyā, gorī gorī sī koī gūjariyā.*
187. *kānha kā pyār kisī gopī ke man meṃ jo pale, kis liye rādhā jale?*

woman with self-esteem, after her man has torn down her self-confidence with his flirtatious behavior.

We also find some echoes of the Rāsa-līlā motif in another song that celebrates the newly confessed mutual love of Gauri and Bhuvan, "Maiṃ ne pyār tujhī se hai kiyā" ("I've come to love only you"). This song is skillfully interspersed with Elizabeth's romp on the theme "I'm in Love." The director has done a wonderful job of juxtaposing Indian and Western perspectives on love (through an Indian lens). While the love of Gauri and Bhuvan is presented as real (or as real as it gets in a Hindi movie song), that of Elizabeth is one of daydreams of her and Bhuvan dancing English-style. The lines blur, though, as in a depiction of happy domesticity of the Indian couple Gauri morphs into Elizabeth, and in a celebration of the Indian couple's signs of happily consummated conjugality (*suratāṃta*), Elizabeth keeps appearing in the picture, dancing in a desert-like landscape. Still, the song ends with a shot of Gauri and Bhuvan alone against the backdrop of a sunset. We are reminded of the television series' Krishna's assertion that in all the women of the world, he sees only his Rādhā—and his emphatic assertion that she just needs to understand that.

It is not till the end of the movie that we finally settle on Elizabeth being identified with Rādhā. As she leaves town in her carriage, the narrator comments: "Elizabeth took Bhuvan's image in her heart when she went back to England. She remained unmarried for the rest of her life, and became Bhuvan's Rādhā."[188] We might well think that she rather conforms to the Mīrā trope of the woman who cannot marry her beloved and never enjoys intimacy with him but remains determined to lead a life of eternally pining for him. This brings us to the topic of the next chapter: the characterization of the cowife, or the threat of the "other woman."

Conclusions: Stand by Your Man

What to conclude? What model do our heroines provide for coping with the first test of their love? The answer is quite clear: these days they all choose, univocally, dharma over love. That was not always the case. Medieval versions stressed bhakti as the major factor in women's decisions to venture outside their "four walls" (*cār-divārī*). While I have been careful to qualify that this message does not necessarily work as liberating for women, the privileging of

188. *Elizabeth apne man meṃ bhuvan kī mūrat lekar vāpas England calī gaī. aur sārā jīvan avivāhit rahkar bhuvan kī rādhā banī.*

love over dharma still had strong potential to do so. Women were shown to argue dharma as it suited their fulfillment in love. Things changed in the televised stories. Sītā is permitted some airtime for making her arguments, but she can be trusted to make the right decisions fulfilling her wifely duties. Even so, Rāma does not deal very well with his wife winning the battle and resorts to ordering her around. As for the Gopīs, when it comes to the screen, their flaunting of dharma has receded to the background. Lip service is paid to it in song, but there is no radicalism in their actions. Their Rāsa-līlā has become more of a leisure activity, after all household duties are properly taken care of. On television, love comes after duty has been fulfilled.

That fits with what we see happening when the Rāsa-līlā moves from Vrindāban to Bollywood. There are some vestiges of love's superiority over dharma and the lovers' disregard of *loka lāja* and *maryādā* in the lyrics of some songs. However, when we put that in the context of the story line, it pales, and appears formulaic. Rādhā and the Gopīs are evoked in dalliance at the beginning of the movies when love is celebrated. But soon the conflict between duty and love takes over, and there is no doubt which one will win. This is not surprising, given the general tendency of Bollywood movies to privilege *farz* over love (see, e.g., Thomas 1995). Bottom line message for girls who might like the spunk of 'spice girl' characters like Nisha in *Ham aap ke hain koun . . . !* There is room for some romping before marriage, but once settled, *maryādā* looms large.

Intuitively, one might blame the tradition for the preoccupation with keeping heroines within *maryādā*. However, we find that exactly the opposite is true. The bhakti tradition privileged love. It is Bollywood that privileges duty. Under the influence of the cinema, it seems, the Rādhā model has become more and more Sītā-ized.

The new cross of the Gopī with the Sītā model could be termed "spice-censorship" (*masālā-maryādā*). We see heroines with a lot of spunk (and modernity) and with some charming, Gopī-like assertiveness. This clearly works to attract desirable matches in the shape of handsome heroes. However, ultimately, happiness is predicated on sacrifice, not spunk. By the end of the movie, Rādhā has to turn into Sītā. She may even have to give up her love, even if he is her husband, in the process, but to dharma she will adhere. In Bollywood movie after movie, we see a phenomenon we could call "the sizzling out of the spice girls."

What we see happening is an interesting redefinition of dharma. In the four movies I have discussed, dharma is narrowed to "family values." This term does not mean what is commonly understood by it in the West, rather, it means placing the interest of the joint family, in particular the husband's family, above one's individual happiness in love. A woman is to do everything, literally everything, in the interest of her husband and his family. In *HAKHK*, we see Nisha ready to sacrifice personal love and marry her sister's widower for the sake of the child in her *sasurāl*. In *Yahi hai zindagi*, we see Radha staying behind in her *sasurāl* because she sides with her in-laws against her own father, who has corrupted her husband. In *Meera ka Mohan*, we see Priti sign divorce papers to make it possible for her husband to remarry. (Not that her refusal would have prevented the second marriage from taking place!) Hers is a total reversal, a sacrifice of the marriage for the sake of her husband's perceived happiness. In *Lagaan*, even the white woman takes on self-sacrifice and remains virginal while allowing her beloved to enjoy happy domesticity with another woman. She is identified with Rādhā without ever enjoying Rādhā's sensual fulfillment—only her pining in love. The very meaning of Rādhā here has been narrowed down to only a chaste aspect.

It is remarkable how in Bollywood, dharma gets ever more conservative for women. It is as if the movies are indulging in a test to see how far they can push the limits of subjugating women. *Strī-dharma* means not just obedience to the husband—it is adherence to a normativity that reflexively values the husband's family's slightest comfort over everything else, even at the cost of the woman's total devastation. The reward in the end is a rehabilitation through nearly supernatural means. The long-suffering heroine will become a goddess herself. In being like Sītā, she will be worshiped like Sītā. But this Sītā after whose model she is to be molded is not the same one of the Sanskritic or the bhakti tradition. It is a truly modernized film version of Sītā that is more conservative than anything before.

We should be vigilant not to vilify Bollywood. The directors work hard to show what the audience wishes to see. Maybe the question should be who constitutes the film audience. One may argue that, especially before the 1990s, the audience in cinema halls has been overwhelmingly male. It is not surprising, then, that the aforementioned perspectives play very well to male fantasies and wishful thinking. This has been well illustrated by the research of Steve Derné (1995a, 2000). One might wonder whether things have changed with the recent return of women to the cinema halls, the advent of video viewing at home, and the broadcasting of movies on television. In this new situation, the female audience becomes more important. What are women's views on the issue?

More research needs to be done, but we can already predict that women's reactions will be diverse. Those who find themselves in oppressive situations in which they have been enduring personal hardship may identify with the characters in the movies and feel vindicated. They may, as Madhu Kishwar

(2001) has argued, feel superior in holding the "moral high ground." In that sense, the Sītā-model is empowering. On the other hand, one may object that relentless self-sacrifice is a high price to pay for respect, and that we should not overemphasize that aspect, lest we los track of and justify what is in the end an oppressive system, as Linda Hess has put it (1999).

In the end, the question is where the patriarchal system of today really is located. It is not necessarily the fault of the old myth or the religion itself. Myths are constantly rewritten. As we have seen, the modern rewritings are more oppressive. How remarkable that an industry like Bollywood, perceived to be modern, rewrites the myth in such conservative ways! How remarkable that the televised versions turn out to be more conservative than the medieval ones—even more remarkable, are a success and hit a nerve—and for both men and for women.

To what extent women are expected to become self-effacing for the husband's greater good will become even more clear when I explore the issue of the "other woman" in the next chapter.

5

The Threat of the Other Woman

Free-Spirited Śūrpaṇakhā and Sophisticated Kubjā

How to Cope with a Rival

In this chapter, we turn to a common crisis many women have to cope with sooner or later: the threat of the "other woman" and the real or imagined unfaithfulness of their man. Our goddesses are no exceptions! There is a plethora of questions to ask. How do these situations arise? Do the men give in to temptation, and if so, do they get away with it? How do their women deal with this situation? Do they find solutions to this problem that are worth emulating? How does the other woman fare in the deal? Does she become the negative example, the anti-role model, whose behavior is interpreted as transgressive? Does she get punished? Can she be redeemed? How far do the mythological stories, usually crafted by male minds, confirm or challenge patriarchal norms? To a large extent, in this chapter, the focus shifts from the goddesses to the "other women," their mirror image, or "alter ego."

Sītā of course is happily married and secure in the knowledge of her husband's exclusive love for her. She has chosen to follow him and initially, they are enjoying something of an eco-honeymoon in the idyllic environs of the forest. Then, the idyll is rudely disturbed when her husband is propositioned by the vamp-like Śūrpaṇakhā, "the lady with the nails like winnowing baskets." She is the ultimate "other" woman, actually a demoness, and as such is racially other, or non-Aryan, as is specified in some versions. Moreover, she is no less than the demon Rāvaṇa's sister, thus—the audience knows—belongs to the inimical camp. Rāma spurns her advances, and sends her to his brother Lakshmana, who has accompanied them in the forest. Lakshmana isn't interested either, but he and his brother indulge in having a little fun at her expense. The episode borders on the burlesque, with the grotesque woman crazed with love for the handsome brothers. When the joke gets out of hand, the mood shifts to horror, as the vamp shows her true demoniacal colors and threatens to devour Sītā. With Rāma's consent, Lakshmana disfigures her. This leads to a major feud with Śūrpaṇakhā's brothers, and eventually the abduction of Sītā.

The focus in the incident is on the other woman. What Sītā may feel remains unaddressed in most sources. She is in fact passive throughout the whole episode. What matters is how the sexually active woman and the men who spurn her advances fare. The Śūrpaṇakhā episode is a case where the threat of the other woman does not lead to the man's unfaithfulness but to a punishment of the other woman for her transgressive behavior. Interestingly, the situation is resolved by the younger brother-in-law. The wife has no hand in this punishment, but it is carried out by what could be seen as her male ally. The focus here is less on how a devoted wife should cope with such a crisis, than on the injury the vamp brings upon herself. Thus we get to hear a great deal about Śūrpaṇakhā's reaction, which differs interestingly over time, as does the treatment the brothers mete out to her.[1]

Rādhā and the Gopīs are in a contrasting situation. The very nature of Krishna's love is nonexclusive; he is the adulterer par excellence. Frequently spending the night with other women, he forces them to cope with their jealousy of each other. Moreover, while Krishna is unfaithful, Rādhā has no rights over him, since they are not married. She has not legal leg to stand on, so to speak, and can only argue that he hurts her feelings. Descriptions of Rādhā's jealousy are colored by the conventions of classical literature (*kāvya*): the theme of the offended woman (*māninī*) comes with its own formulae. In manuscripts of vernacular literature, the poems on Rādhā's jealousy often are grouped under that rubric. In devotional poetry, the *kāvya* conventions and formulaic expressions are adapted for the devotional purposes. We get to hear a lot about the aggrieved woman's perspective, and we become intimately acquainted with her emotions, because she stands for the devotee's longing for an always-unattainable God.

1. It would also be instructive to compare the case of Rāma and Śūrpaṇakhā to that of Bhīma and Ghaṭotkaca's mother in the *Mahābhārata* story. Also fruitful with be a comparison with the case of Ahalyā, the adulteress who is redeemed by Rāma earlier in the *Rāmāyaṇa* story, before his marriage to Sītā. On different versions of Ahalyā's story, see Söhnen-Thieme 1996. For an Indo-Greek comparison, see Doniger 1997.

Rādhā deals with the situation in many different ways. Sometimes her suspicions are shown to be false, and she can reunite happily with her lover; these poems are usually grouped under the rubric of "mistaken pride" (*sambhrama māna*). At other times, his faithlessness is real. Often Rādhā just suffers through it, relieving her pain by confessing in a friend, hovering between envying and abusing the other woman. On occasion, she confronts Krishna about his adultery (*khaṇḍitā nāyikā*). When he comes to her in the morning having spent the night elsewhere, she sarcastically points out the telltale signs that belie his halfhearted excuses.[2] But she rarely can remain upset with him for long. He manages to make her laugh or to make love to him anyway, and they are temporarily reconciled. But Krishna is a repeat-offender: he finds ever more women willing to spend the night with him, especially when he leaves Braj to take up public life in the city, first in Mathurā, later even further away in Dwaraka. There, he contracts multiple marriages, such as the one with Rukmiṇī, and is permanently out of Rādhā's reach. Rādhā retreats in the background as his childhood sweetheart, pining for him but with no hope for her longing ever being fulfilled. We could say that actually here Rādhā herself has become the other woman. She may have been his first love, but she never became the lawfully wedded wife.

Because of Krishna's Don Juan nature, Rādhā and the Gopīs are often confronted with rivals. A well-studied case is the rivalry of Rādhā with Candrāvalī, expanded on famously by Rūpa Gosvāmī (in his *Vidagdha-mādhava* and *Lalita-mādhava;* see Wulff 1984). For the purpose of comparison with Sītā, I will not focus on the jealousy of the different Gopīs for one another but on one case that makes a nice parallel; their first rival from the city, Kubjā. Kubjā is portrayed as deformed, as a hunchback, which puts her on a par with the grotesque Śūrpaṇakhā.[3]

Krishna meets Kubjā after his departure from Braj, when he goes to the big city of Mathurā to assume a public role, killing the tyrant Kaṃsa and restoring the throne to the rightful ruler, Ugrasena, his grandfather. On his way to the task, Krishna enters Mathurā with some fanfare, which causes excitement.[4] He meets a series of marginal characters, subalterns of a sort.

2. For a discussion of the impact of this type of poetry on real-life perceptions of adultery, see Wulff 1997.

3. For interesting reflection on the role and significance of the hunchback in Indian epics, see Sutherland 1992: 246–7.

4. All the city women eagerly observe the arrival of this new, promising young man in town. This again is a *kāvya* convention, a set literary piece, commonly used for the arrival of the hero, as incidentally also for Rāma when entering Mithilā to partake in the Svayaṃvara.

The first one is inimical toward Krishna, but the others become "his first allies" and give him tokens of their devotion.[5] The last in the row is the hunchbacked woman Kubjā, who offers Krishna her costly sandalwood paste unguent.

The episode starts as a prank. Krishna and his brother waylay the hunchbacked servant-woman to extort from her the precious ointment she is carrying. The tone here is humorous, as in the Śūrpaṇakhā episode. Krishna flatters Kubjā so that she spontaneously offers them what they want. In return for her favor, she is delivered from her hunchback and turned into a beautiful woman. She invites Krishna to her home, but he does not come till later. The erotic encounter takes place only after Krishna has killed Kaṃsa.

The stories of Śūrpaṇakhā and of Kubjā have both been studied before but have not been compared. For Śūrpaṇakhā, there is a wonderful essay by Kathleen Erndl (1991), who also includes in her analysis Vālmīki and Tulsīdās, as well as other texts. A comparison of the Kubjā episode in different Sanskrit retellings (with a psychoanalytical interpretation) was carried out by Jeffrey Moussaieff Masson (1980),[6] and a discussion of the *Bhāgavata Purāṇa* version with reference to its commentaries by Noel Sheth (1983). The special contribution of this chapter is the extension of reference to medieval poems and the television series, as well as the comparison of Kubjā with Śūrpaṇakhā and the analytical frame to see this as the role model coping with the other woman.

The Kubjā intermezzo makes for a nice contrast with the Śūrpaṇakhā one. There is an interesting link between Rādhā and Sītā's rivals. In some versions of the story, Kubjā is said to be an incarnation of Śūrpaṇakhā, who did penance in Puṣkar to obtain Rāma's next incarnation, Krishna, for her partner (*BVP 4.62;* see Bulcke 1971: 417, and 4.72.56–7; Sheth 1983: 228). Moreover, like Śūrpaṇakhā, Kubjā is from the inimical camp: she is a servant of Kaṃsa. There are more parallels: Krishna and his brother Balarāma approach her initially in a way that seems to make fun of her, like Rāma and Lakshmana's pranking with Śūrpaṇakhā. The tone then, is that of comedy (*hāsya rasa*). Like Śūrpaṇakhā, Kubjā is taken in by their joking compliments, and she falls in love. We have a bit of the burlesque: a grotesque woman falling for a handsome man. Like Śūrpaṇakhā, Kubjā seems to be a woman of easy virtue, maybe a

5. In the classical version from *Bhāgavata Purāṇa,* there is a washerman first, whom Krishna kills to get new clothes, a weaver, who gives him shawls, and a flower man, who provides him with flower garlands (*BhP* 10.41.32–52).

6. I am grateful to Sally Goldman for alerting me to this work.

courtesan. In any case, she does not hesitate to suggest that Krishna make love to her.

The differences are instructive, too. Rāma's encounter with Śūrpaṇakhā takes place in the forest, Krishna's with Kubjā in the city. Krishna of course is going from the idyllic, bucolic environs of Braj to the city, whereas Rāma makes exactly the opposite trajectory, leaving the city for the forest. Rāma has brought Sītā along, and she is present at the scene of the seduction, whereas Krishna has left Rādhā and the Gopīs behind and they are nowhere near the scene. Kubjā is Śūrpaṇakhā's opposite in many ways. She is not the free-spirited type but rather the sophisticated, professional seducer. She is not a demoness, but she is described as not being naturally pretty and having a physical handicap. In contrast to what happens in the Rāma story, though, Krishna reacts positively to her and promises to consummate the relationship. The mood does not change to horror but instead to the erotic. Moreover, Krishna delivers this woman from her physical handicap. Both women undergo physical transformations: whereas Rāma causes poor Śūrpaṇakhā's disfigurement, "to straighten her out," Krishna straightens out his Kubjā literally, to make her more beautiful.

Still, the stories have something else in common: both have been problematic for their audiences throughout the centuries. Many commentators and translators have worked to justify the cruelty of Rāma and his brother's joke on Śūrpaṇakhā and the punishment meted out to her.[7] Similarly, Krishna's affair with a hunchbacked woman, who seems to have been a courtesan, also has raised enough eyebrows to make for several pages of commentatorial apologetics.[8]

Finally, we should think about how the other women fare outside the story. Unsurprisingly, Śūrpaṇakhā is not worshiped, with the interesting exception of one tribal area.[9] Kubjā, on the other hand, has been the object of verneration.[10] In the Braj area, her image is worshiped alongside that of Krishna even today. One such shrine is found at the area known as Raṅgbhūmi in Mathurā, near Dhanush Tila (Entwistle 1987: 317) and another in the Gatāśram temple near Vishram Ghat in Mathurā, where Rādhā also appears next to Krishna

7. For other versions of this episode, see Erndl 1991.

8. For a discussion of the problems raised by the story, see Sheth 1983.

9. Camille Bulcke states she is worshiped in Nīlgiri and one tribe considers its women to be descendants of Śūrpaṇakhā (Bulcke 1971: 417).

10. I should specify that I mean here Kubjā of the Krishna story, who seems to be entirely distinct from the Tantric goddess usually referred to as Kubjikā (on whom, see Dyczkowski 1995–96 and 2000).

(312). This is not a recent phenomenon; there is evidence of Kubjā worship in the past. The earliest reference to a Kubjā image is in the *Mathurā-mahātmya* in the *Varāha Purāṇa* (465), which is, however, difficult to date. There seems to have been a well named Kubjākūpa in Mathurā (320–1), and there is sixteenth-century evidence of a place on the pilgrimage circuit named Kubjikāsthāna that, according to the mid-sixteenth-century founder of the Braj pilgrimage circuit, Nārāyaṇa Bhaṭṭ, would cure women suffering from deformity or affliction after three years of residence (465). Kubjā, then, has been venerated by those in need of a transformation like hers.

To sum up, the stories of Śūrpaṇakhā and Kubjā make a good contrast. Rāma is approached by Śūrpaṇakhā, who looks like a beautiful woman, but seeing through her appearance, he rejects her and makes her truly ugly. She remains vilified, an antiheroine. Krishna, on the other hand, approaches Kubjā, who is ugly, but he, too, sees through her appearance, and he accepts her, making her truly beautiful in the process. Kubjā becomes the object of veneration in her own right.

The sources for this chapter are as follows. The Śūrpaṇakhā episode is pivotal to the plot and is found in Vālmīki, Tulsīdās, and Sagar's versions of the *Rāmāyaṇa*. Of most interest here is the attempt by the demoness to seduce Rāma rather than the ensuing battles with her brothers. Vālmīki narrates the story in two chapters (*sargas*) in the Araṇya Kāṇḍa (*VR* 3.17–8). Tulsīdās is extremely brief and devotes to the episode not quite one *kaṛavak* (*RCM* 3.17.2–10 and *dohā*). In the television series, the incident is shown in the second part of one episode (vol. 10, episode 29).

The Kubjā episode in *Bhāgavata Purāṇa* comes in two parts: first, Krishna's encounter on the road with Kubjā (here named Trivakrā: *BhP* 10.42.3a), when he delivers her from her physical handicap (10.42.1–12), and second, after his victory over Kaṃsa, when he goes to her house to make love to her (10.48.1–11). Predictably, Sagar shows only the first incident (*TVK* vol. 9, episode 67). As for medieval sources, this episode seems not to have fired the medieval poets' imagination. There are no works devoted to Kubjā alone, and she is only mentioned in passing. Only in the collected works attributed to the devotional poet Sūrdās does she figure more prominently. Sūrdās refers to the first meeting in passing, together with Krishna's feats in Mathurā (*SS* 3665/3047, 3667/3049, and 3669/3051) and in one poem conflates it with the other episode (3668/3050). Krishna's visit to Kubjā's house, though, is treated more elaborately. There is a whole series of poems on the topic, but they are more interpretations than descriptions of the event (3718/3100–3725/3107; again, 3727/3109 mentions it in passing). Sūrdās adds an extra dimension: he dwells at length on the Gopīs' reaction to Krishna's affair (3760/3142–3763/

TABLE 5.1. Comparison of Śūrpaṇakhā and Kubjā

Similarities

Loose women, in love with Rāma/Krishna
Their looks are ambiguous: ugly yet beautiful
Belong to enemy camp
Meet Rāma and Krishna accompanied by brothers
Proposition Rāma/Krishna
Burlesque (*hāsya*)
Rebirth connection (according to *BVP*)
Problematic for commentators

Differences

Śūrpaṇakhā	*Kubjā*
Meeting Rāma in forest	Meeting Krishna in city
Rival present	Rival not present
Demoness takes on beautiful form	Hunchback later straightened
Independent; sister of Rāvaṇa	Servant of Kaṃsa
Approaches Rāma	Krishna approaches her
Propositions right away	Propositions after Krishna straightens her body
Mood turns to horror	Mood turns to erotic
Insults Sītā	Is insulted by Gopīs out of jealousy (in *SS*)
Rāma spurns her	Krishna sports with her
Is disfigured	Is made beautiful
Initiative in sexual love is punished	Initiative in sexual love leads to liberation
Antiheroine	Worshiped in her own right

3155);[11] and even adds a response to this on the part of Kubjā (4061/3443–4065/3447). So thanks to the medieval works, we get to look at the perspectives of both the aggrieved jealous woman and the rival.

Thus we have two scenarios. The Sītā scenario looks at the temptation of the man from the point of view of the married heroine. This leaves not much room for sympathy for the other woman, who comes to a bad end. The Rādhā scenario looks at male infidelity from the point of view of the woman whom he has not married. Here we are privy to both women's feelings, and we may well feel sympathy with both. I will highlight parallels in Hindi movies for both

11. Of all the poems on Kubjā in the *Sūr Sāgar*, only one from this group occurs in the early sixteenth-century manuscripts and makes it into Kenneth Bryant's edition, which is *SS* 3773/3155; which corresponds to his number 189. I am grateful to Jack Hawley for sending me the correspondence table of the forthcoming edition with the Nāgarī Pracāriṇī Sabhā one. I have not seen the critical text or Hawley's translation.

scenarios. Very interesting is Raj Kapoor's 1978 *Satyam shivam sundaram,* about a heroine with a disfigured face. Two movies that are classics of sympathetic treatment of the plight of the other woman are Raj Khosla's 1978 *Main Tulsi tere aangan ki* and Sawan Kumar's 1983 *Souten.* In both cases, the cowife is of lower status (a prostitute in the first movie, a *camār* in the second) and, though she unquestionably loves her lover, she gives way to the legitimate wife. In these movies, we find a happy resolution of the threat of the other woman—that is to say, a happy resolution for the man.

Śūrpaṇakhā: The Vamp Punished

In Sītā's story, the other woman is the free-spirited Śūrpaṇakhā. The way she is portrayed and the treatment meted out to her varies in interesting ways over time. She is a demoness, and in all versions of the story she is truly "otherized." Her outrageous behavior leaves no room for sympathy and leads logically to her punishment. While there is no doubt of her guilt, each version has a subtly different take on what happened.

Demonizing the Lustful Woman

Demonizing the lovelorn Śūrpaṇakhā, Vālmīki's text makes her truly the other. This is patently clear from the string of verses contrasting Rāma and Śūrpaṇakhā at the outset of the story (*VR* 3.17 9b–11), which can be schematized as shown in table 5.2.

This elaborate contrast sets up the impossibility of the match and at the same time lends a humorous tone to the event. It frames the meeting as burlesque: a grotesque older woman is propositioning a handsome young man.

TABLE 5.2. Rāma and Śūrpaṇakhā in *Vālmīki Rāmāyṇa*

Rāma	Śūrpaṇakhā
With handsome face (*sumukham*)	With ugly face (*durmukhī*)
With handsome waist (*vṛttamadhyaṃ*)	With big belly (*mahodrī*)
Big-eyed (*viśālākṣam*)	Ugly-eyed (*virūpākṣī*)
With handsome hairdo (*sukeśaṃ*)	Red-haired (*tāmramūrdhajā*)
Handsome-bodied (*priyarūpaṃ*)	Ugly-bodied (*virūpā*)
Soft-spoken (*susvaraṃ*)	With scary voice (*bhairavasvanā*)
Tender (*taruṇaṃ*)	Terrible and old (*dāruṇā vṛddhā*)
Adroit (*dakṣiṇaṃ*)	Maladroit in speaking (*vāmabhāṣiṇī*)
Of just conduct (*nyāyavṛttaṃ*)	Of vile conduct (*sudurvṛttā*)
Attractive (*priyam*)	Repulsive (*apriyadarśanā*)

Sagar does not follow suit. Instead, his episode is coded as suspense, as signaled by the music, which creates a vaguely threatening atmosphere.

Sagar's Śūrpaṇakhā is not grotesque; she is actually quite pretty as she is first shown, flying through the air in her demoness form, interestingly imagined as tribal. Still, after she spots Rāma, she takes on (midflight) an even more beautiful form that conforms to the Bollywood stereotype of the classical Indian courtesan. Elaborately made up and decorated with jewelry, she sports an outfit that consists of a bustier on top; yet for propriety's sake Sagar has her also wear a shawl draped over the upper part of her body. So she is not all that provocatively dressed. Instead of contrasting her grotesqueness with Rāma's beauty, Sagar contrasts her agitation with Rāma's composure: she is overwhelmed by passion, and he is meditating. Songs expressing Śūrpaṇakhā's passion accompany shots of her impassioned face and of Rāma in meditation.

The verses are in Avadhi, but not actual quotation from the *Mānas*. There is some similarity. Tulsīdās introduces Śūrpaṇakhā as an evil woman, cruel as a snake (*RCM* 3.17.2a),[12] and adds a rather misogynic proverb referring to women's lack of restraint when they see a handsome man:

> Whether brother, father, or son, O Garuda, when a woman sees a handsome man,
> In agitation, she can't stop her heart, the way the sun crystal melts on seeing the sun. (3.17.3)[13]

Sagar throws in a similarly proverbial-sounding line:

> A lecherous woman overpowered by passion, is blind, her bloody mind gone!
> Blind, her bloody mind gone, is a lecherous woman overpowered by passion. (TVR 391)[14]

Sagar's Śūrpaṇakhā is not portrayed as ugly but as a vamp, coded as the opposite of the good heroine. Whereas the good heroine would be shy around a young man, certainly if she has a romantic fancy for the man in question, Śūrpaṇakhā is forward and throughout the scene acts quite sure of herself,

12. *duṣṭa hṛdaya dāruna jasa ahinī*. The reference to the snake (also present in the next verse), evokes the imagery of the snake-woman (*nāginī*). Often this character is portrayed as falling in love with mortal men, who, unaware of her true identity, are lured into a sexual relationship with her. This represents a fear of the seductive feminine as dangerous and belonging to another race altogether. The motif is prominent in South Asian folklore as well as cinema (see Pendakur 2003: chap. 7).

13. *bhrātā pita putra uragārī, puruṣa manohara nirakhata nārī; hoi bikala saka manahi na rokī, jimi rabimani drava rabihi bilokī*. Note the reference to Garuda as "snake-eater."

14. *kāmātura lolupa nārī, bhaī andha gaī mati mārī; bhaī andha gaī mati mārī, kāmātura lolupa nārī.*

boldly asserting herself. She approaches the meditating Rāma without hesitation and shakes her bracelets right in front of his face to rouse him from his meditation.

In Vālmīki's story, Śūrpaṇakhā is on her home turf, so to speak, and she rightfully inquires who these strangers are, who look like a funny mixture of ascetics and *kṣatriya*-householders: Rāma has an ascetic hair arrangement and dress (*jaṭī, tāpasveṣeṇa*), yet she perceptively notices he is with a wife and is carrying a bow and arrows (*sabhāryaḥ, śara-cāpa-dhṛk, VR* 3.17.12). Rāma introduces himself, his wife, and his brother and tells their story. Only then does Śūrpaṇakhā introduce herself.

In Tulsīdās's version, she does not waste words on formal introductions:

> There's no man like you, no woman like me. This meeting has been ordained purposely by Fate.
> A man who's worthy of me in the world, I've searched the three worlds, and not found him.
> For that reason I've remained a virgin till now, but seeing you my heart has taken to you. (*RCM* 3.17.4b–5)[15]

Notwithstanding her forward behavior, Tulsīdās's Śūrpaṇakhā claims to be a virgin. Sagar, by contrast, portrays Śūrpaṇakhā as a mature woman, who offers a straightforward sexual proposal. In Sagar's version, Śūrpaṇakhā is the intruder, the uninvited and ill-mannered guest, who shakes Rāma out of his meditation. Rāma, though disturbed, courteously inquires who she is.[16] Śūrpaṇakhā immediately hints at her sexual intentions, replying that there's no need for formal introductions between the most handsome man and the most beautiful woman in the world (*triloka-sundarī*). After all, "nature" (*prakṛti*) needs no introduction to "spirit," (*puruṣa, TVR* 391).[17] She thus hints that their (she presumes) mutual attraction is entirely natural.

The Irony of High-Register Politeness

Sagar starts out like Tulsīdās, but he preserves some of Vālmīki's dialogue, masterfully infusing it with all the irony the formal Hindi register can lend itself to. When propositioned by Śūrpaṇakhā, Rāma pretends not to get her

15. *tumha sama puruṣa na mo sama nārī, yah saṃjoga bidhi racā bicārī; mama anurūpa puruṣa jaga māhīṃ, dekheuṃ khoji loka tihu nāhīṃ; tāteṃ aba lagi rahiuṃ kumārī, manu mānā kachu tumhahi nihārī.* Literally, the last line means "my heart has come to understand something, gazing at you."

16. *namaskār devi! āp kā paricay?*

17. *vaise prakṛti-puruṣ ke paricay kī kyā āvaśyaktā?*

point, taking refuge into polite formulae. He ironically echoes her own self-description in his address: "O beauty of the three worlds! What service can I provide for you?" (*TVR* 392).[18] As in the *Mānas,* she declares the two of them a match made in haven (392).[19] Though she does not declare herself a virgin, she chastely says she is approaching him as her husband.[20] It may be that Sagar felt the reference to Śūrpaṇakhā's virginity inappropriate, as she is clearly a loose woman. In Vālmīki, she says as much ("I'm roaming alone in this wood," *VR* 3.17.21a).[21]

Sagar then returns to the Vālmīki script, and Śūrpaṇakhā introduces herself, boasting of her lineage. Rāma seems to realize who she really is but remains courteous, though with no small measure of irony, when he says simply "pleased to get to know you."[22] Only then does she ask him to introduce himself, and she remarks on his odd attire, wondering whether he is a *sādhu* or a warrior, as in Vālmīki, although she does not mention the presence of the wife, presumably because Sītā is not present at that very moment.[23] Rāma gives a flattering description of his father, but is not boastful. His family needs little introduction and she seems to recognize his name too.

Rāma then formally inquires about the purpose of her visit, again exploiting the irony inherent in formal Hindi politeness formulae: "What desire for my service has caused this beauty among demonesses to take the trouble to direct her tender feet towards my humble hut?"[24] She restates her passionate intentions. Rāma keeps smiling benevolently, as if he were well-disposed toward her proposal. After all, the audience might well figure, he is God and used to having people declare their devotion to him. At that very moment, Sītā emerges from the hut and walks toward them. Rāma, as yet unaware of Sītā's presence, asks Śūrpaṇakhā in formal language whether she has come to test him: "Respected daughter of demons! O good woman! Have you come to test me?" (*TVR* 393).[25] Sītā arrives only to hear the last part, and looks disturbed. Śūrpaṇakhā denies she is out to test Rāma. Now she is aware of his marital status, since she addresses him as Sīteśa, Lord of Sītā. She then declares she has come to surrender herself to him (*ātma-samarpaṇ*) and proposes a love

18. *he trilok-sundarī! maiṃ āpkī kyā sevā kar saktā hūṃ?*

19. *vidhātā ne ham donoṃ ko ek-dūsre ke lie hī racā hai.*

20. *patibhāv rakhkar maiṃ tumhāre pās āī hūṃ.*

21. *araṇyaṃ vicarāmīdam ekā.*

22. *prasannatā huī paricay pākar.*

23. *tapasvī ke veś meṃ jaṭādhārī deh aur dhanuṣ-bāṇ se suśobhit tum sādhu bhī dikhte ho aur yoddhā bhī. vāstav meṃ tum ho kaun?*

24. *rām se kis kām kī āśā lekar asur-sundarī ke komal caraṇ is kuṭiyā tak āe haiṃ?*

25. *ādaraṇīya asurbālā! he bhadre! kyā tum merī parīkṣā lene āī ho?*

marriage (Gāndharva-vivāha, TVR 393). This proposal, with reference to a type of wedding allowed according to the *Dharmaśāstras*, sounds archaic, but is not from Vālmīki. One might say, though, that it is in conformity with the spirit of the passage in Vālmīki where Śūrpaṇakhā declares in one breath her independence and her marriage proposal (*VR* 3.17.25).[26]

Sagar's Rāma keeps smiling beatifically as he kindly breaks the news that he is married, introducing formally at this point his wife, again in ultraformal Hindi: "I am married. This is my lawfully wedded good wife, Sītā" (TVR 393).[27] This is rather less tender than Vālmīki's hero, who responds to Śūrpaṇakhā's proposal by calling Sītā his "beloved" (*VR* 3.18.2a).[28]

Śūrpaṇakhā's reaction is at first the same as in Vālmīki: she insults Sītā and thinks to devour her. "Hmm. What do you see in this low human child, this stiff and juiceless wooden doll? I'll eat her up right away" (TVR 393).[29] But then she shows, without prompting, an unexpected magnanimity, declaring that if Rāma pities Sītā, she will allow Sītā to stay alive and remain their servant (393).[30] The laws of the jungle, she states, allow for men to be polygamous (393).[31] Rāma then retorts that he has sworn to take only one wife, and besides, she would not want to suffer the ignominy of being a cowife, would she (393)?[32] The inspiration of this may have come from the Parsi Theater versions of the episode. *Rādheśyām Rāmāyaṇa* links the issue of the exclusive wedding vow with noble behavior (*ārya dharma*): "I am not a bachelor. I'm married. But I keep a vow of monogamy. Apart from my own I consider other women mother and sister. In other words, I am unable to observe your command. I am an Aryan man, and can never deviate from Aryan laws."[33] Sagar may have this link of Aryan and un-Aryan conduct in mind when he gives us Śūrpaṇakhā's comment on the laws of her land permitting polygamy.

26. *ahaṃ prabhāvasampannā svacchandabalagāminī, cirāya bhava bhartā me.* One Parsi theater version, the *Rādheśyām Rāmāyaṇa*, also has Śūrpaṇakhā proposing a love marriage: *maiṃ ājñā tumko detī hūṃ, mujhse gandharv vivāh karo* (Kathāvācak 1971: 19; trans. Erndl 1991: 78).

27. *maiṃ vivāhit hūṃ. yah merī pariṇītā dharma-patnī sītā hai.*

28. *kṛtadāro' smi bhavati bhāryeyaṃ dayitā mama.*

29. *hūṃ! kyā rakhā hai is sūkhī-sarī kāṭh kī putalī sī kṣudra mānus-putrī meṃ? ise to maiṃ abhī khā jāūṃgī!* This echoes several lines from Vālmīki: *sītayā kiṃ kariṣyasi* (*VR* 3.17.25), *vikṛtāca virūpā ca na seyaṃ sadṛśī tava,* 3.17.26, *imāṃ virūpām asatīṃ karālāṃ nirṇatodarīm,. . . . bhakṣayiṣyāmi mānuṣīm* (3.17.27a).

30. *hāṃ, yadi tumheṃ is par dayā ātī ho to yah bhī parī rahegī, hamārī dāsī bankar.*

31. *hamāre van-pradeś meṃ ek nahīṃ, anek vivāh racā sakte haiṃ.*

32. *kintu maiṃ ek-patnī-vrat le cukā hūṃ. aur phir tum jaisī strī saut kā sāth kaise sahan karegī.* In the latter remark, Sagar may have taken Vālmīki for his source; see *Tvad-vidhānāṃ tu nārīṇāṃ suduḥkhā sapatnatā (VR* 3.18.2b).

33. *ham kvāre nahīṃ vivāhit haiṃ, phir ek-nārivrat rakhte haiṃ; apnī ko choṛ anya sabko mātā aur bahan samajhte haiṃ; ataeva tumhārī yah ājñā pālan kar sakte kabhī nahīṃ; ham ārya puruṣ haiṃ ārya dharma khaṇḍan kar sakte kabhī nahīṃ.*

Spurning Women, Playing with Fire

In Tulsīdās's version, Rāma glances meaningfully at Sītā, then hands off Śūrpaṇakhā to what he calls his "bachelor" brother (*RCM* 3.17.6a).[34] In Vālmīki, Rāma goes much further and recommends his brother as a suitable marriage partner in glowing terms. This behavior has seemed out of character. It involves a lie—since Lakshmana is actually married, though his wife has not accompanied him into exile—and has set off a flurry of apologetics in the traditional commentaries (see Erndl 1991). Some scholars see it as an indication that in the oldest textual layers of Vālmīki's text Lakshmana was unmarried.

Sagar finds his own solution, which as usual is very carefully crafted. He has Lakshmana arrive on the scene at the critical moment where Rāma has rejected Śūrpaṇakhā. As soon as the demoness sees Lakshmana, she is interested in him. Rāma himself does not have to suggest anything, only answer her questions. She asks who this handsome fellow is and whether he is alone, and Rāma can somewhat ambiguously, but without lying, confirm that indeed his brother is alone in exile (TVR 393).[35] When Śūrpaṇakhā says she'll propose to him, Rāma metaphorically throws up his hands with the rhetorical question "Who can stop a woman with a mind of her own?" (394).[36] Thus, Śūrpaṇakhā is shown to act on her own initiative, which renders her if not a nymphomaniac at least fickle. Her behavior confirms what Tulsī announces women are like at the beginning of his episode.

Lakshmana of course rejects her, too, with the excuse that he is the younger brother, thus a servant, and that she would not be content with playing second fiddle. In Tulsīdās's version, he answers politely, in all seriousness, aware of the fact that this lady is from the inimical camp (*RCM* 3.17.6b–8). Vālmīki has Lakshmana's answer overflow with ironic flattery, even as he is rejecting her. Lakshmana suggests that she should try her chances again with Rāma, who surely would reject miserable Sītā for her sake, repeating the insulting assessment she made of Sītā earlier (*VR* 3.18.11).

Sagar at first follows Vālmīki's lead, again with ironic use of polite-register Hindi. Lakshmana first courteously asks: "Pray tell, what difficulties are you experiencing?"[37] She retorts in the same tone that she has no difficulties but brings a blissful proposition (*TVR* 394).[38] He makes it clear he realizes she has

34. *sītahi citai kahī prabhu bātā, ahai kuāra mora laghu bhrātā.*

35. *hāṃ, ban meṃ to akelā hī hai.*

36. *tum svacchand vicaraṇ karnevālī nārī ṭhahrī. tumheṃ manmānī karne se kaun rok saktā hai?*

37. *kahiye āpko kyā kaṣṭ hai?*

38. *kaṣṭ nahīṃ, maiṃ tumhāre sukh aur ānand kā prastāv lekar āī hūṃ.*

already proposed to Rāma, but she brushes that off, saying that Rāma did not realize the value of her proposal, but surely Lakshmana is more clever than that.

Lakshmana now becomes serious, and less than diplomatic, chiding her for her shortsightedness. He sends her back to his brother to beg for the fulfillment of her desire.[39] His wording is unlucky. By using the term "begging" (*yācnā*), he casts her as a beggar, and that triggers her anger.

Interestingly, in Sagar's version, Śūrpaṇakhā seems to take offense mainly at the idea that she should "beg" for love. She came with a proposal (*prem-prastāv*), as an equal, but is treated as a beggar. One could interpret this scene as rightful feminist disgust with the male insistence on female subservience. Especially as compared to Vālmīki, Sagar's Śūrpaṇakhā seems a strong character. Vālmīki presented her as a simpleton, taking literally Lakshmana's ironic suggestion that she try Rāma again, unaware that they are making fun of her (*parihāsāvicakṣaṇā VR* 3.18.13). Tulsīdās, too, has her go along with being shuttled back and forth between the brothers for another round (*RCM* 3.17.9a). She does not get angry till Lakshmana finally insults her directly: "Marrying you is to throw all self-respect like a straw in the wind" (3.17.9b).[40]

Still, even in Sagar's version, Śūrpaṇakhā does not turn against her male tormentors but instead blames it on Sītā that the two brothers have spurned her. At this point, she threatens to devour Sītā. Rāma remains seated in his meditative pose, but summons Lakshmana. Lakshmana rushes to the demoness, pulls his sword, and cuts her nose. This is nicely ambiguous as to how far Lakshmana's action is approved of by Rāma. In Vālmīki, Lakshmana acts explicitly on Rāma's command. Rāma exhorts him: "You should disfigure this ugly, bad, lecherous, fat-bellied demoness." (*VR* 3.18.20).[41] There was a nice irony in this command, as he echoed Śūrpaṇakhā's assessment of Sītā, but this time applying it to the demoness herself. In the *Mānas,* too, Rāma eggs on his brother (*RCM* 3.17.10).[42] In both cases, Rāma is said to be motivated by concern for Sītā's plight. This less-than-chivalrous behavior by the Lord is again a problem for the commentators (Erndl 1991).

39. *jāo vahīṃ jākar apnī manokāmnā kī yācnā karo.*

40. *tohi so baraī jo tṛna tori lāja pariharaī.* This is rather meek compared to the long lecture Lakshmana gives her in *Rādheśyām Rāmāyaṇa* 20, in which he even suggests she should rather turn to national and social service: "For the sake of service of family, caste and nation, simply become a true ascetic. Reform your sisters. That is the path that leads to your heaven" (*kula jāti deś kī sevā ko bas saccī sanyāsinī ban jā; bahanoṃ kā apnī kar sudhār, yah path hai terī śubh gati kā*); see also Erndl (1991: 78–9) for the full translation.

41. *imāṃ virūpām asatīm atimattāṃ mahodarīm, rākṣasīṃ . . . virūpayitum arhasi.*

42. *sītahi sabhaya dekhi raghurāī, kahā anuja sana sayana bujhāī.*

Śūrpaṇakhā leaves, clutching her nose. Sagar adds a little coda to his story in which he goes out of his way to absolve Rāma of any blame. The play on words here is impossible to translate; it goes something like this: Rāma says: "Poor devil" (*becārī abalā*, TVR 395), and Lakshman retorts: "Devil indeed, brother" (*balā kaho bhaiyā*). Literally, Rāma says "Poor woman," and uses a word for "woman" that means "without power" (*a-balā*). Lakshmana tells him instead to characterize her by using the second part of the word only (*balā*), which has on its own alternate meaning: "calamity," yet also carries the meaning "powerful" thereby suggesting that it was in her "power" to act differently.

Rāma insists that his brother has not acted right,[43] because she is a woman, after all. Lakshmana insists that she is a "despicable bad woman,"[44] and he invokes a precedent: their guru's command to kill the demoness Tāṛakā. He says there's no blame in killing such an evil woman, while he has only cut her nose.[45]

Rāma seems to agree. He confirms a male fear of women's desires: "there is nothing more frightening than when a shameless woman becomes lecherous. When she is rejected, she can totally destroy herself and others."[46] He turns it into a prediction of the future, pointing out that Śūrpaṇakhā will certainly seek revenge. Here he follows again Tulsīdās, lead who calls Lakshmana's act an explicit challenge to Rāvaṇa (*RCM* 17, *dohā*).[47]

It is remarkable that we do not get the slightest idea of Sītā's thoughts during the whole interlude. How did she feel about the challenge posed by Śūrpaṇakhā?[48] In Vālmīki and Tulsīdās's version of the events, we only get to see her proud of her husband after he has slain all the would-be defenders of Śūrpaṇakhā's honor (*VR* 3.30.36–41; *RCM* 3.21.2a).[49] Sagar shows some of her reactions in close-up, but her mime is understated. Mostly, she alternates

43. *phir bhī acchā nahīṃ huā.*

44. *durācāriṇī, duṣṭā thī.*

45. *aisī duṣṭā nārī kā vadh karne meṃ koī doṣ nahīṃ*. Lakshmana here does not refer to the fact that she will never be able to proposition others now, as he does in *Rādheśyām Rāmāyaṇa* 21, see Erndl 1991 for a translation.

46. *ek lajjāhīn strī jab kāmātur ho jāe to usse bhayānak aur koī nahīṃ hotā. vah tiraskṛt hokar apnā aur dūsroṃ kā sarvanāś kar saktī hai.*

47. *lachimana ati lāghavaṃ so, nāka kāna binu kīnhi; tāke kara rāvana kahaṃ, mano cunautī dīnhi.*

48. In *Rādheśyām Rāmāyaṇa*, we get a vivid window into Sītā's thoughts when she first reacts to the arrival fo Śūrpaṇakhā: "Sītā's heart was pierced by anguish: 'if this is the meeting of moon and sun, then my eclipse is complete' " (*sītā kā is soc se hṛday huā kuch cūrṇ, candra sūrya mil gaye to yahāṃ amāvas pūrṇ*, 19). She is referring here to Śūrpaṇakhā's introduction, where she had called her meeting with Rāma as one of the sun and the moon (see Erndl 1991: 78). In the end, she mocks Rāma on his great mercy, approving of her brother-in-law's violent disfigurement (*Rādheśyām Rāmayaṇa* 22).

49. *sītā citava syāma mṛdu gātā, parama prema locana na aghātā.*

between looking disturbed by the demoness with her provocations and glancing fondly at her husband as he replies unfazed. Every now and then she looks despisingly at Śūrpaṇakhā. While temporarily upset when the demoness tries to strangle her, she regains composure remarkably well, remaining silent throughout. Her body language shows her confidence in her husband, quiet pride in her own position in his heart, and contempt for Śūrpaṇakhā's brash ways.

Comparing the Śūrpaṇakhā Episodes

What can be learned from this comparison? It is not Tulsīdās's favorite episode. He renders Vālmīki's two chapters (*VR* 3.17–8) in just ten verses (*RCM* 2.17.2–10 and *dohā*). One gets the distinct feeling that Tulsī's treatment is perfunctory. He seems to have felt compelled to deal with this episode because the plot required it. After all, he needed to explain the motivation of Rāvaṇa to abduct Sītā. Basically, Tulsīdās allows only Śūrpaṇakhā and Lakshmana to speak, with Rāma casting a meaningful glance and uttering barely half a line in response to the proposition.

Sagar, on the other hand, seems to have had fun working on this episode. He forges a felicitous combination of both his main sources' accounts. He fuses the misogynic spirit of Tulsīdās with the dialogues from Vālmīki, which he transforms into his usual high-Sanskritic Hindi. Even Śūrpaṇakhā speaks a highly Sanskritized register, which is quite ironic, given that she is regarded as "un-Aryan" by Rāma in Vālmīki's version (*VR* 3.17.19a). In the process, Sagar reworks the humor inherent in Vāḷmīki's grotesque scene in a more subtle way: less burlesque, more ironic punning.

We see a marked tendency for the later versions of the story to remove as much of the blame for disfiguring a woman from Rāma as possible. However, it does not go hand in hand with more sympathy for Śūrpaṇakhā's plight. Disfiguring a wanton woman is still quite socially acceptable, though it may not be advisable, given how dangerous such a woman can become.

There is definitely a message here about codes of conduct for the sexes. Mainly, the message is for women: a vivid warning against making sexual overtures to men. Women who are sexually assertive cannot expect to be respected. At the very least, they will be the butt of sexual jokes, and they naturally will invite a violent punishment upon themselves. For men, the message is to beware of such women. They may turn dangerous. It seems that killing them is an option, but that a more merciful response is disfigurement, so as to preclude their further sexual assertiveness and neutralize future damage they may cause. However, the rest of the story proves that such a punishment may cause a vendetta with the woman's kin.

TABLE 5.3. Different versions of the Śūrpaṇakhā Story Compared

	VR	RCM	TVR
Context	No disguise; bad match	Ś. takes on pretty form; snake	Ś. Takes on pretty, vamp-like form
	No misogynistic intro	Lustful woman not controlled	Lustful woman blind
Initial Exchange	R's identity unknown	Irony of apparent ignorance	Irony of apparent ignorance
	Ś. asks R. first who he is	no pleasantries	R. asks Ś. first; polite irony
	R. introduces S. and L.	S. present but is not introduced	S. introduced latish; L. comes late
Śūrpaṇakhā's Self-Description	Ś. confident	self-described beauty	Self-described beauty
	Boasts of family	no family mentioned	Boasts of family
	Independent	Has remained *kumārī*	Independent
Śūrpaṇakhā's Proposition	Worthy match	Match made by Creator	Match made by Creator
	Proposes wedding	"Has something in mind"	Proposes Gāndharva wedding
			Ś. proclaims self-surrender
			Ś. confirms bigamy is okay in forest
	Insults Sītā	No insult to Sītā	Insults Sītā but offers her servitude
Rāma's Reasons for Rejection	R. married and loves wife	R. merely looks at Sītā	Rāma married
	Ś. couldn't stand cowife		Ś. couldn't stand cowife
			R. is monogamous
Referral to Brother	R. recommends L	R. suggests brother is bachelor	Ś. spots L. on her own
			R. says he's alone in forest
Brother's Answer	I'm just servant	Rāma is glorious Lord	You could not stand servitude
	Sends her back with irony	Sends her back seriously	Sends her back with irony
			L. upset she asked R. first
	Back to Rāma to devour Sītā	Back to R. and again. to L	L. sends Ś. back to R.
			Ś. feels insulted and doesn't go
Cause of Śūrpaṇakhā's Anger	L. suggested Ś. is problem	L. insults Ś as shameless	L. tells Ś to beg R. to take her
Disfigurement by Lakshmana	R. commands disfiguring	R. hints. L should stop her	R. calls L.'s name in alarmed tone
		For Sītā's protection	When she's about to eat Sītā
Interpretation	No reflection within story	This is R.'s challenge to Rāvaṇa	Reflection on killing woman
			R. feels for her
			L. asserts Ś. was evil
			L. cites precedent (guru's command to kill Tāṛāka)
			R. says shameless woman is dangerous

There is another message sent to men in portraying the mutilation of a woman who is "un-Aryan," that is to say, perceived as belonging to another race. In the context of the depiction of this scene in the *Amar Chitra Katha* comic strip *Valmiki's Ramayana* (no. 100001 in the series), some observers have worried that "the message that may be received—whether intentionally or not—is that it is okay, even morally justified, to physically harm an 'other' woman" (McLain 2001: 35). Against the background of increasing communalization, this is quite problematic, as it may be taken as license to perpetrate atrocities on women of another community.

Another major theme here is that insulting a woman sexually propels her male relatives into action, as it is seen as an insult to their honor. Interestingly, the "non-Aryan" demons are portrayed as following the same code of honor, notwithstanding their purportedly looser morals. One of the ways of revenge is in return to injure the other party's women sexually. In this case, the result of insulting Śūrpaṇakhā will be the abduction of Sītā, to be discussed in the next chapter. This is actually a relatively mild outcome, because it involves an injury less horrific than the usual rape. This logic is in tune with the common cinematic trope of women as the site of battle for male feuds—and, one could add, the reality of gang rape as part of vendetta wars, often in intercaste or intercommunal feuds.

Kubjā: The Ugly Made Beautiful

Now we turn to the Gopīs' rival, the hunchbacked woman from Mathurā who has been rendered beautiful by Krishna's grace. This episode is much more ambiguous. Kubjā is not a villain, yet the feelings she evokes are mixed. There is a marked sense of uneasiness with the whole affair in nearly all versions and only Sagar's version manages to come to terms with the problematic episode.

A Case of Extortion Becomes a Case of Grace

Let us first look at the first meeting of Krishna and Kubjā. We will not have to spend time on the medieval version. In the whole of the expansive *Sūr Sagar,* the first meeting with Kubjā gets only a few lines of passing reference in between Krishna's heroic exploits in Mathurā (*SS* 3665/1047, 11.9–10; 3667/1048, 1.10; 3669/1051, 11.1–4). Comparing the two remaining versions of the meeting with Kubjā, it becomes clear that Sagar is very close to *Bhāgavata Purāṇa,* but with a twist.

Sagar introduces Krishna in the company of his brother Balarāma on his way to the shrine where Śiva's bow is kept. Krishna smells from afar the perfume of the sandalwood the hunchback is carrying, while making her way bent over and leaning on a stick. She is not particularly pretty in the television portrayal, whereas in *Bhāgavata Purāṇa* she has a pretty face (10.42.1).[50] Sagar's Krishna asks what the good smell is, waylaying her in a boyish prank. She reacts upset, with the irritation of someone who has had to endure such pranks many times. Krishna, though, does not insult her, as many other must have. In contrast, he addresses her in flattering terms.

In *Bhāgavata Purāṇa*, the poor woman is taken in by Krishna's gallantry, but in the television series, the hunchbacked woman is hurt at being called "pretty woman" (*sundarī*). She is used to insults, and sketches at some length her humiliation by the people who taunt her. She can cope with that, she says, because after all, it is true, she is a hunchback. However, she finds Krishna's joke a particularly cruel one. Krishna says he's not joking but speaking the truth. He points out he sees beyond her bodily deformity and is referring to the beauty of her soul.[51]

Sagar strikes again! This is a clever way of answering the potential objection that Krishna is acting cruelly in addressing a deformed woman in flattering terms. Sagar's Krishna turns this into an occasion to reflect on the value of beauty. He conservatively points out that ugliness is the result of one's past actions, but that it does not last forever;[52] and he foretells that the end of her curse is at hand. We are not told what the curse is about.

This foreshadowing of Kubjā's delivery is a nuanced and subtle transcreation of *Bhāgavata Purāṇa*. There Krishna links his request for the balm directly with a vague promise of something good: "Give us the perfect body-cream, then before long something good will happen to you" (10.42.2b).[53] There is an odor of extortion to Krishna's words here, but Sagar has reworked it to the extent that Krishna instead is shown to be gracious to her in foretelling the end of her humiliation.

Note that in Sagar's version, there is no hint of extortion. Krishna does not really ask for the sandalwood. Only when Kubjā seems to be upset about having to take it to Kaṃsa, he offers to take it for her. This is close to modern interpretations—in sermons, for instance, where often Kubjā is portrayed as

50. *vilokya kubjāṃ yuvatīṃ varānanāṃ*. In *BVP* 4.72.15–6, Kubjā is not only a hunchback but also old.

51. *maiṃ kisī ke śarīr ko kabhī nahīṃ dekhtā, maiṃ to keval ātmā dekhtā hūṃ.*

52. *śarīr kī kurūptā aur sundartā prāṇī ke apne karmoṃ ke anusār hotī hai. yah sadā nahīṃ rahtī hai.*

53. *dehyā vayor aṅgavilepam uttamaṃ śreyas tataḥ te na cirād bhaviṣyati.*

spontaneously offering her goods to Krishna without his asking for or even wanting them.

Bhāgavata Purāṇa gives the impression that simpleminded Kubjā, happy that someone speaks nicely to her, is the victim of deceit. The poor woman is immediately taken in by the two handsome young men who ask her for the balm, and she hands it to them right away (*BhP* 10.42.3–4). Sagar at once clears his Krishna of any such blame and stretches credulity less—by extending the conversation a bit longer and making her at first suspicious of his intent, only slowly warming up to this unusual young man. Here, Krishna takes her hand, symbolic of his extending his protection to her. When she worries that Kaṃsa will behead her if she does not bring him the balm, Krishna points out that now that he has taken her hand, there is no need for her to go to Kaṃsa. Rather than portraying Kubjā as a victim of Krishna's extortion, Sagar shows Krishna delivering her from her plight of serving a tyrant.

Sagar also deepens the meaning of her handing over the balm to the young men. Lots of shot-counter-shot close-ups suggest that Kubjā has a hunch that Krishna is divine. She is devotionally gazing on the Lord, groping for a way to express her growing realization in words. She says that now it seems to her that she has made the paste just for Krishna, and that in fact she has been waiting for him for many lives.[54] At each point, he confirms her in her impressions. Only then does she offer him the balm, saying that it is nothing, but that her deepest wish is to surrender herself completely to him.[55]

This comes close to the devotional tone we find in some of the poems attributed to Sūrdās, where the whole incident is reported as proof of the Lord's grace (discussed later). However, in Sūr's poetry, the focus is on the low social status of Kubjā, as a maidservant, and the largesse of Krishna's grace, which totally disregards social boundaries.

From Prostitute's Proposition to Ascetic's Boon

The televised episode is quite different in tone from *Bhāgavata Purāṇa*. Consistent with its portrayal of the incident as a boyish prank, *Bhāgavata Purāṇa* shows the two brothers immediately rubbing the paste on their own bodies (*BhP* 10.48.5). Only after they have obtained what they want does Krishna, somewhat ad hoc, decide to straighten Kubjā's body. He reasons that he will do it to show the reward of encountering him (10.48.6–8). In the television

54. *aṃdar se aisā lagtā hai jaise maiṃ kaī janmoṃ se tumhāre hī pratīkṣa kartī rahī hūṃ.*
55. *ātmā ke andar se koī avāz de rahā hai ki . . . apnā sarvasva inke caraṇoṃ par samarpaṇ kar de.*

version, there is no such direct connection between Krishna getting what he wants and returning a favor. Actually, the brothers do not quite get the balm. Kubjā teases them back just a bit. After she first offers the balm to Krishna as a token of her total surrender ("Take this, Lord, this 'all of me' is yours only"),[56] she retreats, charmingly simpleminded in her desire to keep him close, and says she will not give it to him just like that.[57]

Sagar has Kubjā make her request for intimacy right here. Significantly, this is after she has surrendered herself completely to Krishna, but before Krishna makes her pretty. In contrast to *Bhāgavata Purāṇa,* she does not proposition him sexually, which would seem inappropriate for a hunchbacked woman; rather she asks for the more innocent and devotional favor of being allowed to massage the balm onto his body.[58] She uses a humble tone: "Come, Lord, come to my house. Give this servant of yours an occasion to serve you, Lord."[59]

Krishna agrees, but playfully throws her earlier objection back to her: "what if Kaṃsa beheads you?" This prompts a long confession of devotion in which she declares she does not even know of any other "Mahārāj" but him. Now she does not even see anything but Krishna, and in good *advaitic* fashion, she adds: "it's as if my existence is swept away."[60] At this point, the audience has quite forgotten about the balm it all started with. In the end, Kubjā applies a little bit to Krishna's feet, but the container remains in her possession. No one can blame Sagar's Krishna for just being after some good-smelling substances.

In *Bhāgavata Purāṇa,* it is only after she has become pretty that Kubjā asks Krishna to accompany her to her home (10.48.9–10). Krishna half-jokingly promises to do so, with one mischievous eye on his brother and his other friends (10.48.11). He does not seem terribly serious as he somewhat denigratingly calls her house "a place that takes away the agony of men" and her "the last resort of homeless travelers like us."[61] Not very complimentary in any case, and seemingly implying she is a public woman.[62]

In the television version, the tone is much more exalted, and there is no hint that Kubjā might be a prostitute. Moreover, it is only after she has gone

56. *le lo prabhu yah sarvasva tumhārā hī hai.*

57. *nahīṃ, nahīṃ aise nahīṃ dūṃgī.*

58. *jī cāhtā hai āj maiṃ apne hath se tumhāre śarīr par is aṃgarāg kā lep kar dūṃ.*

59. *calo prabhu calo merī kuṭiyā par. Is dāsī ko ek sevā kā avsar do prabhu.*

60. *ab to ātmā ke antar tak keval tumhī tum ho aur kuch nahīṃ. ek prakāś hī prakāś hai, aur us prakāś meṃ jaise maiṃ ḍūbtī jā rahī hūṃ, ḍūbtī jā rahī hūṃ . . . jaisā merā astitva hī nahīṃ rahā.*

61. *te gṛhaṃ . . . puṃsām ādhi-vikarśanam. agṛhāṇāṃ naḥ pānthānāṃ tvaṃ parāyaṇam.*

62. This is picked up by some of the commentators, who try to clean up the sexual reference or claim it is just a joke (Sheth 1983: 230).

through a transforming spiritual experience that Krishna rewards her by straightening her. By the magic of visual special effects, she turns into a beautiful woman, with, incidentally, also a splendid new outfit. Sagar's Kubjā has none of the earthy panache of the one in *Bhāgavata Purāṇa*; she is quite the subservient servant. After glancing happily at her new outfit, she carefully kneels down, with her hands stretched out in supplication. She now somehow feels the need to justify her desire to massage him, arguing that it is something he himself has awakened in her.[63]

Krishna, in all the serious grandness that Sanskritized Hindi can afford, grants her wish: "We approve of your supplication, and solemnly promise that one day we will without fail bestow upon you the opportunity of service."[64] However, he will not immediately gratify her desire. He promises to come later. No winking to his brother here, nothing to demean poor Kubjā, who has after all been shown to be a perfectly respectable devotee. Instead, Krishna explains that he will come to her because he owes it to her. He speaks of a debt (*ṛṇa*) from her previous birth, when she did penance (*tapasyā*) to obtain him.[65] This idea surfaces also in the medieval poems that interpret Krishna's consummation of his relation with Kubjā:

> Kubarī had saved up merit from old penance.
> Śyāma came to her own house, spurning his royal palace.
> First he broke the bow and on his way back she came running to meet him!
> Because of her passion, he came into her power, a love that cannot be explained.
> He promised to come after his divine work and gave her incomparable beauty.
> He glanced at her graciously, and she became Śrī, the Vedas cannot explain this.
> Far from us, [still] attracted by the low, what a compassionate Lord he is!
> Sūr says: having carried out the task the gods gave him, immediately Gopāl came there (to her house). (*SS* 3718/3100)[66]

63. *tum ne svayam hī mere man meṃ yah bhāvnā jagāyī hai.*

64. *hameṃ tumhāre yah saṃkalp svīkar hai, ham vacan dete haiṃ ki ham tumheṃ ek din sevā kā avsar avaśya pradān kareṃge.*

65. *asal meṃ tumhāre pichle janam kā yah ṛṇ hai ham par. tumne hamāre liye baṛī tapasyā kī thī.*

66. *kubarī pūraba tapa kari rākhyau; āe syāma bhavana tāhī kaiṃ, nṛpati mahala saba nākhyau; prathamahiṃ dhanuṣa tori āvata hai, bīca milī yaha dhāī; tihiṃ anurāga basya bhae tākaiṃ, so hita kahyau na jāī; devakāja kari āvana kahi gae, dīnhau rūpa apāra; kṛpā dṛṣṭi citavatahīṃ śrī bhaï, nigama na pāvata pāra; hama taiṃ dūri dīna ke pāchaiṃ, aise dīnadayāla; sūra surani kari kāja turatahīṃ, āvata tahāṃ gopāla.*

Notable here is the saving rather than controlling male gaze—at least, that is the devotional interpretation. The very refrain of this song reiterates the idea over and over again that Krishna's grace was no chance experience but due to Kubjā's penance from old times. Another poem expresses a similar idea:

Kubjā has a lucky fate!
Hari graciously took pity on her. On the spot, he obliged her.
The fruit of a previous life began to blossom. Her heart's desire was fulfilled
The news is on the lips of all the folks of Mathurā. Wherever he goes, a loud "Hurray" arises.
Having killed the demon, he ran there [to Kubjā's house] right away. Fathom his divine ways!
Sūrdās's Lord is bound by love: he met her graciously and brought much bliss. (SS 3725/3107)[67]

In the medieval songs, this interpretation of the event as the result of Kubjā's past penance is presented as the view of devotees, maybe the people of Mathurā or even the Gopīs. In the television version, Krishna himself confirms this interpretation. Plus, he provides more specifics as to the circumstances of this previous penance. He gives Kubjā a clue that it occurred during his previous descent on earth as Rāma. This enigmatic saying is then resolved in the song that follows:

(male voice)
She placed her head at his feet,
Spoke humbly her plea of powerlessness:
"This is not just a cream (*aṅgarāga*),
This is my love's dream (*anurāga*), O Lord."[68]

(female voice)
"I surrender for a glimpse of you,
Your touch brings great rejoicing:

67. *kubijā tau baṛabhāgī hvai; karunā kari hari jāhi nivājī, āpu rahe tahaṃ rājī hvai; pūraba tapa phala bilasana lāgī, mana ke bhāva purāvati hvai; mathurā nara nārini mukha bānī, rahyo jahāṃ tahaṃ jai jai hvai; daitya bināsi turata tahaṃ āe, yaha līlā jānaiṃ pai vai; sūradāsa prabhu bhāvahiṃ kai basa, milata kṛpā kari ati sukha hvai.*

68. *sir dhari caraṇan māhi, binay vivaś bole vacan; aṅgarāg yah hai nāhī, yah hai prabhu mama anurāg hai.*

Lord, gone my body's deformity (*vikṛti*)
Now that I behold your face's dignity (*mukhākṛti*)."[69]

(male voice)
"Always rewarding love's frenzy,
The forest-dweller does not keep debts.[70]
(female voice)
Just like Śabarī patiently,
Scanned the path for Rāma,
Similarly, lifelong, O dark One,
I will scan your path."[71]

Thus, Sagar's Kubjā is really an incarnation of good old Śabarī, the ascetic who waited patiently for Rāma in the forest and treated him as a mother would her son. This interpretation may be Sagar's innovation. He deviates from *Brahma Vaivarta Purāṇa,* where Krishna announces to Kubjā that she is the incarnation of Śūrpaṇakhā and has accumulated *tapas* from this previous birth. The context there is a night visit Krishna pays her. He has to wake her up, and he immediately confronts her with her past:

> Shake off your slumber, lucky lady, make love to me, Beauty!
> Previously, you were Śūrpaṇakhā, Rāvaṇa's sister,
> In my birth as Rāma, you performed for my sake, o lover, austerities.
> Through the influence of your austerities, you get to enjoy me as a lover in my birth as Krishna! (*BVP* 4.72.56–7)[72]

Sagar seems to have liked the idea of Kubjā accumulating merit from *tapas* in a previous life. However, he chose not to make her an incarnation of the vamp Śūrpaṇakhā, instead identifying her with the safely asexual Śabarī.

In conformity with that more humble character, Kubjā meekly agrees that if she has waited for so many lives for the *darśana* of her Lord that she can wait even a bit longer.[73] This sentiment is to some extent also apparent in Sūr's poetry.

69. *tere darśan kī balihāri, terā sparś baṛā sukhakārī; gaī tan kī vikriti svāmī, terī dekh mukhākṛti pyārī.*

70. *sadā prema kā moh cukāve, rin rakhe nā banavārī*

71. *śabarī ne dhīraj dharke, jaise rām kī rāh nihārī; aise hī janam bhar śyām, dekhūṃgī maiṃ bāṭ tihārī.*

72. *tyaja nidrāṃ mahābhāge śṛṅgāraṃ dehi sundari, purā śūrpaṇakhā tvaṃ ca bhaginī rāvaṇasya ca; rāmajanmani mad dhetos tvayā kānte tapaḥ kṛtam, tapaḥ prabhāvān māṃ kāntaṃ bhaja śrīkṛṣṇajanmani.* This was also noted by Jeffrey M. Masson (1980: 114–6).

73. *āj nahīṃ to koī bāt nahīṃ. jab maiṃ ne itne janamoṃ tak pratīkṣā kī hai, tab maiṃ is janam meṃ bhī āj se apnī kuṭiyā maiṃ baiṭhī in caraṇoṃ kī pratīkṣā karūṃgī.*

He turned the hunchback into a beauty queen! . . .
He touched her neck with his hand, put his foot on her back, gave her the beauty of a nymph [like Urvaśī].
Her heart's desire was "let me get Śyāma for a husband right here," but she understood that it could not happen immediately.
(SS 3669/1051)[74]

As is clear from the song quoted earlier, the focus of devotion in the televised version has markedly zoomed in on Krishna's feet. This is apparent also in Kubjā's body language. During the song, Kubjā remains stooping, humbly adorning Krishna's feet with some of her sandal paste. She remains kneeling while he slowly retreats, leaving her in a happy trance of devotion. Sagar has succeeded in turning earthy Kubjā into a meek, subservient woman who is cleanly devoted to Krishna, with not a hint of erotic attachment. Her sexual proposition has been transformed into a plea for a chance to perform *sevā*, which she is granted as a result of her ascetic exertion in previous lifes.

Perspectives on Sexual Fulfillment

Given how he has desexualized the Kubjā episode, it is no surprise that Sagar entirely skips the episode where Krishna visits her and consummates their love physically. It seems a deliberate omission, because the claim is made that the television series covers the first half of *Bhāgavata Purāṇa*'s tenth book. In fact, the series ends with the delivery of Krishna's guru's son from the dead (10.45), leaving out the subsequent chapters on Uddhava's mission to Braj to console all those distressed by Krishna's departure (10.46–7) as well as the episode where Krishna visits Kubjā with Uddhava (10.48), and sends Akrūra to Hastināpura, thus getting involved in the *Mahābhārata* war (10.49). One may safely assume that if Sagar's Krishna has promised to visit Kubjā, he must have done so, but it must have been an encounter of a nonsexual nature. In any case, this has (so far) remained offscreen.[75]

Bhāgavata Purāṇa, on the other hand, describes the visit Krishna pays Kubjā at length. The episode also figures importantly in the collected works attributed to the devotional poet Sūrdās. The material here is less descriptive, more interpretative. Sūr has one poem that conflates the first meeting with the

74. *kūbarī nāri suṃdarī kīnhī . . . grīva kara parasi paga pīṭhi tāpara diyau, urabasī rūpa paṭatarahiṃ dīnhī; cita vākaiṃ ihai syāma pati milaiṃ mohiṃ, turata soī bhaï nahiṃ jāti cīnhī.* An alternative translation would be: "thus happened immediately, in disregard for caste."

75. It should be pointed out that Krishna does not make good on his promise to visit Kubjā in some other classical versions, including *Viṣṇu Purāṇa* (5.20.12; see Sheth 1983: 226 and Masson 1980: 110–24).

second (*SS* 3668/3050) and a series of poems that are interpretations of Krishna's visit to Kubjā's house (*SS* 3718/3100 25/3107, again, 3727/3109 mentions it in passing). Comparing the perspective of the two is revealing.

In *Bhāgavata Purāṇa*, there is a certain sense of unease with the situation, which the commentaries try to explain away. Krishna is accompanied by the wise Uddhava on this visit.[76] There seems to be a bit of criticism inherent in the situation, given that Uddhava has just returned from Braj on a mission to comfort the Gopīs there, Krishna's abandoned lovers. No sooner is he back than he is asked to accompany his friend on an amorous escapade with a city woman. One can read into the texts some indication that he is obliging only grudgingly. There is a curious line specifying that Uddhava does not sit on a bed like Krishna but on the ground instead, though touching a seat (*BhP* 10.48.4a).[77] This can be interpreted as a sign of humility toward Krishna, or that he wishes to avoid offending the hostess (Bryant 2003: 460). The use of the word *sādhu* in this line is interesting. It is used an adverb modifying the verb "received" (*abhipūjito*)—thus "he was well received by her"—but one suspects also a hint of the idea that Uddhava, in contrast to Krishna, behaved like an ascetic (*sādhu*).

In the description of Kubjā's house, there are (as earlier in his promise to her) some clues that seem to indicate it is a house of pleasure, especially in the epithet "equipped with devices for sensuality" (*kāmopāyopabṛṃhitam, BhP* 10.48.2a). And Krishna is said to settle down right away on a rich bed, which is described as "following the ways of the worldly" (*lokācaritāny anuvrataḥ* (10.48.4b). The way Kubjā receives him, dressing herself elaborately and presenting betel and liquors, also evokes the courtesan's behavior: "She approached Mādhava, having prepared herself with bath, makeup, dress, jewelry, garlands, perfumes, betel, liquors, and so on, with playful flirting smiles and beguiling glances (10.48.5).[78]

Sūrdās has redacted all this out. In the poem where he conflates the first meeting with Krishna's visit to Kubjā's house, the tone is not one of sensual gratification but of devotional worship, like that of an image. Thus, Sūr's verse is a good precedent for the televised version of the first meeting:

> "Lord, I've brought sandal for you!"
> Taking Śyāma by the hand, she brought him to her mansion

76. The commentators in fact see the company of Uddhava as an attempt to avoid a scandal. It seems that his reputation of integrity might make him the ideal chaperon (Sheth 1983: 231).

77. *tathoddhavaḥ sādhu tayābhipūjito nyaṣīdad urvyām abhimṛśya cāsanam.*

78. *sā majjanālepa-dukūla-bhūṣaṇa-srag-gandha-tāmbūla-sudhā-savādibhiḥ, prasādhitātmopasasāra mādhavaṃ savrīḍa-līlotsmita-vibhramekṣitaiḥ*

With incense, oil lamps, and sacred food offerings (*naivedya*) she decorated [him]. She had prepared [these] auspicious items carefully.
She washed his feet and took the bathwater, she sang praise of the enemy of demons (Daityāri).
"My life's aspiration was this, that I would massage you with sandalwood"
Sūr's Śyāma delights his devotees, bound by the ties of passionate love. (*SS* 3668/3050)[79]

Sūrdās's list of the substances Kubjā honors Krishna with (*dhūpa, dīpa, naiveda*) picks up the more innocent items in *Bhāgavata Purāṇa*'s description of Kubjā's house, the incense and oil lamps (10.48.2b).[80] Significantly, he adds the "sacred food offerings" (*naivedya*) to the list, as if to overturn the impression created by the betel and liquors she appears with in *Bhāgavata Purāṇa* (10.48.5a; see earlier).[81] Moreover, rather than preparing herself with a bath, she concentrates here on the devotional rite of giving a footbath to Krishna and on drinking the bathwater (something Akrūra is said to have done later in the same chapter in *Bhāgavata Purāṇa* (10.48.15a).[82] One might object that this cleaning-up behavior may just be a cover, dictated by Kubjā herself, since the poem is in her voice, but actually only the refrain (*ṭeka*) and the penultimate line are in the first person. There is a shift to third person in the lines that describe her actions and motivation.

There is a significant omission in this poem: it does not refer to the miracle of Kubjā's transformation. One may presume that it was well-known enough to remain in the background, but even so interestingly the focus has moved totally away from Krishna's curing the misshapen woman to his grace of granting her his presence.

While the reference in the signature (*chāpa*) line of the Sūr poem is to the ties of passionate love (*bhāva raju raṃga*), none of Sūr's poems on the topic actually describes passionate lovemaking. *Bhāgavata Purāṇa* does so in vivid detail, evoking a first encounter between a shy yet passionate woman who has long been burning with unfulfilled desire and a vigorous, self-assured man keen on relieving her agony:

79. *prabhu tumakauṃ maiṃ caṃdana lyāī; gahyau syāma kara apane sauṃ, lie sadana kauṃ āī; dhūpa dīpa naiveda sājikai, maṃgala kare bicāri; carana pakhāri liyauṃ caranodaka, dhani dhani kahi daitāri; merī janama kalpanā aisī, caṃdana parasauṃ aṃga; sūra syāma jana ke sukhadāyaka, baṃdhe bhāva-raju-raṃga.*

80. *dhūpaiḥ surabhibhir dīpaiḥ . . . maṇḍitam.*

81. This is more in tune with the treatment of the episode in *BVP* (4.72. 33–6; see Sheth 1983: 228).

82. *padāvaneja-nīrāpo dhārayañ śirasā nṛpa.*

> He called his lover by his side. She was shy due to the newness of their rendezvous and uncertain of herself. He grabbed her hands, adorned with bracelets, and made her sit down on the bed. Thus, he sported with the passionate woman, whose only virtue was the offer of the ointment.
>
> She wiped out the pain that Cupid had caused in her breasts from her chest, and also from her eyes with the feet of Ananta. With her two arms, she pressed between her breasts her lover, the embodiment of bliss, and shed her long-held sorrow. (10.48.6–7)[83]

Sūrdās is no prude, but he reserves all Cupid's arrows for his descriptions of the love play of Krishna and Rādhā and the Gopīs. The encounter with Kubjā remains quite chaste.

Subverting Doubts

In the course of its account of this passionate encounter, *Bhāgavata Purāṇa* downplays Kubjā's virtue in an offhanded way by using an epithet for her that says she "merely" offered some ointment (*anulepārpaṇa-puṇya-leśayā*, 10.48.6b). This seems a judgmental remark, heightening the impression that the author is only grudgingly reporting on this somewhat disreputable encounter. This ambiguous evaluation of Kubjā's worthiness to sport with the Lord comes through even more strongly in the moralizing judgments that are interspersed in the report of their ensuing conversation:

> By the offering of an ointment, she thus obtained the Lord, Absoluteness in itself (*kaivalya-nāthaṃ*), who is so difficult to reach. Alas, the hapless woman asked the following:
>
> O beloved, you should stay here a few days! Enjoy yourself with me. I cannot bear to leave your company, O lotus-eyed One.
>
> And the obliging one (*mānadaḥ*) granted her heart's desire and obliged her. Together with Uddhava, the Lord of all returned to his own opulent quarters. (10.48.8–10).[84]

83. *āhūya kāntāṃ navasaṅgamahriyā viśaṅkitāṃ kaṅkaṇabhūṣite kare, pragṛhya śayyām adhiveśya rāmayā reme 'nulepārpaṇapuṇyaleśayā; sānaṅgataptakucayor urasas tathākṣṇor jighranty anantacaraṇena rujo mṛjantī, dorbhyāṃ stanāntaragataṃ parirabhya kāntabhānandamūrtim ajahād atidīrghatāpam.*

84. *saivaṃ kaivalyanāthaṃ taṃ prāpya duṣprāpam īśvaram, aṅgarāgārpaṇenāho durbhagedam ayācata; āhoṣyatām iha preṣṭha dināni katicin mayā, ramasva notsahe tyaktuṃ saṅga te 'mburuhekṣaṇa; tasyai kāmavaraṃ dattvā mānayitvā ca mānadaḥ, sahoddhavena sarveśaḥ svadhāmāgamad arcitam.*

There certainly is a sense in *Bhāgavata Purāṇa* that Kubjā is unworthy of Krishna. Sūrdās seems to hint at it in some of his poems:

Śyāma has come to Kubjā's house.
Earlier, Hari had gone away, graciously having turned her into a sensual, pretty woman.
Love has a hold on him. After all he's called: "friend of the poor," and "fond of his devotees."
She met him on her way with sandal paste and her dreams have come true.
Urvaśī is no compare, even Ramā is jealous.[85]
Who understands the greatness of Sūr's Lord? He settles in the house of a maid. (*SS* 3721/3103)[86]

There is a hint of the compound "the woman whose only virtue was the offering of sandal paste" (*anulepārpaṇa-puṇya-leśa*) in the fourth line. However, note that there is no equivalent for the "only" part of the compound. Rather, the emphasis is on the greatness of the Lord for saving someone who is so humble in social rank, not so much someone with little merit.

In Sūr's collection, in fact, things get turned upside down. First Sūr admits that yes, Kubjā is unworthy, but it is because of her social status. Kubjā is a servant, of lower caste. Krishna after all is the prince and king-to-be. His associating with her might be regarded as improper because of the class and caste divide. Thus the unworthiness of Kubjā is transformed into comments on the unevenness of the match. The devotional poet, however, is not bothered by this. Rather, he celebrates this marvel of God's mercy, which disregards social distinctions. There is a series of poems on the subject:

His divine task completed, he went straight to her house!
Man or woman, it's the same to Him. He descended for high and low alike.
Who is servant or maid? Who is Lord or Lordless? The whole world is dwarfed by His bristling body hair.
The heart with true love is Hari's house. It is marked by the fate of God's grace.

85. Literally, "Suffering in Ramā's heart" (*ramā kaiṃ mana tāma*).

86. *kubijā sadana āe syāma; kṛpā kari hari gae prathamahiṃ, bhaī anupama bāma; prīti kaiṃ basa dīnabaṃdhu, bhaktavatsala nāma; milī māraga malaya lai kai, bhaī pūrana kāma; urabasī paṭatarahiṃ nāhīṃ, ramā kaiṃ mana tāma; sūra prabhu mahimā agocara, base dāsī dhāma.*

Śyāma lives by the praise of his servants, female or male. A maid of
Krishna can become equal to the goddess Ramā.
She met him and lovingly massaged Sūr's Lord with sandal paste.
Zillions of rosaries she [must have] prayed, zillions of austerities
in Kāśī.[87] (*SS* 3719/3101)[88]

While socially unworthy, being a mere servant, (*dāsī*), Kubjā is not unworthy of the Lord's grace. The medieval poet chooses not to follow *Bhāgavata Purāṇa*'s disparaging tone in that respect. On the contrary, in the final line, he attributes her gift of grace from Krishna to her adherence to a serious devotional and spiritual regimen. Thus she has become eminently worthy of his attentions. A similar sentiment, that Krishna shows his nondiscriminating grace to the worthy devotee, is expressed in the next poem. Kubjā responds in kind, overcome by joy; yet, aware of her position, she stoops to his feet. This seems in tune with Sagar's treatment of the meeting in the televised version:

The king of the Yādavas is fond of his devotees.
He set foot in Kūbarī's house. Forgot about the rules of caste![89]
She thought her dreams had come true![90] She ran to clasp his feet.
She did not care what she looked like, or her house. Her heart could
not contain the joy.
The Lord took her by the arm and sat her down near him. Happiness
beyond words.
Sūrdās's Lord is always in the power of his devotees. He does not
count king or pauper! (*SS* 3720/3102)[91]

In contrast to *Bhāgavata Purāṇa*, this Kubjā does not care about her house or what she looks like. All the long compounds describing her house and herself in *Bhāgavata Purāṇa* have been obliterated from our memory by the

87. Literally, it reads: "She did crores of rosaries, crores of austerities in Kāśī" (*koṭi*). This can be understood in two ways. Either it equates the massaging with the spiritual exercises or it indicates a causal relationship. I've opted for the latter in the translation.

88. *kiyau surakāja gṛha cale tākai; puruṣa au nāri kau bheda bhedā nahīṃ, kulina akulīna avataryau kākai; dāsa dāsī kauna prabhu niprabhu kauna hai, akhila brahmāṃḍa ika roma jākai; bhāva sāṃcau hṛdaya jahāṃ hari tahāṃ haiṃ, kṛpā prabhu kī mātha bhāga vākaiṃ; dāsa dāsī syāma bhajanahuṃ taiṃ jiye, ramā sama bhaī so kṛṣnadāsī; milī vaha sūra prabhu prema caṃdana caraci, kiyau japa koṭi tapa koṭi kāsī.*

89. Literally, *jāti pāti* means "caste line," a reference to the habit of eating only with members of one's own caste. At public festivals, where people of all castes may be present, one will take care to dine sitting with those of one's own caste only.

90. Literally, "she considered her fate fulfilled" (*pūrana bhāga māni tina apane*).

91. *bhaktabachala śrījādavarāi; geha kūbarī kaiṃ paga dhāre, jāti pāṃti bisarāi; pūrana bhāga māni tina apane, carana gahe uṭhi dhāi; surati rahī nahiṃ deha geha kī, ānaṃda ura na samāi; prabhu gahi bāhaṃ pāsa baiṭhārī, so sukha kahyau na jāi; sūradāsa prabhu sadā bhakta basa, raṃka ganata nahiṃ rāi.*

failure of hers: Sūr says, marvelously simply, "she did not retain awareness of house or body."[92] She is not the accomplished sensual city woman; rather, confronted with Krishna, she turns into a simple Gopī herself.[93]

The commentators on *Bhāgavata Purāṇa* also picked up on its disparaging of Kubjā. They had to work hard to explain why she was called "unlucky" (*durbhagā*, 10.48.8b). Mostly they agree that it was because she merely asked Krishna to gratify her senses, rather than give her liberation (Sheth 1983: 232). Vallabha is quite negative about Kubjā, suspecting that she is a prostitute who approaches Krishna as a worldly customer (232–3). Jīva Gosvāmī, though, reads against the grain. He thinks Kubjā's ill luck refers simply to her earlier state as a hunchback. According to him, she is in fact clever to ask for Krishna himself rather than liberation. He uses all his Sanskrit compound analytic skill to prove that the "mere" gift of an ointment (*anulepārpaṇapuṇyaleśa*) is not denigrating but rather makes her the empress (*īśā*) of devotees (232).

Sūrdās goes a step further. He subverts *Bhāgavata Purāṇa*'s "unlucky" word choice. Turning the tables, he comments on her great luck.[94] In one poem, assuming the voice of the people of Mathurā, he seems to share *Bhāgavata Purāṇa*'s ambiguity, but comes out in the end on the other side of the divide. His Mathurā gazette rhetorically asks who indeed could be luckier than she (in the final line):

> The folks of Mathurā say:
> "Where did that Kubjā with her sandal [paste] meet him? Why did Śyāma show her compassion?
> What austerities had she under her belt? She roamed around all over town!
> She's got no clue. She saw Hari and said right there she'd massage the Lord with love.
> Then He was compassionate and made her beautiful. One can't begin to sing His praise.
> Sūrdās, that's Kūbarī's fate. Who could get a better one?" (*SS* 3723/3105)[95]

92. *surati rahī nahiṃ deha geha kī.*

93. This is in effect what happens to Kubjā in the *BVP* version of the story; she is taken up into Krishna's paradise, Goloka, where she becomes a Gopī by the name of Candramukhī (4.72.66–8; see Sheth 1983: 228).

94. He is on the same wavelength as *BVP* 4.72.56, where Krishna himself calls her *mahābhāge*.

95. *mathurā ke nara nāri kahaiṃ; kahāṃ milī kubijā caṃdana lai, kahā syāma tihiṃ kṛpā cahaiṃ; kahā tapasyā kari ihiṃ rākhī, jahāṃ tahāṃ pura rahai calai; kachū nahīṃ āvata hari dekhī, ihai kahyau prabhu heta malai; tabahiṃ kṛpā kari suṃdari kīnhī, mahimā yaha kahata na āvai; sūradāsa bhāga kūbarī kau, kauna tāhi paṭatara pāvai.*

In another poem, this rhetorical question is the refrain, repeated over and over through the poem, to rub in the point: "What woman is as lucky as Kubjā?" (*SS* 2724/3106). Another assessment of Kubjā as lucky comes from the Gopīs. In the following poem they have just gotten the news of Krishna's new affair. We hear of their first reactions. They say Kubjā has become the happiest bride of all (*suhāginī bhārī*):

> "He met Kubjā, that's what they say.
> His real mother and father is Vasudeva and Devakī." Happy faces, but sad at heart.[96]
> "A mere touch of his hand turned her into a beauty. He made her into the happiest bride.
> Kānha is king and a hunchback is his queen." The women of Braj snicker.
> Their hearts pierced by the curse of this cowife. Totally blown off their feet.
> Sūrdās: "That's the way of the Lord, my friend!" the women told each other. (*SS* 3760/3142)[97]

In short, the devotional interpretation leaves no doubt that Kubjā is lucky and must have deserved her heaven.

The Many Shades of Jealousy

With the last poem we have broached a new series of poems in the *Sūr Sagar,* where Sūrdās dwells at length on the reaction of the Gopīs to Krishna's affair (*SS* 3760/3142–73/3155). There is nothing like this in *Bhāgavata Purāṇa,* or indeed in the television series, which does not look back: once Krishna has left, there is no revisiting Braj.

The Gopīs speak for all women whose beloved has gone away to the city and is reported to have another love. The *Sūr Sāgar* gives a full range of emotion, representing all the shades of jealousy. The snickering in the previously quoted poem dies away soon. Maybe the first reaction is that of utter disbelief:

96. The Braj text is ambiguous as to whom this refers, but it seems most logically to be the women of Braj, who are at once happy about Krishna being a prince, snickering about his falling for a hunchback, and at the same time jealous at this new city love of his.

97. *kubijā milī kahyau yaha bāta; mātu pita vasudeva devakī, mana dukha mukha haraṣāta; suṃdari bhaī aṃga parasata hī, karī suhāgini bhārī; nṛpati kānha kubijā paṭarānī, haṃsati kahatiṃ brajanārī; sauti sāla ura maiṃ ati sālyau, nakhasikha lauṃ bhaharānī; sūradāsa prabhu aisei māī, kahatiṃ paraspara bānī.*

How would Hari do something like this?
Manamohana left Rādhā, to take up with Kaṃsa's maid?
What do you say? She's become his queen? Has he become king just going there?
Throning in Mathurā he does not see anyone? [Doesn't know] who has come, who lives where?
Bought a hunchback? Sold his honor? He's with her all hours of the day?
Sūr says: no one believes it: a prank that thrills the heart. (*SS* 3764/3146)[98]

Denial is the first step, but of course the Gopīs have to find out the truth. The next poem seems to report on a spying expedition to Mathurā:

Have you not seen Kubjā?
I went to Mathurā to sell butter and had a good look around.
She's the daughter of the flower man near the palace! Everyone made fun of her when they saw her.
Do you burn brass again and again? What's the point in testing it over and over?
It's said he turned her into a beauty! And he became pleased with her.
Sūr says: when heart meets heart, what can the *qāzī* do about it? (*SS* 3765/3147)[99]

The last line is meaningful in relation to the theme of the love marriage (explored in chapters 1 and 2). The authorities (here interestingly the Muslim *qāzī*) are powerless in the face of love; they can only ratify matters of the heart. At this point, there is no denying it anymore. The Gopīs now have to come to terms with this new reality. We go through the whole range of feelings with them. The Gopīs are burning with jealousy at the news of Krishna's new conquest; the worst of it is that now there's no more hope that he will come back to them:

When they hear the name Kubjā, the fever of missing him flares up.
A grunt escapes the indignant women, drowning in anger.
Their hope he'd return, gone! Sighs rise up in the air.

98. *kaisaiṃ rī yaha hari karihaiṃ; rādhā kauṃ tajihaiṃ manamohana, kahā kaṃsadāsī dharihaiṃ; kahā kahati vaha bhai paṭarānī, vai rāja bhae jāi uhāṃ; mathurā basata lakhata nahiṃ koū, ko āyau ko rahata kahāṃ; lāja beṃci kūbarī bisāhī, saṃga na chāṃḍata eka gharī; sūra jāhi paratīti na kāhū, mana sihāta yaha karani karī.*

99. *kubijā nahiṃ tuma dekhī hai; dadhi becana jaba jāti madhupurī, maiṃ nīkaiṃ kari peṣī hai; mahala nikaṭa mālī kī beṭī, dekhata jihiṃ nara nāri haṃsai; koṭi bāra pītari jau dāhau, koṭi bāra jo kahā kasaiṃ; suniyata tāhi suṃdarī kīnhī, āpu bhae tākauṃ rājī; sūra milai mana jāhi jāhi sauṃ, tākau kahā kare kājī.*

"That royal maid Kubjā! She took away our hope."
A waterfall of tears from their eyes. Inscrutable. The pain of missing him floods over them like a river.
Sitting or standing, they remember the traits of Sūr's Śyāma. (*SS* 3761/3143)[100]

Losing Krishna feels to the Gopīs like fire and water at the same time, burning them and flooding them, destructive in both cases. They are angry and desperate, all in one breath, or rather one long sigh that turns into songs of remembrance. Jealousy is productively transformed into the devotional practice of "remembrance" (*sumirana*). Then Sūr's Gopīs move into a mood of sad assessment of the situation, seemingly adjusting themselves to their loss:

Śyāma made Kubjā his bride [a lucky woman]. She's got boundless beauty, hard to assess.[101]
He became husband, she his better half. The Gopīs call him "eternally happy."[102]
He is a playboy, she's from the city, and now the two of them have gotten together.
Outdoing each other in splendid qualities. She's sophisticated, he certainly is very urbane.
Whatever she says, Śyāma will do. Night and day he sings her praises.
Life is strange! She stole his heart. Sūraj's Lord will not return to Braj now.[103] (*SS* 3762/3144)[104]

This is the closest Sūrdās comes to *Bhāgavata Purāṇa*, where the Gopīs never mention Kubjā but get occasion to vent their pain in separation from Krishna (*viraha*) most famously to Krishna's city friend Uddhava, when he visits Braj on a mission to comfort them. Though they do not mention Kubjā by name, they make a few jealous remarks about "city women" in general:

100. *kubijā kau nāma sunata, biraha anala jūḍī; risani nāri jhahari uṭhīṃ, krodha madhya būḍīṃ; āvana kī āsa miṭī, ūradha saba svāsā; kubijā nṛpadāsī, hama saba karī nirāsā; locana jaladhāra agama, biraha nadī bāṛhī; sūra syāma guna sumirata, baiṭhī kou ṭhāṛhī.*

101. Or: "caste was not an objection."

102. One gloss for the word *navaraṃgī* in *BBSK* is *sadā sukhī*. This may refer to only Krishna, only Kubjā, or the pair. It seems to be used ironically: the women might outwardly give them their blessing to be forever happily married, but inwardly of course they burn with jealousy.

103. Or: "he stole our heart, but now Sūraj's Lord won't return to Braj."

104. *kubijā syāma suhāgini kīnhī, rūpa apāra jāti nahiṃ cīnhī; āpu bhae pati vaha aradhaṃgī, gopini nāṃu dharyau navaraṃgī; vai bahuravana nagar kī soū, taisoi saṃga banyau aba doū; eka eka taiṃ gunani ujāgara, vaha nāgari, vai tau ati nāgara; vaha jo kahati syāma soi mānata, nisidina vākaiṃ gunani bakhānata; jāni anokhī manahiṃ curāvai, sūraja prabhu aba nahi braja āvaiṃ.*

> Gentle man, does Gada's elder brother sometimes make love—our love—to the city women when they solicit him with their fond, bashful smiles and inviting eyes?

They answer the question themselves, sadly acquiescing:

> Expert in love play, how would he not oblige when invited by the words and coquetry of these choice women?

But they cannot help but persist in hopes he might still also remember them:

> Good man, does Govinda ever remember us, or in the midst of a gathering of city women, mention us, rustic women, in informal conversation? (10.47.40–2)[105]

They seem to accept that they have lost their lover. Only one of the Gopīs uses strong words of condemnation in the famous "song of the bee" (*bhramaragīta*) where she addresses a bee as a stand-in for Krishna. Indirectly, she blames him for being heartless and a cheat. In her despair she puts herself on the same side as other characters maligned by Krishna-Vishnu in this or a previous birth. She forges something of a league of the mistreated, and includes none other than Śūrpaṇakhā in the list:

> [I call him] a libertine (*lubdhadharmā*)![106] Like a hunter he slaughtered the monkey-king (Valin).
> [I call him] a sot of a woman (*strījitaḥ*)! he disfigured a[nother] woman lusting after him!
> [I call him] a crow (*dhvāṅkṣavat*)! Even Bali he dwarfed,[107] after eating what he offered to him (*bali*).
> Enough of these black friendships! It is hard to deny the meaning of these stories. (*BhP* 10.47.17)[108]

105. *kaccid gadāgrajaḥ saumya karoti purayoṣitām, prītiṃ naḥ snigdhasavrīḍahāsodārekṣaṇārcitaḥ; kathaṃ rativiśeṣajñaḥ priyaśca varayoṣitām, nānubadhyeta tad vākyair vibhramaiś cānubhājitaḥ; api smarati naḥ sādho govindaḥ prastute kvacit; goṣṭhīmadhye purastrīṇāṃ grāmyāḥ svairakathāntare.*

106. I have taken some freedom in translating these verses by foregrounding the unflattering comparisons. Literally it reads "like a libertine," "like one conquered by a woman," "like a crow."

107. One of the meanings of the causative *veṣṭaya-* can be "to cause to shrink up" (*MW*).

108. *mṛgayur iva kapīndraṃ vivyadhe lubdhadharmā, striyam akṛta virūpāṃ strījitaḥ kāmayānām; balim api balim attvā 'veṣṭayad dhvāṅkṣavadyas tad, alam asitasakhyair dustyajas tatkathārthaḥ*. The last half-verse can also be translated as contrastive: "however, it is difficult to give up the essence of his story." This is the interpretation of the vulgate.

For Sūr's Gopīs, too, the acceptance is only temporary. Their indignation gets the better of them. They directly accuse Krishna, speaking sarcastically:

You've done well by your love, lotus-eyed heart-breaker!
How come you so lovingly played Holī with us?
And now, in a wink of the eye, you've left us for a maid?
We're better in all ways. Kubjā has a big hunchback.
Just say the word and take us along too. We'll straighten out that hunched back afterwards.
If you've such a roving eye and taste for maids,
Show us your sight, light of our eyes, and make us your maids.
Your fame is growing in the village of Gokul:
All the women of Braj are looking to blame that maid.[109]
Leave the maid, this very moment, King, our Lord and Lover,
Because of that maid, Sūr, there's not a song left in Braj. (*SS* 3773/3155)[110]

Here, their hope has flared up again. Surely, they are better than that hunchback. If he can be seduced by her, they should be able to lure him back. Apparently, it does not work. Then they shift tactics and flaunt an attitude of not caring about it, maybe in hopes that Krishna will return once he gets his sense of adventure out of his system:

"He went off and found a new Kubjā!
He's young, she's young, She has lived in the city and played its games.
He got a maid's love, he's a servant: in love one becomes alike.
Heartless he left us, friends. It's easy [for him] to get many wives.[111]
Just now, Akrūra came to fetch him, he wasted no time obeying."
When they were told about young Kubjā, Sūr's Lord, their heart's pride was wounded. (*SS* 3763/3145)[112]

109. I am interpreting *ciriyā* as a diminutive (probably with denigrating intent) of *cerī*, and *nau* as synonymous with *kau*.

110. *tuma bhalī nibāhī prīti, kamala nayana mana mohana; taba kaisaiṃ ati prema sauṃ, hamaiṃ khilāī phāga; aba cerī ke kāranaiṃ, kiyau nimiṣa maiṃ tyāga; hama tau saba guna āgarī, kubijā kūbara bāṛhi; kahau tau hamahūṃ lai calai, pāchai kūbara kāṛhi; jau pai tumharī rījha hai, cerini so ati nehu; dṛga dyuti darasa dikhāi kai, hama cerī kari lehu; baṛī baṛāī rāvarī, bāṛhī gokula gāṃva; saba braja banitani ḍhūṃṛhi kai, dharyau ciriyānau nāṃva; abahūṃ cerī pariharau, rājan svāmī mīta; yā cerī ke kāranaiṃ, sūra calaiṃ braja gīta.*

111. *Jāni* is glossed in *BBSK* by *patnī, bhāryā*.

112. *kubijā naī pāī jāi; navala āpuna vaha navelī, nagara rahī khilāi; dāsa dāsī bhāva mili gayau, prema taiṃ bhae eka; niṭhura hoi sakhi gae hama taiṃ, jāni sahaja aneka; laina aba akrūra āyau, ko rahata kahāṃ; naī kubijā una sunāī, sūra prabhu mana māna.*

In this poem, they pretend not to care, but they certainly accuse Krishna of being "heartless" (*niṭhura*, l. 3), just like the Gopī in the *bhramaragīta* of *Bhāgavata Purāṇa* (*kitava*, 10.47.12a). They do more: they point out that Krishna was not exactly reluctant to leave them in the first place, suggesting that maybe he smelled adventure. Sūr's Gopīs do not forge an alliance with other outcasts, abandoned and maligned by Krishna, as the Gopī from *bhramaragīta* does—rather the other way around. They get some satisfaction in lumping Krishna with the low and outcast and bring up the allegation that in associating with the lowly you become like them. In loving Kubjā, Krishna has stooped down and become a servant himself, they proclaim gleefully.

From there it is only a small step to start vilifying Kubjā. Soon the Gopīs will stop blaming Krishna and instead turn their anger to Kubjā. At first they just put her down. It is so pathetic, Kūbjā is just a hunchback crawling around on the ground:

> "Do as you please, but you can't change your body's nature."
> "He's a cowherd, she's a maid from the city, what a great pair Fate has made!"
> "Let your mouth not accuse them." "What can I do, how can I say it?"
> "Why blame Śyāma? Or Kubjā? I tell you to make you understand."
> "Why blame Śyāma? Or Kubjā? She's a fickle maid, the laughing stock of town!"
> "Bent over, with a stick, she drags her feet on the ground. Think about it, it's sad," says Sūrajdās. (*SS* 3766/3148)[113]

Their pity verges on mocking. Even that does not last long, though. Pathetic or not, that woman is an obstacle. When they can't get through to Krishna, and she is an impediment, they really get upset. This lady with her lowly origins has become quite impertinent:

> It's Hari who made Kubjā brash!
> She used to serve in every house. [Now] she sits next to him on the throne!
> She was forgotten as soon as she left the door.[114] [Now] she's gotten puffed up with pride.

113. *koṭi karau tanu prakṛti na jāi; e ahīra vaha dāsī pura kī, bidhinā jorī bhalī milāi; aisena kauṃ mukha nāuṃ na lījai, kahā karauṃ kahi āvata mohiṃ; syāmahiṃ doṣa kidhauṃ kubijā kauṃ, yahai kahau maiṃ būjhati tohiṃ; syāmahiṃ doṣa kahā kubijā kauṃ, cerī capala nagara upahāsa; ṭeṛhī ṭeki calati paga dharanī, yaha jānai dukha sūrajadāsa.*

114. *Mukha* can mean *dvār, darvāzā* (*BBSK*).

"No one comes or goes [here]," that's the message she sends:
"Those days are gone, forget him." It's just a matter of ten days!
Sūr's Lord is enticed by a maid! The women of Braj are upset. (*SS* 3767/3149)[115]

They had started out confirming that it is Krishna's fault that this low woman now behaves so impertinently, but by the end of the poem they have come around: he is so besotted by her that she really is the one to blame. This is finely observed: one of the shades of jealousy prompts the women to blame the other woman rather than their man.

Look at the accomplishments of a hunchback!
Now she has herself called the first queen, and Śyāma the big king!
No one calls her "maid," nor him "cowherd."
She insists on being called "princess" and he's become "king of the earth."
A man likes everything [he can get]! What use is a hunchback?
How to get through to Sūr's Lord? He's lost all shame! (*SS* 3768/3150)[116]

Jealousy does not inspire solidarity among women or the downtrodden. It is amazing how when we look through the Gopīs' eyes, we have none of Sūr's earlier lofty sentiments praising the Lord's wonderful power of pitying the lowly. The Gopīs don't look from the perspective of bhakti now, but through the filter of the world. By that book, Kubjā and Krishna are living above their station, and that is not a good thing.

What I've heard now makes me ashamed!
He went to Mathurā and killed Kaṃsa . . . for the sake of an misshapen woman!
That's how people live in the city! They all think it's fine.
No one would ever say a thing in front of Śyāma:
"Here you have made a maid your wife! Look where you've gotten!
You, a powerful king of the Yādavas, got one born a maid!"
And if now she heard anyone say this, Kubjā would exile him.

115. *hari hīṃ karī kubijā ḍhīṭha; ṭahala karatī mahala mahalani, saṃga baiṭhī pīṭha; naiṃkahīṃ mukha pāi bhūlī, ati gaī garabāi; jāta ābata nahīṃ koū, yahai kahaiṃ paṭhāi; vai dinā gae bhūli tokauṃ, divasa dasa kī bāta; sūra prabhu dāsī lubhāne, braja badhū anakhāta.*

116. *dekhau kūbarī ke kāma; aba kahāvati pāṭarānī, baṛe rāja syāma; kahata nahiṃ kou unahiṃ dāsī, vai nahīṃ gopāla; vai kahābatiṃ rājakanyā, vai bhae bhūpāla; puruṣa kau rī sabai sohai, kūbarī kihiṃ kāja; sūra prabhu kauṃ kahā kahiai, beci khāī lāja.*

Sūr says the Gopīs are burning up in the fire of the ugly woman. (*SS* 3769/3151)[117]

The Gopīs' jealous minds have distorted the facts. Or maybe they are just quick to pick up on the city gossip that there is more to the relationship than meets the eye. A scandal. Krishna's real motive in killing Kaṃsa is not to bring justice or to liberate his parents, not even for his family honor. He has done it out of lust for a low and ugly woman. Their jealous outrage has now found a righteous cause to be indignant about.

He killed Kaṃsa for Kubjā's sake!
Could Hari not get any other woman, say? Has he no sense of propriety?
Like a crow taking up with a swan, like garlic with camphor.
As if gold was the same as glass! Like using [an ascetic's] ochre for a [married woman's] *sindoor*!
Like a Brahmin dining with a Śūdra, that's how they look together!
Listen, Sūr's Hari was "Lord of Cows!" Now he's become "Lord of the Hunchback!" (*SS* 3770/3152)[118]

The Gopīs persist in exposing the impropriety of Krishna's new love. This is an intercaste marriage! How ironic that the champions of love here have become defenders of propriety. Far from rejoicing in God's saving power, they mock the Creator's inventiveness in bringing together such an incongruous pair. The offended Gopīs don't relent in their pursuit of their rival. Sometimes it is her low status they mock, other times her ugliness, and always her lack of propriety. They get quite sarcastic;

He's enchanted with dame Kubjā!
A fine princess he got for a wife! Small wonder he's beside himself.
She seduced him with a little sandal paste, on his way to Mathurā.
How to praise her? Such enticing beauty!
He's a cowherd, she's Kaṃsa's maid, a match made in heaven!

117. *yaha suni hamahiṃ āvati lāja; jāi mathurā kaṃsa māryau, kūbarī kaiṃ kāja; loga pura maiṃ basata aisei, sabani yahai suhāta; kabahuṃ koū kahata nāhīṃ, syāma āgaiṃ bāta; kahā cerī nāri kīnhīṃ, kahā āpuna hota; tuma baṛe jadubaṃsa rājā, mile dāsīgota; ajahuṃ kahai sunāi koū, karaiṃ kubijā dūri; sūra ḍahani maratiṃ gopī, kūbarī kai jhūri.*

118. *kaṃsa badhyau kubijā kaiṃ kāja; āi hari kauṃ na milī kahuṃ, kahāṃ gaṃvāī lāja; jaisaiṃ kāga haṃsa kī saṃgati, lahasuna saṃga kapūra; jaisaiṃ kaṃcana kāṃca barābari, gerū kāma siṃdūra; bhojana sātha sūdra brāmhana ke, taisau unakau sātha; sunahu sūra hari gāi caraiyā, aba bhae kubijānātha.*

Sūraj's Lord spurned the women of Braj. Does he inquire about them?[119] (*SS* 3771/3153)[120]

With the last line, we seem to have returned to a more wistful, resigned, *Bhāgavata Purāṇa*–like tone. The Gopīs in that version also eagerly ask Uddhava whether Krishna remembers them at all, and maybe sometimes even speaks about them. A more melancholic tone is also evident in another poem, the only one of the whole cycle that is found in the sixteenth-century manuscripts (included in Kenneth Bryant's forthcoming edition as no. 189):

How would he know what another suffers?
Handsome Śyāma with his lotus-petaled eyes, brother of the Plow-bearer:
A flute on his lips, a peacock feather in his hair, grazing the cows all over the forest.
His complexion is responsible for the Yamunā's color, even now she hangs on to it.
Seeing a hunchback, he forgot even about her. Like we're all erased from his thoughts.
Sūraj, like *cātaks* thirsting for drops, we've perished waiting for him. (*SS* 3772/3154)[121]

In this poem, the Gopīs wistfully remember their beloved. Lovingly they describe him, nostalgic about his past daily activities. There's just a little flare-up of jealousy in the penultimate line, but mostly in the tone of *viraha* rather than sarcastic accusation.

Kubjā's Defense

With all that anger coming her way, Kubjā cannot remain indifferent for long. Again, there is nothing of the kind in *Bhāgavata Purāṇa*, but Sūrdās gives voice to Kubjā. She gets the chance to respond to the allegations. The first poem in the *Sūr Sāgar* on this topic announces that when she hears that

119. It is also possible to read the second half of the line as "when they inquired about him". Yet another possibility, suggested by Swapna Sharma, is "I understood his mind" in the sense "now I understand what is behind why he left us."

120. *bhāmini kubijā sauṃ raṃgarāte; rājakumāri nāri jau pavate, tau kaba aṃga samāte; rījhe jāi tanaka caṃdana lai, madubana māraga jāta; tākī kahā baṛāī kījai, aisaiṃ rūpa lubhāta; e ahīra vaha kaṃsa kī dāsī, jorī karī bidhātaiṃ; brajabanitā tyāgīṃ sūraja prabhu, būjhī unkī bātaiṃ.*

121. *bai kaha jānaiṃ pīra parāī; suṃdara syāma kamala-dala-locana, hari haladhara ke bhāī; mukha muralī sira mora pakhauvā, bana bana dhenu carāī; je jamunā jala raṃga raṃge haiṃ, ajahuṃ na tajata karāī; vhaī dekhi kūbarī bhūle, hama saba gaī bisarāī; sūraja cātaka būṃda bhaī hai, herata rahe hirāī.*

Uddhava is going on a mission to Braj, Kubjā quickly writes him a message for Rādhā:

He (Krishna) wrote a letter and put it in Uddhava's hand. . . .
When she heard "Uddhava's going to Braj," Kubjā called him into her palace.
In her own hand she wrote a letter for Rādhā: "Praise to you and the Gopīs,
You insult me, but it was a case of sudden grace!
Why are you women of Braj angry with me, listen, won't you?" [says] Sūrajdās. (*SS* 4061/3443)[122]

We are privy to the contents of this message. Kubjā does a great job of defending herself. She comes across as humble, notwithstanding all we've heard the Gopīs say about the airs she put on:

"Why are you upset with me, women of Braj?
It's not in anyone's fortune or luck. The Lord's grace is inscrutable."
Kubjā wrote a message for all, very diplomatically.[123]
"I'm just a maid of King Kaṃsa. Look and think for yourself.
I'm the bitter gourd among fruits: thrown out, lying on the garbage pile.
Now I've fallen into the musician-charmer's hands and he's playing a sweet tune.
My body was crooked, everyone knows it, but he touched it, and it became worthy.
Sūrdās's Lord, full of grace, tended me with his own hands." (*SS* 4062/3444)[124]

Here we get yet another reflection on *Bhāgavata Purāṇa*'s "unlucky" epithet for Kubjā that has sparked so much commentary. In this poem (l. 2), Kubjā subverts the interpretation we saw earlier, that it was her luck that

122. *Pātī likhi ūdhau kara dīnhīṃ . . . kubijā sunyau āta braja ūdhau, mahalahiṃ liyau bulāi; apane kara pātī likhi rādhehiṃ, gopini sahita baṛāi; mokauṃ tuma aparādha lagāvati, kṛpā bhaī anayāsa; jhukati kahā mo para braja nārī, sunahu na sūrajadāsa.*

123. The Braj is *kīnhī manuhārī*, which can have a negative connotation of "flattering" or just a neutral one of "being considerate" (*OHED*). I've opted for the latter, as in contrast to the Gopīs' accusations that she is acting up, here she is well aware of her low status.

124. *hama para kāhaiṃ jukati brajanārī; sājhe bhāga nahīṃ kāhū kau, hari kī kṛpā ninārī; kubijā likhyau saṃdesa sabani kau, aru kīnhī manuhārī; hauṃ tau dāsī kaṃsarāi kī, dekhau manahiṃ bicārī; phalani māṃjha jyauṃ karui tomarī, rahata ghure para ḍārī; aba tau hātha parī jaṃtrī ke, bājata rāga dulārī; tanu taiṃ ṭeṛhī saba kou jānata, parasi bhaī adhikārī; sūrajadāsa svāmī karunāmaya, apane hātha saṃvārī.*

Krishna came to her. Her take on it is that no, she is not worthy. God's grace is above all categories of worthiness or luck. We're back to marveling about God's immense saving power.

Another poem too, shows Kubjā's humble side. In a personal message to Rādhā, she says:

> Uddhava, tell this to Rādhā:
> "As Śyāma showed grace on me, would you please do the same?
> You're angry with me without reason, I'm your servant.
> Look for yourself at your heart's virtue: you've reached Kāśī without penance.
> How would you be Śyāma's better half? I am not worthy of you.
> Don't you ask Sūraj's Lord, why he does not go there?" (*SS* 4064/3446)[125]

Here she goes as far as to humbly give Rādhā precedence and declare herself nothing but a servant of Rādhā, too. The last lines are somewhat ambiguous, though, not helped by the many possible readings of the Braj original. The most logical meaning seems to be that Kubjā challenges Rādhā to confront Krishna herself. However, Rādhā has complained that the problem is that she cannot get through to Krishna. Is there some sarcasm in Kubjā's remark? Is she showing her true colors here at the end?

It is true, Kubjā herself is not above jealousy. What we've just heard was only the written and official version of her message. There is an interesting informal verbal comment that she asks Uddhava to convey. Humble as she may be in the letter, she is in the strong position here, and she knows it. And she is not above a bit of revenge. After all the Gopīs have accused her of, she can afford a bit of counter-accusation. It is not in the official letter—she will not get caught by the lawyers, so to speak. But she certainly gives Uddhava an earful as she asks him to deliver her diplomatic letter:

> Uddhava, I beg you, please go to Braj.
> Give this letter into Rādhā's hands, that's what I ask from you
> "Curse me from when you get up in the morning. I keep on hearing that slander:

125. *ūdhau yaha rādhā sauṃ kahiyau; jaisī kṛpā syāma mohiṃ kīnhī āpa karata soi rahiyau; mo para risa pāvatiṃ binu kārana, maiṃ hauṃ tumharī dāsī; tumahīṃ mana maiṃ guni dhauṃ dekhau, binu tapa pāyau kāsī; kahāṃ syāma ko tuma aradhaṃgini, maiṃ tuma sari kī nāhīṃ; sūraja prabhu kau yaha na būjhiai, kyauṃ na uhāṃ lauṃ jāhīṃ.*

'Nanda's darling son went and became king, then he got a deformed woman for his queen!'
Why are you angry with me? Anger can't keep Śyāma.
From when he was little, Mother Yaśodā tied him up, because you said he ate your butter.
You held the ropes, you were the big guys, you too, daughter of Vṛṣabhānu!
Sūr's Śyāma will return to Braj . . . is he such a fool?" (SS 4063/3445)[126]

Now how is that for hitting right on the weak spot? She argues that the situation is not her or even Krishna's fault. The Gopīs have only themselves to blame. They were the ones who chased Śyāma away. They have bullied him since he was a kid. It will take some time for him to get over that. She continues in that vein:

You'll have to listen, Uddhava, and take my message when you go to Gokul,
When you return tell these Gopīs just one word from me:
"Get it in your head that Śyāma came to Mathurā, for love of his parents.
Kānha is not your beloved, just like he is not Yaśodā's son.
Look in your own hearts and think, what happiness have you given him?
He was just a kid, and you, lusty milkmaids, fleeced him completely.
For a cupful of yoghurt or butter, you made him fear Yaśodā.
You all laughingly ran to tie him up, why would he have pity on you?
What Vṛṣabhānu's daughter did there, you all know well in your hearts
Braj's playboy gave up all modesty for her! Now what's she sad about?"
Sūrdās's Lord, hears such matters, his head bowed low on the ground.

126. *ūdhau brajahi jāhu pā lāgauṃ; yaha pātī rādhā kara dījau, yaha maiṃ tumasauṃ māṃgauṃ; gārī dehiṃ prāta uṭhi mokauṃ, sunai rahati yaha bānī; rāja bhae jāi naṃdanaṃdana, milī kūbarī rānī; mopara risa pāvaiṃ kāhe kauṃ, baraji syāma nahiṃ rākhyau; larikāī taiṃ bāṃdhati jasumati, kahā ju mākhana cākhyau; raju lai sabai hajūra hoti tuma, sahita sutābṛṣabhāna; sūra syāma bahurau braja jaihaiṃ, aise bhae ajāna.*

On one side Kubjā, on the other the Gopīs' love. He does not know what to say. (*SS* 4065/3447)[127]

Kubjā gets back at the Gopīs. And she makes the same mistake in interpretation as they. Rather than thinking it marvelous that God shows grace to those who love him, she considers it inappropriate and blames the recipients of living above their station. In other devotional poems, we marvel at God's amazing love, how he dances for butter he does not need, how he allows himself to be tied up, how he flaunts village gossip for love. Now, Kubjā turns it upside down. Instead of praising the Gopīs for their love, she accuses them of impropriety.

The last lines shift the focus to Krishna, who is caught in this crossfire between his lovers-devotees. He is the one who ends up humilied: God on Earth with bowed head. They all see only their side of the story: how they love him so much. And they're blind to the possibility that the other side might love him as much and that his action is just inspired by his surplus of grace. This excess of possessive love (*mamatā*) is exactly what endears his devotees to him, but we get a whiff here that it is somewhat tiring and exasperating, too.

If we come back to the realm of worldly love and the vale of tears cowives have to go through, we may especially cherish this last image, of a man whose loving of too many women backfires. The women get quite vocal in slandering each other. Caught in the crossfire, the adulterer is reduced to speechless watching, with hanging head.

Comparing the Kubjā Episooles

What can we conclude from this close look at different interpretations of Krishna's adultery? The story of Kubjā in *Bhāgavata Purāṇa* raised many problematic issues that commentators, translators, and interpreters felt compelled to address. Why does Krishna make fun of a poor handicapped woman? Is she a courtesan, of ill repute, and if so, why does he associate with her? Why does he go so far as to gratify her desire to make love to him? Does she deserve this good luck?

127. *suniyata ūdhauṃ lae saṃdesau, tuma gokula kauṃ jāta; pāchaiṃ kari gopini sauṃ kahiyau, eka hamārī bāta; mātu pita kau neha samujhi kai, syāma madhupurī āe; nāhiṃna kānha tumhāre prītama, nā jasudā ke jāe; dekhau būjhi āpane jiya maiṃ, tuma dhauṃ kauna sukha dīnhe; ye bālaka tuma matta gvālinī, sabai mūṃḥa kari līnhe; tanaka dahī mākhana ke kārana, jasudā trāsa dikhāvai; tuma haṃsi saba bāṃdhana kauṃ daurīṃ, kāhū dayā na āvai; jo vṛṣabhāna sutā uta kīnhī, so saba tuma jiya jānau; tāhīṃ lāja tajyau braja mohana, aba kāhaiṃ dukha mānau; sūradāsa prabhu suni suni bātaiṃ, rahe bhūmi sira nāe; ita kubijā uta prema gopikani, kahata na kachu bani āe.*

TABLE 5.4. Different Versions of Kubjā's Story Compared

	BhP	SS	TVK
Introduction/Commentary	Pretty but hunchback Hint she's a courtesan	Low-caste hunchback "Ways of city women"	Not pretty hunchback No courtesan allusion
Initial Exchange	K. approaches her	She approaches K.	K. waylays her and she tries to escape
Reaction to Krishna Calling Kubjā "sundarī"	She's flattered	No reaction described	She objects, relates her woes K. explains about inner beauty
Sandal Paste Incident	K. asks for paste He promises good result Kubjā gives, is charmed K. gets sandal paste	She offers paste right away No promises Kubjā gives unbidden K. gets sandal paste	K. does not ask for paste He predicts end of curse Kubjā gives as self-surrender K does not take sandal paste
The Miracle	After she gives sandal paste Reward of *darśana*	After she gives sandal paste Divine grace	Before he gets sandal paste End of curse, thanks to her *tapas*
Interpretation of Miracle	Gratuitious	Penance from previous birth Hints at insults during life	*Tapas* as Śabarī; he owes her Dwells on miserable current life
Kubjā's Proposition	After miracle Sexual No mokṣa	After she gives sandal paste Devotional massage, hint of passion No mokṣa	Before miracle devotional massage Spiritual transformation
Krishna's Reaction	Promises but winks	Promises and comes indeed	Promises when she's still ugly
Fulfillment	Separate episode	Blended with meeting	Not shown
Background of the Rendezvous	House of pleasure Kubjā acts as courtesan Kubjā prepares house and body No hint of marriage	Kubjā's home, neutral Kubjā acts as devotee (touches feet) Kubjā forgets about house and body Jealous interpretation: he has married Kubjā, He killed Kaṃsa for Kubjā	

(continued)

TABLE 5.4. *(continued)*

	BhP	SS	TVK
Idea of Mismatch	Sense of impropriety	Jealous perspective: mismatch by Creator, pathetic	
	Krishna follows “ways of world”	jealous perspective: she leads him to live above status	
Nature of Mismatch	Kubjā is public woman	Kubjā has low social status	
Kubjā’s Worthiness	Kubjā is unworthy	Worthy: penance of previous birth	
	Her only virtue is giving sandal paste	Jealous perspective: she seduced him with sandal paste	
	Kubjā is unlucky	Is extremely lucky	
Reasons for Fulfillment	Lord knows devotees’ wishes	To give grace beyond comprehension	
Gopī Reaction	Jealous about city women	Jealous about Kubjā	
	Resigned: sad and wistful	Gamut of feelings: disbelief, resignation, anger	
	One girl indignant: he is cheat	Krishna cast as Kubjā’s victim	
	Solidarity: league of the maligned	Conformist: opposed to mismatch	
Kubjā’s Reaction	not described	In writing: humble, Rādhā’s servant	
	not described	Orally: insulting back: accuses accusers of cheating God	

In the vernacular devotional milieu, the scandals have been downplayed, and the official take on the last question is that yes, she was deserving, just by her simple love. Her love is portrayed not as that of a courtesan but of a devotee. Even so, she is of lower caste. Thus, Krishna's response to her is transgressive by worldly standards, but, according to the bhakti perspective, this is not a problem; rather, it illustrates the amazing saving power of God, which is beauty- and caste-blind.

However, at the same time, within the same corpus of poetry, there is also a subversive undercurrent to this official interpretation. The reaction of the Gopīs to Kubjā's transgressive love for Krishna is one of ridicule and accusation. They call it pathetic and think Kubjā is living above her station. Moreover, they see her as not only keeping Krishna in Mathurā away from them but also as leading him astray, causing him to murder Kaṃsa and take the throne for himself. Kubjā in turn finds fault with the Gopīs' transgressive love: they abused Krishna, making him dance for a little butter and causing his mother to tie him up.

Thus, the devotee whose love for Krishna is transgressive herself become a spokesperson for conservative morality with regard to others. Devotees seem to have a hard time allowing others the same privileges they enjoy. It is not easy to accept God's caste- and merit-blind love when it comes to those other than oneself. That viewpoint, though, is what receives most of the poet's attention. The female jealousy is explored at length, and all sides get a sympathetic hearing. Why would the devotional poet be so attracted to the less-than-lofty interpretation of Krishna's love? The implication seems to be that this jealousy is worthwhile because it stems precisely from their great love, and in the end endears them to God.

The modern television version has a different focus; it is mainly concerned with absolving Krishna of the accusation of impropriety and with desexualizing Kubjā. Kubjā's ugliness and suffering is stressed; there is no hint that she is a courtesan. Krishna only seemingly teases her, but he is actually serious. He calls her beautiful because he sees through appearances and recognizes her inner beauty. He is not after her sandalwood paste, which he does not even get hold of in the end—he is after her soul. Kubjā's gift of sandal paste stands symbolically for self-surrender. The incident is really a catalyst for Kubjā's spiritual transformation. Her bodily transformation seems secondary. Erotic desire and charming, jealous outbursts have been set aside to make room for humble submission to God. In the process, Kubjā now becomes eminently worthy to receive Krishna's grace. In fact, she has become worthy of him through her penance in an earlier life; more specifically, she can be identified as an incarnation of the old, devoted mother figure Śabarī. God's grace may seem random, but it is not; there is a sense that the cosmic books on merit and sin are being kept carefully. God is really just paying off the debts. Paradoxically, in his attempt to give Krishna a clean sheet of divinity, Sagar ends up reducing his divine grace to cosmic bookkeeping.

What is the message sent here to mortal women whose husbands have gone off to the city and found solace in the arms of another woman? What do women learn about coping with their cowives? Not much, it seems. Men just do what they do, and there is not much that can be done about it. Only in the devotional version is there a lot of attention to the women's perspective. No solutions are offered, but at least all voices are heard. There is space for airing all the grievances, but the adulterous beloved is rarely confronted directly. The women reflexively blame each other. Anger is displaced from the beloved to the rival. This is not going to lead anywhere, just to more tension and acrimony. The only chance for compromise comes with Kubjā's letter, wherein she shows humility and declares herself a servant of Rādhā. The message is obviously that it is up to women to rise above their jealousy, accept the situation, and humbly serve the rival for the sake of peace.

Kubjā and Śūrpaṇakhā Compared

Comparing earlier and later versions of the Śūrpaṇakhā and Kubjā myths, we find that in both cases the tone of these episodes changes. The earliest versions are burlesque, impossible seduction scenes of grotesque women comicly in love with handsome heroes. The contemporary versions are serious; the seductresses are less absurd. There is no more joking around in either case. The musical score sets a different mood: Śūrpaṇakhā has become threatening, Kubjā a serious devotee.

How do the main actors fare over time? The heroes are absolved from blame. Rāma was vulnerable to the reproach that he hurt a woman, Krishna that he consorted with a prostitute. In both cases, the whiff of scandal is downplayed and nearly eliminated in the television series. The heroes have become more solemn and more in control. They do not wince but keep smiling beatifically throughout the episodes.

Śūrpaṇakhā and Kubjā have grown further apart. They have become two different sides of a coin: the first the evil, self-assured seductress, the second the good, humble devotee. Kubjā has become remarkably desexualized. She does not approach Krishna with libidinal intent. If there is a question of sexual attraction, she has channeled her sexual energies toward the higher aim of self-surrender. Interestingly, this trend is already there in the medieval version. Bhakti, it seems, is keen on preserving propriety.

As regards the reactions of Sītā and Rādhā, that is not the focus of attention in most of these scenes. For Sītā, we get the impression that Śūrpaṇakhā is not a serious rival at all. Though Sītā nearly becomes a victim of the aggression of her rival, she is saved in the nick of time in all versions. Her feelings are not expressed. It seems that the good wife is simply to look on without complaint or action and see how the situation evolves. Rādhā is nowhere on the scene when Krishna meets Kubjā, yet her feelings are voiced at length, though only in the medieval version. She is restrained in blaming Krishna, but Kubjā certainly gets a good sauce. And Kubjā responds in kind. All this fits well the stress in bhakti on feelings and in particular on a sense of intimacy with the beloved (*mamatā*).

Sagar has chosen not to pick up on this mutual jealousy and its implications. On the contrary, the scene is totally purged of allusions to a potential sexual encounter between Krishna and Kubjā. Thus there is no intimation that Kubjā could be Rādhā's rival. Kubjā's love is purely spiritual; she engages in austerities (*tapasyā*). As usual, Sagar's instincts fit well with that of popular Hindi movie directors—after all, he is one himself. I will analyze in detail two popular Hindi movies on the theme of female rivalry that confirm this trend toward spiritualization of the love of the other woman.

Śūrpaṇakhā and Kubjā in Popular Cinema

Many Hindi movies tackle in one way or another the theme of the other woman. Love triangles of one man and two women abound. Very often, the hero and heroine are separated for some reason and a second woman, commonly a loose or low-caste woman, comes along to lure the hero away. The hero may be temporarily besotted, or pushed into the other woman's arms by circumstances, in which case we may come close to a Kubjā scenario. Or he may, in good Rāma-like fashion, resist temptation. In any case, the focus is rarely on the man's quandary, because the temptress usually is such an impossible partner—either low-caste or a caricature—that she cannot form a real threat (unless she allegorically stands for the temptations of modernity, Westernization, or crime). Even if she does, rarely are the men confronted with their adultery. The focus is instead on how the heroine suffers but succeeds in winning him back or on what happens to the adulteress.

Śūrpaṇakhā, the Vamp

We find there is no dirth of Śūrpaṇakhā-like characters in Hindi movies. Indeed, the vamp is one of the famous stereotypes of Hindi movies, and played a significant role at least till the 1970s (Virdi 2003: 167–70), with faint echoes still apparent in many contemporary movies. In the Śūparṇakhā vamp scenario, the perspective of the situation tends to be through the eyes of the legitimate wife or fiancée, without much sympathy for the seductress. Just like Śūparṇakhā, she is often otherized and demonized as non-Aryan—in Bollywood, the Anglo-Indian or Westernized woman.[128] A prime example of the contrasting of the good heroine with the bad vamp is of course in the all-time classic *Shri 420* (1955; d. Raj Kapoor), wherein the hero is caught between two women, the upright schoolteacher Vidya ("wisdom") and the crooked trickster-seducer Maya ("delusion").[129] In more recent movies, it may be the NRI woman, raised in the West and sometimes redeemable by an Indian hero.

Let me be clear that I am not trying to argue that the vamp character can be reduced to or finds its origin in the Śūrpaṇakhā story. Obviously, there are resonances with the philosophical concept of *māyā*. Moreover, there is a long folk tradition of stories that warn men about seductive strangers who turn out to be dangerous nonhuman, sometimes vampire-like creatures, sometimes *yakṣīs* or *nāginīs*. They are rumored to seduce men only to devour them. The vamp motif seems to owe something to this popular vampire warning literature with the theme "Men, beware." Still, in some interesting movie scenes, the hero is confronted with a vamp and this is compared within the movie to Śūrpaṇakhā's attempt to seduce Rāma.

An explicit reference occurs in *Hamara dil aapke paas hai*, directed by Satish Kaushik (2000). This movie resounds with *Rāmāyaṇa* references, most prominently the image of the redemption (or nonredemption) of the rape victim.[130] Priti (Aishwarya Rai) is a rape victim, but she is sheltered by Avinash (Anil Kapoor), a rich business man. They love each other, but her past and a series of misunderstandings prevent them from declaring their love to each other. In the second part of the movie, an old youth friend of Avinash, Khushi (Sonali Bendre), shows up, returning from America with the explicit purpose of marrying Avinash. Khushi has heard that Avinash is living with a woman, but shakes that off as something that happens all the time in America. Her first enthusiastic reunion with Avinash takes place in full view of Priti's friend and confidante, Babli (Tanaaz Currim). Priti shyly leads Babli away and pretends

128. For an anlysis of the Anglo-Indian vamp, see Gangoli 2005.

129. Of course, in this movie, the two women characters stand allegorically, as their names indicate, for the right and the wrong path, true Indian wisdom and the tricky foreign way of progress, epitomized in the songs each heroine sings. Vidyā sings: "Traveler, just look back for a minute" (*Jānevāle, muṛke zarā dekhte jānā*). Māyā sings: "Don't look back" (*Muṛmuṛke na dekhnā*).

130. I am grateful to my student Ranjit Saini for bringing this movie to my attention.

not to care, but Babli immediately realizes what is going on and makes the comparison with Śūrpaṇakhā. When Priti pretends she does not care, she offers: "What must have been Sītā's feelings when Śūrpaṇakhā was making out with Rāma?" Priti rejects the interpretation: "Hey, what language you're using! And she seemed a good girl, not a Śūrpaṇakhā." But Babli persists: "If she wasn't a Śūrpaṇakhā, she wasn't a Śabarī either, I'm sorry to say."[131]

The comparison might seem overdone, because Khushi is too much the spoiled, over-exuberant child to be a full-blooded vamp. Her intentions to marry Avinash have, moreover, the sanction of his parents. And she wears glasses, though stylish ones, usually the sign of the intellectual woman rather than the vamp. Otherwise, though, she lives up to the stereotype of the free-spirited woman who takes the initiative sexually. She dresses extremely provocatively and enjoys the male attention she thus gets. She is working for MTV, suggestively crooning love songs. She drops many hints to Avinash to show her love. Finally, she proposes marriage to him, publicly too, in a bowling alley, and Western-style, on one knee, with hands folded. Avinash rejects her, but while up till then their relationship has been a big joke, with lots of romping around, all joking stops here. Avinash takes her aside and seriously declares his love for Priti, and professes that he will marry her and no one else. Without much thought for his dear friend's feelings, he just leaves her after this passionate declaration.

The comparison stops there, or rather, this Śūrpaṇakhā gets the chance to redeem herself. She takes Avinash's tactless rejection well, as she sincerely wants the best for him. Her next move is to visit Priti, offering her a bouquet and telling her that Avinash loves her. The spoilsport in this movie is rather Avinash's mother (Smita Jaykar) who is under the mistaken impression that Priti is the main reason for the estrangement between her husband and son that has led the son to leave the family home to live alone. The mother has been hoping Khushi might be able to bring her son around and work a reconciliation. When she hears Khushi crying because she feels rejected, she decides to take the matter in hand and confronts Priti with her past as a rape victim, declaring that she, the mother, would die if such a disgraced woman became her daughter-in-law. Priti of course takes this the only possible way and sacrifices her own happiness for the sake of the mother of her beloved. Priti plays her part so convincingly that Avinash (who, we remember earlier, declared solemnly he would remain unmarried if Priti rejected him) even agrees to

131. *"are, sītā jī kā kyā hāl huā hogā jab śūrpaṇakhā rāmjī ko paṭā rahī thī." "e, kyā language hai terī. aur vah acchī laṛkī thī, koī śūrpaṇakhā nahīṃ thī." "...lekin ek bāt hai: agar vah śūrpaṇakhā nahīṃ thī, to phir vah śabarī bhī nahīṃ thī, sorry to say."*

marrying Khushi. Luckily, in the nick of time Khushi finds out what has happened. At her own marriage ceremony, she exposes the whole matter, and sends Avinash back to Priti.

The roles are reversed here. Avinash is passed back and forth between the two girls like a hot potato, much as Śūrpaṇakhā is passed between the men in the epic. The crucial difference is that he really is much desired by both girls, and they are each simply sacrificing for what they perceive to be his happiness. Far from being dismembered, the Śūrpaṇakhā character, Khushi, is portrayed as a victor, the mature woman who takes her fate in her own hands, confident that she can stage her beloved one's happiness, even if that scenario does not include herself.

Kubjā, the Other Woman in the City, or the Deformed Lover

Similarly, we can detect in popular Hindi movies a Kubjā-like scenario, where a woman's husband leaves for the city and stays there or comes back with a cowife. One example would be the 1986 *Naseeb apna apna,* directed by T. Rama Rao. In this movie, the wife (Radhika) goes as far as to become a servant in the household her husband (Rishi Kapoor) has established with another woman (see Derné 1995b: 198).

Again, it is not that the Kubjā story itself is the source of such narrative plots. In folklore we see this scenario play out over and over, both in songs and stories. There are multiple songs voicing the longing of the abandoned wife, and stories abound of women whose husbands leave for the city and are lured by clever city women into new relationships, making them forget all about their home, even—worst-case scenario—bringing the woman home as a cowife. In many of the stories, the denouement highlights ways a woman can act to resolve the situation, whether destructively, by taking revenge on the husband or the cowife (as in some Rajasthani folk songs; Raheja and Gold 1994: 142–6), or more positively, by scheming to bring the wayward husband back home (as in *Chabili Bhatiyari;* Sangari 2002: 247–78). Some stories take the perspective of the cowife trying to counter such moves by the legitimate wife (as in *Jungli Rani;* Raheja and Gold 1994: 149–63). Whether from the legitimate or the second wife's perspective, there is not much more sympathy for the other woman than in the Śūrpaṇakhā scenario.[132]

132. The folk themes show up also in "high literature," including Sufi romances that appropriate folk themes, literary versions of folktales, including Dholā-Māru, in court drama, including at the Marāṭha court at Tanjore (even in inscriptions of donations by rival wives, see Peterson 2004), and of course in Brahminical mythology, including Puranic stories about the cowives Gaṅgā and Pārvatī.

Many of these scenarios pop up in Bollywood, but the denouement is usually quite different from the folk scenarios. An example of a movie that stays close to the folk story is the 1975 *Jai Santoshi Ma* (directed by Vijay Sharma), which is based on a women's tale (*vrat-kathā*). The long-suffering heroine, aptly called Satyavati (Kanan Kaushal) patiently waits at home, while her husband, Birju (Ashish Kumar), has gone out to the city in search of work. Suffering from amnesia, he gets involved with a rich merchant's daughter. He regains his memory only through the interference of the goddess—thanks to the heroine's devotional persistence. The other woman disappears from the script without a trace once the husband is safely back home. In other movies, though, we find an interesting twist, very different from the folk versions: a kind of mutual accommodation between the hero's two women (more below).

A direct equivalent of the Kubjā character is not immediately apparent in popular movies, if we are looking for women with physical handicaps, except for Raj Kapoor's *Satyam shivam sundaram.*[133] The heroine, Roopa (Zeenat Aman), due to an accident with cooking oil in her childhood, has a disfigured face, which she keeps veiled. This covering up is more than made up for by the uncovering of her other body parts, in particular, breasts and legs.[134] It is not incongruent, then, that notwithstanding her disfigurement, she manages to marry her hero—but only because she has kept her face veiled from him. At their wedding, when he finds out that she is disfigured, he thinks she is an impostor. He seeks to find again the girl he loves, and the heroine in her despair takes on a double role, continuing her premarital rendezvous with him as his beloved, all the while keeping her face veiled. In playing this double game, she in effect becomes her own cowife. Out of guilt over having disappointed him in her role as wife, she plays the role of the extramarital mistress. In other words, it is out of Sītāesque wifely duty that she can take on a Rādhāesque part. (I discuss the mythological imagery in this movie further in chapter 6).

133. This movie has several explicit links with Rādhā-Krishna mythology. A poignant scene is when the child heroine assists her father in singing a *bhajana* at the Rādhā-Krishna temple for the birthday of the village's landlord's son. The motherless little girl's loneliness and longing for love is vividly portrayed as she observes the boy's doting mother kissing him. The *bhajana* she performs has the refrain "Śyāma asks his mother Yaśodā: 'Mom why is Rādhā fair and I black?' " (*yasumatī maiyā se pūchyau śyāma, maiyā rādhā kyoṃ gaurī maiṃ kyoṃ kālā*). In the film's performance context of the song, the roles are reversed, as it is a girl envying a boy and her frustration is less about appearance and more about luck in life and to some extent social rank. She seems to ask "why is he loved and not I."

134. Her revealing attire seems vaguely justified as tribal dress. Raj Kapoor had a reputation of pushing the limits of what the censor board would allow, and apart from the famous kiss that was no doubt a major crowd puller, Aman's outfits definitely push the borders of decency.

Looking for Kubjā-like seductresses minus the physical handicap, we could turn to the woman of lower social status than the hero. For one, there is the stereotype of the courtesan with the heart of gold who comforts the hero on his sojourn in the city.[135] The most prominent example is maybe in *Devdas,* best known in its 1955 version, directed by Bimal Roy.[136] The hero, Devdas, leaves for the city when his parents discourage a match with his childhood sweetheart, Paro. He finds solace in the arms of the courtesan Candramukhi. Significantly, in the most recent remake of that classic, the 2002 movie by Sanjay Leela Bhansali, the two women in the hero's life, Paro (Aishwarya Ray) and Candramukhi (Madhuri Dixit), get together and come to an understanding inspired by their mutual love for Devdas (Shah Rukh Khan). Earlier versions keep the heroines strictly separate, with barely a look at each other during a chance meeting on the street—which is not even in Saratchandra Chattopadhyaya's novelette, on which the films are based. If the progression in the Devdas remakes is anything to go by, it seems to have become more and more imperative for rivals or cowives to come to peaceful terms in the name of their common love.[137] That impression is confirmed by two other movies focusing on the theme of the other woman.

"Main Tulsi tere aangan ki": Lover Forces Hero to Marry Another

The stereotype of the low-caste cowife is well exemplified by the now almost forgotten but at the time highly successful *Main Tulsi tere aangan ki* (1978; d. Raj Khosla).[138] The main theme here is that of an illegitimate first lover who, out of great love for her man, makes way for the legitimate wife. The movie

135. On the courtesan film genre in general, see Chakravarty 1993: 269–305.

136. The same movie has also the other side of the story, the Gopīs' or Rādhā's perspective, in the theme of the abandoned childhood sweetheart, Paro. Paro's reaction when Devdās leaves the village for the city is reminiscent of the Gopīs' following Krishna's chariot when he rides away to Mathurā.

137. A twist on the theme is the seduced woman whose seducer fully intends to marry her, but circumstances prevent it. Often, the woman becomes a courtesan and ends up performing at the wedding of her seducer. Explicit references to the Rādhā-Krishna mythology may be part of such scenes, as famously in the song "Ek thī Rādhā, ek thī Mīrā," in Raj Kapoor's 1985 Filmfare award–winning *Ram teri Ganga maili.* Here Ganga dances at the wedding of her erstwhile fiancé, who thought she was dead and has been forced by his family to marry another woman, named Radha. Ganga performs the song, contrasting poignantly her own situation with the bride's. Still, Radha ends up being the other woman because her groom, delighted to see his long-lost love back, takes Ganga in his arms and chooses her over matrimony arranged by his parents.

138. It received three Filmfare awards that year: for the best movie (winning over *Muqaddar ka Sikandar* and *Trishul!*), best actress (Nutan, winning over Zeenat Aman in *Satyam Shivam sundaram*), and, interestingly, best dialogue (Dr. Rahi Mazoom Reza) (see http://tamanbollywood.singcat.com/awards/filmfare/ffaeng1978.shtml). The movie states in the credits that it is based on a novel by the Marathi author Chandrakant Kakodkar (b. 1921), *Ashi tujhi preet.* Raj Khosla's bigger hit movie, the 1970 *Do raaste,* was also based on a Kakodkar novel; in fact, Kakodkar received a Filmfare award for best story for that movie.

spans two generations, but I will focus on the first generation, the love story of a runaway prostitute (*tawaif*), Tulsibai (Asha Parekh), and a rich Rajput, Kuṃvarjī (Vijay Anand).

Tulsi is of course a name with Vaishnava connotations; it refers to the goddess of the basil plant, commonly known as Vishnu's second wife and sometimes confused with Vrindā, the goddess of Vrindāban, the site of Krishna's idyllic pastoral sport with the Gopīs. This imagery is explicitly referred to in the movie.

Though Tulsibai is a seductive dancer, she does not wish to partake in the less artistic part of her profession and narrowly escapes an unwanted customer, into whose arms her madam (*mausī*) has driven her. In despair, she runs out on the road and is nearly run over by a car; she is saved by the owner of the car, referred to in the movie as Kuṃvarjī, who gives her shelter in his mansion. Slowly love blossoms between the two. Kuṃvarjī fully intends to wed the unlucky girl, notwithstanding his mother's strong objections.

Tulsi is, however, not the opportunistic seducer one might expect. Rather, she is the long-suffering, self-sacrificing prostitute with a heart of gold. Painfully aware of her low position, she finds her highest happiness in serving those whom she loves, even at the cost of her own happiness. This comes to a climax when Kuṃvarjī's mother, in an argument about her son's affair with a fallen woman, has a heart attack. Tulsi makes up her mind to sacrifice her own happiness. She uses emotional blackmail, not unlike Kaikeyī in *Rāmāyaṇa*, but to a patriarchically sanctioned end: she forces her lover to marry a respectable girl. After extracting a promise from him that he will grant her whatever she asks, she asks him to marry the girl his mother has selected for him. She says:

> Where is there room for a Tulsi in the house, my prince, that I would dream of a house? I have been for birth after birth outside the treshold of the house. I am this era's Vrinda, prince, the harlot Vrinda, whom even Lord Krishna could not bring inside the house. My marital happiness lies in being like the Tulsi plant and staying outside the doors of this house.[139]

She follows up with the paradox "You love me, don't you? Then you will have to marry someone else."[140]

139. *tulsiyoṃ ke liye ghar meṃ jagah hotī kahāṃ hai, kuṃvar jī, ki maiṃ ghar ke sapna dekhtī. maim to janam janamāntar se ghar kī caukhaṭ ke bāhar kharī hūṃ. maiṃ is yug kī vrindā hūṃ kuṃvarjī veśyā vrindā, jise bhagavān kṛṣṇa bhī ghar ke andar na le jā sake. tulsī bankar āp ke darvāze ke bāhar khaṛe rahnā hī merā saubhāgya hai.*

140. *āp mujhse pyār karte haiṃ na, to āp ko kisī aur se śādī karnī paṛegī.*

Her sacrifice is even greater than meets the eye, because she is hiding from her lover the fact of her own pregnancy so as to get him to agree to the match his mother has made for him. After the wedding, Tulsi actively tries to make the relationship between bride and groom work, but Kuṃvarjī can only love her. When Tulsi gives birth to a son, Kuṃvarjī's mother prods the unhappy bride, Sanjukta (Nutan), to throw out this threat to the family honor. Sanjukta confronts Tulsi with her own miserable plight and blames her for it. She asks Tulsi to leave and blurts out that she has remained a virgin since her marriage. Tulsi then takes the ultimate step. She commits suicide, leaving the baby boy, the child of her love marriage. Her swan song is "Main Tulsi tere aangan ki" (nominated for the best lyrics Filmfare award, written by Anand Bakshi, sung poignantly by Lata Mangeshkar), addressed to the legitimate wife of her lover. She swears that she is only the wife's servant, and is nothing to her husband:

> I am the Tulsī of your courtyard,
> I am nothing to your husband.
> On your door, I am thirsting,
> Today the cloud has come and rained on me,
> The thirsty cloud of the rainy season.
> The parting of the hair, the *sindoor* too is yours,
> Everything is yours, nothing is mine,
> I swear by your tears.
> Why are you jealous of me?
> Alas, to me you seem,
> A childhood friend.
> What would I take away from you?
> The little I have I will give you,
> I'm just dust on your path.
> Don't go inside to cry, sister,
> Come outside and look in the street
> At the bier of your cowife.[141]

After her death, finally, husband and wife grow closer to each other, in large part because the wife repents of her resentment and shares her husband's admiration for the prostitute with the great heart. In the second part of

141. *maiṃ tulasī tere āṃgan kī, koī nahīṃ maiṃ tere sājan kī. dvār paṛe paṛe taras gaī, āj umaṛ kar baras gaī, pyāsī badalī sāvan kī. māṃg terī sindūr bhī terā, sab kuch terā kuch nahīṃ merā, mohe saugandh terī ansuvan kī. kāhe ko tū mujhse jaltī hai, āy rī mohe to tū lagtī hai, koī sahelī bacpan kī. maiṃ terā kyā le jāūṃgī, kuch na kuch to hai de jāūṃgī, dhūl maiṃ terī galiyan kī. mat ro bahnā andar jāke, dekh galī meṃ bāhar āke, arthī apnī sautan kī.*

the movie, the wife in turn goes so far in her admiration and love for her former rival that she favors Tulsi's illegitimate son far above her own. Both parts of the movie, then, are about women whose love leads them to extremes of sacrifice in countering the jealousy that is normal between cowives. In the first part, we get the perspective of the prostitute who does all for the happiness of her lover and his family. In the second part, it is the perspective of the wife (now widowed) who does all she can to honor the remembrance of the noble sacrifice of the prostitute.

The movie takes pains to transform the potential threat of the cowife into a constructive force. Notwithstanding the understandable initial tension, both women mature and see their common cause in love for one man and, importantly, for his family. Total submission to their men, to the point of self-annihilation, becomes the prescribed course of action for women: they need to overcome their selfish jealousy to serve the higher patriarchal ends.

"Souten": Radha Marries Another for Shyam's Own Greater Marital Bliss

Sawan Kumar Tak's *Souten* (1983) reinforces this interpretation even more strongly, and the word "self-sacrifice" (*ātma-samarpaṇ*) is written all over it. Here the other woman is not just of lower caste, she is an untouchable (*camārin*), which is interesting, as it is one of the few Hindi movies of the eighties that confronts the issue of untouchability. This movie seems to have been a success, and it received some Filmfare nominations, mainly for its songs. The movie is set in Mauritius. Its plot is dense with many interesting twists on the Rādhā-Krishna relationship. The references to mythology are explicit: the hero is named Shyam (Rajesh Khanna); the woman he marries Rukmani (Tina Munim); and the other woman Radha (Padmini Kolhapure).

Radha's father, notwithstanding being a Harijan, is hired as an accountant by Shyam, the owner of a small shipping enterprise, who treats him as a friend. Radha falls secretly in love with Shyam, but she is acutely aware of her caste status and admires him only from a distance, cherishing private fantasies of playing Holī games with him. And Shyam has a girlfriend, the rich Rukmani (Ruku), who refuses to have anything to do with Shyam's friend the Harijan. When Radha hears about their blossoming love and estrangement on account of her father, she complains in a prayer to her Krishna-image: "Did you have my father call me Radha to see such a day?"[142] She continues, in a

142. *suno kyā aise din ke liye tumne bābā se merā nām rādhā rakhvāyā?*

self-sacrificing vein, "The insults [of Ruku to the Harijan father] may remain unfinished, but my name will become true. There are many different passions in love: worship, sacrifice, and prayer. . . . May Shyam babu get Rukmani's love, and if possible, let me get the right to service."[143] What irony: the sensual, jealous mistress has been turned into a self-sacrificing woman committed to *tapasyā*. Nothing could be further from the medieval erotic Rādhā.

Radha's prayers are answered, and Shyam weds Ruku. However, the marriage goes quickly downhill, for several reasons. The class differences between Ruku and Shyam come to the fore, and Shyam starts feeling irritated when reminded that he married above his class and that he owes his fortune to his wife. Here is an echo of the coda of the Rukmiṇī story in *Bhāgavata Purāṇa*. However, the situation is more complex, as Ruku, behind Shyam's back, gets an operation intended as a temporary means of birth control that unfortunately makes her barren for life. The film here touches on interesting questions of who should control a woman's fertility, as well as the roles of procreation and sex in marriage. In a climactic discussion, he reproaches her: "Ruku, now your body is no longer a temple that allows for the meeting of two loving souls."[144] When she objects that he is insulting her, he retorts: "You are the one who has committed insult, towards that body that can be holy by becoming a mother."[145] Surprisingly, Ruku gets the last word just before the intermission: she gets to respond that he has gone too far, he has insulted womanhood. She blames this on his pride, which is due to his new wealth. She curses him: may he return to his state of "fisherman," in which she first met him and loved him. And she stipulates that it will not be she but God who will take this revenge. This is a remarkable reversal. While our sympathy has been mainly with Shyam, against Ruku's upper-class, selfish negligence of basic human values such as having children, these last words before the intermission succeed in raising doubts. Though she starts out the scene teary-eyed and full of remorse, Ruku turns into an avenging female with power to curse. She seems a Draupadī-like character, reacting fiercely because of an insult to womanhood.

Such marital troubles take their toll, and Shyam is depressed. When he finally meets Radha, he is understandably enchanted by her simplicity and domestic inclinations, so sorely lacking in his glamorous wife. A contrast is set

143. *cāhe apmān adhūre rah jāe par yah nām sac ho jāe. koī bāt nahīṃ, kanhaiyā. pyār ke bahutse raṃg hote haiṃ: pyār, pūjā, tapasyā aur prārthanā. ab is rādhā kī cintā choṛ do kanhaiyā, bas ek hī prārthanā sun lo. śyām bābū ko denā rukmanī jī kā pyār aur ho sake to mujhe pūjā kā adhikār.*

144. *ruku, tumhārā yah badan yah śarīr ab do pyār bharī ātmāoṃ kā milānevāle mandir na rahā.*

145. *apamān to tumne us pavitra śarīr kā kiyā jo ek mā banne kā darjā pātā hai.*

up between the rich, upper-class, selfish Rukmani and the poor, outcaste, selfless Radha. It is quite clear with whom our sympathies should be. Radha is the image of happy, cheerful domesticity. She is also a librarian, thus combining some of the traits of the Sarasvatī/Vidyā image of the good heroine in the Hindi movie of the 1950s, incorporating education and love of wisdom. Radha wants very much to worship Shyam Babu, as she calls him, without asking for anything in return. When Shyam comes to dinner with her and her father at their home, she notices that "storms are brewing in his mind." Keen on providing him with peace of mind (*śānti*), she offers to take all his sorrows onto herself.[146] When he points out that everyone has to carry his own sufferings, she answers: "I've not asked for your happinesses, but for your sorrow. Can you not even give me that?"[147] This draws him irresistibly to her as his relationship with Rukmani worsens. She seems to offer him some comfort with her simple advice: "Smile in your heart and all sorrow will go."[148] Oddly, one of her moves to cheer him up is watching a soccer game together, which seems to work. This Radha is quite a woman of her time, although she is shown literally to worship the dust of his footsteps.

No wonder, then, that after a disaster at work and consequent crisis with his wife, Shyam promptly seeks comfort with Radha. Somehow, he finds her alone at home. In contrast to the self-centered Rukmani, Radha responds with sympathy and plays the part of the servile wife: with soothing sitar music playing on the background (suggestions of Indian tradition), she tends to the wounds he has sustained in a car accident on his way to her, sits at his feet, takes off his shoes and socks, massages his feet, dries his tears, and finally provides a comforting embrace, intended to be innocent. At this point, Shyam, caressing her hair, realizes what this may lead to and frees himself of her embrace. Though a tropical hurricane is brewing outside, he gets up to leave so as not to compromise her reputation. However, Radha does not want to risk his safety and invokes the witness of Shri Krishna to protect her good name (*sab se baṛā gavāh vah hai*). There is some ambiguity in their body language: there is certainly an intimation that they might be headed to a sexual encounter, but there is also the suggestion that Radha's love is pure and her embrace nonsexual and that Shyam is in control of his feelings. We are not privy to what happens that night, but the assumption articulated during the rest of the film is that nothing happened. Thus, Radha is indeed the other woman, as

146. *apne sāre dukh mujhe dījiye.*
147. *maiṃ ne āp kī khuśiyāṃ to nahīṃ, dukh māṃgā hai, kyā āp mujhe ve bhī nahīṃ de sakte haiṃ?*
148. *man meṃ muskurāiye to sāre dukh apne āp cale jāeṃge.*

she is in mythology, but this time around, her love for Shyam does not get fulfilled. All she provides is comfort in a crisis, and no sexual gratification takes place.

Unfortunately, people misunderstand the situation, and Rukmani comes to know about Shyam spending the night with Radha. During a party, where Radha and her father are also present, Ruku makes a big scene. In a cabaret-style dance number, she makes a spectacle of herself. When an excited guest tries to kiss her, Shyam intervenes: "How dare you touch my wife" (in English). Ruku responds: "Well well, someone has touched me and you burn with jealousy, but when you came back having spent the night with another woman, do you know what fire burned my body and soul?"[149] She proceeds to publicly announce that Shyam is carrying on an affair with the Harijan woman, confronting him with Radha. Shyam denies that anything happened that night, but when Ruku puts the question, he admits he loves Radha. A revenge for mythology? Unfulfilled Rādhā's greatest wish finally publicly fulfilled? Unfortunately not.

Shyam tries to make his wife understand the situation but does not manage. Through some complicated twists in the plot, he loses both her and his fortune. Again, this is an ironic reversal of the myth, wherein Krishna leaves Rādhā to go off to fame and wealth. In the movie, Shyam is utterly destitute and stands to lose the adoring Radha, too. Radha's father, unable to suffer any longer the humiliation he has had to endure, decides to depart, taking his daughter with him. A conversation between father and daughter ensues in which Radha asks whether he, too, doubts her purity.[150] He half-heartedly replies that he may believe her but not the world, and certainly not Rukmani. Radha then gets into mythological parallels: "Rukmiṇī always doubted Rādhā, father, she misunderstood the sacred connection between Krishna and Rādhā. As for the world, people did not let even a goddess like Sītā off the hook."[151] Her father retorts: "Sītā proved her truthfulness by undergoing a trial by fire. What trial can you undergo?[152] When Radha assures him she will undergo whatever he says, he asks her to come along with him and get out of Shyam's life. Just then Shyam shows up, in need of Radha's comfort. But Radha's father refuses to open the door, and Shyam, after a sad song,

149. *acchā, kisī ne mujhe chū liyā to āg lag gayī tumheṃ, jab tum kisī gair-aurat ke sāth rāt guzār āye to mere tanman meṃ kaisī āg lagī thī, patā hai tumheṃ?*

150. *āp bhī śak karne lage merī pavitratā par?*

151. *rukmiṇī ne hameśā rādhā par śak kiyā hai bābā. kṛṣṇa aur rādhā ke pavitra riśte ko galat samajhā thā. rahī duniyā kī bāt: duniyāvaloṃ ne to sītā jaisī devī ko bhī nahīṃ choṛā thā.*

152. *sītā ne agniparīkṣā dekar apnī saccāī sābit kī thī. tū kaunsī parīkṣā de saktī hai?*

leaves defeated. Again we have an ironic reversal of the mythology. Radha is asked to go through a trial by fire, and what is asked from her is to disappear from Shyam's life for ever. She is molded in the Sītā model, except that for her there is no happy reunion in store; moreover, there never was a happy union in the first place.

Notwithstanding everything, Radha does not give up on trying to reconcile the estranged Shyam and Rukmani. When given the opportunity, she proposes to make an even greater sacrifice. She is tricked into believing that all suspicions will be removed from Rukmani's mind and Shyam's marriage will be saved if only she will marry someone else. Ever prepared to sacrifice for the happiness of the pair, Radha announces her willingness to marry whomever.[153] When her father objects to such lack of care for her own life, arguing there is no need for such a grand abstinence,[154] she declares that this is not abstaining for her but rather a positive religious praxis.[155] So this Rādhā, for the sake of her love, is married to another! She becomes *parakīyā* after all, but it is for her Syāma's sake that she does so!

As it turns out, Radha's husband is a drunk who leaves her for days on end, takes away all her money, and mistreats her. All this is revealed to the audience in a flashback: a highly pregnant Radha, dressed in widow's white, happens to meet Shyam. At first she does not want to bother him about her personal tragedies, but eventually, when she collapses under incipient labor, he gets the story out of her. The confession takes place in the hospital, with a cross figuring large on the wall behind Radha's hospital bed. She describes her husband's atrocities and her own willingness to swallow all the insults; at one point she even, in order to distract her husband from harming her father, invites him to "do whatever atrocity you want to commit on me."[156] To Shyam she describes her forbearing attitude toward her husband: "I agreed with everything, after all, he was my husband. I never obstructed him, I never stopped him. Whatever he wanted to do, he did."[157] In contrast to her mythological counterpart, this Rādhā is long-suffering, carefully constructed as not enjoying any sensual pleasure, just suffering through it for the sake of her dharma. The contrast with the ever-quarreling Ruku is of course obvious.

153. *unkī khuśiyāṃ vāpas lauṭ sakeṃ to maiṃ kuch bhī karūṃgī. unkā ṭūṭā huā ghar bas sake to maiṃ kisī bhī se śādī kar lūṃgī.*

154. *itne baṛe tyāg kī zarūrat nahīṃ.*

155. *yah tyāg nahīṃ, mere liye tapasyā hai.*

156. *mujhpe jo cāhe zulm kar lījiye.*

157. *mujhe to sab kuch manzūr thā: ākhir vah to mere pati the. maiṃne unheṃ kabhī nahīṃ ṭokā, kabhī nahīṃ rokā. unkī jo marzī meṃ ātā thā kar dete.*

Then Radha describes how she told her husband that she was carrying a child. The situation is exactly the opposite of what happened in Shyam's own marriage. Here the woman insists "Children are God's gift" (*bacce to bhagvān kī den haiṃ*), but the husband complains that he cannot feed another mouth. Moreover, he doubts her: "Low, outcaste woman! Is this the gift of god or of your lover?"[158] The stigma has stuck. Radha cannot escape the consequences of that fatal night. Her husband accuses her of still carrying on an affair with Shyam, says the child is Shyam's and vents his anger by whipping her. Radha is the willing victim, but her father is unable to suffer this, and when he finds out that his son-in-law actually also has another wife, he gets into a fight with him, during which Radha's husband is killed. Irony has run its full course: Radha, having suffered through unwanted sex, has become pregnant, and is now widowed to boot. Nothing could be further from the mythological Rādhā.

Radha's confessions finally prompt Shyam to guiltily inquire: "And for my sake, for my happiness, you had to endure everything. What kind of relationship is there between you and me, Radha?"[159] Radha replies: "Even God Krishna and Rādhā could not find the name of this relationship. All I know is that husband you are to Ruku and for me Lord. I have only worshiped you!"[160] Shyam wonders what kind of worship this is in which the worshiper's whole life gets ruined so badly. But she insists that if one gets burned for the sake of worship, it is cool as precious sandalwood, which is used for cooling effect.[161] This Radha seems intent on upstaging the devotion of her mythological counterpart.[162]

Unfortunately, notwithstanding all Radha's sacrifice, Ruku is about to divorce Shyam, whom she believes on trumped-up charges has married Radha. Shyam says he wants to turn the lie into a truth and will marry Radha. To which the filmī Radha of course reacts with a strong no. But her reason is quite interesting: "If you do that, my god will be called honorless"![163] Radha's first concern is always Shyam, whether Shyam Babu or Śyāma Bhagavān. In any case, he does not listen to her objections and promises her that he will put *sindoor* in her hair and give the baby girl his name so that Radha will not have

158. *kamīnī badzāt! yah bhagvān kī den hai, yā tere yār kī?*

159. *aur tumheṃ mere liye, merī khuśiyoṃ ke liye sab kuch sahnā paṛā! yah tumhārā merā kaunsā riśtā hai rādhā?*

160. *is riśte kā nām to bhagavān kṛṣṇa aur rādhā jī bhī nahīṃ dhūṃṛh pāe śyām bābū. bas itnā jāntī hūṃ ki pati āp ruku jī ke haiṃ aur mere parameśvar. maiṃne to āp kī sirf pūjā kī hai.*

161. *nahīṃ śyām babū, pūjā ke liye agar hāth jal jāye to vah jalan bhī candan jaisī ṭhaṇḍak detī hai).*

162. There is also a hint of her morphing into Mīrā here: her widowhood, and the talk about *pūjā* of an unattainable beloved seem to point that way.

163. *agar āpne aisā kiyā to mere bhagvān be-imān pukārā jāegā, śyām bābū.*

to suffer the world's taunts. He sets off promptly to find a priest. Will Radha finally get married to her Shyam, over her own objections?

The film script determines differently. Radha now takes an active role and pleads with Rukmani to take Shyam back. She even falls at Ruku's well-heeled feet, but Ruku frees herself and runs off, leaving Radha to sing her swan song of dedication and, like Tulsi, eventually take poison. Radha, never jealous of the real wife Rukmani, sings, teary-eyed, "I am your little sister, do not mistake me for a rival. Shyam is yours, and will remain so. I am just his devotee."[164] When Shyam arrives on the scene, it is too late to save Radha from the poison. Still, she is satisfied that "As I'm leaving, I have gotten the dust of your feet. My worship is completed, Shyam Babu."[165]

There is no *sindoor* in Radha's hair as her corpse is prepared for cremation, but there is in Ruku's hair parting when she arrives at the funeral. She pays homage to the dead Radha, and even touches her feet and kisses her cheek. Then she takes the baby from Shyam's arm, and the last image in the film is that of the bier being carried by Shyam with Ruku and the baby right at his side. In this film version, remarkably, Radha has not gotten to enjoy any sensual pleasures; yet, ironically, her function has been to bring Shyam what he has most desired: a baby girl. It is as if the scriptwriter, Kamleshwar, has deliberately set out to subvert the Rādhā-Krishna romance. This has nothing to do with carefree, intense, mutual passion. Instead, this filmī Radha has upstaged even Sītā in selfless devotion, to the point of utter self-annihiliation.

I hardly need to make the point that compared to mythology, these modern films come out quite a bit more on the conservative end on the topic of cowives. There should be no jealousy, and the legally wedded upper-caste and upper-class wife always takes prevalence, even though the lower-caste sweetheart may upstage her in sacrificial spirit. Both should be dedicated to the husband-lover's greater good, which is defined as social status and economic clout. Sensuality is to be kept to a minimum. Ideally, the cowife provides pure, subservient relief from stress, while the wife is the legitimate recipient of the husband's sexual affections and of course of the ensuing progeny. In these film versions, we do not find a displacement of anger from the beloved to the cowife but of love to the legitimate wife and the beloved's honor and family. The submission of the heroine to patriarchy is complete and unquestioning. It inevitably leads to her own annihilation because she herself is a blot on the

164. *maiṃ terī choṭī bahinā hūṃ, samajh na mujhko sautin. śyām tere haiṃ, tere raheṃge maiṃ to unkī jogan hūṃ*. The reference to herself as *jogan* again evokes Mīrā imagery.

165. *jāte jāte āp ke caraṇoṃ kī dhūl bhī mil gayī. merī pūjā pūrī ho gayī śyām bābū*

hero's record. In view of all this one cannot be surprised at Sagar's transformation of low-caste Kubjā with her prostitute connotations into a self-sacrificing woman who will wait chastely for a Krishna who never comes.

Conclusions: Do Not Blame Your Husband

The comparison of three navigational points for the other woman shows that the persistence of attitudes over time is remarkable. There is not much sympathy for the rivals of Sītā and Rādhā in any of the versions I have looked at. Śūrpaṇakhā-type women, who are sexually assertive, are stereotyped as vamps and considered for all practical purposes racially other. There is no doubt they deserve punishment, although increasingly, over time, the hero proper takes his distance from that punishment. The task falls to a hotheaded Lakshmana type, who can be forgiven for doing the dirty job.

While Śūrpaṇakhā represents the negative example, Kubjā can be redeemed. She becomes in the contemporary version a positive example for (low-caste) women who might get involved with a high-caste man. The message is that she should channel her sexuality into safer conduits; a tone of self-surrender and humility should prevail. Sexuality is to be sublimated into long-suffering penance of the *tapasyā* type. Even so, such a woman can never expect the man to reciprocate, let alone fully have him for herself. She can only wait patiently and be grateful for the few rewarding moments she may get—maybe at the point of dying, maybe in another life. Her attitude of humble servitude is not to be reserved for the man but also to be projected onto the (higher-caste) cowife.

We do not actually hear much from the perspective of the legal wife in the Śūrpaṇakhā story. It seems that Sītā has totally bought into the patriarchal way of dealing with the situation—after all, she is portrayed as the ultimate victim of the sexual aggression of the rival. In the end, Sītā smiles, proud of her husband who has defeated all the demons that had come to revenge Śūrpaṇakhā. There is no hint she might reproach him for joking with the woman and thus endangering her and himself.

In the medieval version, we get to hear from the Gopīs. At length. However, these are not documents of female revolt against male abuse. The Gopīs do not reproach Krishna too badly. Instead, they are quick to put the blame squarely at Kubjā's feet. And Kubjā reciprocates in kind, at least in her oral commentary, whatever her official response may say. Had Sagar picked up on this theme, he would no doubt have taken his cue not from Kubjā's oral message but from her letter and her humble tone therein. He would have saved Krishna from the crossfire between jealous lovers by making the Gopīs and Kubjā outdo each other in offering their humble servitude to one another. They would have united, not in protest but in love for their men—like their movie alter egos: Candramukhi and Paro, Tulsi and Sanjukta, Radha and Rukmani.

Self-sacrifice for the interest of one's man is the prescription for wife and lover alike in popular Hindi movies. It is remarkable that while all the attention is on cowives and rivals in love, the man's guilt is glossed over. If anything, he is absolved. Our sympathy is unquestionably with the hero, whose adultery is nonexistent, misunderstood, or attributable to remarkable twists of fate that force him into another woman's arms. His intentions are always perfectly noble. Under the circumstances, his actions are always perfectly understandable. When problematic situations ensue, it is not action on the hero's part that is required to resolve the knot. Rather, the initiative comes from the other woman, who is defined as the one of lower status. Invariably, the action entails self-sacrifice, even to the point of self-annihilation.

The difference in denouement between the folk stories about cowives and the ones in the movies is striking. In both cases, the legally wedded upper-caste wife keeps her husband, but the cowives behave quite differently. The folk stories are often from a female perspective, the point of view of the legitimate wife. They focus on how she wins back her husband through her own cleverness and scores victory over the other woman. By contrast, the movies seem to be a male fantasy world where men can have it both ways. All women are totally dedicated to the man, and the cowife outdoes the wife in sacrificial spirit, even conveniently killing herself when that is what patriarchal society demands. More recently, a marked transformation of the love triangle theme has been noted, in 1990s movies that make sure the hero gets both the women (Deshpande 2005). This phenomenon may not be all that new, as our analysis of a seventies' and eighties' movies suggests, but we can still speak of a triumphant emergence of the bigamous hero.

The phenomenon in the movies is all the more interesting against the background of the calls for a unified civil code by right-wing groups, including the reinstitution of legal polygamy for Hindus. Women involved in right-wing politics seem to endorse such demands, justifying it with hopes that this will keep men home and limit the spread of AIDS (Sarkar 2005). Whether we like it or not, this paradigm seems to strike a chord and appeal to many Hindu women, as well as—less surprising—their husbands.

6

Sexual Harassment

Sītā Abducted and Rādhā Accosted at the Well

How to Cope with Sexual Harassment and Eve-Teasing

In coping with marital challenges, the threat of the other woman has for its obverse that of the "other man." In this chapter we turn to what happens when the woman is propositioned. What are her reactions, or what should they be? What are the repercussions for her marriage and the family's honor? Might she be tempted? If not, how will she resist?

Often, the threat of the other man is unwanted and can be described as sexual harassment. Movies and television series abound with portrayals of such situations. The ultimate example is abduction and rape, but less spectacular is "eve-teasing," that is, verbally or physically accosting women.[1] This phenomenon is pervasive in the

1. While there is some legal and action-directed literature focusing mainly on harassment in the workplace, remarkably little research has been published about this so-called eve-teasing. Notable exceptions are an article reconstructing the history of eve-teasing in the past century (Anagol-McGinn 1994), a sociological study based on interviews with contemporary middle-class women (Puri 1999: chap. 4) an article documenting the portrayal of sexual violence (including eve-teasing) in the popular Indian cinema of the late nineties (Ramasubramanyam 2003), and a reflection on the ethnographer's position when confronted with eve-teasing (Chopra 2004). This lack of interest may be because eve-teasing is less spectacular than rape. Still, it is very much a reality and arguably an important day-to-day problem all women, beyond class and caste barriers, have to cope with. The very term is problematic as it implies the practice is harmless and agreeable to women.

modern public sphere in South Asia. It is perpetrated by so-called Road Romeos, who practice it as a sport. If the physical harassment is accompanied by verbal action, these young men often take their cue from the movies and will express their intentions with reference to popular films, for instance by humming a suggestive love song or spouting a few lines of appropriate filmī dialogue. Thus, it is relevant to study how popular movies narrate these events. I will identify what use the popular Hindi film makes of mythology to identify the messages about sexual harassment sent to men and women. Or rather, what the male authors and directors of our texts, television series, and films think women feel when harassed and how they should react.

Many popular movies make reference to the mythology of Sītā when dealing with women being accosted. Sītā's resistance to the demon Rāvaṇa who approaches her when she is alone in the forest is a prime example of how to deal with unwanted sexual attention. Thus, it is natural to first look in detail at the abduction of Sītā by Rāvaṇa—one of the most powerful moments in the Sītā myth.

This episode was the one Gandhi singled out as a prime example of nonviolent resistance. Scholars have noted that it is at this point that the television Sītā breaks out of the mold of the passive, suffering image with which she is often associated (Zacharias 1994).[2] Still, the episode has attracted relatively little serious scholarly attention[3]—certainly less than the fire ordeal—though it is arguably a moment of great intensity and significance for the rest of the story. It is particularly relevant for the study of Sītā as role model, in that it portrays a very real experience in ordinary women's lives: being propositioned by an unwanted man and finding oneself in a situation where one is powerless. Rather than the proof of purity, this certainly is something most women have to face at some point. Indeed, women cite Sītā's courageous nonviolent resistance as a positive, empowering example (Kishwar 1997).

In the *Rāmāyaṇa*, the abduction episode proper is found in the Forest Book or Araṇya Kāṇḍa (*VR* 3.44–7; *RCM* 3.28.4–29.2; TVR vol. 11, episode 32). Sītā's nonviolent resistance to Rāvaṇa after she has been abducted and is completely at his mercy, as witnessed by Hanumān, is found in the Book of

2. Zacharias, interestingly, posits this assertiveness as a trait of the original Sītā, whom she sees as a fertility goddess (1994: 40–1). She finds resonances of Sītā as earth in the abduction passage in Vālmīkī's *Rāmāyaṇa* (42–3). She acutely observes a strong loss of the erotic in the Sītā of the television *Ramayan:* "the erotic is constantly sublimated into the pious" (43).

3. A notable exception is Sally Sutherland-Goldman's wonderful article insightfully analyzing how Vālmīki constructs womanhood in this passage of Sītā's despair (2001). She goes beyond Sītā's courageous answer to the demon and reflects on woman's dependence on others (*paravaśyatā*).

Hanumān or Sundara Kāṇḍa (*VR* 5.19–22; *RCM* 5.9–10; TVR vol. 15, episode 44). In connection with Sītā's abduction, we should also look at the incident just preceding it, which figures prominently in the popular imagination: Lakshmana drawing around Sītā the protective line that is named for him, the Lakshmana Rekhā. This circle of protection is intended to keep Sītā safe from the *rākṣasas* of the forest. For ordinary women, this line would be one that protects her from unwanted male attention. But she is safe only as long as she remains within its boundaries, so it simultaneously restricts her movements. It is often interpreted as the circle of propriety (*maryādā*) that keeps women confined to the home. Feminists tend to reject the concept as handicapping women. It is illuminating just how little of this commonplace understanding can be traced back to Vālmīki or even Tulsī. The events associated with the Lakshmana Rekhā are found in the Araṇya Kāṇḍa, just before the abduction (*VR* 3.43; *RCM* 3.28.1–3; TVR vol. 11, episode 32).

Finding a parallel for Rādhā-Krishna mythology is tricky. *Bhāgavata Purāṇa* includes a passage where the Gopīs are abducted by a demon, but this episode is little known. It occurs after Krishna has killed the snake Sudarśana (in 10.34.21–32). At the celebraton party, the Gopīs are entranced by Krishna and Balrāma's songs. A Yakṣa, Śaṇkhacūḍa, abuses the situation, and the Gopīs are "herded away as if they were cows" (10.34.26–7). When the women call out for help, Krishna and Balrāma come to their rescue. This mini–abduction episode does not figure much in popular culture, and indeed is not depicted in the television series *Shri Krishna,* nor is this theme taken up by Braj poets.

What figures importantly in the popular imagination is Krishna's own acts as an accoster, as he sexually propositions Rādhā and the milkmaids of Braj. This makes for a good contrasting parallel with Sītā's abduction. However, it seems inappropriate to term Krishna's licentiousness "sexual harassment." Harassment is by definition unwanted, whereas it is problematic to cast Rādhā and the Gopīs as not wanting Krishna's sexual attention, since they seem to welcome it. I will evaluate the issue of the complicity of the women later. For now, I shall refer to Krishna's acts as "eve-teasing," which has a less serious ring (see also Kakar 1989: 36–7).

Sexual propositioning more or less willing milkmaids is a pervasive trait of Krishna's behavior. He finds more than one occasion to do so. The most obvious cover for such activities is the licentious festival of colors, Holī, when the Braj villagers compete to soak each other with colorful substances. In the chase, men may take some liberties with women, and Krishna is the arch–Holī player, not only drenching the milkmaids but also grabbing them and tearing their clothes. Small wonder that lots of Hindi movies use the excuse of Holī celebration for erotic display, often with explicit references to Krishna's mythology, especially in the songs accompanying the images.[4]

Another notable occasion where Krishna sexually propositions the women of Braj is the adult, so to speak, version of his famous butter thievery, the butter tax episode, significantly called the "episode of the gift" (*dāna-līlā*). Here Krishna waylays the milkmaids on their way to the market and demands they give him and his companions a share of their goods as a tax before they can proceed. The bartering is for more than just milk products, as the men do not shy away from molesting the women in the bargain. Like the theme of the little butter thief, that of the adult accoster is immensely popular and is commemorated in Rās-līlās and festivals (Entwistle 1987: 53–4). It has been discussed with all its Freudian implications by Jack Hawley (1983). There are many variants on this theme, including a "boat tax līlā" (*naukā-vihāra*), where a ferryman—Krishna of course—extorts his tax from the milkmaids (55).

A similar episode involves eve-teasing at the place where the village women go to fetch water, known as the *panaghaṭa*.[5] I make this episode the focus of this chapter because of its hold in the popular imagination. The situation is immediately recognizable, for many of India's village women who have to fetch water from the well daily. Women usually carry out this chore in groups, as the well may be located a little way from the hamlet where they live and they prefer to go chaperoned. As they leave the purdah of the home, they are potentially approachable by strangers, hence the need for chaperones. Fetching water then involves a precarious temporary move outside the safe confines of the Lakshmana Rekhā of village control. If they go alone, they risk being harassed by men. The local village youths may well be loitering in the neighborhood in hopes of such encounters. They may exploit the situation, particularly when the women are on their way back home with heavy, full water-pots on their heads, which slows them down and makes it difficult for them to run away.

4. Some researchers have developed a theory that the practice of eve-teasing is an outgrowth of the licentiousness of the Holī festival, facilitated by the anonymity of urban life, suggesting a colonial origin for the practice (Anagol-McGinn 1994: 221–2). The medieval poetry documents similar behavioral patterns of males in precolonial India.

5. More accurate than "well" would be "place for drawing water," as it comes from *pānī*, "water," and *ghāṭa*, "steps leading to a body of water." In the Krishna context, it refers indeed not to a well but the spot at the river Yamunā where people can easily approach the river to draw water. However, since "place for drawing water" is cumbersome, I will throughout use "well."

The more aggressive among the village youth may even throw little stones trying to dislocate the water pot and spill or break it, so that the women get drenched and display the famous wet-sari effect. Waylaying women on the way to or from the well is a common motif in popular movies.

The theme of the woman water-carrier (*panahārin*) is frequently expressed in folk song (for Rajasthani songs, see Joshi 2000). It often involves a meeting at the well with a stranger who tries to seduce the woman with nice or not-so-nice words. Sometimes the stranger is just testing her virtue. He may turn out to be her long-awaited husband who has just returned from abroad and is unrecognizable due to some disguise. He accosts her because he wants to see whether she is faithful to him still. The woman may be annoyed, or flattered and enjoying the attention, engaging in repartee, while at the same time not giving in, as she is acutely aware of the damage it would cause to her good name. Our focus here will be on the portrayals of Krishna's encounters at the well with Rādhā and the milkmaids. In this case, the women do give in to the stranger and choose to throw all caution and all dharma to the wind.

Bhāgavata Purāṇa does not have any episode of the kind, but the *panaghaṭa* theme was popular in medieval Krishna bhakti. *Sūr Sāgar* has thirteen pages of poems under the title "Panaghaṭa līlā" (*SS* vol. 1: pp. 588–601). Nanddās uses the theme more sparingly; there are only four *padas* on the topic in his *Padābali* (80–1 and 83–4), collected with others under the generic heading "Brajabālāoṃ kā prema." In Sagar's *Shri Krishna*, there is no *panaghaṭa* episode proper, but a very similar scene that is something between a *panaghaṭa* and a *dāna-līlā*.

Though their situations are to some extent opposite, Sītā and the Gopīs face a similar problem. Both are approached by an unrelated male when alone: Sītā's husband and brother-in-law have been lured away; the Gopīs have left the village boundaries to go to the Yamunā's banks to fetch water. The harassment can only occur outside the safe boundaries of male protection, made explict in Sītā's case in the transgressing of the Lakshmana Rekhā. The man was approaches them is a stranger: often the Gopīs say they do not know who the charming dark man at the well is. Rāvaṇa approaches Sītā in disguise, and reveals his identity only later. The men try first flattering words to seduce the women, but when they are unsuccessful, they resort to violence: Sītā is dragged by the hair, grabbed by the buttocks, and abducted, but not raped; the Gopīs suffer milder forms of violence but are molested nevertheless, as they are being grabbed and touched in inappropriate places.

The fundamental difference between the scenes is where the teller and the audience's sympathies lie. Actually, both stories are told from the male point of

TABLE 6.1. Comparison of Sītā Being Abducted and the Gopīs Being Accosted

	Sītā Abducted	Gopīs Accosted
General	Sympathy with husband Sexual aggressor is villain	Sympathy with accoster Sexual aggressor is hero
Accosted When Alone	S. has sent husband and brother away Lakshmana Rekhā crossed	Gopīs on way to well Village boundaries crossed
Accoster	In disguise	"Unknown youth"
Reaction to Accoster's Flattering Words	Negative reaction	Play game; feign negative reaction
to Forceful Attack	Resists Calls for help Argues dharma Faithful to dharma and love	Give in Call for more Complain dharma, but secretly enjoy Transgress *dharma* for love

view. In the Sītā scenario, the sexual aggressor is a villain, and the audience is sympathetic to the husband of the accosted woman. In the Rādhā scenario, he is the hero, not a villain, so our sympathy is with the accoster. Consequently, the heroines differ in their basic reactions. Again, they are at opposite sides of the moral universe. Sītā resists the abductor, being a loyal wife. She calls for help. The Gopīs fall for the accoster and become adulterous lovers. They call for more. Sītā defends herself verbally, trying to shame her abductor on the grounds of dharma. The Gopīs may complain about Krishna's ways, and invoke dharma, but the bottom line is they enjoy it. Again we have a prime contrastive example of the complex ways gender and dharma are interrelated: Sītā remains faithful to her love through dharma; the Gopīs have to disregard dharma for their love.

In this chapter, I will first discuss the Lakshmana Rekhā and Sītā's resistance to Rāvaṇa, comparing how different aspects are treated in the classical, medieval and televised sources. Next, I will discuss the Gopīs' reaction to Krishna's eve-teasing. Most of this section will focus on the poems in *Sūr Sāgar,* with a brief discussion of the television series. Finally, I will discuss how these scenarios play out in popular Hindi movies, first looking at *panaghaṭa* references in the songs of three movies: K. Asif's 1960 *Mughal-e-azam,* Raj Kapoor's 1978 *Satyam shivam sundaram,* and Sanjay Leela Bansali's 2000 remake of *Devdas.* Next, I will look at a reworking of Sītā's abduction in Santosh Kumar's 1999 *Lajja,* and finally we will analyze the multiple echoes of Sītā's and Rādhā's temptations in Mehboob Khan's classic 1957 *Mother India.*

Sītā Abducted in the Forest

The abduction of Sītā consists of many scenes. One could go as far back as to link up with the previous chapter and study Śūrpaṇakhā's report to her brother Rāvaṇa. She talks up Sītā's beauty to incite him to take revenge, which is in contrast to her demeaning words about Sītā during her attempted seduction of Rāma (*VR* 3.30–2). She is successful: Rāvaṇa prepares to get the demon Mārīca to take the form of a golden deer to delude Sītā (3.33–40). Alternatively, one could start with the impression this golden deer makes on Sītā, which prompts her to send Rāma out to capture it, while Lakshmana remains behind to protect her (3.41). It is certainly significant that the abduction is made possible by Sītā's desire for the golden deer, which can be said to be her fatal mistake.

I have singled out for study here the incidents that are most prominent for the popular imagination, most relevant for Sītā's agency, and parallel with the Gopīs' reactions. I will first compare the portrayal of the events in the Araṇya Kāṇḍa. First, I look at the incidents associated with the drawing of the Lakshmana Rekhā and how it transpired that Sītā was left alone (*VR* 3.43; *RCM* 3.28.1–3; TVR vol. 11, episode 32). Then I look at the abduction by Rāvaṇa proper and the circumstances that led Sītā to cross the Lakshmana Rekhā (*VR* 3.44–7; *RCM* 3.28.4–29.2; TVR vol. 11, episode 33).[6] Finally, I will look at the scene in Laṅkā where Sītā resists Rāvaṇa's attempts to seduce her. This is in the Sundara Kāṇḍa, just before Hanumān visits her in Aśokavana (*VR* 5.19–22; *RCM* 5.9–10; TVR vol. 15, episode 44). Thus we reflect both on how Sītā was brought into a position where she could be abducted, partly through her own agency, and on her reaction once abducted. Her story can be read as a tale of warning how not to act, as well as an exemplary one of how to resist when powerless to defend oneself.

Sītā Left Alone

Why does Rāma leave Sītā alone in the forest, unprotected? This is one of the central problems with the *Rāmāyaṇa* story, especially if Rāma is understood as divine. If God is all powerfull, how could he allow his consort to be abducted? If he is ominiscient, how could he not know that Rāvaṇa would abuse his

6. The scene where Rāvaṇa is challenged by the loyal bird Jaṭāyu who tries to rescue Sītā is interesting, too, in terms of the help available to the accosted woman. However I do not analyze it here as there is no parallel in the Rādhā-Krishna mythology.

absence? There are many ways the tradition has tried to make sense of this, and it bespeaks a concern and anxiety about the need to protect women in order to preserve men's honor.

One of Tulsī's variations on the Vālmīki story addresses exactly that problem. The answer provided is that Rāma did not leave his Sītā unprotected but allowed only a body double to be abducted. Tulsīdās is not the inventor of the episode; his source text seems to be the *Adhyātma Rāmāyaṇa,* and there are several other earlier versions of this "ruse" (Vaudeville 1955: 191–2). I will look at Tulsī's verses; he inserts them as a little prologue to the abduction story. Rāma and Sītā are alone. Lakshmana has gone to gather roots and fruits in the woods. Tulsī feels the need to specify that even Lakshmana will not be in on this little secret (*maramu, RCM* 3.24.3a). Rāma addresses Sītā:

> "Listen my dear, you are skilled and good at observing vows.
> I'm about to carry out a beautiful charade as part of my mortal appearance (*naralīlā*).
> You should reside in the purifying fire, until I've exterminated the demon."
>
> When Rāma had revealed everything, she entered the fire obediently.[7]
> She left a body double (*pratibimba*), equal to her in beauty, virtue, and humility. (*RCM* 3.24.1–2)[8]

That's it; Tulsī resumes the action immediately. In just five lines he has solved the issue—a quick fix to an age-old problem. Rāma requests Sītā to "reside in the purifying fire" for the duration of the events to come; she obeys promptly. No discussion, no questions asked. A body double is provided to suffer the ignominy in Sītā's stead. Whoever came up with it, it is certainly a brilliant idea. Many problems are solved at once. It resolves all lingering doubts about Rāma's divinity: he knows everything all along and does not allow anything to happen to Sītā. We need no longer worry about Sītā's purity: she is indeed safe all along. It is merely her body double that goes through the tribulations and disgrace of being abducted. Finally, the blow of the fire ordeal, which is to come at the end of the war, when Sītā is liberated, is softened: the outrageous Agniparīkṣā is transformed into a mere burning of the body double

7. Literally: "placing her Lord's feet in her heart."

8. *sunahu priyā brata rucira susīlā, maiṃ kachu karabi lalita naralīlā; tumha pāvaka mahuṃ karahu nivāsā, jau lagi karauṃ nisācara nāsā. jabahiṃ rāma saba kahā bakhānī, prabhu pada dhari hiyaṃ anala samānī; nija pratibiṃba rākhi tahaṃ sītā, taisaï sīla rūpa subinītā*

and reappearance of the original Sītā. It is a move Sagar undoubtedly approves of; he includes this scene in a flashback just before Sītā's fire ordeal (see Hess 1999: 11–4 for an analysis of that scene).[9]

What messages does such a scene send to women in terms of role models for them to follow? Unfortunately, ordinary women, no matter how many austerities (*vratas*) they practise, are not able to literally follow Sītā's example and produce body doubles, as much their husbands might wish they could keep their honor intact by such magic. The message, however, lies in Sītā's obedience, her immediate and unquestioning acceptance of whatever her husband decides as appropriate for preserving her chastity. In that respect, the innovation is not exactly one that is empowering for women.

The "dea ex machina" of the Sītā body double makes such a brief appearance in *Rām Carit Mānas* that it is often overlooked. Indeed, many people who saw the televised *Ramayan* thought that Sītā's sojourn with Agni was an innovation of the film director (Hess 1999: 15). One could be forgiven for not noticing, as Tulsī proceeds with the rest of the narrative as if nothing had happened. Sagar of course introduces us to the secret only in flashback, so the audience will take all the happenings at face value. In that respect, it is justifiable to continue the exploration of Sītā's abduction as if it really happened.

THE AMBIGUOUS RELATIONSHIP OF SĪTĀ AND LAKSHMANA. In contrast to Tulsīdās, who moves swiftly through the action, Vālmīki devotes a whole *sarga* to the first scene, where Sītā and Lakshmana are alone in the forest hut and hear what sounds like Rāma's voice crying out for help. The audience has just witnessed Rāma killing Mārīca, so knows the cry is false, but Sītā, who does not know, is truly shaken. She urges Lakshmana to go and help Rāma, but Lakshmana does not stir. He assures her that no harm can come to Rāma. Tulsī masterfully shortens all the talking into the brevity of the *caupāī*: "How could even in a dream harm come to Him, who causes creation and destruction with a frown of his brow?" (*RCM* 3.28.2b).[10]

Vālmīki's Sītā then gets really upset and wildly accuses Lakshmana of not being a good brother, suspecting him immediately of having designs on her (*VR* 3.45.6b),[11] or being an agent of Bharata (3.45.24b).[12] She warns him that

9. One could, however, also raise the objection that the "solution" brings new moral problems in its wake. Notably, as the students in my class did in autumn 2005, one could wonder whether this means that Rāma's allies, including the monkeys, are misled and fooled into fighting a war for "shadow" reasons.

10. *bhṛkuṭi bilāsa sṛṣṭi laya hoī, sapanehuṃ saṃkaṭa parai ki soī.*

11. *icchasi tvaṃ vinaśyantaṃ rāmaṃ lakṣmaṇa matkṛte.*

12. *mama hetoḥ praticchannaḥ prayukto bharatena vā.*

he should not think she would stoop to becoming his if Rāma died; she would rather die: "That won't happen, son of Sumitrā, neither your [plan] nor Bharata's [will come about]. How could I, who clung to my husband Rāma of blue lotus color with his lotus eyes, desire a mere man like you, son of Sumitra? I will surely die. Without Rāma I will not live a moment on this earth" (3.25.7a).[13]

What is going on here? Sītā's insinuation that Lakshmana has secret designs on her is not that far-fetched. Culturally, a relaxed, sexually tinted relationship between a woman and her younger brother-in-law, called the *devar-bhābhī* relationship in modern Hindi, is acceptable. Traditionally, there is no code of avoidance between them (as there is between a woman and her elder brothers-in-law) but instead an easy familiarity and joking relationship, with apparently a possibility of some sexual intimacy. Kakar has ascribed this to the awareness of the custom of *niyoga,* the practice of marriage of the widow to her deceased husband's brother (1989: 13–4),[14] which is surely relevant here. Indeed, if Rāma were to be slain, it would be natural for Lakshmana to marry his widowed sister-in-law. Sītā declares such a scenario as out of the question, but by bringing up this suspicion, she opens up a tricky issue, so to speak.

Tulsīdās did not like these accusations. He shortens the quarrel between sister- and brother-in-law substantially and just hints at what he calls "subtle," "enigmatic" accusations (*RCM* 3.28.3a).[15] Sagar did not like it either, but he takes care to remain true to the Sanskrit version. He works some Valmikian statements into Lakshmana's words.[16] However, Sagar's Sītā is not overtly suspicious of Lakshmana's sexual or political intentions. Lakshmana gives her no cause for that: during the whole conversation he does not as much as lay eyes

13. *tan na sidhyati saumitre tavāpi bharatasya vā, katham indīvaraśyāmaṃ rāmaṃ padmanibhekṣaṇam; upasaṃśritya bhartāraṃ kāmayeyaṃ pṛthagjanam, samakṣaṃ tava saumitre prāṇāṃs tyakṣyāmy asaṃśayam; rāmaṃ vinā kṣaṇam api naiva jīvāmi bhūtale.*

14. Kakar refers to the mythological case of Sītā and Lakshmana as an illustration. Note, however, that he mistranslates the passage where Lakshmana reports the conversation to Rāma. Lakshmana does not report, and Sītā never said, that she was overcome by love for him. The line in question is *bhāvo mayi tavātyarthaṃ pāpa eva niveśitaḥ, vinaṣṭe bhrātari prāptuṃ na ca tvaṃ māṃ avāpsyase* (*VR* 3.59.17).

15. *marama bacana jaba sītā bola.*

16. Lakshmana says: "No gods or antigods, snakes or demons can defeat your husband. No way that was brother's voice. It's some trick. Do not become so impatient, sister-in-law! Keep faith" (*āp ke svāmī ko dev, asur, nāg, dānav, koī parāst nahīṃ kar saktā. yah kadācit bhayyā kī āvāz nahīṃ hai. yah koī dhokhā hai. āp itnī adhīr na hoṃ bhābhī! dhīraj rakhie, TVR* 425–6). This may well be a reworking of Vālmīki's "There's no doubt, Vaidehī, that your husband cannot be defeated by any one from among gods or men, heavenly beings, snakes, demons, ghosts, heavenly hosts, animals or titans, it unthinkable, pretty lady" (*aśakyas tava vaidehi bhartā jetuṃ na saṃśayaḥ, devi deva-manuṣyeṣu gandharveṣu patatriṣu; rākṣaseṣu piśāceṣu kiṃnareṣu mṛgeṣu ca dānaveṣu ca ghoreṣu na sa vidyeta śobhane,* VR 3. 45.11–2), and "You should unburden your heart and give up agony" (*hṛdayaṃ nirvṛtaṃ te 'stu saṃstāpas tyajyatāṃ tava,* 3.45.15b) and "Clearly that was not his voice, nor of a divine one. It was the magic of that demon, like a mirage" *(na sa tasya svaro vyaktaṃ na kaścidapi daivataḥ; gandharva-nagara-prakhyā māyā tasya ca rākṣasaḥ,* 3.45.16b–17a).

on her. Sagar carefully frames the whole conversation with all its intensity as one in which Sītā is standing on the porch with Lakshmana to her right, at the bottom of the stairs leading to the porch. She is turned toward him, looking at him, begging and taunting, but he is turned away, in profile, and keeps his eyes averted, staring at a point in front of him, while delivering his defense and explaining why he does not act.

Sagar has it psychologically right. His Sītā, in her anxiety about her husband, works herself into a tizzy. She believes the voice she heard is Rāma's and cannot understand why Lakshmana does not run off to help him. First, she accuses Lakshmana of being a coward for not doing so: "Are you not going so as to save your hide out of fear for the monsters? I never thought you would be such a coward!" (TVR 426).[17] When he still does not stir, she says he is always quick to brag, but now, when his heroism would be of use, he does not rise to the occasion. When he acts upset, she taunts him further: Rāma has been as a father to him, and now needs him, but he is too frightened and hides behind his sister-in-law: "Your brother raised you like a son. Now his life is endangered, and you're so afraid that you hide quietly behind your sister-in-law's apron!" (426).[18]

Sagar has managed to desexualize the accusation by setting up Rāma as Lakshmana's surrogate father and Sītā as a surrogate mother. There may still be a hint of sexuality, certainly in the audience's mind, which of course knows about the Vālmikian version, as well as the *devar-bhābhī* relation, but Sagar's Sītā shies away from accusing her brother-in-law falsely of sexual designs on her. In her calling Lakshmana a child, the hint of sexuality is deflected. Sagar has masterfully orchestrated this purification.

Lakshmana answers that his duty is to follow his brother's orders, which means he has to stay at the forest hut and protect Sītā.[19] She now declares that her protection does not mean a thing if Rāma is gone: "My protection? But it's

17. *kyā tum rākṣasoṃ ke ḍar ke māre apne prāṇ bacāne ke lie nahīṃ jā rahe ho? maiṃ ne tumheṃ itnā kāyar kabhī nahīṃ samjhā thā!*

18. *jis bhāī ne tumheṃ apne putra kī bhāṃti pālā hai, āj jab un ke prāṇ saṃkaṭ meṃ ā gae, to ḍar ke māre apnī bhābhī ke āṃcal meṃ chup gae?*

19. Lakshmana's words are again inspired by Vālmīki. In TVR, he says: "I have only one duty, to be obedient to my big brother's Śrī Rāma's command. And he left, telling me that I should remain right here for your protection. That's the reason why I cannot go off and leave you alone, under any circumstances (*merā ek hī karttavya hai, apne baṛe bhāī Śrī rām kī ājñā kā pālan karnā aur ve mujhe kah gae haiṃ ki maiṃ āpkī rakṣā ke lie yahīṃ rahūṃ isliye maiṃ āpko kisī bhī sthiti meṃ akelā choṛ kar nahīṃ jā saktā*, TVR 426). Compare with "You have been entrusted to me by that great soul, Rāma, pretty lady, so I am unable to suffer leaving you here" *nyāsabhutāsi vaidehi nyastā mayi mahātmanā; rāmeṇa tvaṃ varārohe na tvāṃ tyaktum ihotsahe, VR* 3.45.17b–18a). Note that Sagar drops all the flattering epic epithets by which Vālmīki's Lakshmana addresses Sītā (e.g. *varārohe*). Instead, he has him use throughout the kinship term *bhābhī*, and even *mātā* which at the same time makes the situation more recognizable to the audience and avoids the sexual innuendo.

his life that is in danger, [the life] of the one for whom I've left my whole world and chosen to live in the forest, without whom I can't live for even a second. So what's the point in protecting me?" (426).[20] Sagar has nicely worked in here the Vālmikian line where Sītā assures Lakshmana she cannot live without Rāma, while avoiding her accusation about her brother-in-law's sexual intentions.

Next, Sītā asks dramatically what the point of protecting her is if Rāma dies: "if something happens to him, I won't be able to live a moment longer. Then, sure, persist in keeping watch over my dead corpse, and stubbornly obey your brother's command."[21] Sītā now changes tactics and from tearful turns into determined; if he does not go, she will: "If you can't go, then give me your bow and arrow. Every Aryan woman knows very well how to protect her husband."[22] Again, Sītā's doubt of Lakshmana's intentions have been transformed into doubts of his courage and a challenge to his very manhood. When Lakshmana does not give her his weapons, she declares herself prepared to go unarmed and hurries down the stairs.

Note the use of the word *ārya*: Sītā is portrayed as the prototype of the Aryan woman, whose main characteristic is that she defends her husband rather than the other way around! Sagar's Sītā takes on more agency than any of the others. Still, her agency is of course totally a function of patriarchy: a woman's first task is to protect her husband. This resonates with contemporary Hindutva sentiments, where "Sita's sex is coming to the rescue of Ram" (Sarkar 1991: 2058). Note that there is no precedent for this seemingly archaic understanding of women's duty in Vālmīki or Tulsīdās.

In Vālmīki's version, Sītā's suspicions of his intentions hurt poor Lakshmana. Vālmīki puts a few misogynic utterances in his mouth "Unbecoming words are not surprising out of the mouth of women, Maithilī, that's women's nature, evidenced in this world" (*VR* 3.45.29);[23] "women turn away from dharma, are fickle, sharp, and cause quarrels" (3.45.30a.).[24] Lakshmana cannot stand it any longer and resolves to go. He evokes the forest deities as witnesses that she has wrongfully doubted him, and he utters a curse—she will suffer for this: "May all forest-dwellers observe my words as witnesses.... Since I've

20. *merī rakṣā? jiske lie maiṃ sārā saṃsār tyāg kar is van meṃ rahne āī hūṃ, jiske bagair maiṃ ek pal bhī jīvit nahīṃ rah saktī, us ke prāṇ saṃkaṭ meṃ ā gae to merī rakṣā karne se kyā lābh?*

21. *agar unko kuch ho gayā to maiṃ ek pal bhī jīvit nahīṃ rah sakūṃgī. phir mere mṛt śarīr kī rakṣā karte rahnā aur pālte rahnā bhāī kī ājñā.* Note the ironic use of the tense expressing persistence (imperfect participle with the verb *rahnā*).

22. *tum nahīṃ jā sakte to yah dhanuṣ-bāṇ mujhe de do. har ārya strī apne pati kī rakṣā karnā acchī tarah se jāntī hai.*

23. *vākyam apratirūpaṃ tu na citraṃ strīṣu maithili, svābhāvas tv eṣa nārīṇām eṣu lokeṣu dṛśyate.*

24. *vimuktadharmāś capalās tīkṣṇā bhedakarāḥ striyaḥ.*

spoken truly, but you addressed me harshly, I now curse you: you'll come to naught since you have doubted me" (3.45.31a–32).[25] He ascribes her foolishness to "woman's nature" (*strītvam*): "[you suspected me] while I'm obedient to my elder's words, because you're a woman and out of your mean nature" (3.45.33a).[26]

Sagar's Lakshmana, no doubt aware of the possibility that there might be some among the audience who would take offense, does not utter anything so openly misogynistic, but he certainly questions Sītā's mental capacities: "Sister, why don't you understand? . . . what unlucky fate has dimmed your brain?"[27] To which Sītā has her answer ready: "What greater unlucky fate can befall a woman [than that her] husband is in danger of his life?"[28]

Sagar's Sītā, then, is portrayed as irrational when confronted with the danger that her husband's life may be in danger. That is totally understandable, even laudable; thus she is not to be blamed for nagging Lakshmana until he left. She has no false suspicions and remains totally pure, acting in every respect as an ideal wife, well above the suspicions and weaknesses of ordinary family life.

Whatever she says, it is clear in all versions that it is because of Sītā's insistence that Lakshmana leaves and she remains unprotected. All versions see this as her second fatal mistake leading to her abduction. The first fatal mistake is sending Rāma away out of an irrational desire for the golden deer. The second fatal mistake, sending Lakshmana away, is caused by an equally irrational desire to protect her husband. Again, it is Sītā herself who is to be blamed. Or more precisely, it is irrational desires, so typical, for the weaker sex, that make them vulnerable to preying males.

DRAWING THE LAKSHMANA REKHĀ. Thus compelled by Sītā, Lakshmana leaves her alone so as to go and help Rāma. In Vālmīki's version, he invokes the forest deities again to protect her: "I'm off to where Rāma is, may you be well, woman with your beautiful face. May the forest deities protect you, woman with your large eyes" (*VR* 3.33b–34a).[29] He ends with a foreboding that he may not see her again after he returns. Sītā is crying and takes a vow that she will kill herself if Rāma dies rather than touch another male: "Without Rāma, I will drown myself

25. *upaśṛṇvantu me sarve sākṣī ṇo hi vanecarāḥ . . . nyāyavādī yathā vākyam ukto 'haṃ paruṣaṃ tvayā, dhik tvām adya vinaśyantīṃ yan mām evaṃ viśaṅkase.*

26. *strītvād duṣṭasvabhāvena guruvākye vyavasthitam.*

27. *bhābhī āp samajhtī kyoṃ nahīṃ? . . . kis durbhāgya ke kāraṇ āp kī buddhi itnī dīn ho gayī?*

28. *jis ke pati ke prāṇ saṃkaṭ meṃ hoṃ us nārī ke liye is se baṛā durbhāgya aur kyā ho saktā hai?*

29. *gacchāmi yatra kākutsthaḥ svasti te 'stu varānane, rakṣantu tvāṃ viśālākṣī samagrā vanadevatāḥ.*

in the Godāvarī, Lakshmana, or I'll hang myself, or I'll give up this body [jumping] off a precipice, or I'll drink a bitter poison, or I'll enter the fire, but I will not touch another man than Rāmā, not ever!" (3.45.36–7).[30] Lakshmana tries to calm down the hysterical Sītā but she refuses to talk to him, so he finally reluctantly goes to join Rām, looking back again and again (3.45.38–40).

Amazingly, we discover that there is no drawing of the famous Lakshmana Rekhā in Vālmīki's *Rāmāyaṇa*! Sure, Lakshmana entrusts Sītā to the forest gods, but that seems a rather weak precursor of the protective circle he draws in other versions. If one looks at the whole passage, including the semicurse he utters, it seems there is scope to interpret it as an ironic statement: "Very well, let the forest deities protect you," meaning: "You're on your own now." Vālmīki's Lakshmana is exasperated by Sītā's taunts and seems to say that there's no way she can be safe without him.

How about Tulsīdās? Surely he has a Lakshmana Rekhā episode? We are disappointed again. He simply states that Lakshmana's resolve flounders when Sītā accuses him, but the inspiration for this floundering is ascribed to Rāma himself (*RCM* 3.28.3a).[31] This safely takes care of any unresolved doubts about Lakshmana's actions. It is God's divine plan anyway. Tulsīdās quickly dispatches his Lakshmana, who runs off after hastily entrusting everything to the deities of the forest and the guardians of the four directions (3.28.3b).[32]

Still the Lakshmana Rekhā figures importantly in the meta-narrative, what has been called The "Ramayana tradition" or *Rāmkathā* (Richman 2001: 3–52). Thus, Sagar has to work with the modern audience's expectations, and the Lakshmana Rekhā is very much on his mind. His Lakshmana, too, has a foreboding: "Sister-in-law! Don't be so stubborn, something terrible will happen!" (TVR 427).[33] Sītā responds predictably that a terrible thing will happen if he does not go and help Rāma. She gives him a *Gītā*-esque command, telling him to stop talking and act (427).[34] It is her threat to go off to help her husband herself that finally pushes Lakshmana into the fatal decision to go against his brother's command. He asks Rāma to forgive him, after stating dramatically to

30. *godāvarīṃ pravekṣyāmi hīnā rāmeṇa lakṣmaṇa, ābandhiṣye 'thavā tyakṣye viṣame deham ātmanaḥ; pibāmi vā viṣaṃ tīkṣṇaṃ pravekṣyāmi hutāśanam, na tv ahaṃ rāghavād anyaṃ kadāpi puruṣaṃ spṛṣe.*

31. *marama bacana jaba sītā bolā, hari prerita lachimana mana ḍolā.*

32. *bana disi deva saumpi saba kāhū, cale jahāṃ rāvana sasi rāhu.* In calling Rāma the "the mythical planet Rāhu, Swallower of the Moon-Rāvaṇa," Tulsīdās hints at the happy ending of the story, rather than the foreboding of Rāvaṇa's abducting Sītā we see in Vālmīki's and Sagar's versions.

33. *bhābhī! āp haṭh mat kījie, kuch amaṃgal ho jāegā.*

34. *bāteṃ na karo karm karo—karm!*

Sītā: "All right, in order to obey your command, today for the first time Lakshmana disobeys his Lord Rāma's command."[35]

Now follows the dramatic representation of Lakshmana Rekhā. Addressing Sītā as Mother, he asks her to step back onto the porch. We see him reciting mantras and drawing a line around the hut with his arrow, while Sītā looks on in amazement. He announces that he has a special power to build an invisible wall (427–8).[36] "If anyone would have the guts to cross this 'Lakshmana Rekhā' to come inside, he will burn to ashes" (428).[37] With extreme politeness, he urges Sītā to stay within it until Rāma returns: "For that reason, Mother, I have this request for you, that you would not under any circumstance, until brother Rāma comes, place a foot outside this circle" (428).[38]

Sagar then links up this innovation to the authoritative *Vālmīki Rāmāyaṇa* by having Lakshmana invoke the forest deities: "O spirits of the forest! All living beings! I am going away, leaving mother Sītā in your caretaking. Keep her safe!" (428).[39] He then runs off, looking left and right, presumably for fear of attackers. However, Sagar's Lakshmana never looks back to Sītā. That would be out of charcter, as he did not even look at her while speaking to her. Thus, Sagar has succeeded in lending the authority of Vālmīki's version to the narrative of the Lakshmana Rekhā, which is not actually told in *Vālmīki Rāmāyaṇa* nor in the *Mānas.*

In the meta-*Rāmāyaṇa* narrative, that is, as it is popularly remembered, the Lakshmana Rekhā is drawn in a context of suspicion of erotic potential between the sister-in-law and younger brother-in-law. The man who is most suspected of desiring Sītā puts the strictest restrictions on her movement. But in none of our versions are these elements allowed to come together. Why this suppression? Is it to avoid a reading of the episode as a classical case of the male being suspicious of women because of a fear of his own sexual desires? In any case, because all the authors here are male, the drawing of the Lakshmana Rekhā may tell us more about the fears and perhaps desires of men than of women.

35. *acchī bāt hai. āp kī ājñā kā pālan karne ke liye āj pahlī bār lakshman apne prabhu śrī rām kī ājñā ullaṃghan kartā hai.*

36. *guru kī dī huī mantra-śakti se maiṃ ne yahāṃ ek adṛṣya dīvār banā dī hai.*

37. *koī bhī us lakṣmaṇ-rekhā ko pār kar ke andar āne kā sāhas karegā to vah jalkar bhasm ho jāegā.*

38. *is lie mātā merī āp se vintī hai, kisī bhī paristhiti meṃ, rām bhayyā ke āne tak, āp apne caraṇ is rekhā se bāhar na rakheṃ.*

39. *he van ke devtāo! samasta prāṇiyo! maiṃ mātā sītā ko āp kī surakṣā meṃ choṛe jā rahā hūṃ. in kī rakṣā karnā.*

The Stranger in the Woods

Once Lakshmana is gone and the drama of family relationships has played out, we see Sītā alone. Now she is to face the threat from outside the family. The forest again looms large. It is as if the camera zooms out and shows us again the whole canvas: the mysterious forest with its dangers lurking in the shadows, lone Sītā unprotected in the middle of it. Soon indeed the forest will intrude on Sītā's world. Interestingly, though, its danger comes disguised in the shape of the familiar. The world of the threatening unknown enters the world of civilization in the shape of the liminal figure of the ascetic.

BEWARE OF THE BRAHMIN-SĀDHŪ. With Lakshmana gone, Rāvaṇa sees his chance, and he comes in the guise of an ascetic (*VR* 3.46.2b), with all its paraphernalia. Vālmīki indulges in a description of how nature holds its breath when the demon approaches pretty Sītā. Several comparisons build suspense (3.5–10). Tulsīdās turns to comedy by building a contrast between Rāvaṇa's reputation as a warrior and his approaching Sītā surreptitiously: "Gods and demons were so afraid of Rāvaṇa that they could not sleep at night or eat by day. However, that ten-headed demon, like a dog, sneaked up stealthily glancing left and right!" (*RCM* 3.28.4b–5a).[40] This is a comic image, but Tulsī does not fail to draw the lesson from it and adds a bon mot (addressed to the interlocutor, the king of the birds): "If you set out on the wrong path, O Lord of Birds, your body loses its vigor and your mind grows dim" (3.28.5).[41] Sagar's Rāvaṇa, too, once he has taken on the ascetic's guise, has a bit of the comic figure: he spies left and right before entering the enclosure of the ashram, and makes some comical attempts to cross the invisible Lakshmana Rekhā, only to burn his toes and fingers. Even recourse to mantras does not help him across.

In all versions, Rāvaṇa approaches as a mendicant asking for alms.[42] Sagar casts him as a Śaiva mendicant with the appropriate *tilaka* (forehead mark), *rudrākṣa* necklace and bracelet and dressed in a cloth printed with the Mantra Om Nāmāya Śivāya. He utters the Sanskrit formula for begging alms: *bhīkṣam dehi*. In *Vālmīki Rāmāyana*, he is described as uttering sacred mantras (*VR* 3.46.14a),[43] but when he addresses Sītā, his speech is not that of the ascetic. Instead, he addresses her with flattering epithets, wondering whether she

40. *jākeṃ ḍara sura asura ḍerāhīṃ, nisi na nīda dina anna na khāhīṃ; so dasasīsa svāna kī nāīṃ, ita uta citai calā bhaṛihāīṃ.*

41. *imi kupantha paga deta khagesā, raha na teja tana budhi bala lesā.*

42. *bhikṣurūpeṇa*, *VR* 3.46.9a; *jatī keṃ beṣā*, *RCM* 3.28.4a.

43. *brahmaghoṣam udīrayan.*

is a goddess or a nymph (3.46.16–7), singling out each of her body parts for a loving description, particularly her breasts (3.46.18–23). If it were not so inauspicious, his words would provide a great quick study of flattering epithets for the would-be wooer in Sanskrit. Rāvaṇa then dwells on how inappropriate it is for her to be alone in the forest, ironically alerting her to its dangers, including the presence of demons (3.46.24–5a and 29–31). He tells her she deserves better (3.46.25b–26), especially a protective husband, and inquires who her husband might be.

Tulsī summarizes it as "Rāvaṇa made nice small talk of all kinds, he showed some diplomacy, threats, and love" (*RCM* 3.28.60).[44] He does not specify or quote any of Rāvaṇa's flatteries, as if refusing to give the evil demon any airtime. Sagar, too, restrains his Rāvaṇa Possibly he is reluctant to let the sacred Brahmin ascetic, elsewhere celebrated in the series, be dragged down as a lecherous hypocrite. Rather than having him utter compliments to the lady, Sagar concentrates on the irascibility of the ascetic, who is asking for shelter and demands to be treated with respect.

Sagar hits a nerve: there is something unsettling about the ploy of the disguise as an ascetic. We may well wonder why the mighty demon takes the trouble to approach hapless Sītā in disguise, especially in the versions where there is no question of the Lakshmana Rekhā. Why is the danger coming from the forest, from the other, transformed into one that is more of the world of civilization, be it a liminal character in the shape of the ascetic? If we were intent on reading against the grain, we might detect a hint of a suggestion that the threat to women's honor is not necessarily coming from outside the Aryan fold. Should one suspect ascetics of a demonic alter ego rather than the other way round? This would be of a par with reading Sītā's wild accusation of Lakshmana as suggestive that the threat to women's virtue may well come from within the family, within the very Lakshmana Rekhā drawn for her protection. Whatever the value of digging up such subsurface tensions, they are easily submerged in the rest of the story where Rāvaṇa's demonic nature will figure large.

DO NOT CROSS THE LAKSHMANA REKHĀ. In Vālmīki's version, Rāvaṇa's disguise works well. Initially, Sītā's suspicions are not aroused and she falls into the trap. Deceived by his appearance, she immediately offers him hospitality. Vālmīki exonerates his heroine of potential suspicion that she is susceptible to lecherous words by stressing that she is kind to the ascetic because she per-

44. *nānā bidhi kari kathā suhāī, rājanīti bhaya prīti dekhāī.*

ceives him to be a Brahmin.[45] Understood is that she is obligated to lend a Brahmin ascetic special hospitality. Vālmīki says explicitly that she responds to his questions and tells him about herself because she is afraid of being cursed by him (*VR* 3.47.2a).

That is the line of apologetics Sagar follows. His Rāvaṇa does not act the Don Juan in the beginning but sticks to his role of ascetic. It is thus more understandable for Sītā to play the part of the good hostess right away, apparently without suspicions. She innocently tells the ascetic he cannot come into the hut because her husband is not home, a piece of information he of course cherishes. When she brings the food out for her guest, she remembers her brother-in-law's command. She hesitates to cross the Lakshmana Rekhā to take the food to the ascetic, who is seated on a mat a little distance from the hut, and asks him instead to come and take the food from her. Her guest is unwilling to get up, claiming he is tired from his journey and cannot get up again. Annoyed by her refusal to come to him, he accuses her of slighting a guest. Sītā assures him she intends no insult and again straightforwardly tells the ascetic that she cannot leave the hut because of the Lakshmana Rekhā: "The real reason is that my brother-in-law has for my protection drawn a borderline and implored me solemnly not to go outside this borderline of propriety."[46]

Sagar has Rāvaṇa seated facing the camera, but with his back to Sītā. Thus, the audience can see his facial expressions, which betray his true reactions. He is obviously pleased with this information. However, Sītā only hears his voice. Rāvaṇa plays the insulted Brahmin ascetic and lectures her. He is indignant that she first denied him access to her hut, and now wants to throw his food at him: "As if I were some animal. That is how low-castes are treated. When a holy man comes to your door, you respectfully go to him yourself and touch his feet before giving him the alms."[47] He threatens he'll go away and curse her. Dramatically, he gets ready with his water pot, preparing to give his curse binding power by sprinkling water. Sītā stays put but tries to stop him with words, pleading he has misunderstood her. Rāvaṇa says he understands very well, in fact, he knows her husband is chasing a golden deer, which has attacked him already once, and he will curse him with—. . .

The threat of a fatal curse to her husband finally compels Sagar's Sītā to transgress the Lakshmana Rekhā. She tearfully hurries toward the ascetic to

45. *dvijātiveṣeṇa hi taṃ dṛṣṭvā, VR* 3.46.33a; repeated in 3.46.35a and further on, *brāhmaṇavat*, in 3.47.35b.

46. *vāstav meṃ mere devar merī surakṣā ke liye ek sīmā kī rekhā khīṃc gaye haiṃ aur apnī śapat dekar kah gaye haiṃ maryādā kī sīmā ko tyāgkar bāhar na jānā.*

47. *jaise ham koī paśu-pakṣī ho. aisā vyavahār nīc jāti ke logoṃ se kiyā jātā hai. koī sant-mahātmā dvār par ā jāe to baṛe ādar se svayam us ke pās jākar uske caraṇ chūkar bhīkṣā dī jātī hai.*

stop him, begging for forgiveness, again irrational in her worry for Rāma. Immediately Rāvaṇa drops pretenses. He says he will not curse her husband because he cannot stand seeing a beautiful woman in trouble. But Sītā, in her relief, does not immediately catch on to the danger. She innocently thanks him and answers his questions as to her identity.

DROPPING DISGUISES. In Vālmīki's version, too, Sītā is deceived.[48] She meekly answers the ascetic's questions and even tells him her story. At the end, she innocently asks Rāvaṇa who he is. He introduces himself as Rāvaṇa, feared by all, and comes immediately to his point, inviting her to become his first queen (*agramahiṣī, VR* 3.47.28). At this point, meek Sītā turns into a fierce rhetorician. She declares her vow of fidelity to Rāma, repeating solemnly at the end of each of four verses "I am devoted to Rāma" (*ahaṃ rāmam anuvratā;* 3.33–6b). The rest of the verses she fills with epithets for Rāma that are intended to frighten Rāvaṇa. After this impressive declaration of fidelity, she indicates he cannot touch her: "However you, a jackal, desire me, a lioness, impossible to obtain. I can no more be touched by you [than by] the glow of the sun" (3.47.37).[49] She continues with a whole set of comparisons to show the impossibility of the fulfillment of his desires, ending each verse on the word *icchasi,* "you desire," and filling the object slot with equivalents of "the impossible" (3.47.39–44). Then she vehemently argues that the demon is infinitely different from her husband, again using comparisons within a frame of repetition, this time with a relative-correlative construction at the beginning of each half line; "what difference there is between . . . that's the difference between you and Daśaratha's son" (*yad antaram . . . tad antaram dāśarathes tavaiva ca,* 3.47.46–7).

In contrast to the deceived Sītās of Vālmīki and Sagar, Tulsī's Sītā sees right through the ascetic with his Casanova tricks, and she tells him so, too: "Listen you Mr. Holy Ascetic, you speak like a crook" (*RCM* 3.28.6b).[50] When Rāvaṇa then assumes his terrible form, she fearlessly challenges him: "Sītā

48. Vālmīki seems to have deliberately construed Rāvaṇa's seduction parallel with that of Śūrpaṇakhā. Rāvaṇa approaches Sītā in disguise and with seductive intent, as his sister did Rāma. Like Śūrpaṇakhā, he starts the conversation by asking who she is, remarking that her presence in the forest is odd, and Sītā responds, like Rāma, by answering straightforwardly and telling their story. Like Śūrpaṇakhā, Rāvaṇa is blunt in propositioning and sure of his superiority, insulting the rival party, in this case Rāma himself. Like Śūrpaṇakhā, when spurned and angered, he takes on his real demonic form. The difference of course is that Sītā does not joke with the demon and that he can force her to come with him. In the end, whether demon or human, the women are the losers.

49. *tvaṃ punar jambukaḥ siṃhīṃ mām ihecchasi durlābhām, nāhaṃ śakyā tvayā spraṣṭum ādityasya prabhā yathā.*

50. *kaha sītā sunu jatī gosāīṃ, bolehu bacana duṣṭa kī nāīṃ.*

said with great forebearance: 'Stay there, crook, my Lord is coming back in a minute. Like the low hare who desires the lioness, Lord of the Demons, you've invited your death!' " (3.28.7b–8a).[51] Sītā gets the last word here. In contrast to Sagar's irrationally worried Sītā, Tulsī's has total faith in her husband, enough to threaten the demon that Rāma is about to come back. Not only that but Tulsī says Rāvaṇa is impressed with her fidelity. Though he shows anger outwardly, in his heart of hearts he admires her and is pleased (3.28.8b).[52]

By contrast, in Vālmīki's version, Sītā's rejection and her denigrating words do not go down well with Rāvaṇa. He feels the need to reassert his prowess by boasting of his family lineage and advertising the beauties of his Laṅkā (*VR* 3.48.1–13). He assures Sītā that she will quickly forget this Rāma, what use does she have for a prince who has lost his kingdom anyway (3.48.14–6)? He then threatens her that spurning him will do her harm and invokes mythological precedent (not unproblematically, the story of Urvaśī and Purūravas, 3.48.18). Sītā answers him in kind, saying one may be able to get away with abducting Indra's wife Śacī, but not with violating a woman like Sītā (3.48.23–4). In order to convince her of his prowess, Rāvaṇa reveals his true form and boasts he is the only worthy husband for her, further belittling Rāma (3.49.1–14). Interestingly, he promises her that if she is devoted to him, he never will displease her (3.49.12).[53]

All along, it is clear that Vālmīki's Rāvaṇa thinks that Sītā is deluded, sticking with the mere human Rāma because she does not realize the extent of Rāvaṇa's might. There is no hint that he might admire her fidelity or guts to defend herself, although some commentators read much into the text to affirm that Rāvaṇa is really a devotee (be it of the lower variety, a *tāmasa-bhakta*) of Sītā (see Pollock 1991: 315).

To return to Sagar's version, when Sītā tells the ascetic who she is, he expresses his surprise at seeing such a noble and pretty woman in such destitute surroundings. He suggests she is wasting her youth and she should marry a mighty king. She rhetorically asks who could be a better husband than Rāma. He misunderstands it as literally a question, and in response gets up, dramatically recommending the king of Laṅkā, Rāvaṇa. Sītā reacts with disgust and finally realizes he must be a holy man in disguise only. She challenges him and asks him who he is to make such a suggestion. Again, he takes the

51. *kaha sītā dhari dhīraju gāṛhā, āi gayaū prabhu rahu khala ṭhāṛhā; jimi haribudhahi chudra sasa cāhā, bhaesi kālabasa nisicara nāhā.*

52. *sunata bacana dasasīsa risānā, mana mahuṃ carana baṃdi sukha mānā.*

53. *naiva cāhaṃ kvacid bhadre kariṣye tava vipriyam.*

rhetorical question literally and reveals himself, taking on his real form and inviting her to be his queen.

Sītā now gets quite a few good lines of defiance. She indignantly wonders whether he thought she would just come along with him after hearing who he was. She threatens that Rāma will extinguish him and his Laṅkā with one arrow. He boasts of his prowess in Valmikian style. But Sītā reminds him that his brothers have already been defeated. She uses the same jackal simile as in Vālmīki and then simply tells him to leave. Sagar's Rāvaṇa, then, is challenged quite a bit more than Vālmīki's, no doubt to the delight of the audience. He says that no one has challenged him like this before and asks her rhetorically whether she knows what the consequences of challenging him are. Now Sītā gets to answer this rhetorical question with a good one of her own: "And no one has foolishly tried either before to cast such an evil eye on a faithful wife. Do you know its consequences?"[54] This Sītā is far from meek; she stands up against her harasser, sure of herself. However, the reason she is so sure of herself lies in her faithfulness (*pātivratya*). It is obvious that only the woman who is blameless can hold her head high. And it is exactly on this point that Rāvaṇa sees her weakness and manages to gets his way.

Rāvaṇa points out that Sītā is in no position to boast of her faithfulness, since she has just crossed the Lakshmana Rekhā: "Once a woman crosses the line of respectability, it becomes impossible to return."[55] Now Sītā realizes the full extent of her plight. The impossibility of getting back behind the defensive Lakshmana Rekhā is taken quite literally. No matter how Sītā tries to, indeed she cannot return behind the invisible wall. She can only cry out for help, but, somewhat surprisingly, does not try to run away. Rāvaṇa just laughs.

This interpretation of the Lakshmana Rekhā sends a vivid message to women. It is a protection that works only under the condition one stays inside it. Once crossed, there is no returning. A woman who has left the protection of her home cannot expect to be taken back. This is enacted literally on the screen. The magical device has the additional effect of neatly absolving the home of all blame. We are not led to feel that it is heartless of Lakshmana or Rāma to not to allow Sītā back behind the Lakshmana Rekhā. It is an impersonal device that works a certain way, so no one is to be blamed, except Sītā who crosses it, the victim herself. Indeed, Sītā's boast that she is a faithful wife is undermined by this act. Never mind that she crossed the line out of love for her husband; once she has crossed it, she has irrevocably sinned against dharma, and her love is

54. *aur ek pativratā satī kī or aisī kudṛṣṭi ḍālne kī mūrkhtā kisī ne bhī nahīṃ kī hogī; is kā pariṇām jānte ho?*
55. *strī ek bār apnī maryādā kī rekhā se bāhar jā āe phir uskā vāpas jānā asambhav ho jātā hai.*

tainted according to dharmic standards. It is on these grounds that the demon can abduct her.

In all versions, whether Rāvaṇa likes Sītā's devotion to her husband or not, the narrative must run its course. Rāvaṇa forcefully abducts Sītā in his celestial chariot (*RCM* 3.28, *dohā*). The description in Vālmīki's text is very graphic: he grabs her by the hair and thighs (*VR* 3.49.17). This violation of Sītā has been vexing the commentators and has been much discussed (Pollock 1991: 319–20). In Sagar's televised version, there are no words, only action: Rāvaṇa smashes the plate with food she is still carrying and grabs her by the hand. She tries to escape, and they swing around, while she beats on his arm as he holds on to her hand. Finally, he throws her over his shoulder, his right hand indeed touching her thighs, though he does not pull her hair, and then throws her into his aerial chariot, which immediately takes off into the air.

We could say that this is Sītā's first temptation. She resists valiantly, but in Sagar's version, she is overpowered through a mistake of her own: the fatal crossing of the Lakshmana Rekhā. Paradoxically, it is her concern for her husband's welfare that makes her cross the line of good behavior. The message sent to women is a stern one. Even if the concern is commitment to the husband, still the crossing of the lines of *maryādā* is fatal. Sagar's Sītā then puts love before concerns of dharma, and she gets the dire consequence. Here is a warning to women: whatever the circumstances, crossing the line of *maryādā* is taboo. In none of the other versions is there such an issue, as the Lakshmana Rekhā does not figure in these retellings. Sītā is simply overpowered. One could even say that it goes against the spirit of many classical and bhakti stories wherein women are lauded for being willing to even sell their bodies for their husband's sake (see for example the story of the *bhakta* king Pīpā's wife, also named Sītā; Callewaert and Sharma 2000).[56] In any case, only Sagar puts the blame for the abduction on Sītā crossing the protective line. The story as it stands in Vālmīki is more a tale of warning not to trust magic appearances, whether pretty mirages, voices crying for help, or Brahmin ascetics. Sagar's text is a warning not to step outside the magic circle of protection drawn by the family, the Lakshmana Rekhā.

56. Its corollary, women's commitment to fulfilling their husband's wishes, even if they flaunt dharma, is found in several Puranic stories, e.g. the story of the devoted Brahmin wife who carried her disabled husband to a prostitute's house (Citrāv 1964: 21). Such scenarios show up also in the Hindi movie, which tends however to maintain common-sense morality over excess of wifely devotion: when a similar scenario was shown in the movie *Pati Parmeshwar* (1989; d. Madan Joshi), it ran into difficulties with the censors over exactly that scene, although eventually the judges ruled it was not in violation (Gangoli 2005: 145–6).

Sītā's Defiance

After this first temptation, there are two more scenes of temptation to come. So far, I have concentrated on the story as a tale of warning, how women should not behave: minor mistakes, even if committed out of love for the husband, can have huge consequences. Women should abide by the rules restricting their movements, no matter what. Now the intention shifts to showing a role model for behavior. In the next scenes of temptation, Sītā will shine as an example of resisting a seducer-attacker. She is not the powerless heroine who meekly suffers insults in silence but one who proudly takes agency and actively sticks to her fidelity.

SĪTĀ'S FIRST REACTION AND RĀVAṆA'S INSISTENCE. Initially, overpowered by the demon, all Sītā can do is bewail her plight, calling out for help to her husband and brother-in-law. But they are far away. In Vālmīki's version there is a hint of reproach as she calls out to Lakshmana: "O strong-armed Lakshmana, always seeking favor with your elder, don't you know that I am being abducted by a demon, who can change his form at will?" (*VR* 3.49.24). Addressing Rāma, she cries: "Rāghava, who for dharma's sake renounced life and its pleasures, don't you see that I am being abducted in defiance of dharma?" (3.49.25). There is a hint of complaint that her men have let her down. They pride themselves on special virtues, Lakshmana on his loyalty to his brother, Rāma on always pursuing dharma, but now that those need to be applied in a real-life situation concerning Sītā, they are not present.

Tulsī's Sītā, by contrast, while crying out for help, in the same breath absolves Rāma and Lakshmana for their failure to protect her. Her first response is to blame herself instead: "Alas unique hero on earth, king of the Raghu dynasty. What did I do wrong that you have forgotten your spouse?" (*RCM* 3.29.1a).[57] "Alas Lakshman, you are not to blame. I got the just desert for my blind anger" (3.29.2a).[58]

Tulsī has only a hint of criticism when he says: "Vaidehī wailed and lamented, but the dear Lord of abundant grace was far away" (*RCM* 3.29.2b).[59]

57. *hā jaga eka bīra raghurāyā, kehiṃ aparādha bisārehu dāyā.*

58. *hā lachimana tumhāra nahīṃ dosā, so phalu pāyaūṃ kīnheū rosā.* Presumably Tulsīdās finds Valmikian justification for this in the verse "Indeed the result of wrongdoing is not always [immediately] apparent. Time too takes part in this, as in the ripening of grain" (*na tu sadyo 'vinītasya dṛśyate karmaṇaḥ phalam; kālo 'py aṅgībhavaty atra sasyānām iva paktaye, VR* 3.49.27). In Vālmīki, however, that verse seems to refer to the lack of immediate outrage and protest against Rāvaṇa's evil actions (referring to the next line, 3.49.28). Tulsī gives it a twist and has instead applied it to Sītā's self-reproach.

59. *bibidha bilāpa karati baidehī, bhūri kṛpā prabhu dūri sanehī.*

The internal rhyme in this line (*bhūri,* "abundant," with *dūri,* "away") further reinforces the poignancy of the discrepancy between Rāma's reputation and his aloofness at this crucial moment. Note, however, that the criticism is not put in Sītā's mouth. The ideal devotee does not complain. Only the commentator, Tulsīdās himself, does. Sītā adds a nice line summarizing her plight: "Who will tell my Lord about my plight? The donkey wishes to eat the sacrificial cake!" (3.29.3a).[60]

Sagar's Sītā does not reproach the brothers or herself; she simply calls out for help (*ārya! lakṣmaṇa! bacāo!*). Sagar thus leaves aside the thorny issue of why they do not come to her rescue and whose fault it really is that Rāma's wife could be desecrated. As in the other versions, the only one who comes to her help is Jaṭāyu,[61] but Rāvaṇa easily defeats him.[62]

Soon, Sītā will recover and assume some agency to further her own rescue. After Rāvaṇa has emerged victorious from the fight with Jaṭāyu, he takes off once again with her in the air chariot. Now, Sagar's Sītā cleverly drops pieces of her jewelry down in the hope that such will help Rāma track her. In Vālmīki's version, no such agency is initially ascribed to Sītā, who is kept tight in Rāvaṇa's embrace. She keeps struggling against him, though, and in the tussle her jewels fall off.[63] Only later, when she sees the monkeys on a mountain peak, does she throw down a bundle containing her outer upper garment (*uttarīya*) and jewels (*VR* 3.54.1–3). Tulsīdās follows suit in that regard (*RCM* 2.29.13a). Compared to the others, Sagar's heroine takes agency earlier on.

Notwithstanding her weak position, Vālmīki's Sītā also gets to deliver a spirited lecture to the demon in midflight. She taunts her abductor: "Do you not feel shame at this act, vile Rāvaṇa, to steal me away when I was bereft and then to run off?" (*VR* 3.53.3).[64] And sarcastically: "Surely, it shows your great valor, most debased demon! For haven't I been conquered in battle after

60. *bipati mori ko prabhuhi sunāvā, puroḍāsa caha rāsabha khāvā.*

61. The figure of the vulture Jaṭāyu is interesting in its own right. It represents the part of the father-figure type of old man, challenging the abductor to preserve dharma, putting up a good fight when words do not have an impact, and prepared to die for preserving the honor of his "daughter."

62. The fight with Jaṭāyu takes place in the air in Sagar's version. Vālmīki's demon is compelled to leap from his shattered chariot and fight on the ground (*VR* 3.51.16–9). At some point, he has to put aside Sītā whom, he has been holding during most of the fight (3.51.40). However, oddly, Sītā does not flee but watches the fight and rushes to hold the dying Jaṭāyu (3.51.44–6). When Rāvaṇa tries to grab her again, she holds onto a tree (3.52.6–7), but he seizes her by the hair (3.52.8b) and keeps her again in tight embrace until arrival in Laṅkā.

63. The fair woman caught in the embrace of the dark demon is likened to lightning in a rain cloud a (3.52.14 and 24). The rain is her jewelry falling down due to the violence of the embrace, further likened to meteors falling on earth, etc. (3.50.26–33).

64. *na vyapatrapase nīca karmaṇānena rāvaṇa, jñātvā virahitāṃ yo māṃ corayitvā palāyase.*

you disclosed your name? How come you're not ashamed to have done such a contemptible act as abducting a woman for one in a lonely place and moreover belonging to another man? (3.53.6–7).[65] And she continues in a vain attempt to scare him about Rāma's revenge, which is sure to cost him his life.

Tulsī only says she is wailing, without specifying what she says (*RCM* 3.29.12b), but Sagar reworks Vālmīki a bit to good effect. Sītā confronts her abductor with the cowardice of his act: "Are these the signs of heroic men, that like thieves they sneak in and steal the wife when her husband is not at home? Is your prowess only so big that you can attack a woman when she is alone?" (TVR 436).[66] It may seem macho to abduct a woman, but it is after all easy to overpower those who are weak. Good lines, but to no avail. The abductor just laughs. This is very much in the line of what film villains do when their victims appeal to their humanity.

Once in Laṅkā, Sītā finds herself amid enemies and exposed to the seductions of luxury and sensuality. Rāvaṇa does all he can to bring Sītā around. However, she steadfastly resists all temptation. *Vālmīki Rāmāyaṇa* has two scenes that treat this topic: one just after Rāvaṇa brings her to Laṅkā (*VR* 3.55–6), and another one, later on, witnessed by Hanumān just before he approaches Sītā with his encouraging message from Rāma (5.19–22). Sagar has faithfully preserved these two different scenes (vol. 11, episode 32 and vol. 15, episode 44). Tulsīdās only elaborates on the latter scene.

Vālmīki devotes a whole *sarga* to Rāvaṇa's attempt at seduction upon arrival in Laṅkā (*VR* 3.55). The demon shows Sītā his kingdom in all its splendor and offers her rule over it and his heart. He points out the hopelessness of her situation were she still to entertain hopes of Rāma rescuing her. He portrays her arrival in this "heaven" as a reward for her hardships in the forest (3.55.27b–28a) and even asserts that he has acted in conformity with the Vedas (3.55.35). He acts the submissive lover, even bowing to her feet, stressing that he does not do so lightly (3.55.36–7a). Tulsīdās does not elaborate on the first scene beyond saying that Rāvaṇa threatened and flattered her but she would not yield (*RCM* 3.29, *dohā* a). In the second scene he singles out especially Rāvaṇa's offer to make her mistress of all his queens. Apparently, it is imagined that such would appeal to womanly pride in superiority over other women

65. *paramaṃ khalu te vīryaṃ dṛśyate rākṣasādhama, viśrāvya nāmadheyaṃ hi yuddhe nāsmi jitā tvayā; īdṛśaṃ garhitaṃ karma kathaṃ kṛtvā na lajjase, striyāś cāharaṇaṃ nīca rahite ca parasya ca.*

66. *kyā vīrpuruṣ ke yahī lakṣaṇ hote haiṃ? jab pati ghar meṃ na ho to us kī patnī ko coroṃ kī bāṃtī ākar curākar le jāe? ek akelī strī par ākramaṇ karnā hī tumhārī śūrvīrtā hai?*

(5.9.2b–3a).[67] Thus, where Vālmīki's Rāvaṇa declares himself her slave, Tulsī's Rāvaṇa makes his wives her slaves.

Sagar's Rāvaṇa has a more insidious argument going: he suggests that Sītā is just a small-town dreamer and should raise her ambitions above just being a poor man's wife: "Don't dream of being a beggar's wife like an ignorant girl . . . if you are going to dream, then follow the ambition of becoming Laṅkā's empress (TVR 441).[68] Like Vālmīki's Rāvaṇa, he offers her his kingdom and his heart, pointing out that he does not bow in front of anyone but her (442).

The last scene of temptation in Sundara Kāṇḍa has a different setting. Here Rāvaṇa, intoxicated, approaches Sītā in the company of his harem in the early morning.[69] He is pained to see her grieve and languish, he thinks she could be very happy with him. He argues that her youth is wasting away. He restates his offer of power and richess and even comes up with a novelty, offering his kingdom to her father, Janaka (*VR* 5.20.18b). In his pride he cannot imagine Rāma could be in any way preferable to him, as he is so clearly superior. Sagar follows quite literally the argumentation of Vālmīki's Rāvaṇa, though he does not take up the offer to make her father rich. Maybe he felt that even the suggestion of such a buying off of the father of the girl would be an insult to Janaka.

SĪTĀ'S FIRM RESISTANCE. In her reply to Rāvaṇa's cajoling, Sītā becomes a role model for the Indian woman who is forced to respond to unwanted sexual attention. In Vālmīki and Tulsīdās, the first thing she does is keep her distance and seek shelter in a symbolic purdah. She places a grass blade (*tṛṇam*) in between herself and her accoster (*VR* 3.56.1b; 5.21.3; *RCM* 5.9.3b). However ineffective in real terms, the psychological effect is great, as it is apparently the recommended action for a woman in case she needs to speak to an unrelated man (on potential variant readings and what the commentaries have to say, see Pollock 1991: 331). It will become clear later how Sītā uses this in her strategy to resist Rāvaṇa. Sagar's Sītā at first takes resort to a more mundane gesture: she draws her veil (*ghūṃghaṭ*), but then she, too, takes the symbolic blade of grass. Throughout the scene, she does not look into Rāvaṇa's eyes but stares away from him at a point in front of her.

Vālmīki's Sītā's line of defense is mainly to try and impress on Rāvaṇa the gravity of the consequences of his act. She points out these will not be limited

67. He may be following Vālmīki's Sundara Kāṇḍa in that matter, where Rāvaṇa likewise offers Sītā to hold sway (*aiśvaryaṃ kuru*) of his harem (*VR* 5.20.31–2).

68. *ek añjān bālikā kī bhāṃti ek bhikhārī kā sapnā mat dekh . . . sapnā dekho to laṃkā kī sāṃrājñī banne kā . . .*

69. For an incisive analysis of the scene where Hanumān finds Sītā and the contrast between the erotic and the ascetic, see Sutherland-Goldman 2004: 126–31.

to his own death but the destruction of his whole city. She then tries to make him see the sacrilege he has committed in laying hands on a pure woman. She uses sacrifical terms: "An altar centrally placed at the sacrifice and adorned with ladles, consecrated with Brahminical mantras cannot be trampled by an untouchable (*caṇḍāla*)" (*VR* 3.56.18).[70] "Similarly, I, the lawful wife of a lawful man, firm in my vow, cannot be touched by a sinner, o vile demon!" (3.56.19).[71] Finally she makes clear the impossibility of what he wants: that she would of her own accord yield to him. It is as impossible as a mating of two different species: the lofty swan who sports among lotuses and the lowly diver bird that lives among grass tufts (3.56.20). She says she does not care whether he ties up her body or puts it to death, because it is not worth keeping it alive, and she just cannot abuse it as he would want her to. She declares herself incapable of transgressing dharma: "On this earth I will not be able to abuse myself" (56.22a).[72]

Sagar's Sītā gets some good lines of her own. When Rāvaṇa first brags about his power, she answers that all the goods he has have been corrupted by his sins (TVR 441). Interestingly, she adds that even the gods (Brahmā and Śiva) who granted him power have become corrupt because of his sins. This is an interesting reminder of superiors' responsibility for the deeds of those they have helped climb the ladder; even the gods cannot be absolved of responsibility! Sītā voices a firm conviction: "Remember: when power gets corrupted and its gods tainted, then there's no force left in that power. The truth may stand alone, but it still conquers endless armies of corrupt powers opposing it" (441).[73] She warns him that he has not yet been confronted with a woman's *satya,* or miraculous power of truth as a consequence of her loyalty to her husband (441).[74] Yet her boast sounds somewhat hollow, as she as much as grants that he has been able to touch her, and she still has to refer him to her husband's forces to save her: "Ego-driven fool! Sustained by sin you have been able to touch me once with your sinful hands, but just that mistake is sufficient cause for your destruction. My heroic and virtuous husband with his poisonous arrows will surely root you out completely" (441).[75]

70. *na śakyā yajñam adhyasthā vediḥ srugbhāṇḍamaṇḍitā; dvijātimantrasampūtā caṇḍālenāvamarditum.*

71. *tathāhaṃ dharmanityasya dharmapatnī dṛḍhavratā, tvayā sraṣṭuṃ na śakyāhaṃ rākṣasādhama pāpinā.*

72. *na tu śakyam apakrośaṃ pṛthivyāṃ dātum ātmanaḥ.*

73. *yād rakho, jab śakti bhraṣṭ ho jāe aur uske devtā kalaṃkit to śakti meṃ bal nahīṃ rahtā. satya akelā ho to bhī bhraṣṭ śaktiyoṃ kī apār senā uske sāmne parājit ho jātī hai.*

74. *ek pavitra pativratā nārī ke satya-bal se terā sāmnā nahīṃ huā.*

75. *ahaṃkārī murkh! tūne pāp vṛtti se ek bār apne pāpī hāthoṃ se merā aṃg-sparśa kiyā hai itnā hī doṣ tere nāś ke lie paryāpt hai. mere śūrvīr aur dharma-parāyaṇ pati ke viṣaile bāṇ niścay hī terā samūl nāś kar deṃge.*

Sometimes, Sagar's Sītā seems to be less addressing the demon than the women in the audience. She turns her own decision into a lesson for ordinary women: "No one can be lower than a woman who deluded by splendor, power, wealth forgets her vow of fidelity to her husband" (442).[76] She continues to curse him, and his mother, and his whole lineage of ancestors, yet, amazingly, rates the woman who falls for temptation beneath everyone, including the man who tempts her. That is actually the opposite line of argument to the one Sītā takes in Vālmīki's Sundara Kāṇḍa, where she urges Rāvaṇa to follow the course of conduct of the virtuous and not to approach other men's women, as such behavior by a king leads to ruin for the whole kingdom (*VR* 5.21.6–12). The context there is different, as Rāvaṇa has approached Sītā in the company of his harem, and she may be seen to appeal to those women at the same time.

In Sundara Kāṇḍa, too, Sītā rejects all Rāvaṇa's offers as resolutely as before, arguing on the grounds of dharma: "This deed cannot and will not be done by me, it is reprehensible to a loyal wife, because I am born in a great family and have married into [another] virtuous family" (*VR* 5.21.4b).[77] It is interesting that she gives a collective argument for her virtue. It is not her individual choice but her family background that determines her action. Still, Sītā speaks of her unique bond with Rāma: "I cannot be seduced by power or money. I'm unwaveringly devoted to Rāghava like sunlight to the sun. Having been at the righteous arm of the Lord of the three worlds, how could I really take the arm of another?" (5.21.16).[78] She uses Brahminical imagery here, too: "I am lawfully the wife of him, the Lord of the world, just as wisdom belongs to a Brahmin who has taken his vows, his ceremonial bath and realized his potential (*ātman*)" (5.21.17).[79] She offers Rāvaṇa a face-saving olive branch if he will restore her to Rāma, and paints a picture of doom if he does not accept that (5.21.19–34).

Tulsīdās's Sītā does not get to say all that much, but she surely is majestic in her utter despising of the demon. She minces no words:

> "Listen, with your ten heads, you're like a firefly. Has the lotus ever opened up to its light?
> Understand this heart," said Jānakī. "Rogue! Don't you have any idea of Rāma's arrows?

76. *vaibhav, śakti, sampatti ke moh meṃ ākar jo strī apnā pati-vrat dharm bhūl jāe usse adham aur koī nahīṃ ho saktā.*

77. *akāryaṃ na mayā kāryam ekapatnyā vigarhitam, kulaṃ samprāptayā puṇyaṃ kule mahati jātayā.*

78. *śakyā lobhayituṃ nāham aiśvaryeṇa dhanena vā, ananyā rāghaveṇāhaṃ bhāskareṇa yathā prabhā; upadhyāya bhujaṃ tasya lokanāthasya satkṛtam, kathaṃ nāmopadhāsyāmi bhujam anyasya kasyacit.*

79. *aham aupayikī bhāryā tasyaiva ca dharāpateḥ, vratasnātasya vidyeva viprasya viditātmanaḥ.*

> Sinner! You snatched me away in his absence. Shameless vile man!
> Don't you have any sense of shame?" (*RCM* 5.9.4–5)[80]

She nearly spits out the despising terms, clearly articulating her utter contempt for the demon and his pretensions. Sagar's Sītā, too, shows utter contempt for Rāvaṇa, and incorporates Tulsīdās's firefly (here *juganū*) line (TVR 591).

Mostly, though, Sagar follows Vālmīki very closely: his Sītā, too, extends an olive branch, incorporating several of the expressions of Vālmīki's Sītā to make Rāvaṇa understand her commitment to Rāma. Predictably, Sagar elaborates most on Vālmīki's line on the impossibility of the Aryan woman commiting adultery: "I am a loyal wife. I have been born in a great family and was entrusted to a holy family. It is impossible for me to commit an act censored by people" (*TVR* 591).[81] Sītā's example to women who consider themselves of good families is clear: always remember your family, never act in a way that people might disapprove of.

WHY DOES HE NOT RAPE HER? In all versions, Rāvaṇa is enraged by Sītā's defiance and issues an ultimatum that he will wait for her for a year to change her mind, and if she has not come around, he will eat her for breakfast (*VR* 2.24b–25, *RCM* 5.10.5a). Rākṣasas are imagined as cannibals eating human flesh, so this threat is appropriate. In Vālmīki's Sundara Kāṇḍa, he points out that she is lucky that he does not kill her for disrespecting royal authority, and he repeats his ultimatum (*VR* 5.22.1–6). Tulsī has Rāvaṇa so enraged at Sītā calling him a firefly that he actually draws his sword, threatening to kill her (*RCM* 5.9, *dohā* and 10.1). Sītā declares that to be a welcome solution, saying she wishes either her husband's arms around her neck or the demon's sword (5.10.2b).[82] He would have killed her were it not for the intervention of his queen Mandodarī, who manages to calm him down (5.10.4a). Sagar incorporates this scene, too (TVR 502–3).

Before that, however, back in Araṇya Kāṇḍa, Sagar's Rāvaṇa has done even worse: he has been on the verge of raping Sītā: "In Laṅkā, if anyone refuses of their own volition to give in to the king's wishes, then the king knows how to

80. *sunu dasamukha khadyota prakāsā, kabahuṃ ki nalinī karaï bikāsā; asa mana samujhu kahati jānakī, khala sudhi nahiṃ raghubīra bān kī; saṭha sūneṃ hari ānehi mohī, adhama nilajja lāja nahiṃ tohī.*

81. *maiṃ ek pati-vratā hūṃ, maiṃ ne ek baṛe kul meṃ janma liyā hai. merā ek pavitra kul meṃ sambandh huā hai. mujh se koī lok-nindit kārya sambhav nahīṃ ho saktā.*

82. *syāma saroja dāma sama sundara, prabhu bhuja kari kara sama dasakaṃdhara; so bhuja kaṃṭha ki tava asi ghorā, sunu saṭha asa pravāna pana morā.*

get his desires fulfilled by his own power" (TVR 442).[83] With these words, he approaches her clearly with the intent of raping her. Of the three versions, the televised one is the only one where Rāvaṇa threatens to rape Sītā. None of the other versions ascribes such intent to Rāvaṇa; rather, Vālmīki's Rāvaṇa stresses that he does not wish to approach her against his will (*VR* 5.20.6). One reason for Sagar's addressing the rape issue may be the contemporary context in which the series was aired. The eighties saw an abundance of movies about rape, so the threat was foremost in the audience's mind (Virdi 2003: 159–67).

The question of why Rāvaṇa stops short of raping Sītā is not new, though, and certainly occurred to the commentators (see Pollock 1991: 331). The standard answer is that Sītā was so pure he could not touch her. There is some textual support for this argument in the Sundara Kāṇḍa when Hanumān finds Sītā and she is described as "protected by her own virtue" (*VR* 5.17.27b).[84] Sītā herself, too, boasts she could burn Rāvaṇa to ashes herself but does not do so, in deference to Rāma: "I won't turn you to ashes by my burning glow (*tejas*), o ten-headed beast" (5.22.20b).[85] She says why she does not do so: "because I did not get Rāma's permission, and so as not to deplete my asceticism (*tapas*)" (5.22.20a).[86]

A related erudite reflection as to why he did not rape her is by reference to the last book of Uttara Kāṇḍa, where the story of Rāvaṇa's own karmic history is told. After raping a nymph, he was cursed: if he rapes any more women, he will be punished by immediate death (*VR* 7.26).

Sagar combines both arguments and has it both ways.[87] When Rāvaṇa approaches her, Sītā lifts a blade of grass, holds it in protection in front of her, and warns him not to cross that boundary: "Watch out, you sinner! Don't you dare to cross this wall" (TVR 442).[88] Rāvaṇa downplays her act, pointing out that women can conquer men only with the arrows of love, not with blades of grass: "Pretty lady, a male's heart can be melted only through the flower arrows of Cupid" (443).[89] Sītā bravely persists: "This is not a blade of grass, it is the flaming arrow of a true woman's virtue and truth. It is the unbreakable wall of Sītā's

83. *laṅkā meṃ laṅkāpati kī icchā yadi koī svecchā se pūrī nahīṃ kartā to laṅkāpati svayaṃ apne bal se apnī icchā pūrī karnā jāntā hai.*

84. *rakṣitāṃ svena śīlena sītām.*

85. *na tvāṃ kurmi daśagrīva bhasma bhasmārhatejasā.*

86. *asaṃdeśāt tu rāmasya tapasaś cānupālanāt.*

87. Interestingly, he does not refer to Sītā's own prehistory as a victim of Rāvaṇa's lasciviousness in her former incarnation as the chaste Vedāvatī (*VR* 7.17). Sagar does not seem to like the idea that her current incarnation is her revenge: she is coming back to bring about his destruction. Though such an approach would have fit the contemporary *filmī* climate with an abundance of rape-and-revenge movies, Sagar may have felt this to be out of character for his Sītā, who is pure in every incarnation.

88. *sāvdhān pāpī! is prācīr ko pār karne kā sāhas na karnā.*

89. *sundarī! kāmdev phūloṃ ke bāṇoṃ se puruṣoṃ ke hṛday bhedte haiṃ.*

truth. A screen of grass is sufficient to shield a loyal woman from a strange man" (443).[90] She takes refuge in Anasūyā, the wife of the sage Atri, endowed with special powers, whom Sītā has met shortly before (Pauwels 2001), swearing: "If in heart, word, and deed I have been loyal in my love to my husband, then, Mother Anasūyā, embodiment of righteousness, may this sinner be burned to ashes as he crosses the line" (443).[91] Thus Sagar has confirmed the first argument: that Mother Sītā was protected by her absolute loyalty to her husband.

However, that is not enough. Rāvaṇa ridicules this "kiddie theatre" (*baccoṃvālā nāṭak*) and rushes to drag her off by her hair. At this point, however, he hears a voice in the air (*ākāśvāṇī*), which reminds him of how he was cursed by Nalakubera after he raped his wife. It is not clear whether this is a miraculous event or merely a flashback playing in Rāvaṇa's head. In any case, it causes him to change tack. He suddenly drops his threat and decides to give Sītā another chance, because sooner or later she will come around, he figures. It is ambiguous, then, why Sagar's Rāvaṇa does not rape Sītā. Those inclined to believe so may well argue it is because of her miraculous powers as a loyal wife, but it may also be because of the curse Rāvaṇa brought on himself. Thus it may be because of her virtue as well as of his sins.

FEMALE SOLIDARITY, DIETARY CONCERNS, AND THE TRUE GANDHIAN SĪTĀ. Vālmīki incorporates an element of female solidarity between victims of male transgression. The ladies of Rāvaṇa's harem, who have suffered the same fate as Sītā, are portrayed as reassuring, indicating by their facial expressions that they are supportive of her resistance (*VR* 5.22.10–1). Even Rāvaṇa's main queens protect her against their husband's anger (5.22.39–43). As we have seen, the same was also the case in Tulsīdās and Sagar. We get, then, an interesting glimpse of female solidarity, which goes even beyond that with fellow victims, since even the (presumably lawfully wedded) queens protect Sītā's life. Whereas Rāvaṇa plays on Sītā's sense of jealousy among females, the women respond exactly the opposite way, as if to belie the male stereotype.

A different set of females, the low-class prison guards, who are hideous monsters, get the role of Sītā's opponents. Rāvaṇa now leaves it up to them to bring Sītā around. They first act collectively, trying to impress Sītā so she would surrender to their king (*VR* 5.23.2–19, 24.1–5; TVR 593–4). Sagar's demonesses then do a good cop, bad cop routine. After a group of them frightens Sītā,

90. *yah tinkā nahīṃ, yah ek dharmparāyaṇ strī ke śīl aur satya kā agnibāṇ hai. yah sītā ke satītva kī abhedya dīvār hai. ek satī aur par puruṣ ke bīc ek tinke kī oṭ bhī bahut hotī hai.*

91. *yadi maiṃ ne man, vacan, karm se apne pati se ananya prem kiyā hai to he nārī dharm kī mūrtimān devī mātā anusūyā, is tinke ko pār karte hī yah pāpī bhasm ho jāe!*

Trijaṭā comes in as the good cop and approaches Sītā with admiration so as to win her trust, in which she succeeds.

Still, of course, Sītā resists giving in to the demon, insisting that a union of a human woman with a demon is unnatural (*lok-viruddh*, TVR 594). Sagar highlights the one verse in Vālmīki wherein she says that even though she is destitute, her husband remains venerable to her, which sounds like a piece of good advice for women in general: "He's my husband, even though he may have been humbled and bereft of his kingdom, still it remains for me to worship him" (594).[92] The demonesses then change tactics and start threatening her (*VR* 5.24.13–47; TVR 594). They seem to be at the point of devouring Sītā when good cop Trijaṭā comes in and relates her dream, predicting the victory of Rāma (*VR* 5.27; TVR 595). In Tulsī's version, Trijaṭā is a devotee of Rāma (*RCM* 5.11.1a), which explains why Sītā would bond with a prison guard. Sagar follows suit. In any case, even among the evil women in Laṅkā, there is at least one who is on Sītā's side. This female bonding in the enemy's camp is a remarkable contrast to the female jealousy Rāvaṇa thinks he is playing on when he tries to woo Sītā.

The vulgate *Rāmāyaṇa* has at this point an interpolation of a chapter from the Northern *Rāmāyaṇa* recension (*prakṣiptaḥ sargaḥ*), where Indra offers Sītā divine sustenance so she can remain alive till Rāma will come and save her. This chapter shows a typical Brahminical preoccupation with dietary prescriptions. It addresses a doubt (*śankā*) about how Sītā could survive such a long captivity without compromising herself by partaking in the food of the demons. And the answer is unequivocally that she did not eat anything untoward but survived courtesy of the old Vedic gods.

Sagar, too, stresses Sītā's refusal to partake of food or drink while in captivity. His interpretation of Sītā's resistance may be colored by Gandhian interpretations, not only the experiments with food that preoccupied so much of Gandhi's thinking but also the idea of the hunger strike. When Rāvaṇa comes to visit Sītā in Aśokavana, the demoness guard reports to him that Sītā neither eats nor drinks and is in danger of dying (TVR 440–1). This worries Rāvaṇa, but he cannot convince Sītā to give it up, and he is in any case more interested in getting her to sleep with him than to eat. It is, however, a concern to Sītā's prison guards.

92. *jo mere pati haiṃ ve dīn haiṃ athavā rājyahīn haiṃ, ve mere lie pūjanīya haiṃ*. This line is based on *dīno vā rājyahīno vā yo me bhartā sa me guruḥ, taṃ nityam anuraktāsmi yathā sūryaṃ suvarcalā* (*VR* 5.24.8). Vālmīki continues with a list of mythological examples of faithful women, including (somewhat inappropriately) Indra's wife Śacī, Vasiṣṭha's wife Arundhatī, the Moon's Rohiṇī, Agastya's Lopāmudrā, Cyavana's Sukanyā, Satyavān's Sāvitrī, Kapila's Śrīmatī, Saudāsa's Madayantī, Sagara's Keśinī, and Nala's Damayantī.

When Trijaṭā talks to her, she convinces Sītā that she has to eat something to remain alive by phrasing it as doing it for the sake of her husband. She points out that there is a contradiction in Sītā's professions of trust in her husband and her wish to die (TVR 445). She even chides her gently that this is no way for a loyal wife to talk (445).[93] Sītā points out that she cannot eat the food of this region but only, like her husband, vegetarian fare (*kaṃd-mūl,* 446). Trijaṭā agrees that now she is talking according to her *strī-dharma* and promises to bring her some pure fare (*sāttvik,* 446). This establishes a mother-daughter relation between the two.

Meanwhile, more female bonding is going on in Sagar's version: Mandodharī, too, defies all stereotypes of the jealous cowife and sends fresh clothes to Sītā in deference to rules of hospitality (447). Sītā, however, sends them back, arguing that her clothes, which she received from the ascetic Anasūyā, are magical and never get dirty. Moreover, she will not dress in splendor as long as her husband is dressed in ascetic garb. There may be an echo of *swadeshi* in the refusal to wear foreign clothes as long as she is not liberated. Sītā also gives Mandodharī the good suggestion that she plead with her husband to set Sītā free. Sītā thus starts to reform the household of sinful Rāvaṇa from within, taking all clues of goodness that come her way and answering them in kind, convincing her jailers of her virtue and working to reform them. Indeed, she brings about a wonderful change of heart in some of the women around her. Sagar's Sītā is a true Gandhian in that respect, too.

Different views of Sītā's Abduction

How liberating has bhakti proven to be for Sītā as role model in this scene? Tulsī's devotion to Sītā has led him to take out the unbecoming words she spoke to Lakshmana. Tulsī does not report speech he does not like. He even cuts any of Sītā's words that might have a hint of blaming Lakshmana and Rāma and has her blame herself for the abduction instead. The ideal devotee clearly is not to complain. Furthermore, in Tulsī's view, Sītā is not deceived by the demon and sees immediately through his disguise, giving him a spirited lecture about how an ascetic should behave. When her situation seems hopeless in Laṅkā, she encourages Rāvaṇa to kill her. Tulsī does not give Rāvaṇa much of a chance to woo Sītā, in fact, he is shown to be secretly pleased that she is so steadfastly loyal to Rāma, as in Tulsī's universe, the demon himself is also a devotee. Ultimately, that detracts from the scene, it becomes

93. *kyā tum pativratā strī dharm ke anukūl bāt kar rahī ho?*

TABLE 6.2. Comparison of Sītā's Abduction in Three Sources

	VR	RCM	TVR
Lakshmana Rekhā	S. speaks harsh words to L.	Alluded to	S. calls L. coward
	S. accuses L. of wanting her	Not explicit	S. says L. clings to her skirts like child
	L. utters misogynistic words	N/a	thinks Sītā's mind is dimmed by bad luck
	L. curses Sītā	N/a	N/a
	L. asks *vanadevatā* to protect S	L. entrust Sītā to *vanadevatā*	Lakshmana Rekhā linked with *vanadevatā*
Abduction	Mood: suspense	Mood: comic/līlā	Mood: comic/suspense
	R. woos elaborately	Short	No wooing; R. is irascible ascetic
	S. believes him initially	Sees through him	Believes him initially
	S. is afraid he'll curse her	S not afraid	S transgresses, fearing curse on Rāma
	S. rhetorically rejects R.	Confidently rejects R.	Confidently rejects R.
	R. is furious	R. secretly admires S.	R. furious because treated as untouchable
	R. grabs her	R. grabs her	R. points out she cannot return to Lakshmana Rekhā
Sītā's Resistance	S. calls for help: reproach	Self-reproach	Simple call for help
	Spirited speech	Wailing	Sarcastic speech
	"You should be ashamed"	"Should be ashamed"	"Shameful is woman who gives in"
	No threat of rape	No threat of rape	Threat of rape
	Unclear why no rape	Unclear why no rape	Reason: Sītā's virtue + Rāvaṇa is cursed
	Gods send food	N/a	Trijaṭā provides appropriate food

irrelevant for real-life situations: in the end this is all unreal, a *līlā*. The accosting of Sītā is ultimately not a real threat. That deflates the liberating potential of Sītā as role model.

Reading the televised version against its professed primary sources also reveals its contemporary concerns. Overall, it represents a return to Vālmīki, bypassing some of the bhakti innovations. One such return to Vālmīki is that Sagar's Sītā is deceived by Rāvaṇa's disguise as an ascetic, whereas Tulsī's Sītā sees right through that. Another has to do with Vālmīki's Sītā's angry words when she interprets Lakshmana's hesitation to help Rāma as his having designs on her. Tulsī chose to bypass this, merely alluding to Sītā's angry words.

Sagar, too, finds this problematic, but he follows Vālmīki in letting Sītā be suspicious of her brother-in-law, minus the sexual innuendo. Sagar transforms Sītā into the Aryan woman ready to take up weapons herself to protect her husband, if need be. Lakshmana, then, is prompted into action because his masculinity is questioned, not his sexual intentions.

Sagar succeeds in sounding authentic, while bending Vālmīki's text to his own message. Thus he makes it a point to quote from Vālmīki lines that drive home a conservative message, for example the collectivist argument that the Aryan woman cannot commit adultery because she is born and married into a pure family. Sagar adds more conservative pseudoquotations in the same vein, including lines to the effect that a woman who gives in to this temptation is the lowest creature on earth. On the other hand, this is compensated for to some extent, in that Sagar grants his Sītā more agency and gives her some good lines of defiance, too.

Significantly, Sagar shows Rāvaṇa actually threatening to rape Sītā. The question of why he does not rape her has certainly come up before, but is not addressed explicitly in the two source texts. Sagar's solution is an ambiguous combination of Sītā's inviolability as a loyal woman and Rāvaṇa's own bad karma. The latter reason is a sad comment on the state of affairs in case of repeat offenders: it took many rapes before Rāvaṇa was finally cursed. Certainly Sagar shows a strong deterrent effect for capital punishment for rapists (with the proviso that the punishment is believed to be immediate). The issue of Sītā's inviolability is a two-edged sword. The argument that gives loyal women miraculous powers to defend themselves against aggressors may seem empowering at first but also works against women. The other side of the coin is that women who are raped are by definition deemed not virtuous. They can be blamed without investigation of the circumstances, because had they been virtuous, they could not have been touched. Thus we have a conundrum that condemns the rape victim because she is a rape victim.

The last important difference between the televised text and its sources is that Sagar chooses to incorporate the Lakshmana Rekhā, an episode that is not present in the two other versions. This results in adding a third fatal mistake to Sītā's list of mistakes, the first sending Rāma after the golden deer, and second sending Lakshmana to save him. This third mistake comes as the climax of the other two, and thus acquires a special significance. The abduction, then, is ultimately blamed on Sītā's transgression of the line. The message sent to women is a warning never to trespass the rules of the patriarchal family. Since Sītā does so for fear of her husband's life, the implication is that under no circumstances should one break *maryādā,* not even for love of the husband. What is remarkable is the contrast to how the Lakshmana Rekhā is commonly understood. Generally, "crossing the line" is seen as committing adultery in itself, or at least leaving the boundaries of *maryādā,* refusing to toe the family line. Sītā, though, notwithstanding her crossing the magic line, still upholds all rules of *maryādā* and remains absolutely true to her husband. Even so, she is blamed. Once again, Sagar has established firmly the superiority of dharma over bhakti.

Rādhā Accosted at the Well

If Sītā is blamed, notwithstanding resisting her accoster, what to say of Rādhā's way of dealing with Krishna's sexual advances? She may initially be hesitant and unwilling, but eventually she will submit to her accoster, Krishna, with whom she is secretly in love. That is true for all of Krishna's eve-teasing. We focus here on the *panaghaṭa līlā,* where Krishna surprises the Gopīs on their way back from the well.

There is no classical precedent for this scene. Neither *Bhāgavata Purāṇa* nor *Brahma Vaivarta Punāṇa* have any episode of the kind. The closest match in *Bhāgavata Purāṇa* is the song of the Gopīs describing the enchanting effect of Krishna's flute (*BhP* 10.35). The water-carriers frequently blame Krishna's flute playing for their seduction, and they say he casts a spell on them. In *Bhāgavata Purāṇa,* the Gopīs sing their song when Krishna is in the woods tending the cows, while they are back in the village eagerly awaiting his return at the "hour of the cow" (*go-velā*), late afternoon toward dusk, when the cows return from the pastures. They do not refer to any meetings near the well.

The *panaghaṭa* theme, though, was popular with the Krishna *bhaktas* of the sixteenth century, at least judging by the twentieth-century collections of their work. *Sūr Sāgar* includes a whole section of poems under the title "Panaghaṭa līlā".[94] Given that there is no precedent in *Bhāgavata Purāṇa,* the compilers had to determine where to insert the poems on this theme. They did so, along with many others not in the classical scripture, after the action of Krishna's demon-killing is over and just before his departure from Braj (which in the classical sources is *BhP* 10.36). As is usually the case with such collections, some of the songs included under this heading are only tangentially connected to the "water-carrier" theme and are actually elaborations on the love the Gopīs feel or descriptions of Krishna's beauty. I will concentrate here on the songs that are

94. It should be pointed out that none of these poems has sixteenth-century attestation, and only one poem arranged under the *panaghaṭa* theme in the Nāgarī Pracāriṇī Sabhā edition (*SS* 2076/1458) makes it into the forthcoming edition of Kenneth Bryant (as no. 75). Incidentally, that poem does not explicitly relate to the water-carrier theme, so I do not discuss it here.

explicitly connected with the theme of harassment at the well (*SS* 2017/1398, 2021/1403–2016/1443, 2065/1447–2068/1450, 2070/1452–2071/1453, 2075/1457). Some of these poems form a miniseries; when grouped together, they provide a short narrative. For Nanddās, the situation is different. He has only four *padas* on the topic in his *Padābali* (80–1, 83–4), collected with others under the generic heading "The Love of the Young Women of Braj" (*brajabālāoṃ kā prema*). I will discuss them as they fit in with the issues raised in Sūr's cycle.

I will first discuss the medieval poems, starting with those that sketch the situation: the titillation of a meeting with women outside the village boundaries. This first section is mostly from Krishna's point of view. Then I will look at the point of view of the women, and whether they are to be considered victims or willing partners. This brings us to the complaints brought before Krishna's mother, Yaśodā, and her reaction. Finally, I will look at how the Gopīs relate to the Lakshmana Rekhā issue, their awareness of the affair compromising their honor, and their willingness to cross the line knowingly. In the last section, I discuss how the episode is dealt with in the televised *Shri Krishna* (vol. 5, episode 35).

Profiling a Case of Harassment: "Rashomon" in Sūrdās's Poems

First I will look at poems that provide the context. How does the *Sūr Sāgar* frame this series of scandalous poems? What is the setting and what actually transpires? Do we get a view of what the participants feel? Sūr's poems do not represent a simple, omniscient third person report. There is no single narrator as in *Rām Carit Mānas*. Instead, multiple voices interpret the events. As in the 1950 Akira Kurosawa movie *Rashomon,* this case, of molestation too, is not as clear-cut as may appear at first sight. We get many different and somewhat contradictory perspectives. In addition, it is not always clear who is doing the speaking, whose perspective is provided. Thus, I'll have to offer some suggestions as to whose reported speech I am looking at. In Krishna's world, there is not an authoritative Tulsīdās-like reporter. Things are much more subjective. We get a nearly postmodern profile of a case of harassment.

POLISHING THE POTS: VICTIMS TRANSFORMED INTO WILLING PARTNERS. The compilers of *Sūr Sāgar* start with a disclaimer. They see fit to put in first some kind of preventive apologetics, in case one might object to the whole titillating affair on dharmic grounds. The voice in this poem definitely belongs to the commentator; it is an extradiegetical voice, a theologian expounding scripture. Basically, the line of argument is that though it might appear so, Krishna is not a lecher. The motivation of his acts is not his own desire. He is God, so without desire himself. However, he fulfills the desires of his devotees. He performs this *līlā* moved by love for his devotees. In the end, such a thing is incomprehensible for humans.

> Hari is the Lord of the world. He has all desires fulfilled and fulfills all desires.[95] He is all-pervasive, dwelling within each being [in every vessel].
> Considering the love of the young ladies of Braj, he extended his sports along Yamunā's banks.
> He spilled one girl's little water pot, snapped[96] the pot carrier of another.
> He grabbed and broke the big jar of one girl and stole another's heart with flirtatious glances.
> Thus he won the hearts of all. No one can fathom Śyāma's ways. (*SS* 2017/1398)[97]

In its very first line, this poem cleverly uses the image of God dwelling in each being, using the word "vessel" (*ghaṭa*). This announces the theme of the *panaghaṭa* and at the same time adds a level of irony that God, dwelling in all vessels, would himself break these very vessels. One can see here a profound theological musing about the need to transcend the material world in order to come closer to God, to break material boundaries to reach the highest goal. In any case, the poem is intended to frame the set of poems that follows. Whereas the water-carrier assault theme is potentially scandalous, this poem mitigates that at the outset by providing a philosophical interpretative frame. We could say it is a kind of theological tone-setter for the rest of the work.

This philosophical poem is followed by some descriptions of Krishna and the entrancing effect of his flute. This may be to connect this cycle with *Bhāgavata Purāṇa*, by evoking the songs of the Gopīs describing the effect of Krishna's flute (10.35). Then we plunge right into the action. The scene is outside the village boundaries, where women venture at the risk of encountering harassers. Krishna and his friends are hanging out near the place to fetch water near the Yamunā, bored because no Gopī has arrived yet to fetch water today.

95. The Braj term *pūranakāmī* can have both connotations.

96. *Phaṭkār-* can mean "to whip," "to snap" (*OHED*).

97. *hari triloka-pati pūranakāmī, ghaṭa ghaṭa byāpaka aṃtarajāmī; braja-juvatini ko heta bicāryau, jamunā kaiṃ taṭa khela pasāryau; kāhū kī gagarī ḍharakāvaiṃ, kāhū kī iṃḍurī phaṭakāvaiṃ; kāhū kī gāgarī dhari phoraiṃ, kāhū ke cita citavata coraiṃ; yā bidhi sabake manahiṃ manāvaiṃ, sūra syāma-gati kou na pāvai.*

Kanhāī keeps stopping them at the well.
No one manages to fetch water from the Yamunā, seeing him, they turn back.
Then Śyāma thought up a trick, he himself remained hidden.
He called his friends who were standing on the banks to come with him.
He made the cowherds sit down under a tree. He himself remained on the lookout.
It took a long time, no one came, Sūr's Śyāma mulled this over in his mind. (*SS* 2021/1403)[98]

Again, this is the reporter's voice. But this time, there are no theological musings, just a vignette of village India, with young men loitering near the well, keen on meeting women. This seems a straight-out-of-life situation, and we can well imagine that the Gopīs' reaction will provide a scenario for how ordinary women should behave. Indeed, the Gopīs see the boys from a distance, and turn around. Undaunted, Krishna, the leader of the gang, comes up with the idea of hiding nearby.

Here I will turn to one of the poems by Nanddās, in which he, too, sketches a rustic world. He paints a little village vignette in his *kavitta*:

The water-carriers of Gokul set off to the river. Their wide eyes lined with kohl,
Wrapped in flowery saris, brilliant from top to toe, flower bracelets on their arms so fair.
They walk amid a group of friends, giggle and chat, oblivious to how they look, water pitchers on their head.
On their way they meet the Mountain-bearer: glancing flirtatiously they totally lose the way. Nanddās capitulates. (*NP* 83)[99]

Here, Nanddās, too, has taken on a reporter's (or photographer's) stance. He sketches an ordinary, everyday village sight: a group of women departing for the well—picturesque in their colorful saris, chatting away, unaware that they are being spied on. When they meet Krishna, though, things become out

98. *panaghaṭa roke rahata kanhāī; jamunā-jala kou bharana na pāvai, dekhata hīṃ phiri jāī; tabahiṃ syāma ika buddhi upāī, āpuna rahe chapāī; taṭa ṭhāṛhe je sakhā saṃga ke, tinakauṃ liyau bulāī; baiṭhāryau gvālani kauṃ druma-tara, āpuna phiri phiri dekhata; baṛī bāra bhaī kou na āī, sūra syāma mana lekhata.*

99. *gokula kī panihārī paniyā bharana cālī, baṛe-baṛe naina tāmeṃ khubhi rahyo kajarā; pahiraiṃ kasūbhī-sārī aṃga aṃga chabi bhārī, gorī gorī bāṃhana meṃ motina ke gajarā; sakhī saṃga liyauṃ jāta haṃsi haṃsi karata bāta, tana hūṃ kī sudhi bhūlī sīsa dharaiṃ gagarā; naṃdadāsa balihārī bīca mile giridhārī, nainani kī sainani meṃ bhūli gaī ḍagarā.*

of the ordinary. They lose their way; everything is turned topsy-turvy. Nanddās has no words for it.

The actual encounter with Krishna is described in Sūr's poems quite a bit later in the series. We witness what happens at the well when a girl arrives alone. Again, the speech is that of a reporter, and the tone is very earthy. Krishna is attracted by her sensuous body. We have strayed quite a bit from our philosophical introduction. Indeed, without the reference to Krishna, this song could be a more bawdy folk song along the lines of "boy spots pretty girl at well."

> A young lady came to fetch water from the Yamunā.
> Looking her pretty body all over, prince Kanhāī was attracted:
> Fair body, red sari,[100] hairlocks scattered on her forehead,
> On each wrist she has four bracelets,[101] at her lower arms, her bangles glisten.
> Her body adorned by the bloom of youth: her Maker took care of her "make up"!
> She set off with her full water pot, all a-jangling. Sūr's Śyāma himself approached. (*SS* 2065/1447)[102]

This poem admits quite brazenly that Krishna is attracted by the woman's physical charms, and a married woman at that, as she is wearing bangles and a red sari. It flies unapologetically in the face of our first theological interpretation. This Krishna seems to be quite lustful, far from having all his desires satisfied (*pūranakāmī*). The woman is objectified, and Krishna's is the lustful male gaze. The poem seems to be from his perspective. But then there is an ironic reference to the Creator who did a good job on her. The comment could be reflecting Krishna's musings, but of course, Krishna himself is the Creator! If we were for a moment fooled into seeing Krishna as a lustful male, this reference jolts us out of commonplace understanding. It serves as a little reminder of his divinity. This is no ordinary male's gaze!

Things do not remain restricted to gazing. Krishna gets quite physical and accosts the woman. The action is continued in the next poem of the series,

100. The term used is *cūnarī*, which refers to a specific type of cloth that is partly dyed and usually red (*OHED*).

101. The word choice, *ḍārani*, or "branches," can also mean "wrist." I am grateful to Prem Pahlajrai for providing insight into this line.

102. *jubati ika jamunā-jala kauṃ āī; nirakhata aṃga-aṃga prati saubhā, rījhe kuṃvara kanhāī; gore badana cūnarī sārī, alakaiṃ mukha bararāī; ḍarani cari cari curī virājati kara kaṃkana jhalakāī; sahaja siṃgāra uṭhata jobana tana, vidhi nija hātha banāī; sūra syāma āe ḍhiga āpuna, ghaṭa bhari calī jhamakāī.*

which seems to be there to respond to the audience's curiosity. It fills out what happens when a solitary woman is on her way back from the well:

> The milkmaid left a-jangling, having filled her water pot.
> Suddenly Śyāma grabbed her hair, asking: "What's so burning hot?"
> Mohana's hand on the locks on the woman's face. . . . For good comparisons, your brain rack:
> Rāhu stealing nectar from the moon,[103] and Hari arrived to stop him [in his track].
> He touched her breast and drew her close, hearts rejoicing [as he her modesty wrecks].
> Sūr's Śyāma pretends to search for nectar vessels: looks her over and takes his tax.[104] (*SS* 2066/1448)[105]

In its first couple of lines, this may well be interpreted as a warning poem: "Beware when alone at the well." The last two lines specify that you may lose more than just your water and your pot. However, in the third line, the earthy tone is transformed to a fancier mythological one. The poet interrupts the narrative and comes up with the image of the demon Rāhu violating the moon for the sake of nectar, an apt mythical allusion. Such elaborations are like little moments of *darśana*, "verbal icons" (Bryant 1978) meant to help the audience visualize the happenings. The dark locks of hair look like a demon's fingers, grabbing the fair woman's moon-like face. Krishna grabs her hair, as if stopping the demon who is about to snatch her nectar. Ironically, Krishna turns into accoster himself; under cover of saving her nectar, he actually takes some for himself. In the last line, he grabs her breasts, and looks them over, as if in search for vessels of nectar. It cleverly extends the metaphor of the demon caught at pilfering nectar from the moon. Now Krishna takes over the vessels of nectar he has saved from the demon's hands. A delightful development indeed, Krishna enjoys it fully, and so does the audience. But does the woman?

The text is ambiguous about who is enjoying it in line 5. Is it Krishna alone, or does the poet intend to transmit that the girl, too, is secretly

103. Rāhu is the mythological planet held responsible for eclipses of the moon. The story is that he was a demon who disguised himself as a god in order to get a taste of the nectar of immortality. The Sun and the Moon realized what happened and told Vishnu, who promptly decapitated him. However, because he had drunk of the nectar, his head was immortal, and it chases the Sun and Moon, occasionally managing to swallow them.

104. The word for tax, *kara*, can also mean "hand"; "he brought/took [the vessels] in his hand." The two "vessels" are standard poetic comparisons for breasts.

105. *gvāri ghaṭa bhari calī jhamakāi; syāma acānaka laṭa gahi kahī ati, kahā calī aturāi; mohana-kara tiya-mukha kī alakaiṃ, yaha upamā adhikāi; manau sudhā sasi rāhu curāvata, dharyau tāhi hari āi; kuca parase aṃkana bhari līnhī, ati mana haraṣa baṛhāi; sūra syāma manu amṛta ghaṭani kauṃ, dekhata haiṃ kara lāi.*

happy with the situation? She will definitely feign something else in the next song:

> "Mohana, let go of my hair!
> Aren't you ashamed to touch my breast over and over! O why have I come here without companions?
> Some girl might come and see us," she said, frowning her brow.
> "Again and again I implore you by brother,[106] you don't listen to my plea!"
> "You're taking an oath for such a slight offense? I came to behold your face."
> Sūr's Śyāma's sophisticated lady was done in, overpowered she went home, but not angry. (*SS* 2067/1449)[107]

In this poem, we get to witness the actual exchange between the accoster and the Gopī. At the surface level, the woman is upset and appealing to Krishna's sense of shame. However, if we feel so inclined, we may well think that she is only pretending she is afraid someone might see them. She frowns, but that may be intended coquettishly. The dialogue between the two is ambiguous; it is not clear who says what. She seems to appeal to his sense of propriety by invoking his (or maybe her) brother. Krishna seems to be out to charm her by saying she is quick to abuse him and that he intends nothing improper, he just wants to see her angry. In any case, by the end of the song, Krishna has won, and the girl goes home "overpowered" (*bibasa*) but not angry, at least so specifies the commentator, Sūr. Here we are back to the third person reporter. The audience may well be left wondering what the Gopī really felt. The next poem, in response, further clarifies her state of mind.

> She went home, her heart abducted by Hari
> She goes two steps, stops, looks back. Her heart wonders: "what did Hari do?"
> She forgot which way she had come. She doesn't recognize the way she came.

106. The term *bīra-duhāī* can mean "oath by the brother" or "calling for help for a friend." It can be interpreted as the girl's brother or friend. However, the Hindi paraphrase by Bāhrī and Kumar (1974: 981) specifies this as referring to Balarāma, Krishna's brother, which is another possibility. The line is ambiguous. If Krishna is addressing the girl, one could translate also: "again and again [your friends] implored you, but you did not listen to their plea." In that case, the next line would be the girl's answer "I came to make them swear," meaning "to annoy my friends."

107. *chāḍḥi dehu merī laṭa mohana; kuca parasata puni puni sakucata nahiṃ, kata āī taji gohana; juvati āni dekhihai koū, kahati baṃka kari bhauṃhana; bāra bāra kahī bīra-duhāī, tuma mānata nahiṃ sauṃhana; itanai hīṃ kauṃ sauṃha divāvati, maiṃ āyau mukha johana; sūra syāma nāgari basa kīnhī, bibasa calī ghara koha na.*

Annoyed and irritated, she shakes her hairlocks. The very ones that
Śyāma's hands had released!
She drowns in an ocean of love. Her heart captured and colored by
Hari's passion
Her thoughts stuck on Sūrdās's Lord, she did not come home,
wavering whether to trust this path or that.[108] (*SS* 2068/1450)[109]

Whatever she might have felt at the moment of the encounter, afterward this milkmaid seems to have come around to liking it. The poem is a third person account, but it presents a fine insight into the woman's psychological state and portrays a chain of small events. At the beginning, she resolutely sets off on her way home, but she is totally upset, trying to make sense of what has happened. She has lost all sense of direction, even literally, to the point where she cannot find her way back home, which upsets her further. Irritated with her own irresoluteness, she shakes her head, which loosens some hair locks. This reminds her of Krishna's touching them. That thought plunges her in "an ocean of love," and now passion overwhelms her. She does not know what to make of her usual world anymore. The meeting with the divine totally unsettles the world of everyday experience, it alienates us from our usual ways. It throws us literally off track and forces us to reevaluate who we are.

We have caught this Gopī in a suspended state of agitation, unsure of what happened, unsure of how she feels about it, yet irresistibly attracted. In the next poem we see her regain her wits.

Then home and family intruded in her mind.
Now her eyes recognized the road home. She became ashamed at
heart.
Somehow or other she reached her home, but Kanhāī wouldn't
budge from her mind.
Her friends started to question her: "How come you lingered at
Yamunā's banks?
You got in some strange state. Why don't you tell us what
happened?"

108. Literally: "she did not come, trusting this way and that way," or "she did not manage to trust (*āvata nahiṃ . . . patīnau*) here nor there." This may refer to the path she is to take home, or metaphorically to the moral path she will take: join Krishna or stay home.

109. *calī bhavana mana hari hai līnhauṃ; paga dvai jāti ṭhaṭhaki phiri herati, jiya yaha kahati kahā hari kīnhauṃ; māraga bhūli gaī jihiṃ āī, āvata kai nahiṃ pāvati cīnhauṃ; risa kari khojhi khojhi laṭa jhaṭakati, syāma bhujani chuṭakāyau īnhauṃ; prema siṃdhu maiṃ magana bhaī tiya, hari kauṃ raṃga bhayau ura līnau; sūradāsa-prabhu sauṃ cita aṃṭakyau, āvata nahiṃ ita utahiṃ patīnau.*

"What can I say? I can't speak. Sūr's Śyāma has put a spell on me."
(SS 2069/1451)[110]

Here the poet shows the heroine trying to regain composure. She becomes all at once aware of her house and elders, thinking of what they may say about the incident. That sobers her up. The familiar world of ordinary, everyday experience takes over again. However, the meeting with the divine causes a profound alteration. When the milkmaid gets home, she finds it still impossible to put Śyāma out of her thoughts. And now her friends have gotten wind that something happened. In the next, somewhat enigmatic poem in this cycle, she relates to her friends what has happened. As she articulates the incident, it gets altered: she puts her own spin on it.

"Listen friend, there on Yamunā's banks
I was filling water alone at the well, and Śyāma grabbed my hair.
I put the water pot on my head, set out on the road. He was wearing this yellow garb . . .
He looked so handsome, I got desirous. The jingling of the waist-belt on top of the garment."[111]
The milkmaids were secretly pleased, proud in comportment like great conquerors, victorious in battle.
Caught in Sūr's Gopāla's embrace, her destiny was fulfilled, her vessels gilded.[112] (*SS* 2070/1452)[113]

Our heroine starts out telling a straight story, but then she gets off track. As she remembers how good Krishna looked, she becomes somewhat incoherent, but she admits she was more than willing. She is less explicit about what happened next. The reference to the sound of the waist-belt is enigmatic. Is it

110. *ghara gurujana kī sudhi jaba āī; taba māraga sūjhyau nainani kachu, jiya apanaiṃ tiya gaī lajāī; pahuṃcī āi sadana jyauṃ-tyauṃ kari, naiku na cita taiṃ ṭerata kanhāī; sakhī saṃga kī bhūjhana lāgīṃ, jamunā-taṭa ati gahara lagāī; aurai dasā bhaī kachu terī, kahati nahīṃ hama sauṃ samujhāī; kahā kahauṃ kachu kahata na āvai, sūra syāma mohinī lagāī.*

111. It is not clear what is meant with *kāch banī*; it seems to be a compound verb with the first part *kāch-*, which is a transitive verb meaning to "put on a loincloth." The colloquial expression *kāch kholnā* means "to loosen the loincloth," i.e., "to have sexual intercourse" (*OHED*); something in that vein may be the intended meaning. Bahadur (1999: 301) translates this line simply with reference to the sound of the waist belt and interprets it as Krishna's waist belt. The Hindi paraprase of Bāhrī and Kumār (1974: 983) is similar. However, in the light of the reference to victory in the following line, I'm inclined to read it as a reference of the sound of her girdle, a veiled allusion to love play with the woman on top (see the discussion).

112. This translation is slightly free. Literally: "her golden vessels bore fruit." Bāhrī and Kumār interpret this as her breasts (*kucoṃ*) (1974: 983).

113. *sunahu sakhī rī vā jamunā-taṭa; hauṃ jala bharati akelī panighaṭa, gahī syāma merī laṭa; lai gagarī sira māraga ḍagarī, una pahire pīre paṭa; dekhata rūpa adhika ruci upajī, kācha banī kiṃkini-raṭa; phūla hieṃ gvālini kaiṃ jyauṃ rana jīte phirai mahābhaṭa; sūra lahyau gopāla-āliṃgana, suphala kiye kaṃcana-ghaṭa.*

Krishna's waist-belt resounding because he dances? Or might she be implying it is hers? If the latter, this maybe an allusion to lovemaking with the woman on top (*viparīta rati*).[114] It seems that this Gopī is suggesting obliquely to her friends that she made love with Krishna, while being on top. That would explain her friends' reaction: they feel victorious, as if they have been on a conquest. Often, lovemaking is compared to a battle between the man and the woman (*surata yuddha*) and the woman on top is interpreted as a victory for the woman.

Are we witnessing here the Braj variant of women boasting about their sexual experiences? Maybe the woman-on-top interpretation is far-fetched (or for the initiated only). In any case, the Gopī has transformed the unsettling experience at the well into one from which she emerges victoriously. Her friends approve, and so does the poet. He ends by putting his own, theological spin on the event: she has found her destiny fulfilled. The term used, *suphala,* literally means "bore good fruit"; here the intended meaning is "reached the summum bonum." This poem seems to hearken back to the very first poem, both in its theological interpretation and in the play on the word *ghaṭa*. The first meaning of this polysemantic term is "vessel," so there is a reference to the water pitchers the milkmaid brought to the well. "Her vessels have become golden" alludes to her ordinary experience of going to the well being transformed in a wondrous one. Second, as the woman's breasts have been compared to vessels filled with nectar (*SS* 2066/1448), another level of meaning of "golden vessels" may be an allusion to physical fulfillment. Finally, *ghaṭa* can also mean "body," "mortal frame." The milkmaid's golden body has found its destiny, has become fulfilled in the encounter with her Lord. Here we have a more philosophical interpretation. The compilers of *Sūr Sāgar* have definitely succeeded in gilding the pots—in upgrading an earthy incident with a shiny theological polish and transforming titillating folk songs into vehicles for divine revelation.

Thus, we started out this sequence of poems from the point of view of the accoster: we followed Krishna's lustful male gaze and saw him approach the woman alone at the well. We also got a hint that she might have enjoyed it. When we followed the woman home, we got to explore her perspective. We witnessed how she gradually processed the experience, to the point of seeing herself not as a victim, but as a victor in the battle of love. She could even share the experience with her friends triumphantly. The claim in the initial theological tone-setter poem seems proven: Krishna plays this role of accoster to fulfill the women's secret wishes.

114. Whereas the sound of anklets is indicative of lovemaking in the "missionary position," the tinkling of the girdle belt is supposed to evoke *viparīta rati* (see, e.g., Ingalls 1965: 510, n. at 592).

RĀDHĀ FIGHTS BACK. Does all this mean that the Gopīs offer women an example of minimal resistance to accosters, even license to indulge? In comparison to Sītā's example, this Gopī's reaction seems rather meek indeed. In the end, though, she has not taken Krishna's harassment lying down. She starts out as the victim, but she comes around to being a victor, if only in her own mind. She shares her experience with others, who now in turn will be emboldened to react. They make for stronger assertive role models: women standing up against eve-teasing.

Rumors have spread, and everyone knows now about Krishna and his gang tyranizing women who dare go to the river. We've seen already how this leads to more caution on the part of the women, and Krishna and his friends tiring from waiting for hapless victims to show up at the well (*SS* 2017/1828). The following poem gives the sequel. Now the women come to the well prepared for what may happen. One woman somehow shows up, but she is determined not to be scared off:

> One young lady arrives. Śyāma sees her.
> Hari keeps himself hidden in the tree. The woman walks the Yamunā's banks.
> The water ripples as the lass fills her pot of brass. Then she puts it on her head.
> She is about to go home, but from behind her, he makes the pot spill over her head.
> Quick-witted, the milkmaid grabs Śyāma's hands. She gets hold of his golden stick.
> "You keep teasing the others, Kanhāī, but now you've encountered me!"
> He smiles and puts her pot back in the milkmaid's hands. "I won't take an empty pot,
> Sūr's Śyāma, you fill it with water and bring it here, only then will I hand your stick back!" (2022/1407)[115]

This milkmaid is no pushover. She quickly assesses the situation and gets right back at Krishna, grabbing his stick. She wants him to make up for spilling water from her pot. Who is this daring lady? There is a hint that this Gopī may be Rādhā, as she invokes the power of Vṛṣabhānu in the next poem:

115. *juvati ika āvati dekhī syāma; druma kaiṃ oṭa rahe hari āpuna, jamunā taṭa gaī bāma; jala halori gāgari bhari nāgari, jabahīṃ sīsa uṭhāyau; ghara kauṃ calī jāya tā pāchaiṃ, sira taiṃ ghaṭa ḍharakāyau; catura gvāli kari gahyau syāma kau, kanaka lakuṭiyā pāī; aurani sauṃ kari rahe acagarī, mosauṃ lagata kanhāī; gāgari lai haṃsi deta gvāri-kara, rītau ghaṭa nahiṃ laihauṃ; sūra syāma hyāṃ āni dehu bhari, tabahi lakuṭa kara daihauṃ.*

"If you'll fill my pot with water, then I'll give back your stick.
So what if Nanda is a big shot? I swear by Vṛṣabhānu, I won't be afraid!
We have to live in one village, in one spot. It's you or me. Why would I take this laying down?
Sūr's Śyāma, I won't be afraid of you. I'll answer your questions!" (*SS* 2023/1405)[116]

If Krishna's father, Nanda, is an important figure in the village of Gokul, Rādhā's father, Vṛṣabhānu, has no less clout in Braj. We have a person speaking here who is sure of herself, secure in the knowledge that she is of equal standing to Krishna. But Krishna knows how to treat such girls:

"Fill my pot with water. Then I'll give back your stick.
I'm the daughter of an important man. I won't be afraid of you!"
"Give me my golden stick, I'll fill your pot with water.
Have you forgotten that day when I took away your clothes?"
Hearing such talk the milkmaid was overpowered, she forgot herself completely.
Sūr says: she did not realize the stick had fallen out of her hand, Śyāma put a spell on her. (*SS* 2024/1406)[117]

Her allusion to her father being an important man, together with the reference to Vṛṣabhānu in the previous poem, makes us suspect that it is indeed none else than Rādhā who is taking on troublesome Krishna. However, he is not to be outsmarted so easily. He pretends he'll do as she wants him to and acts submissively, but then he reminds her of a secret they share: his prank of stealing the Gopīs' clothes. That totally throws her off, and reliving the memory, she forgets everything. The stick just slips out of her hand. Krishna certainly has an uncanny ability to enchant the milkmaids out of their wits. We find out what happens next in the following song:

Śyāma filled the pot with water and lifted it [for her].
She did not have any bodily awareness, went off, in full view of Braj.

116. *ghaṭa merī jabahīṃ bhari daihau, lakuṭī tabahīṃ daihauṃ; kahā bhayau jau naṃda baṛe bṛṣabhānu-āna na ḍaraihauṃ; eka gāṃva eka ṭhāṃva bāsa, tuma kai hau kyauṃ maiṃ saihauṃ; sūra syāma maiṃ tuma na daraihaum, jvāba svāla kau daihauṃ.*

117. *ghaṭa bhari dehu lakuṭa taba daihauṃ; hauṃ hūṃ baṛe mahara kī beṭī, tuma sauṃ nahīṃ ḍaraihauṃ; merī kanaka lakuṭiyā dai rī, maiṃ bhari daihauṃ nīra; bisari gaī sudhi tā dina kī tohiṃ, hare sabani ke cīra; yaha bānī suni gvāri bibasa bhaī, tana kī sudhi bisarāī; sūra lakuṭa kara girata na jānī, syāma ṭhagaurī lāī.*

Handsome Śyāma filled her eyes, and she kept him there and brought him along.
Wherever she turned her eyes, everywhere she saw Kanhāi.
A friend came by, asking: "where did she get lost?
Sūr, just now she came smiling, and went by, lost somewhere." (*SS* 2025/1407)[118]

Thus, feisty Rādhā is totally taken in by handsome Krishna. She does not even greet her friends on the road, totally immersed in her own world of love. Her friends want to know why she is so absentminded, and she explains herself in the next poem:

"Friend, Śyāma put a spell on me!
Just now I went to get water alone. Hari's glances pierced my heart.
What to say, I can't utter anything; the arrowhead has hit my weak spot.
Sūrdās's Lord took my heart, I've lost it, friend." (*SS* 2026/1408)[119]

Rādhā blames Krishna for putting a spell on her. Nanddās, too, presents a first person account in this *pada,* where the Gopīs complain about Krisna's magic:

"I came with water from the Yamunā.
Someone's dark son, with crooked glances made me loose my way.
Mohana said: 'I don't recognize you as one of Braj.'
I was spellbound, struck with magic. Ever since, I'm restless, can't bring out a word.
From the day he looked at my body, I was lost to him.
My heart went to Nanddās's Lord, like water to the well." (*NP* 84)[120]

This watter-carrier claims that "some dark lad"—and of course we know who that is—has put a spell on her. Krishna's words, that she seems to be from a different village, are significant, because by saying so he suggests the woman is not "like a sister," as the women of one's village should be treated. Instead, as

118. *ghaṭa bhari diyau syāma uṭhāi; naiku tana kī sudhi na tākauṃ, calī braja-samuhāi; syāma suṃdara naina-bhītara, rahe āni samāi; jahāṃ-jahaṃ bhari dṛṣṭi dekhai, tahāṃ-tahāṃ kanhāi; utahiṃ tai ika sakhī āī, kahati kahā bhulāi; sūra abahīṃ haṃsata āī, calī kahā gavāṃi.*

119. *rī hauṃ syāma mohinī ghālī; abahiṃ gaī jala bharana akelī, hari citavani ura sālī; kahā kahauṃ kachu kahata na āvai, lagī marama kī bhālī; sūradāsa prabhu mana hari līnhau, bibasa bhaī hauṃ ālī.*

120. *āvata hī jamunā bhari pānī; syāma rūpa kāhū koṃ ḍhoṭā, bāṃkī citavana merī gaila bhulānī; mohana kahyo tumako yā braja meṃ, nahiṃ jānī pahicānī; ṭhagi sī rahī ceṭaka soṃ lāgyo, taba taiṃ byākula phurata na bānī; jā dina tai citayo rī mo tana, tā dina taiṃ una hātha bikānī; naṃdadāsa prabhu yau mana mili gayo, jyoṃ sāraṃga meṃ pānī.*

a stranger she becomes sexually available to him. This Gopī does not have a witty repartee ready to go. She is simply at a loss for words, she says. Yet she manages to bring out an apt comparison in the last line.

The image the Gopī evokes of her heart flowing automatically to Krishna as water to a well is very applicable indeed. It stresses the inevitability of the goings-on. In a way, it absolves all parties from blame: what is happening is just natural. Krishna is attracted to the women and they to him. It is as crystal-clear as water. At the same time, it is an ironic comment on the *panaghaṭa* theme. Women are drawn to Krishna as water to the well. What better way to express this than by the theme of the chance encounter of the water-carrier and the stranger at the same well? This is another instance where the *panaghaṭa* poems are self-reflective and hint at explanations of why the theme of the water-carrier is so apt for the *bhakta*.

L'ARROSEUR ARROSÉ: KRISHNA IN LOVE AND WORKING HARD TO SEDUCE RĀDHĀ. Some Gopīs as role models may encourage assertiveness in the face of the accoster as they resist and put up a fight. Yet they are not successful at keeping their accoster at bay. Try as they may, in poem after poem the women are taken in by Krishna. He charms them out of their wits. On the other hand, though, it is not only the milkmaids who loose their cool. One time, at least, Krishna, too, is seriously in love. This is a case of *l'arroseur arrosé:* the sprinkler, the expert at getting the Gopīs soaked, is now drenched himself in the liquid of love. And this time, the lady in question is unambiguously identified as Rādhā:

> Rādhā called her friends and went off:
> "Come, let's go to fetch water from the Yamunā." All went off happily.
> All took a pot and quickly reached [the river].
> There they saw young handsome Śyāma and the young girl was pleased in her heart.
> Seeing Nanda's darling son attracted, they kept staring at him with enchantment.
> Sūr's Lord's dear Rādhā smilingly filled her pot. (*SS* 2054/1436)[121]

We hear of the effect of Śyāma's appearance on all the women, but Rādhā seems to be a different case. She just goes about her business smilingly. Krishna on the other hand is majorly affected:

121. *rādhā sakhini laī bulāi; calau jamunā jalahiṃ jaiyai, calīṃ saba sukha pāī; sabani ika ika kalasa līnhau, turata pahuṃcī jāi; tahāṃ dekhyau syāma suṃdara, kuṃvari mana harașāi; naṃda-naṃdana dekhi rījhe, citai rahe cita lāi; sūra prabhu kī priyā rādhā, bharati jala musukāi.*

They went home, [their pots] filled with water.
Pretty Rādhā looked splendid in the midst of her friends. Hari fell in love.
She looked gorgeous as she moved slowly, her shawl flapping [in the breeze].
Mohana was enchanted, and kept them company on the way.
There are no words to describe how her braid kept swaying on her buttocks.
Under the spell of this sweet girl, Sūr's Śyāma tasted passion in every pore [of his body]. (*SS* 2055/1437)[122]

No philosophy here. It surely is Rādhā's physical charms that attract Krishna. Now he is the one under a spell. He just cannot keep his eyes off her. It is his turn to be a victim of Cupid's arrows:

The pretty lass fetched water with her jar [of brass].
Pot on head, among her friends, she cast at him a glance.
Her neck sways, her nose ring picks up the pace. Slowly she comes this way.
Her brow's the bow, her glance the arrow, she aims at Hari all along the way.
His mere glance once burned Cupid's body. Now Cupid strikes him back.
Sūr's Śyāma, gazing at the sweet girl's beauty, calls himself blessed. (*SS* 2056/1438)[123]

Krishna is so taken in with this pretty girl that he gets really fancy with a Homeric simile, comparing her to the elegant royal elephant (*SS* 2057/1439). More significantly, this time, Krishna does not play the accoster. In fact, he is nearly falling over his feet to please her:

There comes the smart girl amid her friends.
Seeing her beauty, Nanda's darling son is attracted. He seeks to attract his darling in [his] heart.

122. *gharahiṃ calīṃ jamunā-jala bhari kai; sākhini bīca nāgarī birājati, bhaī prīta ura hari kaiṃ; maṃda maṃda gati calata adhika chabi, aṃcala rahyau phahari kai; mohana kauṃ mohinī lagāī, saṃgahiṃ cale ḍagari kai; benī kī chabi kahata na āvai, rahī nitaṃbani ḍharikai; sūra syāma pyārī kaiṃ basa bhae, roma-roma rasa bhari kai.*

123. *nāgari gāgari jala bhari lyāvai; sakhiyani bīca bharyau ghaṭa sira par, tāpara naina calāvai; ḍulata grīva laṭakati naka-besari, maṃda-maṃda gati āvai; bhṛkuṭī dhanuṣa kaṭāccha bāna, manu puni puni harihiṃ lagāvai; jākauṃ nirakhi anaṃga anaṃgita, tāhi anaṃga baṛhāvai; sūra syāma pyārī chabi nirakhata, āpuhiṃ dhanya kahāvai.*

Sometimes in front, sometimes behind, he tells her about all the shades of his love.
Rādhā guesses as much: "Hari is out to steal my heart."
He's walking ahead with his golden stick, clearing a path for her.
Wherever he sees the shadow of his beloved, he makes the stick [or: his own shadow] touch it.
Gazing at her beauty, he'd give up his body, that's what he wants the smart girl's heart to understand.
He makes her feel like she would like to cover her head with [his] yellow sash.[124]
He wraps his sash to show her,[125] with that excuse he comes near.
Sūr's Śyāma with such desires attracts Rādhā's heart. (2058/1440)[126]

Here, Krishna is not harassing Rādhā but rather making a path for her through the jungle thickets. Krishna is going out of his way to please her. She senses his intent, and remains alert so as not to fall for him. Instead of grabbing her, as is his wont, he does not touch her body but touches her shadow instead. Then he comes up with some excuse to get close to her; apparently he offers her his yellow sash to cover her beauty, so as to ward off the evil eye, caused by his excessive admiration. At the end of the poem, it is said "he attracts Rādhā's heart," so he seems to be finally gaining some ground. Or is he? The next poem starts on a discouraging note:

Śyāma does not manage to get his love to stick.
Then he hit on a way: this surely is to awaken desire in the body of his beloved!
With some excuse he came close and inspected her face. He threw his yellow sash to cover her head (to ward off the evil eye).
With such a trick Kanhāī stole her heart. He overwhelmed the pretty princess with desire.

124. This line is unclear. I've taken it that Krishna's admiration causes Rādhā in her natural modesty to want to draw a veil over her head, yet her desiring his garment to do so indicates at the same time a contradictory desire to be close to him. I've read *vārata* here literally as "covering." An alternative interpretation, with similar implications, would read it as "warding off evil, surrendering." So one can read "He surrenders, yellow sash on head, to make her want him," or "she would like the yellow-sashed youth to ward off evil from her head."

125. An alternative interpretation would read "She draws her veil, and goes to show him."

126. *sakhiyani bīca nāgarī āvai; chabi nirakhata rījhyau naṃda-naṃdana, pyārī manahiṃ rijhāvai; kabahumka āgaim kabahuṃka pāchaiṃ, nānā bhāva batāvai; rādhā yaha anumāna karai, hari mere citahiṃ curāvai; āgaiṃ jāi kanaka lakuṭī lai, paṃtha saṃvāri banāvai; nirakhata jahāṃ chāṃha pyārī kī, tahaṃ lai chāṃha chuvāvai; chabi nirakhata tana vārata apanau, nāgari-jiyahiṃ janāvai; apane sira pītāṃbara vārata, aisaiṃ ruci upajāvai; oṛhi uṛhaniyāṃ calata dikhāvata, ihiṃ misa nikaṭahiṃ āvai; sūra syāma aise bhāvani sauṃ, rādhā-manahiṃ rijhāvai.*

Her body shivered, her bodice burst, the joy in her chest made her shawl flutter.
Aiming for her jug, he started throwing pebbles, their rebound hit his darling's body.
With Mohana's spell on her heart, she came home amid her girlfriends.
Sūrdās's Lord had tied up her heart, and made her forget home and hearth.[127] (*SS* 2059/1441)[128]

Well, yes, Rādhā falls for his tricks. It seems that his gesture of wrapping his yellow sash so as to cover her beauty is what finally wins her over. Her reaction is very physical: her hair standing on end, her bodice bursting, her shawl fluttering with her heart's movement. It is as if all markers of womanly virtue have automatically become undone. Krishna catches on right away to these telltale signs of sexual desire and he promptly falls back into his accoster ways: he starts pellting her with pebbles. Interestingly, it is physical abuse that he indulges in, not lovemaking. Rādhā continues on her way home, but what has happened has eradicated all sense of home and body.

What to make of all this? We've witnessed some of the events at the well, but they have come filtered through many voices. The official version is that it is all about God fulfilling his devotees' wishes. We are to fit everything in the theological perspective of God showing his grace. The Gopīs are role models for the devotee; their all-encompassing love is to show us the path to God.

However, the situation of the encounter at the well is all too recognizable for ordinary women. Notwithstanding the theological framing, there is no around the fact that this is an affair of physical attraction: the description of the Gopīs' physical charms leave nothing to the imagination as to what Krishna is supposed to be attracted by. And what they report to be attracted by is Krishna's dark handsomeness.

What kind of subtextual message, then, does this send to women? Does the religiously sanctioned flirtatious behavior of the Gopīs open the door for women to express their own desires, even if extramarital? Does it hold out the possibility of a mutually agreeable relationship in which a woman can be an

127. Literally: "body and house."

128. *laga lāgana nahiṃ pāvata syāma; taba ika bhāva kiyau kachu aisau, pyārī-tana upajāyau kāma; misa kari nikaṭa āi mukha heryau, pītāṃbara ḍāryau sira vāri; yaha chala kari mana haryau kanhāī, kāma bibasa kīnhī sukumāri; pulaki aṃga aṃgiyā darakānī, ura ānaṃda aṃcala phaharāta; gāgari tāki kāṃkarī mārai, ucaṭi ucaṭi lāgati priya-gāta; mohana mana mohinī lagāī, sakhini saṃga pahuṃcī ghara jāi; sūradāsa prabhu sauṃ mana aṃṭakyau, deha-geha kī sudhi bisarāi.*

assertive partner and not hierarchically subjugated? The answer of expounders of the scriptures will undoubtedly be in the negative.

Indeed, if we look at the nature of the relationship itself, we may well raise some questions. Krishna expresses his affection in rather physically abusive ways: throwing pebbles, breaking pots, grabbing the women by their hair, and molesting them. The Gopīs are not always pushovers, but in the end, they always loose. Krishna has this way of putting a spell on them. They are unable to defend themselves, hopelessly lost. Only one time does Krishna himself get lost, too, and go out of his way, to woo Rādhā. But once he senses victory, he is back to his old ways of abuse.

If there is a message sent to women, it is not about the permissibility of extramarital affairs, or lessons in how to react assertively when accosted. Rather, it lies in how their reactions are perceived in the case of sexual harassment. How is this harassment judged? Who is to blame? Whose perspective is presented in such judgments?

Deciding Where to Put the Blame

Sūr Sāgar, in framing these songs with a theological master narrative, supports the assumption that the devotees actively want and enjoy this type of relationship with God. Transposed to the real world, this may imply that physical abuse is what women really want. This begs the question whether the women really enjoy the harassment. The panoply of voices and perspectives does not make it easier to decide what we should conclude from these poems. We must assemble the evidence and decide about whether or not the women come out as victims of harassment, or whether they are acting of their own volition and thus can be blamed, at least partially, themselves.

THE WILLING VICTIM. The big difference, then, with Sītā's situation is the ambiguity in the Gopīs' reaction to the sexual harassment they are confronted with. It is not immediately clear whether they are willing or unwilling victims. The poems do not give us a straightforward answer. In his editorial voice, Sūrdās says explicitly that one of the milkmaids is delighted to meet Krishna at the well. As if to back up his assessment, he reports a conversation between the accosted woman and her friends and has the woman herself confess that such an interpretation is correct. The story is spread over three poems in *Sūr Sāgar*:

> Hari met with the girl and gave her bliss.
> Her fever subdued when she tasted love, she was lost in passion.
> She could not move a step on the path, the clever lady, forgot all
> about home.

The women of Braj on their way to fetch water called out when they saw her:
"Where are you going, you left the path?" They told her, "Come here."
Drenched in Sūr's Lord's passion, she just stares, her heart hopelessly lost.[129] (*SS* 2028/1410)[130]

"Someone has put a spell on you!"
"Your friends are inquiring, but you don't listen a bit!" "What drug did you eat?"
She started, as if waking up from a dream. Then she told her friends everything:
"I met a dark-hued lad, he put a spell on me.
I came this way with my water, when he all at once caught me in embrace."
Sūr: in front of her friends, the milkmaid told everything, as if she had lost all shame. (2029 /1411)[131]
"I'm coming here with water from the Yamunā.
A dark boy, I don't know whose son, but when I saw his body, I forgot the way home.
I gazed at his body, he at mine, right there I was sold to him.
My heart aflutter, under his fixed stare my body was restless, not a single word coming out of my mouth.
Mohana said: 'Enchanting lady, who are you? I haven't had the pleasure of your acquaintance yet.' "
One look at Sūrdās's Lord Mohana and she was lost like a drop in the ocean.(2030/1412)[132]

Thus, at least one Gopī acknowledges among friends in her first person report that she was totally taken in by Krishna. This is not platonic love. She

129. Literally: "she keeps staring, her mind applied."

130. *mili hari sukha diyau tihiṃ bāla; tapati miṭi gī prema chākī, bhaī rasa behāla; mṛga nahīṃ ḍaga dharati nāgari, bhavani gaī bhulāi; jala bharana brajanāri āvati, dekhi tāhi bulāi; jāti kita hvai ḍagara chāṃḍe, kahyau ita kauṃ āi; sūra prabhu kai raṃga rāṃcī, citai rahī cita lāi.*

131. *kāhū tohiṃ ṭhagaurī lāī; būjhati sakhī sunatai nahi naikuhuṃ, tuhīṃ kidhauṃ ṭhagamūri khāī; cauṃki parī sapanaiṃ janu jāgī, tab bānī kahi sakhini sunāī; śyāma barana ika milyau ḍhuṭaunā, tihiṃ mokauṃ mohinī lagāī; maiṃ jala bhare itahiṃ kauṃ āvati, āni acānaka aṃkama lāī; sūra gvāri sakhiyani ke āgaiṃ, bāta kahati saba lāj gaṃvāī.*

132. *āvati hī jamunā bhari pānī; syāma barana kāhū kau ḍhoṭā, nirakhi badana ghara-gaila bhulānī; maiṃ una tan una mo tana citayau, tabahīṃ taiṃ una hātha bikānī; ura dhakadhakī ṭakaṭakī lāgī, tana byākula mukha phurati na bānī; kahyau mohana mohini tū ko hai, mohi nāhīṃ tosauṃ pahicānī; sūradāsa prabhu mohana dekhata, janu bāridha jala-būṃda hirānī.*

describes a physical sensation: she is gazing at the handsome man's body, he at hers. Physical attraction is writ large over the incident. Again, in this case, Krishna stresses he does not know her (yet), and she seems not to know whose son he is, so we have a subtle suggestion that she is from "out of town" and thus sexually available to him.

Instead of being scared off by these tales of harassment, the Gopīs react in quite the opposite way. In the following poem, this news causes a group of women to rush off to the river.

> When they heard that that was the matter, the girls felt all aflutter.
> They took her [the milkmaid who had been accosted] by the arm and led her home. Then they themselves went for water to the Yamunā.
> When they got there, they saw Hari wasn't there, wherever their keen eye fell.
> They filled up with water, lingered, but set off for home, regretting about Hari over and over.
> When he saw the milkmaids thus distressed, Hari came out of hiding. He happily cooled the fire in their bodies.
> Sūr's Śyāma embraced them, because he could read their mind. (*SS* 2027/1409)[133]

The women are agitated, but not with righteous anger. They set off for the Yamunā and are disappointed when they find that Krishna is not there. They linger, they look around, and then, just when they are about to give up and express regret, he shows up. Here, clearly, it is because of their desire that Krishna approaches them. His motive is fulfilling his devotees' longings. We are reminded here of the theological framing poem at the beginning of the series.

So a first assessment seems to provide evidence for the Gopīs being willing victims. They even actively seek out the experience of being harassed by Krishna, after they have heard one Gopī's report. Krishna merely acts out of kindness toward them when he obligingly accosts them. They would have been disappointed had he not. However, there is also some counter-evidence.

133. *sunata bāta yaha sakhi aturānī; tāhi bāṃha gahi ghara pahuṃcāī, āpu calī jamunā kaiṃ pānī; dekhe āi vahāṃ hari nāhīṃ, citavati jahāṃ tahāṃ bitatānī; jala bhari ṭhaṭhukati calī gharahiṃ tana, bāra-bāra hari kauṃ pachitānī; gvālini bikala dekhi hari pragaṭe, harasa bhayau tana tapati bujhānī; sūra syāma aṃkama bhari līnhī, gopī-aṃtaragata kī jānī.*

THE MORALLY OUTRAGED. Who will stand up against Krishna's harassment? Sometimes a Gopī is portrayed as genuinely outraged by the reports of Krishna's harassment. In the following poem, she sets off resolutely with the intention to lecture that Krishna with his wily ways. However, her motives may not be so pure either:

> "Kanhāī does not budge from my thoughts.
> For one I keep savoring the dark one's passion. On top of that she told us her story."
> She sent her [the accosted woman] off with words of warning. Then she herself went, keen for water.
> A peacock crown on his head, a yellow sash wrapped around: she saw the young man is Nanda's son!
> Earrings flashing on his handsome cheeks, beautiful, large, pleasant eyes.
> She said: "Sūr's Lord, you've learned some manners! You're going around enchanting other men's wives!" (*SS* 2031/1413)[134]

This Gopī lectures Krishna about what he is doing and confronts him with the moral implications of his acts. Still, she, too, seems irresistibly drawn to the handsome stranger in the woods. Though she keeps up a tone of moral outrage, Krishna is ready with a good answer. He shifts the burden of proof to the women:

> "Whom have I enchanted, did I trick you?"
> "Why not, you may still enchant me. I've seen how you've enchanted others"
> "Speak up, say her name, how did I enchant? I keep hearing this accusation.[135]
> Tell me what the evidence was for this deceit? What were the wounds of this attack?"
> "Well, hear the evidence of deceit from me: with sweet smiles you steal hearts!

134. *naiṃku na mana taiṃ ṭarata kanhāī; ika aisaiṃhi chaki rahī syāma-rasa, tāpara ihiṃ yaha bāta sunāī; vākauṃ sāvadhāna kari paṭhayau, calī āpu jala kauṃ aturāī; mora mukuṭa pītāṃbara kāche, dekhyau kuṃvara naṃda kau jāī; kuṃḍala jhalakata lalita kapolani, suṃdara naina bisāla suhāī; kahyau sūra-prabhu ye ḍhaṃga sīkhe, ṭhagata phirata hau nāri parāī.*

135. Literally: "they keep telling this story."

Sūr's lord, you go around glancing meaningfully and you twist your
body like a dancer."[136] (*SS* 2032/1414)[137]

Krishna presses for specifics about the identity of his victims. In reply, this Gopī drops a hint that she herself may still fall victim to him. While she poses as a would-be savior of women's virtue, her accusation does not amount to much of an argument to stand in court, and she herself seems rather taken in by Krishna's flirtatious glances. We can only guess what happened next, but we may have a strong suspicion that this woman, too, fell a willing victim to Krishna's charms, which she so eloquently describes. At other times, however, there is real moral outrage in the women's voices:

"Śyāma your mischief is too much:
You snatch pot carriers, you break water pots.
Let us fill up with Yamunā's water. Stop your naughty talk.
No one dares to walk the road. You keep stopping them with your
gang on the path.
Spying the road, stepping ahead, girls arrive dying of fear.
Sūr's Śyāma, you'll get scolded, whichever of us comes to your
house!" (*SS* 2033/1415)[138]

These women sound exasperated. They have had enough of this constant harassment and hit on the right tactic to subdue him: they will go to his house and complain to his elders. Krishna might act tough far away from the control of village rules, but it remains to be seen what he will do when he is confronted with the consequences of his behavior back home. The Gopīs have had to face the consequences all along. Their mothers and sisters have already been complaining. And they do not fail to tell Krishna:

"Bring back the pot carriers that aren't yours.
What do you care?[139] But my sister and mother will quarrel with me.
Others went with me to fetch water. From every house, they've
returned.

136. Literally: "in *tribhaṅga*."

137. *kahā ṭhagyau tumharau ṭhagi līnhau; kyauṃ nahiṃ ṭhagyau aura kaha ṭhagihau orahi ke ṭhaga cīnhauṃ; kahau nāma dhari kahā ṭhagāyau, suni rākhaiṃ yaha bāta; ṭhaga ke lacchana māhiṃ batāvahu, kaise ṭhaga ke ghāta; ṭhaga ke lacchana hama sauṃ suniyai, mṛdu musukani cita corata; naina-saina dai calata sūra prabhu, tana tribhaṃga kari morata.*

138. *atihiṃ karata tuma syāma acagarī; kāhū kī chīnata hau iṃḍurī, kāhū kī phorata hau gagarī; bharana dehu jamunā-jala hama kauṃ, dūri karau ye bātaiṃ laṃgarī; paiṛe calana na pāvai koū, roki rahata larikani lai ḍagarī; ghāṭa-bāṭa saba dekhati āvati, juvatī ḍarani marati haiṃ sagarī; sūra syāma tehiṃ gārī dījai, jo kou āvai tumharī bagarī.*

139. Literally: "What will anyone do to you?"

Sūr's Śyāma, give back the pot carrier, or else we'll tell mother
Yaśodā." (*SS* 2035/1417)[140]

When Krishna takes away their pot carriers, the milkmaids get into trouble at home. The family cannot afford to lose so many pots and pot carriers daily. The Gopīs get blamed for the loss. Never mind it was not their fault, their mothers and sisters blame them all the same. Between the lines we read how women are always held responsible for preserving their honor. The village suspicion is that if these girls are saying they are being harassed, still they may be at fault for having invited such trouble. Now, they decide to turn the tables and let Krishna suffer his family's censure. In the last line, they threaten to tell his mother, Yaśodā. They make their threat more explicit in another poem:

"You don't give me my pot carrier? All right.
Well, we'll take you and confront mother Yaśodā. Come girls, let's go as a group.
No one can put the fear in Kanhāī. On the road, on the steps, everywhere you harass us.
You swept away the pot carrier at Yamunā's pool, you broke all our pots and jugs.
You've had your fun, prince Kanhāī, today we'll root out your naughtiness!"
Sūr [says]: They confronted mother Yaśodā, all the women of Braj, with their complaints. (*SS* 2034/1416)[141]

The Gopīs decide to get together as a group. Krishna's victims unite. They are determined to change his ways now, by confronting the only one with authority over Krishna, his mother. Here surely they set a wonderful role model for ordinary women coping with male harassment: they have to make common cause, identify who has authority over the harassers, and file a complaint all together. But will they be successful?

EXCUSES AND ACCUSATIONS: KRISHNA EXPOSED BEFORE MOTHER YAŚODĀ. When they bring their complaints before Mother Yaśodā, the Gopīs get to build the

140. *āni dehu geṃḍurī parāī; terau koū kahā karaigau, larihaiṃ hama sauṃ bhaginī māī; mere saṃga kī aura gaī lai jala bhari, ghari ghara taiṃ phiri āīṃ; sūra syāma geṃḍurī dījiye, na tu jasumati sauṃ kaihauṃ jāī.*

141. *nīkaiṃ dehu na merau giṃḍurī; lai jaihaiṃ dhari jasumati āgaiṃ, āvahu rī saba mili ika jhuṃḍarī; kāhūṃ nahīṃ ḍarāta kanhāī, bāṭa ghāṭa tuma karata acagarī; jamunā-daha giṃḍurī phaṭakārī, phorī saba maṭukī aru gagarī; bhalī karī yaha kuṃvara kanhāī, āju meṭihaiṃ tumharī laṃgarī; calīṃ sūra jasumati ke āgaiṃ, urahana lai braja-tarunī sagarī.*

case for their innocence and Krishna's insolence. On this occasion, they refrain from portraying themselves as willing victims, but unfortunately, they betray themselves in minor ways. Krishna points out right from the start that it might well be argued that it is not he who is harassing them but they who are harassing him. In the first poem in the cycle, he does just that. Thus the threats to expose him to his mother leave Krishna undeterred. In the first poem, we witness a comical incident: it seems that Krishna's mother has appeared on the scene, catching him red-handed. But he cleverly turns the tables:

> He climbed up the tree in a hurry!
> Twisted face, brows risen, shouting loudly, swearing by Nanda.[142]
> "Go, tell in front of mother. Fine, all gang up and tie me down."
> "They ganged up to beat me. Then [they] threw the pot carrier [at me].[143]
> That's what was going on when you found me. As if I am to do their jobs for them!"
> "Sūr's Śyāma has made you forget those days: when you brought the mortar to tie him up." (*SS* 2036/1018)[144]

In this poem, it seems that Yaśodā has arrived at the scene.[145] Krishna is quick to save himself. Within his mother's hearing range, he addresses the women, accusing them of ganging up on him. To his mother he says the women were beating him and treating him like a servant. He seems to say that they threw the pot carrier at him to make him go to the well and fetch the water for them. The Gopīs get the last word, but they have no good defense. Gasping at Krishna's quick wit, they can only invoke precedent. They remind Yaśodā how her boy used to steal butter and she had to tie him down to the mortar. That little reminder of the Gopīs is intended to encourage Yaśodā to punish her son this time as she did in the past. Yet at the same time it is a also reminder to the audience of Krishna's miraculous act when he was a toddler,

142. This line could refer to Yaśodā arriving on the scene, although she would not actually pronounce her husband's name but would swear by "your father." One could also read this line as referring to the Gopīs.

143. One could also read this as "I threw it back at them." Krishna has shifted from talking to the Gopīs in the previous line to addressing his mother here.

144. *āpuna caṛhe kadama para dhāī; badana sakora bhaumha morata haiṃ, hāṃka deta kari naṃda-duhāī; jāi kahau maiyā ke āgaiṃ lehu, sabai mili mohiṃ baṃdhāī; mokauṃ juri mārana jaba āīṃ, taba dīnhī geṃḍurī phaṭakāī; aisaiṃ kari mokauṃ tuma pāyau, manu inakī maiṃ karauṃ cerāī; sūra syāma ve dina bisarāe, jaba bāṃdhe tuma ūkhala lāī.*

145. This interpretation is not shared by Bāhrī and Kumār (1974: 969), who see the whole poem as simply Krishna's angry words to the Gopīs. However, the problem with such an interpretation is that the penultimate and last lines do not fit that scenario.

tied to the mortar: he started crawling dragging the heavy mortar around and uprooted two trees in the process, thereby liberating the tree-spirits from a curse.

The last line of the poem, then, does not only function at the level of the quarrel between Krishna and the Gopīs. It also involves a minor epiphany, a sudden revelation, or a drawing of the curtain as Bryant has insightfully called it (1978: 112). This appeal to Yaśodā's memory reminds us of something else: the level beyond the goings-on, beyond the issue of who is harassing whom; of Krishna's divinity.

With Krishna on the scene, the Gopīs do not get to make their case very well. In another poem, they are clever enough to tell him not to come along and go to talk to Yaśodā on their own:

> "You stay here and I'll do the talking, Kanhāī!"
> They went off to tell mother Yaśodā. They went off swearing by Nanda to Śyāma.
> Mother was churning butter in her house, meanwhile all the women gathered.
> She remained staring at women trickling in, could bring out: "what a crowd!
> I know that Hari has pestered them. That's why they've all come running with complaints."
> Sūrdās: the milkmaids were full of anger: "Such insolence your son commits, mother!" (*SS* 2037/1419)[146]

We are transported right there, on the scene, with Yaśodā in the midst of her daily chores as the women arrive. She is amazed at how many keep trickling in and can only bring out: "What a crowd!" But she immediately guesses what it is all about. We are privy to her feelings of unhappy anticipation of what she will hear next.

This time, the Gopīs get to voice their complaints at more length. They use different lines of argument. There are several poems that voice their complaints, and we can imagine that each is spoken by a different woman:

> "Listen mother, your dear boy has gone over the line with his teasing.

146. *ihaṃhi rahau tau badauṃ kanhāī; āpu gaīṃ jasumatihiṃ sunāvana, dai gaīṃ syāmahiṃ naṃda-duhāī; mahari mathati dadhi sadana āpanaiṃ, ihiṃ aṃtara juvatī saba āīṃ; citai rahī juvatini kauṃ āvata, kaha āvati haiṃ bhīra lagāī; maiṃ jānati inakauṃ hari khijhayau, tātaiṃ saba urahana lai dhāīṃ; sūradāsa risa bharī gvālinī, aisau ḍhoṭha kiyau suta māī.*

We went to fetch water from the Yamunā. He stops us on the path.
Makes our water spill from our heads, breaks all our water pots.
Throws away our pot carriers. What Hari is doing is harassment!
All the time he acts like that and he calls us sluts.
Now there's no place to live here in your township of Braj."
He went and climbed on the *kadamba* tree, they all kept an eye [on him].
"Sūr's Śyāma for ever keeps quarreling with us like that." (*SS* 2038/1420)[147]

These women argue that Krishna is harassing them, but they undermine their own case when adding that he calls them sluts (*dhagaṛī* means "adulteress" [*OHED*]). Inadvertently, this gives voice to Krishna, who might well answer the complaints by turning the tables and saying they are not so virtuous themselves. The slur compromises the Gopīs and raises the suspicion that they may have been "asking for it." Moreover, all the while, as they are voicing their complaints, they keep an eye on Krishna in the nearby tree, thus betraying that they cannot keep their eyes off him. Another woman also pleads with Yaśodā to take her son in hand:

"Scold your son, mother, and keep him [home].
He does not let anyone go on the path. He smashes [pots] and throws them on the road.
You don't know your son's vice, while with us you fight.
He takes some ten cows for an alibi,[148] and stops in Braj playing [his flute].
Hari stands on Yamunā's banks. When we see [him] we get afraid again.
Give Sūr's Śyāma a good scolding, he's causing too much of an outcry." (*SS* 2039/1421)[149]

147. *sunahu mahari terau lāḍilau ati karata acagarī; jamuna bharana jala hama gaī tahaṃ rokata ḍagarī; sira taim nīra ḍharāi dai horī saba nagarī; geṃḍuri daī phatākārī kai hari karata ju laṃgarī; nita prati aise ḍhaṃga karaiṃ hamasauṃ kahai dhagarī; aba basa-bāsa banai nahīṃ ihi tuva braja-nagarī; āpu gayau caṛhi kadama para citavata rahīṃ sagarī; sūra syāma aisaiṃ hi sadā hama sauṃ karai jhagarī.*

148. One of the meanings of *lālaca* can be "bait" (*OHED*), but here the intended meaning seems to be more "alibi" or "excuse."

149. *suta kauṃ baraji rākhahu mahari; ḍagara calana na deta kāhuṃhiṃ, phori ḍarata ḍahari; syāma ke guna kachu na jānati, jāti hama sauṃ gahari; ihai lālaca gāi dasa liye, bajati haiṃ braja ṭhahari; jamuna taṭa hari dekhi ṭhāṛhe, ḍarani āvai bahari; sūra syāmahiṃ naiṃku barajau, karata haiṃ ati cahari.*

Here Krishna stands accused of using cowherdng for an alibi while really being out to stop the women on their way to the well. Yaśodā does not see through it; she does not know what her son is up to; she does not know his vices. The word used I have translated as "vices" (*guṇa*) really means "qualities." It can be neutral or positive. Here the meaning is ironical: "bad manners." For the audience, there is an additional irony because Krishna is of course God, and what we are doing in singing this song is singing about God's "qualities," praising him for them. However, in the eyes of the Gopīs, these "qualities" are "vices."

Another Gopī takes yet a different tack. She indicates they have been reluctant to tell Yaśodā till now so as not to hurt her feelings. But things have gotten out of hand now:

> "We're hesitating to tell you this, mother.
> You don't know your son's vice, while with us you fight.
> Has it not come to your ears what an outcry Hari creates?
> Nobody gets to fill up with water. He keeps [us] stopped on the path
> He commits insolence, that Mohana. He threw [my] pot carrier in the deep river."
> What lesson have you taught Sūr's Lord, scolded by angry girls? (*SS* 2040/1422)[150]

This woman echoes the line from the last poem about Krishna's mother being ignorant of Krishna's vices. She is amazed, though, that Yaśodā can claim to be ignorant because she surely should have heard about it, as Krishna has created such an outcry in the village. The last line shifts to the perspective of the mother and sums up the irony of Yaśodā's quandary: how can she teach Krishna a lesson? We know it is all the more difficult because how, indeed, can one scold the Lord of the universe?

YAŚODĀ'S RESOLVE AND ITS RESOLUTION. In the next series of poems, the perspective shifts. We see things through the eyes of the establishment, that is, Krishna's mother. How does Yaśodā react to these complaints? What is her verdict? For one, it is not easy being the mother of God, or any mother for that matter. Yaśodā is torn; her feelings swing all directions. She is willing to

150. *tuma sauṃ kahata sakucatiṃ mahari; syāma ke guna kachu na jānati, jāti hama sauṃ gahari; naikuhūṃ nahiṃ sunati sravanani, karata haiṃ hari cahari; jala bharana kou nāhiṃ pāvati, roki rākhata ḍahari; acagarī ati karata mohana, phaṭaki geḍuri dahari; sūra prabhu kauṃ kahā sikhayo, risani juvatī jhahari.*

punish Krishna, but she points out that the Gopīs have not shown themselves firm in their resolve to see Krishna punished in the past:

> "What am I to do? You all, tell me!
> If I catch him, I'll show him to you. But you'll all be crying 'woe, woe.'
> You too know Hari's vices, but [remember] when [I] tied him to the mortar?
> When I took the stick and started to beat him, you all scolded me!
> Since his youth, he acts like that. I've known his vices since then.
> Sūr, [you'll see] how I shall punish him![151] I'll catch Hari in a minute when he comes." (*SS* 2041/1423)[152]

Yaśodā pleads helplessness. She knows how the Gopīs will react when she tries to punish Krishna, even if she catches him red-handed. They did not like it when she gave him a beating when he committed butter theft. In the last line, Yaśodā seems to have made up her mind: she is ready to punish Krishna. She has come around to the milkmaids' point of view:

> "I know Kanhāī's insolence!
> But first let Syām come home. [You'll see] what a trashing I'll give him.[153]
> Let Mohana be rude to me, I'm his mother
> He does not listen to anyone else. He'll hesitate just a bit in the presence of brother Balarāma.
> Now if I go, where would I find him? Who will fetch him for me?
> Sūr's Śyāma is getting more naughty every day, let me erase that behavior." (*SS* 2042/1424)[154]

Notwithstanding the refrain admitting his insolence, Yaśodā is ambivalent. On the one hand, she realizes Krishna may have gone too far and she takes responsibility as his mother to lecture him. On the other hand, she is postponing:

151. The expression *hāl karnā* means "to punish" (*BBSK*). This seems to be a rhetorical question (Bāhrī and Kumār 1974: 971).

152. *kahā karauṃ mosauṃ kahau sabahīṃ; jau pāūṃ to tumahi dikhāūṃ, hā hā karihai abahīṃ; tumahūṃ guna jānati hau hari ke, ūkhala bāṃdhe jabahīṃ; saṃṭiyā lai mārana jaba lāgī, taba barajyau mohiṃ sabahīṃ; larikāī taiṃ karata acagarī, maiṃ jāne guna tabahīṃ; sūra hāla kaise kari hauṃ dhari, āvai tau hari abahīṃ.*

153. The word *sajāī* is attested as a variant of *sazā* (*BBSK*). Again this is a rhetorical question.

154. *maiṃ jānati hauṃ ḍhīṭha kanhāī; āvana tau ghara dehu syāma kauṃ, kaisī karauṃ sajāī; mosauṃ karata ḍhiṭhāī mohana, maiṃ vākī hauṃ māī; aura na kāhū kauṃ vaha manai, kachu sakucata bala bhāī; aba jau jāuṃ kahā tihiṃ pāūṃ, kāsauṃ dei dharāī; sūra syāma dina dina laṃgara bhayau, dūri karauṃ laṃgarāī.*

she is inclined to wait till he gets home, or wonders how to get hold of him. Still, she seems to be determined to at least lecture her son about his behavior. The Gopīs go home satisfied. But then, on the way, they encounter Krishna, who is on his way home:

> She explained to the girls, and sent them all home:
> "Forgive me for that insult, that's what I say, mothers."
> As all the milkmaids left for their houses, young Kanhāī came from the other side.
> On his way, Hari ran into the girls. When their eyes met, they were ashamed.
> "Go Kānha, your mom calls you. We've just been singing your praises."
> One look at their face and Sūr's Śyāma smiled: "I'll make my mom understand." (*SS* 2043/1425)[155]

Yaśodā has apologized to the milkmaids, but when they run into Krishna, they feel bad about telling on him. They ironically say they have been singing his praise. Well, indeed they have been talking about his "qualities." Krishna can tell from their faces what is going on, but he is confident he will get his mother's ear. The next poem, by contrast, shows Krishna somewhat unsure of himself:

> Syām went home, hesitating a bit.
> From the doorstep he could see: Mom is engaged in her work.
> She was saying: "Where has Kanhāi gone off to?"
> He was standing right behind his mother, listening attentively.
> "The girls don't manage to fill up with water, they're being stopped on the well steps.
> Sūr: everyone had their pot smashed," and Śyāma fled in a hurry.[156] (*SS* 2044/1426)[157]

155. *juvati bodhi saba gharahiṃ paṭhāī; yaha aparādha mohiṃ bakasau rī, yahai kahati hauṃ merī māī; ita taiṃ calīṃ gharani saba gopī, uta taiṃ āvata kuṃvara kanhāī; bīcahiṃ bheṭa bhaī juvatini hari, nainani jorata gaīṃ lajāī; jāhu kānha mahatārī ṭerati, bahuta baṛāī kari hama āī; sūra syāma mukha nirakhi kahyau haṃsi, maiṃ kaihauṃ jananī samujhāī.*

156. I'm taking *parāī* as derived from the verb *parā-*, which can mean *bhāg-* (*BBSK*). Alternatively, one can read the fleeing as part of Yaśodā's speech: "He smashed their pots and ran off in a hurry." This is the interpretation of Bāhrī and Kumār (1974: 971). Maybe both meanings are intended at the same time.

157. *sakucata gae ghara kauṃ syāma; dvārehīṃ tai nirakhi dekhyau, jananī lāgī kāma; yahai bānī kahata mukha taiṃ, kahāṃ gayau kanhāi; āpu ṭāṛhe janani-pāchaiṃ, sunata haiṃ cita lāi; jala bharana juvatī na pāvaiṃ, ghāṭa rokata jāi; sūra sabakī phori gāgari, syāma jāi parāi.*

This poem does not follow logically after Krishna's confident smile in the previous one. Its beauty here lies in the realism of the description. The young child sneaks in, to try to assess the situation. Unaware that he is back, his mother voices the complaints. Once he knows he has been found out, he quickly runs off, fleeing the inevitable punishment. In the last line we taste the irony of God fleeing to avoid a punishment.

In case we have wondered why Yaśodā is talking out loud, we find out in the next poem that she is discussing the situation with Rohiṇī, Krishna's aunt, who is cooking inside.

> Speaking her mind, mother Yaśodā got angry.
> Rohinī was cooking inside, she told her everything she had heard:
> "He insulted our daughters and daughters-in-law. They came running here.
> 'Fie, fie' they all say. I'm alone, how am I to get them off my back?[158]
> What outrage to caste and lineage!" Saying this, she threatened her son.[159]
> "I've gotten defeated in lecturing Sūr's Śyāma. Even a beating does not get him ashamed." (*SS* 2045/1427)[160]

In this poem, again, Yaśodā seems to be outraged by what she has heard of Krishna's behavior. She is on the side of the village's daughters and daughters-in-law. She wants to protect her caste and lineage, and speaks of worries about what people might say. Clearly, dharma concerns prompt her to punish her son. But in the very next poem, Krishna makes her doubt again who is to blame and who should feel shame (*lāj*):

> "You know whether to beat me.
> Who knows about their character? You accept what they say.
> They call me from the *kadamba,* down on the banks, and start their sweet talk.
> While flirting their water pots fell from their heads. Now they are intent on such a scheme!"
> She turned and saw him: "Where were you? Say, don't I know you?"

158. The expression *khuṃṭa churāv-* seems to be equivalent with *pīchā churā-* (Bāhrī and Kumār 1974: 973).

159. The verb *dhirānā* can mean "to bully," "to threaten" (*OHED*).

160. *jasumati yaha kahi kai risa pāvati; rohini karati rasoī bhītara, kahi-kahi tāhi sunāvati; gārī deta bahū beṭini kauṃ, vai dhāī hyāṃ āvati; hā hā karati sabani sauṃ maiṃ hīṃ, kaisaiṃhu khūṃṭa chuḍāvati; jāti pāṃti sauṃ kahā acagarī, kahi sutahiṃ dhirāvati; sūra syāma kauṃ sikhavati hārī, mārehuṃ lāja na āvati.*

Sūr: as soon as she saw her son, her anger dissipated. She pulled
him to her chest and kissed him. (*SS* 2046/1428)[161]

It does not take much for Yaśodā to come around. She is just as helpless before her son as the milkmaids are. He has quickly turned the tables on them and said they are so fond of him they flirt with him, break their own pots, and then blame him. It is the classic defense of the male accoster: "They were asking for it, and now they blame me." Yaśodā falls for it right away and takes over his discourse entirely:

"They falsely blame my son, these cheats!
I know their ways well, they get together and make up something.
They're all crazed with youth's excitement. My Kanhāī is still small.
They broke the pots on their heads themselves, and come to
complain here.
Why do you go near them, they are bad, each and every woman!
Sūr's Śyāma: now take to heart what I said, they're all insolent
peasant women." (*SS* 2047/1429)[162]

So Yaśodā ends up teaching Krishna quite a different lesson from anticipated: to stay away from the milkmaids all right, not because he is insolent but because they are. She mouths effortlessly the mysogynistic discourse that all women are bad. As all mothers do, she still sees her son as a little boy, even though she should know better:

"They like Mohana, my little Govinda, what does he know of
falsehood?[163]
Those young girls all come with their complaints, joining in
fabricating false stories.
One says he took her pot carrier, another he broke her water pot.
Another one reports about her necklace and bustier! Sure, they're
more innocent than my Kānha!
If they now come again with their complaints, I'll send them off
with hanging face.

161. *tū mohīṃ kauṃ mārana jānati; unake carita kahā kou jānai, unahiṃ kahī tū mānati; kadama-tīra taiṃ mohiṃ bulāyau, gaṛhi-gaṛhi bātaiṃ bānati; maṭakata girī gāgarī sira taiṃ, aba aisī budhi ṭhānati; phira citaī tū kahāṃ rahyau kahi, maiṃ nahiṃ tokauṃ jānati; sūra sutahiṃ dekhatahī risa gaī, mukha cūmati ura ānati.*

162. *jhūṭhahiṃ sutahiṃ lagāvatiṃ khori; maiṃ jānati unake ḍhaṃga nīkauṃ, bātaiṃ milavatiṃ jori; vai saba jobana-mada kī mātī, merau tanaka kanhāī; āpuna phori gāgarī sira taiṃ urahana līnhe āī; tū unakaiṃ ḍhiga jāta katahiṃ hai, vai pāpini saba nāri; sūra syāma aba kahyau māni tū, haiṃ saba ḍhīṭhi gaṃvāri.*

163. This interpretation is based on Bahri and Kumar (1974: 973).

> Sūr says: here's my Kanhāī, a little boy, and they are in the prime of youth!" (*SS* 2048/1430)[164]

This is the first time in the confrontation with Krishna's mother that we hear of broken necklaces or bustiers. The Gopīs themselves seem to have shied away from mentioning the sexual aspect of Krishna's harassment, apart from their mentioning that Krishna calls them sluts. They probably figured they would get more sympathy if they stuck with the material damage: how he broke their pots and impeded them in their daily chores. But here Yaśodā in her eagerness to defend her son shows she has understood what lies behind the complaints. She brings up herself the most scandalous part of the molestation—only to dismiss it in the next breath as a fabrication of girls acting innocent, while her Krishna of course can commit no mischief.

So much for female solidarity. Even united, Yaśodā and the Gopīs do not stand strong. We may well suspect that even if the Gopīs made a better case, it be to no avail. The judge is not in favor. Nothing has been accomplished by this appeal to the authorities. Even the female judge does not take the women's side. Krishna has managed to convince his mother that it is not his fault.

Yaśodā's verdict is clear. What is ours? We know that Krishna is not really the innocent little boy his mother understands him to be. We've seen enough of his deeds to know he is having some adult fun. Yet we cannot help being charmed by the young boy running away from his house as soon as he hears his mother has got wind of his tricks. And he can argue so innocently, turning the tables in a wink. It is hard to stay angry with him.

Are the Gopīs the poor victims at the end of the day? Now that they stand accused in turn, what do they have to say for themselves? Do they plead guilty? We have seen that they as much as admit to each other that they have enjoyed Krishna's harassment themselves. In some cases, they seem to have been hanging out just a bit longer than needed at the well in hopes of being caught by Krishna. And they are as weak, when push comes to shove, as Mother Yaśodā. They cannot quite put together a decent line of defense without being distracted by Krishna's charms. The whole point of the poems is that Krishna charms everyone out of their wits. No one cares about reason anymore. Nor about dharma. Love for him, bhakti, overrides all other concerns. This does not come easy: we see the Gopīs' inner struggle in a series of poems where they are pondering whether to give in to their strong feelings for the young man or not.

164. *mohana bālagubiṃdā bhāī, merau kaha jānai khori; urahana lai juvatī saba āvatiṃ, jhūṭhī batiyāṃ jori; koū kahati geṃḍurī līnhī, kou kahaiṃ gāgari phorī; koū colī hāra batāvati, kānhahuṃ taiṃ ye bhorī; aba āvaiṃ jauṃ urahana lai kai, tau paṭhavauṃ mukha mori; sūra kahāṃ merau tanaka kanhāī, āpuna jobana-jori.*

Rādhā Steps outside the Lakshmana Rekhā

There is an epilogue to the story at the well. The Gopīs may have gotten up in arms, but to no avail. Still, they could stop going to the well. That is what their relatives would like them to do. They enforce this by confining them to the house and courtyard. We could say that they have been imprisoned within a Lakshmana Rekhā, a code of family morality. This is quite the opposite from Sītā, who cannot go back once she has crossed the line. These women have been seduced; they have stepped outside the code of marital fidelity. Yet their relatives take them back, perhaps unaware of the extent of what has already taken place. They try to keep them confined, try to make them toe the line. How will the Gopīs react? We hear the wagging tongues of village gossip, and then how Rādhā and the Gopīs struggle about what to do.

THE VILLAGE GOSSIP MILL IN ACTION. Krishna may have managed to convince his mother that it is not his fault. However, the damage is done. Rumors have spread far and wide:

> In every house of Braj the rumor is spreading:
> "Mother Yaśodā's son is committing insolence. No one manages to get water from the Yamunā.
> Darkish hue, dance master's dress on his body. On his flute he plays a monsoon tune.
> The brilliance of his earrings outshines the sun's rays. His [peacock] crown outdoes Indra's rainbow.
> He does not listen to anyone. Bent on teasing, he grabs waterpots and spills the water on the ground."
> Mother and father together lecture Sūr's Śyāma: "Such ways are not ours."[165] (*SS* 2049/1431)[166]

Apparently, Yaśodā has persisted somewhat in her promise to the Gopīs, and has enlisted the help of her husband. But to no avail. Their parental

165. I have interpreted *āpunahiṃ* as the two words *āpu* and *nahiṃ*. Alternatively, one can take *āpunahiṃ* as a third person pronoun of respect, referring to Krishna, as do Bāhrī and Kumār (1974: 973). The line can also be read as addressed to the Gopīs: "Mother and father lectured about Sūr's Śyāma, [stressing that] such ways are not ours."

166. *braja-ghara-ghara yaha bāta calāvata; jasumati kau suta karata acagarī, jamunā jala kou bharana na pāvata; syāma barana naṭavara bapu kāche, muralī rāga malāra bajāvata; kuṃḍala-chabi rabi-kiranahuṃ taiṃ duti, mukuṭa iṃdra-dhanuhūṃ taiṃ bhāvata; mānata kāhu na karata acagarī, gāgari dhari jala bhuṃi ḍharakāvata; sūra syāma kauṃ māta pita dou, aise ḍhaṃga āpunahiṃ paṛhāvata.*

authority is flaunted. Krishna persists in his harassment. The description of his antics is presented lovingly. Whoever is spreading this rumor has had the pleasure, it seems, of seeing Krishna at it. The complainant is clearly infatuated with this handsome man in the woods.

> He's gone too far with teasing, Lord Nanda's [boy].
> With his friends he's sitting on the banks of the Yamunā. People don't get across the path.
> [Relatives] may get irritated and scold all they want, but the young ladies are in trance.
> In deed, word, and thought, they don't know anything but handsome Śyāma.
> Śyāma is engaged in all this playful activity (*līlā*), for the sake of Braj's young ladies.
> Sūr: whatever way you approach Krishna, you will be rewarded in kind. (*SS* 2050/1432)[167]

It is not clear who is spreading this rumor. This time, it is not one of the Gopīs, but someone who can comment on their state of mind. It seems that some elders of the village are lamenting the effect Krishna has on the women of Braj. The commentator in the last two or three lines seems to be someone with the theological insight that Krishna is doing all this for their sake, that it is a reward for their devotion. He must be a pundit who knows the scriptures, as the last line seems to refer to the *Bhagavad Gītā* (7.21: *yo yo yāṃ yāṃ tanuṃ bhaktaḥ śraddhayārcitum icchati, tasya tasyācalāṃ śraddhāṃ tāmeva vidadhāmy aham*). Maybe this is the sage Śuka commenting on the action, as he does on several occasions in *Bhāgavata Purāṇa*, downplaying scandal by providing theological justification. Another gossiper ends up wondering philosophically who can escape Krishna's tyranny:

> No one manages to fetch water from the Yamunā.
> He has climbed the *kadamba* tree, sits on a branch and calls everyone names.
> He grabs a water pot and breaks it. He spills the water over another girl's head.
> Another one he approaches lovingly. With meaningful glances he steals her heart.

167. *karata acagarī naṃda mahara kau; sakhā liye jamunā-taṭa baiṭhyau, nibaha na loga-ḍagara kau; kou khījhau koū kina barajau, juvatini kaiṃ mana dhyāna; mana-baca-karma syāma suṃdara taji, aura na jānatiṃ āna; yaha līlā saba syāma karata haiṃ, braja juvatini kaiṃ heta; sūra bhajai jihiṃ bhāva kṛṣṇa kauṃ, tākauṃ soi phala deta.*

All at once, he embraces another one. He gives his heart to yet another.
Sūr's Śyāma has gone too far with his teasing. But no one can catch him by any means. (*SS* 2051/1433)[168]

This song confirms that Krishna is tyrannizing the village, and no one can get him. It might well be a Gopī's complaint. As she sketches the situation, with some moral outrage, she points out he is unstoppable. Indeed, how could anyone stop God? A similar complaint stresses Krishna's unruliness when he is accompanied by his whole gang of friends:

No one can go out in the environs of Braj.
With his cowherd friends he runs amok, shouting loudly wherever they run
He throws away a pot carrier. He spills someone's water pot,
He calls another names and runs off. Then he draws yet another in his embrace.
Within Braj, he does not listen to anyone. He's infamous as Lord Nanda's son.
Sūr's Śyāma, a dance master's dress on his body, plays his flute on the banks of the Yamunā. (*SS* 2052/1434)[169]

This may well be an appeal to Nanda to do something about his son who is creating so much havoc. However, the last line again reveals a loving doting on Krishna. So the rumor mill betrays a condoning attitude: everyone is enchanted by this handsome young man, he is totally out of hand, but no one has the power—or indeed the will—to stop him.

While the village gossip complains of Krishna, it shows an awareness that the women who have been pestered actually are drawn to him. Again we hear the theological argument with which it all started: the Gopīs get what they want, or what they deserve, depending how you look at it. It is the way you approach God that determines how he will answer you. There is a hint again that it is the women who want him erotically, not he them.

168. *jamunā-jala kou bharana na pāvai; āpuna baiṭhyau kadama-ḍara caṛhi, gārī dai dai sabani bulāvai; kāhū kī gagarī gahi phorai, kāhūṃ sira taiṃ nīra ḍharāvai; kāhū sauṃ kari prīti milata hai, naina-saina dai citahiṃ curāvai; barabasa hī aṃkavāri bharata dhari, kāhū sauṃ apanau mana lāvai; sūra syāma ati karata acagarī, kaisaihuṃ kāhū hātha na āvai.*

169. *braja-gvaiṃḍe kou calana na pāvata; gvāla sakhā saṃga līnhe ḍolata, dai-dai hāṃka jahāṃ tahaṃ dhāvata; kāhū kī iṃḍurī phaṭakārata, kāhū kī gagarī ḍharakāvata; kāhū kauṃ gārī dai bhājata, kāhū kauṃ aṃka bhari lāvata; kāhūṃ nahiṃ mānata braja bhītara, naṃda mahara kau kuṃvara kahāvata; sūra syāma naṭavara-bapu kāche, jamunā kaiṃ taṭa murali bajāvata.*

RĀDHĀ'S CHOICE. How do the Gopīs themselves evaluate their behavior? When they venture outside the village boundaries, that seems to amount to crossing a Lakshmana Rekhā of sorts. Do they make a choice to flaunt dharma for the sake of love? To some extent, we could say it is the other way around: it is being molested by Krishna that pushes the girls to the margins of orthodox society. It is after they have been willy-nilly seduced by him that they decide to flaunt the rules of appropriate behavior. Even so, the decision is a heartrending one to make.

The Sūr cycle develops as follows. First we follow the story of Rādhā, who has been seduced by Krishna. She is discovered by her friends and coaxed out of her strange state:

> The milkmaids went back to the Yamunā
> Jointly they said to her "come." They talked a bit, entreating her.
> "The smart lady does not answer us." "She keeps her face turned away."
> "She's under a spell!" "What does she think?" "Someone must have stolen something."[170]
> Putting their hand on her arm they say: "Let's go. He won't come now, that fraud!"
> The girlfriends can vouch for Sūr's Lord's past, their eyes rolling. (*SS* 2060/1442)[171]

We see the Gopīs wondering what happened to Rādhā, but they know well enough who is responsible for her state. They know his old tricks, his "record" (*carita*). When Rādhā is woken up from her trance, she gives an elaborate first person account of what happened. We hear a recap of what we have seen happening to her earlier: how Krishna went out of his way to seduce her at the well and she was taken in by his gesture of throwing his yellow sash as a veil over her head. Here follows Rādhā's own take on what happened:

> "The dark one doesn't leave the path, how can I go to the well?
> Here I'm standing, hesitating, afraid someone might call me names.
> Wherever I look, I see him, that sensuous son of Nanda.

170. The last two lines can be taken as statements the Gopīs addressed to each other, or as directed to Rādhā; the latter is the interpretation of Bāhrī and Kumār (1974: 977).

171. *gvārini jamunā calīṃ bahori; tāhi saba mili kahatiṃ āvahu, kachuka kahatiṃ nihāri; jvāba deti na hamahiṃ nāgari, rahī ānana mori; ṭhagi rahī mana kahā socati, kāhu liyau kachu cori; bhujā dhari kara kahyau calahi na āvaiṃ abahīṃ khori; sūra prabhu ke carita sakhiyani, kahati locana ḍhori.*

Furtively glancing all over [my body], he welcomed me with a wink.
Stick in hand, he goes ahead, clearing the way.
'Show some mercy on me. Turn and look at me with a smile.'[172]
When I had filled the pot with Yamunā water and put it on my head,
The border of my bodice was lifted up. He noticed, his heart lusted [for me].
He threw a stone at the jug, but it hit my body.
He remained standing in the middle of the path, teasing those who come and go.[173]
I couldn't say anything, in my shame, for fear of what people might say.
Touching my body, the breeze passed by and went on to embrace him.
He came close, inspected my face. I was shy then looked up.
In his style[174] he wrapped his shawl around me: he covered me with his yellow sash.
When his love did not stick with me, he was upset.
But he persisted and touched my shadow with his.
Who knows where my house and elders' honor got lost?[175]
My heart is tied up in a knot, with the border of his yellow sash.
Till then I was standing there hesitating. Now I'll show my passion.
I'll play with him intimately. I'll take it that's my fate.
What do I care what all the people of Braj call me in every house?
I'll let my hidden love shine through, throwing out family values.
Until I met him, heart to heart, I've been dancing a dance of desire,
[But now,] I'll stay with Sūr's Śyāma alone. I'll make my heart's longing transpire." (*SS* 2061/1443)[176]

172. This line is enigmatic. I take it to be Krishna asking Rādhā to turn her face toward him and smile at him. It could, however, also be Rādhā reporting on how Krishna turned to her as he went in front: "Showing mercy on me [flattering me], he turned and smilingly looked at me." This is the interpretation of Bāhrī and Kumār (1974: 979).

173. Or: "teasing me as I was trying to come or go." This is the interpretation of Bāhrī and Kumār (1974: 979).

174. I've interpreted *au* as *vā*. Bāhrī and Kumār take it as *aura* (1974: 979).

175. One of the meanings of *sora* is "name" (*BBSK*). Bāhrī and Kumār take it as *śora* (1974: 979), which could be translated in English as "Who knows what hell broke loose."

176. *gaila na chāṃḍai sāṃvarau, kyauṃ kari panaghaṭa jāuṃ; ihiṃ sakucata ḍarapati rahauṃ, dharai na koū nāuṃ; jita dekauṃ tita dekhiyai, rasiyā naṃda-kumāra; ita uta naina durāi kai, palakani karata juhāra; lakuṭa liyai āgaiṃ calai, paṃtha saṃvārata jāi; mohiṃ nihorau lāikai, phiri citavai musukāi; jamunā-jala bhari gāgarī, jaba sira dharauṃ uṭhāi; tyauṃ kaṃcuki aṃcarā uṛai, hiyarā taki lalacāi; gāgari mārai kāṃkarī, lāgai meraiṃ gāta; gaila māṃjhi ṭhāṛhau rahai, khūṭai āvata jāta; hauṃ sakucani bolauṃ nahīṃ, loka-lāja kī saṃka; mo tana chvai*

Well, Rādhā's feelings are somewhat ambiguous. By her own interpretation, it took her a while to come around. She is embarrassed when Krishna first stops her. But she manages to go about her business. However, as she lifts the pot on her head, her blouse creeps up and reveals part of her breast. He notices. She notices he notices. She is deeply embarrassed. He throws a stone at her pot, but misses, and it hits her body. We get a hint that she is getting sexually aroused as she poetically describes how the wind touched her body and then went on to embrace him. Sensing her arousal, he comes closer and wraps her in his shawl. Even so, Rādhā says she did not give in to him. Eventually, it is his touching her shadow with his shadow that seems to have melted her resistance. That is different from the interpretation in the previous report of the same events, where it was the wrapping of the shawl that did the trick. We see multiple interpretations of Rādhā's feelings. The poems present a multiverse of meanings, of shades of love.

Now that she has given him her heart, Rādhā has lost all sense of shame. She articulates how her love for Krishna transcends the rules of dharma. She no longer cares about wagging tongues, or "family values" (*kula kī kāni*). That all represents a world of unfulfilled desires that keep people dancing around. Quite philosophically, Rādhā ends with the observation that desiring Krishna instead fulfills the heart's deepest longing.

Sūr Sāgar's Rādhā seems to know pretty much right away to choose the path of love over dharma. However, in some other poems, we find the women affected by Krishna in a quandary: should they stay within *maryādā* or just throw such concerns to the wind and meet with Krishna? In Nanddās's *Panaghaṭa* songs, the Gopīs are shown caught on the horns of this dilemma. One Gopī is unable to decide between love for Krishna and fear for her family's name. This poem poignantly describes her state of mind in the *kavitta* meter:

> She went to draw water and lost her senses. She came back having drawn love. Now she's keen to see him again.
> [On one side] desire for Mohana, [on the other] fear for the family elders. [In between] she's frozen like a picture. She tells her friends it's languor.

---

baihara calai, tāhi bharata hai aṃka; nikaṭa āi mukha nirakhi kai, sakucai bahuri nihāri; au ḍhaṃga auṛhai oṛhanī, pītāṃbara muhiṃ vāri; jaba kahuṃ laga lāgai nahīṃ, vākau jiya akulāi; taba haṭhi merī chāṃha sauṃ, rākhai chāṃha chuvāi; ko jānai kita hota hai, ghara gurujana kau sora; merau jiya gāṃṭhī baṃdhyau, pītāṃbara kauṃ chora; aba lauṃ sakuca aṃṭaki rahī, pragaṭa karauṃ anurāga; hili mili kai saṃga khelihauṃ, māni āpanau bhāga; ghara ghara brajabāsī sabaiṃ, kou kina kahai pukāri; gupta prīti pragaṭa karauṃ, kula kī kāni nivāri; jaba lagi mana milayau nahīṃ, nacī copa kaiṃ nāca; sūra syāma-saṃgahī rahauṃ, karauṃ manoratha sāṃca.

Her necklace broken, her dress torn, tears are trickling from her
eyes. A crowd assembled at the well. Her pitcher [in the water]
forgotten.
Thus grew deeper her love for Nanddās's Lord. The news spread of
her desires [ill-begotten]. (*NP* 80)[177]

This girl is immobilized, unable to make a decision, knowing full well she is acting against her family's interest, but unable to control herself. She is so out of her mind she even forgets her pitcher at the well. Moreover, here we see the telltale signs of Krishna's handiwork: the broken necklace, the torn clothes—elements we have heard Yaśodā refer to. No wonder gossip is already spreading about her.

In another of Nanddās's poems, the Gopī is even more explicit about privileging love over dharma. This milkmaid has made up her mind in this *kavitta:*

Cursed that sense of propriety, what do I get from it? The lotus-eyed
comes and I don't even really see him.
He appeared from the forest, I met him on the way. I was shy,
because of those people.
I tried many ways, but got defeated: it's hard beholding Mohana.
From the cover of my veil I tried [to sneak a peak].
Since that day, says Nanddās's Lord's beloved, my eyes have stayed
with him, immersed in the color of passion. (*NP* 81)[178]

This beloved of Krishna may well be Rādhā. She complains she tried to stay "behind the veil," but that has impeded her in beholding Krishna. And then she has taken the big step and ventured outside the boundaries of propriety—outside the Lakshmana Rekhā, we might say. She goes so far as to curse her sense of propriety for inhibiting her love for Krishna. This breaking of the Lakshmana Rekhā seems to be on its way to becoming an epidemic in Braj. It is spreading fast; woman after woman steps outside her enchanted cirle. We could nearly speak of a movement of civil disobedience.

177. *jala kauṃ gaī sudhi bisarāī neha bhar lāī, parī hai caṭapaṭī darasa kī; ita mohana gāṃsa uta guru-jana trāsa, citra so likhī ṭhāṛhī nāuṃ dharata sakhi arasa kī; ṭūṭe hāra phāṭe cīra nainani bahata nīra, panaghaṭa bhaī bhīra sudhi na kalas kī; naṃdadāsa prabhu soṃ aisī prīti gāṛhī bāṛhī, phaila parī caracā cāyana sarasa kī.*

178. *jara jāo rī lāja mero aisai kauna kāja, āvata kamala-naina nīkaiṃ dekhana na dīne; bana teṃ ju āvata māraga meṃ bhaī bheṃṭa, sakuca rahī rī hauṃ ina logana ke līne; koṭī jatana kari hārī mohana nihāribe koṃ; acarā kī oṭa dai-dai koṭa srama kīne; naṃdadāsa prabhu pyārī vā dina taiṃ mere naina, unahīṃ ke aṃga saṃga raṃga rasa bhīne.*

SHOULD I STAY OR SHOULD I GO? Once the women fall for Krishna, they fall hard. Now the question is whether they will become "repeat offenders." Will they defy all propriety and return to the well, in full knowledge that Krishna will harass them again? Here is the musing of a Gopī in the *kavitta* meter:

> In the neighborhood of Gokul, there's a dark-hued lad. He sneaked into my eyes and blocked the road to my heart.
> I don't get rest for a moment. My house feels like the woods. He took away my body and heart, my life and money too!
> My home holds no respite. My courtyard is too small. I'm sighing, see what state has he reduced me to!
> Sūrdās's Lord is he! He softly hums a tune, so sweet it seems that he has honey in his flute. (*SS* 2053/1435)[179]

This Gopī describes her restlessness; ever since Krishna has blocked her way to the well, it seems like he is still blocking the road to her heart. She cannot find peace in her own house, her courtyard is too small for her, it is as if the four walls are closing in on her. In the end, it is Krishna's flute playing that has this magic effect, as if it has cast a spell. Another woman describes a similar sentiment: her house feels like a prison, her awareness of family honor holds her back, but her love is stronger than all this:

> How can I go to fetch water?
> My path is blocked, O friend, by a boy of the name Kānha.
> I can't slip out of the house. I'm restrained by what people might say.
> My body is here, but my heart has gotten stuck where Nanda's son appears.
> I can't stand to remain sitting here at home.
> Give me some good advice, so I'll find a way out.
> I can't go out, but neither stay inside the house.
> Mohana has put a spell on me, I tell you for sure, friends.
> Propriety and good name, give my heart pause before I act.[180]
> Without him my body is lifeless, so what's this brain for? Worthless!

179. *gokula ke gvaiḍai eka sāṃvarau sau ḍhoṭā māī, āṃkhini kaiṃ paiṃḍaiṃ paiṭhi jīke paiṃḍe paryau hai; kala na parata chana gṛha bhayau bana-sama, tana-mana-dhana-prāna- sarabasa haryau hai; bhavana na bhāvai māī, āṃgana na rahyau jāi, karaiṃ hāya hāya dekhau jaise hāla karyau hai; sūradāsa prabhu nīkaiṃ gāvata madhura sura, mānau muralī maiṃ lai pīyūṣa-rasa bharyau hai.*

180. *jiya lauṃ* after can mean "till the heart" or "compared to the heart."

I am getting convinced in my heart: I need to stop this quandary!
I'll go and make love with Sūr's Śyāma. I'll nip this sense of shame in the bud. (*SS* 2071/1453)[181]

We are privy to the decision-making process of these milkmaids, torn between their "family values" and their strong fascination with Krishna. In the end, their resolve is a strong and unequivocal choice for their love, for bhakti over dharma. There are a few more poems in this vein, without clear references to the *panaghaṭa* theme (*SS* 2072–4), and finally this one, which illustrates the complete identification of Rādhā and Krishna:

"I'm bewitched by the dark one, friend. I can't make up my mind for home or forest.
I go to the Yamunā to fetch water. Śyāma is there casting his spell.
I'm wearing a yellow shawl and a red skirt.
He flirts with sharp-edged brows. One look and he conquers me.
He's splendid with his peacock crown, sweet words on his lips.
So dear are Hari's looks, he's gotten stuck in my eyes.
I'm entranced by his handsome looks. Let them gossip whether it's right or wrong."
She's found the Lord of Sūrdās: two bodies, but their hearts are one. (2075/1457)[182]

This milkmaid, too, is torn between home and the forest. Yet her choice is clear. Whether it is right or wrong, whether people gossip, it all does not matter. Like Sītā, the Gopīs are compelled by their love to transgress these boundaries. Sītā had to suffer severe consequences, but these women do not, at least not yet. What is the use for morality, what is the relevance of punishment, when one has united with the Lord? There is no need for Lakshmana Rekhās in the all-absorbing love of the Gopīs for Krishna. Dharma pales in the light of love.

In summary, the message sent to women in the *Sūr Sāgar* poems is heavily colored by bhakti discourse. It is intended to illustrate the overriding power of

181. *kaisaiṃ jala bharana maiṃ jāuṃ; gaila merau paryau sakhi rī, kānha jākau nāuṃ; ghara taiṃ nikasata banata nāhīṃ, loka-lāja lajāuṃ; tana ihāṃ mana jāi aṃṭakyau, naṃda-naṃdana-ṭhāuṃ; jau rahauṃ ghara baiṭhi kai tau, rahyau nāhiṃna jāi; sīkha taisī dehi tumahīṃ, karauṃ kahā upāi; jāta bāhira banata nāhīṃ, ghara na naiku suhāi; mohinī mohana lagāī, kahati sakhini sunāi; lāja aru marajāda jiya lauṃ, karati hauṃ yaha soca; jāhi binu tana prāna chāṃḍe, kauna budhi yaha poca; manahiṃ yaha paratīti ānī, dūri karihauṃ doca; sūra prabhu hili mili rahauṃgī, lāja ḍārauṃ moca.*

182. *mohī sajanī sāṃvaraiṃ mohiṃ, gṛha bana kachu na suhāi; jamuna bharana jala maiṃ tahaṃ, syāma mohinī lāi; oṛhe pīrī pāmarī hô, pahire lāla nicola; bhauṃhaiṃ kāṃṭa kaṭīliyāṃ mohiṃ, mola liyau bina mola; mora-mukuṭa sira rājaī ho, adhara dhare mukha baina; hari kī mūrati kauṃ basa bhaī, aba bhalo burau kahai koi; sūradāsa prabhu kauṃ milī kari, mana ekai tana doi.*

love for God, which eradicates barriers of morality. That does not mean that the example of the Gopīs is as such transferable to day-to-day scenarios of sexual harassment. The message is not that women can participate in sexual banter with strangers without moral repercussions. Rather, the opposite. The matrix of perspectives in which the transgression is embedded illustrates abundantly an unsympathetic perspective on the woman who is sexually abused, an ambiguity about whether she is a victim or a willing participant. The assumption seems to be that women enjoy this kind of eve-teasing. The theological understanding that it is a reward for the Gopīs can easily be transferred to the assessment that women who are thus vexed are actually getting what they wish, or what they deserve.

Krishna's Harassment Caught on Screen

In Sagar's *Shri Krishna* there is no *panaghaṭa* episode proper where water pots are broken at the well. This is in contrast to the popular Homi Wadia movie *Shri Krishna leela* (1970), where the first meeting of Rādhā and Krishna actually takes place as she is fetching water at the well. Krishna first hears the jingling of her anklets as she is on her way to the river. Enchanted, he asks his friends who she may be. They tell him she is the wife of Aney, one of the more influential milkmen of the village. The camera shifts to Rādhā fetching the water, but when she hears Krishna's flute, she is completely entranced and leaves her water pot to float in the river. She dances to Krishna's tune and subsequently has a first meeting with him, where she confesses she has heard from others about him, and has wondered what he is like. The loving meeting is cut short by her "Svāmī," as she calls her husband, Aney.

The sound of the anklets of a woman on her way to the well reminds us of the medieval poems we have read, where the women were "all a-jingling," and of Rāma's first awareness of Sītā in Tulsī's Flower Garden episode. Rādhā forgetting her pot also is a motif we are familiar with from the Braj poems, as is the combination of the enchantment of the flute and the theme of the water-carrier. However, there is a significant difference. The filmī Rādhā is not immediately ready to give up considerations of her worldly duties and her good name (*loka-lāja*) for her Krishna. Just as quickly as she was drawn in by Krishna's flute, she runs off when she hears the sound of her husband's bullock cart coming. She leaves Krishna instantly. We hear her plead with her husband to go back home for breakfast, but he does not listen, and we see her left disappointed. *Maryādā* surely comes before bhakti in this incident.

The television series *Shri Krishna* incorporates a scene where Krishna and his friends smash the milkmaids' pots. The only difference is that the pots are not water but milk pots, and the women are not coming back from the well but on their way to the market. Krishna is not demanding a tax, so the incident is not a *dāna-līlā,* or tax-levy, episode proper. It falls somewhere between a *panaghaṭa* and a *dāna-līlā*. There are quite a few interesting elements, especially the scene where the women complain to Yaśodā.

Sagar does not provide all the shades of meaning and subtleties of voice of the Braj poems. Instead, we get the camera's seemingly objective eye, the director's version of events. Sagar deals with the episode of Krishna smashing the Gopīs' pots in the context of Krishna's *bāla līlā* (vol. 5, episode 35). At the beginning of the episode, Krishna is still a toddler, and the Gopīs are so fond of him that they want to kiss him all the time. One Gopī comments that she thinks he was her lover in a previous birth. The women's love, then, is portrayed as tinged with some erotic feelings, although the boy is still very little and seems unaware of all this doting having an erotic tint. The little actor playing Krishna actually seems rather baffled by all the attention.

Next we see a Krishna who has grown up to grade school age, and we get to witness some of his butter-stealing episodes. The Gopīs are portrayed as luring Krishna into their houses with alluring, strategically placed pots of butter. They admit as much to each other. Still, they voice complaints about Krishna's butter thievery. When his mother confronts Krishna with these complaints, he manages to convince her that he is innocent. Once back among his friends, they all brainstorm about how to get back at the Gopīs for telling on them. They come up with the plan to break their milk pots as they are on their way to the market. There is no hint of demanding a tax, as the boys are only seeking revenge. Sagar also leaves out any hint of sexual assault.

The incident itself is short. The boys are ready, hidden among the branches of a tree. As the women file past the tree, the boys manage to grab the little dishes used to cover the milk pots on which there is butter. They eat the butter and then get out their catapults and shoot stones at the women from behind, breaking their pots. The Gopīs get drenched with their milk. They quickly spot the boys, who flee on Krishna's command. Only young Krishna remains behind. He denies having been involved, but the women insist he come down. They tie his hands and smear his face with butter, the better to make their case that he stole their butter. Then they take him to Yaśodā to complain. This time, Krishna has been caught red-handed, and Yaśodā promises to give him a stiff punishment. But now the Gopīs feel bad, and they are reluctant to leave him helplessly in his angry mother's hands.

The Gopīs' glee at catching Krishna red-handed and their threats to take him to his mother were there in the Braj poems. So was Yaśodā's exasperation at the Gopīs' request for punishment, and her pointing out that they actually have been the first to cry woe whenever she has tried to punish him in the past. However, the television-series Yaśodā is not so quickly convinced of her son's innocence.

Yaśodā locks Krishna up in a dark room and is looking for a stick to beat him with, when Krishna cries out that he feels a snake slither over his feet. Yaśodā opens the doors back up, and indeed, there is a cobra right in front of them. While she holds out the stick, threatening the snake, she urges Krishna to run, but Krishna nobly says he will not leave his mommy alone. He prays to the snake to go away and promises Mother will place some milk for him near the tree in the evening. This of course charms his mother to the point where she cannot bring herself to give her son a thrashing. So eventually, Sagar's Yaśodā's heart melts, just as in Sūr's version. However, in the television series, she persists in being upset and does not want to talk to Krishna, resorting to moral blackmail: keeping a vow of silence (*mauna vrata*). Krishna manages to tease her out of that by telling her that his brother teases him as "having been bought at the market" and not being his mother's real son. The whole argument is enacted in song and mime. That of course sets Yaśodā off, and she promptly forgets about Krishna's punishment, instead gearing up to punish her other son.

While there are many echoes of Sūr-like poems, in the television interpretation, the crucial difference is that Krishna is still a child. The whole episode is part of the butter wars between the Gopīs and the village kids. The boys are getting back at them for telling on them about their previous butter thefts. Everything is very childlike. There is no question of molesting the women, just grabbing their butter and smashing their pots. Krishna allows himself to be caught by the women, who gleefully take him to Yaśodā. Compared to Sūrdās's cycle, the Gopīs have a strong case to make, and Yaśodā is appropriately convinced. Contrary to Sūr's Yaśodā, who quickly wavered, this one has no doubt in her mind that Krishna is guilty, and she sets out to give him a severe beating as well as locking him up in a dark room. Ironically, in this version the Gopīs get what they asked for, but now they feel bad for Krishna and try to save him, though to no avail. After they have gone, it is the incident with the snake that saves Krishna. Her son's heroic behavior and his instinctive defense of his mother softens Yaśodā's resolve, though she still will punish him by not speaking to him, till he teases her out of that, too.

Sagar's version, then, remains within the boundaries of dharma by keeping Krishna's acts childlike and nonerotic. The Gopīs desire Krishna's butterthefts, but their desires are not in conflict with dharma. After Krishna teases them by smashing their pots, they rightfully ask for a punishment, and Yaśodā follows dharma in her resolve to punish him. The Gopīs' love for

Krishna makes them regret their action, but such is hardly counter to the norms. Yaśodā, too, softens, charmed as she is by her boy's handling of the snake, though she remains convinced of his guilt and seeks to punish him by other means. We can conclude that in the television series, dharma remains preserved, though carrying out the actual punishment is difficult because of love. This does not mean that the Gopīs get off scot-free. They are unambiguously enjoying the butter wars with Krishna, and confess as much to each other, even speaking of seeing in the child Krishna a lover from previous births. But in the end, Sagar succeeds in having bhakti and keeping dharma too.

Different Views on Rādhā Being Harassed

Compared to the medieval poems, the television version excludes any element that could be used to build a case for sexual harassment. Krishna is depicted as a child, and his teasing is devoid of erotics. If there is a hint of erotics, it is only in the Gopīs' perception, not in Krishna's. Significantly, there is no Rādhā among these Gopīs. Rādhā is Krishna's age, while these Gopīs are all older than little Krishna.

As in the medieval version, the television Gopīs complain about Krishna—here his childlike pranks—but Yaśodā takes their complaints and her own responsibility to teach her child manners seriously. In theory, the irresponsible child is to be punished, although in practice, Yaśodā's excessive love for her son intervenes, and he succeeds in escaping punishment here, too. In the medieval poems, Krishna's teasing is of a sexual nature, but his mother believes in his innocence and refuses to punish him. Krishna's behavior is not bound by rules of dharma, it seems, so he transcends the duality between good and bad behavior, and is not punished. The Gopīs, by contrast, are portrayed as enmeshed within that duality. They are the ones breaking the norms of dharma, and transgressing the lines of decorum. And they do so willingly for their love.

So is bhakti liberating for the Gopīs as role models? They are allowed some agency and are portrayed as the subjects of sexual desire, choosing to transcend moral boundaries and enjoying their sexuality. However, it surely is turned against them "in court," where it is decided who is to blame. Even when they unite and make an appeal to older women to come to their help, they fail and are not taken seriously. The mother figure believes in her son's innocence and concludes that all women are sluts. That seems to be the consensus of village gossip, too. If there is a message to women, it is certainly that affairs outside the Laksmana Rekhā will cost them dearly in terms of respectability.

That message definitely confirms the intuition of many contemporary women who are suffering eve-teasing and are worried about what it will do to their "respectability." Even if such incidents are totally unprovoked, women hesitate to relate them to their families, out of fear of what their parents might think of them, as is shown by a sociological study of urban middle-class women in India (Puri 1999: 77–8, 87–8, 92). Blaming the victim is something we see in the medieval songs (presumably about rural situations) as well as in contemporary urban narratives (see also Derné 1995a: 34, Rajan 2000: 50–3). At the same time, the theme of letting the accoster off the hook, which appears in the medieval songs, persists today. Eve-teasing nowadays is often carried out publicly and is tolerated by bystanders as "innocuous" (Anagol-McGinn 1994: 222). The public's evaluation of the perpetrators as harmless and love-stricken has ancient precedent in Braj, as we have discovered. It may not be too far-fetched to see the modern Road Romeos as inheritors of Krishna's legacy. That will become more obvious as I look at movie depictions of eve-teasing incidents in the following sections.

Sītā and Rādhā Compared

How do Sītā and Rādhā compare as they cope with harassment? First let us look at the situation in which the women find themselves, which has made them vulnerable to the harassment. Sītā finds herself alone, due to some important mistakes (sending her husband for the golden deer and sending Lakshmana to help Rāma). It could be said that she is vulnerable through her own doing. Rādhā and the Gopīs, by contrast, have gone to the well to carry out their daily chores; their venturing outside the village boundaries is necessitated by their tasks as women, by their dharma. At this point, Sītā can be held responsible for getting herself into a difficult situation, but not the Gopīs. If we look at the harassment itself, that by Rāvaṇa is serious and violent; his goal is to abduct Sītā and keep her forever. Krishna's is playful, and he just wants a fleeting affair. He is not offering to take the women outside their own world. The woman's response differs accordingly. Sītā responds by resisting with all her might and calling for help. She tries to discourage the accoster by arguments that are dharma based. Even in hardship, she manages to remain true to her love and within the borders of dharma. Rādhā and the Gopīs either feign resistance or find themselves helpless, unable to resist. They worry about dharma, but in the end find themselves following the call of their love, even at the cost of dharma.

Both women cross a Lakshmana Rekhā for the sake of love. The way Sagar portrays it, Sītā in crossing the line is paradoxically inspired by her love for Rāma. She is deceived by the demon's disguise and fears for her husband's life. It is not really a transgression. Yet while it is perfectly understandable, even honorable, in its intent, it is fatal. Once she has crossed the line, she cannot return within the magic circle. The Gopīs' case is different. They have to leave the magic circle to go toward their beloved, who is outside of it. They seem to have the option to return within the fold, to reenter the Lakshmana Rekhā, but they choose not to. Though they could, they find themselves unwilling to go back to the world of dharma. They are not deceived but fully aware of what they are doing. Theirs truly is a transgression, and they are ready to pay the price. For them dharma and love are incompatible.

Thus, both heroines choose for love, but for Sītā it means maintaining dharma, and for the Gopīs breaking it. Surprisingly, in the rest of the story, we see the consequences Sītā has to face for her fatal crossing, in the form of her need to prove her innocence through a trial by fire (Agniparīkṣa) and banishment. In the case of the Gopīs' transgression, however, we never witness any punishment for their breaking the rules of dharma. Yes, Krishna leaves them, and they are left longing for him, but their husbands and in-laws never seem to take the measures that surely would follow in real life if a woman committed adultery.

What message is sent to women here? How does this relate to women coping with everyday eve-teasing and the threat of rape they may encounter? Surely the message is not that they are allowed to enjoy a fleeting affair but cannot leave the home for good. I would argue that the Sītā scenario is aimed at a female audience and the Krishna one at a male one. Sītā's story sends a strong message to women discouraging them from crossing boundaries of propriety and alerting them to the dire consequences of even well-intentioned mistakes. Rādhā's story, on the other hand, illustrates how males view casual affairs. Let us look at the Gopīs' case more closely.

Even though my reading of the poems has been sensitive to all the subtleties of voice switching, the evidence is overwhelmingly that by and large the Gopīs do not seem to mind Krishna's teasing, certainly not after the fact. When all is said and done, they enjoy it and seek it out. They have acted as Sītā's opposites.

So if the Gopīs do not care about being harassed, should we? Here it is important to keep in mind that the other major difference is that between the harassers: in contrast to Rāvaṇa, Krishna not only gets his way with the women but gets off scot-free. At worst, he will get scolded by his mother, maybe his father, but no one is able to control him. What signals are being sent when Krishna is never punished, always excused on grounds of cuteness? When women are perceived to be actually enjoying and asking for the sexual harassment? When even if they get their act together and complain, they are weak in love? When even when united, they find no ear with the authorities? And when in the end, they end up asking for more?

Such a portrayal of events in the mythological realm may well have some unwarranted real-life repercussions. It seems overly sympathetic to the harasser, willing to let him off the hook on the slightest pretext. After all, what can one expect from men "in their youth"? And it seems dangerously close to blaming the eve-teasing or rape victim. If theologically, the *panaghaṭa līlā* is interpreted as Krishna answering the love of the women in kind, the argument is not far off from the one that when women are harassed, they get what they deserve. We get close to the all too common interpretation that women who get groped or raped must have asked for it. Remarkably, whereas the Gopīs display behavior opposite to that of Sītā, the results are the same. The old prejudice that women who are harassed actually deserve it seems to raise its ugly head again. And that is exactly what we see worked out over and over again in the popular movies.

Sexual Harassment in Popular Film

The topic of sexual harassment figures importantly in Hindi movies. Often the image of the violation of a woman carries strong political overtones. "Woman" often stands for the self-esteem, the honor (*izzat*), of a community, and sometimes the nation-state.[183] A woman's reaction to an offender and the reaction of the males around her is not just an issue of how to cope with a practical problem but comes to stand symbolically for outrage against injustice. Sometimes the offender is clearly identified; sometimes the references are more oblique.

There are many variations and twists on this important theme. The movies offer the same two scenarios I have been discussing: a sexual harassment and an eve-teasing one. The first is the Sītā scenario, with an attempt at abduction or rape by a villain, and the second is the Rādhā scenario, with a seduction scene by a playboy type, who may be the hero.[184] Sexual harassment sets in motion

183. This can also be said to be the case for the televised *Ramayan*. Zacharias argues perceptively that its narrative may be read as a metaphor for the violation of the motherland by the enemy, never named yet understood to be "Muslim" (1994: 39).

184. I do not mean to limit the film scenarios to just two. Here I focus on what is relevant for this chapter, but there are many more possibilities. Another important epic reference is found in violation scenarios that include disrobing, a reference to the episode of Draupadī's public disrobing that sets in motion the wheels of revenge leading to the fratricidal war of *Mahābhārata* (see Rajan 2000b). Another seduction-harassment scenario hearkens back to the *dastān* tradition and involves the crazed lover type, the *majnūn* type of hero, who will go to extreme lengths to draw the heroine's attention. A delightful comical example is the Akbar character (Rishi Kapoor) in Manmohan Desai's *Amar Akbar Anthony* (1977); a macabre example is the Rahul (Shahrukh Khan) character in Yash Chopra's *Darr* (1993). In addition, there is a whole genre of rape-cum-victim-revenge movies that became de rigeur in the 1980s (Virdi 2003: chap. 5; Gopalan 2000). Here the references are frequently to the mythology of the goddess Kālī.

the wheels of vengeance: the heroine's honor needs to be avenged. Eve-teasing involves mostly an unmarried woman and sets in motion the wheels of matrimony, with a happy marriage hopefully ensuing toward the end of the movie. This scenario often involves a scene near a well, confirming the romantic-everyday overtones of the *panaghaṭa līlā*. I will first discuss generally the occurrence of these two scenarios in Hindi movies, before offering a detailed analysis of the relevant scenes from selected movies.

For the sexual harassment scenario, the focus is on the aggrieved party seeking revenge. Villains may kidnap with explicit reference to Sītā, as when in the 1986 *Karma* (Past action; d. Subhash Ghai) the villain announces his abduction of the hero's wife by saying: "I'm taking Sītā Mātā to Laṅkā" (discussed by Derné 1995b: 201–3). This theme in particular lends itself to political messages, as is the case with the 1988 *Tezaab* (Acid), directed by N. Chandra, who earlier made a Shiv Sena propaganda film (*EIC* 487). This movie transposes Sītā's kidnapping to contemporary Bombay. The hero is coded Maharasthrian, and the kidnapper is an outsider, thereby giving a Shiv Sena chauvinist understanding to the scenario of the Aryan Rāma protecting the Aryan women from the *rākṣasa*-outsider aggressor.

It is interesting that in the Sītā scenario, often there are explicit or oblique references to the Lakshmana Rekhā. The heroine is invariably shown to have trespassed on a rule of public decency, some transgression of the "boundaries of propriety" is involved. This may be a flagrant flouting of decency, for example dancing seductively in a rock concert in *Tezaab,* or flamboyantly wearing a minidress, often considered an invitation to rape, as in the 1994 hit *Mohra* (Pawn; d. Rajiv Rai).[185] Or the trespassing may be involuntary, such as returning home late from the office and getting drenched in the rain, as in the 1996 movie *Hamara dil aapke paas hai,* directed by Satish Kaushik. Other movies refer to the transgression of dharma along those lines (See Virdi 2003: 126–36). For the purpose of detailed analysis, I will take a close look once again at Kumar Santoshini's *Lajja,* this time focusing on a different story within the film.

There have also been movies that explore what happens if a Sītā like character, a married woman gives in to a seducer. Most notably in its explicit referencing *Rāmāyaṇa* mythology is B.R. Chopra's *Gumrah* (1963), the story of Meena (Mala Sinha), who is in love with the painter Rajinder (Sunil Dutt) but after the sudden death of her sister feels compelled to marry her sister's

185. This movie also has an interesting reference to a Lakshmana Rekhā of sorts: when the heroine is pursued by prison inmates, the hero saves her from rape by drawing a Lakshmana Rekhā between her and him on one side and the would-be rapists on the other side (Bagchi 1996: 5).

widower, Ashok (Ashok Kumar). She chooses to do so in order to take care of her beloved niece and nephew. The story focuses on the psychology of the young woman in an unsatisfactory marriage with an older lawyer, gradually giving in to the lure of desire for a meeting of hearts with her former artist-lover. Eventually, she forsakes this extramarital relationship and returns to proper matrimony by her own decision. This movie is actually prefaced by an enactment of Lakshmana drawing the invisible line around Sītā. The husband, Ashok, refers to the myth in his moralizing sermon at the end of the movie. He reveals to his wife that he has known of her affair but—and here is the big difference from the *Rāmāyaṇa* scenario—offers his wife a choice. He is prepared to either take her back, if she comes of her own choice, or to make way for her and let her go, if she chooses for her lover. Although one might argue that the heroine of the movie has to go through a kind of trial-by-fire scenario, still, she is offered a real choice. Moreover, when she chooses for the husband, she is able to get back within the enchanted circle. This Sītā has actually transgressed the Lakshmana Rekhā by allowing herself to be seduced, yet she can return to the world of *maryādā,* even after her transgression.

For the Rādhā scenario, the focus is usually on the playboy hero's perspective. The heroine is mostly ambiguous in her reaction to his eve-teasing. Initially, she may make a pretense of a Sītā-like resistance, which may be stronger or weaker, depending on the movie. Yet the hero's persistence will pay off, and eventually the heroine will come around and find herself loving him. One example is David Bhawan's 1992 *Bol Radha bol:* the hero, the rich Kishan, dreams of his Rādhā, and when he finally meets her, in the village where he is to start a new factory, she is not at all receptive to his attempts to woo her. In fact, she gets the villagers to beat him up (due to a misunderstanding). Even when—much later in the movie—he honorably asks her father for her hand, he is publicly humiliated, as Radha still does not wish to get involved with him. Eventually, of course, even this Rādhā comes around and starts to appreciate him. Not all Road Romeos have such serious intentions, though. In the second half of Raj Khosla's 1978 *Main Tulsi tere aangan ki,* the playful, spoiled son of Kuṃvarjī, Pratap, now a grown man, hides in a tree as the village women file past on their way to the well. In an interesting variant of Krishna's *panaghaṭa līlā,* he throws a tomato, hitting the girl he fancies, Geeta, on her behind. She is not amused, and later takes her revenge by hitting him with oranges. He uses the occasion to declare himself "crazy for her" (*terā divānā*), enacting the role of the madman. His repeated pestering finally wears down her resistance, and in the end it is Geeta who, helped by some *bhang,* takes the initiative in seducing him. Of course she becomes pregnant, and while promising all will be all right, Pratap is not prepared to honor his commitment, but instead uses her as a pawn in his own politics. In this movie, Pratap starts out as one of the two heroes, but increasingly takes on a villain-like character, and it is at that point that the playful Krishna relationship takes a more Rāvaṇa-like turn, though in the end, of course, he has a change of heart and becomes a good man again.

Complaints of Molestation as Titillation: "Satyam shivam sundaram," "Devdas," and "Anarkali"

Interestingly, sometimes songs referring to Krishna's eve-teasing are performed in movies to attract the hero, who then falls in love with the heroine. One example is in Raj Kapoor's 1978 *Satyam shivam sundaram* (already referred to in the previous chapter). The heroine, Roopa (Zeenat Aman), daily worships in the temple in the morning and sings a song on her way back from bathing in the river. One morning, she is overheard by a young and handsome engineer, Rajeev (Shashi Kapoor), who has newly arrived in the village in connection with the opening ceremony of the newly built dam. He immediately falls in love with her voice. When he hears her sing again, in the morning as she goes to the well, he follows her and catches a glimpse of the seductive beauty of her body. The song is steeped in Krishna imagery. It is a song on the theme of being accosted at the well:

> When dawn comes, at the well,
> Naughty Krishna teases me.
> My shawl clings and gets stuck.
> What can I do, O God! Alas!
> When dawn comes, at the well.[186]
> No girlfriend, no chaperone with me, I'm alone.
> If anyone sees me, they will say:
> On pretext of getting water, she lifted the waterpot,
> And Rādhā is going to meet her Śyāma, alas!
> When dawn comes, at the well.[187]
>
> A gust of wind comes, crushes my every limb.
> Secretly, silently,
> He is sitting somewhere, quietly,

186. *bhor bhaye panghaṭ pe, mohe naṭkhaṭ śyām satāye; morī cunariyā lipṭī jāye, maiṃ kā karūṃ, hāy rām, hāy hāy; bhor bhaye panghaṭ pe.*

187. *koī sakhī sahelī nahīṃ saṅg maiṃ akelī; koī dekhe to yah jāne, paniyā bharne ke bahāne gagarī uthāye, rādhā śyām se milne jāye, hāy; bhor bhaye panghaṭ pe.*

Gazes and smiles, he's shameless, he doesn't feel shame!
When dawn comes, at the well.[188]
If I don't meet him on the path,
He will come to my house.
I can scold him, tease him,
Not open the closed window,
But if I fall asleep, he will wake me by throwing pebbles.
When dawn comes, at the well.[189]

Rajeev follows Roopa from a distance, hiding behind the bushes, just like Śyāma in the song. Effortlessly, he steps in the footsteps of "naughty Krishna", although he will not force her against her will, he will certainly seduce her.

Echoes of the meeting-at-the-well theme are apparent in many movies. One classic is the famous relationship between Devdas (Dilip Kumar) and Paro (Suchitra Sen) in the 1955 *Devdas*, by Bimal Roy. They have several rendezvous near the well, including the famous one where Devdas hits her with his cane for her insolence. This may bring out a certain masochistic streak in the heroine, who is ready to bear the hero's abuses, ascribing them to his violent love for her. The theme of eve-teasing at the well is also apparent in the recent (2002) remake by Sanjay Leela Bhansali, though in a different way. Two interesting songs bring up the theme. The first scene is the picturisation of the song "More Piyā" (sung by Jaspinder Narula and Shreya Ghosal), which evokes the Rāsa-līlā theme.[190] At the same time, Paro (Aishwarya Rai) and Devdas (Shah Rukh Khan) act out a meeting at the river, and the song also includes a complaint about harassment, though Paro seems more than willing in the picturization:

Don't talk so much, I'm feeling shy.
Yes, leave me alone, I swear by you.
No, don't insist, let me go, my love.
Look, I will scold you, crazy.
Go, off with you, don't torment me, my beloved.
My beloved, look, my heart is afraid.[191]

188. *āye pāvan jhakorā, ṭūṭe aṅg aṅg morā; corī corī cupke cupke, baiṭhā kahīṃ pe vah cupke; dekhe musakāye, nirlajj ko lāj na āve; bhor bhaye panghaṭ pe.*

189. *maiṃ na milūṃ ḍagar meṃ, to vah calā āye ghar meṃ; maiṃ dūṃ gālī, main dūṃ chiḍkī, maiṃ na kholūṃ band khiḍki; nīndiyā jo āye, to vah kaṅkar mār jagāye; bhor bhaye panghaṭ pe.*

190. *"dhumak dhumak kar nāc rahī thī merī rādhā pyārī hāṃ, jāne kahāṃ se rās racāne āyā chail girdhārī"* and "*kare kṛṣṇa rās rādhā ke saṅga.*"

191. *na bayān dharo, āti hai mujhe śaram; hāṃ, choḍ do tumko hai merī kasam; na, zid na karo jāne do mujhe balam; dekho, dūṃgī maiṃ gāliyāṃ bhāṃvare; calo haṭo satāo na more piyā, more piyā ḍarta hai dekho morā jiyā.*

The enactment also involves his removing thorns from her feet and then kissing her feet, a very erotic moment, also reminiscent of the reversal of roles with humble Krishna at Rādhā's feet in the mythological stories. Devdas also breaks Paro's bangles and necklaces, though in a restrained, not violent, way. Most interesting here is that the song is actually sung by Paro's mother, which has the effect of a maternal consent to this premarital Rāsa-līlā.

The second reference to the *panaghaṭa* theme is the song used for the courtesan Candramukhi's (Madhuri Dixit) first performance for Devdas. This scene seems to be filmed deliberately as an ode to Anarkali's dance in *Mughal-e-azam,* which I shall discuss later, yet there is an interesting twist. This song sets up Candramukhi's love as similar yet contrasting to Paro's, which was celebrated using the same metaphor of the seduction at the well. The Devdas-Paro encounter was private and intimate, and the dialogue was direct between the woman and her accoster. The Devdas-Candramukhi encounter is a public one, where she is the spectacle and he one among many spectators, and the incident at the well is reported in indirect voice. In Paro's case, there is happy fulfillment in love; not so in Candramukhi's.

The song starts as Candramukhi approaches Devdas,[192] performing several pirouettes right in front of him, her veil slapping his face. Irritated, he grabs it. At this point, she starts with an appropriate line, quickly reversing the situation, as if he is harassing her instead of the other way around:

> "Śyāma ran up and stopped me, suddenly kissed my face.
> My shawl slipped from my head, lower, lower, and lower . . ."
>
> "Why did he tease me," sang the wife, "why did he tease me,
> Nanda's prince, so brazenly? He forced himself on me and took my honor [*lāj*].
>
> Vrindā's Śyāma did not heed [my words].
> Whom to tell this to? I can't even listen to my own heart, friend.
>
> With a pot full of curds I walk the path.
> I hear a sound, my heart stopped, and pounded, pounded."[193]

192. As a prelude, Devdas's friend Cunni Lal Babu describes the courtesan poetically: "Braided with jasmin, her sweet curls crowding her face, flashing like lightning, her gait is intoxicating" (*māltī gundhāī kaisī pyārī ghūṅghar bhare, mukh dāminī sī damakat cāl matvārī*).

193. *dhāi śyām rok le rok le, aur acak mukh cūm le; sar se morī cunarī gaī, sarak sarak sarak. kāhe cheḍ mohe gharvāl gāī, kāhe cheḍ mohe; nandakumār aiso ḍhīṭh, barbas morī lāj līnhī. brindā śyām mānata nāhīṃ, kā se kahūṃ maiṃ apne jiy kī sunat nāhīṃ māī. dadhi kī bharī maṭkī le jāt rahī ḍagarī bīc; āhaṭ sun jiyā rag gaī aur dharak dharak.*

As Candramukhi is mimicking the action of her song (*abhinaya*), she smiles seductively. This suggests that the outrage of the heroine is just for show: she really enjoys the game of cat and mouse that Krishna is playing with her. At this point, the last line of the song, she starts complaining about Krishna's more physical action:

> "He grabbed my hands and broke all my bangles, o friend."[194]

The last line of the poem, with the reference to breaking the bangles, is an allusion to passionate lovemaking. Such explicit references are allowed in movie songs under the cover of a bhakti song for Krishna, the references to Śyāma and Nandakumāra ensuring that the song is understood as a Krishna *bhajana*.

Indeed, there are many resonances with the medieval songs I have analyzed. As in them, the atmosphere is very earthy and physical, especially the way the song starts out, with a beautiful woman walking seductively to the well. Krishna does what he always does: stages a surprise attack and embraces the woman, "taking her honor." In the second half, we see a repeat offense, this time when the woman is carrying a pot of curds on her head, so presumably more of a *dāna-līlā* context. Again, he sneaks up on her; she is helpless, standing with beating heart as she anticipates what is coming; and he forces himself on her. As in the medieval songs, all this is framed as a Gopī's complaint to another Gopī. She is baffled, still does not know what to make of it. Yet, through the dancer's *abhinaya,* we suspect the speaker may have enjoyed what happened, an impression the medieval songs also conveyed.

Within the movie, this is part of a seduction scene. Reality mixes with the script evoked by the song. When Candramukhi acts the last line, she approaches one of the drunk patrons of her performance, who sees his chance to grab her hand in fact. In the playful introduction, the obverse took place. Devdas grabbed her veil, and she compared it to Krishna stopping Rādhā on the way to the well. There, the roles were reversed. Whatever the song said, we could see that the woman was teasing the man. Poor, pursued Devdas was the one who really felt harassed. The courtesan made a show out of being harassed, but she signaled she enjoyed it.

Thus, the risqué topic of seduction at the well is appropriated here for the context of the courtesan's performance. The tale of the seduction of a woman is appropriated to seduce men. The complaint of the Gopīs is used to titillate real-life (well, reel-life) patrons. This may say something about the performance

194. *kar pakaṛat cūṛiyāṃ sab karkī karkī o māī.*

context of the *panaghaṭa* songs, and the way they spill over in secular domains and are appropriated for commercial ends. Whether indeed historically such songs were performed by courtesans or not is beside the point here. What is instructive is that their occurrence in the film context illustrates the abiding influence on the imagination of this type of song and the interpretation of sexual relationships between men and women it provides.

In the end, the seduction does not work. Devdas spoils all the fun by rudely leaving the performance. When Candramukhi tries to hold him back, he has a little sermon for her that could have come straight from the pen of the Gandhian Hindi writer Premcand: "You are a woman, Candramukhi. Recognize yourself. Woman can be mother, sister, wife, or friend. When she is nothing else, then she is a courtesan. You can be something else, Candramukhi."[195] The reform agenda has intruded. One is reminded of the modern Hindi poetry project of leaving the dreams of Braj for a nationalist awakening that calls for the rehabilitation of the fallen woman (Ritter 2005). The Hindi film has had it both ways: using the Braj lyrics for titillation as well as incorporating the reform through the resistance of the hero and his refusal to be seduced. Remarkably, it is the hero who resists the seductive Krishna scenario. The heroine, on the other hand, enacts a reverse scenario of that of the Gopīs. Attracted as irresistibly to Devdas as the Gopīs to Krishna, she will break with her former life, just as they do with theirs. Instead of leaving behind dharma for love, though, her love will motivate her to choose the path of dharma. In the Hindi film world, the path of love—it seems—can be no other than that of dharma.

Another famous example of allusion to the theme of pestering at the well in song, for the sake of seduction, is a classic scene from *Mughal-e-azam* (d. K. Asif, 1960). Prince Salim (Dilip Kumar) falls in love with Anarkali (Madhubala) as she performs a Krishna Janmāṣṭamī dance number. The song is sung by Lata Mangeshkar (music by Naushad, lyrics by Shakeel Badayuni):[196]

> At the well, I was teased by Nandalāla,
> He twisted my delicate wrists.
>
> He threw pebbles at me, broke my water pot,
> My simple[197] sari was drenched.

195. *tum aurat ho candramukhī. pahcān jā apne āp ko. aurat mā hotī hai bahin hotī hai patnī hotī hai dost hotī hai. aur jab vah kuch nahīṃ hotī to tavāif hotī hai. tum kuch aur ban saktī ho candramukhī.*

196. The song has been attributed to Raghunath Brahm Bhatt, who wrote it originally for a Gujarati play in 1920 (in.nri.yahoo.com/041115/156/2hymn.html), though it may go back to the court of the Lucknow Navabs.

197. The use of the word *anāṛī* here may be a play on the name of the dancer, Anarkali. She means to express that she is simple and innocent.

With the magic of his eyes, he enchanted my soul.
My veil opened to his gaze.[198]

Anarkali here performs a Krishna *bhajana,* as is befitting for the occasion. Prince Salīm himself has invited her to take the part of Rādhā for the Janmāṣṭamī performance, suggesting to his father that she "will be fitting for the part of Rādhā."[199] The dance is preceded by a sequence showing the *pūjā* of the child Krishna in the palace. However, when the performance of the dancers begins, the tone changes to a more erotic atmosphere, befitting the theme of *panaghaṭa līlā*. Although the queen is also present, witnessing the performance as a religious festivity, it is intended mainly for the men.

In mock complaint, the dancer describes herself as victim of Krishna's teasing, describing all the usual actions we are very familiar with: Krishna throws pebbles, and breaks the water pot, which causes the famed wet-sari effect, here only evoked in words. Finally, he puts a spell on his victim, she is lost to him, and her veil opens up to his gaze. "Twisting wrists" stands as a code word for molestation, but she stops short of describing the more sexual embraces (*aṅka bharanau*) we heard about in some of the bhakti songs. It is as if the veil discreetly opens up only for the beloved, but then hides the couple from the spectators' (and our) gaze.

The beauty of the song is in its ambivalence, in the playful alternation between complaint and surrender. The body language (*abhinaya)* interpreting the words leaves the listener guessing about what is not said explicitly. There is also a voyeuristic element, a glimpse into a woman's very private life, the effect of an overheard conversation that stirs the soul.

The addressee of the song is ambiguous. One could imagine one Gopī confiding to another, but the choice of the vocative particle *re* instead of *rī* suggests rather a male interlocutor. This fits with the performance context, where the song is performed for the emperor and his retinue. The slave girl then speaks under pretext of a complaint about her molestation by Krishna to another male. The effect is one of titillation, and indeed, she is successful. The emperor is pleased and showers the dancers with coins. Prince Salim falls in love with her dramatically.

This seduction works. However, there still is a reform agenda at work. In the rest of the movie, Anarkali is shown consistently as suffering for love, rather than enjoying the few stolen moments she has with her lover. She is

198. *mohe panghaṭ pe nandalāla cheḍ gayo re; morī nāzuk kalaiyā maroḍ gayo re. kankarī mohe mārī gagariyā phoḍ ḍālī, morī sāṛī anāṛī bhigoyī gayo re. nainoṃ se jādū kiyā jiyarā moh liya, morā ghūṅgaṭ nazariyā se khol gayo re.*

199. *rādhā ke liye munāsib rahegī.*

painfully aware of her social position and hardly dares admit her love. Her sister, Suraiya, tries to tease her out of this attitude, but to little avail. Anarkali's view of love as suffering is taken up again and again, but it may be most explicitly stated in her song contest with her rival, Bahar. Bahar aspires to marrying Salim and sees Anarkali as her rival. Her love is functional: she wishes to become the empress. Her jaded conception of noble love comes out in her song, where she typifies it as "trembling, quietly turning into a mere sigh and dying a death of suffocation."[200] She prophetically foretells that this perception will turn out to be the realistic one, as she says she will watch the fun and have the last laugh.[201] The prince rewards her as the winner of the contest with the rose. Anarkali equally prophetically professes her view of love: "I concede that love ruins one's life, but it is not a small accomplishment the world remembers one in death. I too will let the world ruin me for my love and see."[202] Perceptively, the prince bestows on her the thorn, which she accepts gratefully, as thorns do not wither as roses do. Anarkali then is not one to celebrate her love, like a Gopī, flaunting rules of dharma. Rather than enjoying it, she is painstakingly aware of her transgression, and ready to suffer for it even before the enjoyment. This ideal lover certainly has a masochistic streak.

All these examples illustrate a preoccupation with woman as a willing victim of sexual abuse. The Krishna songs per se do not encourage such an interpretation—one could even argue the opposite and see them as a celebration of love. However, their filmic prevalence in the performance context of the courtesan's *mujrā* (seductive performance) adds an extra dimension. The woman speaking admits she has already been molested, which opens up the possibility for the male in the audience to molest her again. Victimization breeds more victimization. Her attitude toward the abuse is interpreted as a willing invitation, even enjoyment, of suffering. This construction of a masochistic sexual partner seems the logical counterpart of a sadistically inclined male. If these women serve as role models in any way, it seems to be one carefully constructed to serve a male preoccupation. "Films seem to say, then, that harassment and force are the way to a woman's heart" (Derné 2000: 152; for a psychoanalytical explanation, see Kakar 1989: 33–7).

200. *taṛapnā cupke cupke āh bannā ghuṭke mar jānā,*

201. *kisī din yah tamāśa muskarākar ham bhī dekheṃge.*

202. *muhabbat ham ne mānā zindagī barbād kartī hai, yah kyā kam hai ki mar jāne pe duniyā yād karte haiṃ, kisī ke iśq meṃ duniyā luṭākar ham bhī dekheṃge.*

This streak is abundantly clear in some more recent movies, where we find an interesting combination of both the Sītā and Rādhā scenarios, as in the 1990 hit *Dil*, directed by Indra Kumar already referred to in Chapter 3.[203] In this movie, the playboy hero Raja (Aamir Khan) and the heroine Madhu (Madhuri Dixit) are studying at the same college. Initially, they are sworn enemies, and do everything to make each other's life miserable. The harassment here definitely goes both ways, with Madhu scheming just as hard to waylay Raja as he her. Though there is no love lost between them, and the tone is more serious than the war of the sexes in the Krishna myths, there is a hint that he may actually desire her. This comes to the fore during a boxing match she arranges for him to get beaten up. At the outset, he insists that the prize for fighting will be that if he is the winner, he will get to kiss her. She agrees reluctantly, assuming he will lose anyway. When he actually wins, against all odds, he moves closer to her, and they come close to kissing, but at the last minute he turns his head and leaves her doubly dishonored: nearly publicly kissed *and* publicly spurned. Madhu seeks revenge, and the climax comes during an overnight school trip to a mountain station. Madhu tricks Raja to come into her room and then accuses him of trying to rape her, for which he is expelled from the camp. Raja, now utterly provoked, seeks revenge by abducting Madhu from her room and threatening to rape her for real. Again, he stops short from the actual act, a replay of the kissing scene at the end of the boxing match. His claim is somewhat surprisingly that he did all this not out of revenge but rather so as to make her feel what it really is like to be a rape victim and to show how immoral it was for her to use the ruse of a rape to hurt him. By falsely accusing him of rape, she has dishonored other women who truthfully have been in such a situation. Raja here does an amazing tour de force, transforming from a near-rapist into a champion of rape victim's rights. He has it both ways: he asserts his power over the woman and poses as a defender of the weak. The underlying assumption seems to be that a lot of rape victims are actually women who are out to vilify the accused man, and that it is difficult to distinguish between them and the few rightful victims there might be.

Most telling about implicit gender prejudices is that the exact scene contains the seeds of Madhu's love for Raja. After he turns away from her and explains his behavior, we see her gaze at him with a softening that betrays incipient love. Sure enough, in the next scenes she takes the initiative in

203. See also n. 105 in chapter 2. This movie is also analyzed by Derné 2000: 152–3.

courting Raja, inviting him to meet with her privately. All this confirms that our worries about the implications of the *panaghaṭa līlā* on the assumption that women really like it rough were not misplaced. Not only is there scope to interpret these bhakti songs in that way, we see these scenarios play out fully in the movies.

There is yet something else going on in many of these scenarios. The hero is coded as a playboy, a wayward, *junglee* kind of character, and has to be transformed by the end of the movie into either a responsible citizen settling into happy domesticity or a tragic hero succumbing to a heroic demise. In other words, the hero's *junglee*-ness needs to be reformed or erased. The project of such a transformation is taken on by the heroine. So we see that it is via the agency of the Rādhā character that the hero is turned from irresponsible Krishna into Rāma. In the process, Rādhā changes, too. Her character is turned into either a savior or a punisher of wayward males. This theme fits well with similar projects going on in early Hindi literature, where the call for reform from the dream world of Krishna's flute into rallying songs for the motherland is heard frequently. A movie where the transformation of Rādhā into an agent for the nation is remarkable is the classic *Mother India*, which has both scenarios and is well worth a detailed analysis.

Sītā Standing up to Sexual Harassment: "Lajjā"

First I focus on an illustration of the Sītā scenario. Kumar Santoshini's *Lajja* is a delightful recent reworking of the issues related to Sītā's abduction in the light of sexual harassment of women. I have already discussed scenes from this movie in connection with Sītā's wedding. The frame story features Vaidehi (Manisha Koirala), who is pregnant and fleeing her abusive husband. In the course of her flight, she meets several characters, all named after Sītā. Here I will explore the story of Janaki (Madhuri Dixit), an actress in a *nauṭaṅkī* company in a small town where Vaidehi seeks temporary shelter.

The first meeting of the two women is significant. When Vaidehi drops in at the theatre company, Janaki is performing a scene from the play *Mughal-e-azam*. She is enacting Anarkali's song "Jab pyār kiyā to ḍarnā kyā" ("When you've loved, what is there to fear?"). This immediately defines her as defiant of societal norms. The song also foreshadows events to come, as Janaki indeed has loved outside of wedlock and will reap the dire consequences. But first we get to appreciate Janaki for her spunk and sheer love of life, regardless of what people may think of her. Vaidehi is attracted to her carefree devil-dares-all spirit and becomes friends with her. She learns to whistle at the movie star

Shah Rukh Khan in the dark cinema hall.[204] The audience shares her fascination with Janaki, celebrated in the saucy song "Bābā kyā hai muśkil" ("Man, what's so difficult").

Complications soon surface, though. It turns out that Janaki is in love with her fellow actor, Manish, whose child she is carrying and whom she is hoping to marry after the run of the play ends. However, someone else has designs on her: the company's director, who is the Rāvaṇa character, though ironically he is named Purushottam, "the best of men," an epithet of Rāma. Though he is married and insists on his wife keeping strict purdah, he does not miss a chance to romance Janaki. Janaki is dependent on him as he is her director, but she resists his attempts to seduce her. We see her keeping the older man at a distance with a decisiveness that shows she does not take him very seriously as a sexual aggressor. Part of her strength in resistance derives from the fact that she is secure in the love of Manish.

Purushottam then resorts to subterfuge. He strikes at the heart of Janaki's confidence by creating discord between the lovers. First, he convinces Manish and Janaki to stay for the run of the next play—none other than an enactment of the *Rāmāyaṇa*. The lovers are convinced to stay on, on the grounds that it is very inauspicious to turn away from the *Rāmāyaṇa*. It will prove exactly the opposite: it will be disastrous for them to reenact the *Rāmāyaṇa*. That message is not lost on the viewer. Interestingly, there are two plays within the movie. On the one hand, there was *Mughal-e-azam*, with its strong message of defiance to patriarchal rule, epitomized in the song "Jab pyār kiyā to ḍarnā kyā," which Janaki performed earlier. On the other hand, we have the *Rāmāyaṇa*, here perceived as a play that embodies the oppression of women.

Once the two lovers have committed to stay on, Purushottam makes his next move. He suggests to Manish that he has a relationship with Janaki himself and manages to sow the seeds of mistrust in Manish's mind about whether the child Janaki is expecting is really his. This Rāvaṇa, then, is not a threatening figure; he is an old man who does not really pose a threat to Janaki, and is not a plausible seducer of women. However, his sneakiness is all the more dangerous, and we see that he actually succeeds in seducing Manish away from his love.

The climax comes in the midst of a very emotionally loaded performance of the *Rāmāyaṇa*. Behind the curtains, Manish informs Janaki that he does not

204. There is a lot of cinema self-referencing in this episode, as when Janaki encourages Vaidehi to wear one of her saris that will make her look like Karisma Kapoor—whereas the actress is Manisha Koirala.

want to marry her if she keeps the child. Janaki immediately grasps that he is suggesting abortion and understands why he is doing so. She refuses the abortion, not so much on moral grounds but because she feels her pride and love is at stake. Back on stage, she transforms the fire ordeal scene by infusing it with her own pain at being rejected. As Sītā, she points out that she followed Rāma in his exile and that throughout she has remained loyal to him. Does she deserve this plight? Rāma-Manish grandly claims he is rejecting her for the sake of such ideals as protecting virtue in the world (*sadācār kī rakṣā*). Janaki then oversteps her role, asking Rāma-Manish whether he loves her. Startled by the deviation from the script, he falls back on a standard monologue about the need to show society, but she cuts him short: "The question is addressed to you, not to society. You tell me whether you're with me or not!"[205] Behind the curtains, Vaidehi, who functions as *souffleur*, is speechless. someone tells her "She's speaking the wrong lines," but Vaidehi closes the script book and whispers: "She's got it right." [206] On stage, the Lakshmana character tries to interfere, spouting lots of sonoric epic vocatives, in an attempt to calm Janaki down. But Janaki turns against him, pointing out that his disfigurement of Śūrpaṇakhā is what caused Rāvaṇa to abduct her in the first place. We can applaud her directing attention to the root cause of the abduction, putting the blame with the men, whereas we have seen the television version stressing Sītā's fatal mistakes leading up to the abduction, put the blame on the victim herself.

Janaki spits out that men always show their macho-hood by taking it out on women. When Lakshmana gets angry, she rebukes him: "I'm the one who should be angry because it's my character that is being questioned."[207] She points out how heroically she has withstood Rāvaṇa on her own, while the brothers had to gather an army first before they could come to her rescue. But what signifcance would that army have had had she not withstood the tyrant? Her description of her rejection of Rāvaṇa brings to mind her rebuttals to Purushottam: "Is this the reward of my courage, my patience, my trust, and my love that today in public I am insulted and abandoned?"[208] Sītā's anger here is not directed at the Rāvaṇa character but at the men who claim to rescue her from the aggressor and then cast doubt on her reputation, becoming aggressors themselves.

205. *praśna āp se kiyā hai samāj se nahīṃ! āp batāiye: āp mere sāth haiṃ yā nahīṃ.*

206. *"vah galat dialogue bol rahī hai," "sahī bol rahī hai."*

207. *krodhit mujhe honā cāhiye kyoṃki mere caritra kā savāl uṭhā hai.*

208. *mere sāhas, mere dhairya, mere viśvās, mere prem kā yahī phal mil rahā hai ki āj baṛī sabhā meṃ merā apamān, merā parityāg?*

We may like it, but in the film, the audience watching Janaki's Sītā interpretation is getting restless; they do not appreciate the turn the story is taking. Lakshmana is at a loss and comically tries to save the situation in an aside to the stage assistant: "Hey man, quickly open the fire pit,"[209] and he as much as tries to push Sītā in the pit. Lakshmana has it right; he is catering to what the audience demands. However, to the great outrage of the public, Janaki flatly refuses: "No, I'm not going to prove something in which I don't believe! I don't need to prove anything to someone who doesn't believe my word."[210] She insists that Rāma-Manish take the fire ordeal with her: "We'll take a trial by fire together."[211] But Manish refuses. Significantly, in the film, the audience is with him. Everyone wants to see a meek Sītā jumping into the fire. The actors nearly push her into the fire in an attempt to save the situation, but to no avail; the performance is lost, and the public protests. They demand that Sita act as she should and commit her immaculate self-sacrifice. Only Vaidehi applauds Janaki's actions. The curtain falls, and the public starts to riot.[212]

Behind the curtains, in the dressing room, Janaki rages to Vaidehi: "Keep telling them what they like and what attracts their heart, then they will put you on their shoulders, worship you and say you're a goddess. But tell them what you think, and they'll call you a slut of disreputable character."[213] Vaidehi approves of Janaki's rewriting of Sītā's story. She muses: "If only Sītā had acted the way you have, then today every man would not [be able to] ask trial by fire of any woman."[214] But she points out that it is not the *Rāmāyaṇa* that is to blame; Janaki, too, has committed a mistake: she should not have trusted Manish. Janaki quickly retorts, pointing out that respectably married Vaidehi, too, is in the same state: "a child in the womb, and exiled."[215] She is referring to the events of the last book of *Rāmāyaṇa,* the Uttara Kāṇḍa, where Sītā is exiled on grounds that she is tainted and that her return to Rāma's house sends the wrong signal to his subjects. Sītā's situation, pregnant and exiled, epitomizes

209. *are jaldī se cittā khol do yār.*

210. *are mujhe kuch sābit-vābit karnā nahīṃ, jise mujh par bharosā nahīṃ, jise merī bāt par bharosā nahīṃ, uske liye mujhe kuch sābit karnā nahīṃ.*

211. *ham donoṃ agni parīkṣā deṃge.*

212. These scenes are reminiscent of the real-life rioting in cinemas in Delhi and Bombay that showed the movie *Fire* (1996) by the Canadian director Deepa Mehta. The objection there was similar: that the character with the name Sita acted in ways uncharacteristic of the mythological Sītā.

213. *jo bāt inke kānoṃ ko acchī lage, inke man ko ricāe, vahī bolte raho, to sir par biṭhākar pūjā kareṃge, kaheṃge devī hai. aur apne man kī kaheṃge, to kaheṃge kulaṭā hai, caritrahīn hai.*

214. *kāś sītā jī ne bhī vahī kiyā hotā jo tum ne kiyā hai, to āj har mard kisī aurat kī agniparīkṣā kī māṃg nahīm kartā.*

215. *kokh meṃ baccā lekar banvās.*

every woman's plight. After men have had their fun, they leave you, and there you are: pregnant and rejected. She is voicing a common understanding that explains the resonance Sītā's story has for many women.

While outside a demonstration against Janaki takes place, Purushottam comes to offer his services. He has the temerity to confirm that it is all Janaki's fault, as she has committed an offense against dharma (*dharma kā apamān*). In his view, the mistake is that she has not "acted her part." Janaki gets furious when she hears his hypocritical sermon. She points out that he himself daily accosts her while keeping his wife behind purdah. Isn't that a greater offense? Purushottam tries to make use of her vulnerability to blackmail her into becoming his mistress, but she furiously refuses: better to go to the insane asylum than submit to such vile desires. He then sends her into the crowd, where she is insulted and beaten, to the point that she loses the child.

This movie's agenda is to stand up against the oppressive discourse perceived to be epitomized in the *Rāmāyaṇa* story. Its creative engagement with the story illustrates the pervasiveness of the Sītā trope. In its attempt to rewrite Sītā's lines, in particular during the infamous Agniparīkṣā, the movie playfully appropriates the right to rethink the story. Does it overstretch the boundaries in rewriting Sītā by incarnating her in an actress who is pregnant before marriage? How far can one go before the vessel breaks? When does Sītā cease to be Sītā (Rao 2004)? In building in this critique within the movie—in the audience's reaction to the play—the director acknowledges he is swimming against the tide. Indeed, this self-prophecy came true. *Lajja* was declared to be a subversion of the *Rāmāyaṇa,* and there were attempts to have it banned. Just as in the movie, where the rioters burn posters of the actress playing Sītā, BJP workers in Bhopal burned posters of Madhuri Dixit in her role as Janaki playing Sītā, as well as effigies of the director (Aklujkar 2007).

Even had the audience liked it, Santoshi's reworking of *Rāmāyaṇa* might be thought to fail on a deeper level. As was the case with Maithili, we see again a woman who speaks out but is utterly ruined, with no way out, in the end. While these women's courage and defiance surely goes a long way to create an alternative example, their dire helplessness in the end is a strong deterrent to following that example. These scenes of protest serve to offer the audience some relief of its pent-up anger, but in the end, the status quo is maintained. The only redeeming feature is that Vaidehi goes and confronts Purushottam in front of his obedient wife, who now turns against him, saves Vaidehi from his rage, and accompanies her to the station. There is a brief satisfaction and sense of closure here. However, beyond speculation that the power dynamics in Purushottam's household might be slightly altered, there is no future for this wife either. At the end of the movie, there is no happy resolution as there was for Maithili's story, however brief and unconvincing. Within the movie, Janaki is utterly irredeemable. She is a fallen woman. Once fallen, once she has crossed the Lakshmana Rekhā, there is no saving her. Her carefree attitude is shown up. Her protest has utterly failed. It has not opened up alleys of alternative lifestyles. It has only brought disaster. The movie has failed, then, to write a plausible alternative to Sītā's story.

In the end, the whole project of consciously rewriting *Rāmāyaṇa* has the wrong focus. What is the point of blaming an old story and its characters? Why should we blame Sītā for the way she reacted? The blame lies not with Sītā or with the story. The story has been reworked many times for different needs. The more modern versions are not the less oppressive ones—rather the opposite. What is driving women into bad situations is not an outdated religion but simply the lack of human kindness. The problem is not with the gods but with men and women who do not step up to their responsibilities, who claim the dharma high ground while acting otherwise, and with those—men and women—who condone such behavior and fail to show up their hypocrisy. The problem is not with the film industry either. There is indeed a courageous movie that shows a counter-example of somebody standing up to sexual harassment of women. Surprisingly, it is a classic movie dating from the fifties: *Mother India.*

Rādhā Stands Up to Punish Krishna's Harassment: "Mother India"

When we look at scenarios of sexual harassment in popular movies, there is one movie we cannot neglect: *Mother India.*[216] This epic film can of course not be reduced to only issues of sexual harassment,[217] but they figure prominently. It is interesting, too, that the movie was directed by Mehboob Khan—a devout Muslim, who shows a deep and insightful engaging with Hindu mythology. When confronted with the apparent paradox of his reworking Hindu mythology as a Muslim, he is reported to have said that these stories are "in our blood" (Gayatri Chatterjee, personal communication, February 18, 2006). The

216. The movie was successful at the time of its release: it received several Filmfare awards—best film, best cinematography (Faredoon Irani), best director, best actress, and best sound (Kaushik)—and was nominated for the Oscars. It was also a huge international success, especially in the then USSR and South America. Due to the place it holds in the Indian imagination, it has created a mythology of its own (see Thomas 1989).

217. For a wonderfully insightful analysis of the movie, see Chatterjee's book-length study (2002), which also deals with some mythological elements. I want here to take up Chatterjee's invitation to study the mythological references (2002: 73–4) but will do so less with reference to Krishna rather to Rādhā and Sītā.

movie in fact contains an interesting take on both the Sītā and the Rādhā scenario.

First, a comment on the name of the mythic heroine of this national epic: Radha. This may be surprising. Why would a strong, long-suffering peasant woman, who symbolizes the nation and indeed Mother Earth, be named after the delicate erotic heroine best known for her expertise in love play and melancholic longing and pining for an absent beloved? It seems all the more incongruent because the movie is intended to be something of a nationalist epic. It was first released to coincide with the celebration of the first decade of Indian independence in 1957.

The nationalist movement had felt itself worlds apart from the feminine world of Rādhā's Braj. It heralded a move away from decadent Rādhā-Krishna-type topics in literature and toward a more robustly masculine patriotic literature, involving more Rāma-type characters and frequent references to powerful goddesses like Durgā, equated with cosmic power, or *śakti* (King 1994). It has been noted that whereas Rādhā was a popular figure in the poetry of the prenationalist period, she more or less disappears from the literary map from the end of the nineteenth century onward. This is well expressed in the title of an article on the topic of literature of the period: "Where Have All the Radhas Gone?" (Schomer 1982). The one notable exception is Ayodhyā Singh Upādhyāy Hariaudh's *Priya-pravāsa,* a Sanskritic reinterpretation of the Krishna mythology, which moves Krishna from philandery to philanthropy, one could say. In this new universe, Rādhā is shorn of sensuality and transformed into a chaste social worker (see Ritter 2005).

However, the fact is there: in popular cinema, squarely in the foreground of this nationalist film, we have a Rādhā, not a delicate lover or a chaste social reform worker but a bread-and-butter mother, toiling in India's red earth, literally carrying the weight of her children on her shoulders in the midst of a flood. Mehboob succeeds in updating Rādhā. In this movie incarnation, she is a down-to-earth ordinary woman but rises to superhuman strength to save the future of the nation. She seems unrecognizable at first glance, but if we look closely we find that some of the features of the traditional Rādhā persist, with some very interesting twists.

At first sight, one might wonder why she is not named Sītā, as she might be closer to preconceptions of Sītā rather than the erotic Rādhā. This is the case right from the beginning of the movie, which starts auspiciously with Radha's wedding. It is quite the traditional village affair; there are plenty of cows and oxen, signifying auspiciousness and fertility (throughout the film, cattle play an important role in the family's fortunes) as well as evoking the pastoral world of Krishna's Braj. However, the tone at the wedding is not joyous and spontaneous, as in the Braj depictions of Rādhā's wedding. Rather, everything is serious and solemn, as it would be observed from the perspective of the young inexperienced bride about to embark on a journey into an uncertain future. Some shots show only the feet of the couple, as if through the eyes of the bride, who shyly keeps her head bowed. We get a glimpse of the wedding ceremony's Brahminical ritual highlights and then the leavetaking. This occasion prompts the first song of the movie, a *bidāī* song, expressing the sorrow of the family of the bride at seeing her leave "Piy ke ghar āj pyārī dulhaniyā calī" ("The pretty bride left for her beloved's house today"). The tone on the sound track remains tragic, even when the scene changes to the arrival in the groom's house and the camera registers the joy and playfulness of the women there. This is in contrast with the shy uncertain bride's feelings, which continue to be poignantly expressed in the song. Still, the wedding represents the erotic mode (*śṛṅgāra*), and we do get a glimpse of the excitement of the groom at the prospect of the wedding night. Significantly, as the groom opens the bride's veil, the lines of the song are: "I have no special qualities, ways, or anything; the honor of my bangles [symbolizing the marital state] now rests with you; I've come to be with you for a lifetime."[218] The lines are humble (ironically, given the actress, Nargis's splendid looks) and voice the surrender of the bride to her new groom: whatever she may be, their marital bliss all depends on him; his approval or disapproval is the determining factor. This is marvelously acted by Nargis, as she keeps her eyes closed but totally surrenders to her groom's touch, while he ardently, somewhat awed, gazes at her face and touches her for the first time. The beautifully framed, glamorous Nargis evokes the erotic atmosphere magically (see Chatterjee 2002: 24–5), yet the last shot of this scene is of her falling at the feet of her groom. The audience is not going to miss the point that this Radha is right from the start more of a Sītā type.

Sure enough, all too soon the erotic gives way to duty. Radha is depicted as putting the role of the proverbial good *bahū* first and only secondarily that of the erotic young wife. As soon as she hears about the mortgage her mother-in-law took out for the wedding, she takes off her jewelry and gets to work. She coyly dodges her enamored husband Shyamu's affection for fear of what people might say (*śaram*), but that heightens his desire only more. One early scene is reminiscent of Rādhā and Krishna's love play. In the morning, catching her at work in the stable, he wants to put her jewelry back on so he can admire her beauty. She protests that he should sell it to pay off the loan, but he

218. *koī guṇa ḍhaṃg na mujhmeṃ koī bāt hai, morī cuṛiyoṃ kī lāj ab tore hath haiṃ, tore saṃg maiṃ jīvan bhar ko sajnā calī.*

insists. She succumbs to the moment and teases that she'll take it off every day, just so she can have the pleasure of him putting it back on. This evokes images of Krishna adorning Rādhā. However, the love scene gets interrupted by the arrival of the mother-in-law, who reminds them of wagging tongues in the village, and the tone changes to comedy as the lovers, scolded by her, clumsily try to resume their household tasks. Mother-in-law gives the new *bahū* a good piece of advice: "Don't let him have his way or he'll be a good-for-nothing." We are squarely back to "Dharma comes first." A later scene reminiscent of Krishna mythology shows the couple at work in the fields when it starts raining and they seek shelter under a tree, huddling under one cover. However, the erotic potential of the moment is not exploited, as we are now focusing on the injustice of the hard work the farmer has to endure while the treacherous moneylender takes most of his hard-gotten harvest.

The actress Nargis is certainly glamorous, even while going about household tasks, including churning butter like a true Gopī, and she exudes erotic power even when covered with mud and earth. Still, erotics are hardly the order of the day. Even in the beginning, the songs celebrating Radha and Shyamu's love are work songs, and they are depicted harvesting rather than dallying about. In contrast to her namesake goddess, Radha also gives birth to children; her two surviving sons appropriately are named Ramu and Birju. The oldest son is named after the epitome of dharma, the second after carefree, naughty Krishna. Right from the beginning, they enact perfectly their characters: Ramu is obedient, self-controlled, and hard-working; Birju is self-willed, impulsive, and a rebellious loafer (wonderfully acted by precocious little Sajid). He is disobedient to parental authority yet strongly attached to his mother (see Chatterjee 2002: 45). Like Krishna, he is mother's favorite. She cannot punish him. There are some wonderful vignettes of the delight of parenthood (*vātsalya bhāva*) as everyone enjoys the children's pranks (*bāla līlā*). At this point, the references to the mythology of Krishna shift from the erotic focus on the couple to the child Birju, and Radha transforms into the Yaśodā character of Krishna's mother rather than the erotic partner.

Soon, though, disaster strikes. In an accident, Shyamu loses both his arms and is totally incapacitated—read impotent. Unable to bear this, Shyamu flees the house in despair, leaving Radha to fend for their children. Before leaving, Shyamu obliterates the *ṭīkā*, or auspicious cosmetic mark on the forehead of the sleeping Radha. This is significant as it symbolizes her happily married status (*suhāg*). When Radha wakes up, she frantically tries to get her husband back and sets to search for him. Here the image of the erotic Rādhā shifts to that of Mīrā. Radha is shown wandering from temple to temple in hopes of finding her husband somewhere among the beggars at the temple entrance, because without arms, that is how he would need to subsist. Against the backdrop of a *bhajana*-like song, this evokes the image of pilgrimage, in particular that of Mīrā to the temple city of Dwaraka, crazy in her devotion to Krishna. The song definitely sounds like a Mīrā *bhajana:*

> From town to town from door to door, I am looking for the dark one.
> Crying out over and over: "Beloved, beloved," I've gone mad.
>
> My beloved heartlessly has blown me into the fire of sorrow.
> Pining for my love sets aflame[219] my happiness: unlucky am I.
> Every moment my heart weeps, turning my eyes into brimming waterpots.
>
> When I came, what dreams of love did I bring in my eyes.
> Now I'm going with tears and all aspirations squashed.
> In the riotous confusion of the world, the backpack of my life got plundered.
>
> These two eyes hungering to see you will not sleep lifelong,
> [But will remain] spread open in welcome for you. We'll cry night after night.
> Now, O God [Rāma], I don't know how I'll spend my life.[220]

It is ambiguous who is the "dark one" of the song: is it Radha's husband, Shyamu, or Mīrā's beloved God, Krishna? The last line seems to indicate it is God himself, here addressed as Rāma. However, the song's picturization gives a twist to the Mīrā image. Radha is still in her red shawl and colorful outfit, clearly not the widow in white Mīrā is often portrayed as. Moreover, she is accompanied by her two older sons. While the last verse is sung, the camera shows her two sons leading her back home, and the song's formulaic reference to the woman's two hungry eyes acquires a whole new meaning. We are reminded of the hunger of the two children, which is not a hunger to see God or even their father but a very real down-to-earth hunger for food.[221] Then, in retrospect, the "mercilessness" (*bedardī*) of the beloved takes on another

219. Literally: "the spark of pining [*viraha*] falls into the married happiness [*suhāga*] of an unhappy one."

220. *nagarī nagarī dvāre dvāre ḍhūṃṛūṃ re sāṃvariyā, piyā piyā raṭate maiṃ ho gaī re bāṃvariyā; bedardī bālam ne mohe phūṃkā gam kī āg meṃ, birahā kī cingārī paṛtī dukhiyā ke suhāg meṃ, pal pal manavā roe chalke nainoṃ kī gāgariyā; āī thī āṃkhiyoṃ meṃ lekar sapne kyā kyā pyār ke, jātī hūṃ to āṃsū lekar āśāeṃ sab hārke, duniyā ke mele meṃ luṭ gaī jīvan kī gaṭhariyā; darśan ke do bhūkhe nainā jīvan bhar na soeṃge, bichṛe sājan tumhāre kāraṇ rātoṃ ko ham roeṃge, ab na jāne rāmā kaise bītegī umariyā.*

221. This seems intentional, because the lyricist has chosen the image of "hunger" rather than the more common one of "thirsting eyes" (*pyāse nainana*).

meaning. It becomes an outcry against men dodging family responsibilities. Why do men value their pride more than their families? Why are they so easily influenced to let go when they have lost their honor and choose to leave their own families in the lurch? By extension, it raises the question of why God is so irresponsible as to leave women to fend for their families. This song very subtly, but surely, undermines some traditional bhakti tropes, while using their appeal and popularity. We could interpret it as a socialist-inspired appropriation of Mīrā-style bhakti.

Radha returns home to shoulder full responsibility for the family. However, she refuses to let go of her husband and keeps wearing the signs of the auspicious marital state, convinced he will return one day. Chatterjee has perceptively observed that this is crucial for the movie, as it enables Radha to remain a sexually active woman and embodiment of *śakti,* which could not have been possible had she been widowed (Chatterjee 2002: 48).[222] In this respect, Radha truly is modeled after her mythological namesake, as she faithfully remains pining for her absent husband, always waiting, always expecting him back. The visions she has of him returning and her fond memories of marital bliss in flashbacks serve to reinforce that theme.

Still, there are several echoes of Sītā's story. The movie also has scenes of sexual harassment reminiscent of the Sītā scenario. That is particularly the case in the first part of the movie, where the village moneylender, Sukhilala, has a lecherous eye on Radha, who has recently arrived in the village as a new bride. He is an old lecher, far from a romantic alluring flute player, but still we encounter him first as he is making passes at the village women on their way to the well. He pretends to be concerned about their safety, telling them to watch out not to slip lest their pots break, a statement full of sexual innuendo. But Rādhā's friend gets back to him with quick repartee: "Women do not slip like men do." She adds, criticizing his practice of moneylending, asking rhetorically: "With you around, who can afford copper pots?" Radha does not speak to the moneylender and asks her friend not to pay attention to him (the scene is described in Chatterjee 2002: 41).

Later on in the movie, Sukhilala becomes something more of the Rāvaṇa character. After Shyamu becomes incapacitated, Sukhilala taunts him in hopes of making him leave town. Indeed, he succeeds, and Shyamu leaves Radha. Now Sukhilala sees his chance and tries to force Radha into submission. He tries to seduce her, now destitute, with promises of wealth, suggesting she

222. See also Chatterjee 2002: 50–1 for more reflection on the absence and failure of the husband in the light of the postcolonial predicament.

deserves better than the penury in which her husband has left her. Radha does not give in to him but literally stands—and plows—her ground. She is shown doing so while also feeding and raising her family, to the strains of the famous song "Duniyā meṃ ham āe haiṃ to jīnā hī paṛegā" ("We've come to the world, so we have to go on living"). The song propounds the main concern most explicitly in the line:

> It's woman on whom depends the shame of the world.
> In this vale of tears, women are the keepers of honor.[223]
> Who lives in honor, will also die in honor.[224]

The song then articulates a discourse valuing women's honor above all. It applies the principles of *Rāmāyaṇa* to a real-life situation, but makes the point that it may not always work out. While the song ends in firm resolve, Radha is to be further tested, not by fire, like Sītā, but by flood. A devastating flood destroys all they own. Radha is desperate to feed her children, and as she struggles to make a meal with nothing but mud, her youngest baby dies. As she stands with the dead baby in her arms, covered with mud from the flood, Sukhilala chooses this moment to appear and repeat his offer to "protect" her. He offers her surviving, starved children some food (*cannā*). Radha forbids the children to accept anything from the moneylender. Sukhilala withdraws but repeats that his offer remains valid and he will wait patiently. Once Sukhilala is gone, her favorite son, Birju, faints from hunger, and Radha is frantic that she might lose this son, too. Desperate to feed her children, she runs to Sukhilala's house, ready to take him up on his offer. In this version, then, Radha-Sītā succumbs to Rāvaṇa, but only because of her children. The memorable scene of her (aborted) seduction in Sukhilala's house deserves detailed attention, as it is contains many hints of Radha's divine alter ego, the goddess (see also Chatterjee 2002: 55–7).

Radha does not have to say anything. Sukhilala knows why she is there. He greets her with mock humility in an ironic reference to the divine Rādhā, stressing the incongruence of her arrival, something he had not hoped for just yet: "May you be blessed. The feet of the goddess Rādhā have reached Sukhilala's house. Blessed is my fortune!"[225] Another goddess, however, has blessed Sukhilala—the goddess of wealth, Lakṣmī, and she is given pride of place in his house. When Radha sees this silver image, she becomes furious

223. Literally: "She is [truly] woman who is the shame (*śarm*) of the world. In this world, woman's duty (*dharma*) is just her honor (*lāj*)."

224. *aurat hai vah aurat jise duniyā kī śarm hai, saṃsār meṃ bas lāj hī nārī kā dharm hai; zindā hai jo izzat se vahī izzat se maregā.*

225. *dhanya ho devi. rādhārāṇī ke caraṇ aur sukhīlāl kā ghar! dhanyabhāg!*

and throws the symbols of her wedded state, her "wedding necklace" (*maṅgalsūtra*) and bangles, at the image. Sukhilala promptly proceeds to put a new "wedding chain" around her neck, saying gleefully that she has done well to come to him; she will benefit, because he is so generous that he will put golden chains even around the neck of his dog. As he ties the chain, he says admiringly: "I swear by God (Rāma), you look like a Lakṣmī. Come Lakṣmī,"[226] and he pulls her toward the bed. Radha bitterly repeats, "I look like Lakṣmī,"[227] tasting the full bitter irony of the situation, and she directs her anger again at the goddess image. "Goddess, are you not ashamed manifesting yourself in Radha's body? You've become embodied in me, now watch how your own honor is being robbed."[228] Challenging Lakṣmī as if the goddess were a person, she says: "Don't laugh. You'll lift the burden of the world, goddess, but the burden of motherhood is to be upheld too. First become a mother yourself, then see how your feet too will falter.[229] Meanwhile, Sukhilala is trying to remove the image of Lakṣmī, keen not to have his goddess of good fortune offended. But Radha stops him: "The goddess gave you fortune and brought me to you by making me unfortunate. I will tell this goddess! It's easy to show the path, but very difficult to follow it. It's easy to sit on a seat and watch the spectacle. But becoming the spectacle yourself and living your life that way is very difficult, very difficult."[230] In her despair, she vows to show the childless Lakṣmī what she cannot understand: "I'll tell this goddess what a mother when pushed can do for her children. How far she can fall, how deep. Goddess of power, if you don't give me power, then take my shame [and be ashamed of yourself]! I cannot sacrifice my poor children."[231]

There is a great deal of bitter irony in this scene. For one, Radha is indirectly trying to shame Sukhilala, but she knows he is a lost cause. Still, she can manipulate this superstitious man by insulting his goddess of fortune. To some extent, she succeeds. Sukhilala tries to move the image away, so his goddess will not become displeased with him. At the same time, there is also a direct appeal to the goddess herself, trying to shame her. At the basic level,

226. *rām kasam, lakṣmī lagtī ho, lakṣmī, āo.*

227. *lakṣmī lagtī hūṃ.*

228. *devi rādhā ke rūp meṃ āte hue lāj na āī? merī rūp meṃ āī ho, to apnī lāj luṭe hue bhī dekh lo.*

229. *haṃso nahīṃ. saṃsār kā bhār uṭhā logī devī mamtā kā bhoj na uṭhāyā jāegā. mā bankar dekho. tumhāre pā̃v bhī ḍāgmagāeṃge.* I am grateful to Munni Kabir for clarifying the Hindi.

230. *devī ne tumheṃ dhan diyā aur mujhe nirdhan banākar tumhāre sāmne lāyī. maiṃ devī ko batāūṃgī: rāstā dikhānā sahaj hai par rāste par calnā bahut kaṭhin. sthān par baiṭhkar tamāśā dekhnā āsān. tum khud tamāśā bankar jīnā bitānā bahut muśkil hai, bahut muśkil.*

231. *maiṃ devī ko batāūṃgī ki ek majbūr mā apne baccoṃ ke liye kyā kar saktī. kahāṃ tak gir saktī, kahāṃ tak gir saktī. devi, śakti nahīṃ de saktī, devī. to lāj le lo. maiṃ apne baccoṃ kā balidān nahīṃ kar saktī devi.*

Radha's speech is triggered by Sukhilala's remark that she looks like Lakṣmī. If Radha has turned into Lakṣmī, then the irony is that he is about to rape Lakṣmī herself. Lakṣmī, the goddess image, will have to watch her own disgrace. In the background is also the avatar theology, holding that Lakṣmī manifested herself on earth in the form of the goddess Rādhā, for whom Radha is named. How can she now stand seeing her namesake being abused this way? How can the goddess of love stand seeing love so abused? At another level, there is a more socialist-inspired critique. Radha is venting her anger by trying to shame the goddess about her lack of evenhandedness. She has blessed Sukhilala; whatever he touches seems to turn into gold. Now even Radha is part of that miracle. How unfair it is that the goddess manifests herself so abundantly in the house of this man, while staying away from the farmer's hovel and thus forcing hard-working mothers to sell their bodies. Radha is addressing the goddess in good bhakti tradition, which allows for this type of blackmailing of the god, and it pays off. Finally, there may also be a metacriticism here about filmī denigration of women becoming a spectacle for the public. It is easy for us to sit and watch this sexual harassment take place and feel moral outrage. But Radha asks, do we something about it or do we just watch the fun? This scene seems to interpellate the audience that they should not just chime in with the song we've just heard and join the rhetoric about women having to protect the honor of the world and "show the way" but that they should also take the much more difficult road and "walk the path,"—show in action how to remain honest in the face of adversity. It is easy to preach, the filmmaker seems to say, but how about doing something about it?

The miracle Radha prays for happens. The goddess gives her power (*śakti*) to stand up and walk out on the deal. It is not a spectacular miracle (as in the earlier film *Aurat*, of which *Mother India* was a remake, see Chatterjee 2002: 57) but one that is in the eye of the believer. In the tussle with Sukhilala, who is trying to move the image, Radha finds her *maṅgalsūtra* again, which she had earlier tossed at the goddess. She sees this as a sign from the goddess and recovers her belief that her husband will come back and things will turn out well in the end. Sukhilala, ironically, tries to appeal to her sense of dharma, arguing that her first duty is not her absent husband but her children, who will die if she does not go through with his deal. But Radha now is convinced that the goddess is on her side, and she is determined to leave. He tries to overpower her, but she fights him off. We get some comic relief when Sukhilala falls and gets stuck in cotton jar, and some real relief when Radha finds a stick to beat him up with.

No men are needed to wage war against this Rāvaṇa; Radha fights the battle on her own. The only help she needs is *śakti* from the goddess: the power to stand up against injustice, the conviction that she is fighting the right fight. More than that, Radha's conviction to stand her ground is a transformative one. Not only does she stay put and toil on her land for a better future; she manages to transfer her resolve to the whole village. As they are about to make an exodus from their flood-devastated fields, her powerful example convinces them to stay. The personal victory over tyranny is turned to a collective benefit. It is in the song "O jānevālo" that Radha first takes on the role of Mother with capital M. She calls the villagers back, appealing to them in the name of Mother Earth.

> O emigrants, don't leave your house behind:
> Mother is calling you with folded hands.[232]
>
> This town is yours, its lanes, its neighborhoods are yours,
> Where are you going leaving all this behind?
> It's nothing, yet it's a million, the earth is your mother.
> You won't find happiness in the world by breaking your mother's heart![233]
>
> Stop, your fields are calling you back.
> The sky says you have to live right here.
> Come back, so that Mother's sighs won't stick with you.
> Stop, where are you going, turning your back?[234]

At the last repetition of the refrain, Radha stoops and scoops some mud from the ground; she reaches out with earth in hand as she repeats that Mother Earth is calling them. And this is the real miracle: her plea stops the villagers from leaving. They return to their lands to toil side by side with her. Her identification with the earth is complete, as her body is totally covered in mud.[235]

In the next, upbeat song "Dukha bhara dina bīte re bhayā" ("Days of sorrow are gone"), the identification gets subtly shifted to one with Mother India. First, the turning wheel of the bullock cart that signifies the passing of time (announcing a flashback) is also reminiscent of the *cakra* in the Indian flag. Then comes the famous striking image of a map of India its borders traced

232. *o jānevālo jāo na ghar apnā choṛke, mātā bulā rahī hai tumheṃ hāth joṛke.*

233. *nagarī tumhārī galiyāṃ tumhārī ye bastiyāṃ, in sab ko choṛkar are jāte ho tum kahāṃ; kuch nahīṃ hai lākh phir bhī hai dhartī tumhārī mā, duniyā meṃ sukh na pāoge dil mā kā toṛke.*

234. *ṭhahro pukārtī hai tumhārī zamīn tumheṃ, kahtā hai āsmān hai jīnā yahīṃ tumheṃ; lauṭ āo mākī hāy lage nā kahīṃ tumheṃ, ruk jāo jā rahe ho kahāṃ pīṭh moṛke.*

235. Of course, as many observers have noticed, this is also a reversal of the exodus of Partition, in 1957 still fresh in people's memory. In the light of the atrocities and rapes accompanying the event, it is notable how the filmmaker predicates the return to one's land on a woman standing up against sexual tyranny.

with haystacks and chiseled in the earth. In fact, the map shows pre-Partition India, including Sri Lanka, Pakistan, and parts of Burma. In the light of the previous song, which pleaded with emigrants not to heed the call to move, it seems to be a criticism of the separate-homeland "solution." In any case, Radha is now transformed into the mother of the village, and by extension of the whole of India.

In this movie, then, the Sītā scenario has been rewritten in a powerful way. This Sītā is an active agent, fighting for her family, to keep her children alive. Her priority is not her chastity but her children: she is tempted to give in to the seducer only when she is desperate and sees no other way. There are no men around to save her, but she finds strength in the goddess, and in herself and her self-esteem to resist and keep up the fight. This transformation is not only for the benefit of her family but also her village and, it is suggested, the nation. The resistance to sexual harassment is what transforms Radha into Mother India.

In the second half of the movie, Radha is called upon to preserve not only her own chastity but that of all the village women. As her children grow up, Radha assumes more and more the role of doting mother. Like Yaśodā, she is indulgent toward her favorite son, happy-go-lucky Birju, who was the rebellious child, a little trickster whose pranks evoked at one point the butter thief. In a scene early in the movie, he snatches some sweets (*canā-guḍ*) from the moneylender's daughter, Roopa. Now that he has grown into an adult, he has become quite the Krishna playboy character, forever teasing girls. In good Krishna tradition, we see him breaking their pots of water as they come back from the well, making passes at them, and indeed succeeding in capturing quite a few hearts, including that of Sukhilala's daughter. Roopa is the girl foregrounded among these Gopīs, and she is shown to proudly threaten Krishna-Birju with the consequences of his actions, secure in her position as the daughter of the village's richest man. This is reminiscent of the Rādhā poems I have discussed, where Rādhā threatens Krishna that her father, Vṛṣabhānu, is a powerful man in the village.

One of the most explicit references to Krishna mythology is a scene where Roopa and her friends complain to Radha about Birju's behavior. The girls complain (as far as we know falsely) that Birju spied on them while they were bathing and (rightly) that he always breaks their pots, each in turn testifying "he broke three, four, five, six . . . pots of mine." The last girl sadly remarks that he has not broken any of hers.[236] This makes it clear that the girls actually

236. *merī ghaghṛī to phoṛtā hī nahīṃ.*

secretly like Birju's passes. In that respect, they resemble very much the Gopīs in Sūrdās', poems and Sagar's television series *Shri Krishna.*

However, the big difference is in the reaction of the mother. Whereas Yaśodā always ends up taking her son's view and casting doubt on the women's character, this Radha takes the women's complaints very seriously. She makes it clear to Birju that she cannot tolerate this behavior. We hear a new discourse now, Radha is adamant that Birju should not sexually assault girls from his own village.[237] We saw Sūr's Yaśodā mentioning this just once, briefly, and then immediately being persuaded by Krishna's counter-arguments. There seems to be some ambivalence, too, about whether the Gopīs at the well are perhaps from different villages, as Krishna suggests in the way he addresses them. Of course in Sagar's series, there is no question of the child Krishna sexually assaulting the women; the erotic desires are ascribed to the women, not to Krishna. In any case, what is new here is the mother's insistence that her son not mess with the village women. Ironically, it is *mother* Radha who insists on this propriety.

In the movie, Birju at first manages to avoid being punished by convincing his mother, in good Krishna fashion, that it was not he who teased the girls but they who teased him. He gets the girls off his back by creating havoc with a snake. That is similar to what happens in the television series with little Krishna. There too the snake shows up at just the right moment to distract his mother. Here, Birju has the snake hidden under his jacket and shows it to the girls, who are scared into saying what he wants them to and admitting they are wrong. His mother has not seen this happen and is tricked into believing her son has done no harm. Just seconds later, though, she sees the snake peek out from under his jacket, which frightens her. Birju throws the snake out, to create panic and distraction. In this first incident, then, the mother's anger is dissipated by the snake, just as in *Shri Krishna.*

However, just like Yaśodā in the television series, Radha is not convinced, and tries the age-old strategem of silence (*mauna vrata*) and a hunger strike. After some back and forth between her and her two sons, it gets resolved playfully. In the television series, too, Krishna manages to distract his mother from her sulking protest (with reference to his brother's teasing). However, in the film, Radha's memory is not so short. She comes back to the issue and warns her son that she will kill him if he damages the honor of one of the village women: "I will not forgive you as long as I live if you stain the honor of

237. *āj maiṃ sacmuc uskā sar toṛ ḍālūṃgī. gāṃv kī laṛkiyoṃ ko ciṛhtā hai, apnī bahinoṃ ko ciṛhtā hai.*

any girl of our village. I will kill myself and you."[238] That warning turns out to be prophetic.

More Krishna references ensue. First there is a good-natured reversal of roles, in a delightful scene where Birju is offering to go to the well instead of his pregnant *bhābhī*, his brother's wife. As he comes back with several pots full of water on his head, the girls are waiting for him and take their sweet revenge by breaking them. We have not seen any such scene in *Sūr Sāgar* with regard to the *panaghaṭa-līlā*, but it is totally consistent with the playful tone of role reversal in many other scenes. So far, things are friendly. However, Roopa makes it a game to egg on Birju. She knows she can really make him mad by wearing the golden bangles (*kaṃgan*) that Birju bought for his mother and Sukhilala managed to take from him. This is a constant reminder for Birju of his mother's shame and his own impotence to do anything about it. The bangles totally spoil the relationship with Roopa. Even the celebratory Holī song ("Holī āyī re Kanhayī," also with Krishna references) ends in a fight when Roopa taunts him by sporting his mother's golden bangles.

His mother thinks he has harassed the girl and is ready to beat him mercilessly, but luckily his brother, Rāmu, speaks up for him. Radha, like mother Yaśodā, accepts that it was Roopa who provoked her son. In this case, we know that the mother is right not to blame her son. Yet Birju is not let off the hook so easily. Wily Sukhilala points out that Birju has been teasing all the girls of the village and that not all of them have provoked him. This turns the village against Birju. Sukhilala senses victory and eggs Birju on with the taunt that he has noble dreams of giving his mother golden bangles but that he just should ask him, Sukhilala, to do that job. He is insinuating that Birju cannot protect his mother's sexuality and she should just give in and become the moneylender's mistress. This predictably sets off Birju and he tries to attack Sukhilala. Sukhilala has cleverly managed to deflect attention from the sexual character of his daughter to the collective propriety of the village and in addition has cast doubt on the propriety of the perpetrator's mother's character, knowing full well that this will cause Birju to lose his cool.

This is an interesting variant on the scenario of complaints about sexual molestation from the Krishna mythology. Krishna is always playful about warding off complaints about his molesting of women. However, here the complaint is turned around, and the suggestion is that his mother can be

238. *magar yah marte dam tak nahīṃ māf karūṃgī ki tū gāṃv ke kisī laṛkī kī izzat par hāth ḍāl le. terī aur apnī jān ek kar dūṃ.*

sexually molested. This is not a complaint that is to be taken in jest. Birju's anger now turns murderous.

When Birju tries to attack Sukhilala, the whole village beats him up and decides to exile him. But Radha makes her plea, promising "If he teases any girl, I myself will kill him."[239] The warning she has given Birju in private has now been solemnized in front of the village. This Yaśodā has stepped out of the traditional script. Her role is no longer only doting on her beloved son, the savior-to-be of the village. Instead she takes on the strong role, that of the parent who determines what the rules are, and what is the framework within which the village can be saved. Radha here sets her son limits: he can under no circumstance molest a woman of the village.

Birju is too enraged, though, to listen to reason. Barely recovered from the trashing, he steals a gun. When his mother questions him, he swears to kill Sukhilala and sacrifice his own life to liberate the village from Sukhilala's tyranny. While it is clearly Sukhilala's taunt and threat about his mother's sexuality that has set him off, Birju frames his personal rage as something of communal benefit, giving it a social revolutionary justification. The discourse now shifts; the question is whether violence can be justified in service of a just cause. One could say that the background of psychological transgression of the honor of the mother turns all this into an academic exercise, which is beside the point. The audience's sympathy is with Birju, as the insult he has suffered is the ultimate one.

His mother tries to convince him that violence does not help: "Nothing will come from a gun. You won't be able to cover the heads of the village women by means of a gun. No food will come in their house by means of a gun. Their cooking fires can't be lit by means of a gun. Look at me . . . We'll toil, we'll labor. God will turn the tide for us, for the whole village He will turn the tide."[240] This is good Gandhian advice, not the type that Yaśodā would have given, though she, too, tried to keep her son from killing the tyrant. But there the argument was her mother love and how she could not live without him. Radha starts out that way, but she progresses toward the debate so prominent during the struggle for independence whether violent or nonviolent resistance is the way to fight an oppressor.

239. *agar isne kisī laṛkī ko ceṛhā, to maiṃ uskī jān le lūṃgī.*

240. *bandūk se kuch nahīṃ hogā. bandūk se tū gāṃv kī auratoṃ ke sir nahīṃ ḍhak saktā. bandūk se unke ghar meṃ anāj nahīṃ āegā. bandūk se unke cūlhe bhī nahīṃ jaleṃge. mujhe dekh lo . . . ham mahnat kareṃge, majdūrī kareṃge. bhagvān hamārā din badal degā, sāre gāṃv kā din badal degā.*

Predictably these arguments are to no avail. Birju is not convinced. He is the hotheated rebel (indicated iconographically by his reddened complexion). He shakes off his mother and runs off to murder Sukhilala. However, Birju does not succeed and has to flee. Pursued by the whole village, he gets trapped in the fire they set to the haystacks. Radha attempts to save him and runs frantically in the fire. In the end it is he who saves her, only to leave her in safety and run off himself.

With Birju gone, Radha's health deteriorates quickly. She sees no purpose in life anymore. She is physically ill from missing her son, and we see her emaciated, feverish, continuously muttering his name. Here we are back to the erotic Rādhā. She has all the symptoms of the classical lovelorn heroine in the advanced state of lovesickness called *vyādhi,* the penultimate stage of love in separation (*viraha*): fever, emaciation, pale complexion, constant repetition of the beloved's name like a mantra. However, the man who is so missed is here not her lover but her son. This pain of separation is greater than what she was shown to suffer when her husband absconded.

Meanwhile, Birju steals a horse and becomes a bandit. He gathers a whole gang of outlaws around him, and they rob wedding parties on their way back with bride and dowry to the groom's house. On the day of Roopa's wedding, Sukhilala comes to Radha to beg her to prevent her son from attacking his daughter's wedding party. The moneylender now addresses Radha as "sister," indicating he has finally given up his designs on her and Radha's friend tells him he should call her *mā*. Indeed, what he asks for requires a forgiveness only mothers can muster. The roles are totally reversed now. Sukhilala comes to beg Radha to protect his *izzat*: "I am asking you for the alms of my good name. Sister Radha, please forgive me, I fall at your feet."[241] Radha, in a world-weary voice, says she forgives him. Ramu is shocked that she can say this so easily, after all that has transpired. However, Radha has gone beyond this old enmity; all she cares about is her missing son. What really pushes her into action is the firm resolve that he should not break the rules she has set him. In her eyes, not so much Sukhilala's *izzat* but her own and that of the whole village is at stake. Paradoxically, Radha can only be roused from the depth of her despair over her son by this sense of duty; her love is upstaged by dharma—as duty forces her to punish him.

Radha goes off and tries to stop Birju on the way to the robbery, but he does not listen. He races past her to take his revenge on Sukhilala. After all the

241. *maiṃ tumse apnī izzat kī bhīkh māṃgtā hūṃ, rādhā bahin, mujhe māf kar do, maiṃ tumhāre pāṃv paṛtā hūṃ.*

injustice the moneylender has put Birju through, it is immensely satisfactory for the audience to see him cower before the hero. Birju succeeds in recovering his mother's golden bangles and setting all the exploitative accounts on fire. Eventually he kills the man who brought his family to penury, caused his father to leave, and nearly took his mother's honor. All this seems justified, and no one really makes a move to stop him.

However, when Birju tries to abduct Roopa, the bride, he meets stiff opposition, not least from his own brother, who professes that his goal is to make sure, as good Rāmas do, that his parent (in this case mother) can stick to her word and does not see her promises broken. Still, Birju manages to capture the bride and gallops off with her on his horse. Now comes the amazing climax. Birju is on the road to freedom, only to find his mother blocking his path, gun in hand. She threatens to kill him, but exhilarated by his success, he just laughs and says she will not do that, as she is his mother. She answers "I am a woman" (*Maiṃ ek aurat hūṃ*); he reiterates: "I am your son." She retorts: "Roopa is a daughter of our whole village. She is my honor. Birju, I can give a son, but not my honor."[242] He brushes it off and sets off once again, the veiled Roopa in his arms. Radha aims the gun and shoots him in the back—her own beloved son. Roopa runs off to safety, leaving mother and son alone for the denouement. Birju dies in Radha's arms as the golden bracelets he recovered for her fall out of his lifeless hands.

Radha has come full circle, from being prepared to give up her own *lāj* to the moneylender, arguing with the goddess that she could not sacrifice her children for *lāj*, to doing exactly that: sacrificing her son for the *lāj* of the village. It is an amazing transformation, yet entirely believable. The movie has shown Radha evolve from the erotic wife, the dutiful *bahū,* the devoted mother, the toiling mother, the abandoned mother, ready to sacrifice for her children even her own sexual purity, to a defier of the village tyrant, savior of the village, Mother India, the excessively doting mother of grown sons, loving grandmother, and finally, the protector of the village women's honor. We have been zooming in and out the public aspect of Radha, foregrounding her private family life. But here, in the final scenes, she makes the horrible choice, like Rāma, privileging her public over her personal role. It is as if Mehboob is revisiting the *Rāmāyaṇa* scenario where Rāma banishes his beloved wife for the sake of his subjects. Radha, too, chooses for the public good, and she

242. *"maiṃ terā beṭā hūṃ." "rūpā sāre gāṃv kī beṭī hai. vah merī lāj hai. birju, maiṃ beṭā de saktī hūṃ lāj nahīṃ de saktī hūṃ."*

sacrifices her beloved son. We know what that sacrifice costs her personally. We know how much she dotes on particularly this son and he on her. His last act is to give her back her bangles. The sacrifice of the one who was ready to sacrifice so much for her is all the more terrible. Radha was identified with Mother Earth, as she was covered with mud; now she has become truly Mother India, as she is covered in the blood of her own son, killed by her own hand.

In the last scene of the movie, the blood on Radha's hands colors the water of the dam as it is released by the same, now older hands. This completes the flashback with which the movie began. Now the future can start. In the blood spilled for the nation, we see the blood of Partition, the trauma of which was still vividly on people's minds ten years later, at the release of this film. The film heralds a new epoch, a call to leave the unspeakable past behind and press on to a bright and better future. Yet at the same time, the film is wholly about the past, an attempt to come to terms with its haunting sacrifices. It is an exercise to exorcize the indentured state of colonialism, but even more an expiation of past sins, of the brother-against-brother violence and the rape of one's own sisters that have rocked the newly independent state. The wounds are still raw; there is no soothing balm. The horror is transferred, but it is still there. Watching the film, it is as if we can see the nation struggle with its past, as we gaze on the last scenes, cathartic through the riveting effect of unspeakable sacrifice.

What enables Radha to preside over the future is the sacrifice of her own son. Radha becomes Mother India by killing her Krishna. Mother India eats her own sons. Goddesses like Durgā are known to require terrible sacrifices for victory. Here it is the goddess who makes the sacrifice herself. One could nearly read it as a Christian solution: God herself makes the sacrifice to atone for our sins. There is definitely something of Christian iconography in the promotion still, showing Radha lifting the plow on her shoulder, looking like a woman lifting the cross. In the film, the visual reference to Christ and his cross comes at the end of the song "O jānevālo," when Radha falls under her plow-cross. However, this imagery is truly Indianized in a wonderful transformation. The next shot is of her now grown boys lifting her out of the mud. This image reverts then to the Hindu iconography of the incarnation of Vishnu, Varāha, who saves the earth from the mud after a flood. Here Radha is firmly identified with Mother Earth, or Bhūdevī.

At another level, we find the theme of the conflict between bhakti and dharma. Radha is the epitome of bhakti. Here she has absorbed not only the lover's fervor (*śṛṅgāra*) but also the mother's boundless love for her son (*vātsalya*), which is, if anything, portrayed as the strongest love.[243] Yet the same Radha, in order to make her way to modernity, leaves all bhakti behind. Precisely because the bond between mother and son is so strong, the sacrifice is all the more dramatic. Bhakti is validated, but is thoroughly subjugated to dharma. It is the "honor" (*lāj*) of the community that should be the ultimate criterion, not love. This honor is embodied in the character of the moneylender's daughter, the least worthy of all women in the village to be saved from Birju's hands, as we know she was secretly in love with Birju and, moreover, her father was the oppressor of all. Is the honor of such a girl worth sacrificing one's son for? Emphatically, the movie says yes, linking the release of this woman with the release of the waters that bring abundance, not devastation. The threat to Radha's *lāj* was tied up with the devastating flood; Roopa's release is connected with live-giving channeled waters.

In this movie, terrible sacrifices are required from Radha. She struggles and toils for those she loves, and eventually kills her Krishna with her own hand. There could be no stronger way to put the imperative that bhakti is to be subjugated to dharma. But the result is overpowering: she is transformed in a truly modern goddess for this age: Mother India. The filmmaker Mehboob has succeeded where the Hindi poet Hariaudh failed. In writing *Priyapravās,* Hariaudh sought to create a new Rādhā for the nation, but his Sanskritic and somewhat prim Rādhā never became popular, always was felt to be somewhat of an oddity, a literary exercise in rewriting the tradition (Ritter 2005: 201). Yet Mehboob's Radha became the symbol of the nation. Film succeeded where literature failed.

Conclusions: The Victim Will Be Blamed

I have shown that the way movies digest the mythological messages are multiple and complex. The Sītā scenario tends to be the one most straightforwardly targeted to the female audience. It offers an inspiring model for resistance to unwanted sexual attention. Sītā's steadfastness in her devotion to her love, and her indignant, self-confident retort to her tempter is exemplary for women everywhere in all ages. Her chastity entitles her to extraordinary

243. There is yet another level to this, since in real life, the actress Nargis married Sunil Dutt, who played Birju in the movie. There was (and still is) a lot of comment on this "scandalous" wedding of mother and son (Thomas 1989). This confusion of maternal and erotic love is all the more interesting in the light of the ambiguous relationship of Rādhā and Krishna in several of the sources. Real life, reel life, and mythological life get intertwined in interesting twists.

power, which may inspire the women in the audience who have had to cope with harassment in real life.

At the same time, her story certainly has a deterrent function: women cannot fail to get the message that the slightest breach of decorum can be fatal. We find a strong preoccupation with the Lakshmana Rekhā in the popular movie, which is remarkable, given that there is so little scriptural authority for that aspect of the story. In the movies, there is hardly any possibility of returning to happy matrimony once the line is transgressed. Sītā's story is relentlessly reworked in the Hindi movie and gets conflated with the rape victim scenario.

There is no reflection as to the psychology of the rapist; he is demonized and acts the way he does because he is evil. He is always the other, a member of a group that is set up as the enemy. The woman is the symbol of the violated right of the group we are sympathetic to. The violation automatically leads to the need for vengeance. This focus on the rape is actually not inherent to the Sītā story. As we have seen, Rāvaṇa refrains from raping Sītā in all our mythological versions. However, whether the heroine is actually violated or not, she still is considered to have lost her chastity. This perception is perpetuated in the popular domain. We should hasten to add, though, that there are movies that treat the issue differently. *Lajja* is an excellent example of a counter-movie. Still, it sparked controversy, which tells us something about what the audience wants (or does not want) to see.

The Rādhā scenario, on the other hand, seems to be targeted to a male audience. It condones eve-teasing, implying that the woman really enjoys such attention. In this view, her protest is feigned, is a mock resistance. In the end, the woman will fall for her accoster. The movies cast this scenario as one that is attractive to men. Women are portrayed as aware of the lure of such stories of violation and they manipulate it in seduction scenes. The focus is ordinarily not on resisting or punishing the accoster, as it is in the Sītā scenario. In fact, here the seduction usually succeeds.[244] On the other hand, there is one highly

244. On the other hand, there is also an argument that the eve-teasing is a way of teaching a woman who has become "too proud for her own good" a lesson (Rajan 2000b in the context of the story of Draupadī). In the movies, we are reminded of the scenario of *Dil,* where proud and rich Madhu is "taught a lesson" by Raja. In real life, this is also clear from the targeting of women who are perceived as Westernized (Anagol-McGinn 1994). There is also a class issue in real life: on the one hand, the more aggressive forms of harassment (such as stripping and publicly parading) tend to be perpetrated on members of low castes to "teach them a lesson" (Rajan 2000b: 52–3); on the other hand, middle-class women often interpret eve-teasing as coming from lower-class males (Puri 1999: 100–101). I am not sure how to square that information with the mythology of Rādhā, except that as we have seen, in some instances Rādhā is interpreted to be the proud daughter of her village's headman. In such cases, the mythology of Draupadī seems more revealing (no pun intended).

successful movie that insists on a punishment for the accoster: *Mother India.* In this movie, though, the responsibility for the young man's transgressive actions is squarely placed on the shoulders of none other than his doting mother. We could read this as holding women responsible for the violation of other women, not the men! It is also interesting that it is not the man's eve-teasing per se that is condemnable but his doing so with women who are not available to him, the women of his own village. This aspect might be fruitfully explored further. Implicit in the Rādhā scenario as well as the Sītā one seems to be an awareness that the threat of violation may come from inside the group rather than outside. Maybe it is not insignificant that the context of the Lakshmana Rekhā is one of suspicion of the sexual desires of the brother-in-law for his sister-in-law. Such a transgression though is too unspeakable to surface openly, or if it does, as in Birju's teasing the women from his own village, it is to be punished by the terrible breaking of another taboo: the mother killing her own son, taking the life she herself gave.

Conclusion

Approaching Sītā

Why is the little girl on the cover of this book crying? Is it the shadow cast by Sītā on the wall, who stands for a tradition perceived to be oppressive? Or are the scary glasses of the foreign viewer, a metaphor for alien interpretative lenses, perceived to be intrusive? Is there anything wrong with the Sītā model? Or are we looking at her the wrong way?

Sītā and the Women's Movement

I began this study by contrasting two opposing views of Sītā, both from within the women's movement in India. To some extent, I created a false dichotomy. The Indian women's movement itself is varied, and has a complex and interesting relationship with the Hindu religious tradition in general,[1] and Sītā in particular. Women activists have appealed to Hindu beliefs and values for justifying women's causes at many times in history; feminists of the "first wave" in the late nineteenth and first three-quarters of the twentieth century tended to do so frequently, and later less, those of the "second wave," from the mid-1970s onward, seem to have done the opposite

1. See Robinson (1999) for a good overview and Chaudhuri (2004) for some important landmark essays on the topic.

(Robinson 1999: 196–7). At the root lies an assessment of the Hindu tradition as either irredeemably misogynic or potentially beneficial to women and potentially instrumental for building a better world for them.[2]

I will first sketch briefly how the movement has engaged with Sītā historically. Somewhat surprisingly, this goddess has a long history of being promoted by women activists. We find glowing evaluations of her right from the start. This is not limited to the male reformers taking up the cause of uplifting women to transform society—including Gandhi (Forbes 1996: 124–5).[3]

At the turn of the twentieth century, Pandita Ramabai Ranade, while condemning the misogyny of the Indian tradition that expected unquestioning loyalty of the wife, still finds room to praise Sītā in her *Stri Dharma Nīti* (Kosambi 1995: 83–5). Chimnabai, the maharani of Baroda, judged Sītā to be an example of women's partnership with men in the public sphere in the glorious golden age of ancient India (Robinson 1999: 69). Sītā is, with some selective reinterpretation of her story, quoted as a lofty example for emancipation of the "modern Indian woman," notably by Sarojini Naidu (Alexander 2000: 98–9) and Annie Besant (Robinson 1999: 96–102). In the late 1920s, activists of the All India Women's Movement, such as one-time president Kamaladevi Chattopadhyaya, spoke reverentially of Sītā as role model (108). As many have observed, this positive evaluation is possible in the context of a nationalist equation of women as the symbol of India's past glory, where women bear the burden of saving the nation. The accompanying rhetoric emphasizes women's duties rather than rights.

It was not till the women's movements of the seventies, which tended to reject the entire Hindu tradition as irredeemable in its oppression of women (Robinson 1999: 156), that Sītā became persona non grata. Thus we find that the report *Towards Equality*, produced by the Committee on the Status of Women in India in 1975, deplores the references to submissive heroines like Sītā in school textbooks "since they tend to perpetuate the traditional values regarding the subordinate and dependent role of women. This results in the

2. Whichever position is favored, the desire to establish indigenous sources or features for Indian feminism is persistent throughout its history (Chaudhuri 2004: xxii–xxviii). The journal *Manushi* is a good illustration: it had a special issue on women *bhakta* poets (January–June 1989) and regularly features research as well as creative writing on goddesses, in particular Sītā.

3. Such nationalist admiration of Sītā by men has been criticized. An example is Uma Nehru's criticism of Hindu male nationalists who held up Sītā as a role model for women in order to preserve the tradition, while men can imitate the West (in the journal *Stri Darpan*, quoted in Talwar 1989: 228). Such a criticism would not hold good for Gandhi, though. But others have criticized Gandhi for other reasons, particularly his extending an essentializing discourse of "separate spheres" (Patel 2000).

development of social attitudes among even many educated persons, men and women, who accept women's dependent and unequal status as natural order of society" (Guha 1975: 282).

By the midseventies, though, and especially in the eighties, voices were raised advocating a rethinking of theory and pactice in the women's movement, foregrounding indigenous concepts, for example *strī śakti,* as a corrective against Marxist positions (Rajan 2000a: 275–6). Here Sītā does not figure importantly; instead attention shifted to Mahādevī, in particular in ecofeminism, and as we have seen, Western scholarship has followed suit in singling out the independent Great Goddess for research. More recently, other women activists have called for a reevaluation of Sītā's empowering characteristics rather than a morbid focus on her self-immolation (Chitnis [1988] 2004: 20). Kishwar makes a similar appeal, pointing out how ordinary women find strength in invoking Sītā's example (1997). Others contrast male-authored Sanskrit texts that portray a meek Sītā with the folk tradition, where women speak out and project onto her their sorrows and resistance (Sen 1998).

At the same time, women in right-wing Hindutva movements also cite Sītā as a role model, in a return to the earlier discourse of woman as nation, a move that sometimes takes a vindictive stance against Muslim women (Robinson 1999: 186–91). In some cases, this leads to a reappropriation of the Sītā model along lines advocated by Kishwar, as for instance when the prominent BJP (Bhāratīya Janatā Party) spokeswoman Uma Bharati said:

> In India, women are oppressed because people are uneducated and deceived into believing that religion dictates women's inferiority. I am very religious and I don't believe that is what Hinduism says. After all, look at Sita. She did not always obey. Sita went her own way and committed suicide in the end rather than following her husband's orders. So why should women demean themselves? (quoted in Basu 1995: 168)

Sītā's example is here cited as one of defiance of even the patriarchy of the husband, and in the same breath, her "suicide" is upheld as an act of resistance. Even more problematic is that Uma Bharati and Sadhvi Rithambara are well known to be brilliant interpreters of Tulsīdās's *Rām Carit Mānas,* and in particular for their use of it in anti-Muslim rhetoric to excite Hindu men to communal violence, which lead to the rape of Muslim women (Basu et al. 1993: 99–102). Thus, when Sītā functions as empowering for some women within Hindutva, this power may be used to the detriment of women outside the community. This is true not only of Bharati's interpretation of Sītā; it has been observed that the power of *śakti* has been directed externally against outsiders rather than internally to the amelioration of the Hindu community (Agnes 1995: 141).

If we look at the women's movement's engagement with Rādhā, we find a remarkable silence. Of course, nineteenth- and twentieth-century social reformers minced no words in censuring her erotic allure, both those advocating "the woman's cause" and those not (Gupta 2005: 30, 39). One of the most remarkable features of literary change is indeed the sudden collective loss of interest in the ruling lady of medieval poetry in the early reform-minded Hindi literature, as aptly expressed in the title of an influential essay: "Where Have All the Rādhās Gone?" (Schomer 1982). Rādhā seems to be beyond redemption, and forced attempts to rehabilitate her as a modern heroine, like Hariaudh's, are painfully doomed to obscurity (Ritter 2005). The same attitude is found in the women's movement. Rādhā is an inconvenient inheritance of a remote past, not even on the radar of most studies of women in India, as a quick glance at the word indices will prove.

This overview leads to the question of whether the women's movement should engage with traditional role models and if so, how. It seems imperative to do so today, with Hindutva appropriating some of the women's movement's causes, while at the same time condemning feminism as derivative of the West (Robinson 1999: 189). To counter the latter reproach, it is good to be able to speak the language of tradition in a knowledgeable way. Some advocate mining the tradition for useful symbols that can be manipulated for feminist causes. However, that seems tantamount to approaching the tradition with an imperialist attitude, not to mention the women thus manipulated. And one should also beware of an overoptimistic, romantic assessment of the tradition. Sometimes, in seeking alternative spaces of feminism outside the West, there may be a tendency to perceive these traditional sites as "pure uncontaminated entities outside the structure of modernity" (Chaudhuri 2004: xxix). Obviously, contemporary interpretations are deeply impacted by modernity, even those that claim or seem to be traditional. In a way, Indian feminists are caught between a rock and a hard place. Whereas many ally themselves with third-world feminism and the desire to complicate the subjectivity of the third-world woman beyond that of the victim, yet they may feel compelled to cast women as victim as they counter a "right wing discourse that falsely proposes women's total freedom" (Mani 1990: 37). Despite a strong awareness of this, it remains a challenge to find "political possibilities distinct and antithetical to fundamentalist assertions" (Chaudhuri 2004: xxviii).

Maybe, at the end of this exploration, I have to say that my initial question about whether Sītā is a feminist, and who is right, her defenders or detractors, is beside the point. We should not fall in the trap of anachronistically passing feminist judgment on Sītā. However, it is fair to question whether particular portrayals of the goddess are oppressive or not. The attitude I have tried to take in this book is to approach the tradition with respect—with a listening, empathetic, yet critical ear, paying attention to the multiplicity of voices, seeing each in its own context. There is a beauty of its own in doing that, a joy in getting to know this rich and wonderful tradition better in its awesome diversity, and I hope I have been able to share some of that. I must say I have been surprised—some results went against my intuitions. I was particularly surprised by how conservative the televised Sītā is underneath it all. Yet I have seen it as my task to make available this information in all its complexity, without uncritically privileging what fits my own prejudices, so as to allow others to make an informed choice and become truly informed agents of their own destinies.

How Liberating Are the Bhakti Role Models for Women?

So what to conclude? By contrasting Sītā with Rādhā and siting her at different moments in time, some patterns have emerged. I shall first look at the results from the medieval sources before assessing their contemporary relevance. As compared to the Brahminical Sanskrit texts, does the vernacular bhakti context afford a more liberating role model for women? At first glance, one might be inclined to say yes. The medieval sources have a devotional agenda, which makes them automatically foreground love and seemingly downplay the rules of dharma. In privileging emotion, they offer much play for women's subjectivity. First of all, there seems to be room for woman's choice in matrimony. Whereas in the Sanskrit *Ramāyaṇa* Sītā was not even present when Rāma won her hand, Tulsīdās added the episode of Sītā falling in love, opening up the possibility of a love marriage (chapter 1). This romantic element also comes to the fore in Tulsī's description of Rāma stringing the bow, where Sītā prays ardently that this handsome young man may win the competition. In the devotional version of the Rukmiṇī story by Nanddās, Rukmiṇī's decision to invite Krishna to elope with her is ascribed to inspiration from the Gopīs' model. Rukmiṇī, too, disregards patriarchy, or at least the arranged marriage she does not like. Thus, elopement seems to be a valid alternative to the arranged marriage if the groom is not one the bride can live with (chapter 2). When I explored the marriage ceremonies themselves (chapter 3), I found some more positive elements. The medieval descriptions of Rādhā's folk wedding and Sītā's society wedding paid much attention to harmony between the bride's and groom's parties, certainly a welcome role model for real-life marriages. Hierarchy was subjugated to loving informality, and this went hand in hand with a foregrounding of women's folk rites. Further, the move out of purdah seems to make a strong case for women's liberation (chapter 4). Sītā and Rādhā adroitly use arguments of dharma to get what they want. Tulsīdās's Sītā makes her decision to leave the palace and live in exile against not only her husband's but also her mother-in-law's wishes. While she is constrained by rules of etiquette, still her voice comes through, thanks to the poet's artistry. The decision not only to come out of purdah but also to flaunt patriarchy is yet stronger in the Rāsa-līlā, where the whole point is that the Gopīs value love above morality. The first Braj reworking by Harirām Vyās, which I explored in detail, certainly is unequivocal in that regard. Krishna declares himself outdone by these women, as their strong love disregards dharma. Looking at the threat of the other woman (chapter 5), I showed that the Gopīs are allowed to voice their jealousy at length, Kubjā gets to respond, and Krishna is caught in the middle. Sītā, on the other hand, does not get much of a voice; in fact, Tulsīdās treats the whole Śūrpaṇakhā episode stingily, as "seduction" does not fit well in his agenda of love. When it comes to the threat of the other man (chapter 6), Tulsīdās completely subverts the classical scenario by making Rāvaṇa a secret devotee of Sītā and Rāma who just happens to play the role of the villain. Moreover, Sītā is not really abducted; her body double, the *chāyā* Sītā, is. Yet Sītā is a powerful role model for women who have to cope with sexual harassment; she is not fooled by the demon's disguise and by no means cowers but speaks strong words of rejection. Rādhā, too, is portrayed as braving Krishna's eve-teasing, and in general, the *panaghaṭa* cycle in *Sūr Sāgar* pays much attention to female subjectivity. The Gopīs giving in to Krishna's sexual propositions can be seen as a celebration of love, it certainly seems to be a loving, sympathetic description of women's emotions, their hankering for true love and their plight of being contained within the four walls of domesticity.

However, my analysis has shown that things are more complex. Although there is a hint of a love marriage, Tulsīdās makes sure Sītā and Rāma's meeting in the Phūlvārī receives divine sanction and remains free from eroticism. Nanddās, possibly inspired by Tulsīdās, also adds an element of divine legitimization to the Vastraharaṇa episode, as well as a more serene tone (chapter 1). With this, Nanddās's Gopīs have come to resemble Tulsīdās's Sītā. Both first fall in love with their grooms but then seek sanctification of the match from divine agents—a scenario that becomes very popular in the movies. The elopement of Krishna and Rukmiṇī similarly receives divine sanction in Nanddās's version. He also glosses over the sacrifice Rukmiṇī has to make to be united with her beloved (chapter 2). She does not even get to voice her agony about her brother's humiliation by her husband-to-be, and no one apologizes to her, as Balarāma does in *Bhāgavata Purāṇa*. In his description of Rāma stringing the bow, Tulsīdās stresses propriety, and Sītā actually prays that she may be Rāma's servant (*dāsī*), while Rāma keeps his cool and acts only when commanded by his guru and being moved by "compassion" for Sītā. The wedding scene itself marries Brahminical and women's rites, taking care to assert the orthodoxy of the event (chapter 3). As for the decision to leave purdah, though they win, the arguments of Sītā and the Gopīs remain male-focused. While they are willing to break dharma, it is only to follow their men. Even so, they cannot expect much support in return, as the men are ready to turn them back home on grounds of dharma. The women have to persist and show themselves willing to completely sacrifice everything for their love before the men accept them (chapter 4). A close comparison of Tulsī's Sītā with Vālmīki's reveals that she is a stronger character in the Sanskrit text. The presence of her mother-in-law in Tulsī's version may account for part of that. Still, he portrays a much meeker heroine. As for the other woman (chapter 5), Tulsīdās has not much sympathy for Śūrpaṇakhā, with some misogynic phrases to boot. Sūrdās, too, shows a nonflattering picture of jealous women in giving voice to the mud-slinging between Kubjā and the Gopīs. Neither party confronts Krishna; instead they take their anger out on each other. Not an uplifting example for women, though maybe a fine realistic observation. Sūr also deeroticizes Kubjā and turns Krishna's prank and somewhat disreputable visit to her into an act of grace, all of which has the effect of domesticating the temptress. Finally, in describing the goddess's reaction to the other man (chapter 6), there is underlying this issue a patriarchal concern about women's chastity, whereas such is not the case for the men under temptation in the previous chapter. Moreover, the assumption is that the women are the ones to be blamed for transgressions. Tulsīdās censures Vālmīki's Sītā's reproach to Rāma and Lakshmana about their inability to save her, and instead has her blame herself for what happened. Sūrdās leaves ample scope for ambiguity about whether the women are really so upset about the eve-teasing they experience or whether they enjoy it. The theological frame of the poems is that they get what they deserve. Ultimately, they lose the argument about who is bothering whom, and are outsmarted by Krishna.

What to make of all this? The picture is mixed at best. One should not uncritically see bhakti as woman-friendly. There are many positive points that may inspire women to stand up for what they believe in. On the other hand, there is a strong confirmation of a patriarchal status quo. Basically, bhakti positively values emotions over duty and gives scope to the subjectivity of women. Still, the relationship with the men remains fundamentally hierarchical. If the woman is the devotee and the man stands for God, there remains a basic inequality. I hasten to add that the panoply of voices and perspectives we are exposed to in the bhakti poems does not make it easier to decide what we should conclude on their basis. Moreover, some poets are more conservative than others. My selection here is to some extent idiosyncratic, especially in choosing the more progressive Vyās for his recreation of the *Rās Pañcādhyāyī*. Finally, it is difficult to determine which poems are original and which are later elaborations. Some of the attitudes here presented as medieval devotional may actually be as late as the nineteenth century. In short, it is not easy to generalize about bhakti.

How Modern Are Sītā and Rādhā on the Screen?

Things are less ambiguous as to Sītā and Rādhā as role models in modern times. From the film and television versions, young women get a fairly unambiguous message. Surprisingly, our analysis shows that it is by and large more conservative than that of the earlier versions, except on one count. On a political plane, we find that women can speak up and take on male roles in times of crisis—that is, if it is in defense of their husband's family's interests and, by extension, what Sagar referred to as the "Aryan nation." Women's initiative, then, is encouraged if framed by obedience to elders and holy men and a firm commitment to patriarchal values. This is clear in the televised *Ramayan,* especially in the episodes where Sītā insists on following her husband into exile and where she resists the seductions of her abductor. It is also foregrounded in the Lakshmana Rekhā episode, where Sītā declares herself prepared to take up weapons to defend Rāma, as an Aryan woman should. The strong woman holding up her family—and by extension the nation—is in sync with what we see in the movies. Examples abound of women who take agency, yet always in order to sacrifice their personal good for the greater good of the patrilocal family, the village, or the nation. Strong women, then, are encouraged to voice protest and take action, but always strictly for the sake of patriarchal values.[4]

For the rest, the picture is conservative. For coping with love, Sītā is the recommended role model. Young women are advised against following Rādhā's free-style loving ways, which get toned down significantly in the television series. There are no concessions to modernity here. Under the glossy veneer of *masālā,* we find iron *maryādā*. Premarital feelings are to be strongly controlled.

4. This problem of what could be called a false sense of empowerment has also been noted in the field of development studies, see Bagchi 1999.

One has to carefully consider whether the beloved is one's "true" partner, both on a cosmic level—love from previous births, with divine sanction—and a societal level, as arranged by the family, with parental sanction. As for courting behavior, even the Sītā model has become more conservative. Compared to the older versions, there is a marked loss of the erotic. As one observer of Sagar's series puts it, "the erotic is constantly sublimated into the pious" (Zacharias 1994: 43).[5] In the movies, there is seemingly more indulgence in scenes of premarital courtship yet the ubiquitous rendition of the accompanying songs in Lata Mangeshkar's adolescent girl falsetto style can be interpreted as domesticating and infantilizing of the potentially threatening, free-agent woman cavorting in the public sphere (Srivastava 2006: 130, 140, 146). Here, too, Rādhā finds herself Sītā-ized.

In any case, whether there is premarital love or not, the proper match is to be arranged or at the very least confirmed by the parents. Elopement is not encouraged, and the preferable outcome evidently is the wedding, publicly celebrated with proper decorum, to the greater good of the joint family. Vows are colored by patriarchy. Dowry is auspicious and adds prestige to the celebrations, but the most important gift the parents can give the bride is instruction in total submission to the husband and his family. The joint family is ideally one that welcomes the young bride with loving understanding, that is, if the young woman is prepared to totally submit herself to its ideals.

In times of distress, a woman's loyalty should be unquestionably with her husband and his family. She should not fall back on her parental kin. If another woman were to come into the picture, the ideal course is selfless persistence in working for the husband's and his family's greater good. Indeed, this is expected also from the other woman, with whom an alliance for the common—patriarchal—goal is recommended. In fact, forbearance and a sacrificing spirit can redeem the woman who loves a married man. Thus there is a certain tolerance of adultery, but then only on the man's part and if it comes close to respectable bigamy, that is, if the other woman behaves like a wife, totally submitting herself to the husband's family. In contrast to the men, women should under all circumstances remain within the Lakshmana Rekhā, the boundaries of propriety of the family. Harassment by other males may occur, and is ultimately to be blamed on the woman's shortcomings rather than her family's inability to protect her. In any case, it is to be strongly and

5. Zacharias, interestingly, posits Sītā's assertiveness as a trait of the original Sītā, which she sees as a fertility goddess (1994: 40–1). She finds resonances of Sītā as Earth in the abduction passage in Vālmīki's *Rāmāyaṇa* (42–3).

courageously resisted. If women are to show their fierce form, it is in resisting other males. To be sure, the heroines are shown to be spunky and have some veneer of Western emancipation, but even these more Rādhā-esque characters unfailingly must conform sooner or later to the Sītā mold if they are to find their way to the happy ending. With some minor exceptions, the contemporary picture is remarkably uniform. Notwithstanding some triumphant proclaiming that "This is the era of women" (*kuṛiyoṃ kā hai zamānā* in *HAKHK*), it is still the guys who hold the ropes.

While Sītā and Rādhā initially seem to occupy opposite ends of the spectrum of moral landmarks, in the contemporary versions, they have become alike. The erosion of the Rādhā model seems to have built up the Sītā one yet further. If we make the assumption of a historical evolution (which is not unproblematic), the Gopīs have moved to the middle, abandoning their leftish position. The mainstream of modern Hinduism, if that is what the television versions represent, pushes counterculture-ish heroines to the margins. Is what we are witnessing a process by which voices of protest and alternative role models are absorbed within the ever-larger-than-life Sītā image? Even Sītā seems to have slid more to the right, identifying emphatically with her in-laws and concerned about *maryādā* at every turn. Are we witnessing an ever more reactionary model being forged for women?

One observer, commenting mainly on the television *Ramayan*'s sequel showing Sītā's abandonment, sums it up provocatively:

> The Sagar Ramayana reconstitutes patriarchy, re-legitimates political power in the hands of the ruling elite, and reconsolidates hegemonic ideologies despite serious contestations to all three. Sagar may have drawn his narrative from a dozen Ramayanas but the means by which he has returned the advantage to the hegemonic Ramayanas is entirely his brainchild. . . . By using a popular medium and with a more sympathetic treatment of Sita, Sagar has managed to give the impression that his version is an alternative version; however, the central feature of the alternative versions available in popular traditions is their critique of Rama's unfair treatment of Sita. By making Sita the agent of her own abandonment, Rama's upholding of patriarchal institutions is made to disappear and his actions are now above reproach. (Chakravarti 2005)

Our investigation of the love scenes of Sītā's life confirms this, as does the comparison with Rādhā: the television series seem progressive and women-friendly in giving a lot of airtime to women's subjectivity, yet at the core, the message is a reconfirmation of the patriarchal status quo.

This scenario is not one feminists typically like to see. We should not forget, though, in our focus on women, that other role models are set up here, too, for men and for families. Sagar definitely has a message to joint families, which comes through especially in the episodes leading up to and culminating in Sītā's wedding. The wedding wave movies follow suit. Families should welcome young brides and not exploit the superiority of the groom's family at the expense of the bride's. Young men are also given a wonderful example in Rāma's loving behavior toward his wife, including his vow of monogamy. All this is of course seriously bracketed by patriarchal values and predicated on the given that the young woman complies with the family ideals. But even so, it is an enlightened patriarchy that is advocated.

In conclusion, we see a decisive victory of Sītā on television and in the movies. Sensuous Rādhā has become domesticated and Sītā-ized. *Maryādā* wins out over bhakti on both the small and big screen. Some elements of this trend can be traced already in sixteenth-century devotional sources, in particular the concern to downplay eroticism and seek legitimization for women's apparently defiant behavior, but it is certainly more pronounced in twentieth-century film and television. Love is no longer stronger than dharma. True love totally conforms to *maryādā*. We could speak of an increasing domestication of our goddesses.

Sagar's Success: A Case of Saffronization?

The picture we get from Sagar's series fits well with the Hindu Right's construction of Hindu women. While the Hindu Right offers an empowering self-image for women, yet this remains in service to the ultimate cause of the Hindu nation, which is inherently patriarchal (Jaffrelot 1996: 426–8). Is there a "saffron" agenda in Sagar's series? The *Ramayan* particularly seems suspect, given that its success coincided with a surge of interest in the controversy about the birthplace of Rāma, the so-called Rāma-Janmabhūmi campaign, often seen as the reason that the Hindu Right gained influence and political power. No tightly argued case has been made yet, though many are convinced of the connection (Farmer 1996: 101–8, 114–5).

Certainly there are some elements in Sagar's *Ramayan* that seem inspired by ideas usually associated with Hindu nationalism. First, there is an Aryan rhetoric. Of course, we can find Aryan rhetoric in Vālmīki's *Rāmāyaṇa*, particularly in the conflict with the *rākṣasa*. However, this is not stressed in Tulsīdās's version, which absorbs even the non-Aryan other into the bhakti family by the extension of divine grace to the enemy. Sagar, then, has revived

Vālmīki's Aryan chauvinism, even adding some passages with no parallels in the earlier sources.[6] This came to the fore in the wedding scenes, where Vasiṣṭha sanctioned Sītā and Rāma's wedding as the union of two important Aryan powers. In the Lakshmana Rekhā episode, Sītā is prepared to take up arms to defend her husband "as any Aryan woman would do," which evokes of Hindutva ethos, where "Sita's sex is coming to the rescue of Ram" (Sarkar 1991: 2058). We can see here an element of what has been called the "feminizaton of violence," which is strikingly in conformity with what is professed by members of woman's organizations of the Hindu Right, such as the Rāṣṭrīya Sevikā Samiti and the Sādhvī Śakti Pariṣad (Bannerjee 2005: 111–37) and reminiscent of the activism of women in the Rāma-Janmabhūmi campaigns (Basu 1998: 179).

Less explicit but maybe more pernicious is that throughout the series, there is an overwhelming stress on obedience to gurus and holy men; even kings bow to them, to the point that all agency seems to be transferred from the political rulers to holy men. This fits again well with the political agenda of Hindu nationalism.[7] Hindutva women are frequently exhorted to make it their goal to instill in their children obedience to authority (Sarkar 1995).[8] This fits Sagar's privileging of societal and political welfare above individual happiness.

Finally, the series stresses chastity in women and discourages premarital affairs and has an element of blaming the victim for rape. All these aspects have been observed to be prominent in Hindutva women's discourse (Bannerjee 2005: 146–7), although they may also be part of a broader cultural pattern.

However, is that enough grounds to posit a hidden Hindutva agenda in Sagar's series? It was Rajiv Gandhi who gave the go-ahead, and Congress certainly tried to get political mileage out of the series (Tully 1991: 146–7). The commissioning secretary of the ministry of information and broadcasting, S. S. Gill, vigorously denies any intent of seeking to promote Hinduism (Farmer 1996: 107), but there is no denying that the Congress government had an "Ayodhya strategy" of its own (Hasan 1996: 91–2).

It is unclear where Sagar's own political sympathies lay. He credited Rajiv Gandhi with the permission to broadcast on Doordarshan at a ceremony in his

6. Note though that Sagar generally inculcates respect for the Tamil culture that Rāvaṇa represents (Lutgendorf 1990: 156–7).

7. Sagar makes frequent use of the term *saṃskāra*, which is a key term for the Hindu Right (Sarkar and Butalia 1995: 189).

8. Significantly, women activists are called "woman-servant of the nation" (*rāṣtrasevikā*), not "volunteer of the nation" (*rāṣṭrīya svayaṃsevikā*) (Sarkar and Butalia 1995: 184).

honor, presided over by Swāmī Viśveṣ Tīrth, a stalwart of Hindu nationalism (Jaffrelot 1996: 390 n. 81). It has been documented that Sagar participated in Vishva Hindu Parisad (World Hindu Council)-staged events (Rajagopal 2001: 326 n. 48). He is inspired by Morari Bapu, an influential Hindu saint who is closely associated with the Sangh Parivar or umbrella of Hindutva-inspired organizations (Lutgendorf 1995: 228).[9] No one has paid much attention to this issue, and certainly it is in need of more serious research.

There is no doubt that the *Ramayan* series created a nationwide audience sensitized to *Rāmāyaṇa* matters, at a time when the BJP was using the Rāma-Janmabhūmi campaign for political propaganda (Rajagopal 2001). At the same time as Sagar was recasting Tulsīdās's *Rām Carit Mānas,* it figured prominently in the speeches of BJP rhetorician Uma Bharati, which unabashedly excited Hindus to violence against Muslims (Jaffrelot 1996: 388). Yet one has to balance this with the fact that Muslims and Christians also enjoyed the television series and wrote fan letters to Sagar (Tully 1991: 143–4 and 150–1). Indeed, it seems to have been popular even in Pakistan. Some observers have characterized the series' engagement with Hindu politics as "a dialogic interrelation" (Zacharias 1994: 37–8). In short, it is unclear what the causal link is between the series and the rise of the Right in India.

One could also see Sagar less as a sinister agent than a product of his times. All indications are that he was as surprised as anyone else by the remarkable success of his first series. Certainly, many others jumped on the mythological bandwagon without hesitation. Another similar expression of the zeitgeist is found in treatises about the proper role of Hindu women published by the Gita Press in the wake of Rāma-Janmabhūmi agitation (Basu 1998: 175–6). This seems to be a case of unexpectedly hitting a nerve. It is in the end a chicken-or-egg question whether Sagar was a trendsetter or merely responsive to trends. I have shown that the series fits a lot of the conventions of Hindi cinema, the genre in which Sagar had been working all his life. There are remarkable convergences with the portrayal of women in the movies even of the seventies and eighties and yet before. One could also see a foreshadowing of *Ramayan*'s success in that of the 1975 devotional movie *Jai Santoshi Maa.* Sagar may just have tapped a market that had been there but was relatively ignored. Still, in any case, the enormous impact of his series makes it a force to be reckoned with.

9. Morari Bapu, for instance, participated in a Sangh Parivar staged "Shabri Kumbh Mela" for the reconversion (*śuddhīkaraṇa*) of tribals from Christianity in February 2006 (see Kumar 2006).

The issue is too complex to do justice to in a few paragraphs at the end of this book. The question certainly begs for more focused attention from political scientists. In short, though, I think we can confidently say that the message of the television *Ramayan* is considerably more to the right and on the conservative side than its ancient and medieval sources and that it resonates with the Hindutva agenda. One may postulate that both appeal to the same audience, namely the disenchanted, upper-caste middle class, well-educated but with few employment opportunities, who have felt disenfranchised by the secular state, which is perceived to be selling out to minorities (Jaffrelot 1996: 428–31).

For the newer series and the movies of the nineties, one might postulate a more marked influence of a Hindu Right mentality. Some have argued a definite Hindutva influence at work in *Hum aap ke hain koun . . . !*, which has been characterized as the picture of the ideal Hindutva family that comes at the cost of certain erasures (Kazmi 1999: 150–63). A recent article about the impact of the Right on the film industry "rejects the widely held view that any depiction of Hindu practices in Hindi film is connected with the rise of Hindutva ideologies. However, while these signs are not inherent in the text it is possible that audiences and politicians may see them and manipulate these signs for such reading" (Dwyer 2006: 208). It remains difficult to put one's finger on whether indeed there is a trend toward a saffronization of the screen, and if so, if that is the result of manipulation by agents with a political agenda. Certainly more research into the financing and artistic inspiration of particular films would be necessary (and is not immediately forthcoming). In the absence of such studies, maybe it is more fruitful to concentrate on the broader picture.

Whether we like it or not, the bottom line is that Sagar's interpretations have been a runaway success, taken up in movie after movie, whereas more feminist interpretations and contestations, like *Lajja*, are controversial. That does not mean that women acquiesce and do not contest the abuses of patriarchy, but whatever the reality may be, when it comes to entertainment, there seems to be a real hunger for traditional ideals, a desire to see these scenarios with happy endings played out over and over again. It seems that both men and women like to see their heroines traditional at the core. Whether we approve or not, we have to conclude that people want it. Why is that so?

Sītā and Soaps: Publicity and Pride in Tradition

The success of the televised series and of the movies of the nineties tells us something about shifting trends in society as a whole. It can be situated in the particular conjunction of circumstance, a paradox of sorts. On the one hand, we see a resurgent pride in Indian tradition and a desire to make women the carriers of this pride, which is reminiscent of the nationalist period. On the other hand, there is a concern to ensure that this does not conflict with the appropriation of certain Western ideals and the consumption of luxury goods. This fits the context of India's newly emerging middle class and its economic successes. We could term this is a nouveau chauvinism, a *masālā-maryādā* core cum—veggie—McDonald's or, for more cachet—at the cost of loosing the alliteration—cum Starbucks. The movies show both heroes and heroines at ease in a cosmopolitan environment yet proud in their tradition. There is a marked feeling of superiority to what is perceived to be Western decadence and moral deficit. Sagar's series surely helped instill a pride in tradition. At the same time, the opulence of the lifestyle of its main characters paved the way for what in the movies comes out as a hip gloss of Western consumerism.

In the movies of the nineties, we detect a winning combination of Sītā *and* slick consumerism. This goes back to her appearance on television. Indeed, the television *Ramayan* was conceived with the dual purpose of raising national consciousness and reaping a harvest of high advertising revenues (Gupta 1998: 51). It is easy to forget, when watching the epics on video or DVD, that they were first broadcast and made their major impact on the small screen, shoulder to shoulder with advertisements for consumer goods. Often the success of the series is measured by the increasing price of the advertisement slots bracketing it. Thus we see a series privileging tradition and the communal good (here imagined as the Aryan nation and its local representative, the patriarchal family) cheek-by-jowl with advertisements playing on individual desires and satisfaction of the individual good. As they share the same space, it is no wonder that the two need to accommodate one another and come to converge. As ads take on elements of chauvinism, the epics need to come to terms with the newly uncorked, centrifugal forces of individualism. With the proliferation of television channels at the same time as the opening of India for foreign consumer goods, this convergence has become even more pertinent. An analysis of television ads of the nineties shows a distinct proclivity for a message that promotes believing in oneself, and being a confident, happy, modern India that takes its place on the world stage (Dasgupta 2006; Gupta 1998: 101–2).[10] This may be seen as a result of Hindutva discourse.[11] In the

10. This type of juxtaposition is not limited to the moving image. An analysis of recent posters advertising Gujarat, land of Krishna, as a site of investment to NRIs illustrates what could be termed "Rāsa-līlā cum Paisā-līlā" (Mukherji 2005).

11. Fareed Kazmi quotes an ad for salt (Annapurna Namak) that picks up *HAKHK* as well as Hindutva rhetorics: *Vāh bhābhī! Garv se kahtā hūm maiṃne āp kā namak khāyā hai!* (Kazmi 1999: 162).

advertisements, women are interpellated as the "new Indian woman," carefully constructed as modern but not Westernized, as Rajeswari Rajan has so eloquently shown (1999: 130–3). No wonder we will see a Sītā and Rādhā with an—at times—emancipated air: self-confident but firmly rooted in *maryādā*. No wonder film heroines resemble them.

The very medium on which *Ramayan* was broadcast puts it also in the context of soap series, which partook in current debates about such modern issues as the advantages and disadvantages of traditional arranged marriages and joint-family living. Examples of such series, explicitly intended to be entertainment cum education, yet funded by commercial companies, were the family-oriented *Hum log* and its successor, the more nationalist *Buniyad,* which were both, incidentally, about a family named Ram (see Gokulsingh 2004: 29–47, 55–60; Mankekar 1999: 110–113).[12] These serials were intended to promote respectful treatment of women and show a wide range of social roles for them.

The situation is parallel for *Shri Krishna*. Although by the late 1990s, the tone of the serials aired on Doordarshan had changed dramatically, probably under the influence of the competition of channels such as ZeeTV (Gokulsingh 2004: 59–60). The new soaps more boldly foregrounded problems like rape (the serial *Shanti* aired in 1994) and extramarital affairs (*Swabhiman* in 1995)—both in shows sponsored by leading companies (see 55–6). The new entertainment channel Metro had meanwhile also been airing soap operas, most notably *Dard,* the heroine of which, named Radha, is a woman engaged in an extramarital affair. She ends up being widowed, but instead of marrying her lover, she chooses to devote her life to raising her child—a decision much applauded by those critical of the earlier part of the series (57). Female desire and adultery seem to be big issues these series wrestle with.

Whereas the traditional subject of the mythological series does not leave much room to explicitly discuss these issues, they still loom large in the background. They constitute, so to speak, the unspoken "problematization" (*pūrvapakṣa* or *śaṅkā*) to which the actual portrayal in the series can be read as an answer or "dousing of doubt" (*śaṅkā-samādhāna*). The ubiquity of the happy-within-*maryādā* ending is remarkable for both the soaps and the tele-

12. Interestingly, these series sometimes featured an explicit social comment at the end of each episode; for *Hum Log,* this was delivered by the well-respected actor Ashok Kumar (Gokulsingh 2004: 31). In that light, it is not surprising that we find Sagar also appearing after certain episodes and delivering his own comment on the narration. Of course, he is also following more classical examples, notably that of Vālmīki, who appears as an agent in his *Rāmāyaṇa*.

vised epics, but not until after the modern alternative has been fully explored for the voyeuristic pleasure of the viewer.

If the medium of television is defined by ideologies of liberalism, secularism, and individualism, the broadcasting of epics on this medium is balled up with an "ideological contradiction at play in the creation of the modern" (Gupta 1998: 94). If modernity is typically characterized by individualism, it comes into conflict with a traditional culture where typically the individual is conditioned to conform to the social will. The issue of coping with love, of the arranged versus the love marriage, is symptomatic of this conflict, and hence it is not surprising that it assumes such an important place in the scenarios of many movies and television series (94–6). Love becomes the battlefield for competing values, a site for contestation, where we see audience and film directors rework traditional ideals to accommodate new values, and vice versa. It has been perceptively pointed out that in Hindi movies, "modernity is disavowed even as it is endorsed, tradition is avowed even as it is rejected" (Mishra 2002: 4). There is no one-size-fits-all but multiple solutions. Some are more successful, others less. Some are more agreeable to feminists, others less. It is by no means sure that the individual values will win out; rather, we see different degrees of appropriation and adjustment. We could well apply here what has been said with regard to the televised *Mahabharat:* that there are "multiple interpretive frames" at work and that the series "can be appropriated for both hegemonic and subversive purposes" (Majumder 1996: 213).

Sītā as Barometer for Women's Suffering

Is this a bleak picture for feminists? We might be outraged that women are lured into the Sītā mold with the promise of a surfeit of consumer goods at the happy ending as their just "desserts," after a long-suffering, stale (*bāsī*) main course. Is this opium for the masses to keep them in line, working for hunger wages toward an India that will remain "shining" only for the privileged few? Rajeswari Sunder Rajan has problematized the interpellation of women as "the new woman" by television and advertisements which she deems a surreptitious form of undermining feminist discourse and its revolutionary project (1999: 13–3).[13] Women are offered seemingly slick solutions to feminist

13. Rajan also warns against the hijacking of feminist agendas by other interest groups, in particular the Hindu Right (1999: 136–7).

problems, all to be purchased for a price of course. Conflict and discomfort are minimized; products are substituted for processes of change. We certainly can apply this sentiment to the feel-good movies of the nineties. They may not be such innocent entertainment after all.

Some observers have complained that the Sītā ideal is conducive to the glamorization of suffering, divine justification for keeping women in place. One can turn this argument on its head and see it as a way to understand her appeal, as has been insightfully argued in a recent study:

> One can understand why Sita is the favourite mythical woman in India, the ideal woman. Sita has lent dignity, even glamour, to suffering. When there is no escape from suffering, one prefers to accept it with grace. Sita helps one do just that. She is a victim who suffers in grandeur, without being vengeful. (Sen 1998)

In this view, Sītā functions as a kind of cultural capital, a source of strength women can turn to when needed. In a better world, then, there will be no more need for such suffering. Could Sītā, then, be a kind of barometer for women's oppression: as long as she is needed, women are still suffering injustices?

Madhu Kishwar goes further and argues that Sītā's perfection in suffering puts Rāma to shame. She says her story is "a reminder that men need to be seriously reformed in order to become worthy of Sītā" (2003b: 24). She might be seeing a vision of an ideal future society, much like Sagar's and the world of *Hum aap ke hain koun . . . !*, where ideal *bahūs* are treated with respect in ideal joint families. In reality, the women are coming close to conforming to the utopian ideal, but the men need more work. One wonders, though, whether men share that vision. There may be a rhetoric of admiration, praising women for their superiority in suffering, but are men serious about emulating them, or even treating them with more respect in real life? Do these retellings of the Sītā story really function as an interpellation to men to do better? Basically it suits men well that women are held to Sītā-style ideals. Anthropological work has shown that male cinema-goers emphatically prefer the status quo. Notwithstanding being bombarded with the modernist messages of film, they do not come away with progressive ideas (Derné 2000). If the films men watch carry "feminist" messages, the men are not reluctant to express their disagreement (Derné 1995b: 208–12). This should caution us about taking the films as indicators of normative behavior. People may like what they see, but they are not necessarily swayed; they make up their own minds.

Indeed, it seems that if we take feminism and democracy seriously, we should also value women and people's agency, their ability to make their choices for themselves. Role models are not necessarily the root of all evil.

People can buy into them or not and recreate them for their needs.[14] It has been argued that

> Sita and Sāvitrī have reached us as *pativratas* because their stories have been selectively told.... A history of Sita's life will show us a woman who walked out of a safe home to face the dangers of the world, a woman who had to overcome sexual harassment... all conditions familiar to many women today.... In short, Sita is a wonderful ideal not because of who she is married to but because of who she is.
>
> The problem that women today have had with Sita as traditional role model has always been that she is cast as a goddess, a heroine-victim, or a *pativrata*. In these symbolic forms she has served male rather than female history. It is not she but her representation in Indian literary, oral, and now audio-visual and political tradition that has been counterproductive to the women's movement and the achievements of contemporary Indian women. If Sita were recast as woman, perhaps the ideal Indian woman and the modern one would not need to be at such odds. (Barua 1996: 232–3)

By siting Sītā, I have sought in this book to provide the necessary information to make such feminist-friendly recasting of Sītā possible, to help see possibilities where one might have thought there were none, to expose the silences and moments that have been suppressed. If we reveal the male voices that have spoken—and are speaking—through Sītā's mouth, we may help women regain their own, much as Basanti in *Sholay* realized it was not Śiva dictating that she marry Veeru but he himself. What woman do with that knowledge is up to them. Like Basanti, they may still want to submit to the hero and sacrifice for love. Women can choose and compose their own meaningful portfolios of memory, their own selections of Sītā's words and deeds that are meaningful to their circumstances. One can hardly begrudge them that they seek out a happy ending.

A Test Case: The Dowry Issue (*Kasauti Dahej kī*)

Should we condemn the screen versions because they may be politically tainted or commercially exploitative? Or should we hail them as truly democratic, as

14. A wonderful contemporary recreation of myth to empower women by a male author is Bhīṣam Sahnī's play *Mādhavī*. This "decentering" patriarchal myth is analyzed at length by Singh and Jaidev 1999.

they are apparently so popular? The first interpretation would be in line with the Frankfurt School's critiques of mass culture, seeing the masses, in this case women in particular, as the victims of exploitation by economic and political forces.[15] However, recent scholarship has stressed that meaning-making is a two-way street. Since there is a dialogic relationship between the media and its consumers, audience reaction is foregrounded as crucial. Yet maybe that pernicious popularity should encourage us to question the message all the more vigorously, because we may be partaking in some mass delusion. When we want to, we are easily fooled into believing that things have changed, even as the status quo endures.

Crucial is the question whether change for the better is really forthcoming. This is not the place to evaluate progress made in India's legal system (for which see Robinson 1999: 180–3). In fact, legal progress is only half the story. We can take for a case study the issue of dowry. The controversial Dowry Prohibition Act stipulates stiff punishments for demanding, giving, or taking dowry, but is easily circumvented by "voluntary gifts" to the marrying couple. This is totally within the Sagar spirit, where dowry is present but not named: it is present under cover. If illegal, it remains an unspoken requirement, which is open to misunderstanding and abuse. It is hard to evaluate whether the Act has made things worse or better for the bride and her party. The fact seems to be that the praxis of bride-gift has been spreading regionally, as well as socially: over more regions and to more and more castes. The monetary value of dowries has been rising disproportially to people's incomes. It is hard to assess whether legal progress has paid dividends in societal praxis.

Still, by good Bollywood convention, I would like to end on a hopeful note that there are some possible, if faint, indications that the tide may be turning. In the media at least, brides are being shown to "put their foot down" in instances of abuse. An inspiring example that received much media attention in 2003 was an educated, middle-class, upper-caste bride named Nisha Sharma from Noida (New Delhi). She was celebrated as Miss Anti Dowry because she called the police on her cell phone when her future in-laws, at this last minute, in an arrogant way, demanded a cash amount on top of a very lavish dowry (Brooke 2003b). This case received a lot of media attention; she reportedly received many alternative marriage proposals, and indeed married another groom in a simple ceremony a few months later (Brooke 2003a). We

15. Fareed Kazmi has a more nuanced view, seeking to lay bare the series of interpellations that neutralize the potential antagonism between the power bloc and the people it seeks to control, which, for the movies he discusses, he sees as the lower middle class (1999: 67–72).

might well say that this Maithili has found a happy ending, at least for the time being.[16]

It is tempting to attribute this event to the influence of *Lajja*-like images in popular culture. Maybe that is too facile a conclusion. On the contrary, Nisha's mother has insisted that her daughter had not been exposed to "subversive" media elements. About her children's television watching, she is reported to have said: "We let them only watch *Discovery, National Geographic* and *Kasauti zindagi ki*" (quoted in Majid 2003). The reference to the soap series foregrounding matrimonial (mis)alliances between two families is revealing. One wonders also about the feel-good fare of the nineties. Was Nisha strengthened in her resolve by the role models of the spunky heroines of the wedding wave movies? Or was it the obvious contrast between these *filmī* ideals of joint families and the less-than-exemplary behavior of her in-laws-to-be that led her to take action?

Whether subversive or not, the media have been quick to catch on to the exemplary nature of her story, as there has been talk about her story being used for a comic strip as well as for movie scripts (Kak 2003). Maybe Sharma has already had an impact; it is tempting to relate her story to another more recent case that involved a less-educated, lower-class bride from Patiala, appropriately named Sita, who sent back the *barāt* of her groom after some of its members misbehaved with her sister.[17] Whatever the case may be, the potential is there for this real-life Maithili to inspire others, especially because the happy endings of these stories are more encouraging than the dramatic *filmī* ones. Sometimes, life writes its own scenarios, which no script writer might dare to broach for fear of being branded too unrealistic or too predictable.

Maybe it does not matter all that much why Nisha and Sita took a stand against their grooms' parties' arrogance. Zooming out from the specifics, in general it is difficult to say to what extent a changing zeitgeist (perceived or real) may be the long-term effect of an aggregrate of efforts or may be triggered by more immediate events. It is difficult to evaluate whether the legal progress has fostered societal improvement and what the influence may have been of past feminist, religious, political, and other initiatives that have been undertaken to raise awareness against the dowry practice in particular and to reform marriage ceremonies in general. There certainly have been many efforts to

16. Critics have pointed out that the issue here was not the dowry demand as such, as a huge dowry had already been provided. Some have also pointed out that the girl ended up marrying an old boyfriend and that there may have been more to the story than reported in the Western media.

17. As reported in an editorial of the *Tribune*, January 17, 2005, www.tribuneindia.com/2005/20050117/edit.htm#1.

reform the marriage rites, such as Gandhi's, those of the Brahmo Samaj in Bengal, and the Self-Respect ceremonies in Tamil Nadu, to name only a few. Sagar's series is itself part of a long series of events great and small that may foster a certain impact—or not. Untangling a web of motivations is always a complex undertaking.

What may be more productive is to look at the data anew, reassess the problem, and learn the lessons for raising awareness about social problems. If popular movies and television seem to have appeal, whereas years of feminist activism have failed to stir people, this surely merits a closer look. The problem is not with the appeal of the Sītā-Rāma-*vivāha* fashion, not even with the gifts as such, but more with the mentality that sees the *bahū* as a cash cow (*kāmadhenu*) for her in-laws. Madhu Kishwar (2005) has recently proposed a new, sensitive approach to counter the abuses of the dowry system. She also recommends rewriting the script of the actual marriage ceremony, involving a public vow whereby both bride and groom pledge their promises to love and cherish one another in front of the community, making explicit the terms of the marriage. Wife-battering so as to get more dowry becomes more difficult if one has promised to cherish and take care of one's bride. One may quibble about what should be written into the vows. One may question how far one can go in thus forcing grooms, and especially their families, to negate traditional privilege. Still, the idea seems solid. In the light of the predominance of the concept of *izzat,* this makes sense. It could be a wonderful homeopathic way to cure the evil, by appealing to the same principle that causes the problems. If the root of the problem is that the groom's family seeks to aggrandize itself in the eyes of the community, why not turn societal awareness into something that works for the better? Why not appeal to people's strong sense of "shame" (*lajjā*) and indeed rewrite the scripts to be more in conformity with the proclaimed values?

If we feel a new version of Sītā's wedding and her ways of coping with love is needed to start the trend, Bollywood may be willing to put its weight behind it in a positive way. Of course, we will always have to reckon with its limits. After all, as it is put at the end of *7 1/2 Phere:* "It's all about entertainment."

Windows and Widows

This book has made some contributions in siting Sītā, but we are still a long way from mapping her. I have been able to concentrate only on certain aspects of Sītā's story as compared with Rādhā. It is appropriate to end by opening up further windows for research. First, there is more that can be done using the methodology of siting Sītā and Rādhā, by focusing on other moments in their stories.[18]

One element I have not touched on is the issue of the goddess's youth. The stories of Krishna and Rāma as children are widely popular, and the places associated with their childhoods are flourishing pilgrimage centers. Similarly, Rādhā's birthplace in Barsānā is one (Entwistle 1987), and so is Sītā's Janakpur, which was "discovered" only in the eighteenth century (Burghart 1983). At these places, the birth of the goddess is celebrated in a festival by singing birth celebration songs (*janmabadhāī*). This is in striking contrast with the lack of such celebration at the birth of a nondivine female. This issue would be worth further study. One could take as a point of departure Raj Kapoor's 1978 film *Satyam shivam sundaram,* in which the heroine is born on Janmāṣṭamī, the festival of Krishna's birthday. Her father, the village pundit, is singing in the Krishna temple in front of the Rādhā-Krishna images when the news that his child has been born is signaled to him by a little messenger. While everyone in the temple sways and chants in ecstasy, he hastens home, only to find that the baby is a girl. Particularly poignant is the contrast between the singing of celebratory songs for the commemoration of the mythical event of the birth of Krishna and the lamentations in the real-life event of the birth of a baby girl.

Another important issue that could be fruitfully researched is Sītā as mother. Why are there hardly any happy family portraits of both her and Rāma and the children? In the story, indeed, as soon as Lava and Kuśa regain their father, their mother disappears forever. This aspect of Sītā's story seems problematic from a feminist perspective. Is she surrendering to patriarchy by returning the sons to their rightful family after nursing them for the first years? On the other hand, her sons are in many versions portrayed as avengers of the injustices their mother had to suffer. That is again problematic, as it strengthens the belief that it is only men who can redeem women. Sītā's eventual return to the earth may also be read as a protest against the continuing questioning of her character and a confirmation of her identity with her parental family. These issues, however, are downplayed in the televised series. The motherhoods of Hindu goddesses in general is an issue that would be fruitful to research. One *filmī* point of departure could be the diatribe of the

18. Originally, I also envisioned including in this book a chapter on "songs of separation" dealing with the issue of longing for the absent beloved. Another chapter would be the reverse: the celebration of love in union and the erotic relationship of the lovers, something that happens prudently offscreen in all of Sagar's series, but features prominently in the classical and medieval literature.

heroine of *Mother India* to Lakṣmī when she is forced to give in to the lecherous moneylender, challenging the goddess to understand a mother's plight.

Related to Sītā as mother is the image of Sītā in the kitchen, an important omission in the normative texts presented here, and recently studied by Phyllis Herman (see also Gandhi 1992).

Even for the aspects of Sītā's life I have portrayed here, there are many more points of reference; I have only been able to look at successful, high-prestige texts and movies from the North. Especially fruitful would be to look at sources that show the impact of the colonial intervention and the nationalist movement's rewritings of the epics in response; the Parsi theater of Rādheśyām Kathāvācak is an especially interesting case (see Kapur 1995). I have only marginally been able to touch on the rich theatrical adaptations or Rām- and Rās-līlā and Parsi theatre, and have not even mentioned puppet theatre (see Blackburn 1996). Moreover, more attention to how these texts are expounded in oral discourse may also reveal welcome new aspects (Wulff 1985). Many scholars are working on regional variants on the basis of both folk and regionally prestigious texts, which enable cross-region comparisons. Particularly helpful would be a study of reworkings of the epics in Tamil cinema, and indeed their entanglement with the politics of Tamil Nadu.[19]

My selection of movies has been limited to Hindi popular movies in which the stories of Rādhā and Sītā have functioned as intertexts. Even with regard to Rādhā-Sītā references in films, I have only covered the tip of the iceberg, and I have not even touched on diaspora movies, for example Canadian director Deepa Mehta's controversial *Fire* (1999), about which much more can be said (see Desai 2004: 159–91). Further, there are other trends afoot in Hindi popular cinema that could make for a good contrastive study (see, e.g., Gargi 2005). Comparisons of cinema and soaps would also be useful. Soaps are widely recognized to provide role models for women, but are vastly understudied (Sultana 2005).

Incorporating folk epics in the equation is another desideratum, as a wealth of information is already beginning to surface about folk *Rāmāyaṇas* or better *Sītāyanas* (see Nilsson 2001, Rao 1991 and 2003, and a host of articles in *Manushi*, e.g. Sen 1998), and even older texts are being unearthed (*Candrāvatī Rāmāyaṇa*, see Sen 2000). There is a tendency to oppose the empowering Sītā of women's folk songs to the Brahminical oppressive one of Sanskrit texts that is perhaps not altogether justifiable (Vanita 2005: 39). This fits an often heard

19. For Jayalalitha, see Pandian 1993. For some remarks about Rādhā-Krishna imagery in Kannada movies, see Nagaraj 2006: 95.

general assessment of Hindu culture as consisting of a Brahminic paradigm that is less and an alternative one that is more woman-friendly (Robinson 1985). Such an assumption deserves to be carefully argued and backed up after surveying a wide variety of folk materials, with an honest assessment of what fits the argument and what does not.

Finally, to fill out the picture, it would be necessary to bring in something that has been woefully absent in this book: visual representations, classical sculptures, miniatures, modern paintings (Sirhandi 1999), as well as folk art (Heinz 2006), God-posters (Pinney 2004), and comic strips (McLain 2001).

Beyond the siting methodology, I hope this study will inspire anthropologists to take up the challenge of seeing how Sītā and Rādhā's stories may be used in narrating life narratives (Heinz 2000; Jacobson 1978). The variants presented in this book may also be useful in starting discussions on issues such as choice of marriage partner, dowry, patrilocality, bigamy, and sexual harassment and eve-teasing. Movies and myth may provide useful conversation starters to elicit people's opinions on these issues, as well as their reflections on how the role models actually influence or are irrelevant to their real-life decisions. Are the role models merely "out there"? Is this different for men or women, for older or younger women, for married and unmarried ones? Is there a class, caste, or other social divide with regard to the issue of how relevant the "national" role model is? What are alternative role models (Draupadī and Pārvatī seem obvious choices), maybe regional or caste specific ones?

Maybe there is also a useful pedagogical function to the comparisons featured in this book, which might be fruitful to generate class discussions. There have been arguments that textbooks for school children should not contain references to Sītā, as she is perceived to be a negative role model (Guha 1975). Such radical omission and rejection of an important cultural icon seems unwarranted. Rather, one might teach students about the multiplicity of voices portraying Sītā and encourage them to express their opinions about "whose Sītā" is most inspiring for their day-to-day life. May be some would like to see her "rewritten" on the screen, or rewrite her themselves in their own lives.

For students of religion, there is a lot more work to be done in charting women's worship of Sītā images both in temples and in private houses, and how this relates to her role model function. It would be useful to compare with her worship by males, including ascetics. The different forms of worship of the branches of the Rāmānandīs and the role Sītā plays in each would certainly help to contribute to the understanding of Sītā as a role model more generally. The influence of the Śrī-Sampradāya on South Indian views of the goddess also needs more attention (Narayana 2000). It is remarkable how little research has been done in this area.

Further, there is the striking fact that ashrams for widows in places of pilgrimage tend to be focused on Rādhā-Krishna worship. The widows are—at least ostensibly—encouraged to focus on detachment (*vairāgya*) and discouraged from thinking of themselves as erotic; they are not supposed to wear jewelry and are encouraged to don plain white saris and shave their heads. Looking at these old, destitute women, one would indeed be hard-pressed to think of Rādhā as a role model.[20] This situation might at first glance seem reminiscent of the burlesque of the demoness Śūrpanakhā in love with Rāma and the hunchback Kubjā inviting Krishna to make love to her. How the women themselves make sense of this would be an interesting anthropological study. One could also bring into the picture Deepa Mehta's controversial, award-winning 2005 film *Water*. This movie juxtaposes the widows' asceticism with erotic Krishna imagery, notably in the songs, as well as in many explicit references by the protagonists. The Krishna imagery is mainly in reference to the young and attractive widow, Kalyani (Seema Biswas), the only one of the widows who is sexually active. First she is lured into prostitution. Later, she falls in love with a bespectacled Gandhian reformer named, meaningfully, Narayana (John Abraham), who—unlikely as it may seem—embodies Krishna for her. While her identification as Rādhā is nearly exclusively in the romance with Narayana, there is a hint of a suggestion that the erotic Rādhā-Krishna lyrics may create a longing for love in the widows, which is then manipulated to lure them into prostitution. On the way to her—presumably—first client "across the river," Kalyani is in a boat rowed by her procuress, the *hijra* Gulabi, who is singing a song ("Maiṃ kā karūṃ rām," "What can I help it, Rāma!"). A dreamy Kalyani interrupts her to ask whether Krishna sometimes comes down on earth as a man.[21] Gulabi says he does so in the yearly *nautanki* performance to celebrate Krishna's birthday, where she herself plays a Gopī. The *hijra* here deftly plays to Kalyani's longings in order to ensure her cooperation in the "deal."[22] This blatant abuse of divine role models for women is a *filmī* interpretation, and one by a diaspora filmmaker who has already been much maligned for her "abuse" of Hindu tradition. Still, the issue she raises demands a careful exploration and study of contextualization; while a full dis-

20. I am grateful to Professor Monika Horstmann for suggesting this issue to me.

21. *kyā krishna jī ādmī ke rūp meṃ dhartī par āte haiṃ?*

22. This psychological game is confirmed later in the movie, when the *hijra* plays along with the head of the ashram to lure the little girl Chuhiya, who thinks she's being taken home, into the same situation.

cussion is well beyond the scope of this work, we may venture that the problem lies not with the role model herself but with the manipulation of it by shrewd agents with, in this case, certainly less-than-noble intent.

One conclusion is clear. It will no longer do to blame a timeless mythological Sītā, or Rāma, or Vālmīki, or *Rāmāyaṇa* for women's woes. While the Sanskrit text certainly is steeped in patriarchal principles, it leaves still some maneuvering room for Sītā as a strong character. There are nuances, but on the whole, the conclusion is inescapable that in the television version, Sītā is meeker and buys into and promotes patriarchal structures more actively. At the same time, the alternative models of the Gopīs and Rādhā, available at least at some points in the past, have been substantially submerged. There's no longer a real Rādhā alternative; Rādhā has undergone a total transformation of domestication. We could say that Sītā has carried out thoroughly the pioneering project of domestication of the wilderness: she has colonized Vrindāban, even Bollywood. But then, there are many Sītās on the walls of Indian houses. Let us wait for the sequel. After all, there has been one "amazing," rewrite: the *Adbhūta-Rāmāyaṇa* where Sītā herself slays a demon worse than Rāvaṇa (Vanita 2005). There may be more sequels. No doubt new trends are on the horizon. There always is an answer to each *Rāmāyaṇa:* women might well have a surprising, new Uttara-sītāyana or sequel to Sītā's story in the making.

References

EDITIONS WITH TRANSLATIONS

Bāhrī, Hardev, and Rajendra Kumār, eds. 1974. *Sūrasāgara Saṭīkā*. 2 vols. Allahabad: Lok Bhāratī Prakāśan.

Bāpū, Morārī. 1986. *Rām Carit Mānas-kathā*. Bombay: Prācīn Saṃskṛti Mandir.

Bechert, Heinz, ed. 1976. *The Bhagavata Purana: The Birch Bark Manuscript in the State and University Library in Göttingen (with a Concordance by Maheshwari Prasad)*. New Delhi: International Academy of Indian Culture.

Bhagvāndīn and Brajratnadās, et al., eds. 1973. *Tulsī Granthāvalī*. vol. 1. Benares Nāgrī Pracārinī Saabhā.

Brajratnadās, ed. [1949] 1957. *Nanddās Granthāvalī*. Nāgarī Pracāriṇī Granthmālā 39. 2d ed. Benares: Nāgarī Pracāriṇī Sabhā.

Chopra, B.R. and Ravi Chopra. *Mahabharat*. DVD Set. Harrison, N.J.: Indo-American Video Corporation.

Goswami, Chinmanlal, ed. 1969. *Śrīmad Vālmīki-Rāmāyaṇa, with Sanskrit Text and English Translation*. 3 vols. Gorakhpur: Gita Press.

Goswami, Chimman Lal, and M. A. Śāstrī, eds. [1971] 1982. *Śrīmad Bhāgavata Mahāpurāṇa, with Sanskrit Text and English Translation*. 2 vols. 2d ed. Gorakhpur: Gita Press.

Kanhaiyālāl, Munśi, ed. 1979. *Caurāsī Vārtā: Śrīmadācāryyāṇa Paramānukampāsthada Bhāgavadīya Caturāśitisaṃkhyākabaiṣṇavānāṃ vārtā*. Bombay: Mumbāī Ula Ulūm.

Kathāvācak, Rādheśyām. 1971. *Rādheśyām Rāmāyaṇa*. 7th ed. Śrī Barelī: Rādheśyām Pustakālay.

Kṛṣṇadās, Gaṅgāviṣṇu, ed. [1958] 1986a. *Caurāsī Vaiṣṇavan kī Vārtā*. Reprint. Bombay: Lakṣmī Veṅkaṭeśvar Steam Press.
———, ed. [1958] 1986b. 252 *Vaiṣṇavan kī Vārtā*. Reprint. Bombay: Lakṣmī Veṅkaṭeśvar Steam Press.
Mahārāj, Śrī Govindlāljī, and Ānandīlāl Śāstrī, eds. 1968. *Śrī Nāthjī kī Prākaṭya Vārtā (Gosvāmī Śrī Harirāy Mahānubhāv Kṛt)*. Nāthdvārā: Vidyāvibhāg.
Mizokami,Tomio, and Girish Bakhshi, eds. 1992. *Ramayana: A TV Serial by Ramanand Sagar*. Osaka: Osaka University of Foreign Studies.
Parīkh, Dvārikādās, ed. 1970 (2027 VS). *Caurāsī Vaiṣṇavan kī Vārtā*. Govarddhan Granthmālā 45. Mathurā: Śrī Govarddhan Granthmālā Kāryālay.
Pauwels, Heidi Rika Maria. 1996b. *Kṛṣṇa's Round Dance Reconsidered: Harirāma Vyās's Hindī Rās-pañcādhyāyī*. London Studies on South Asia 12. Richmond, U.K.: Curzon Press.
Poddār, Hanumānprasād, ed. [1942] 1990. *Śrīmadgosvāmī Tulsīdāsjīviracita Śrīrāmcaritmānas*. Gorakhpur: Gītāpress.
Ramanan, T, trans. 2003. *Śrīsubodhinī*. Collected Works of Shri Vallabhācārya Series 18. Delhi: Satguru Publications.
Rāmdās, ed. 1983. *Do Sau Bāvan Vaiṣṇavan kī Vārtā*. Reprint. Bombay: Lakṣmī Veṅkaṭeśvar Steam Press.
Rānade, Puruṣottoma Govinda, ed. 1935. *Brahmavaivartapurāṇam, etat pustakam Vāsudeva Śāstrī Mārathe ity etaiḥ saṃśodhitam*. Ānandāśramasaṃskṛtagranthāvalīḥ 102. 2 vols. Pune: Ānandāśrama Mudranālaya.
Ratnākar, Jagannāth Dās, et al., eds. 1972–76. *Sūr Sāgar*. 2 vols. 2d ed. Benares: Nāgarī Pracāriṇī Sabhā.
Sagar, Ramanand. 1987. *Ramayana*. Video set. Bombay: Sagar Video International.
———. 1991a. *Shri Krishna*. DVD set. Mumbai: Sagar Enterprises.
———. 1991b. *Shri Krishna*. Video Set. Mumbai: Sagar Enterprises.
Śaran, Anjaninandan, ed. 1925–56. *Mānas pīyūṣ*. 12 vols. Ayodhya: Mānas Pīyūṣ Kāryālay.
Śarmā, Śrīrām, ed. 1970. *Brahmavaivartapurāṇa, sarala Hindī bhāṣya sahita*. 2 vols. Bareilly: Sanskrit Sansthān.
Śāstrī, Jagdīś Lāl, ed. 1983. *Bhāgavata Purāṇa of Kṛṣṇa Dvaipāyana Vyāsa: With Sanskrit Commentary "Bhāvārthabodhinī" of Srīdharasvāmin*. Delhi: Motilal Banarsidass.
Tapasyānanda, Swami, ed. and trans. 1985. *Ādhyātma Rāmāyaṇa: The Spiritual Version of the Rāma Saga. Original Sanskrit with English Translation*. Madras: Sri Ramakrishna Math.
Upādhyāy, Rāmkiṅkar. 1974. *Mānas-Muktāvalī*. 4 vols. Calcutta: Biralā Academy of Art and Culture.

TRANSLATIONS

Bahadur, Krishna P. 1999. *The Poems of Sūradāsa*. New Delhi: Abhinav.
Brockington, John, and Mary Brockington, trans. 2006. *Rāma the Steadfast: An Early Form of Rāmāyaṇa*. London: Penguin Group.

Bryant, Edwin F. 2003. *Krishna: The Beautiful Legend of God: Śrīmad Bhāgavata Purāṇa Book X*. London: Penguin.

Burnouf, M. Eugène, (Hauvette-Besnault, and R.P. Alfred Roussel), trans. [1840–96] 1981. *Le Bhâgavata Purâṇa ou Histoire Poétique de Krĭchṇa*. 5 vols. Paris: Jean Maisonneuve.

Coleman, Tracy 2003. "The Abduction of Rukmiṇī." *Journal of Vaishnava Studies* 12.1 (Fall): 25–56.

Goldman, Robert. 1984. *The Rāmāyaṇa of Vālmīki: An Epic of Ancient India. Bālakāṇḍa*. vol. 1. Princeton, N.J.: Princeton University Press.

Growse, Frederic S, and R. C. Prasad. 1978. *The Rāmāyaṇa of Tulsī Dāsa*. Delhi: Motilal Banarsidass.

Hill, W. Douglas P. 1971. *The Holy Lake of the Acts of Rāma: A Translation of Tulsī Dās's Rāmacaritamānasa*. Bombay: Oxford University Press.

McGregor, R. S. 1973. *Nanddas: The Round Dance of Krishna and Uddhav's Message*. London: Luzac.

Pollock, Sheldon. 1987. *The Rāmāyaṇa of Vālmīki: An Epic of Ancient India. Ayodhyākāṇḍa*. Vol. 2. Princeton, N.J.: Princeton University Press.

———. 1991. *The Rāmāyaṇa of Vālmīki: An Epic of Ancient India. Āraṇyakāṇḍa*. Vol. 3. Princeton, N.J.: Princeton University Press.

Vaudeville, Charlotte, trans. 1977. *Le Rāmāyaṇa de Tulsī-Dās, Texte Hindi Traduit et Commenté*. Paris: Société d'Édition "Les Belles Lettres."

OTHER WORKS

Agnes, Falvia. 1995. "Redefining the Agenda of the Women's Movement within a Secular Framework." In *Women and Right-Wing Movements: Indian Experience*, ed. Tanika Sarkar and Urvashi Butalia, 136–57. London: Zed Books.

Aklujkar, Vidyut. 2001a. "Crying Dogs and Laughing Trees in Rāma's Kingdom: Self-Reflexivity in the *Ānanda-rāmāyaṇa*." In *Questioning Ramayanas: A South Asian Narrative Tradition*, ed. Paula Richman, 83–103. Berkeley: University of California Press.

———. 2001b. "Sita as Rama's Advocate: Propriety in the *Ananda-Ramayana*." *Manushi* 125 (July–August): 38–42.

———. 2007. "Family, Feminism, and Film in Remaking *Rāmāyaṇa*." In *Indian Literature and Popular Cinema: Recasting Classics*, ed. Heidi Pauwels, 42–53. London: Routledge.

Alexander, Meena. 2000. "Sarojini Naidu: Romanticism and Resistance." In *Ideals, Images and Real Lives: Women in Literature and History*, ed. Alice Thorner and Maithreyi Krishnaraj, 91–103. Hyderabad: Orient Longman.

Anagol-McGinn, Padma. 1994. "Sexual Harassment in India: A Case Study of Eve-Teasing in Historical Perspective." In *Rethinking Sexual Harassment*, ed. Clare Brant and Yun Lee Too, 220–34. London: Pluto Press.

Anderson, James A. 1998. "Qualitative Approaches to the Study of the Media: Theory and Methods of Hermeneutic Empiricism." In *Television, and Social Behavior*, ed. Joy Keiko Asami and Gordon L. Berry, 205–36. Thousand Oaks, Calif.: Sage.

Appadurai, Arjun, and Carol Breckenridge. 1992. "Museums Are Good to Think: Heritage on View in India." In *Museums and Communities,* ed. I. Karp, S. Levine, and C. M. Kreamer, 34–55. Washington, D.C.: Smithsonian Institution Press.

Archer, W. G. 1985. *Songs for the Bride: Wedding Rites of Rural India.* New York: Columbia University Press.

Asami, Joy Keiko, and Gordon L. Berry, eds. 1998. *Research Paradigms, Television, and Social Behavior.* Thousand Oaks, Calif.: Sage.

Babb, Lawrence, A. 1981. "Glancing: Visual Interaction in Hinduism." *Journal of Anthropological Research* 37.4: 47–64.

Bacchetta, Paola. 2004. *Gender in the Hindu Nation: RSS Women as Ideologues.* New Delhi: Women Unlimited.

Bagchi, Amitabha. 1996. "Women in Indian Cinema." www.cs.jhu.edu/~bagchi/women.html.

Bagchi, Jasodhara. 1999. "Women's Empowerment: Paradigms and Paradoxes." In *From Myths to Markets: Essays on Gender,* ed. Kumkum Sangari and Uma Chakravarti, 368–79. New Delhi: Manohar.

Bailey, Greg, and Mary Brockington. 2000. *Epic Threads: John Brockington on the Sanskrit Epics.* New Delhi: Oxford University Press.

Bakhshi, Rajni. 1998. "Raj Kapoor: From *Jis desh mein Ganga behti hai* to *Ram teri Ganga maili.*" In *The Secret Politics of Our Desires: Innocence, Culpability and Indian Popular Cinema,* ed. Ashish Nandy, 92–133. Delhi: Oxford University Press.

Banaji, Shakuntala. 2005. "Young British-Asian Viewers Discuss Sexual Relations on and off the Hindi Film Screen." *South Asian Popular Culture* 3.2 (October): 177–92.

Banerjee, Sikata. 2005. *Make Me a Man! Masculinity, Hinduism and Nationalism in India.* Albany: State University of New York Press.

Banerjee, Sumanta. 1993. *Appropriation of a Folk-Heroine: Radha in Medieval Bengali Vaishnavite Culture.* Socio-Religious Movements and Cultural Networks in Indian Civilization, occasional paper 3. Simla: Indian Institute of Advanced Study.

Barua, Mahasveta. 1996. "Television, Politics, and the Epic Heroine: Case Study, Sita." In *Between the Lines: South Asians and Postcoloniality,* ed. Deepika Bahri and Mary Vasudeva, 216–34. Philadelphia: Temple University Press.

Basu, Amrita. 1995. "Feminism Inverted: The Gendered Imagery and Real Women of Hindu Nationalism." In *Women and the Hindu Right: A Collection of Essays,* ed. Tanika Sarkar and Urvashi Butalia, 136–80. New Delhi: Kali for Women.

———. 1998. "Hindu Women's Activism in India and the Questions It Raises." In *Appropriating Gender: Women's Activism and Politicized Religion in South Asia,* ed. Patricia Jeffery and Amrita Basu, 167–84. New York: Routledge.

Basu, Tapan, Pradip Datta, Sumit Sarkar, Tanika Sarkar, Sambuddha Sen. 1993. *Khaki Shorts, Saffron Flags.* Hyderabad: Orient Longman.

Beck, Guy. 2005. "Krishna as Loving Husband of God: The Alternative Krishnology of the Rādhāvallabha Sampradāya." In *Alternative Krishnas: Regional and Vernacular Variations on a Hindu Deity,* ed. Guy Beck, 65–90. New York: State University of New York Press.

Belafante, Ginia. 2005. "Courtship Ideas of South Asians Get a U.S. Touch." *New York Times*, August 23, 2005.

Bharucha, Rustom. 1995. "Utopia in Bollywood: *Hum Aapke hain koun . . . !*" *Economic and Political Weekly* 30 (April 15): 801–4.

Bhasin, Kamla, and Ritu Menon 1988. "Sati: A Symposium on Widow Immolation and Its Social Context: The Problem." *Seminar* 342 (February): 12–3.

Bhasin, Kamla, Ritu Menon, and Nighat Said Khan, eds. 1994. *Against All Odds: Essays on Women, Religion and Development from India and Pakistan*. New Delhi: Kali for Women.

Blackburn, Stuart. 1996. *Inside the Drama House: Rāma Stories and Shadow Puppets in South India*. Berkeley: University of California Press.

Booth, Gregory. 1995. "Traditional Content and Narrative Structure in the Hindi Commercial Cinema." *Asian Folklore Studies* 54.2 (October): 169–90.

Bose, Mandakranta, ed. 2003. *The Rāmāyaṇa Culture: Text, Performance, and Iconography*. New Delhi: D. K. Print World. (Rev. ed. of *A Varied Optic: Contemporary Studies in the Rāmāyaṇa*. Vancouver: Institute of Asian Research, University of British Columbia.)

———. 2004. *The Ramayaṇa Revisited*. New York: Oxford University Press.

Breckenridge, Carol A., ed. 1995. *Consuming Modernity: Public Culture in a South Asian World*. Minneapolis: University of Minnesota Press.

Brockington, John L. 1984. *Righteous Rāma: The Evolution of an Epic*. Delhi: Oxford University Press.

———. 1998. *The Sanskrit Epics*. Leiden: Brill.

———. 2000. "Sanskrit Epic Tradition IV: Svayaṃvaras." Paper presented at the Eleventh World Sanskrit Conference, Torino, Italy, April 3–8.

Brooke, James. 2003b. "Dowry Too High: Lose Bride and Go to Jail." *New York Times*, May 17, 2003.

———. 2003a. "Anti-dowry Woman Weds." *New York Times*, November 20, 2003.

Brosius, Christiane. 2005. *Empowering Visions: The Politics of Representation in Hindu Nationalism*. London: Anthem.

Brown, Cheever Mackenzie. 1974. *God as Mother: A Feminine Theology in India: An Historical and Theological Study of the Brahmavaivarta Purāṇa*. Hartford, Vt.: C. Stark.

Bryant, Edwin F. 2002. "The Date and Provenance of the *Bhāgavata Purāṇa* and the Vaikuṇṭha Perumāl Temple." *Journal of Vaishnava Studies* 11.1: 51–80.

Bryant, Kenneth E. 1978. *Poems to the Child God: Structures and Strategies in the Poetry of Sūrdās*. Berkeley: University of California Press.

Brzezinski, Jan. 2000. "Rādhā and Kṛṣṇa's First Meeting as Found in Jīva Gosvāmī's *Gopāla-Campū*." *Journal of Vaishnava Studies* 8.2 (Spring): 27–42.

Bulcke, Camille. [1950] 1971. *Rāmkathā: Utpatti aur Vikās*. Allahabad: Hindī Pariṣad Prakāśan.

Burghart, Richard. 1983. "The Discovery of an Object of Meditation: Sūr Kiśor and the Reappearance of Janakpur." In *Bhakti in Current Research, 1979–1982*, ed. Monika Thiel-Horstmann, 53–63. Berlin: Dietrich Reimer Verlag.

Caldwell, Sarah. 1999. *Oh Terrifying Mother: Sexuality, Violence, and the Worship of the Goddess Kālī.* New York: Oxford University Press.

Callewaert, Winand M., and Swapna Sharma. 2000. *The Hagiographies of Anantadās: The Bhakti Poets of North India.* Richmond, U.K. Curzon Press.

Chakravarti, Uma. 2005. "The Making and Unmaking of Tradition: The *Ramayana* Narrative in Two Moments." In *Traditions in Motion: Religion and Society in History,* ed. Satish Saberwal and Supriya Varma, 72–101. New Delhi: Oxford University Press.

Chakravarty, Sumita. 1993. *National Identity in Indian Popular Cinema 1947–87.* Austin: University of Texas Press.

Chatterjee, Gayatri. 2002. *Mother India.* London: British Film Institute.

Chaudhuri, Maitrayee, ed. 2004. *Feminism in India.* New Delhi: Kali for Women.

Chitgopekar, Nilima. 2002. *Invoking Goddesses: Gender Politics in Indian Religion.* New Delhi: Shakti Books.

Chitnis, Suma. [1988] 2004. "Feminism: Indian Ethos and Indian Convictions." In *Women in Indian Society: A Reader,* ed. Rehana Ghadially, 81–95. New Delhi: Sage. Reprinted in *Feminism in India,* ed. Chaudhuri Maitrayee, 8–25. New Delhi: Kali for Women.

Chopra, Anupama. 2002. *Dilwale Dulhania Le Jayenge.* London: British Film Institute.

———. 2005. "Bollywood's Good Girls Learn to Be Bad." *New York Times,* July 24, 2005.

Chopra, Radhika. 2004. "Encountering Masculinity: An Ethnographer's Dilemma." In *South Asian Masculinities: Context of Change, Sites of Continuity,* ed. Caroline Radhika Chopra and Filippo Osella. New Delhi: Kali for Women.

Chowdhry, Prem. 2004. "Private Lives, State Intervention: Cases of Runaway Marriage in Rural North India." *Modern Asian Studies* 38.1: 55–84.

———. 2005. "Imagined Lovers: Ideology, Practice and Social Hierarchies." In *Women of India: Colonial and Post-colonial Periods,* ed. Bharati Ray, 110–38. History of Science, Philosophy and Culture in Indian Civilization 9.3. New Delhi: Sage.

Citrāv, Siddheśvar Śāstrī. 1964. *Bhāratvarṣīy Prācīn Caritra Koś.* Poona: Bhāratīy Caritrakoś Maṇḍal.

Coburn, Thomas. 1995. "Sita Fights While Ram Swoons." *Manushi* 90: 5–16.

Dalmia-Lüderitz, Vasudha. 1991. "Television and Tradition: Some Observations on the Serialization of the *Rāmāyaṇa.*" In *Rāmāyaṇa and Rāmāyaṇas,* ed. Monika Thiel-Horstmann, 207–28. Wiesbaden: Otto Harrassowitz.

Das, Veena. 1998. "Narrativizing the Male and the Female in Tulasidas' *Ramacharitamanasa.*" In *Social Structure and Change,* ed. A. M. Shah, B. S. Baviskar, and E. A. Ramaswamy, 66–92. Religion and Kinship, vol. 5. New Delhi: Sage.

Dasgupta, Sudeep. 2006. "Gods in the Sacred Marketplace: Hindu Nationalism and the Return of the Aura in the Public Sphere." In *Religion, Media, and the Public Sphere,* ed. Birgit Meyer and Annelies Moors, 251–72. Bloomington: Indiana University Press.

De, Suniti Kumar. 1961. *The Early History of the Vaishnava Faith and Movement in Bengal.* 2d ed. Calcutta: Firma KLM.

Derné, Steve. 1995a. *Culture in Action: Family Life, Emotion, and Male Dominance in Banaras, India.* Albany: State University of New York Press.

———. 1995b. "Market Forces at Work: Religious Themes in Commercial Hindi Films." In *Media and the Transformation of Religion in South Asia,* ed. Lawrence Babb and Susan Wadley, 191–216. Philadelphia: University of Pennsylvania Press.

———. 2000. *Movies, Masculinity, and Modernity: An Ethnography of Men's Filmgoing in India.* Westport, Conn.: Greenwood Press.

Derné, Steve, and Lisa Jadwin. 2000. "Male Hindi Filmgoers' Gaze: An Ethnographic Interpretation." *Contributions to Indian Sociology* 34.2 (May–August): 243–69.

Desai, Jighna. 2004. *Beyond Bollywood: The Cultural Politics of South Asian Diasporic Film.* New York: Routledge.

Deshpande, Sudhanva. 2005. "The Consumable Hero of Globalised India." In *Bollyworld: Popular Indian Cinema through a Transational Lens,* ed. Raminder Kaur and Ajay J. Singha, 186–203. New Delhi: Sage.

Dimock, Edward C., Jr. 1966. *The Place of the Hidden Moon.* Chicago: Chicago University Press.

Doniger, Wendy. 1997. "Sita and Helen, Ahalya and Alcmena: A Comparative Study." *History of Religions* 37.1: 21–49.

Dwyer, Rachel. 2000. *All You Want Is Money, All You Need Is Love: Sex and Romance in Modern India.* London: Cassell.

———. 2006. "The Saffron Screen? Hindu Nationalism and the Hindi Film." In *Religion, Media, and the Public Sphere,* ed. Birgit Meyer and Annelies Moors, 273–89. Bloomington: Indiana University Press.

Dyczkowski, Mark S. G. 2000. *Kubjikā, Kālī, Tripurā and Trika.* Nepal Research Centre Publications 22. Stuttgart: Franz Steiner Verlag.

———. 1995–96. "Kubjikā the Erotic Goddess. Sexual Potency, Transformation and Reversal in the Heterodox Theophanies of the Kubjikā Tantras." *Indologica Taurinensia* 21–2: 123–40.

Entwistle, Alan W. 1987. *Braj: Centre of Krishna Pilgrimage.* Groningen: Egbert Forsten.

Erndl, Kathleen. 1991. "The Mutilation of Surpanakha." In *Many Rāmāyaṇas: The Diversity of a Narrative Tradition in South Asia,* ed. Paula Richman, 67–88. Berkeley: University of California Press.

Farmer, Victoria L. 1996. "Mass Media: Images, Mobilization, and Communalism." In *Contesting the Nation: Religion, Community, and the Politics of Democracy in India,* ed. David Ludden, 98–115. Philadelphia: University of Pennsylvania Press.

Forbes, Geraldine. 1996. *Women in Modern India.* The New Cambridge History of India 4.2. Cambridge: Cambridge University Press.

Gabriel, Karen. 2002. "Draupadi's Moment in Sita's Syntax: Violations of the Past and the Construction of Community in Kamal Haasan's *Hey! Ram.*" In *Women and the Politics of Violence,* ed. Taisha Abraham, 76–124. New Delhi: Shakti Books.

Gandhi, Ramachandra. 1992. *Sita's Kitchen: A Testimony of Faith and Inquiry*. New Delhi: Penguin Books.

Gangoli, Geetanjali. 2005. "Sexuality, Sensuality and Belonging: Representations of the 'Anglo-Indian' and the 'Western' Woman in Hindi cinema." In *Bollyworld: Popular Indian Cinema through a Transsational Lens,* ed. Raminder Kaur and Ajay J. Singha, 143–62. New Delhi: Sage.

Gargi, Charu. 2005. "Women's Sexuality in Films: On Making Empowered Choices." In *Women and Media: Challenging Feminist Discourse,* ed. Kiran Prasad, 81–108. Delhi: Women Press.

Gillespie, Marie. 1995. "Sacred Serials, Devotional Viewing, and Domestic Worship: A Case-study in the Interpretation of Two TV Versions of The Mahabharata in a Hindu Family in West London." In *To Be Continued: Soap Operas and Global Media Cultures,* ed. Robert Clyde Allen, C. Allen Robert, 354–80. London: Routledge.

Gokulsingh, K. Moti. 2004. *Soft-Soaping India: The World of Indian Televised Soap Operas*. Stoke on Trent, U.K.: Trentham Books.

Goldman, Robert. 2000. "The Ghost from the Anthill: Vālmīki and the Destiny of the Rāmakathā in South and South East Asia." In *A Varied Optic: Contemporary Studies in the Rāmāyaṇa,* ed. Mandakranta Bose, 11–32. Vancouver: Institute of Asian Research.

———. 2004. "Resisting Rāma: Dharmic Debates on Gender and Hierarchy in the Work of the Vālmīki *Rāmāyaṇa*." In *The Rāmāyaṇa Revisited,* ed. Mandakranta Bose, 19–46. New York: Oxford University Press.

Gopalan, Lalitha. 2000. "Avenging Women in Indian Cinema." In *Making Meaning in Indian Cinema,* ed. Ravi S. Vasudevan, 215–37. New Delhi: Oxford University Press.

Guha, Phulrenu, ed. 1975. *Towards Equality: Report of the Committee on the Status of Women in India*. New Delhi: Government of India, Ministry of Education and Social Welfare.

Guha, Ranajit. 1992. "Dominance without Hegemony and its Historiography." In *Subaltern Studies VI: Writings on South Asian History and Society,* ed. Ranajit Guha, 47–60. Delhi: Oxford University Press.

Gupta, Charu. 2001. *Sexuality, Obscenity, Community: Women, Muslims, and the Hindu Public in Colonial India*. Delhi: Permanent Black.

———. 2005. "Gains, Losses and/or Potential Possibilities: Gender and Social Reforms in the United Provinces." In *Exploring Gender Equations: Colonial and Post Colonial India,* ed. Shakti Kak and Biswamoy Pati, 29–56. New Delhi: Nehru Memorial Museum and Library.

Gupta, Nilanjana. 1998. *Switching Channels: Ideologies of Television in India*. Delhi: Oxford University Press.

Haberman, David L. 1988. *Acting as a Way of Salvation: A Study of Rāgānugā Bhakti Sādhana*. New York: Oxford University Press.

———. 2003. *The Bhaktirasāmṛtasindhu of Rūpa Gosvāmin*. New Delhi: Indira Gandhi National Centre for the Arts.

Hardy, Friedhelm. 1983. *Viraha Bhakti*. New Delhi: Oxford University Press.

Hasan, Zoya. 1996. "Communal Mobilization and Changing Majority in Uttar Pradesh." In *Contesting the Nation: Religion, Community, and the Politics of Democracy in India,* ed. David Ludden, 81–97. Philadelphia: University of Pennsylvania Press.

Hawley, John Stratton. 1983. *Krishna, the Butter Thief.* Princeton, N.J.: Princeton University Press.

———. 1984. *Sūr Dās: Poet, Singer, Saint.* Publications on Asia of the Henry M. Jackson School of International Studies 40. Seattle: University of Washington Press.

———. 1995. "The Saints Subdued: Domestic Virtue and National Integration in *Amar Chitra Katha.*" In *Media and the Transformation of Religion in South Asia,* ed. Lawrence Babb and Susan Wadley, 107–34. Philadelphia: University of Pennsylvania Press.

———, ed. 2002. "Bibliography of D. Dennis Hudson." *Journal of Vaiṣṇava Studies* 11.1 (September): 189–93.

———. 2005. *Three Bhakti Voices: Mirabai, Surdas, and Kabir in Their Time and Ours.* New Delhi: Oxford University Press.

Hawley, John Stratton, trans., and Kenneth Bryant, ed. Forthcoming. *Sūr's Ocean.* Oxford: Oxford University Press.

Hawley, John Stratton, and Shrivatsa Goswami. 1981. *At Play with Krishna: Pilgrimage Dramas from Brindavan.* Princeton, N.J.: Princeton University Press.

Hawley, John Stratton, and Mark Juergensmeyer. 1988. *Songs of the Saints of India.* Oxford: Oxford University Press.

Hawley, John Stratton, and Donna Marie Wulff, eds. 1982. *The Divine Consort: Rādhā and the Goddesses of India.* Boston: Beacon Press.

———. 1996. *Devī: Goddess of India.* Berkeley: University of California Press.

Heinz, Carolyn Brown. 2000. "Sita Was a Mithila Girl: Narratives of Text and Self in North Bihar." Paper presented at the Ninety-ninth annual meeting of the American Anthropological Association, November 19.

———. 2006. "Documenting the Image in Mithila Art." *Visual Anthropology Review* 22.2: 5–33.

Herman, Phyllis K. 1998. "Relocating Ramarajya: Perspectives on Sita's Kitchen in Ayodhya." *International Journal of Hindu Studies* 2.2 (August): 157–84.

———. 2000. "Sita in the Kitchen: The *Pativrata* and *Ramarajya.*" *Manushi* 120 (September–October): 5–11.

——— 2003. "Remaking Rama for the Modern Sightseer: It's a Small Hindu World after All." *South Asian Popular Culture* 1.2 (October): 125–40.

Hess, Linda. 1999. "Rejecting Sita: Indian Responses to the Ideal Man's Cruel Treatment of His Ideal Wife." *Journal of the American Academy of Religion* 67.1: 1–32.

———. 2001. "Lovers' Doubts: Questioning the Tulsi *Rāmāyaṇ.*" In *Questioning Ramayanas: A South Asian Narrative Tradition,* ed. Paula Richman, 25–47. Berkeley: University of California Press.

Hiltebeitel, Alf, and Kathleen Erndl, eds. 2000. *Is the Goddess a Feminist? The Politics of South Asian Goddesses.* New York: New York University Press.

Hirst, Jacqueline Suthren, and Lynn Thomas, eds. 2004. *Playing for Real: Hindu Role Models, Religion, and Gender*. New Delhi: Oxford University Press.

Humes, Cythia Ann. 1997. "Glorifying the Great Goddess or Great Woman." In *Women and Goddess Traditions in Antiquity and Today*, ed. Karen L. King, 39–63. Minneapolis: Fortress Press.

Ingalls, Daniel, trans. 1965. *An Anthology of Sanskrit Court Poetry: Vidyākara's "Subhāṣitaratnakoṣa."* Vol. 1. Harvard Oriental Series 44. Cambridge, Mass.: Harvard University Press.

Jacobson, Doranne. 1978. "The Chaste Wife: Cultural Norm and Individual Experience." In *American Studies in the Anthropology of India*, ed. Sylvia Vatuk, 95–138. New Delhi: Manohar.

Jaffrelot, Christophe. 1996. *The Hindu Nationalist Movement and Indian Politics: 1925 to the 1990s*. London: Hurst.

Jeffery, Patricia, and Robert Jeffery. 1996. *Don't Marry Me to a Plowman! Women's Everyday Lives in Rural North India*. Boulder, Colo.: Westview Press.

John, Mary E., and Janaki Nair. 1998. "Introduction: A Question of Silence? The Sexual Economies of Modern India." In *A Question of Silence? The Sexual Economies of Modern India*, ed. Mary E. John and Janaki Nair, 1–51. New Delhi: Kali for Women.

Joshi, Sarasvati. 2000. "La Femme et l'Eau: O Ma Belle, Donne-Moi Deux Gorgées à Boire." In *Le Rajasthan, Ses Dieux, Ses Héros, Ses Homes*, ed. Annie Montaut, 63–80. Paris: Inalco Publications Langues'O.

Kak, Smriti. 2003. "Common Girl with Uncommon Grit." *Tribune*, May 25, 2003.

Kakar, Sudhir. 1981. *The Inner World: A Psycho-analythical Study of Childhood and Society in India*. 2d ed. Delhi: Oxford University Press.

———. 1989. *Intimate Relations: Exploring Indian Sexuality*. New Delhi: Viking.

Kane, Pandurang Vaman. 1974. *History of Dharmaśāstra: Ancient and Medieval Civil Law in India*. Vol. 2.1. Poona: Bhandarkar Oriental Research Institute.

Kapur, Anuradha. 1990. *Actors, Pilgrims, Kings, and Gods: The Ramlila at Ramnagar*. Calcutta: Seagull.

———. 1993. "Deity to Crusader: The Changing Iconography of Ram." In *Hindus and Others: The Question of Identity in India Today*, ed. Gyanendra Pandey, 74–109. New Delhi: Viking/Penguin India.

———. 1995. "The Representation of Gods and Heroes in Early Twentieth-Century Drama." In *Representing Hinduism*, ed. Vasudha Dalmia and Henry von Stietencron, 401–19. New Delhi: Sage.

Kazmi, Fareed. 1999. *The Politics of India's Conventional Cinema: Imagining a Universe, Subverting a Multiverse*. New Delhi: Sage.

King, Christopher Rolland. 1994. *One Language, Two Scripts: The Hindi Movement in Nineteenth-Century North India*. Bombay: Oxford University Press.

King, Karen L. 1997. *Women and Goddess Traditions in Antiquity and Today*. Minneapolis: Fortress Press.

Kinsley, David. 1988. *Hindu Goddesses: Visions of the Divine Feminine in the Hindu Religious Tradition*. Berkeley: University of California Press.

Kishwar, Madhu. 1985. "Gandhi on Women." *Economic and Political Weekly* 20.40: 1691–1702.

———. 1990. "A Horror of 'Isms': Why I Do Not Call Myself a Feminist." *Manushi* 61 (November–December): 2–8.

———. 1997. " 'Yes to Sita, No to Ram!' The Continuing Popularity of Sita in India." *Manushi* 98 (January–February): 20–31.

———. 2001. " 'Yes to Sītā, No to Rām': The Continuing Hold of Sita on Popular Imagination in India." In *Questioning Ramayanas: A South Asian Narrative Tradition,* ed. Paula Richman, 285–308. Berkeley: University of California Press.

———. 2003a. "The Essential Oneness of Amar, Akbar, Anthony: Bollywood's Response to Globalisation, Religious Conflicts and Terrorism." Plenary address for the conference Contesting Religion and Religions Contested: The Study of Religion in a Global Context, Emory University, Atlanta, November.

———. 2003b. "Of Humans and Divine: Feminine Role Models in the Hindu Tradition." *Manushi* 136 (August–September): 17–30.

———. 2005. "Strategies for Combating the Culture of Dowry and Domestic Violence in India." Paper prepared for the Expert Group Meeting entitled "Violence against Women: Good Practices in Combating and Eliminating Violence against Women," UN Division for the Advancement of Women, Vienna, May 17–20. www.un.org/womenwatch/daw/egm/vaw-gp-2005/docs/experts/kishwar.dowry.pdf.

Kishwar, Madhu, and Ruth Vanita, eds. 1984. *In Search of Answers: Indian Women's Voices from Manushi.* London: Zed Books.

Kosambi, Meera. 1995. *Pandita Ramabai's Feminist and Christian Confessions Focus on Stree Dharma-Neeti.* Bombay: Research Centre for Women's Studies, S.N.D.T. Women's University.

Kripal, Jeffrey J., and Rachel Fell McDermott, eds. 2003. *Encountering Kali in the Margins, at the Center, in the West.* Berkeley: University of California Press.

Kumar, Nitin. 2005. *Sita—The Silent Power of Suffering and Sacrifice.* www.exoticindiaart.com/article/sita.

Kumar, Vinay. 2006. "Kumbh Mela: Centre Asks Gujarat to Maintain Law and Order." *Hindu,* February 3.

Kurtz, Stanley N. 1992. *All the Mothers Are One: Hindu India and the Cultural Reshaping of Psychoanalysis.* New York: Columbia University Press.

Lele, Jayant. 1981. "The Bhakti Movement in India: A Critical Introduction." In *Tradition and Modernity in Bhakti Movements,* ed. Jayant Lele, 1–15. Leiden: Brill.

Lorenzen, David. 1995. "The Historical Vicissitudes of Bhakti Religion." In *Bhakti Religion in North India: Community, Identity and Political Action,* ed. David Lorenzen, 1–32. New York: State University of New York.

Lutgendorf, Philip. 1990. "Ramayan: The Video." *Drama Review* 34.2: 127–76.

———. 1991a. "The 'Great Sacrifice' of *Rāmāyaṇa* Recitation: Ritual Performance of the *Rām Carit Mānas.*" In *Rāmāyaṇa and Rāmāyaṇas,* ed. Monika Thiel-Horstmann, 185–205. Wiesbaden: Otto Harrassowitz.

———. 1991b *The Life of a Text: Performing the "Rāmcaritmānas" of Tulsidas.* Berkeley: University of California Press.

———. 1991c. "The Secret Life of Rāmcandra of Ayodhya." In *Many Rāmāyaṇas: The Diversity of a Narrative Tradition in South Asia,* ed. Paula Richman, 217–34. Berkeley: University of California Press.

———. 1994. "The Quest for the Legendary Tulsīdās." In *According to Tradition: Hagiographical Writing in India,* ed. W. M. Callewaert and R. Snell, 65–85. Khoj: A Series of Modern South Asian Studies 5. Wiesbaden: Otto Harrassowitz.

———. 1995. "All in the (Raghu) Family." In *Media and the Transformation of Religion in South Asia,* ed. Lawrence Babb and Susan Wadley, 217–53. Philadelphia: University of Pennsylvania Press.

———. 1999. Like Mother, Like Son: Sita and Hanuman. *Manushi* 114: 22–35.

———. 2002. "Jai Santoshi Maa and Caste Hierarchy in Indian Films" and "A 'Made to Satisfaction' Goddess: Jai Santoshi Maa Revisited." *Manushi* 131 (July–August): 10–16, 24–37. www.indiatogether.org/manushi/issue131/index.htm.

———. 2007. "Bending the *Bhārata:* Two Uncommon Cinematic Adaptations." In *Indian Literature and Popular Cinema: Recasting Classics,* ed. Heidi Pauwels, 19–41. London: Routledge.

Majid, Sabita. 2003. "Guts in the Time of Dowry." *Women's Feature Service,* June 1. www.wfsnews.org/.

Majumder, Sanjoy. 1996. "From Ritual Drama to National Prime Time: *Mahabharata,* India's Televisual Obsession." In *Between the Lines: South Asians and Postcoloniality,* ed. Deepika Bahri and Mary Vasudeva, 204–15. Philadelphia: Temple University Press.

Mani, Lata. 1990. "Multiple Mediations: Feminist Scholarship in the Age of Multinational Reception." *Feminist Review* 35 (Summer): 24–41.

Mankekar, Purnima. 1993. "National Texts and Gendered Lives: An Ethnography of Television Viewers in a North Indian City." *American Ethnologist* 20.3 (August): 543–63.

———. 1999. *Screening Culture, Viewing Politics: An Ethnography of Television, Womanhood, and Nation in Postcolonial India.* Durham, N.C.: Duke University Press.

Manuel, Peter. 1993. *Cassette Culture: Popular Music and Technology in North India.* Chicago: University of Chicago Press.

Martin, Nancy Kershaw. 1995. "Mīrābāī: Inscribed in Text, Embodied in Life." *Journal of Vaishnava Studies* 5 (Fall): 5–44.

Masson, J. M. 1980. *The Oceanic Feeling: The Origins of Religious Sentiment in Ancient India.* Dordrecht: Reidel.

McDaniel, June. 2000. "The Tantric Rādhā: Some Controversies about the Nature of Rādhā in Bengali Vaishnavism and the Rādhā Tantra." *Journal of Vaiṣṇava Studies* 8.2 (Spring): 131–46.

McGregor, Ronald Stuart. 1973. *The Round Dance of Krishna and Uddhav's Message.* London: Luzac.

———. 1976. "Tulsīdās's *Śrīkṛṣṇagītāvalī.*" *Journal of the American Oriental Society* 94.4: 520–7.

———. 1984. *Hindi Literature from Its Beginnings to the Nineteenth Century.* A History of Indian Literature 8.6, edited by Jan Gonda. Wiesbaden: Otto Harrassowitz.

———. 1992. "The Padas Attributed to Nanddās." In *Devotional Literature in South Asia: Current Research, 1985–1988,* ed. R. S. McGregor, 237–46. Cambridge: Cambridge University Press.

McLain, Karline. 2001. "Sita and Shrupanakha: Symbols of the Nation in the Amar Chitra Katha." *Manushi* 122 (January–February): 32–9.

Miller, Barbara Stoler, ed. 1997. *Love Song of the Dark Lord: Jayadeva's Gitagovinda.* New York: Columbia University Press.

Minturn, Leigh, and Swaran Kapoor. 1993. *Sita's Daughters, Coming out of Purdah: The Rajput Women of Khalapur Revisited.* New York: Oxford University Press.

Mishra, Vijay. 2002. *Bollywood Cinema: Temples of Desire.* New York: Routledge.

Mitra, Ananda. 1993. *Television and Popular Culture in India: A Study of the Mahabharat.* New Delhi: Sage.

Mody, Parveez. 2006. "Kidnapping, Elopement and Abduction: An Ethnography of Love-Marriage in Delhi." In *Love in South Asia: A Cultural History,* ed. Francesca Orsini, 331–59. Cambridge: Cambridge University Press.

Molina, Alfonso. 2002. *Assessment of Project SITA: Computer Skill Training Program for Low-Income Women in India.* Edinburgh: School of Management, University of Edinburgh. www.sustainableicts.org/infodev/SITA.pdf.

Mukherji, Parul Dave. 2005. "Gendered Bodies and Cultural Claims: Visuality in Public Culture." In *Rethinking Modernity,* ed. Santosh Gupta, Prafulla Kar, and Parul Mukherji, 168–77. New Delhi: Pencraft International.

Murphy, Anne, and Shana Shippy. 2000. "Sita in the City: The Ramayana's Heroine in New York." *Manushi* 117 (July): 17–23. www.india.together.org/manushi/issue117/sita.htm.

Nadkarni, Durgaprasad S. 1975. *Textual Restoration in the Bhāgawata-Purāna, with Special Reference to Metrical Analysis.* Bombay: Popular Prakashan.

Nagaraj, D. R. 2006. "The Comic Collapse of Authority: An Essay on the Fears of the Public Spectator." In *Fingerprinting Popular Culture: The Mythic and the Iconic in Indian Cinema,* ed. Vinay Lal and Ashis Nandy, 87–121. New Delhi: Oxford University Press.

Narayana, Vasudha. 2000. "All Compassionate and All Powerful: Sita of South Indian Stories." *Manushi* 118 (May–June): 24–7.

Nilsson, Usha. 2001. " 'Grinding Millet but Singing of Sita': Power and Domination in Awadhi and Bhojpuri Women's Songs." In *Questioning Ramayanas: A South Asian Narrative Tradition,* ed. Paula Richman, 137–58. Berkeley: University of California Press.

Niranjana, Tejaswini. 1992. *Siting Translation: History, Post-structuralism and the Colonial Context.* Berkeley: University of California Press.

———. 2000. "Nationalism Refigured: Contemporary South Indian Cinema and the Subject of Feminism." In *Community, Gender and Violence,* ed. Partha Chatterjee and Pradeep Jaganathan, 138–66. Subaltern Studies 11. New York: Columbia University Press.

O'Flaherty, Wendy Doniger. 1980. *Women, Androgynes, and Other Mythical Beasts.* Chicago: University of Chicago Press.

Olivelle, Patrick. 2005. *Manu's Code of Law: A Critical Edition and Translation.* New York: Oxford University Press.

Orsini, Francesca. 2006. *Love in South Asia: A Cultural History.* Cambridge: Cambridge University Press

Pandian, M. S. S. 1993. "Jayalalita: 'Desire' and Political Legitimation." *Seminar* 401: 31–4.

Pandurang, Mala. 2003. "Conceptualizing Emigrant Indian Female Subjectivity: Possible Entry Points." In *South Asian Women in the Diaspora,* ed. Nirmal Puwar and Parvati Raghuram, 87–95. Oxford: Berg.

Parry, Jonathan. 2002. "Anakalu's Errrant Wife: Sex, Marriage and Industry in Contemporary Chhattisgarh." *Modern Asian Studies* 20: 783–820.

Patel, Sujata. 2000. "Construction and Reconstruction of Woman in Gandhi." In *Ideals, Images and Real Lives: Women in Literature and History,* ed. Alice Thorner and Maithreyi Krishnaraj, 288–321. Hyderabad: Orient Longman.

Pauwels, Heidi. 1996a. "The Great Goddess and Fulfilment in Love: Rādhā Seen through a Sixteenth-Century Lens." *Bulletin of the School of Oriental and African Studies* 59.1: 29–43.

———. 2000. "Three Ways of Falling in Love: Tulsīdās's Phūlvārī Episode and the Way It Is Portrayed in Contemporary Electronic Media." In *A Varied Optic: Contemporary Studies in the Rāmāyaṇa,* ed. Mandakranta Bose, 55–100. Vancouver: Institute of Asian Research, University of British Columbia. (Reprinted in Mandakranta Bose, ed., *The Rāmāyaṇa Culture: Text, Performance, and Iconography.* New Delhi: D. K. Print World, 2003.)

———. 2001. "Educating Sītā: Anasūya's Advice Compared in Three Rāmāyaṇas." *Rocznik Orientalistyczny* 54.1 (Fall): 173–88.

———. 2004a "Is love still stronger than *dharma?* What ever happened Sita's choice and the Gopis's voice?" In *Playing for Real: Hindu Role Models, Religion, and Gender,* ed. Jacqueline Suthren Hirst and Lynn Thomas, 117–140. Delhi: Oxford University Press.

———. 2004b. " 'Only You': The Wedding of Rāma and Sītā, Past and Present." In *The Rāmāyaṇa Revisited,* ed. Mandakranta Bose, 165–218. New York: Oxford University Press.

———. 2007. "Stealing a Willing Bride: Women's Agency in the Myth of Rukmiṇī's Elopement." *Journal of the Royal Asiatic Society* 17.4: 407–41.

Pendakur, Manjunath. 2003. *Indian Popular Cinema: Industry Ideology and Consciousness.* Creskill, N.J.: Hampton Press.

Peterson, Indira. 2004. "Theater and the Court in Maratha Tanjavur." Paper presented at the Thirty-third Annual Conference on South Asia, Madison, Wisconsin, October 24.

Pfleiderer, Beatrix and Lothar Lutze. 1985. *The Hindi Film: Agent and Re-Agent of Cultural Change.* Delhi: Manohar.

Pinney, Christopher. 2004. *'Photos of the Gods': The Printed Image and Political Culture in India.* New York: Oxford University Press.

Pintchman, Tracy. 2001. *Seeking Mahādevī.* Albany: New York State University Press.

Prasad, Mishra. 1998. *Ideology of the Hindi Film: A Historical Construction.* Delhi: Oxford University Press.

Puri, Jyoti. 1999. *Woman, Body, Desire in Post-colonial India.* New York: Routledge.

Raghavendra, M. K. 2006. "Structure and Form in Indian Popular Film Narrative." In *Fingerprinting Popular Culture: The Mythic and the Iconic in Indian Cinema,* ed. Vinay Lal and Ashis Nandy, 24–50. New Delhi: Oxford University Press.

Raheja, Gloria Goodwin. 1994. "Women's Speech Genres, Kinship and Contradiction." In *Women as Subjects: South Asian Histories,* ed. Nita Kumar, 49–80. Charlottesville: University Press of Virginia.

———. 2003. "Negotiated Solidarities: Gendered Representations of Disruption and Desire in North Indian Oral Traditions and Popular Culture." In *Songs, Stories, Lives: Gendered Dialogues and Cultural Critique,* ed. Gloria Goodwin Raheja, New Delhi: Kali for Women.

Raheja, Gloria Goodwin, and Ann Grodzins Gold. 1994. *Listen to the Heron's Words: Reimagining Gender and Kinship in North India.* Berkeley: University of California Press.

Rajadhyaksha, Ashish. 2000. "Viewership and Democracy in the Cinema." In *Making Meaning in Indian Cinema,* ed. Ravi S. Vasudevan, 267–96. Delhi: Oxford University Press.

Rajagopal, Arvind. 2001. *Politics after Television: Religious Nationalism and the Reshaping of the Indian Public.* Cambridge: Cambridge University Press.

Rajan, Rajeswari Sunder. 1999. *Real and Imagined Women: Gender, Culture and Postcolonialism.* London: Routledge.

———. 2000a. "Real and Imagined Goddesses: A Debate." In *Is the Goddess a Feminist? The Politics of South Asian Goddesses,* ed. Alf Hiltebeitel and Kathleen M. Erndl, 265–84. New York: New York University Press.

———. 2000b. "The Story of Draupadi's Disrobing: Meanings for Our Times." In *Mapping Histories: Essays Presented to Ravinder Kumar,* ed. Neera Chandhoke, 39–60. New Delhi: Tulika.

———. 2004. "Is the Hindu Goddess a Feminist?" In *Feminism in India,* ed. Maitrayee Chaudhuri, New Delhi: Kali for Women.

Ramasubramanian, Srividya. 2003. "Portrayals of Sexual Violence in Popular Hindi Films, 1997–99." *Sex Roles* 7–8 (April): 327–36.

Rao, Velcheru Narayana. 1991. "A *Ramayana* of Their Own: Women's Oral Tradition in Telugu." In *Many Rāmāyaṇas: The Diversity of a Narrative Tradition in South Asia,* ed. Paula Richman, 114–36. Berkeley: University of California Press.

———. 2003. "Sita Locked Out: A Telugu Women's Song of Sita." *Manushi* 139 (November–December): 26–30.

———. 2004. "When Does Sītā Cease to be Sītā? Notes toward a Cultural Grammar of Indian Narratives." In *The Rāmāyaṇa Revisited,* ed. Mandakranta Bose, 219–41. New York: Oxford University Press.

Rayaprol, Aparna. 1997. *Negotiating Identities: Women in the Indian Diaspora.* Delhi: Oxford University Press.

Redington, James D. 1983. *Vallabhācārya on the Love Games of Kṛṣṇa*. Delhi: Motilal Banarsidass.

Richman, Paula, ed. 1991. *Many Rāmāyaṇas: The Diversity of a Narrative Tradition in South Asia*. Berkeley: University of California Press.

———, ed. 2001. *Questioning Ramayanas: A South Asian Tradition*. Berkeley: University of California Press.

———. 2005. "Kumudini's *Ramayana:* A Woman's View of Raghukul Politics." *Manushi* 148 (May–June): 22–9.

Ritter, Valerie. 2005. "Epiphany in Rādhā's Arbor: Nature and the Reform of Bhakti in Hariaudh's *Priyapravās*." In *Alternative Krishnas: Regional and Vernacular Variations on a Hindu Deity*, ed. Guy Beck, 177–208. New York: State University of New York Press.

Robinson, Catherine A. 1999. *Tradition and Liberation: The Hindu Tradition in the Indian Women's Movement*. Richmond Curzon Press.

Robinson, Sandra P. 1985. "Hindu Paradigms of Women: Images and Values." In *Women, Religion, and Social Change*, ed. Yvonne Yazbeck Haddad and Ellison Banks Findley, 181–215. Albany: State University of New York Press.

Rodrigues, Hillary Peter. 2003. *Ritual Worship of the Great Goddess: The Liturgy of the Durgā Pūjā with Interpretations*. Albany: State University of New York Press.

Sarkar, Tanika. 1991. "The Woman as Communal Subject: Rashtrasevika Samiti and the Ram Janmabhoomi Movement." *Economic and Political Weekly* 26: 2057–62.

———. 1995. "Heroic Women, Mother Goddesses: Family and Organisation in Hindutva Politics." In *Women and the Hindu Right: A Collection of Essays*, ed. Tanika Sarkar and Urvashi Butalia, 181–215. New Delhi: Kali for Women.

———. 2001. *Hindu Wife, Hindu Nation: Community, Religion, and Cultural Nationalism*. London: Hirst.

———. 2005. "Between laws and faith: 19th century debates on widow immolation in colonial Bengal." Seminar sponsored by the Simpson Center of the University of Washington, Seattle (Nov. 22).

Sarkar, Tanika, and Urvashi Butalia, eds. 1995.*Women and the Hindu Right: A Collection of Essays*. New Delhi: Kali for Women.

Śāstrī, Kaṇṭhamaṇi Viśārad. 1954. *Śrī Nanddās kṛt Manjarī-pañcak par ek dṛṣṭi nikṣep*. Kankroli: Vidyā Vibhāg.

Schomer, Karine. 1982. "Where Have All the Rādhās Gone?" In *The Divine Consort: Rādhā and the Goddesses of India*, ed J. S. Hawley and D. M. Wulff, 89–115. Boston: Beacon Press.

Sen, Geeti. 2002. *Feminine Fables: Imaging the Indian Woman in Painting, Photography and Cinema*. Ahmedabad: Mapin.

Sen, Nabaneeta Dev. 1998. "When Women Retell the *Ramayan*." *Manushi* 108 (September–October): 18–27.

———. 2000. "*Candrāvati Rāmāyaṇa* Feminizing the Rāma-Tale." In *Faces of the Feminine in Ancient, Medieval, and Modern India*, ed. Mandakranta Bose, 183–91. New Delhi: Oxford University Press.

Sharma, Arvind. 2005. *Goddesses and Women in the Indic Religious Tradition.* Leiden: Brill.

Sheth, Noel. 1983. "The Justification for Krishna's Affair with the Hunchbacked Woman." *Purāṇa* 25.2 (July): 225–34.

Shulman, David. 1991. "Fire and Flood: The Testing of Sītā in Kampaṉ's *Irāmāvatāram.*" In *Many Rāmāyaṇas: The Diversity of a Narrative Tradition in South Asia,* ed. Paula Richman, 89–113. Berkeley: University of California Press.

Singer, Milton. 1966. "The Rādhā-Krishna *Bhajanas* of Madras City." In *Krishna: Myths, Rites, and Attitudes,* ed. Milton Singer, 90–138. Chicago: University of Chicago Press.

Singh, Pankaj K., and Jaidev. 1999. "Decentering a Patriarchal Myth: Bhisham Sahni's Madhavi." In *From Myths to Markets: Essays on Gender,* ed. Kumkum Sangari and Uma Chakravarti, 3–17. New Delhi: Manohar.

Sirhandi, Manuella C. 1999. "Manipulating Cultural Idioms." *Art Journal* 58.3: 40–7.

Söhnen-Thieme, Renate. 1996. "The Ahalyā Story through the Ages." In *Roles and Rituals for Hindu Women,* ed. Julia Leslie, 39–62. Delhi: Motilal Banarsidass.

Srivastava, Sanjay. 2006. "The Voice of the Nation and the Five-Year Plan Hero: Speculations on Gender, Space, and Popular Culture." In *Fingerprinting Popular Culture: The Mythic and the Iconic in Indian Cinema,* ed. Vinay Lal and Ashis Nandy, 122–55. New Delhi: Oxford University Press.

Stasik, Danuta. 1995. "The Divine Marriage: The Nuptials of Rāma and Sītā as Seen by Tulsī." In *Proceedings of International Conference on Sanskrit and Related Studies (Cracow, September 23–26, 1993).* ed. P. Piekorski et als. Cracow Indological Studies 1. Crecon: Institute of Orient Philology.

———. 1999. "Text and Context: Two versions of Tulsīdās's *Rām-lalā-nahachū.*" In *Studies in Early Literature in New Indo-Aryan Languages: Proceedings of the Sixth International Conference on Early Literature in New Indo-Aryan languages (Seattle 1994),* ed. A. Entwistle et al., 379–92. New Delhi: Manohar.

Sternfeld, Michael. 2005. "The *Ramayana* in Modern Media and Performance." *Journal of Vaishnava Studies* 13.2 (Spring): 161–208.

Sultana, Waheeda. 2005. "Women in Indian Soap Operas." In *Women and Media: Challenging Feminist Discourse,* ed. Kiran Prasad, 109–22. Delhi: Women Press.

Sutherland, Sally J. M. 1989. "Sītā and Draupadī: Aggressive Behavior and Female Role-Models in the Sanskrit Epics." *Journal of the American Oriental Society* 109.1: 63–79.

———. 1992. "Seduction, Counter Seduction, and Sexual Role Models: Bedroom Politics and the Indian Epics." *Journal of Indian Philosophy* 20.2: 243–51.

Sutherland-Goldman, Sally J. M. 2001. "The Voice of Sita in *Vālmīki's Sundarakāṇḍa.*" In *Questioning Ramayanas: A South Asian Narrative Tradition,* ed. Paula Richman, 223–38. Berkeley: University of California Press.

———. 2004. "Gendered Narratives: Gender, Space and Narrative Structures in Vālmīki's *Bālakāṇḍa.*" In *The Rāmāyaṇa Revisited,* ed. Mandakranta Bose, 47–85. New York: Oxford University Press.

Talwar, Vir Bharat. 1989. "Feminist Consciousness in Women's Journals in Hindi, 1910–20." In *Recasting Women: Essays in Indian Colonial History,* ed. K. Sangari and S. Vaid 204–32 New Brunswick, N. J.: Rutgers University Press.

Taylor, Woodman. 2002. "Penetrating Gazes: The Poetics of Sight and Visual Display in Popular Indian Cinema." *Contributions to Indian Sociology* 36.1–2: 297–322.

Thapar, Romila. 1999. *Śakuntalā: Texts, Readings, Histories.* London: Anthem Press.

Thiel-Horstmann, Monika. ed. 1991. *Rāmāyaṇa and Rāmāyaṇas.* Wiesbaden: Otto Harrassowitz

Thiruchandran, Selvy. 1999. *Women, Narration and Nation: Collective Images and Multiple Identities.* New Delhi: Vikas.

Thomas, Rosie. 1989. "The Mythologization of Mother India." *Quarterly Review of Film and Video* 11.3: 11–30.

———. 1995. "Melodrama and the Negotiation of Morality in Mainstream Hindi Film." In *Consuming Modernity: Public Culture in a South Asian World,* ed. Carol E. Breckenridge, 157–82. Minneapolis: University of Minnesota Press.

Tully, Mark. 1991. *No Full Stops in India.* New Delhi: Viking.

Uberoi, Patricia. 1998. "The Diaspora Comes Home: Disciplining Desire in *DDLJ*." *Contributions to Indian Sociology* 32.2: 305–36.

———. 2001a. "Imagining the Family: An Ethnography of Viewing *Hum Aapke Hain Koun . . . !*" In *Pleasure and the Nation: The History and Politics of Popular Consumption in India,* ed. Rachel Dwyer and Christopher Pinney, 186–211. Delhi: Oxford University Press.

———. 2001b. "A Suitable Romance? Trajectories of Courtship in Indian Popular Fiction." In *Images of the "Modern Woman" in Asia: Global Media, Local Meanings,* ed. Shoma Munshi, 169–87. Richmond, U.K.: Curzon Press.

van der Veer, Peter. 1988. *God on Earth: The Management of Religious Experience and Identity in a North Indian Pilgrimage Centre.* London: Athlone Press.

Vanita, Ruth. 2005. "The Sita Who Smiles: Wife as Goddess in the Adbhut Ramayana." *Manushi* 148 (May–June): 32–39.

Vasudevan, Ravi. 2000. "The Politics of Cultural Address in a 'Transitional' Cinema: A Case Study of Indian Popular Cinema." In *Reinventing Film Studies,* ed. Christine Gledhill and Linda Williams, 130–64. London: Arnold.

Vaudeville, Charlotte. 1955. *Étude sur les Sources et la Composition du Rāmāyaṇa de Tulsī-Dās.* Paris: Adrien Maisonneuve.

Virdi, Jyotika. 2003. *The Cinematic ImagiNation: Indian Popular Films as Social History.* New Brunswick, N. J.: Rutgers University Press.

Viśārad, Kaṇṭhamaṇi Śāstrī. 1954. *Śrīnanddās Kṛtaḥ Mañjarī-Pañcaka par Ek Dṛṣṭnikṣep* Kāṃkrolī: Vidyā Vibhāg.

Whaling, Frank. 1980. *The Rise of the Religious Significance of Rāma.* Delhi: Motilal Banarsidass.

Wulff, Donna Maria. 1984. *Drama as a Mode of Religious Realization: The Vidagdhamādhava of Rūpa Gosvāmī.* Chico, Calif.: Scholars Press.

———. 1985. "Images and Roles of Women in Bengali Vaiṣṇava *Padāvalī Kīrtan*." In *Women, Religion, and Social Change*, ed. Yvonne Yazbeck Haddad and Ellison Banks Findley, 217–45. Albany: State University of New York Press.

———. 1997. "Radha." In *Women and Goddess Traditions in Antiquity and Today*, ed. Karen King, 64–83. Minneapolis: Fortress Press.

Young, Katherine K. 1996. "Theology Does Help Women's Liberation: Śrīvaiṣṇavism, a Hindu Case Study." In *Vaiṣṇavī: Women and the Worship of Krishna*, ed. Steven Rosen, 235–94. Delhi: Motilal Banarsidass.

Zacharias, Usha. 1994. "The Sita Myth and Hindu Fundamentalism: Masculine Signs of Feminine Beauty." In *Ideals of Feminine Beauty: Philosophical, Social, and Cultural Dimensions*, ed. Karen Callaghan, 37–52. London: Greenwood Press.

Index

Adhyātma Rāmāyaṇa, 33, 51, 102*n*10, 103*n*13, 104, 253, 386
agency, 154, 514
  bride's, 96, 99, 100*t*
  family context of, 504
  Gopīs', 458
  Hindu nationalism and, 508
  males', 136
  marriage and, 87, 113
  Rādhā's, 472
  Rukmiṇī's, 119, 127–29, 132, 136, 139, 157
  Sagar v. VR, 113, 113*n*33
Agniparīkṣā. *See* fire ordeal
Ahalyā, 109, 314*n*1
allies, new brides', 141, 182–84
Āḻvār, 14*n*15
Amar Chitra Katha (comic strip), 297
Anasūyā, 101, 109, 168, 189, 231, 409, 411
Andaaz, 295, 298
Arādhāna, 166, 223–25
archetypes, text v. film, 27–28
arousal, sexual, 449–52
Aryans, 504, 507–8
asceticism *(tapas),* Sītā's, 408
assisted marriage, 95
atman (Self), 271, 279–80
audience, 26, 35, 37, 91, 317–18, 460
Avadhī, 53

Bahri, Hardev, 37
Balrāma, 114, 381
banvās/vanavāsa, 243, 265
barāt, 112, 123, 167, 169, 170, 177, 179, 183, 185–86, 199, 210, 234, 517
Barjatya, Sooraj R., 43, 147–50
BDS. *See Bhāsā Dasama Skandha*
Bhāgavata Purāṇa (BhP), 31, 34, 51, 414, 502–3
  BDS Vastraharaṇa v., 60–66, 67*t*
  eroticism in, 78
  Gopīs/forest setting in, 247–48
  Gopīs in, textual versions and, 31–32
  Krishna-Rukmiṇī elopement in, 98
  Kubja in, 318
  Kubja in TVK/SS v., 330–61, 357*t*–358*t*
  Nanddās'/TVK Rukmiṇī elopement v., 115–41, 137*t*–138*t*
  Rādhā-Krishna in Braj/TVK/*Brahma Vaivarta Purāṇa* v., 201–2, 220–22, 221*t*
  Rādhā-Krishna love-marriage rites in, 201, 206
  Rāsa-līlā in, 244
  Rukmiṇī's/elopement in, 113, 114–15, 370
  Sangam's Vastraharaṇa v., 85
  Sītā's abduction parallel in, lack of, 382
  transcreations of, 37, 244, 331
  TVK v., 78
bhajana, 37, 69, 467

bhakti (devotion), 221
classical, 199
dharma and, 197–201, 413–14
Gopīs struggle over, 445–46
Krishna and, 60–66, 67*t*, 97, 129, 217, 245, 285
liberation through, 15–16, 45, 501–4
Mīrā-style, 482
Rādhā-Krishna, 206
role models of, 66–68, 501–4
Sītā's abduction and, 412
tradition of, love privileged over duty in, 309
Tulsī/Nanddās role models for, 66–68
Tulsī/Vyas on, 245, 502
two camps of, 16
Bharati, Uma, 499–500
Bhāsā Dasama Skandha (BDS) (Nanddās), 34–36, 60–66, 67*t*
Bhasin, Kamla, 8–9
Bhawan, David, *Bol Rādhā bol,* 463
BhP. *See Bhāgavata Purāṇa*
bidāī, 161, 167, 181–82, 231, 479
blame, 431–46, 494–96
Bobby, 150, 226
Bollywood, 292
Andaaz theme in, 295, 298
caste and, 369–76
dowry in, 226–27, 228–31
duty theme in, 143–47, 292–310
elopement theme in, 140–41
Kubja variants in, 364–77
love/dharma in, 292–308
love-marriage arranging, 141–61
panaghata theme in, 461–72, 461*n*184
Rāsa-līlā and, 292, 296, 305, 307–8
sensuality message in, 373, 375
sexual harassment/eve-teasing theme in, 461–94, 461*n*184
sexuality message of, 376–77
Sītā's abduction theme in, 472–77
society weddings theme in, 222–39
Śurpaṇakhā in, 361–64
temptation addressed in, 361–77
Bol Rādhā bol, 463
Bose, Mandakranta, vii, 11*n*11
bow sacrifice (Dhanuryajña), 100–112, 111*t*
bracelet rite, *see* kaṅkaṇa
Brahma, 206–7
Brahma Vaivarta Purāṇa, 32, 166, 414
Rādhā-Krishna mythology in, 201–2, 203–8, 220–22, 221*t*
TVK/BVP/Braj poetry v., 201–2, 220–22, 221*t*
Braj Bhāsā poetry, 14, 33–38. *See also* Gopīs of Braj
classical v., 60
pride rubric in, 315
Rādhā-Krishna, 201–2, 220–22, 221*t*
rivals in love in, 315
Braj region, Kubja worship in, 317–18
bride(s). *See also* sati
agency of, 96, 99, 100*t*
allies for new, 141, 182–84
brother-in-law of, *devar-bhābhī,* 301, 388, 393
burning of, 18
dowry of, 181–84, 200, 215, 515–18
equality between parties of groom and, 167–71, 230, 237
groom's family alliance with family of, 156–61, 164
ideal, in-laws and, 188–92, 199–200
in-laws and, 141, 182–84, 188–92, 199–200
parental farewell to, 184–88
Bride and Prejudice, 232

caste, 132, 134, 147, 151, 197–98, 369–76
ceremony. *See* rites/rituals; wedding ceremony
Chabili Bhatiyari, 364
Chadha, Gurinder, 232
chastity, 508
sensuality v., 13
chāyā (shadow), 4
child groom, Krishna as, 204–5
child marriage, 194–95
Chimnabai, 498
Chopra, B. R., 462–63
Mahabharat, television series, 17, 41–42, 114, 136–40, 137*t*–138*t*, 158–59, 289
Chopra, Ravi, 41
class, social, 179, 298, 375. *See also* caste
contextualization, Sagar's, 41
creativity. *See* innovations
cross-dressing motif, Krishna's, 285, 300

daily life, epics and, 19
dāna-līlā (gift episode), 382, 456, 467
Dard, 512
darshan, 56, 102, 108, 198–201
Bollywood portrayals of, 293
Krishna, 130
Rāma/Sītā, 173–76
Sītā/Gopīs desire for, 277–78
Tulsī and, 173–76
Daśaratha, 169–71

decorum, feelings v., 175–76, 200, 266–67
delusion (māyā), 362
demonizing
  of lustful women, 313–14, 320–22
  of Sūrpanakhā, 313–14
demon-style wedding (Rākṣasa-vivaha), 98–99, 100*t*, 116, 209*n*99
Derné, Steve, 310, 462
devar-bhabhī relationship, 388, 389
Devdas, 366, 465–68
devotee, 68
  Tulsī's ideal, 401–2
devotion, 6, 15, 50. *See also* bhakti
  medieval poetry, 14, 33–38, 60, 166, 201–2, 220–22, 221*t*, 315, 458–59
  Nanddās and, 66–68
  Tulsī and, 66–68, 173–76
  wedding ceremony and, 173–76
Dhanuryajña. *See* bow sacrifice
dharma. *See also* decorum; duty
  bhakti and, 197–201, 413–14
  Gopīs and, 288, 304
  Krishna's transgression of, 52
  Lakshmana Rekha and, 399–400, 413–14, 452, 460
  love transcending, 451
  love v., 16, 73, 86–87, 245, 272–74, 281, 292–308, 479–80
  love within bounds of, Bollywood's message of, 292–308
  Phūlvārī/Flower Garden and, 53–60
  redefinition of, Bollywood's, 309–10
  Strī-, 310, 411, 498
Dharmaśāstra, 7, 96
Dil, 166, 225–27, 471–72
Dilwale dulhania le jayenge, 43, 149, 151–56, 223, 292
director, role/innovations of, 24
domestication, 507, 523
doormat Sītā, 9
Do raste, 19
dowry, 181–84, 200, 215, 515–18
  Bollywood exploring, 226–27, 228–31
  monetary value of, rising, 516
Draupadi, Sītā and, 13*n*12
Durgā, 8, 78, 147*n*105, 478, 493
Durgāsaptaśatī, 174, 178
duty (*maryādā*), 89, 90–91. *See also* decorum; dharma
  bhakti tradition privileging love over, 309
  Bollywood focus on, 143–47, 292–310
  eroticism giving way to, 479
  Gopīs v. Sītā in renunciation of, 248–50
  happy-within-, modern endings as, 512–13
  in-law relations as woman's first, 294–95
  love v., 144, 301, 451, 455
  married women, 188–92, 200, 294–95
  Sītā's forest decision and, 277
  touching husband's feet, 108–9
  TVK/Sagar emphasis on, 75–76, 78
  TVR/Sagar emphasis on, 68–75, 103, 108
  women's *strī-dharma* as, 310, 411, 498

East-West theme, 144, 161
elopement
  aftermath of, 133–36
  battle after, 128–33
  Bollywood portrayal of, 140–41
  Dharmaśāstra and, 96
  Dil and, 225–27
  invitation of, 119–23
  private v. public affair of, 130
  Rukmiṇī's, 97–98, 113–41, 137*t*–138*t*, 370
emotion. *See* feelings
empowerment, of women, 244. *See also* agency; women's movement, Sītā and
  film/TV message of, 504–7
  illusory, 200–201, 308–11
engagement, *Rāmā-Sītā* style, films with, 142–47
epics. *See also* texts
  appropriation of, innovations in, 20, 66, 87
  changing messages/versions of, 21–23
  daily life and, 19
epithets, 228, 472, 473
equality. *See also* gender equality
  bridal party, 168–69
  in-laws, 167–71, 230, 237
  UN report on, 16, 498
eroticism, *see* śṛṅgāṛa
eve-teasing, 379–84, 379*n*1, 458–59, 461–94, 461*n*184
  Panaghaṭa Līlā and, 415–31
extortion, 330–32

falling in love, 49–52
  film versions of, 82–89
  Gopīs' Vastraharaṇa and, 60–66, 67*t*, 97
  Krishna's, 427–31
  Sītā's Phūlvārī and, 53–60
  Tulsī/Nanddās bhakti and, 66–68
family, 181–92, 282, 425, 436–45
  agency in context of, 504
  bride/groom, 156–61, 164
  love and, 156–61
  marriage involving, 141

feelings
decorum v., 175–76, 200, 266–67
Nanddās poems and, 213–14
Rādhā's, ignoring, 86
Rāma's, lack of emphasis on, 71, 72
Sagar message against excess, 188, 198–99
Tulsī's emphasis on, 173
females. *See* women; women's movement, Sītā and
feminism, 7, 8–12, 514–15
films, 19–21. *See also* Bollywood; *specific films*
1950s, 371
1980s, 147–51
1990s, 151–56
audience of, 26, 310, 460
caste and, 369–76
date of, 42
duty emphasized in, 143–47
elopement in, 140–41
eroticism and, 83*n*60
falling in love portrayed in, 82–89
Gāndharva-vivāha weddings in, 223–27
Holi festival in, 83*n*60
impromptu weddings in, 223–27
love/dharma in popular, 292–308
love/society weddings in popular, 222–39
mythology and, 19–20
patriarchal status quo maintained by, 44, 159, 237, 238, 494
Rāmāyaṇa subversion criticism of, 476
religion and, 26–27
rituals surrounding making of, 222*n*138
scholarship on, 19–20, 25–28, 43
selection of, 520
Sītā scenario-turned sour in, 227–32
soundtrack of, weddings use of, 222–23
successful, 232–33
svayaṃvara counterpoints in, 157–60
text v., archetypes in, 27–28
traditional weddings in, subversion/affirmation of, 227–32
use/focus of, 42–44
vamp stereotype in, 361–64
wedding wave in, 1990s, 232–39, 517
women in TV and, 504–7
fire ordeal (Agniparīkṣā), 8, 18, 42, 121
Bollywood variants of, 299
Rāma's counterpoint to, 107
scholarship focus on, 11
Tulsī's treatment of, body double of Sītā in, 386–87
Flower Garden scene. *See* Phūlvārī
forest
danger of, 259–60, 262–63
Gopīs v. Sītā decision to go to, 244–91, 246*t*, 287*t*
in-law relations and, 275–76
Sītā leaving purdah for, 243–46, 246*t*
suicide threat and, 278–80

Gāndharva-vivāha, 211–13
"filmi," 223–27
Gandhi, Mahatma, 244, 380, 498, 517–18
Gandhi, Rajiv, 39, 508–9
Gaurī Pūjā, 78, 176, 288
gender equality, 29, 167, 191, 264
Ghai, Subhash, *Pardes*, 160
ghaṭa (vessels), 415–23
gift exchange
dāna-līlā episode as, 382, 456, 467
wedding ceremony, 164
Gītagovinda (Jayadeva), 203–4
goddesses
domestication of, 507, 523
falling in love, 49–52
prayers to, variations in, 58, 62, 70, 73, 78, 125–28
wedding attendance by, 213
women's movement and, 500–501
Goddess, Great (Mahādevī), 8
gods, 206–7
love-marriage rite attendance by, 213
rustic portrayal of, 177
Goldman, Robert, 31*n*27
Goldman, Sally, 11*n*11, 316*n*6, 380*n*3
Gopālacampū (Jīva Gosvāmī), 166
Gopīs of Braj. *See also* Kubja
agency of, 458
age of, Rādhā v., 458
audience and, 460
Bhāgavata Purāṇa and, 31–32, 247–48
bhakti struggle of, 445–46
categorization of, 64–65
dharma and, 288, 304
dilemma of, 453–55
falling in love with Krishna, 60–66, 67*t*, 97
forest decision of, Sītā comparison to, 244–91, 246*t*, 287*t*
goddess prayer of, 62, 78
jealousy of, 351–52, 502
Krishna rejection by, Bollywood's, 300–302
Krishna steals clothes of, 51, 52, 52*t*, 60–66, 67*t*, 75, 76, 78, 80–81, 81*t*, 82, 83–86, 97, 211

Gopīs of Braj. (*continued*)
mental state of, worldly concerns and, 248–50
moral outrage of, 434–36
Panaghaṭa Līlā and, 382, 415–31
Rādhā-Sītā contrast through, 14, 14*n*15
reciprocity of love between Krishna and, 284–86
reformed, 300
restlessness of, 453–55
rivals of Rādhā and, 315–16, 319*t*
sexual harassment and, 431–33
Sītā v., women's voices and, 265–81
tone/body language of, 265–69
TVK's Krishna and, 246–91, 455–58
as unmarried, 78, 79, 288
village gossip and, 446–48
as willing victims, 431–33
gossip, Panaghaṭa Līlā village, 446–48
Gosvāmī, Jīva, 51, 165, 252*n*20, 253, 343
Gosvāmī, Rūpa, 51, 166, 253, 315
Gowarikar, Ashutosh, *Lagaan*, 246, 302–8
grace, extortion becoming, 330–32
groom. *See also* bow sacrifice
bride's family alliance with family of, 156–61, 164
child, 204–5
equality between parties of bride and, 167–71, 230, 237
testing of, 148–50, 160
Gumrah, 462–63
guru, 508
Sagar's, 73–74

hagiography, 16, 35, 35*n*38, 36, 67, 68
Hamara dil aapke paas hai, 362–64
Hanumān, 256*n*30, 380–81, 385, 403, 408
Hawley, Jack, 382
Heinz, Carolyn Brown, 3–4
Hess, Linda, 311
Hindi, polite-register, 322–24, 325–26
Hindu
nationalism, 10, 507–10
women, liberation for, 15–16, 45, 291, 308–11, 501–4
Hindutva, 45, 499, 500, 508–10
Holī festival, 83*n*60, 202, 300, 381–82
home videos, *Shri Krishna leela*, 455–58
Hum aap ke hain koun . . . !, 42–43, 52, 142–47, 161, 223
love within dharma message of, 300–302
Phūlvārī in, Rādhā and, 87–89
westernization/tradition mix in, 233–35
Hum Log (television series), 96–97, 512
husband
subjugation to, 308–11
touching feet of, 108–9

icebreakers, wedding, 180, 218
in-law relations, 188–92, 199–200, 275–76
brides and, 141, 182–84, 188–92, 199–200
brother-sister-, 301, 388, 393
devar-bhābhī/brother-, 388
equality and, 167–71, 230, 237
forest substitutes for, Sītā's, 275–76
wedding ceremony and, 167–71
as woman's first duty, 294–95
innovations
archetypes portrayal, 27–28
bride/in-laws, 189, 191, 199–200
director's, 24
epic appropriation with, 20, 66, 87
kāvya tradition and, 50
Phūlvārī, 87–89
Rukmiṇī episode, 114
Sagar's, 81*t*, 171, 252–53, 280–81, 284–86, 321
Vastraharaṇa, overview of, 81*t*
interaurality, 25
International Society of Krishna Consciousness (ISKCON), 40, 41
intertextuality, 22, 238
ISKCON. *See* International Society of Krishna Consciousness

Jai Santoshi Maa, 26, 509
Janaka, Daśaratha first meeting with, 169–71
Janakī Maṅgal (Tulsīdas), 165
Jaṭāyu, 402, 402*n*61
Jayadeva, *Gītagovinda*, 203–4
jayamālā, 100, 108, 111
jealousy, 252, 280, 305–6, 314–15, 351–52, 502
jhāṇkī, 51, 108, 173, 290
Jhoot bole kauva kate, 155–56
Jungli Rani, 364

kabaḍḍī (game), 160
Kaikeyī, 180, 185, 196, 243, 247, 270, 291, 367
kajli, 51
Kaṃsa, 115, 315–16, 318, 319t, 331–33, 345, 350–51, 353, 359
kaṅkaṇa, 218–20
Kapoor, Raj
Bobby, 150, 226
Ram teri Ganga maili, 157–59
Sangam, 43, 52, 83–87

Satyam shivam sundaram, 365, 464–65
Shri, 362
Kaushik, Satish, 362–64
kāvya, 50, 53, 82–83, 187, 314
Khan, Mansoor, 150, 151
Khan, Mehboob, 477–94
Khosla, Raj, 19, 366–69, 463–64
Kishwar, Madhu, 9, 10, 10*n*9, 518
Krishna
answer from, Rukmiṇī awaits, 123–25
bhakti and, 60–66, 67*t*, 97, 129, 217, 245, 285
as child groom, 204–5
childhood of, texts and, 42
cross-dressing motif of, 285, 300
dāna-līlā/gift episode of, 382, 456, 467
darśana of, 130
dharma transgressed by, 52
disappearance of, forest episode and, 284
eve-teasing by, 381
falling in love by, 427–31
forest dangers presented by Rāma and, 259–60, 262–63
Gopīs and, TVK's, 246–91, 455–58
Gopīs' falling in love with, 60–66, 67*t*, 97
Gopīs rejection of, Bollywood's, 300–302
Gopīs tested by, ironic speech and, 260–61
Kubjā and, 317–20, 319*t*, 330–61, 357*t*–358*t*
love of, nonexclusive nature of, 314
marriages of, 133
mother of, 436–45
physical abuse by, 431
Rādhā accosted by, 414–31
Rādhā's seduction by, 427–31, 449–52
Rādhā tests, 252, 280
"Rāma-izing" of, 302, 472
Rāma v., forest and, 259–60, 281–86
reciprocity of love between Gopīs
Rādhā and, 284–86
Rukmiṇī elopement with, 97–98, 113–41, 137*t*–138*t*, 370
Rukmiṇī's letter to, 119–23
Sagar's, 280–81, 284–86
as Self, 271, 279–80
sexual propositions by, 381–82
Sītā's wedding v. Rādhā and, 165
superiority of Sagar's, 280–81, 285–86
Sūrdas's disclaimer for, 415–23
village gossip and, 446–48
wedding of Rādhā and, 165, 166, 166*n*6, 201–22, 221*t*, 239
Krishna steals Gopīs' clothes. *See* Vastraharaṇa
Kubjā
BhP/TVK/SS versions of, 330–61, 357*t*–358*t*
Bollywood variants of, 364–77
defense of, 352–56
source texts for, 318
Śurpaṇakhā v., 313–20, 319*t*, 357*t*–358*t*, 360–61
kuladevī, 175, 198
Kumar, Indra, 166, 225–27, 471–72
Kumar, Rajendra, 37
Kurosawa, Akira, 415

Lagaan, 43, 246, 302–8
Lajja, 167, 227–32, 462, 472–77, 510
Lakshmana, 314, 327, 387–91
Lakshmana Rekha, 399–400
Bollywood and, 462
drawing, 391–94
Rādhā steps outside, 446–55
sexual harassment and, 382–83
Sītā's crossing of, 395–97, 413–14, 460
Sītā's v. Gopīs,' 460
Lalita-mādhava (Rūpa Gosvāmī), 166, 316
liberation, 15–16, 45, 291, 308–11, 501–4
love. *See also* falling in love
coping with, women's three ways of, 45
within dharma, 300–302
dharma transcended by, 451
dharma v., 16, 73, 86–87, 245, 272–74, 281, 292–308, 479–80
divine sanction of, 66–67, 77–78, 80, 88, 139, 176–77
duty v., 144, 301, 451, 455
erotic, 56, 59, 67, 75–81, 83*n*60, 90, 194, 207, 248, 448, 456–57, 479
family first in issues of, 156–61
illicit, 201–2
Krishna's nonexclusive, 314
mythology and, 5–8
premarital, 89–93, 505–6
primordial, 171
romantic, 51, 89–93
South Asian codes of, 6, 6*n*3
subjectivity and, 14, 115–16, 123
love marriage, 97–98
arranging, 95–161
Bollywood and, 141–61
in popular films, 222–39
Rādhā-Krishna rite of, 165, 166, 166*n*6, 201–22, 221*t*, 239
Lutgendorf, Philip, 18, 164*n*2, 170*n*16, 224, 227*n*164

Mahabharata, Drapaudi-Sītā contrast and, 13*n*12
Mahabharat, television series, 41–42, 158–59, 289
date/popularity of, 17
Rukmiṇī's elopement with Krishna comparison of, 114, 136–40, 137*t*–138*t*
Mahādevī (Great Goddess), 8
Mahāvīracarita, 53
Maine Pyar Kiya" (Barjatya), 147–50
Main Tulsī tere aangan ki" (Khosla), 366–69, 463–64
males
agency of, 136
guilt of, 377
mythologies as created by, 313
politics of, female subjectivity v., 115–16, 123, 136–40, 137*t*–138*t*
rejection by, 258–65
women's sexual overtures to, 328, 368, 468, 505
Mangeshkar, Lata, 82
māninī, 315
Mankekar, Purnima, 28
Manushi (magazine), 9, 11*n*11, 498*n*2, 520
marriage. *See also* love marriage; matrimony
agency and, 87, 113
assisted, 95
child, 194–95
as family affair, 141
multiple, 133, 315
polygamy, 324, 377
sermon on, Tulsī's bhakti v., 172–73
women's duty in, 188–92, 200
marriage, arranged, 18
defiance of, 116–19
problem with, 232
maryādā. See duty
matrimony, 171–73
māyā (delusion), 362
media scholarship, 23–25
medieval sources/texts, 29, 32–38, 60, 165, 166, 201–2, 220–22, 221*t*, 315
eve-teasing theme in TV v., 458–59
kāvya and, 50
Rāma/Krishna in television v., 263–65
television Rādhā v., 82
women prevalent in, 222
Meera ka Mohan, 292, 295–300
Mehta, Deepa, 520, 522
Menon, Ritu, 8–9
Mera gaon mera desh, 19
methodology, siting Sītā Rādhā, 21–23, 25, 29
Minturn, Leigh, 11*n*10, 14*n*13
Mīrā, 482
Rādhā-, Sītā and, 295–300
misogyny, 498
Mistry, Babubhai, 290–91
Mithila, 3, 4
modernity, tradition v., 6, 9, 510–13
Mohra, 462
monogamy, 68, 196–97
Monsoon Wedding, 12–13, 232
morality, 271
darśana and, 198–201
Lakshmana Rekhā as, 446–55
moral outrage, Gopīs', 434–36
mother
Krishna's, 436–45
Rāma and, 282
Mother India, 477–94
Moussaieff Masson, Jeffrey, 316
Mughal-e-azam, 468–70, 472
Mukherjee, Hrishikesh, 155–56
mythology, 27–28. *See also* Rādhā-Krishna mythology; *specific myths/texts*
Bollywood's Krishna, 292–95, 301–8
as created by males, 313
film and, 19–20
love and, 5–8
multiple versions of characters in, 30, 30*n*25
versions of, sources and, 29–44

Nair, Mira, 232
nakha-śikha, 57, 71, 102, 175, 199
Nanddās, 34–36. *See* also *Rukmiṇī Maṇgal*
Bhāsā Dasama Skandha, 34–36, 60–66, 67*t*
BhP variants of, 35
Padabali, 415, 417
Rādhā-Krishna of, 201, 213–17, 221*t*
Tulsī and, 66–68
Naseeb apna apna (Rao), 364
naukā-vihāra, 382
nirguṇa bhakti, 16
NP. *See Padabali*

organization, 44–46
other woman, 13, 45, 313–77, 502, 503, 505, 507–8
Kubjā as, 330–61, 357*t*–358*t*, 364–77
Śurpaṇakhā as, 313–30, 319*t*, 329*t*, 357*t*–358*t*, 360–61

Padabali (Nanddās) (NP), 415, 417
panaghaṭa, 382–83
"Panaghaṭa Līlā" (Sur Sagar), 382, 414–61

Bollywood, 461–72, 461n184
"ghata" in, 416, 423
Gopīs' dilemma/restlessness in, 453–55
Gopīs' moral outrage in, 434–36
multiple perspectives in, 415–16
Rādhā's choice in seduction, 449–52
TVK variation of, 455–58
victims/willing partners in, 415–23
village gossip in, 446–48
Yasoda, Gopīs visiting, 436–40
Yasoda's ambivalence/resolution in, 440–45
panahārin (wet-sari effect), 383
parakīyā, 13, 56, 66, 77, 78, 81, 85, 248, 253, 258, 273, 286, 305, 373
Pardes, 160
parents
bride farewell of, 184–88
love of, dowry and, 231
Svayamvara approval by, 109–12
Partition, 38, 486–87, 493
Passages to India (radio show), 10n8
passion, 120
passivity, 140, 265, 314
patriarchy, 128, 136, 159, 308–11, 376–77, 506–10, 523
status quo of, 16, 44, 51, 159, 237, 238, 476, 494, 503
wedding ceremony and, 223–25
Phalke, Dadasaheb, 113
Phūlvārī (Flower Garden scene), 50, 53–60, 139
Hum aap ke hain koun...!, 87–89
popular film version of, 144
Sholay's counterpoint in, 91–93
texts containing/not containing, 51, 53
Tulsī's, 53–60
Vastraharaṇa compared to, 52, 52*t*
physical abuse, 431
politeness, high-register Hindi, use of ironic, 322–24, 325–26
politics, 39
male, female subjectivity v., 115–16, 123, 136–40, 137*t*–138*t*
polygamy, 324, 377
pots, as ghaṭa/ vessels, 415–23
Prasannarāghava, 53
prayer, goddess, 58, 62, 70, 73, 78, 125–28
Gauri Puja, 78, 176, 288
premarital romance, 89–93, 505–6
private wedding vows, 194–97
psychology
rapist's, 495
women's, Rāmāyaṇa influence on, 8
public vows, 192–93
purdah, leaving, 125–28, 277–81
decision to go to forest, Gopīs v. Sītā, 244–91, 246*t*, 287*t*
forest danger and, 259–60, 262–63
joyous v. tearful background for, 246–48
male rejection of decision for, 258–65
outcome of, Krishna/Rāma agreeing, 281–86
Sītā, overview of, 243–46
speaking one's mind and, 253–58
suicide and, 278–80
TVK and, 130
VR version, 244, 254–55
women's voices and, 265–81
pūrvarāga, 50–52, 75

Qayamat se qayamat tak, 150–51

Rādhā. *See also* Rādhā-Krishna mythology
accosted at well, 414–61
agency of, 472
choice of, 449–52
father of, 425
feelings of, ignored, 86
film portrayals of, multiforms in, 19–21
Gopīs and, 14, 14n15, 315–16, 319*t*
Gopīs v., age of, 458
harassment of, TV v. medieval poetry on, 458–59
jealousy of/Krishna test by, 252, 280
Krishna's seduction of, 427–31, 449–52
Lakshmana Rekhā crossed by, 446–55
medieval v. contemporary, 82
Mīrā variant of, 295–300
other woman and, 315–16, 319*t*
Phūlvārī of, 87–89
reciprocity of love between Krishna and, 284–86
as role model, 12–15, 45, 504–7
Sangam version of, 83–87
Sītā and, contrasted/compared, 12–15, 14n15, 45, 165, 201, 222, 286–91, 287*t*, 431, 459–61, 504–7
"Sītā-izing" of, 67, 81, 86, 89, 252, 301–2, 504–5
temptation in Sītā scenario v., 319–20, 319*t*
tone/body language of, 267–68
village gossip and, 281
wedding ceremony comparison of, overview, 220–22, 221*t*
wedding of Sītā contrasted with, 165
Rādhā accosted at well, 414–61
pot-polishing/victim-partner and, 415–23
Rādhā fights back in episode of, 424–27

Rādhā accosted at well (*continued*)
  Sītā's abduction v., 431
  source texts for, 414–15
  victim-partner and, 415–23
"Rādhā kalyāṇam," 165
Rādhā-Krishna mythology
  love-marriage rites, 165, 166, 166*n*6, 201–22, 221*t*, 239
  Nanddās version of, 201, 213–17, 221*t*
  parallel in, Sītā's abduction, 381–84, 384*t*
  Rāsā-līlā and, 201–2, 205, 209–11
  Souten references to, 369–76
  text sources of, 201–2
  TVK and, 202–3
Rādhāvallabha, 37, 166
Raj, Baldev, 41
rāksasa, Aryan/other and, 507–8
Rākṣasa-vivāha (demon-style wedding), 116, 209*n*99
  svayaṃvara v., 98–99, 100*t*
Rāma
  bhakti and, 245
  Bollywood and, 295, 299–300
  bow lifting by, motive for, 107–8
  in control, 283
  darśan of, 173–76
  epithets of, 473
  feelings of, lack of emphasis on, 71, 72
  forest dangers presented by Krishna and, 259–60, 262–63
  Krishna made into, 302, 472
  Krishna v., forest decision and, 259–60, 281–86
  mother and, 282
  Sagar's, matrimony according to, 171–72
  Sītā's choosing, question of, 100–102
  Sūrpanakhā and, 313–14, 317, 322–24, 326–27
  TVR/RCM v. VR's, 283
  wedding night of Sītā and, 195–97
  wedding of Sītā and, 167–201, 198*t*
Rāmāyaṇa
  feminism and, 7, 8–12, 514–15
  Hamara dil aapke paas hai references to, 362–64
  psychology of women influenced by, 8
  rewrite of, 523
  subversion of, film criticized as, 476
  tradition, 392
  versions of, multiple, 30, 30*n*25
Ramayan, televised (TVR), 39–40
  abridged version of, 17
  actors in, 39
  bride farewell of parents in, 185–86, 187–88
  date/popularity of, 16–17
  gender equality and, 264
  Hindu nationalism and, 507–10
  Rāma's sermon on wives in, 195–97
  RCM *v.*, 68–75
  Sampoorna Rāmayan v., 290–91
  Sītā-Rāma wedding in RCM/VR and, 167–201, 198*t*, 208
  Sītā's abduction in VR/RCM and, 385–414, 412*t*
  Śūrpanakhā and, comparison of RCM/VR, 320–30, 329*t*
  Vālmīki's/Tulsī's Sītā svayaṃvara v., 100–112, 111*t*
  wedding vows in, Rāma/Sītā, 192–97
Rām Carit Mānas (RCM) (Tulsīdās), 32–33, 68–75, 499–500, 502. *See also specific episodes*
  bridal farewell in, parents and, 185–87
  darśana/devotion in, 173–76
  films taking on, 89
  Gopīs/forest of Vyas/Sagar and, 246–91
  Phūlvārī/Flower Garden of, 53–60
  Rāma's forest danger speech in, 262–63
  Sītā-Rāma wedding in TVR/VR and, 167–201, 198*t*, 208
  Sītā's abduction in VR/TVR and, 385–414, 412*t*
  Sītā speaks her mind in TVR/VR and, 254–58
  Śurpaṇakhā in, comparison of TVR/VR, 320–30, 329*t*
  television series' use of, 28, 51
  Vālmīki/Sagar Sītā's svayaṃvara v., 100–112, 111*t*
Rām Nahchū (Tulsīdās), *165*
Ram teri Ganga maili, 157–59
Ranade, Pandita Rāmabai, 498
Rao, T. Rāma, 364
rape, 413, 462, 470
  rapist psychology and, 495
  Sītā's abduction and, 407–9, 413
Rās-līlā (theatrical tradition), 37, 382, 520
Rāsa-līlā (Krishna's Round Dance with Gopis), 31, 165, 205, 244–45, 502, 511*n*10
  and Vastraharana, 52, 66, 78
  in movies, 82, 159, 224, 292, 296, 300, 302, 304–5, 307–9, 465–66
  secret wedding vows, 201, 209–13, 221–22
  comparison in BhP, RP, TVK, 247–48, 251–52, 258, 263–64, 267, 272, 280, 283–84, 288
  televised *Mahabharat* version of, 289–90

Rashomon, Sūrdās's poems and, 415
rasika, 166, 263
Rās Pañcādhyāyī (Vyās), 37–38, 244, 502
  Gopīs/forest of Sagar/Tulsī and, 246–91
Rāvaṇa
  as Brahmin-Sadhu, 394–97
  disguise dropped by, 397–400
  not raping Sītā, 407–9
  queens of, 409–11
  Sītā's abduction and, 385, 394–95, 401–4, 407–9, 413
Ravishankar, K., 292, 295–300
RCM. *See Ram Carit Manas*
reductionism, 27
reform, Sagar's agenda for tradition, 168, 169, 182
religion, 6, 19–20, 232. *See also* Hindutva; rites/rituals
  film and, 26–27
renunciation, 61
  duty, 248–50
research. *See* scholarship
Richman, Paula, 11*n*11, 18
rites/rituals
  bracelet, 218–20
  film-making, 222*n*138
  Gāndharva weddings and, 211–13, 223–27
  Gaurī Pūjā, 78, 176, 288
  goddess prayer, variations in, 58, 62, 70, 73, 78, 125–28
  Vedic v. women's/folksy, 173, 177–81, 217
  women's/folksy, 217–20
rivals
  coping with, 313–20, 319*t*
  Gopīs/Rādhā and, 315–16, 319*t*
  Kubjā as, 330–31, 357*t*–358*t*
road Romeos, 380, 459, 463
role models
  bhakti, 66–68, 501–4
  contrasting, Sītā/Rādhā as, 12–15, 45, 165, 201, 222, 286–91, 287*t*, 504–7
  mythological, love, 5–8
  Sītā as, 9, 73–74, 140–41, 411–14, 504–7
  Sītā/Rukmiṇī, 140–41
role reversal, 285, 300
  Rāma/Sītā wedding and, 180–81
romance, 51, 89–93
Roy, Bimal, 366, 465–68
Rukmiṇī
  agency of, 119, 127–29, 132, 136, 139, 157
  awaits Krishna's answer, 123–25
  Bollywood, 151–56
  elopement comparison of, TVK/RM/BhP, 115–41, 137*t*–138*t*
  elopement of, 97–98, 113–41, 137*t*–138*t*, 370
  elopement with Krishna, 97–98, 113–41, 137*t*–138*t*, 370
  goddess prayer of, 125–28
  letter to Krishna from, 119–23
  Sītā contrasted with, 130, 140–41
  Sītā-izing of, 125–28
Rukmiṇī Maṅgal (RM) (Nanddās), 114, 115–41, 137*t*–138*t*

saffronization, 507–10
Sagar, Ramanand, 17–18, 24, 38–40, 73–74. *See also Rāmayan,* televised; *Shri Krishna,* televised
  agency and, 113, 113*n*33
  background of, 38–39
  contextualization by, 41
  dharma/bhakti of, 199–201
  duty emphasized by, 68–76, 78, 103, 108
  feelings downplayed by, 188, 198–99
  guru of, 73–74
  in-laws' equality and, 167–71
  innovations of, 81*t,* 171, 252–53, 280–81, 284–86, 321
  Krishna of, 280–81, 284–86
  Mistry v., 290–91
  patriarchy promoted by, 506–10
  Rāma on matrimony and, 171–72
  rape issue addressed by, 408–9
  reformist agenda of, 168, 169, 182
  Sītā-Lakshmana relationship changes by, 389–91
  Sītā's abduction message of, 400, 406
  Sītā's speech of, 406
  success of, saffronization in, 507–10
  Śurpaṇakhā innovation of, 321
  television series' of, background on, 17–18, 40–41
  Vālmīki direct quote by, 193
  wedding preparation innovation of, 171
saguṇa bhakti, 16
Samanta, Shakti, 166, 223–25
Sampoorna Ramayan, Rāmayan/TVR v., 290–91
sanction, divine, 299, 305
  love, 66–67, 77–78, 80, 88, 139, 176–77
  wedding, secret, 211–13
Sangam (Kapoor), 43, 52, 83–87
Sanskrit, vernaculars v., 15–16, 53, 174, 178, 208, 501, 503, 523
Sanskshipt Rāmayan, 17

Santoshini, Kumar, 167, 462, 472–77
sari. *See* wet-sari effect
sati (widow burning), 8
sasurāl, 110–11, 128, 167, 181–82, 189, 231, 234, 279, 310
Satyam shivam sundaram, 365, 464–65
Sāvitrī, 227, 515
scholarship, 7, 9, 10, 11, 499
  film, 19–20, 25–28, 43
  fire ordeal focus of, 11
  future, 513–23
  gender discourses in, 29
  hagiography and, 16, 35, 35*n*38, 36, 67, 68
  media, 23–25
  Rādhā/Gopīs, 14, 14*n*15
  Rādhā's marriage debate in, 13
  religion-film, lack of, 26–27
  sexual harassment, 379*n*1
  Sītā, 11*n*11
  Sītā leaving for forest episode, 244
  Sītā's abduction and, 380
  Śurpaṇakhā/Kubja, 316
  television and, 17, 18
secrecy, 201–2, 211–13, 221, 222, 223–24
Seeta's Wedding, 164, 164*n*2
self-choice. *See* svayaṃvara
Self (*atman*), Krishna as, 271, 279–80
self-sacrifice, 367–68, 369–76, 493–94
sensuality, 373, 375
  chastity v., 13
Sethumadhavan, K. S., 292–95
7 1/2 Phere, 232, 235–39
sexual harassment, 379–84, 404. *See also* eve-teasing
  blame placement in, 431–46
  Bollywood and, 461–94, 461*n*184
  Gopīs' reaction to, 431–33
  Nanddās poems on theme of, 415, 417
  poetry on, 415, 458–59
  Rādhā accosted and, 414–61
  of Rādhā, TV v. poetry on, 458–59
  Rādhā v. Sītā and, 431
  road Romeos and, 380, 459, 463
  scholarship on, 379*n*1
  Shri Krishna leela and, 455–58
  Sītā's abduction and, 381–414, 412*t*
  Sūr Sāgar and, 415–61
  victims of, blame on, 494–96
sexuality, 376–77
  Bollywood message on, 376–77
  Gopī/Krishna relations as, 432–33
  Rādhā and, 449–52, 458–59
  Sītā-Lakshmana relationship and, 387–91
  of women, 376–77
  women making overtures of, 328
shadow. *See* chāyā
Sheth, Noel, 316
Shiva, 305
Shiva lingam, 223
Sholay, Phūlvārī counterpoint in, 91–93
Shri, 362
Shri Krishna leela (home video), 455–58
Shri Krishna, televised (TVK), 17–18, 40–41, 75–81, 455, 512
  actors in, 40
  Brahma Vaivarta Purāṇa/BVP/Braj poetry v., 201–2, 220–22, 221*t*
  eroticism avoided in, 456–57
  Gopīs/forest in RCM/Vyas and, 246–91
  Krishna/Gopīs in, 246–91, 455–58
  Krishna smile of superiority in, 284–86
  Kubjā in BhP/SS v., 330–61, 357*t*–358*t*
  Rādhā-Krishna in, 202–3
  Rāsa-līlā in, 263–65
  Rukmiṇī's elopement in BhP/Nanddās v., 115–41, 137*t*–138*t*
Sītā, 9. *See also* Phūlvārī; Sītā's abduction
  asceticism of, 408
  as barometer for women's suffering, 513–18
  body double of, Tulsī's, 386–87
  darśan of, 173–76
  defiance of, abduction episode, 401–11
  Draupadi and, 13*n*12
  epithets of, film using, 228, 472
  falling in love by, 53–60
  feelings of, 175
  film portrayals of, multiforms in, 19–21
  fire ordeal of, 11, 42, 107, 121, 386–87, 499
  forest decision of, Gopīs comparison to, 244–91, 246*t*, 287*t*
  Gopīs v., women's voices and, 265–81
  Jatāyu and, 402, 402*n*61
  Lakshmana and, 387–91, 411–12
  Lakshmana Rekha around, 391–94, 395–97, 413–14, 460
  "lapse" of, in-law equality and, 168–71
  prayer of, 58, 70, 73
  purdah and, 243, 244–91
  Rādhā and, contrasted/compared, 12–15, 14*n*15, 45, 165, 201, 222, 286–91, 287*t*, 431, 459–61, 504–7
  Rādhā-Mīrā turns into, 295–300
  Rāma chosen by, question of, 100–102
  rebellious thoughts of, 106

as role model, 9, 73–74, 140–41, 411–14, 504–7
Rukmiṇī contrasted with, 130, 140–41
Sagar's use of, 73–74
Seeta's Wedding and, 164, 164*n*2
soap series and, 510–13
sons of, 519
speaks her mind in RCM/TVR/VR, 254–58
speech to Lakshmana of, 411–12
Śurpaṇakhā and, 314
svayaṃvara of, 96–97, 100–112, 111*t*, 157–60
televised, 501
temptation in Rādhā scenario v., 319–20, 319*t*
tone/body language of, 265–69
wedding night of Rāma and, 195–97
wedding of Rādhā/Krishna contrasted with, 165
wedding of Rāma and, 167–201
women's movement and, 497–501, 515
"Sītā-izing"
of Rādhā, 67, 81, 86, 89, 252, 301–2, 504–5
of Rukmiṇī, 125–28
Sītā-Rādhā
Bollywood and, 292–95, 308
Yahi hai zindagi,
Sītā-Rāma wedding, 167–201, 198*t*, 208
divine guests attending, 177
textual sources for, 165, 166
VR/TVR/RCM versions of, 167–201, 198*t*, 208
wedding night and, 195–97
Sītā's abduction
Bollywood variant of, 472–77
Brahmin-Sadhu in, 394–97
comparing versions of, 385–414, 412*t*
Lajja and, 472–77
Lakshmana Rekha crossed in, 395–97, 413–14, 460
Rādhā accosted v., 431
Rādhā-Krishna parallel of, 381–84, 384*t*
Rāvaṇa drops disguise in, 397–400
Rāvaṇa not raping Sītā in, 407–9, 413
resistance of temptation in, 403–7
Sāgar's message to women in, 400, 406
Sītā left alone episode in, 385–93
Sītā's defiance, 401–11
Sītā's first reaction/Rāvaṇa's insistence in, 401–4
source texts for, 380–81, 411–14, 412*t*
siting, methodology of, 21–23, 25, 29
soap series, Sītā in, 510–13
society weddings, 222–39
solidarity, women's, 409–11, 436–45
sons, Sītā's, 519
soundtrack, film, 222–23
sources. *See also* medieval sources/texts
classical, 29–32
film, 42–44
Kubjā, 318
myths and, multiple versions of, 29–44
Rādhā accosted at well, 414–15
Rādhā-Krishna love-marriage rites, 201–2
Ramayan, televised, 39–40
Sītā's abduction, 380–81, 411–14, 412*t*
Śurpaṇakhā, 318
television series, 38–42
Souten, 369–76
South Asia, 6, 6*n*3
spoofs, 159, 235
"Shri Krishna Vivaha Varnana," 201–2
śṛṅgāra, 67, 370, 373
downplaying/avoidance of, 56, 59, 75–81, 90, 194, 207, 456–57, 505
duty overtaking, 479
films and, 83*n*60
Panaghaṭa Līlā, 448
status quo, patriarchal, 16, 51, 308–11, 476, 503, 506–10
films maintaining, 44, 159, 237, 238, 494
Strī-dharma, 310, 411, 498
subjectivity
love and, 14, 115–16, 123
women's, male politics v., 115–16, 123, 136–40, 137*t*–138*t*
subjugation, patriarch and, 308–11, 376–77
subordination, women and, 188–91
suffering, Sītā as barometer for women's, 513–18
Sufi poetry, 53, 53*n*2
suicide
Bollywood rival themes with, 368–69
threat of, forest decision containing, 278–80
Śuka, 14*n*14, 252, 447
Sūrdās (poet), 34, 36–37, 209–11. *See also Sūr Sāgar*
Kubjā in works of, comparison of, 318–19, 330–61, 357*t*–358*t*
"Panaghaṭa Līlā" of, 414–61
"Rashomon" perspective of, 415
Śurpaṇakhā
Bollywood variants of, 361–64
comparing episodes of, 328–30, 329*t*
demonizing of, 313–14
Kubjā v., 313–20, 319*t*, 357*t*–358*t*, 360–61

Śurpaṇakhā (*continued*)
politeness in Rāma's first meeting with, 322–24
RCM/TVR/VR versions of, 320–30, 329*t*
source texts for, 318
spurning of, 325–28
as vamp stereotype in films, 361–64
Sūr Sāgar (SS)
Kubjā in BhP/TVK v., 330–61, 357*t*–358*t*
"Panaghaṭa Līlā", 382, 414–31
sexual harassment and, 415–31
"Shri Krishna Vivaha Varnana," 201–2
svakīyā, 13, 56, 72, 165*n*5, 248, 253, 258, 286, 287*t*, 303, 305
svayaṃvara (self-choice) wedding, 3–4
comparison of, supposed love marriage and, 112–13
film counterpoint to, 157–60
parental approval for, 109–12
Rākṣasa-vivaha v., 98–99, 100*t*
Sītā's, 96–97, 100–112, 111*t*, 157–60
spoofs on, 159
Vālmīki's/Tulsī's/Sāgar's versions of, 100–112, 111*t*

Tak, Sawan Kumar, 369–76
Tantra, 14*n*15
tapas. *See* asceticism
television, 16–18. *See also Rāmayan,* televised; *Shri Krishna,* televised
bhakti missing in, 222
eve-teasing theme in medieval poetry v., 458–59
Hum Log on, 96–97, 512
Mahabharat on, 17, 41–42, 114, 136–40, 137*t*–138*t*, 158–59, 289
medieval Rāma/Krishna v., 263–65
Rādhā in medieval texts v., 82
Rām Carit Mānas in, 28, 51
scholarship and, 17, 18
series, 38–42
viewers and, 23–24, 25
women in film and, empowerment of, 504–7
temptation
Bollywood themes of, 361–77
luxury/sensuality, 403–4
Sītā's abduction and, 403–7
Sītā v. Rādhā scenario of, 319–20, 319*t*
texts. *See also* epics; medieval sources/texts; sources; *specific episodes; specific texts*
classical, 29–32, 60, 199
film v., archetypes in, 27–28
interaurality and, 25
interpretation of, 24
Krishna's childhood and, 42
Phūlvārī, 51, 53
Rādhā accosted at well, 414–15
Rādhā-Krishna love-marriage rites, 201–2
Rādhā-Krishna wedding, 166
Sanskrit v. vernacular, 15–16, 53, 174, 178, 208, 501, 503, 523
sexual harassment theme in, 380–81, 414–15
Sītā's abduction in, 380–81
versions of, multiple, 21–23, 29–44, 30, 30*n*25
wedding ceremony, 165, 166
Thiel-Horstmann, Monika, 18
Towards Equality (United Nations report), 16, 498
tradition. *See also* kāvya
bhakti, love privileged over duty in, 309
Brahminical/folk, 173–81, 217
love in, 6
modernity v., 6, 9, 510–13
pride in, Sītā/soaps and, 510–13
reform of, Sāgar's agenda for, 168, 169, 182
scholarship and, 9
Vallabhan, 35, 36, 61, 63
Westernization and, trendy mix of, 233–35, 239, 511–13
transcreations, *Bhāgavata Purāṇa,* 37, 244, 331
translators, Kubjā as problematic for, 356, 359
Trijata, 410–11
Trivedi, Isshaan, 232
Tulsī. *See* Tulsīdas
Tulsīdas (Tulsī), 28, 32–33, 245, 502. *See also specific episodes of Ram Carit Manas*
Gopīs/forest of Sagar/Vyas and, 246–91
ideal devotee and, 401–2
Janakī Maṅgal, 165
Nanddās and, 66–68
Rāma bhakti of, Vyas's Krishna bhakti v., 245
Rām Carit Mānas, 28, 32–33, 51, 53–60, 89, 100–112, 111*t*, 172–76, 208, 246–91, 320–30, 329*t*
Ram Nahchu, 165
solution to problem of Sītā's abduction, 386–87
speech editing by, Sītā's Lakshmana, 411–12
TVK. *See Shri Krishna,* televised
TVR. *See Rāmayan,* televised

UN. *See* United Nations
unfaithfulness, 313
United Nations (UN), 16, 498
untouchability, *Souten* and, 369–76

vadhū-vara-guṇaparīkṣā, 97
"vah vah Ramji," 143–44
Vallabha, 35, 36, 61, 63
Vālmīki Rāmayana (VR)
additions to, 30
bhakti and, 15–16
bridal farewell in, 184–85
bridal party equality in, 168–69
dating/use of, 30
multiple versions of myths and, 30, 30*n*25
Rāma's forest danger speech in, 262
Sāgar's direct quote from, 193
Sītā forest episode in, 244, 254–55, 259, 262, 266, 269, 275, 282, 286
Sītā forest episode v. Gopīs/TVK/RCM and, 244–91, 287*t*
Sītā-Rāma wedding in TVR/RCM v., 167–201, 198*t*, 208
Sītā's abduction in RCM/TVR and, 385–414, 412*t*
Śurpaṇakhā and, comparison of RCM/TVR, 320–30, 329*t*
Tulsī's/Sāgar's Sītā's svayaṃvara v., 100–112, 111*t*
vamp
film stereotype of, 361–64
punished, Śurpaṇakhā as, 320–30, 329*t*
Varāha Puraṇā, 318
Vastraharaṇa (Krishna steals Gopīs' clothes), 51, 97, 211
BhP v. BDS, 60–66, 67*t*
film versions of, 82
innovations in Sāgar's, overview of, 81*t*
Phūlvārī compared to, 52, 52*t*
Sangam, 83–86
TVK version of, 51, 75, 76, 78, 80–81
Vedic rites
folk traditions and, 173–81, 217
women's and, 177–81, 217
vernaculars, Sanskrit v., 15–16, 53, 174, 178, 208, 501, 503, 523
vessels, panaghaṭa theme use of, 415–23
victims
rape, 413, 417
sexual harassment, blame on, 494–96
Sītā's example of, 514–15
transformation of, willing partners, 415–23
willing, Gopīs as, 431–33
Vidagdha-mādhava (Rupa Gosvami), 315
videos, home, *Shri Krishna leela*, 455–58
viewers, television and, 23–24, 25
viparīta rati, sound of, waist-belt symbol of, 422–23
vīra rasa, 99, 100*t*
Viśvāmitra, 72, 100–2, 105, 109–11, 168, 182*n*49, 51, 183*n*52, 184–85
vows, wedding
private, 194–97
public, 192–93
Rāma/Sītā, 192–97
secret, 201–2, 221
VR. *See Vālmīki Rāmayana*
vrata. *See* prayer, goddess
vyāhulau utsava, 166
Vyāsa, 114
Vyās, Harirām, *Rās Pañcādhyāyī*, 37–38, 244, 246–91, 502

waist-belt, 422–23
wall painting, 3, 5
water fetching motif (panaghaṭa), 382–83
wedding(s)
actual v. subversive, 201–2
bride/parents farewell and, 184–88
demon-style, 98–99, 100*t*, 116, 209*n*99
dowry and, 181–84, 200, 215, 226–27, 515–18
films on, 1990s wave of, 232–39, 517
Gandharva-vivaha, 211–13, 223–27
in-law relations and, 188–92, 199–200, 275–76
matrimony meaning and, 171–73
Rāma/Sītā's, night of, 195–97
secret, 201–2, 211–13
Sītā/Rāma, 167–201, 198*t*, 208
society, popular films on love and, 222–39
textual sources for, 165, 166
wedding ceremony, 163–67
devotion/dharma in, balancing, 173–81
icebreakers for, 180, 218
impromptu, 223–27
in-law relations and, 167–71
layers of, 163–64
Rādhā-Krishna, 165, 166, 166*n*6, 201–22, 221*t*, 239
Rādhā's, comparing versions of, overview of, 220–22, 221*t*
Rākṣasa-vivaha, 98–99, 100*t*, 116, 209*n*99
real-life, 179
secret, 221, 223–24
Sītā/Rādhā comparison of, 165
VR/TVR/RCM versions of, 167–201, 198*t*, 208
wedding vows, 192–97
private, 194–97
public, 192–93
secret, 201–2

wedding vows (*continued*)
well. *See* "Panaghaṭa Līlā"
Westernization, 150, 301
  tradition and, trendy mix of, 233–35, 239, 511–13
wet-sari effect *(panaharin)*, 383
widow burning (sati), 8
widows, 522
wives, TVR Rāma's sermon on, 195–97
women, 195–97. *See also* other woman
  coping with love by, three ways of, 45
  devotees compared to, Tulsī/Nanddās, 68
  duty of married, 188–92, 200, 294–95
  empowerment of, 200–201, 244, 308–11, 504–7
  feminism and, 7, 8–12, 514–15
  folk rites and, 178, 217–20
  liberation for, 15–16, 45, 291, 308–11, 501–4
  lustful, demonizing, 313–14, 320–22
  medieval text prevalence of, 222
  men as only redeemers of, 519
  premarital romance message to, 89–93, 505–6
  as rape victims, 413, 470
  rights of, arranged marriage defiance and, 116–19
  rites of, 177–81
  role of, Rāsa-līlā, 211
  self-sacrifice of, Bollywood and, 367–68
  sex/lovemaking position of, "Panaghaṭa Līlā" and, 422–23
  sexuality of, 376–77
  sexual overtures to men by, 328
  solidarity between, 409–11, 436–45
  spurning of, Śurpaṇakhā and, 325–28
  strī-dharma as duty of, 310, 411, 498
  subjectivity of, male politics v., 115–16, 123, 136–40, 137*t*–138*t*
  subjugation of, 188–91, 310
  submission of, 113, 121–22, 140
  suffering of, Sītā as barometer for, 513–18
  television viewership, 17
  village, 382–83
  voices of, forest decision and, 265–81
women's movement, Sītā and, 497–501, 515
worship, Kubjā, 317–18

Yahi hai zindagi, 292–95
Yashoda, 436–45